The Diaries
of Giacomo Meyerbeer

Frontispiece: Meyerbeer in the mid-1820s. Lithograph by C. Constans, after a drawing by Pierre Roche Vigneron (Paris, c. 1825).

The Diaries
of Giacomo Meyerbeer

Volume 1
1791–1839

Translated, Edited,
and Annotated
by Robert Ignatius Letellier

Madison • Teaneck
Fairleigh Dickinson University Press
London: Associated University Presses

Associated University Presses
440 Forsgate Drive
Cranbury, NJ 08512

Associated University Presses
16 Barter Street
London WC1A 2AH, England

Associated University Presses
P.O. Box 338, Port Credit
Mississauga, Ontario
Canada L5G 4L8

The paper used in this publication meets the requiremts of the American National Standard for Permanence of Paper for Printed Library Materials Z39.48-1984.

Library of Congress Cataloging-in-Publication Data

Meyerbeer, Giacomo, 1791–1864.
    [Diaries. English]
    The diaries of Giacomo Meyerbeer / translated, edited, and annotated by Robert Ignatius Letellier.
      p. cm.
    Translation of the untitled and unpublished German diaries.
    Includes index.
    Contents : v. 1. 1791–1839
    ISBN 0-8386-3789-2 (alk. paper)
    1. Meyerbeer, Giacomo, 1791–1864—Diaries. 2. Composers—France--Diaries. I. Le Tellier, Robert Ignatius. II. Title.
ML410.M61A3   1999
782.1'092—dc21
    [b]   98-52129
                                           CIP
                                         MN

PRINTED IN THE UNITED STATES OF AMERICA

Contents

SONNET TO MEYERBEER

Some high Poets' genius into our times
    Transfused, meseems as chanting to thy notes,
    From Heaven shot them forth, unto all climes,
    True Art by thee was startled, on it dotes;
For, thy philosopher's vers'd fancy chimes
    In the loftiest text; thy harp, too, denotes
    Thy soul, which self-examen's love sublimes;
    Robert, the Prophet, th'African, Huguenots,
Are superior numbers, so grand, so true,
    That the spirit God's, through them, I'll extol,
    Who did bless thy conceptions, and bedew
The world, with deep as mellow airs that thrall
    The vulgar, Study task, all minds imbue,
    And cause Fame, thee immortal to enrol.
                    —James Pincherle

I hear those odes, symphonies, operas,
I hear in the *William Tell* the music of an arous'd and angry
    people,
I hear Meyerbeer's *Huguenots*, the *Prophet*, or *Robert*,
Gounod's *Faust*, or Mozart's *Don Juan* . . .
. . . .
Give me to hold all sounds, (I madly struggling cry,)
Fill me with all the voices of the universe . . .
. . . .
Then I woke softly,
And pausing, questioning awhile the music of my dream,
And questioning all those reminiscences, the tempest in its
    fury,
And all the songs of sopranos and tenors . . .
. . . .
And I said, moreover,
Haply what thou has heard O soul was not the sound of
    winds,
Nor dream of raging storm, nor sea-hawk's flapping wings
    nor harsh scream,
Nor vocalism of sun-bright Italy,
Nor German organ majestic, nor vast concourse of voices,
    nor layers of harmonies,
Nor strophes of husbands and wives, nor sound of marching
    soldiers,
Nor flutes, nor harps, nor the bugle calls of camps,
But to a new rhythmus fitted for thee,
Poems bridging the way from Life to Death, vaguely wafted
    in night air, uncaught, unwritten,
Which let us go forth in the bold day and write.
              —Walt Whitman, *Proud Music of the Storm*

Illustrations and Maps

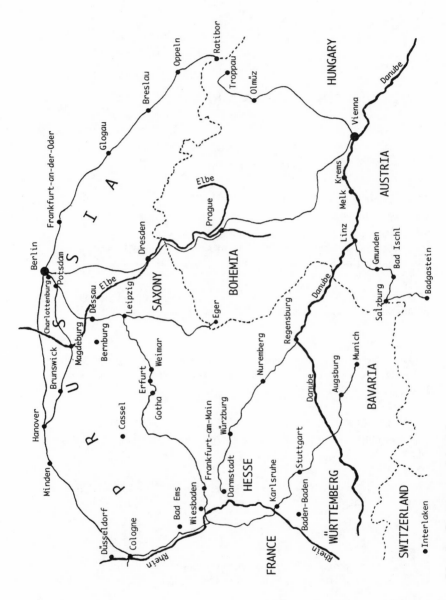

Map 1 – Germany and Austria

Map 2 – France, Belgium, and England

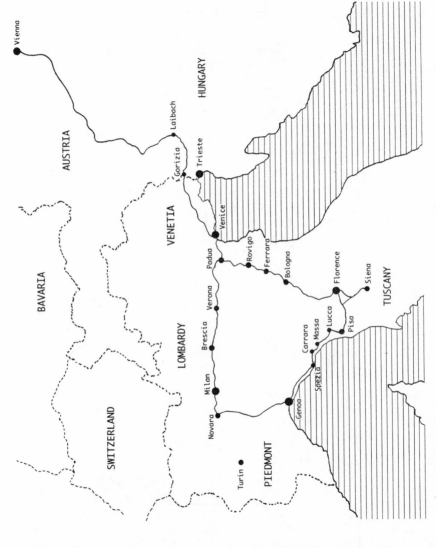

Map 3 – Northern Italy

Musical Examples

Foreword:
Meyerbeer and the *Grand Opéra*

BY HEINZ BECKER

The spectacular première of the five-act *Robert le Diable* on the evening of 21 November 1831 in the Académie Royale de Musique in Paris carried the name of the composer Giacomo Meyerbeer around the world. On the same night, still over-come by the deafening applause that had engulfed Meyerbeer in the opera house, the famous naturalist Alexander von Humboldt, full of regard and enthusiasm, wrote to his now illustrious compatriot in French: he could not sleep before he had expressed his admiration for Meyerbeer—and in the same language that had entranced him all evening. He rejoiced with the composer, delighting in the fame of his friend, seeing it as a boost to the renown of their common Prussian father-land. Jean-François Le Sueur, the grand old man of the Parisian music scene, per-ceived in this première a sea change: with an eye to Rossini, he wrote that the age of charming musical decoration had now finally given way to an era of power and energy.

The period of mythological and biblical themes had passed, a period in which an educated noble class had delighted in recognizing customary and familiar figures, and relished innumerable settings of the same kind of libretto. After the July Revolution of 1830, the world in Paris was profoundly transformed: at the head of the newly elected Parlement stood a banker, Jacques Lafitte, while the opera house was dominated by the parvenus, the strengthened bourgeoisie, the industri-alists, the civil servants, littérateurs and journalists. But then there were also the little people, the *lorettes*, the ladies of fashion, the grisettes, the seamstresses, with their *galants* in the gallery: *tout Paris!* They yearned for realistic stories in which they could perceive something of their own world. The fight on the barricades had steeled their resolve: there was no longer any need for the *lieto fine*, the happy resolution. Indeed, the new form of *grand opéra*, originating in the five-act, through-composed *tragédie lyrique*, had already been heralded in two important works: Auber's *La Muette de Portici* (1828) and Rossini's *Guillaume Tell* (1829). But only in *Robert le Diable* by Meyerbeer was it given decisive character. While Auber remained resolutely in the sound world of the *opéra comique*, Rossini had

15

evolved a new, revolutionary sonority in the impressive Oath of the Cantons. But it was Meyerbeer who went even further with his *musique caracteristique*, his *couleur locale*.

It is as though a higher power was governing stagecraft: Meyerbeer's *Robert le Diable* was the first big new work that the director of the Opéra, Louis Véron, presented to the public after the July Revolution—as musical followed on political event. "I was astonished by the size and originality of subject," Véron later recalled in his *Mémoires*. Meyerbeer had found in Eugène Scribe, the experienced playwright, his ideal librettist. Scribe possessed an extraordinary sense of the theater—of what would be dramatically effective, stage-worthy, stimulating, and refined—as well as an instinct for big crowd scenes. Above all, he had a feel for political topicality, so important to the age. Heinrich Heine acknowledged the preeminent political meaning of *Robert le Diable*, even though the story was based on a medieval French legend: Robert was the faltering hero, who, like Louis-Philippe, did not know exactly what he wanted and shifted uneasily between virtue and vice. The heroes of the *tragédie lyrique*, blameless and single-minded, had played themselves out: Scribe and Meyerbeer created a new kind of hero, wavering and all too human, with all his contradictions, with all his strengths and weaknesses. Robert, Raoul, John of Leyden, and Vasco da Gama all embody the same type.

The psychological believability of such a protagonist was something Meyerbeer and Scribe often debated at length in their collaborative deliberations about their works, as is witnessed in the surviving plans and drafts, the *remarques* and *brouillons*, and most especially in Meyerbeer's diaries. One of the consistent consequences was the emergence of an element new to opera, and one typical of trends in contemporary literature: eroticism. The mythological heroes of the *tragédie lyrique* were motivated by a peerless love. But now Meyerbeer and Scribe shocked their spectators and audiences with the famous Ballet of the Nuns, a daring seduction scene by the ghostly Abbess Hélène. Later, the authors challenged all conventions in their handling of the love story in *Le Prophète*, where the chief female protagonist is the mother of the Prophet, and not the radiant soprano heroine. Fidès's contralto reflects the very darkness of the subject matter itself.

With *Les Huguenots* (1836), in which the bloody massacre of St. Bartholomew's Eve (1572) forms a background to a tragic love story between a Protestant nobleman and the Catholic wife of the comte de Nevers, Meyerbeer turned to great historical and religious themes. In *Le Prophète* (1849) Scribe placed the figure of John of Leyden on the stage: with the Anabaptists, a sectarian group of enthusiasts and demagogues, he went about propagating pseudomessianic ideas in the wake of the Lutheran Reformation (1535). A private family story, a conflict between mother and son, is woven into the actual events of this troubled period.

Various *observations* and notes in his diaries illustrate just how active a role Meyerbeer played in the conception of *L'Étoile du Nord* (1854), a reworking of his Prussian festival opera *Ein Feldlager in Schlesien* (1845). He was anxious to develop the credibility of the protagonists in this episode from the life of Peter the Great, an episode set against the historical background of the Swedish War (1712). In Scribe's draft Peter had been too crude, too brutal, and unredeemed by moments of magnanimity, while Catherine had been lacking in sensibility and tenderness.

Meyerbeer would characteristically add an outstanding sense of context to the psychological illumination of his protagonists, to their dramatic truthfulness. Thus in *L'Africaine* (1865), Meyerbeer's last great work, which was not fully completed at the time of his death, the story of Vasco da Gama is used to raise the politically explosive question of the conquest of foreign lands for selfish ends, and in fact amounts to a critique of colonialism. The actual theme of the opera is racial conflict, the struggle between black and white. It is exemplified in Vasco da Gama, a hero drawn, for different reasons, to the Portuguese Ines, on the one hand, and to the exotic slave Sélika, on the other. The latter is actually a queen, who, in her turn, wavers between her own subject, Nelusko, and the alien explorer Vasco. Meyerbeer, as an unbaptized Jew, suffered very much from the society of his day. The fact that Sélika and Nelusko are more strongly delineated than Vasco and Ines may well have been experienced as provocative in his time, but the "foreigners" are the actual agents of the drama. In the tragic, but reconciliatory, conclusion of the opera—in which Sélika, by renouncing her own happiness, bestows freedom on Vasco and Ines, and herself finds salvation in death—one confronts the heart of Meyerbeer's message: the liberating power of forgiveness.

It is the moving themes of history that still lend Meyerbeer's works their enduring topicality. But big subjects demand correspondingly big structures. In the old Italian operas and French *tragédie lyrique*, arias, duets, and ensembles, interrupted by recitatives, had followed one after the other, like pearls strung on a necklace. Now Meyerbeer embedded these separate numbers in great choral scenes and, with ballets closely integrated to the action, fused these various elements into grandiose tableaux. Even Meyerbeer's sharpest critics, like Robert Schumann and Richard Wagner, could not deny the overwhelming effect of the Blessing of the Daggers in act 4 of *Les Huguenots*. Here, preeminently, Meyerbeer's special gift for the structuring of impressive crowd scenes is apparent. In the Blessing of the Daggers, priests consecrate the weapons of conspirators with holy gestures, as throne and altar unite in an unholy mésalliance; naked blood lust appropriates the sign of the cross, the whole impregnated with Meyerbeer's music, which still reverberates with the political rhythms of the French Revolution. The effect of this scene is intensified by contrast with the intimate duo between Raoul and Valentine that immediately follows. Such contrasts—a feature designed to *épater le bourgeois,* "astound the bourgeoisie"—characterize the very nature of *grand opéra.*

This celebrated love duet also does not follow the conventional concepts of form: the lines are broken in an impassioned dialogue. In fraught confrontation between love and duty, Raoul and Valentine interact with each other and are eventually united blissfully in the famous G-flat major melody, later called the melody of the century. "Meyerbeer schrieb Weltgeschichte, Geschichte der Herzen und Empfindungen, er zerschlug die Schanken der Nationalvorurteile . . . er schrieb Taten der Musik" [Meyerbeer wrote world history, a history of heart and feelings, shattering national prejudices . . . he wrote deeds of music], acknowledged no less a critic than Richard Wagner.

The July Revolution of 1830 and the uprising of 1848 shook the ordinary citizens from their lethargy and assigned them a new, active role. And likewise, on the opera stage, the chorus was no longer merely a prop, but now assumed the role of "the people". No one understood this transference of the masses to the stage better than Meyerbeer. Powerful choruses, often in concerted *unisono*, articulated the voice of the crowd. And Meyerbeer certainly did not eschew terrifying sounds if the action demanded it. This is a malleable art!

The innovative reality of such choral scenes, which even today lack nothing in topical effect, is perhaps most strikingly illustrated by the opening of act 4 of *Le Prophète*. The people of Münster, suffering under the tyranny of the false prophet and his soldiers, give only apparent obedience. The terrified populace whisper their actual opinions, but whenever the Anabaptist *patrouille* appears, they shout out their hypocritical enthusiasm, crying, "Long live the Prophet, long live his soldiers." But once the soldiers are out of earshot, the chorus mutters, "Down with the Prophet."

In the conception of his operas, Meyerbeer followed the demands of Victor Hugo for *couleur locale*, which he formulated in 1827 in the preface to his drama *Cromwell*. Not only must every work have a definite local color, but also every act, indeed every scene. Picturesque images characterize Meyerbeer's operas: knightly halls and bowers, monastic ruins and cloisters, a lonely cross in a remote landscape (which appeared on the operatic stage for the first time in act 3, scene 4, of *Robert le Diable*), the mighty cathedral and the idyllic winter landscape around the city of Münster (in *Le Prophète*), the caravel in the tumultuous seas in *L'Africaine*. Of course it required considerable financial resources to realize Meyerbeer's new costumes and stage designs, but his operas guaranteed the directors the highest box-office takings. In the archives of the Paris Opéra, colored costume designs for the characters and so-called *maquettes en volume*, "stage models," allow one to appreciate the beauty of the *mise en scène* that transported the audiences into the very times of the action. Various stage effects elicited breathless admiration. When, in the act 3 finale of *Le Prophète*, John of Leyden, in the gray morning light, incited his troops to attack the city of Münster, the sun began to rise gradually until its light flooded the very auditorium: for the first time in the history of opera, electric light was used in a production. The famous physicist, Léon Foucault, had specially constructed the light machine for this stage-sun. The elaborate machinery for the ship in *L'Africaine* was also a technical marvel. Thus, the *grand opéra*, as developed by Meyerbeer, is a spectacular form uniting every potential and resource of the opera house.

The colorful stage scene corresponded to the vividness of the orchestral sound. Just as Meyerbeer varied the vast choral tableaux with intimate mood pictures, so in his scores powerful al fresco sound masses of concentrated voices and orchestra alternate with the almost esoteric tenderness of unaccompanied voices, or the sound of a single, distinctive instrument. The effect of the "singing" andante cantabile violoncellos in the Abbess Hélène's famous seduction scene was so enduring that it served as the model for innumerable languishing salon pieces at the fin de siècle. In *Les Huguenots,* for example, there is Raoul's delicate romance ("Plus blanche que la blanche ermine"), accompanied by a solo viola d'amore, which beguiles with its refined and caressing tones. Conversely, one is alienated by the deployment of percussion, bassoons, piccolos, and contrabasses in Marcel's ferocious Battle Song ("Piff, paff"). The bass clarinet, newly invented by Adolphe Sax, was heard for the first time during the Nuptial Blessing in act 5 of *Les Huguenots.* Meyerbeer in fact was a master of instrumentation, and always looking for new and original tonal combinations and effects. In the last act of *Robert le Diable,* for example, he had added the organ to the operatic orchestra. Later, in act 5 of *Le Prophète,* in the scene in which the mother awaits her son, he ventured to use divided contrabasses in dissonant combinations: in this deep register they merge into a diffuse and tense web of sound, full of anxiety and foreboding. Many details would be altered during orchestral rehearsals after careful experimentation. Meyerbeer, moreover, can be said to have developed the music of tumult and the notion of space-through-sound by his many echo effects.

In Meyerbeer's *grand opéra*, German harmony, French rhythm, and innovative orchestration, were united with the techniques of Italian bel canto at an exceptionally intensive level. From the very beginning it was Meyerbeer's belief that only in Italy could one learn to write effectively for the voice. From 1816-1824 he gained crucial experience in Italy, and composed six operas in the Italian style. The title role of the final and most successful of these, *Il Crociato in Egitto* (1824), was written for the last great castrato, Giovanni Battista Velluti. Until the end, Meyerbeer composed the roles of his protagonists with specific singers in mind. He had learned in Italy that a role should suit a singer like a well-made garment, something Mozart also understood perfectly. Meyerbeer would carefully consider the strengths and weaknesses, the character and specific timbre, of the voice in question, in order to realize its fullest potential. He made the highest demands on his singers, and required perfect virtuosity as well as intensity of expression, in the interests of dramatic credibility. He possessed an unerring instinct for the singing voice, but also showed great trust in the judgment of his singers, and was accordingly prepared to alter, even to jettison, what had already been composed. In 1837 he spoke to the tenor Adolphe Nourrit, the creator of Raoul, about "our *Huguenots*" and told him he had done more for the opera than its authors. It had been Nourrit's dissatisfaction with aspects of act 4 that had led to the creation of the famous "Tu l'as dit" section of the love duet. In the same way he transposed the soprano role of the Page in this opera for the famous alto, Marietta Alboni, and wrote her a second aria (the engaging act 2 rondo "Non, non, vous n'avez jamais je gage") as a mark of appreciation for her assumption of this part at Covent Garden in 1848.

Meyerbeer's diaries thus afford one a glimpse into the working methods of one of the most famous and successful composers of the nineteenth century, a man preoccupied with the perfection of his art, which he would refine and alter down to the last moment. His often closely observed journal entries provide a privileged insight into the world of *grand opéra* and the multifarious problems associated with the creation and production of this complex and stimulating art form.

(Translated by R. I. Letellier)

Preface

On 29 January 1861, the composer Giacomo Meyerbeer confided to his diary: "[T]he attacks against my art, and also on me as a person, in newspapers and books from all quarters . . . have left me incapable of working." Some things never seem to change! Earlier, on 6 January 1859, he had observed: "Everywhere I look I see enemies, never friends". These sad reflections came at the end of a life devoted to music and drama, which had been acknowledged and honored by crowned heads, universities, musical academies, and the theatergoing public all over Europe, and indeed throughout the world.[1] They are a puzzling, but prescient, perception of the controversy that even the mention of Meyerbeer's name was later able to provoke. This attitude continues right up to the present, even among people who may not know a note of his music. Few other composers have this power to unsettle, even to disturb, and to understand the reasons for it would require extensive sociological, as much as aesthetic, investigation. No other major artist has suffered more from the vagaries of prejudice, propaganda, and fickle taste.

And yet the truth is always rather more complex, and enlightening, and interesting, than received stereotypes. On 29 October 1848, the composer wrote from Paris to his mother, Amalia Beer, in Berlin:[2]

> I have received a letter from our poor Rossi in Verona[3] that moved me to tears; he and his three children are almost dying of hunger. I sent him 150 francs and wanted to send more, but I have just dispatched 150 francs to the poor old Sina,[4] who is also so sadly in the direst straits. Perhaps you would send the wretched Rossi something as well? It is a great *mitzwe*.[5] Good-bye, dearest beloved Nonna.[6]

This letter is a touching and revealing example of the composer's generous, thoughtful and religious character. For much of this century his star has been in eclipse: he has been vilified and scorned as a parsimonious old impostor who, by some incredible fluke, was able to deceive the musical world and the canons of good taste until World War I, but was inescapably exposed and scornfully consigned to appropriate oblivion. The opera house, concert hall, record catalogs, and musical press still bear testimony to this. But justice based on new scholarship,

21

and the relentless processes of reaction, if nothing else, will exercise their inevitable offices, and perhaps the time has come for an unprejudiced music-loving public to investigate, read, and listen for themselves.[7]

The English translation in this edition is the first full text of Meyerbeer's diaries in any language. I hope that it can play some part in helping to rediscover the life and work of a great composer, indeed a luminary of the operatic firmament, who for too long has been misunderstood and unjustly overlooked.

NOTES

1. See the list of honors awarded to Meyerbeer on pp. 27–28.

2. See Heinz Becker and Gudrun Becker, eds., *Giacomo Meyerbeer: Briefwechsel und Tagebücher* (Berlin: Walter de Gruyter, 1985), 4:451.

3. The librettist Gaetano Rossi.

4. A Viennese businessman fallen on hard times.

5. Hebrew: "commandment," i.e., a holy injunction to charity (*ha-torah we ha-mitzwot adonai,* "the Law and Commandments of the Lord," as in Exod. 24:12).

6. Italian: "Grandmother"; the term used for Amalia Beer by her whole family.

7. It is perhaps worth recalling the perspicacious words of Edward J. Dent: "Meyerbeer has been so much abused by later historians and critics, both as a musician and as a man, that it is worth while stating here that in his younger days he was regarded as an incredibly fascinating and lovable character. Both Weber and Felice Romani (Bellini's librettist), who knew him very intimately, spoke of him in terms of the most ardent affection; they also recorded their gratitude to Meyerbeer's parents, who must have been ideal examples of those cultivated wealthy Jews to whom German musical life has always owed its chief support" (*Opera* [Harmondsworth, U.K.: Penguin, 1940], p. 70).

A Note on the Translation
and Critical Apparatus

The text presented in this book is a full and faithful translation of the transcription, made by Wilhelm Altmann, of the original manuscript of Meyerbeer's diaries, which is now missing. The Altmann transcription is part of the Meyerbeer Archive held in the Staatsbibliothek zu Berlin-Preussischer Kulturbesitz, Musikabteilung mit Mendelssohn-Archiv, and is numbered N.Mus.Nachl. 97, B/7.

The style and content are straightforward, unpretentious and without literary self-consciousness. Every effort has been made to reflect Meyerbeer's prose in all its simplicity and occasional awkwardness. The composer's daily entries are usually short, often in the truncated manner typical of a journal, i.e., with omitted subjectival pronouns and/or "silent" predicates. For example, use of the German preposition *an*, "to," invariably presupposes the missing verb ("wrote"). Purple passages are virtually nonexistent, and extended descriptions very rare; they are usually confined to enthusiastic travel impressions, or some cogent musical observation. His descriptive vocabulary is limited and sometimes repetitious, "interesting" and "lovely" being typical examples.

One of the more unusual features is a reflection of Meyerbeer's polyglot propensities. The language is infused with foreign elements, French words being by far the most common (e.g., *applaudissement*, "applause"; *succès*, "success"; *droits d'auteur*, "royalties"; *traité*, "contract"). Gallicisms also abound (a recurrent instance is *coupuren*, "abridgments"—the French *coupure* with the German plural marker *-n*). The standard Italian musical vocabulary is ever present (e.g., *coloratura*, "vocal embellishment"), but in addition, during his years in Italy, and on later visits, Meyerbeer was inclined to sprinkle his language with Italian words (e.g., *impresa*, "management"). In an effort to convey this very intrusive characteristic, many of the foreign words or hybridizations that are translated in the text have been marked and quoted in the notes.

Meyerbeer consistently used German throughout his diaries and private family correspondence. Just occasionally, in his jottings or notes made in the *Taschenkalender* (appointment books) for ordinary rehearsals, he wrote in French. These passages have been retained in their "extraneous" linguistic form—in order to reflect the original. These rare instances are rendered into English in the endnotes.

Germanization of French verbs occurs often, especially as past participles, in which the "foreign" verb is transformed into the German medium by the suffixed inflection -iert (e.g., déjeuniert, "dined," from the French déjeuner; souteniert, "supported," from the French soutenir). It must be observed that this tendency, very typical of Meyerbeer's written style, was also fairly widespread in the eighteenth and nineteenth centuries, when French was the language of polite society.

Proper nouns and nomenclature relating to the social and professional spheres of Paris and Berlin inevitably resist successful translation. Names of institutions like the Singakademie, the Domchor, and the Commission des Auteurs et Compositeurs Dramatiques have been retained in their original form and romanized. Professional titles, especially German ones, are also generally left untranslated. There are numerous types of civil servant, like *Regierungsrat, Hofrat,* and *Legationsrat* (administrative, courtly, and diplomatic counselors, respectively), and retention of the original helps convey the social and hierarchical characteristics of the German-Austrian terms. Retention of the original form of a term like *Landgutbesitzer* (a form of "lord of the manor"), moreover, conveys something of the formal, and sometimes pedantic, nuance of social implication. This is also true of vocatives, where use of the French *Monsieur* and *Madame* and the German *Herr, Frau,* and *Fräulein* helps to convey the flavor of the style and the changing reflection of social and geographical scenes. In any case, the recurrent form of *Demoiselle* is now archaic, and its rendition as "Miss" would be flat and pedestrian.

Proper names such as Friedrich and Wilhelm have been left as they occur in the original. Common practice has been to Anglicize them, but the recent tendency in historical writing is to retain the German originals. The exception here is "Frederick the Great," who is known to history by his English appellation. The same is the case with the currencies, where consistent reference is made to the hybrid "friedrichs d'or" (= 5 *Reichstaler*), Prussian "thalers" and "silberlings," Austrian "gulden," and French "francs" and "louis d'or."

The critical apparatus is designed to be of maximum helpfulness. All notes endeavor to illumine the text, whether by indicating geographical or historical circumstances, by amplifying or explaining points where necessary, or by providing immediate reference to the operas, ballets, and plays that are referred to constantly. This helps to chronicle the theatrical history of the midyears of the nineteenth century. Each work is listed by genre, with number of acts, details of authorship (musical, literary and choreographical, as necessary) with city, theater, and date of original performance, and any other useful details of performing history.

In order to help provide an overall perspective, the individual titles are grouped together generically in the glossaries, divided into dramatic works (operas, ballets, and plays) and nondramatic works, both musical (orchestral, chamber, instrumental, choral, vocal) and literary (novels, travelogues, works of reference, and musical criticism).

No biographical details of the many hundreds of persons who appear in the diaries are included in the notes. These are listed in the register of names, where entries vary in length according to the importance of the character concerned, the nature of his or her relation to Meyerbeer, or simply the availability of information about them. Obviously in references to people of the stature of Bach, Beethoven, Goethe, Mozart, or Shakespeare there is hardly need for biographical detail; instead, I try to indicate Meyerbeer's attitude to them or the role they played in his artistic life.

A special glossary is devoted to Meyerbeer's work, with a listing of all references to his compositions—including their geneses, rehearsals, and performances—that occur in the diaries.

The bibliography is based on the documents and texts referred to in the translation and the explanatory notes, but aims at an even broader inclusiveness, and hence usefulness, for the student of music, theater, and social history. Sections are devoted to the life and criticism of Meyerbeer, his family and individual works, his contemporaries, the general theater history of the nineteenth century (with a particular emphasis on opera), the historical background (German, French and European) and the particular role of the Jewish people.

In this edition the following abbreviations are used:

BT	Heinz Becker and Gudrun Becker, eds., *Briefwechsel und Tagebücher* (Berlin: Walter de Gruyter, 1960 [vol. 1]; 1970 [vol. 2]; 1975 [vol. 3]; 1985 [vol. 4]).
Richel	Veronica C. Richel, *The German Stage, 1767-1890: A Directory of Playwrights and Plays* (Westport, Conn.: Greenwood Press, 1988).
Tgb.	*Tagebuch* (Diary).
Tk.	*Taschenkalender* (Pocket appointment book).
Wicks	Charles Beaumont Wicks, *The Parisian Stage, 1800–1900: Alphabetical Indexes of Plays and Authors* (University: University of Alabama Press, 1950–79).
*	See Register of Names.

Honors Awarded to Meyerbeer

12 Feb. 1813	Accorded the title Hof- und Kammerkompositeur by Grand Duke Ludwig of Hesse-Darmstadt.
27 July 1820	Elected a Member of the Accademia Filarmonica in Bologna.
5 Feb. 1830	Awarded the Order Imperial do Cruzeiro (of the Southern Cross) by the Emperor Pedro I of Brazil.
22 April 1830	Elected Member of the Institut de France, Académie des Sciences, Paris.
21 Jan. 1831	Appointed Member of the Commission d'Enseignement du Conservatoire de Paris.
19 Jan. 1832	Created Chevalier de l'Ordre Royal de la Légion d'Honneur by King Louis Philippe of France.
11 Aug. 1832	Accorded the title of Hofkapellmeister by King Friedrich Wilhelm III of Prussia.
2 May 1833	Elected Member of the Akademie der Künste in Berlin.
18 Jan. 1840	Awarded the Ritterkreuz des Sachsen-Ernestinischen Haus-Ordens by Duke Ernest I of Saxe-Coburg-Gotha.
16 April 1840	Awarded the Ritterkreuz des Ordens Heinrich des Löwen by Duke Wilhelm of Brunswick.
10 May 1842	Created a Knight of the Nordstjärneorden (Order of the North Star) by King Oscar I of Sweden.
31 May 1842	Nominated Ritter der unter dem heutigen Tage gestifteten Friedens-Classe des Ordens Pour le Mérite für die Wissenschaften und Künste by King Friedrich Wilhelm IV of Prussia.
11 June 1842	Accorded the title Preussischer Generalmusikdirektor by King Friedrich Wilhelm IV of Prussia.
9 April 1843	Awarded the Goldene Medaille für Künste by King Friedrich Wilhelm IV of Prussia.
July 1843	Elected a Member of the Royal Academy of Music in London.
Feb. 1843	Elected a Member of the Académie des Beaux Arts in Brussels.
25 Sept. 1847	Elected an Honorary Member of the Prague Conservatoire.
4 May 1849	Nominated Commandeur de la Legion d'Honneur by the minister Léon Faucher.

20 Jan. 1850	Awarded the Ritterkreuz des Königlichen Sächsischen Verdienstorden by King Friedrich August of Saxony.
10 July 1850	Elected an Honorary Doctor of the Faculty of Philosophy of the University of Jena.
1 Nov. 1850	Created a Ritter des Österreichischen Franz Joseph-Orden by the Emperor Franz Joseph of Austria.
21 Jan. 1851	Elected a Member of the Philharmonic Society of St. Petersburg.
Aug. 1851	Elected a Member of the Senate of the Prussian Akademie der Künste, Berlin.
18 July 1851	Elected an Honorary Member of the Akademie der Tonkunst, Vienna.
28 Nov. 1853	Awarded the Orden der Kunst und Wissenschaft by King Maximilian II of Bavaria.
30 Sept. 1854	Awarded the Kommandeurkreuz des Ordens der Württembergischen Krone by King Wilhelm I of Württemberg, with automatic elevation to the nobility.
Oct. 1854	Awarded the Ordekruis van de Eikenkroon (Order of the Oak Crown) by the queen of the Netherlands.
10 Feb. 1855	Awarded the Comthurkreuz des Albrechtsordens von Johann Nepomuk by Maria Joseph, queen of Saxony.
9 April 1855	Awarded the Kommandeurkreuz 1. Grades mit Stern des Ernstinischen Hausordens by Duke Ernst II of Saxe-Coburg-Gotha.
Feb. 1857	Elected a Member of the Accademia dell'Arte in Florence.
21 Oct. 1861	Awarded the Preussische Kroneorden 2. Klasse by King Wilhelm I of Prussia.
June 1862	Elected an Honorary Doctor of Music by the University of Cambridge (unaccepted)

Acknowledgments

This work was begun in January 1992 in a small flat on the coast of Natal, perched high above the glorious Indian Ocean. It was continued in a quiet room overlooking a secret garden in the middle of London, and concluded in the midst of two other beautiful gardens—one in leafy Buckinghamshire, and the other hidden in the heart of Cambridge. My undertaking was made possible only through the support and help of my late stepfather, Dennis Stanley Jeffray, my cousin Terry Letellier, and my late friend Margaret Pole. Terry devoted hours over the years helping to check my typescript and translation, and advising on the nuances of French. She also shared the joy of my visit to the celebration of Meyerbeer's bicentenary, when we were guests of the German president at Schloss Bellevue in Berlin. Margaret was always one of the most stalwart supporters of my work on Meyerbeer; indeed, our friendship grew out of a very special afternoon in late January 1980 when our mutual friend, Rodney Edgecombe, brought her to meet me, and I played her some of Meyerbeer's beautiful music.

But my gratitude goes back even further. It was my late mother, Dagmar Adeline Halsted, whose devoted trust enabled me to possess the first two volumes of Meyerbeer's *Briefwechsel und Tagebücher* nearly thirty years ago, even though she did not quite understand my devotion to a remote and forgotten composer, and even though in those days I could hardly read German. I owe everything to her love, and it was she who provided the circumstances in which my rapt involvement with the world of opera could grow and flourish.

To Prof. Heinz Becker I owe the example of scholarship, and trust in the power of patient research to reveal the truth about Meyerbeer. This has been in the face of skepticism and indifference, and even hostility, on the part of so many in the musical and publishing establishments. I first corresponded with Prof. Becker in the late 1970s, and then met him in Bochum in 1984. His friendship, and later also that of his wife, Dr. Gudrun Becker, has been a privilege, and an incentive always to continue my lonely work. And it is my particular honor that Prof. Becker has agreed to write a foreword to this edition, in which he discusses Meyerbeer's very special artistic achievement as the principal exponent of French *grand opéra*.

It was Frau Hertin-Loeser of the Staatsbibliothek in Berlin who allowed me to have my own copy of the Altmann transcription of Meyerbeer's Diaries: its arrival brought much joy to my bed of illness in Jerusalem in 1990. Dr. Hans-Günther Klein subsequently sent me further texts, and granted the permission to pursue my translated edition; he has always been so kind and responsive to my requests.

My very special thanks go to Peter Lamb, who prepared the musical examples with exquisite care; and to Mr. Adams of the Rhodes University Library, who over twenty years ago helped in the photographing of many of the items in my private collection. More recently, Mark Scudder and Paul Gurner of the Cambridge University Library have prepared several of the illustrations used in this edition. Mr. Les Goodey, also of the photography department, prepared my hand-drawn maps for publication with beautiful clarity.

Dr. Gerwin Strobl of the London School of Economics spent many wearisome hours with me helping me to decipher some of the more intractable examples of nineteenth-century German handwriting.

Dr. Simon Owens of Trinity Street, Cambridge, advised me on medical matters.

I can never forget the friendship and helpfulness, from my school days on, of the late Hermann Baron of Willesden Green and of his partner, Miss Christel Wallbaum, who found me so many of Meyerbeer's scores, lithographs, and autograph letters. Miss Julia Tredwell and Terry Parsons of Blackwell's Music Shop were also so helpful to me over the years. Michael G. Thomas and John Carter found me many rare and private recordings of Meyerbeer's music, which still suffers from the indifference of the recording industry.

A special word of thanks goes to my friend, His Grace Maurice Couve de Murville, archbishop of Birmingham, who encouraged me and devoted so much time reading my introduction and making many valuable suggestions about style and content.

A most special thanks goes to Walter de Gruyter of Berlin, who has so kindly granted me permission to cite (in translation) from the Beckers' edition of Meyerbeer's *Briefwechsel und Tagebücher*.

Others generous in their permissions are Dr. Helmut Hell of the Staatsbibliothek in Berlin, Heidrun Klein of the Bildarchiv Preussischer Kulturbesitz in Berlin, and Prof. Dr. Giersberg of the Stiftung Preussischer Schlösser und Gärten in Potsdam.

I am particularly grateful to Andrew Lindesay of the Golden Cockerel Press in London for his kind encouragement, and to my publisher, Julien Yoseloff, in Cranbury, N.J., for his assiduous professionalism.

I would like to record my admiration and gratitude for the artistry of that stupendous trio—Joan Sutherland, Marilyn Horne, and Maestro Richard Bonynge; the glorious tenors Nicolai Gedda and Placido Domingo; and the work of Patric Schmidt and the late Don White of Opera Rara. All of them, more than any others in the world of music-making over the last thirty years, have acknowledged Meyerbeer's achievement and kept his name fresh in the few recordings available to us.

It was my privilege to meet and become the friend of Elisabeth Beare, Meyerbeer's great-great-granddaughter, in Berlin in 1991. Knowing her is a special link for me with the composer himself.

I have loved Meyerbeer since I was a child; even then, I soon found, to my mystification, that his name alone was (and indeed still is!) capable of eliciting extraordinary reactions, even though his music was no longer played, and his life hardly known. No two books seemed to agree about him. He has been dismissed as a serious artist, and yet his work is filled with treasures of melody and harmony, with overwhelming dramatic power, and shows a splendid mastery of the complex art form we call opera. It is he, finally, I must thank for the music.

The Diaries
of Giacomo Meyerbeer

Introduction

The composer most frequently performed in Covent Garden and at the Paris Opéra during the nineteenth century was neither Mozart, nor Verdi, but Giacomo Meyerbeer.[1] His operas dominated the international repertoire with a popularity that seemed unassailable.[2] Yet now he has all but passed out of popular consciousness. His operas are not only rarely performed but the general public are not even properly able to hear his music, once so beloved.[3] The average music lover comes across his name only in reading about Richard Wagner, and the role he played in Wagner's path to glory.[4] The intellectual and popular perception of Meyerbeer is something of a historical phenomenon, a sociological as much as a musicological matter, an example of the perplexing power of prejudice.[5] And yet the former ubiquity and longevity of his art suggests an intrinsic worth far beyond his historical significance as a precursor of the sublime achievements of Wagner and Verdi. But the materials for a proper reappraisal of both the man and his music, let alone any curiosity about him or a sense of justice about his treatment, are singularly lacking, most especially in the English-speaking world.

This extraordinary situation *is* nonetheless bound up with Wagner. His following has come close to resembling a religious cult, and his words have often had the effect of scriptural utterances on the Wagnerians of this world—be they musicians, critics or ordinary music lovers.[6] His repudiation of Meyerbeer has had the effect of a ban, and like so many of his ideas, they have exerted a pernicious effect far beyond their innate worth. It is small wonder that Meyerbeer, with some prescience, could never, in later life, hear Wagner's name mentioned without a grimace passing over his face. In his famous biography of Wagner, Ernest Newman observes that "if ever Meyerbeer's diary is published in full, it ought to make interesting reading."[7] Knowledge of Meyerbeer's perspective of events in this fraught relationship,[8] and, indeed, of virtually everything else on the contemporary operatic scene, has long been a serious omission, preventing a fuller understanding of the musical world of the nineteenth century. These diaries are the primary material that take one to the heart of Meyerbeer the man and the composer. His life, like his operas, is well worth investigating for its own sake, and the opportunity for this should be at the disposal of all those who love beautiful music, who have an interest in the rich and complex world of *ottocento* opera and its social context, and who have a concern for the fair reassessment of a life and reputation lost in the *Nacht und Nebel* of partisanship and opprobrium.

With the appearance of this edition, Newman's hypothetical situation has at last become a reality. After languishing in oblivion for more than 130 years, Meyerbeer's diaries are now made available in English. This mysterious, half-forgotten composer, whose operas were once performed in the remotest corners of the globe,[9] can now speak for himself in the unadorned simplicity of the chronicle of his own life and times.

THE MEYERBEER PAPERS OR ARCHIVE [*NACHLASS*]

When Meyerbeer died on 2 May 1864 he left specific instructions that his private papers, particularly his letters and diaries, should remain in the private possession of his family, and not be published.[10] His wishes were honored by his wife and daughters, letters were bought back, and not a word appeared in print. While this was typical of Meyerbeer's self-effacing attitude to his private life and his desire to protect his colleagues, it was a serious setback to his posthumous reputation. Nothing written about the composer had the advantage of research based on firsthand or primary biographical material.[11] In fact his life was to become shrouded in the fog of myth, hearsay, and largely hostile critical (often pseudocritical) opinion.[12] Like the disastrous neglect of Meyerbeer's musical *Nachlass*,[13] the record of his life was seriously damaged by the ban on investigation of his papers. Indeed there *is* an "essential Meyerbeer" waiting to be recovered for the world[14] behind the image of the devious Shylock so beloved of much critical opinion up to the present.[15]

After Minna Meyerbeer's death, the youngest daughter, Cornelie Richter (1842–1922), entrusted the safekeeping of her father's papers to the Moravian Community. Her son Raoul Richter became official custodian in 1895, but he died (12 May 1912) without making appropriate arrangements for a suitable trusteeship. The executors therefore negotiated with Adolf von Harnack, director of the Königliche Bibliothek in Berlin, with the result that in 1914, against Meyerbeer's stipulations, his musical manuscripts, diaries, and substantial library (in sixteen boxes) were loaned to the Royal Library in Berlin for ninety-nine years,[16] although the letters and personal documents remained in the family's possession.[17] The musicologist and director of the music department at the library, Wilhelm Altmann, read the composer's diary and made a transcript of it (1916),[18] but the planned publication never took place because of objections from Cosima Wagner.[19] The heirs thereupon withdrew permission for publication of the diaries, and Cornelie Richter bought the transcript from Altmann. The action was providential, since Meyerbeer's own manuscript, together with many other of his musical autographs and sketches, was lost during the upheavals of World War II,[20] when many of the treasures of the Staatsbibliotek in Berlin were secreted in apparently safe places in Silesia and Poland,[21] and were only partially recovered when peace returned.[22] But for the Altmann *Abschrift* that had remained with the family in Berlin, Meyerbeer's journal would have disappeared forever, and with it the modest but invaluable daily record of the life of one of the great figures of operatic history, a person of decisive influence in the musical world of the nineteenth century.

The next stage of this extraordinary story brings the German musicologist, Professor Heinz Becker, into the picture. Having just been promoted to a university post in 1952, he had commenced research on the clarinet, and came across Meyerbeer as the composer of a clarinet quintet.[23] He felt further drawn to investigate this musician, judged with such contradiction in musical criticism and outlawed during the Nazi period, and he planned to edit a collection of his letters and documents. The idea took shape at the very time that Luise Richter (née Kurschat; d. 1978) entrusted a significant part of Meyerbeer's papers to the care of Alfred Berner, curator of the Institut für Musikforschung, Stiftung Preussischer Kulturbesitz, in Berlin. She had acted on the instructions of her ailing husband, Hans Richter (d. 1955), the composer's last surviving grandson. Becker made Richter's personal acquaintance when he visited his home on the Hohenzollernstrasse, Berlin-Wannsee, and received his unconditional permission to examine and edit all the Meyerbeer papers. Luise Richter took Becker up to the attic of the house, and there Becker discovered further notebooks and parcels of letters, as well as Wilhelm Altmann's transcription of the diaries, arranged neatly on the shelves.[24] These were also transferred to the Institut für Musikforschung. Conditions were now appropriate for the commencement of work on the planned edition of the correspondence, and Becker could begin the vast process of editing the mass of material. Working first alone, and then with his wife, Dr. Gudrun Becker, he began a work that would occupy his every free moment for nearly forty years. In 1960 the first volume of the *Briefwechsel und Tagebücher* appeared, published by the Berlin publishing house of de Gruyter; volume 2 followed ten years later in 1970, volume 3 in 1975, and volume 4 in 1985, bringing the chronology up to June 1849.[25] So, slowly but surely, Meyerbeer's letters, diaries, and appointment books have been appearing in a scholarly edition with annotations, but almost all are still available only in the German original. A selection of the letters was translated into English and printed in 1989,[26] thereby supplementing Becker's own small biography of 1980, which was the first to be based directly on the primary sources of the composer's life.[27]

But the completion of the work appeared to be in danger when in October 1984 Meyerbeer's descendants unexpectedly decided to withdraw the Meyerbeer *Nachlass* from the Preussisches Institut für Musikforschung and denied further access to interested scholars. The material next appeared on auction at Sotheby's;[28] fortunately it was secured (at £160,000) on 23 May 1987, for Germany and the world, by Dr. Rudolph Elvers of the Staatsbibliothek in Berlin, where it is now in the public domain.[29] Included in the Archive was the transcript of the diaries,[30] which initially seemed lost[31] but, on closer searching prompted by the present editor, was recovered among the papers, jumbled in transit but safe. Thanks to the kindness of Frau Dr. Hertin-Loeser the Altmann *Abschrift* was made available to him in March 1990, and with Dr. Hans-Günther Klein's permission, the translation and editing of the diaries progressed apace over the years that followed (1992–96), and the outcome is now presented to the English-speaking world.

THE DIARIES

Meyerbeer's diaries exist (unless the original is one day recovered) solely in the transcript made by Wilhelm Altmann in 1919. This consists of 640 pages, the first 239 of which are typed, and the rest written in a small, close handwriting that is often very difficult to decipher. In one way or another, it covers most of the composer's life, from 1812 to 1864, with the exception of the 1820s. Meyerbeer apparently began keeping a diary in Darmstadt (1811) while studying with the Abbé Vogler: he refers to it in the following year, but it is now lost. The journal begins in very ambitious style in Munich, where the young artist spent eight months of 1812 (May to December) trying to launch his career as a concert pianist and preparing his first two operas for performance. It was the decisive year of passage in his career, something he seemed fully aware of, and that, in his youthful enthusiasm, he recorded in detail: it was to be one of the fullest diaries he ever kept, and shows that the propensity to maintain a journal was there from the start of his career.

The remaining years of the 1810s are variable. The fervor of 1812, which had been severely curtailed by the news of the death of his maternal grandfather, Liepmann Meyer Wulff, in August of that year, was resumed with gusto at the beginning of 1813. Meyerbeer's river trip to Vienna and his firsthand impressions of the city have come down to us in vivid detail, but only for the first four months of the year, before the daily discipline of the journal was submerged in the overwhelming impressions of his new adventures. (The 1813 diary is, exceptionally, not part of the Altmann *Abschrift*: it survives on its own as a fragment in the Meyerbeer Papers held in the Bibliothèque de l'Opéra in Paris.) What follows are further glimpses of life in Vienna (1813–14), Paris at the moment of the Restoration (1815), and London, where he spent a few weeks with his brother Wilhelm prior to his departure for Italy in 1816.

As for the famous years in Italy, they do indeed seem to have bewitched the young composer;[32] his life seems just to have been too full for him to keep a journal, and the 1820s are entirely lacking in any form of autobiographical daily record. Here one is entirely dependent on his letters for primary documentation. Only a tantalizing glimpse of a diary exists for the beginning of 1818; Meyerbeer's reactions to the Carnevale in Milan (1817–18) provide his fullest recorded musical observations in some detail. In September 1818, however, he did write a very long letter to his brother Michael, who had recently left to return to Berlin, and it provided him with a detailed chronicle of the musical scene in Italy. The letter is really an epistolary diary, and in its length and detail presents a unique record of operatic life all over Italy during the first half of that year, and considerable instances of Meyerbeer's musical reactions and artistic opinions. It offers an excellent example of the heady nature of the Italian years, and for that reason has been included in this edition.[33] Fortunately, the genesis of *Il Crociato in Egitto* is described in a large number of Gaetano Rossi's letters to the composer; the pity is that none of Meyerbeer's correspondence with Rossi has come to light as yet. The whereabouts of Rossi's papers remains another tantalizing mystery in the history of the documentation of Meyerbeer's life.

From 1827 the situation changes completely, and in some form or another there is an almost daily record of some aspect of the composer's life and work. In the 1830s he kept a full-scale journal only for the first few months of 1831; as with the 1812 diary, it is among the most detailed records Meyerbeer ever kept. In the main, though, the account of this decade is dependent on the *Taschenkalender*, or pocket appointment books. While providing nothing more than names and the specifications of various meetings, letters written, details of rehearsals and performances, addresses of friends and acquaintances, and miscellaneous notes and ideas, they provide an immense amount of information about the composer's activities, movements, and social contacts, and sometimes almost assume the nature of a journal.[34] Only the years 1828 and 1830 are entirely without either *Tagebuch* or *Taschenkalender*—which is unfortunate, since the period 1827–30 marks the gestation of *Robert le Diable*. However, the history of the genesis of this legendary opera is picked up just before rehearsals became too demanding for Meyerbeer to maintain the levels of commentary he had sustained from January to April 1831. The year 1834 is also limited to a few travel notes in November and December, so depriving us of the details of the composition of *Les Huguenots*, particularly in Nice (late 1833 to March 1834). The appointment books for 1835–36 provide a comprehensive, if somewhat truncated, table of the rehearsals and première of Meyerbeer's most famous opera.

In 1840 and 1841 Meyerbeer began keeping a fuller diary for the first time since the early days of 1831. While the entries for these years vary in length, the compulsion to keep a daily record was growing in the composer's mind. Only in the years 1843 and 1845 did the pressures of his post as *Generalmusikdirektor* to the king of Prussia limit his freedom; there is a consequent need to refer to the *Taschenkalender*, which, nonetheless, once again provide a surprisingly full picture of the events of Meyerbeer's busy official life.[35]

The turning point in the story of Meyerbeer's diaries is 1846. This year begins with a preamble that sets out his "theory" of keeping a diary. He undertook a daily record of significant events in his life, not as an *apologia pro vita sua* with an eye to future publication, but more as an *aide mémoire* for his own retrospective assistance and pleasure. His technique was to use loose leaves that could be carried easily in his notebooks, so as to be able to note down events almost on the spot, if necessary. No matter what the pressures, Meyerbeer was to abide by this resolution until the months before his death, when ill-health finally sapped his remaining strength.

With few exceptions, the daily record that ensued is a complete chronicle of Meyerbeer's life, from January 1846 until January 1864; it presents an almost unique record, warts and all, of the last fourteen years of a famous composer's life. Voluminous correspondence survives from Mozart, Beethoven, Wagner, Verdi, Donizetti, and Tchaikovsky, but to find a diary among the opera composers is a great rarity. The existence of *Mein Leben* (1870) is a case in point: Wagner's presentation of his life is a profoundly self-conscious and political presentation of selected aspects of his own experience, a classic piece of self-projection, even a type of propaganda.[36] Delacroix's journal is full of opinion and speculation that also seems to look to an anticipated readership.[37] Other forms of autobiographical reminiscence by composers are very romantic mixtures of journalism and the first-person novel. In Weber's *Tonkünstlersleben* (1809–27),[38] Spohr's *Selbstbiographie* (1860–61),[39] and Berlioz's *Mémoires* (1865),[40] episodes from the artists' lives are recounted with witty fleetness of incident and a running critical commentary on people and events, the effect of which is a certain picaresque provocativeness, again with an eye to publication and the reading public.

THE STYLE AND CONTENT: A PREOCCUPATION WITH THE THEATER

Meyerbeer's diaries give an entirely different impression. Since they were never intended to be published, they are devoid of any ostentation or self-consciousness, and provide a straightforward account of where he went, whom he met, and what he did. The overall impression is of minimal commentary—and certainly he was not given to developing his critical opinions at length. This general impression is mistaken. The earlier years are full of extensive passages where he describes his reactions to Winter,[41] Poissl,[42] Boieldieu,[43] Spontini,[44] Cramer,[45] Pacini,[46] and Nicolini,[47] for example. Later he reacts to composers ranging from the obscure (like Labarre),[48] through better-known personalities (like Halévy,[49] Adam,[50] and Auber[51]), to the household names (like Bach,[52] Beethoven,[53] and Wagner[54]). Sometimes he exasperatingly remains silent about his feelings.[55] At other times he expresses interest without further qualification,[56] or perplexity that is neither dismissive nor eulogistic.[57] To express his highest admiration, he sometimes offers laconic praise (the oft encountered *wunderschön*).[58] Whatever his feelings or reactions, though, his unrelenting, if not passionate, concern with everything musical meant that he attended all forms of music-making wherever he was, all his life long. It is the scrupulous record of such performances, whether dramatic or nondramatic, vocal or orchestral, symphonic, chamber or instrumental, which provides the consistent points of reference and historical interest in his journal.

But perhaps the most important aspect of Meyerbeer's diaries is the record of his own music-making. Apart from his Italian works, the composition of all his operas are chronicled; from *Le Prophète* onwards, there are references to every stage of development, interest in various subjects, discussion with his librettists, the processes of composition, rehearsal, modification and presentation. Indeed, the compositional histories of *Le Prophète, L'Étoile du Nord, Le Pardon de Ploërmel,* and *L'Africaine* provide one of the most comprehensive accounts available of a composer's working methods.

Meyerbeer's observation of the musical world around him presents a detailed firsthand narrative of the artistic life in the major centers of European culture over a period of fifty years. And this does not refer only to musical events, but to dramatic activity as a whole. He was beyond all else a man of the theater: he breathed its atmosphere and, nearly every day of his life, attended the opera house or the playhouse. He loved the theater indiscriminately: no performance of any work was passed over if he was free to attend. The level of his involvement with literature is surprising, but it must be remembered that he was both cosmopolitan and polyglot. German was his first language and the medium of his most intimate personal expression, as husband, father and citizen. But French was the language of his greatest artistic creativity, his huge operatic success, and his dealings with Scribe. Italian was the medium of his operatic apprenticeship, and remained one of his greatest literary loves. English was also an ever-present factor; he took English lessons all his life and was always working at it, from his first visit to London in 1815 to his last in 1862. He attended plays in German, French, Italian, and English—works ranging from Shakespeare,[59] Racine,[60] Goethe,[61] and Goldoni[62] through Beaumarchais,[63] Dumas (*père*[64] and *fils*[65]), and Sardou, to contemporary vaudevilles and *Lokalpossen* by playwrights whose names are forgotten today (like Bayard[66] and Kalisch[67]). The number of performances he attended was immense, and to follow up even the titles of the works he saw is to have the history of the European theater in the nineteenth century opened to one. Nothing was too ordinary or outré for him, and we see him watching tightrope walkers and acrobats,[68] going to circuses,[69] or investigating the stage machinery of the Viennese theaters.[70] His passionate interest covered many important developments in the life of the theater of his time, like attending Dumas's Théâtre Historique[71] and making the acquaintance of actresses like Rachel,[72] Rose Chéri,[73] Virginie Déjazet,[74] and Adelaide Ristori[75] and of actors like Davison[76] and Fechter.[77]

WORDS AND MUSIC

One of the most interesting things to emerge from Meyerbeer's love of drama is evidence of the very close relationship between the theatrical and musical worlds in the nineteenth century. The hegemony of Kotzebue in the early years of the century[78] and of Scribe in the middle years[79] illustrates this: both were as famous for their plays as for their libretti; many of their plays were identical with libretti;[80] and their sheer narrative and thematic fecundity made them into principal sources of dramatic inspiration. The European scale of theatrical activity, and the transference of ideas and plays through translation[81] and touring companies,[82] contributed to a generic fluidity at the borders between opera and drama.

Meyerbeer's interest was essentially dramatic, and he looked at every story or play in terms of its potential for operatic adaptation. Significantly, he never considered even a fraction of the libretti that were constantly presented to him throughout his life,[83] and he never accepted any libretto uncritically, but would always need to see several drafts, would always make suggestions for changes, and would invariably have to employ a littérateur to attend to the modifications or expansions he required.[84] The figures of Émile Deschamps and Charlotte Birch-Pfeiffer are central here: the former, a Parisian romantic poet, and the latter, a very successful Berlin dramatist, were essential to Meyerbeer's adaptations of the libretti provided for him by such famous names as Scribe and Barbier & Carré. Germaine Delavigne performed such a role in *Robert le Diable*, as Scribe's official collaborator;[85] Deschamps was vital for the final form of *Les Huguenots* and *Le Prophète*. While his work on the former opera was publicly recognized,[86] his work on the latter was kept secret.[87] Birch-Pfeiffer's contribution to the books of *Dinorah*[88] and *L'Africaine*[89] was equally extensive, and is also unacknowledged. Most interestingly of all, Meyerbeer's concern for words and dramatic situations prompted his own textual contributions to his libretti (for example, most of Sélika's *Liebestod* is entirely his own, text as well as music).[90] He needed the services of a bilingual man of the theater, like Joseph Duesberg, a German translator living in Paris, to complete *Vasco da Gama*.[91]

The fusion of musical and theatrical interests is perhaps best summed up in the figure of Ludwig Rellstab, the Berlin poet and critic, who was generally regarded as the librettist of *Ein Feldlager in Schlesien*. The scenario for this "Prussian patriotic opera" had in fact been devised by both Meyerbeer and Scribe,[92] and only translated by Rellstab,[93] who performed similar services in fitting German words to the composer's French *chansons*.

Indeed, the literary response to music, the musical response to literature (so typical of Berlioz), and the constant need to secure appropriate French and German words for his conceptions remain ever-present features of Meyerbeer's life.[94] The very last pages of his diary, written in the midst of his final labors on finishing the closing scene of *L'Africaine*, are filled with restless consideration of new ideas for libretti and his insatiable curiosity for all things theatrical.[95]

The commingling of music and theater is illustrated by many of the plays recorded in the diaries that use incidental music: Beethoven's *Egmont* and Mendelssohn's *A Midsummer Night's Dream* make several appearances.[96] One of Meyerbeer's last labors was his music for Henri Blaze de Bury's *La Jeunesse de Goethe*, which included his settings of scenes from several of Goethe's plays (both songs and melodramas).[97] This work was never produced in the composer's lifetime, and is sadly among his missing *Nachlass*.

But Meyerbeer's most striking tribute to the theater is the incidental music he provided for his brother Michael's play *Struensee*. This work was especially commissioned by King Friedrich Wilhelm IV, both as a posthumous tribute to the tragically short-lived poet and to honor his much-loved mother, Amalia Beer.[98] The play and its music enjoyed considerable popularity in the German-speaking countries during Meyerbeer's lifetime, while the overture remains his finest orchestral achievement. It was also the king's earnest wish that Meyerbeer set the choruses from Aeschylus's *Eumenides*, but this was a project that he never felt able to undertake.[99]

THE OPERATIC EMPHASIS

Of course, it is as a composer of music drama that Meyerbeer secured his fame, and the depiction of the world of opera is the central focus of all his activities. If his interest in the theater was extraordinary, his involvement with opera was total. He attended every opera and ballet that circumstances would allow, seeing works that had already established themselves as repertory, over and over again (like *Don Giovanni* and *Il Trovatore*).[100] As with the straight theater, the diaries present a whole series of forgotten works which were the current fare of opera houses at the time, from vaudevilles, through *opéras comiques* and *Singspiele,* to *grands opéras*. From his earliest entries in Würzburg (May 1812) to his last days in Paris (January 1864), opera was his very raison d'être. It is fascinating to observe the changing contours of the repertoire over half a century, the establishment of universal favorites, the ubiquity of opera as an art form in even the smallest towns throughout Europe, the fluid and fervent interchange between the operas of France and Germany, the progressive hegemony of Italian opera, the unassailable position of Mozart's principal works from the early nineteenth century, and the growing triumph of Verdi and Wagner. Again, no work was too unimportant to be missed: he saw everything, and traveled distances even to see the works of his avowed enemies (like Wagner's *Tannhäuser* in Hamburg in 1855, and Schumann's *Genoveva* in Weimar in 1855). His insatiable curiosity meant that even in the weary last months of his life he attended Berlioz's *Les Troyens à Carthage* no fewer than eight times.[101]

Accompanying these annals of opera in the diaries are constant details of the creation and production of Meyerbeer's own works. These were at the very heart of the repertory until the First World War. Even afterwards, Germany remained loyal to Meyerbeer until the advent of Nazism: *Les Huguenots* was removed from the stage of the Berlin State Opera by express instructions of Göring in 1933.[102] The geneses of his works are described in detail, and the diaries show Meyerbeer the indefatigable traveler moving among the great operatic centers of Europe, supervising performances of his work.[103] Apart from the detailed accounts of the rehearsals, premières, and first performances of *Le Prophète*,[104] *L'Étoile du Nord*,[105] and *Dinorah*,[106] there are vivid descriptions of his visits to Vienna for *Vielka*[107] and *Der Prophet*,[108] to London for *La Stella del nord*[109] and *Dinorah*,[110] and to Stuttgart for *Der Nordstern*[111] and *Die Wallfahrt nach Ploërmel*.[112] One encounters a host of names (both major and minor) from the world of opera: impresarios, conductors, stage designers and especially singers. Perhaps Meyerbeer's greatest single passion was the human voice, and more than any other subject in his diaries, the strengths and weaknesses of singers and their lyrical and histrionic abilities are a constant source of observation and comment.[113] Also listed scrupulously are approaches from various opera house managements,[114] requests for performing permissions,[115] systems of royalties (especially in France),[116] house practices, rehearsals, and the records and criticism of performances.[117] All this creates a detailed picture of the purpose and practice of opera in the middle decades of the nineteenth century.

Nondramatic Music

Meyerbeer also showed great interest in all other forms of music. His tastes were catholic, and no form of music-making was overlooked in the daily course of events. The diaries present a record of attendance at hundreds of different recitals and concerts that cover the gamut of musical genres. The musical life in Paris and Berlin especially emerges in great detail: his account of the Concerts du Conservatoire in the French capital and the Symphonie-Soirées and recitals by the Domchor in the Prussian, as well as of music-making in London, Vienna, Dresden, and various spa resorts, provides a detailed record of the general repertoire across half a century.

The range of composers mentioned is very extensive, from established masters like Mozart, through a host of almost forgotten names, to vibrant contemporaries like Berlioz. The paramount importance of Beethoven emerges clearly, with his symphonies and string quartets the most regularly recurring objects of Meyerbeer's concertgoing.[118] Mozart follows closely,[119] with the other Viennese masters, Haydn and Schubert, trailing considerably behind. Mendelssohn was by far the most performed of all his contemporaries, with Berlioz, Liszt, and Schumann also well-represented. Once again one notices that Schumann's personal aversion to him did not prevent Meyerbeer from genuinely admiring his music.[120] He also showed a consistent loyalty to and interest in the work of Berlioz and Liszt; even though he was not always able to grasp Berlioz's vision, he was appreciative of his orchestral virtuosity and imagination,[121] but a work like Liszt's Piano Sonata seems to have mystified him.[122] Other once-famous contemporaries appear often, like Spohr and Gade, and he was attentive to lesser figures of the Berlin scene like Dorn, Grell, Redern, Rungenhagen, and Taubert.

One of the most interesting features of musical life in the Prussian capital was the vigorous choral tradition practiced by the Singakademie and by the Domchor. Their repertoire of religious music was exceptional, extending from Palestrina, Lassus, and the Gabriellis, through Schütz, Schröter, Stradella, Eccard, Lotti, Caldara, Jomelli, Marcello, Durante, Fasch, Fioravanti, and Zelter, to contemporaries like Schmidt and Blumner. A recurrent feature of Meyerbeer's experience was the Lent and Easter performances of works like Graun's *Der Tod Jesu*[123] and J. S. Bach's *Passion According to Matthew*[124] which he attended nearly every year. Indeed the perennial return of the Bach *Passion* provides a perspective on the unfolding of the Bach revival, which runs like a strand through Meyerbeer's life. As early as 1834 he was reading Bach cantatas as part of his musical preparation for *Les Huguenots*; in Berlin he constantly attended Bach concerts: his admiration for the Mass in B Minor was overwhelming, and the year before his death he was introduced to the *Passion According to John*.[125] He also heard a surprising amount of Bach's chamber and instrumental music, and he studied the *English Suites* at length.[126] His knowledge and love of Handel was similarly extensive, and he was familiar with ten of the oratorios. He studied *Jephtha*[127] and *Joshua*[128] while he was preparing *Le Prophète*, and loved the *Messiah* all his life long.[129]

MUSICIANS AND SINGERS

Bound up with this intensive experience of the musical life was constant contact with performing musicians. Not only was he approached by numbers of singers seeking his approval, direction, and private coaching (very often in roles from his own operas, like the months of study with Mario in 1838), but other composers and performers sought him out relentlessly in the years of his fame after *Robert le Diable* and *Les Huguenots*. Being a fine pianist himself, he had done the same in his youth, as his visits to E. T. A. Hoffmann,[130] Winter,[131] Salieri,[132] Kalkbrenner,[133] and J. B. Cramer[134] illustrate. He never stopped attending the concerts of the brilliant instrumentalists who so dominated the musical scene of the nineteenth century. It was the age of Paganini and Liszt, both of whom were his personal friends, and virtuoso pianists and violinists were an ever-present feature of his daily experiences; among them were Kéler-Béla, Chéri, Ehrlich, Eitner,

Fränzl, Fumagalli, Herz, Hummel, Jansa, Joachim, Kontski, Laub, Mayseder, Moscheles, the Milanollo sisters, Musard, Pixis, Polledro, Rode, Rosenhain, Rubinstein, Clara Schumann, Singer, and Thalberg. Players, theoreticians, teachers, heads of conservatoires, secretaries of musical societies and musical amateurs were always writing to him and calling on him, and he was the recipient of constant invitations to compose works for special occasions (like the Birmingham Festival), or of honors from various musical institutions in France, Belgium, Russia, England, and Italy. In addition to this, he occupied important consultative and administrative roles in the conservatoires and academic bodies of both Paris[135] and Berlin.[136]

LITERARY CONCERNS

Meyerbeer's diaries reflect the culture of his age and embody the mainstream of the Western European musical tradition. His love of the theater shows him abreast of the literary traditions of his time, an aspect of his intellectual life adumbrated by his wider reading. Meyerbeer's record of the books he read show him to have been an avid reader of all forms of literature, although he does not note his reading nearly so carefully as his operatic, theatrical, and musical activities. The early months of 1831 present a vivid picture of the literary scene in Paris. In the salons of the intelligentsia he met Chateaubriand, [137] and he later recorded reading some of the famous man's books.[138] At the same time he was investigating James Fenimore Cooper's historical romance *The Red Rover*.[139] Regular reading was one of his preoccupations, and he resolved often at New Year's to maintain a daily diet of classical literature. Sometimes he carefully noted down what he was reading, like Goethe's *Wilhelm Meisters Lehrjahre*, one of his favorite books,[140] or Rousseau's *Confessions,* to which he responded in exceptional detail.[141] At other times he read as part of his preparation for his own musico-dramatic composition (Marot's metrical translations of the Psalms for *Les Huguenots*,[142] the Book of Jeremiah[143] and Sir Walter Scott's *Old Mortality*[144] for *Le Prophète*, Camoës's *Os Lusiads*,[145] and Soltikoff's *Voyage dans l'Inde*[146] for *L'Africaine*), or as potential subject matter for musical setting (Lord Byron's *Hebrew Melodies*).[147] As with the plays he saw, he was always assessing the feasibility of operatic adaptation (Fouqué's novella *Das Galgenmännlein*,[148] tales by Musäus,[149] or George Sand's *Le Drac*[150]). Otherwise his interests ranged from novels (Tieck's *Vittoria Accrombona*,[151] Janin's *La Religieuse de Toulouse*[152]), through biography (Eberty's lives of Scott and Byron),[153] history (Schiller's *Geschichte des Abfalls der Niederlände*),[154] natural history (Michelet's bird guide)[155] to political-social commentary (Varnhagen's *Diaries*).[156] Closely related to his biographical and historical interests was his reading in musical literature; Nissen's *Biographie Wolfgang Amadeus Mozarts nach Originalbriefe* appears to have been his favorite book on his favorite composer,[157] but he also mentions Mosel's life of Salieri,[158] Marx's study of Gluck's operas,[159] and Oettinger's comic novel based on the life of Rossini.[160]

MUSICAL CRITICISM

The analysis of Meyerbeer's musical reading leads to the controversial topic of music criticism. Much of the composer's attention and energy was devoted to close scrutiny of the musical press. He read Berlioz's *Traité d'Instrumentation*,[161] and consulted Halévy's musical writing for a wider discussion on the debate about the lowering of the pitch of the tuning fork.[162] Indeed, he was always well-informed about the latest critical publications: Griepenkerl's *Die Oper der Gegenwart*[163] and Fétis's *Biographie universelle des musiciens*[164] are typical examples of new critical or standard works of musical reference he investigated.

But, of course, it was musical journalism that was notoriously a source of anxiety, if not anguish, for him. The relation between Meyerbeer and the musical press remains to this day an unresolved and inadequately investigated issue. Critical responses to his work had been divided since the appearance of *Robert le Diable*, but the sensitivity of his reactions can perhaps be symbolically related back to 1838 and his encounter with the Escudier brothers (the founders of *La France musicale*), who, in the guise of friends, interviewed him for an article to appear in their periodical.[165] When this biographical article appeared it was a barely disguised attack on the composer, and initiated a critical stance that was thereafter maintained with ideological consistency. For whatever reason, the Escudiers remained inimical, supporting Verdi and Italian interests, as opposed to Meyerbeer, Schlesinger, and Schlesinger's review *La Gazette musicale,* which was devoted to German music.[166] Meyerbeer would marvel when, later in life, Marie Escudier suddenly went out of his way to show himself friendly, presumably in order to further the particular interests of his pianist-wife, Rosa Kastner.[167] An intense suspicion and fearfulness of the press became second nature to Meyerbeer. He experienced hurt, or even feelings of betrayal, in dealings with Ludwig Rellstab,[168] Alexandre Dumas,[169] Hector Berlioz,[170] Henri Blaze de Bury,[171] and, most famously, Heinrich Heine whose tortured relations with the composer are a subject all their own.[172] Heine was initially devoted to Meyerbeer's artistic interests—or at least appeared to be, since he knew little about music and cared even less for it; but when the composer refused endless requests for money, his benevolence turned to deadly enmity,[173] and resulted in vitriolic attacks on Meyerbeer, both in his critical writings and in his later poetry. He leveled charges of bribery, egoism, and manipulation that have damaged the composer's reputation to this day.[174]

Heine was himself Jewish, and his animosity was motivated by personal envy and disappointment. Critical hostility to Meyerbeer on purely anti-Semitic grounds is a more sinister matter altogether. Because of it he suffered distress from men he regarded as friends (like Liszt),[175] from men he had most generously assisted in their artistic careers (like Wagner),[176] and from complete strangers who launched racially biased attacks from a position of supposed intellectual integrity (like Schlüter).[177]

THE PRESS

The status of Meyerbeer as man and musician was and remains a critical bone of contention. His vivid, powerful style and overwhelming success have always had a provocative effect on the press. While not given to answering allegations made against him in the papers, he was determined not allow the power of journalism to go unchecked. He understood the damaging and wasteful power of malevolent journalism, and was determined, if not to beat the press at their own game, then at least to try and understand how journalism worked, and to use it to his own advantage.[178] The diaries show him in constant touch with critical opinion in the papers: his agent Gouin in Paris, and his secretary Burguis in Berlin assembled all the latest press releases about him, his music, and his family. The composer himself did his best to maintain cordial relationships with influential critics: if Castil-Blaze was an inveterate foe on the Parisian scene over the years,[179] then Meyerbeer developed a very different association with his son, Blaze de Bury, and nurtured cordial connections with important critical figures like Girardin and his literary wife.[180] He was glad to use for his own advantage any opportunities that arose for reconciliation with a hostile journalist; thus, he exercised his proverbial diplomacy with the Dresden critic Banck,[181] and he actively promoted a reconciliation with the husband-and-wife team of the Mundts.[182] He was certainly not averse to using his great wealth to facilitate positive relationships (like helping the Viennese critic Zellner in his difficulties),[183] or supporting particular journals by subscription.[184]

One of the most persistent myths about Meyerbeer is that he regularly bribed the press, and the diaries now make it possible to investigate the allegation.[185] He was remarkably frank about his financial transactions, and as always, the situation is not as simple as the popular perception has had it. There is limited evidence of regular payments to two critics.

The first of these is the Parisian writer Pier-Angelo Fiorentino,[186] whose articles were more satirical social essays than musical critiques. Meyerbeer, for some reason, seems to have felt the need to secure the cooperation of this second-rate journalist—and not necessarily out of fear of his pen. Fiorentino seems to have agreed to act as a kind of agent for the composer: for example, when he wished to discourage performance of *Il Crociato in Egitto* at the Théâtre Italien in 1860, he employed the active influence of Fiorentino behind the scenes.[187] It nonetheless remains unclear why Meyerbeer made so many large payments to Fiorentino[188] when there were obviously many more important figures whom he could more appropriately have "bought" (if that is what he was actually doing).

The other journalist was Jules Leconte, the Paris correspondent of *L'Indépendance belge* and a littérateur,[189] whom Meyerbeer encountered at the home of Brandus,[190] and often met socially. The instances here of some sort of subsidy are far fewer and the specific reasons less clear: they were either to encourage him in his literary career, or to secure a friendly voice in the Belgian press.[191]

Meyerbeer's alleged attempts to win over the critics by entertaining them to expensive meals have also gone down in legend.[192] The diaries do contain many examples of these apparently notorious occasions, but very few of them, if any, can be construed as a form of bribery. He hosted most of these meals in the Hôtel des Princes in the rue Richelieu, where he regularly stayed in Paris, and most of them were arranged to celebrate the advent of some friend (like Paganini when he came to Paris in 1831),[193] or to bring together a certain group of friends or collaborators,[194] or to express his thanks for services rendered (like the relays of supper parties for members of the orchestra after the premières of *L'Étoile du Nord*[195] and *Le Pardon de Ploërmel*[196]). He also gave such dinners in Berlin, and there they played a more obviously important function in the life of a wealthy man with social, artistic, and family commitments. A good example is his welcome of Scribe to Berlin in 1852.[197]

Perhaps Meyerbeer's most interesting and important contribution to the history of journalism, and the best evidence of his desire to control or influence it in some way, was the role he played in organizing what can only be called press conferences. These seem to have emerged from an intention he shared with the directors of the Paris Opéra (Duponchel and Roqueplan) to clarify certain issues before the première of *Le Prophète*,[198] and before the first Viennese performance of *Der Nordstern*. Here the main issue was free access of journalists to the dress rehearsal.[199] In this instance, Meyerbeer's role as an intermediary between the press and the ministerial/theater management represents a high point in his peculiarly modern media awareness, and illustrates the exercise of his patient diplomacy in public relations.

NEGATIVE REPUTATION: HEINE, SCHUMANN, WAGNER, AND MENDELSSOHN

It is the explosive combination of journalism, Judaism, and nationalism that encapsulates the essential problems that have so seriously dogged Meyerbeer's reputation, both as man and artist, in his lifetime, and even more especially in the twentieth century. He was a wealthy, successful German Jew whose operas exercised a cosmopolitan appeal until the 1930s; his most active and dangerous enemies happened to be three artists who, whether accurately or not, appear to capture the very essence of "high German Art," and certainly continue to enjoy the status of folk popularity: Heinrich Heine, Robert Schumann, and Richard Wagner. All three were masters of their art, all three were enthusiastic writers and propagandists, and all three harbored an enduring hatred of Meyerbeer. The situation is rich in irony. The Jewish Heine, one of Germany's most perfect lyric poets, so satirically perceptive of injustice and human fallibility, was himself a purveyor of national anxieties and personal prejudice;[200] Wagner, who aspired to a universal world order redeemed by love, and who may well have had a Jewish father,[201] was the high priest of German nationalism and a spiritual father of Nazism; and Schumann, who cared so much for artistic integrity and justice,[202] was blinded by an obsessive personal and racial prejudice, perhaps a symptom of his congenital mental instability.[203] The first two resented Meyerbeer's reluctance to finance them indefinitely, and Schumann would probably have felt very differently about Meyerbeer, whom he never even met, if Meyerbeer had not been rich and famous, and the master of a dramatic art form that had always eluded Schumann.

The case of Mendelssohn, likewise an implacable adversary of Meyerbeer,[204] was different and is more difficult to understand. He was also of a wealthy Israelite family and also enjoyed unqualified success, but perhaps his Christianized respectability, and his sanitized, nondramatic music was really too bland to disturb German artistic sensibilities, or to offend national idealism.[205] Ironically Mendelssohn appeared to despise Meyerbeer as much as the other three: perhaps their social situation—so similar in many ways,[206] so different in others[207]—and their divergent artistic attitudes were a source of inverted rivalry, even jealousy, for Mendelssohn.[208]

In any case the pity is that all these adversaries wrote negatively about Meyerbeer, and that these opinions, whether intrinsically valuable or not, have become the standard points of critical reference about him: they have entered the popular canon of good taste and, as such, are quoted ad nauseam in any account of Meyerbeer's life or art.[209] Meyerbeer's reputation has been severely damaged, if not ruined, in the minds of critics and the public by the negative comments of these four revered artists: Heine's satirical verse, Schumann's diatribe against *Les Huguenots*[210] (which includes his notorious quip, "I place him with Franconi's circus people"), Wagner's dictum "effects without causes"[211] (also the nasty observation that he was "a Jew banker who happened to write music"), and Mendelssohn's prissy letter from Paris in 1831 inveighing against the immorality of the Parisian stage and the "heartlessness" of the music of *Robert le Diable*.[212]

The situation has not been helped by Berlioz, another unassailable hero of modern musical political correctness. He was in regular and often close contact with Meyerbeer, chose the latter as his sponsor when elected to the Légion d'Honneur,[213] and enjoyed his help and hospitality on two artistic journeys to Berlin.[214] Meyerbeer's interest and concern extended even to Berlioz's mistress, Marie

Recio.[215] But this did not prevent Berlioz from adopting a decidedly ambiguous, even contemptuous, attitude towards Meyerbeer, for example when he praised Verdi's "gentlemanly" bluntness at the expense of Meyerbeer's "snakelike flexibility," a weighted and emotive phrase, ever since quoted as the decisive confirmation of Meyerbeer's alleged insincerity.[216]

However, it is surely very significant that the enlightened Liszt, who loved and championed Schumann and Wagner and Berlioz, was big-hearted enough to love Meyerbeer too. To the end Liszt delighted in his music,[217] and famously quarreled with Schumann and Wagner about their intransigent prejudice toward Meyerbeer.[218] Unfortunately, the journalistic power of all these artists, their caustic critical articulateness, the appeal of their own aesthetic achievements, and their prestige in the European (especially German) pantheon, have damaged Meyerbeer incalculably. Only a profoundly fresh reassessment of the man and his art will change this, and enable a truer appreciation of his greatness to emerge.

ANTI-SEMITISM

The Jewish question has had a general significance that reaches beyond the reputation of a single artist. For Meyerbeer it was no doubt the determinative factor, if not trauma, of his life.[219] He would later write to Heine: "What can one do? . . . not all the waters of the bath of baptism can restore the little piece of foreskin which is robbed from us on the eighth day of our existence; and whoever has not bled from this operation on the ninth, will nonetheless bleed from it all his life long, even beyond death itself."[220] The circumstances of his origins affected his very conception of self-identity, and not necessarily as some psychological compulsion. With his large nose and dark complexion, Meyerbeer had a distinctly Semitic appearance, and it was the cause of prejudiced observation. As a youth he was personally rejected by people who did not know him: the mockery of two girls in a tavern in 1812, and his wounded reaction, prefigured a lifelong situation ("When will I eventually learn to accept peacefully what I have so long known to be inevitable?").[221] Even when a famous composer, he could be treated crudely by people ignorant of his identity: in 1841 he recorded an instance of racial insult from fellow diners in a Heidelberg inn: "There at a neighboring table . . . I heard an instance of *Richesse* [anti-Semitism] directed against me personally."[222] Most disturbing was the ostracization by elements of the establishment, at the height of his social prestige. In 1847, for example, at Franzensbad, General von Hannecken invited all the Prussians at the resort to a dinner in honor of the king's birthday, but pointedly excluded Meyerbeer, even though he was a Berliner, a celebrated composer, and *Generalmusikdirektor* to the royal household. The action can only be construed as an unkind social slight, motivated by anti-Semitism ("It is the same old story . . .").[223] The situation was enough to undermine his self-confidence, or sense of social standing. He always saw the matter clearly for what it was, and prophetically for what it would be. The words he wrote to his brother Michael in September 1818 reveal the depth of his perception, and quite justifiable suspicions about the magnitude of popular prejudice, and the uncertainty of social attitudes, even in the manifestation of good will: "Never forget the iron word *Richesse*. From individual to individual the word can be forgotten for a while (although not for long), but by the collective public never, since it requires only one who remembers to bring it back into general consciousness again."[224]

It must be remembered that anti-Semitism in Germany, France, and Italy drastically worsened in the later nineteenth century, with the inexorable rise of jingoism and the emergence of harbingers of racial hatred, like Georg von Schönerer in the Austria of the 1880s, who proposed solutions to the "Jewish problem" that would find their logical culmination in the horrors of the Holocaust.[225] The Franco-Prussian War (1870) marks a frightening watershed in the changing perceptions of nationalism in both Germany and France. The Dreyfus affair[226] and the pseudo-philosophical racial theories of Houston Stewart Chamberlain[227] punctuate a deteriorating condition in the psyche of a civilization that would need to pass through the traumatic knowledge of Auschwitz and Treblinka before the problem could be adequately grasped and honestly confronted. It must never be forgotten that Richard Wagner was the author of the notorious tract *Das Judentum in der Musik* (1850), which distinguishes between "Aryan" and "Jewish" music,[228] and the teasing question remains: did Wagner hate Meyerbeer because he was a Jew, or did he hate Jews because Meyerbeer happened to be one?[229] Racialism and aesthetics seem commingled in the minds of many, just as Meyerbeer's wealth and success cloud perception of the man and his achievement.[230] It is interesting to speculate that if *Le Prophète* had been written at Theresienstadt by a struggling composer living in the shadow of death, the work would no doubt be honored now as *entartete Musik*, and the whole of his oeuvre long since committed to subsidized recording.[231]

RELIGION AND ATTITUDE

While Meyerbeer remained faithful to Judaism all his life, he did not practice orthodoxy. His father, Juda Herz Beer, was a leading member of the Reform Movement in the early years of the century;[232] his mother was prominent in the Jewish community and social circles, and decorated for her charitable work.[233] His brother Wilhelm was also a valued member of Berlin society, and gained considerable civic influence.[234] Like all civilized Prussian Jews until the advent of Nazism, Meyerbeer regarded his religion (at a conscious level, anyway) as a denominational rather than racial one. He was a Freemason[235] and open to all appeals from his coreligionists; he was interested in the presence and activity of other Jews, but also apparently quite open and accepting of Christianity. He celebrated Christmas with his children, attended Easter musical celebrations, funerals, and other memorial services, both Catholic and Protestant, in Paris and Berlin, and accepted his daughter Blanca's conversion to Catholicism with equanimity.[236]

The recurrent subject matter and themes of his operas also suggest an intensely religious sensibility.[237] Perhaps it is the frank consideration of matters of faith and affiliation, with the appropriation of a variety of Christian symbolism, that makes his operas extremely uncomfortable for many. This may also be one of the principal reasons why the strong Jewish element in the international musical scene has done nothing to revive, restore, promote, or even reassess his musical reputation (that and the ironically defensive stratagem of avoiding anyone of artistically pariah status).[238] And yet Wagner, who did so much to promote such depth of anti-Semitic feeling, is revered, constantly performed, and credited with impeccable good taste.[239]

HISTORICAL QUESTIONS: THE PRUSSIAN STATE AND THE LIBERAL IDEAL

There can be little doubt that popular perceptions of Meyerbeer's critical fortunes reflect interesting sociohistorical attitudes as much as, if not more than, aesthetic ones. This is particularly true of the ambiguities associated with the Prussian State. Frederick the Great had established a polity characterized by Enlightened ideals of good government, but it needed the advent of Napoleon to disseminate the Revolutionary ideas of liberty, equality, and fraternity—at least as far as the Jews were concerned. Certainly Prussia's defeat at the Battle of Jena (14 October 1806) impelled Friedrich Wilhelm III to confront a massive programme of reform and modernization.[240] What Karl Freiherr von Stein and Fürst Karl von Hardenberg accomplished in a few years through social, educational, juridical, and agricultural restructuring remains one of the miracles of modern European history, and it opened Prussia to the genuine intellectual enlightenment heralded by Immanuel Kant and Moses Mendelssohn.[241] Preeminent among the reforms was the emancipation of the Jews,[242] and Meyerbeer's parents were at the forefront of enthusiastic Jewish response to new developments in trust and progress, personally noticed by the monarch, and religiously, socially, and culturally prominent in the new "Athens on the Spree" the king sought to found. The new Berlin was to symbolize the efflorescence of much that was noble and commendable in Western thinking and practice.[243] Political and cultural enlightenment was to flourish until the 1870s and 1880s, when the wars against Denmark,[244] Austria,[245] and France,[246] and the tragic death of the Emperor Friedrich after a reign of only three months,[247] heralded the advent of an aggressive and ugly nationalism that was to cost the world dearly, with consequences of which affect us still.[248]

The courts of Friedrich Wilhelm III, Friedrich Wilhelm IV, and Wilhelm I, especially their exceptional ministers like the Humboldt brothers, represented the best in Prussian thinking and liberal idealism. These monarchs showed no racial or religious prejudice; all three held the Beer family in the highest regard. The young Meyer Beer[249] knew the future King Friedrich Wilhelm IV as a child[250] and was an intimate of his court. He also knew the circles of his brother, Prince Wilhelm (later king and then emperor), Princess Augusta, and Prince Karl at Glienecke. Meyerbeer's intimacy with the Prussian royal family is a matter of almost daily record in his Berlin life from the 1840s to the 1860s. Their friendship and love for the composer was sustained and genuine:[251] many of Meyerbeer's works were the direct result of royal commands, and much of his artistic career, including his freedom to write and travel, was affected by the often burdensome honor of his royal appointment to the post of *Generalmusikdirektor* in 1842, and then to the directorate of the Court Concerts, a function he performed until the last months of his life. These positions meant that he was constantly at the palace and in personal contact with the royal family. Indeed, the chronicle of the Court Concerts provides a fascinating perspective on aspects of court life and musical taste and practice in the middle decades of the nineteenth century.[252]

The fact that Meyerbeer was chosen to write the *Krönungsmarsch*, played at the coronation of King Wilhelm I at Königsberg in 1861, says all that can be said about Meyerbeer's social and artistic triumph in the old Prussia. Ten years later the scene and atmosphere had changed irrevocably: the new march for the new emperor of the Second Reich, proclaimed in the Hall of Mirrors at Versailles on 18 January 1871 in the face of a defeated France, was composed by Richard Wagner.[253]

A similar situation applied in France, where, in the nineteenth century, Meyerbeer was the most performed composer at the principal opera house, the Paris Opéra, the veritable image of the nation. The fact that he was both German and Jewish did not matter in France for most of the century. But openness and tolerance noticeably waned in the wake of the Franco-Prussian War,[254] which ironically established a German (actually Wagnerian) intellectual hegemony among French musicians, the most "self-respecting" of whom turned away from opera and preferred to concentrate on instrumental music.[255] After World War I the situation deteriorated disastrously, and Meyerbeer disappeared entirely from the hearts and minds of the nation who had raised him on the shield of adulation,[256] the nation whose legends and history had found perfect expression[257] for nearly a century[258] in the operas of a Prussian Jew.[259] The Restoration, the July Monarchy, the Second Republic, and the Second Empire, for all their political differences, had provided a positive context for the Revolutionary-Napoleonic ideals of emancipation and fraternity, while avoiding the corrosion of a narrow nationalism.[260] Napoleon's vision was of a united Europe. Meyerbeer, the alien, could be regarded as a national institution;[261] he was admired by Louis Philippe[262] and treated as a personal friend of Napoleon III and the Empress Eugénie.[263] Anxiety about the production of *L'Africaine* was a matter of enduring ministerial concern for more than a decade,[264] and the composer's death before its première a cause for national mourning.

Emancipation and liberalism, or liberalization, were thus major determinants in Meyerbeer's life. Without any self-conscious political commentary, or even undue political perception, he responded to the climate of his times and those great events which were portentous for everyone. His travels in 1812–13 could not escape the final showdown with Napoleon, and in 1815 he witnessed the return of Louis XVIII to Paris. But most remarkable was his firsthand experience of the 1848 Revolutions: he lived through the events in Paris, responded to the disturbing reports from Berlin, and was caught up in the periphery of the June uprising in Prague. The dismissal of the liberal ministers and the crisis for emergent democracy that ensued in Prussia (18 March 1862)[265] elicited the clearest statement of Meyerbeer's political concerns and ideals: "I have copied out Uhland's 'Gebet eines Württembergers' . . . and will compose it when there is an elected return to the constitutional path" (19 November 1862). These developments were indeed of the most serious consequence for Prussia. They signaled deleterious changes in the body politic and heralded a resurgent militarism that would lead inexorably to 1914 and 1939.

A LIFE OF WANDERING

The story of Meyerbeer's life, as the diaries show, is a tale of two cities, Berlin and Paris. His artistic triumph and legendary status were achieved in Paris, and he will always be remembered as the chief exponent of French *grand opéra*. But he never abandoned Prussia, especially his home city of Berlin.[266] Indeed, it was of the utmost importance for him that he should repeat there the artistic successes won in the French capital (which he did, albeit in a minor key), and that he should be socially and professionally accepted there as man and artist. The whole complicated nexus of motivation, wealth, professional fluency, and artistic and social success were drawn together in his friendship and high office with the Prussian royal family. Contrary to popular belief, Meyerbeer never lived permanently in Paris; he only rented rooms there. His home was in Berlin. He returned after the death of his father, after his marriage, and especially after the triumphs of *Robert le Diable* and *Les Huguenots,* which gave him international artistic prestige.[267]

Meyerbeer's whole later career was determined by the constant and regular movement between these two poles of his existence. The rattle of his coach and, after 1841, the clatter of his train journeys became the underlying rhythm of his life. He lived in each city with an energy and fervor characteristic of both his personality and his music. The diaries record his activities in Paris and Berlin in such detail that it conjures up the intellectual and artistic life of both cities, and indeed of the whole period. His journeys were for his art, and his restless enthusiasm also took him to many other major European centers. His regular trips to Dresden and Vienna, and to a lesser extent London and Stuttgart, add further dimensions to the cultural evocation of the times. His Italian sojourn (January–March 1856) is intensely interesting to the historian, as is his retreat in Nice (December 1857–March 1858). Meyerbeer's straightforward and unselfconscious observations provide a tissue of details on modes of transport, the nature of nineteenth-century travel, the climate and weather, the kind of money used, the quality of inns, and various local customs. He combines with these observations descriptions that conjure up vividly the appearance of road and landscape, particularly voyages along the Danube[268] and Elbe,[269] past the lakes and mountains of the Salzkammergut,[270] and along the Ligurian coast[271] and the French Riviera.[272] He provides vignettes of German cities like Hanover,[273] Magdeburg,[274] Nuremberg,[275] and Munich,[276] and chronicles unique episodes in special places (like attending the lord mayor's banquet in London),[277] and visits to resorts, museums, and exhibitions.[278] All this cumulatively fleshes out the events of his life and creates something approaching a chronicle of the period.

QUESTIONS OF HEALTH

Another constant aspect of Meyerbeer's traveling are the various health resorts and spas that he visited regularly from the 1830s onwards. This stems directly from his ill-health, another source of rumor and speculation. The popular perception (assiduously developed by Heine in some of his most waspishly satirical late poems)[279] is that Meyerbeer was an impossible hypochondriac. But was he? The recurring symptoms of his alimentary complaint first described in January 1831[280] are consistent with medical understanding of a chronic disease like ulcerative colitis. The illness is hardly mentioned until the 1840s, when it becomes more recurrent, while during the 1850s[281] and 1860s[282] it reaches moments of acute crisis. But there are whole months, even years, when he seems to have been free of it. It appears to have been a genuine physiological affliction, no doubt exacerbated by a highly nervous psychological disposition. The condition and its proposed treatment (the favorite nineteenth-century panacea of "taking the waters") necessitated virtually annual visits to a gamut of European resorts, not only Spa (virtually his summer home in the 1850s), but also Alexisbad,[283] Franzensbad,[284] Bad Gastein,[285] Bad Ischl,[286] Boulogne,[287] Dieppe,[288] Nice,[289] Wiesbaden, Schwalbach and Bad Ems.[290]

The evocation of Spa is of particular interest.[291] This little town, buried in the greenery of the Ardennes, identified deeply with Meyerbeer's loyalty to the place and responded gratefully by building a famous memorial to the composer, an honor not extended to him by even his native city. Spa is also fascinating because of its mixture of French and Belgian elements, reflecting in miniature the society and theatrical life of Paris and Brussels. It was a place frequented by celebrities, and Meyerbeer inevitably met elements of Parisian society transposed from the metropolitan milieu. He invariably socialized with the author Jules Janin, as well as with Fétis and other visiting officials. His descriptions preserve the record of many other charming local people, places, and customs—like the kindly director of the casino, Davelouis,[292] the donkey attendant Henri Dedoyard,[293] members of the local wind band,[294] the little playhouse,[295] the evenings of chamber music,[296] and a songbird competition.[297]

More serious is the perspective afforded on nineteenth-century attitudes to medicine and healing. Many of Meyerbeer's water cures are recorded in some detail, as are his dealings with doctors, especially Dr. Schönlein, the composer's preferred physician, even when the latter left Berlin for Bamberg. Ill-health, or fear of illness, certainly haunted the Meyerbeer family, probably because of the tragic infantile deaths of the first two children, Eugénie[298] and Alfred.[299] Any hint of sickness provoked the specter of bereavement,[300] and there is an elegy weaving its way through the diaries as Meyerbeer witnessed the deaths of his father, his firstborn children, his three brothers, and his mother; in the later years this becomes a threnody, as so many of his close friends and colleagues (preeminently his confidant, Gouin,[301] and his principal collaborator, Scribe)[302] died. The evocation of encroaching debility and ill-health intensify after the première of *Dinorah,* which seems to have seriously exhausted him. Swollen feet, tinnitus, failing eyesight, hernia, and the deterioration of his bowel complaint, with the essentially ineffectual handling of the medical situation,[303] give the last years of the diaries an air of weariness, and a sometimes oppressive atmosphere.

FAMILY MATTERS

The subject of ill-health leads directly on to one of the great enigmas of Meyerbeer's life, his wife Minna Mosson (1804–86), who was his first cousin, the daughter of his mother's sister. He married her quite suddenly in 1826 after his father's death, as if to fulfill his duty in becoming the head of a Jewish family.[304] Although the union hardly began as a love match, it certainly appears to have become one: his devotion to Minna was enduring and constantly expressed. Visitors to the Meyerbeer home testified to its love and affection, the warmth and closeness shared between the parents and the three daughters who survived their first two unfortunate siblings.[305] The deaths of the latter were no doubt an enduring trauma for Minna, whose own health seems to have taken a permanent turn for the worse in the mid-1830s. While supportive of her husband's great fame, she could not adapt to life in Paris, and preferred always to live in Berlin, in her own *gemütlich* German world of family and friends.[306] After 1839, she does not appear to have returned to Paris in her husband's lifetime, not even for the glittering premières of his operas. The correspondence, however, shows her to have been alert, intelligent, abreast of every development in Meyerbeer's artistic career, and often functioning as an intermediary for him in difficult or sensitive negotiations (as with Caroline von Weber).[307] Indeed, after Meyerbeer's death, she had to oversee the editing and production of *L'Africaine*, which she entrusted to Fétis.

In the 1840s Minna began yearly pilgrimages to the watering places of Europe in a vain attempt to cure her unspecified illness: Carl Baermann regarded her as having a weakness of the chest, and doomed to an early death;[308] later the problem appears to have been gynecological.[309] Nonetheless, despite all appearances, she outlived her husband by ten years and died at the fine old age of eighty-two. There appears to have been a wide degree of independence in the marriage. The couple lived apart from each other for a large, sometimes the greater, part of the year. Meyerbeer enjoyed the freedom of being an itinerant artist, but always maintained the most dutiful and tender correspondence with his wife, and always returned to the bosom of his loving family. During Minna's prolonged absence at Interlaken in 1846, he wrote her over twenty letters in the space of a few weeks, and had to take on himself the burden of the whole domestic scene, including the deteriorating mental and physical condition of his mother-in-law and the direction of his eldest daughter's education.[310] He needed to keep a Berlin housekeeper (Bertha Arndt) to maintain his household during his wife's prolonged absences. He became used to acting on his own, and Minna did not accompany him to any official, social, or theatrical functions.[311] This role was gradually assumed by his daughters as they became older.[312] But the well-being and safety of his family was a constant concern for Meyerbeer, especially the serious illness of his daughter Caecilie in 1848, during the preparations for the première of *Le Prophète*.[313] There are only hints of any actual tension between Giacomo and Minna, as when he felt the burden of her long absences,[314] or in the debate in 1860 about the necessity of maintaining their Berlin home at 6a Pariser Platz.[315] Occasionally there are glimpses of a true domestic happiness, as in the vignette of the composer's special journey to Vienna to celebrate with Minna their twenty-fifth wedding anniversary,[316] or his sojourn in Bad Ischl in July–August 1848 where he completed *Le Prophète*, or the months in Nice (December 1857–March 1858), which includes the touching episode of Minna's long, lonely journey from the resort to Berlin and back in order to be present at Blanca's confinement.[317]

Meyerbeer's domestic circle was thus a strange amalgam of touching devotion and determined individualism expressed in the prolonged absences in pursuit of either the artistic life, or in Minna's case, elusive (illusive?) cures. Perhaps this was her way of adjusting to life with a famous composer who lived principally for his art.[318]

The three daughters appear to have been gracious and charming, and educated with all the cosmopolitanism and diplomacy of their illustrious father. The eldest, Blanca (1830–96), evinced a high-spiritedness that was a source of concern to Meyerbeer, especially when he was shown her youthful diary.[319] Her independence of mind found expression in her conversion to Catholicism (in spite of the shock this would cause her formidable grandmother, Amalia).[320] Her marriage to the Prussian officer and gentleman Baron Emanuel von Korff was a sign of her family's social prestige,[321] but the financial and legal problems caused by the young man's gambling was of profound concern to Meyerbeer in the late 1850s,[322] and introduces the only real note of domestic drama into the composer's otherwise peaceful family circle.[323] His obvious joy in his grandson, Fritz von Korff, seemed to make up for any distress, though.[324]

The second daughter, Caecilie (1837–1931) seems to have inherited her parents' disposition to chronic ill-health; she was suddenly struck down by a wasting illness that seemed to have potentially serious consequences (perhaps it was a type of anorexia nervosa?).[325] Ironically, though, she was to outlive her other sisters. In 1869 she married the Austrian diplomat Freiherr Andrian zu Werburg; her son, a friend of Hugo von Hoffmannsthal, became director of the Burgtheater in 1918. Caecilie became something of a legend in her later years and died only in her advanced old age.[326]

Meyerbeer's delight in the affection of his youngest daughter, Cornelie (1842–1922), is very touching,[327] and his efforts to shield her from the relentless importunings of her many suitors (rather like the agitated Dr. Bartolo in *The Barber of Seville*) adds a rare note of humor to the domestic dimension of the diaries.[328] Cornelie would eventually marry the court painter Gustav Richter,[329] and, in time, the onerous duty of preserving the *Nachlass* would fall to her and her children.

On the whole, the wider family was also a benign and gentle circle. Meyerbeer was always devoted to his brothers; his words written to Michael Beer in September 1818 reveal an almost passionate devotion that was posthumously sustained in his loving work on the tragedy *Struensee*. The second brother, Wilhelm, who effectively became the head of the family in Berlin, distinguished himself on active service during the War of Liberation, and subsequently achieved great personal prestige as an astronomer, businessman, financier, and local politician.[330] He was devoted to his brother's fame; his premature illness and death were a great blow for Meyerbeer's interests.[331] Unlike his brother's family, all Wilhelm's children remained Jewish and married into the world of high finance.

Holding all together was the matriarch, Amalia Beer, who outlived all her sons, except her eldest; her presence, strength, and intelligence were perhaps the greatest single source of personal support enjoyed by the composer.[332] Her longevity is a happy exception in his domestic scene, and meant that he survived her by only ten years.[333]

Meyerbeer's wistful little aside during his visit to Genoa in February 1856, recalling the last time he, his parents, and his brothers had all been together as a family,[334] is a touching moment in a life that sought relief in work and tried to channel all grief into fervent artistic activity.[335]

FRIENDSHIP AND HONOR

Meyerbeer's propensity to friendship is another characteristic emerging from his diaries: he certainly inspired considerable loyalty and devotion in the hearts of several men. After Minna, the most enigmatic personality who played a central role in his life was his confidant and *homme d'affaires* in Paris, the obscure postal official Louis Gouin. He acted as Meyerbeer's agent in every way during the composer's long absences from Paris, exercising the power of attorney and keeping a close eye on every aspect of his artistic interests there, with all the intrigues and politics that this implied. He reported on opinions and the changing scene at the Paris Opéra, administered the royalties deriving from the operas, and acted on Meyerbeer's behalf in negotiations with Scribe, the Opéra management, and various attorneys. Their correspondence provides one of the most detailed accounts of the inner world of opera in the Paris of these decades.[336] Gouin seems to have been entirely self-effacing and unacquisitive in his devotion to Meyerbeer's interests.

Another friend of similar loyalty and dedication was the Viennese lawyer and littérateur, Dr. Joseph Bacher, who came into Meyerbeer's life before and after the production of *Vielka* in 1847,[337] and thereafter devoted himself to the composer both as friend and artistic agent. Karl Kaskel in Dresden[338] and the critics Charles Grüneisen[339] and James William Davison[340] in London were similarly dedicated, if to a lesser extent. After Gouin's death in 1856, the publisher Brandus took over his role on Meyerbeer's behalf.[341] The famous playwright and librettist Scribe was not only his principal collaborator, but also seems to have been his friend, although he was too busy and independent an artist himself to have developed undue personal involvement.

The man in Berlin who retained Meyerbeer's greatest trust and admiration was the famous naturalist and privy councillor Alexander von Humboldt, a devoted friend to the Beer family and to the composer personally.[342] Meyerbeer turned to him on innumerable occasions for special presentation of his particular concerns and requests to the king, and he remained a beacon of idealism and disinterested graciousness on the Prussian scene.[343]

Meyerbeer's friendships included other composers and artists, like Carl Maria von Weber, most famously,[344] and Heine, most painfully.[345] The composer's dealings with the poet reveal his great capacity for forgiveness, and his visit to the sick and decrepit Heine, after all the guile shown him by the latter, is very touching.[346]

The diaries record many deeds of immense kindness, contradicting another myth about Meyerbeer's alleged meanness. These stories persist and are tirelessly repeated, even in the latest writings about him.[347] What is clear is that Meyerbeer was a restrained man. In spite of his great personal wealth and huge artistic success, he lived with Spartan simplicity, eating frugally when alone,[348] maintaining a discreet wardrobe, invariably dressing in simple black suits, renting modest lodgings in Paris as close to the opera houses as possible, and eschewing owning his own carriage. He was an astute businessman, drawing up precise contracts with his artistic collaborators, theater managements, and publishers, keeping records of his artistic income, and separate cash-books of expenditure, carefully controlling his fortune by financial advisers and agents,[349] providing his children with their own accounts and making provision for their future. He exercised discretion in his financial allowances to them[350] and in his choice of gifts for his family.[351]

While Meyerbeer was jealous of his artistic achievements, and concerned about the acknowledgment of this in the many orders and honors he received throughout his life, he did not pursue social preferment for its own sake. The knighthood bestowed on him by the king of Württemberg carried automatic elevation to the nobility, but he never sought to use this, and never added the *von* to his surname.[352] The amassing of honors was not an end in itself, and he did not clutch at the honorary doctorate the University of Cambridge wished to bestow on him, when, for reasons of health, he was unable to attend the degree ceremony.[353] Early in his life he himself observed: "Nothing is more distasteful to me than pushing for higher social status."[354] Being a man of wealth and a composer of renown, the only just and suitable acknowledgment could be the recognition of his artistic worth and influence. He refused to be treated as a lucky amateur or a deferential professional craftsman. In his breathtaking refusal of gifts (jeweled snuff boxes) from both the emperor of Austria[355] and the king of Württemberg,[356] he made a statement about the role and meaning of the artist in society. The age of patronage was gone forever. This process had begun with Beethoven's unconventional social attitudes; and Meyerbeer's actions, in their own way, were just as radical. He too assumed a special social superiority based on purely artistic grounds, as was evinced even more provocatively in the behavior of Liszt, Berlioz, and Wagner.

It is extraordinary how genuine modesty and self-denial can be confused with hypocrisy and parsimony, especially when the record of thoughtful generosity to others is incontrovertible. At no possible social or material gain to himself, Meyerbeer made regular financial gifts to a number of former associates or destitute artists—the old Viennese businessman Sina;[357] the aged composer Gyrowetz;[358] the hapless poetess Helmine von Chezy,[359] the blind author Lyser,[360] and his old Italian librettist, Gaetano Rossi.[361] His support for the latter amounted to paying him a pension, while he also agreed to help maintain Dr. Bacher in an institution after his friend suffered a mental breakdown.[362] Other gestures, like his spontaneous acts of charity to poor French[363] and Austrian[364] children, those in need,[365] or his annual alms for both the Jewish and Christian poor of Munich on the anniversary of Michael Beer's death,[366] further attest to an exceptional personal compassion.[367]

Meyerbeer's diaries reveal an abstinent man of simple tastes, whose life was devoted to art: the propagation of his own music, and the unstinting contemplation and admiration of the achievements of others. His little superstitions (like a fear of Fridays), his childlike resolutions, and his prayers and blessings on his birthdays and at New Year's (for his family, his work, his reputation, and the good of mankind) are the endearing traits of an anxious and diffident character. As an artist he brought much joy and loveliness into the world, and as a person he suffered much from prejudice and his own human limitations. But his kindness and generosity are beyond doubt, and his musical achievements very considerable indeed.

Certainly the many acts of homage and popular acclaim that so regularly punctuated his experiences, and that he recorded with such naive delight,[368] were the just rewards of a life devoted to dramatic truth, enduringly expressed in the lyrical beauty of song.

NOTES

1. See Harold Rosenthal, *Two Centuries of Opera at Covent Garden* (London: Putnam, 1958), pp. 679–776; and Stéphanie Wolff, *L'Opéra au Palais Garnier, 1875–1962* (Paris: Entr'acte, 1962), pp. 23–228, for the seasonal statistics.

2. Meyerbeer's operas were an almost annual feature of the repertoires of Covent Garden, the Metropolitan, and La Scala from 1870 to 1910.

3. There is, for example, at the time of writing (mid-1997), no commercial recording of either *Robert le Diable* or *L'Africaine*, two of the most famous operas ever written—and this when the catalogs now boast extensive exploration of the most obscure composers.

4. The cue has been taken from Hugo Riemann's famous dictum: "History will point to Meyerbeer as one of the most important steps to Wagner's art" (*Musik-Lexikon* [1882; reprint, Berlin: M. Hesse, 1929]).

5. Franz Werner Halft is right in describing most popular and critical responses to Meyerbeer as "eine Anhäufung von Vorurteilungen" [a heap of clichés] (*Fono Forum*, 1975, p. 1109).

6. Even during his life he was referred to as "der Messias von Bayreuth" (Theodor Goering, 1881). George Bernard Shaw's *The Perfect Wagnerite* (1899) is a famous attempt at analyzing the emotional and intellectual intensity of Wagnerolatry.

7. Ernest Newman, *The Life of Richard Wagner,* vol. 2, *1848–1860* (London: Cassell, 1933; reprint, Cambridge: Cambridge University Press, 1976), p. 607. The page number is to the reprint.

8. Ibid. See his appendix 1, "Wagner and Meyerbeer," in which Newman discusses five letters from Wagner to Meyerbeer published by Kinsky on 15 November 1934 in the

Schweizerische Musikzeitung. Examination of these letters led Newman to conclude that "in the Meyerbeer case it becomes more and more difficult to put up any defence against the oft repeated charge against Wagner of ingratitude to his benefactors" since "[it] seems probable Meyerbeer had really done him several services out of pure kindness of heart" (pp. 607–8). Newman is actually referring to Henri Blaze de Bury, *Meyerbeer et son temps* (Paris: Michael Lévy Frères, 1865): "One single name had the privilege of irritating him; it was the name of Richard Wagner. He could not hear it pronounced without experiencing a disagreeable sensation immediately. He did not bother to hide it, who was ordinarily so discreet . . ." (p. 215).

9. See, for example: *Il Crociato in Egitto* (Oporto, 1827; Havana, 1828; Corfu, 1838; Constantinople, 1839), *Robert le Diable* (Calcutta, 1836; Port Louis, 1841; Valparaiso, 1847; Melbourne, 1861), *Les Huguenots* (New Orleans, 1839; Odessa, 1843; Batavia, 1851; Sydney, 1863), *Le Prophète* (Reval, 1856; Mexico City, 1861; Buenos Aires, 1873; Cairo, 1875), *L'Étoile du Nord* (New Orleans, 1855; Algiers, 1856; Liverpool, 1889; Buenos Aires, 1889), *Dinorah* (Lemberg, 1861; Constantinople, 1870; Rio di Janeiro, 1878; Santiago, 1883), *L'Africaine* (Sydney, 1866; Alexandria, 1869; Montevideo, 1869; Tiflis, 1872).

10. Meyerbeer actually requested that his papers be passed on only to a musical member of his family, or heir, otherwise they were to be destroyed.

11. The letters quoted in Jean F. Schucht's biography (*Meyerbeers Leben und Bildungsgang, seine Stellung als Operncomponist im Vergleich zu den Tondichtern der Neuzeit* [Leipzig: H. Matthes, 1869]) have never been authenticated by any autograph source, and must be presumed to be forgeries. Although the study is otherwise favorable to Meyerbeer, it is unreliable.

12. A classic example is that of a certain A. E. Brent Smith, who wrote the article "The Tragedy of Meyerbeer—1791–1864," *Music and Letters* 6 (1923): 248–55, in which Meyerbeer is treated as "a tragic figure" unable to live up to his early promise and high calling. The reasons are variously given as ambition, a passion for "effect," a compulsive lapse into the commonplace, and serious ethical pusillanimity. The article is not only devoid of proper musical analysis, but reads like a moral tract: "It is because Meyerbeer's courage and judgment were not those of a great man that he was prepared to barter away his soul for a mess of admiration [!]" (p. 252). The concluding statement of this extraordinary exercise veers into fantasy: "Wagner, with all his faults, was an improver, an idealist, who dreamed dreams that ranged from earth to heaven, while Meyerbeer, not valuing his gifts [!], sold his birthright for immediate success [!]. Then at last in his closing years as he wrestled [!] with his opera 'Africaine', he tried to reclaim the splendid promise of his youth only to realise that he could find in his heart no place for repentance [!], though he sought it earnestly and diligently for the labour of five sorrow-laden [!] years. That, perhaps, is the true tragedy of Meyerbeer." It is this same tone of high *moral* disdain that infects so much of the critical reactions to Meyerbeer, especially in the English musical establishment, from Hubert Parry and Donald Tovey down to Winton Dean in our own day. Generations of music students have been indoctrinated against Meyerbeer by Edward Dannreuther in the old *Oxford History of Music* (vol. 6), and by Donald Grout in his *History of Opera*. One should note, however, that the philosopher Herbert Spencer, the composers Charles Villiers Stanford, Ralph Vaughan-Williams, and Edward Elgar, the composer-critics Bernard van Dieren and Cecil Grey, and the critic Edward J. Dent were positive in their assessments of Meyerbeer, although their opinions have never been widely quoted (see, for example, Michael Kennedy, *Portrait of Elgar* [1968; reprint, Oxford: Oxford University Press, 1993], p. 76). Today some English scholars, like David Charlton and Mark Everist, are in the forefront of serious Meyerbeer scholarship.

13. Apart from the autographs of his four principal *grands opéras*, the whereabouts of his other manuscripts and sketches remains unknown. Two of his nonoperatic stage works, *Das Hoffest in Ferrara* and the incidental music to *La Jeunesse de Goethe*, appear to be lost.

14. The (presumably sarcastic) phrase belongs to Winton Dean, who, it would seem, doubts any such fundamental (and by implication, sincere or genuine?) core of identity: "It is worth examining his Italian operas to determine how much of the essential Meyerbeer (if we can assume that such a thing exists) antedated his arrival in Paris, at Rossini's invitation, in 1825." (*Essays on Opera* [Oxford: Oxford University Press, 1992], p. 174.)

15. See, for example, Nigel Douglas, *The Joy of Opera* (London: André Deutsch, 1996), who refers to "the new-fangled concoctions of Monsieur Meyerbeer" (p. 56). The tone of contempt is unmistakable, and the inference is one of a bogus, calculating aesthetic manipulation.

16. The provision was that the unpublished portion (manuscripts and the diaries) was to be closed to inspection and scholarly investigation until 1935.

17. See Edgar Istel, "Meyerbeer's Way to Mastership," *Musical Quarterly,* January 1926, p. 73: "Unhappily, the Meyerbeer family, in their shortsighted obstinacy, choose to withhold from public access until 1933 by far the greater part of the master's literary remains. . . ."

18. Altmann's work was of immense importance for research. See Istel again: "After wearisome negotiations the Director, Dr. Altmann, has succeeded in releasing only the manuscripts of the dramatic works produced during the German-Italian period from 1811 to 1822. But these very works now made accessible and compared with other sources, render it possible—although Meyerbeer's letters and diaries are still withheld from examination—to provide a most interesting view of the way in which Meyerbeer arrived at mastership . . ." (ibid., p. 73). Little did he know how prophetic his words written in 1926 would soon prove: "Only in this way can much be rescued for future research, which otherwise would have fallen a prey to the evils of the times" (p. 73 n. 1).

19. Not only did Cosima dissuade the heirs from giving permission for the publication of the diaries, but she tried to obtain possession of the documents in Meyerbeer's papers relating to Wagner.

20. For an account of the history of the musical *Nachlass* prior to its disappearance, see *BT,* 1:7–10.

21. See Carlton Smith, "Music Manuscripts Lost during World War II," *Book Collector* 17 (1968): 26–36; and P. J. P. Whitehead, "The Lost Berlin Manuscripts," *Notes* 33 (1976): 7–15.

22. Given the hatred Meyerbeer was subjected to during the Hitler era, it is surprising that any document relating to him survived at all. Fortunately, though, the sixteen boxes of Meyerbeer papers remained closed during this period, but were not destroyed. In 1943 they were removed with other treasures of the library by concerned members of the staff, who acted against orders, to protect them from the aerial onslaught on Berlin that had just begun. The greater part was taken to Furstenau in Pomerania, where it disappeared. A smaller section (including the autographs of the four *grands opéras*) was hidden in the Silesian monastery of Grüssau (now Krzeszow near Kaminia Góra); it was discovered in 1977 and placed in the Biblioteka Jagiellónska in Cracow. There the four *grands opéras* were first examined by Sieghart Döhring in 1981. See Nigel Lewis, "The Great Music Find," *Sunday Times,* 3 April 1977, p. 17; idem, "More Treasures in Polish Art Hoard," *Sunday Times,* 1 May 1977, pp. 1, 3; and esp. Sieghard Döhring, "Die Autographen der vier Hauptopern Meyerbeers: Ein erste Quellenbericht," *Archiv für Musikwissenschaft* 39:1 (1982): 32–63.

23. See 9, 11, 13 July 1812.

24. The musicologist Emil Vogel had arranged Meyerbeer's correspondence and private papers in proper order in 1880, resulting in a Meyerbeer Archive consisting of some three thousand documents.

25. Volume 5 edited by Sabine Henze-Döhring (Marburg) and Hans Moeller (Paderborn), was published by de Gruyter in March 1999.

26. Heinz Becker and Gudrun Becker, *Giacomo Meyerbeer: A Life in Letters,* trans. Mark Violette (Portland, Ore.: Amadeus Press, 1989).

27. Heinz Becker, *Giacomo Meyerbeer: In Selbstzeugnissen und Bilddokumenten,* Rohwolts Monographien (Reinbek bei Hamburg: Rowohlt Taschenbuch Verlag, 1980). This was followed by Reiner Zimmermann's large-scale monograph, *Giacomo Meyerbeer: Eine Biographie nach Dokumenten* (Berlin: Henschel Verlag, 1991).

28. See Sotheby's Auction Catalogue for May 1987, no. 455: "The Meyerbeer Archive: a vast collection of upwards two thousand six hundred letters written by or sent to Meyerbeer, diaries, note-books, contracts, drafts, autograph manuscripts, draft libretti, printed libretti, sketches, working papers for all Meyerbeer's most important operas, first and early editions of his music (some inscribed), ephemera, newspaper-cuttings and other material relating to Giacomo Meyerbeer . . ." (pp. 193–211).

29. The fullest account of the history of the Meyerbeer *Nachlass* is provided by Heinz Becker, "Das Archiv Giacomo Meyerbeers: Erwerbung durch die Staatsbibliothek Berlin," *Neue Zürcher Zeitung,* June 1987; idem, *"Fata sua habent documenta:* Zur Erwerbung des Meyerbeer-Archivs für die Staatsbibliothek," *Jahrbuch Stiftung Preussischer Kulturbesitz 1987* 24 (1988): 277–300.

30. The Sotheby's Catalogue lists the Diaries as follows: "No. 455 **C. Diaries and Journals,** II. JOURNALS AND NOTEBOOKS, (d) DR WILHELM ALTMANN'S TRANSCRIPTION (CORRECTED TYPESCRIPT AND MANUSCRIPT) OF MEYERBEER'S APPARENTLY LOST AND SUBSTANTIALLY UNPUBLISHED TAGEBÜCHER (journals), 1812–1844, and 1846–1864, A DOCUMENT OF GREAT IMPORTANCE, *over 700 pages, somewhat frayed.*"

31. Hence the statement by Zimmermann: "Ungeklärt ist die Verbleib der Altmann-Abschriften; vermutlich sind sie zurückgehalten worden und nicht in die Auktion gelangt" [The whereabouts of the Altmann transcript is not explained; presumably it was held back, and did not form part of the auction] (*Giacomo Meyerbeer,* p. 9).

32. The phrase "bewitched in a magic garden" refers to the eight years 1816–24 during which the composer lived in Italy, a period decisive to his artistic development. The phrase is quoted in a letter from Meyerbeer to his biographer, Hermann Mendel, in *Meyerbeer: Seine Leben und seine Werke* (Berlin: L. Heimann, 1869). Although the genuineness of this letter has been called into question, the phrase has endured as an accurate evocation of the effect this period exerted on his life. See Andrew Everett, "Bewitched in a Magic Garden: Giacomo Meyerbeer in Italy," *Donizetti Society Journal* 6 (1988): 163–92.

33. This letter, by its unique character, has always remained separate from the rest of the correspondence, and as such, was catalogued with the diaries and journals by Sotheby's as "No. 455, **C. Diaries and Journals,** II. JOURNALS AND NOTEBOOKS, (b) Autograph journal in the form of a long letter to Meyerbeer's brother, Michael, covering the period 1–17 September 1818, *13 pages, 4to.*"

34. They exist for the years 1827, 1829, 1831, 1832, 1833, 1834, 1835, 1836, 1837, 1838, 1839, 1840, 1842, 1843, 1845, 1846, 1847, 1848, 1849, 1850, 1851, 1852, 1853, 1854, 1856, 1858, 1859, 1860, 1861, 1862, 1863, 1864.

35. The only instance where both the diary and the appointment books are used in conjunction with each other is for the period January to April 1849. The purpose is to throw as much light as possible on the creation and rehearsals of *Le Prophète*.

36. Wagner distributed private editions of *Mein Leben* to his close friends with a tacit understanding of confidentiality. After his death Cosima recalled these gifts, and intended a radical editing of the text. Only the fact that Mary Burrell had obtained a secret copy of the original, laid aside by the publisher Bonfantini in Basel, prevented Cosima's full-scale revision. The official 1911 edition hence contained few omissions and alterations (see Robert Gutman, *Richard Wagner: The Man, His Mind and His Music* [Harmondsworth, U.K.: Pelican Books, 1968], pp. 320–21).

37. Delacroix kept his journal from 1822 to 1824, and again from 1847 to 1863. It is a source for his life and work, as well as a commentary on the social, intellectual, and artistic world of Paris. See *Journal de Eugène Delacroix: Nouvelle édition publiée d'après le manuscrit original,* ed. André Joubin (Paris: Librarie Plon, 1932); English trans. Walter Pach, *The Journal of Eugène Delacroix* (London: Jonathan Cape, 1938).

38. See John Warrack, *Carl Maria von Weber* (Cambridge: Cambridge University Press, 1968), pp. 92–97: "Weber . . . despite his lively prose style and quick ear for parody, is no novelist. *Tonkünstersleben* was as much diary and common-place book as novel; yet he impressed his contemporaries with his literary ability . . ." (p. 97). The full text is published in Weber's *Sämtliche Schriften,* ed. Georg Kaiser (Berlin: Schuster & Loeffler, 1908).

39. Louis Spohr, *Selbstbiographie,* 2 vols. (1860–61; reprint, ed. Arnold Schmitz, Cassel: Bärenreiter, 1954). Anonymous trans. "from the German," *Louis Spohr's Autobiography* (London: Longman, Green, Longman, Roberts & Green, 1865).

40. *Memoirs of Hector Berlioz from 1803 to 1865, comprising his Travels in Germany, Italy, Russia and England,* first published in 1870, has been translated by Ernest Newman (New York: Alfred A. Knopf, 1932), and David Cairns (London: Victor Gollancz, 1969).

41. See his description of Winter on 4 May 1812.

42. See his reactions to *Ottaviano in Sicilia* on 27 June 1812.

43. Reactions to *Jean de Paris* on 2 April 1813 are exceptionally detailed.

44. His account of *Fernand Cortez* on 3 April 1813 is most critically articulate.

45. See 24 December 1815.

46. See the analysis of *Adelaide e Comingio* in January 1818.

47. See his reaction to *Balduino* on 3 January 1818.

48. See the discussion of *Les deux Familles* on 17 January 1831.

49. See the discussion of *Le Guitarero* on 19 October 1841.

50. See reaction to *Giralda* on 28 September 1850.

51. See his enthusiasm for *Manon Lescaut* on 25 August 1856.

52. See his reactions to the cantata *Ich habe viel Bekümmernis* on 10 February 1861.

53. See his description of the Piano Sonata no. 28 in A Major on 3 January 1862.

54. See his reactions on first hearing *Tannhäuser* on 29 April 1855.

55. As on his examining the vocal score of *Tristan und Isolde* on 26 January 1861.

56. See his account of Berlioz's *La Damnation de Faust* in Berlin on 19 June 1847.

57. See his description of Beethoven's String Quartet no.14 in C-sharp Minor on 14 November 1856.

58. His reaction to the Mendelssohn Violin Concerto on 4 November 1856.

59. From *Othello* on 10 December 1812 to *A Midsummer Night's Dream* on 26 August 1863.

60. E.g., *Phèdre* on 13 October 1849.

61. He saw, for example, *Egmont* regularly from 20 August 1812 to 1 January 1856.

62. He saw *La Locandiera scaltra* during September 1818, and attended many of Goldoni's plays during the first four months of 1856.

63. *Le Barbier de Séville* on 14 December 1815.

64. E.g., *Charles VII* on 5 January 1831.

65. E.g., *La Dame aux camélias* on 25 July 1852.

66. E.g., *Jeune et Vieille* on 7 January 1831.

67. E.g., *Hunderttausend Taler* of 3 February 1853.

68. See 1 July 1813 and 8 May 1846.

69. See 20 January 1853 and 18 April 1856.

70. See April 1813 and 13 January 1847

71. See 2 October 1847.

72. See 30 April 1847.

73. See 25 November 1847.

74. See 6 February 1848.

75. See 6 September 1855.

76. See 25 January 1855.

77. See 10 May 1862.

78. Meyerbeer saw twenty-four of Kotzebue's plays between 1812 and 1850.

79. He attended fifteen of Scribe's plays between 1831 and 1858.

80. E.g., Kotzebue's *Deodata* and *Der Kreuzfahrer*, and Scribe's *Yelva* and *Adrienne Lecouvreur*, not to mention over one hundred libretti.

81. This is particularly true of the ancient Greek theater and Shakespeare.

82. See the visit of Ristori's Italian company to Berlin, 20–29 October 1856.

83. See proposals by Barbier & Carré, Birch-Pfeiffer, Heugers, Levy, Lucas, Rellstab, Saint-Georges, Scribe, and Taillade.

84. An account of Meyerbeer's involvement in the textual genesis of his principal operas is provided by Christhard Frese, *Dramaturgie der grossen Opern Giacomo Meyerbeers* (Berlin: Robert Lienau, 1970). John Howell Roberts, "The Genesis of Meyerbeer's 'L'Africaine'" (diss., University of California at Berkeley, 1977), also looks at length at Meyerbeer's working methods (esp. chap. 3, "Meyerbeer and the Libretto," pp. 88–135).

85. See 13 January, 27 December 1827; 9, 10, 22 January, 4 February 1831.

86. See 4 March, 26, 29 June, 16, 20, 25 July, 8 August, 14 October, 12 November, 17, 30 December 1835.

87. See 14, 16, 17, 18, 19, 20, 22, 23, 24, 28, 30 March, 5 October, 27 December 1848; 12, 17, 20 January 1849.

88. See 4 May 1859.

89. See 30 March, 2, 5, 13, 17, 24 April, 3, 13, 28 May, 6, 13 May 1863.

90. See 27, 28, 29 October, 5, 8, 24, 27, 28, 29 November 1863.

91. See 23, 24, 25, 26, 27 October, 19 December 1862; 26 January, 1 March, 3, 5, 6, 24, 26 April, 29 May, 27 October, 6, 15 November, 3, 12 December 1863; 13 January 1864.

92. See 28 October, 2, 13, 25 November 1843.

93. See 1, 16, 18 March, 11 May, 8 July, 7, 8 October, 12 December 1844.

94. See Heinz Becker, "Giacomo Meyerbeers Mitarbeit an den Libretti seiner Opern," *Kongress-Bericht Bonn, 1970* (Cassel: Bärenreiter, 1973), pp. 155–60, for an account of the composer's working methods.

95. See 24 November 1863 to 17 January 1864.

96. *Egmont,* six times between 1841 and 1856; and *A Midsummer Night's Dream,* three times between 1844 and 1863.

97. See 24 November 1859, 31 July, October and November, 12, 19 December 1860, 27 August, 30 September, 9 November 1861, 11 February, 9 May, the whole of August, 6 September, 9 and 13 December 1862.

98. See 23, 28 April, 11 May, 15 June 1846.

99. See 12 February 1852.

100. These two operas emerge as the most performed works attended by Meyerbeer in his lifetime: he saw *Don Giovanni* twenty-nine times between 1812 and 1862, and *Il Trovatore* thirty-four times between 1855 and 1864. This would bear out Gustav Kobbé's assertion that Verdi's opera was the most popular in the world during the nineteenth century: "[F]or a long time [it] could be accounted the most popular work in the operatic repertory of practically every land" (*Kobbé's Complete Opera Book,* ed. and rev. the earl of Harewood, 9th ed. [London: Cassel], pp. 561–62).

101. See 5 November to 20 December 1863.

102. Saul Friedländer, *Nazi Germany and the Jews* (London: Weidenfeld & Nicholson, 1997), pp. 130–35, describes the "de-Judaization of music in the Reich." Schlösser, writing to the theater council on 9 March 1934, referred to "the joke about . . . *The Huguenots:* Protestants and Catholics shoot at each other and a Jew makes music about it. Given the unmistakable sensitivity of the wider population about the Jewish question, one has, in my opinion, to bear such an important fact in mind" (p. 134). And yet, between 1929 and 1 April 1933, when Hitler prohibited Jews from appearing on the radio, the tenor Joseph Schmidt, for example, broadcast nearly every week from Berlin; among the forty-two operas he sang in were *L'Africaine, Robert le Diable,* and *Dinorah.* During the Nazi period Meyerbeer was systematically denounced. Joan L. Thomson quotes from the curriculum vitae of Dr. Hans Richter, Meyerbeer's grandson, which had to be presented to the military authorities after the War by those needing food and fuel: "Meyerbeer's descendants 'had to endure silently that the reputation of our grandfather was constantly defiled in the press', while the Meyerbeer Foundation, originally intended for the education of young German musicians, was taken and 'used to indoctrinate hatred . . . for Jewish music'" ("Meyerbeer and his Contemporaries" [diss., Columbia University, 1972], p. 79). (This document is now in the Beer-Meyerbeer Collection at the Leo Baeck Institute in New York.) Manfred Haedler put it succinctly: "Bis zu den 20er Jahren dieses Jahrhunderts gehörten die Hauptwerke Meyerbeers zum ständigen Repertoire der Lindenoper. Erst der faschistische Rassenhass liess Giacomo Meyerbeers Musik verstummen" [Until the 1920s, Meyerbeer's principal works were part of the permanent repertoire of the Linden Opera. Only the racial hatred of the Fascists silenced Giacomo Meyerbeer's music] (in "Meyerbeer in Berlin," *Das Linden-Blatt,* August/September 1991). The fullest examination of Nazi policy towards music and its implementation in the politics and administration of the Hitler era is provided by Michael Meyer, *The Politics of Music in the Third Reich* (New York: Peter Lang, 1993). Meyer points out that the racist musicologist Blessinger "had characterized Meyerbeer as an 'unscrupulous business Jew and most powerful exponent of the second phase in the process of forging the appropriated heritage through Jewry'" (p. 269).

103. Mina Curtiss captures something of his energy and dedication: "A man of work he certainly was. No one deserves the title more. He was preoccupied with what he had done, after what he had done, with what he would do. He nursed his fame with indefatigable zeal. . . . He went alone to see his works, sitting at the back of a little box. He would arrive in time for the first act and leave only after the last note. He had but one thought—his music, again

his music, and always his music" (in *Bizet and His World* [New York: Alfred A. Knopf, 1958], p. 149).

104. See 11 November 1848 to 4 July 1849.

105. See 12 September 1853 to 27 May 1854.

106. See 26 October 1858 to 14 June 1859.

107. See 10 December 1846 to 3 April 1847.

108. See 2 February to 4 March 1850.

109. See 14 June to 26 July 1856.

110. See 20 June to 31 July 1859.

111. See 9 September to 1 October 1854.

112. See 1 December to 22 December 1859.

113. He was closely associated with singers like Velluti, Nourrit, Falcon, Mario, Duprez, Tuczek, Lind, Viardot, Roger, Battaille, Cabel, Faure, Lucca.

114. Most especially that of the Opéra (Lubbert, Véron, Pillet, Duponchel, Roqeplan), the Opéra Comique (Perrin), Berlin (Küstner), Dresden (Lüttichau), Vienna (Lanckoronski), London (Monk Mason, Bunn, Lumley, Gye).

115. See 13 and 23 December 1858.

116. The returns from his French operas are recorded in detail.

117. The commentary on the many opera houses and performances during the Italian visit (January—April 1856) provides many good examples.

118. All nine symphonies feature regularly from 1831 to 1859, and eight of the string quartets from 1831 to 1856.

119. Mozart is represented in all genres—operatic, orchestral, chamber, instrumental and religious.

120. See, for example, his pleasure in the Overture, Scherzo, and Finale on 5 December 1862.

121. See his reactions to *La Damnation de Faust* (19 June 1847) and the *Requiem* (20 and 22 October 1852).

122. See 28 January 1857.

123. In 1853, 1855, 1857, and 1861.

124. In 1851, 1853, 1857, 1860, 1861, 1862, and 1863.

125. See 29 March 1863.

126. See 1–6 June 1846.

127. See 3 January and 9 May 1841.

128. See 25–26 March 1840.

129. He heard the work from 1818 to 1862.

130. See 13 April 1812.

131. See 4 May 1812.

132. See 28 March 1813.

133. See 19 December 1815.

134. See 24 December 1815.

135. The Commission de la Surveillance de l'Enseignement and the Commission des Auteurs et Compositeurs Dramatiques.

136. A member of the Senate of the Academy.

137. See 2 February 1831.

138. See 14 October 1849 where he refers to *Atala* and *René*.

139. See 7 and 24 January 1831.

140. See 6 October 1841 and 13 August 1856.

141. See 19 August and 4 September 1850.

142. See 1 May 1841.
143. See 16 March 1840.
144. See December 1838.
145. See 21 October 1850.
146. See 15 October 1850; 27 and 30 June 1852.
147. See 16 November 1851.
148. See 16 June 1856.
149. See 16 July 1847.
150. See 17 January 1864.
151. See 5 May 1841.
152. See 16 September 1850.
153. See 22 August 1861 and 13 June 1863.
154. See 16 July 1847.
155. See 4 August 1856.
156. See 13 January 1862.
157. See 2 November 1829, 4 November 1841.
158. See 7 June 1857.
159. See 23 February 1862.
160. See 14 October 1850 and 22 June 1858.
161. See 14 July 1863.
162. See 30 May and 2 June 1862.
163. See 20 September 1847.
164. See 12 November 1858.
165. See 11, 12, 21 January 1838.
166. The matter is discussed fully by Paul Henry Lang in *The Experience of Opera* (London: Faber & Faber, 1973), pp. 182–86: "The influential publishers, the brothers Escudier, having been unable to secure the publishing rights to the opera [*Les Huguenots*], left no stone unturned to hurt it. . . . Escudier used the poet [Heine] to try to woo Meyerbeer away from Schlesinger, but when that proved to be impossible, the publisher assigned him the task of promoting the cause of a possible rival. In 1847 Heine was writing for the same German paper he once used to ingratiate himself with Meyerbeer [the *Augsburger allgemeine Zeitung*], only this time he sang the praises of the still-unknown Verdi. . . ."
167. See 25 July 1862.
168. See 26 November 1860.
169. See 17 January and 11 April 1854.
170. See 18 April 1855.
171. See 27 June 1856, 25 March and 28 August 1857.
172. See Heinz Becker, *Der Fall Heine-Meyerbeer* (Berlin: Walter de Gruyter, 1958).
173. See Lang, *Experience of Opera,* p. 185: "The poet and the composer became fast friends, but Heine's unsavoury money operations—surprisingly similar to Wagner's—eventually led to a complete break between them." The poet's financial insecurity plagued him constantly. Meyerbeer loaned him money which was never repaid (see 19 February 1846), and interceded on Heine's behalf with his uncle Salomon and later with his cousin Carl. Heine had hoped to share in Meyerbeer's financial prosperity in Paris, both by becoming his unacknowledged press-agent there, and by having the composer set more of his poetry. His disappointment in these two areas led to the first attack in an anonymous article in the *Augsburger allgemeine Zeitung* (7 February 1847)." See the chapter "Meyerbeer and Heine" (pp. 233–44) in Thomson, "Meyerbeer and His Contemporaries," 1972).

174. Vol. 3 of Heine's collected writings included the poem *Lutetia* (1854–55), an exercise in devastating satire, in which he attempted to interpret French life and letters to the Germans, and in which Meyerbeer's achievements were maliciously discredited: it was suggested that he had paid an Italian to rewrite his early works and Gouin to compose the French ones, before having him committed to a mental asylum to prevent the truth from coming out. The best analysis of Heine's satirical mode remains Siegbert S. Prawer's *Heine: The Tragic Satirist* (Cambridge: Cambridge University Press, 1961).

175. See 3 November 1859 and February 1860.

176. See 24 November 1851 and 5 December 1858.

177. See 13 November 1863.

178. Minna Wagner's comment to the painter Ernst Benedikt Kietz (on the rehearsals for the Paris performance of *Tannhäuser*), written on 1 February 1861, is apposite in its perception of a very real problem, and the challenge to deal with it: "I cannot but believe that it [*Tannhäuser*] will appeal to the superficial French—the open-minded unprejudiced public, that is. The press is another matter, they simply horrify me—and to suborn the rabble as Meyerbeer would—well, we haven't got the money and it would be rather beneath Richard's dignity." See Herbert Barth, Dietrich Mack, and Egon Voss, *Wagner: a Documentary Study* [London: Thames & Hudson, 1975], p. 194).

179. See 19 October 1855, 21 July 1856, and 15 December 1857.

180. See 5 January 1831 and 19 November 1847.

181. See 13 January 1855.

182. See 26 April and May 1850.

183. See 27 July 1854; 11 February, 30 October, 1 and 3 November 1855.

184. Verdi, reminiscing to Italo Pizzi, provided his own perspective: "'[H]e was a great banker,' he added, 'and made money. He also set great store by praise and took infinite pains to obtain it. He subscribed to numerous journals, and if one was about to go bankrupt, he either gave his own help or became a shareholder on the board. He was thus assured of that journal's praise. Journalists on suitable occasions would often beg financial assistance from him." See *Interviews and Encounters with Verdi*, ed. Marcello Conati, trans. Richard Stokes (London: Victor Gollancz, 1984), p. 344.

185. Typical of such allegations are those made by Harold C. Schonberg in *The Lives of the Great Composers* (London: Abacus, 1994), a popular miscellany of biographies that gratuitously and mischievously perpetuates the legend: "There were critics . . . who had been in receipt of large pensions from Meyerbeer since 1831. Meyerbeer did not content himself with giving them pensions and good dinners. He also made it a point of duty to give them costly presents on their birthdays and on New Year's Day" (p. 207). Such statements are made without a shred of evidence being mustered: who were the critics in question? On the other hand, see Lang, *Experience of Opera*, p. 184: "Meyerbeer was exceedingly sensitive about criticism, and it was rumoured that he spent large sums to keep the Paris critics in line. Not the slightest evidence could be uncovered by a number of conscientious researchers to substantiate this charge or any other charge of unethical dealings."

186. See 28 July 1849. Schonberg is accurate in pointing out that "the critic who carried extortion to a fine art" was P. A. Fiorentino who wrote for *Le Moniteur*, *La France* and *L'Entr'acte*. Schonberg quotes Spiridion: "He levied blackmail with a ferocity unknown even in this capital of blackmail. . . . The managers of the Italian, Lyric and Opéra-Comique paid him considerable sums annually . . . Meyerbeer always paid him a large pension with government punctuality" (*Lives of the Great Composers*, p. 207).

187. See 3 and 10 November 1859; 21 February and 30 March 1860.

188. There were actually fourteen payments to Fiorentino, as follows: 28 July 1849 (500 fr.), 28 September 1852 (1000 fr.), 26 July 1853 (unspecified), 11 April 1854 (unspecified), 19 October 1854 (1000 fr.), 21 September 1855 (unspecified), 7 October 1858 (unspecified), 6 November 1858 (unspecified, but described by Meyerbeer as blackmail, *chantage tout pur*), 8 March 1859 (2000 fr.), 27 July 1859 (unspecified), 10 November 1859 (1000 fr.), 21 February 1860 (1000 fr.), 4 September 1860 (1000 fr.), 30 December 1861 (1000 fr.). The payments are irregular, but involved large sums, and were presumable made ad hoc according to the service required (two in 1854, two in 1858, three in 1859, two in 1860) or pressure exerted (see especially 6 November 1858, where Fiorentino used his personal enmity with Roqueplan as the means of extortion). Declining health and concerns about *Dinorah* and the proposed production of the *Crociato* made 1859 a particularly anxious period for Meyerbeer.

189. He tried his hand at libretti (25 February 1855) and drama (see 10 November 1858).

190. See 22 November 1852.

191. There were five occasions: on 19 October 1854 (600 fr.), 20 October 1855 (600 fr.), 17 October 1857 (600 fr.), 7 October 1858 (undisclosed), 29 November 1859 (600 fr.). The regularity of the same payment each year gives it the appearance of some kind of annuity. On two of these occasions (19 October 1854 and 7 October 1858) the visits to Fiorentino and Leconte were combined.

192. It is once again Schonberg who sustains the myth: "The careful Meyerbeer, anxious to keep the press on his side, would always invite the critics, before every one of his premières, to a splendid dinner at the Hotel des Princes or the Trois Frères Provençaux. No critic is on record as ever having turned down the invitation" (*Lives of the Great Composers,* p. 207).

193. See 21 March 1831.

194. Some other dinners arranged for critics were on 4 January 1853, 20 March 1854, 21 October 1857, 12 January 1859, and 7 October 1863. None of these occurred just before the première of any of his operas.

195. See 5 and 21 January 1854.

196. See 11 and 29 February 1859.

197. See 28 May 1852.

198. See 9–10 December 1848, and 30 March 1849. The publisher Dufour did the same before the première of *Dinorah* (see 14 March 1859).

199. See 4 December 1855.

200. Heine's poetry inclined more and more towards satire, a tendency born out of his own sense of self-division. He felt himself to be the archetypally homeless poet, a Jew among Germans, a German among Frenchmen, and a Hellene among Jews.

201. On the possible paternity of Ludwig Geyer, see Newman, *Life of Wagner,* 2:608–13, and Gutman, *Richard Wagner,* pp. 24–29: "That hysterical anti-Semitism which continued unabated throughout his life may well have grown from attempts to evince an Aryan purity."

202. Schumann liked to see himself as a musical David fighting alone against the Philistines of the artistic world.

203. Schumann's personal hatred was motivated nationalistically, religiously, and racially. "Schumann the Protestant was offended by the adaptation of Lutheran church music and history to the operatic stage" (see Thomson, "Meyerbeer and Schumann," pp. 223–32). "Schumann, by this religious susceptibility, and this aversion for the Hebrew race, is totally

in the German tradition . . ." (Adolphe Jullien, *Musiciens d'aujourd'hui* [Paris: Librairie d'l'Art, 1894] p. 76). Frieder Reininghaus, "Der Ton der (Schein-)Heiligen in *Les Hugue-nots* and *Le Prophète*, Thurnau Symposium, 1991, investigates Schumann's attitude to Meyerbeer from a psychological, if not Freudian, perspective, and speculates on the former's possible jealousy of Meyerbeer's successful integration of the public and private dimensions of his life.

204. Meyerbeer in fact regarded him as "the most dangerous and intriguing of all my enemies . . . who hates me mortally" (see 16 January 1842).

205. Mendelssohn's involvement with religion, in the public and solemn mode of oratorio, was regarded as serious and respectable. Praise for *Paulus* at the expense of *Les Huguenots* was in fact the starting point of Schumann's notorious critique.

206. Not only did they share a common ancestry in the families Oppenheim and Wilner, but they were also related through marriage, Mendelssohn's cousin Betty Meier having married Heinrich Beer. See G. Ballin, "Die Ahnen des Komponisten Giacomo Meyerbeer," *Genealogie* 6 (June 1966): 228.

207. The Mendelssohn-Bartholdys were prominent converts to Lutheranism, whereas the Beers remained staunchly Jewish.

208. See Thomson, "Meyerbeer and Mendelssohn," pp. 220–22. "Although Mendelssohn never competed with Meyerbeer in the sphere of opera, their musical careers in Germany overlapped. Meyerbeer in Berlin and Mendelssohn in Leipzig held the two most prestigious positions in the German musical world. Their names were linked by Schumann in his well-known review of *Les Huguenots*, when their works were performed within a few days of each other. Their Jewish ancestry was a focal point of the anti-Semitic diatribes of Richard Wagner. Their wealth, their backgrounds, their achievements resulted in publicity and envy. Although Mendelssohn may have felt nothing in common with the author of *Robert le Diable*, the Germans connected them as late as the Nazi era when their works were banned and equated as undesirable." The relationship between the composers is also discussed by Frieder Reininghaus, "Zwei Emanzipationswege aus Berlin: Anmerkungen zum Verhältnis Meyerbeers und Mendelssohns," in *Giacomo Meyerbeer: Musik als Welterfahrung,* ed. Sieghart Döhring and Jürgen Schläder (Munich: Ricordi, 1995), pp. 223–36.

209. See Schonberg, who in his brief discussion of Meyerbeer (*Lives of the Great Composers,* pp. 203–8) quotes Mendelssohn on p. 205, the standard Schumann and Heine on p. 206, and Wagner on p. 208 (the last three cited at length). Most of the rest of the "biography" is devoted to other negative or ridiculing opinions from the contemporary Parisian press.

210. Originally published in the *Neue Zeitschrift für Musik* 6 (1837): 74. The tone of the article is captured in the vicious emotionalism of the following: "But what is all this in contrast to the vulgarity, the distortion, to the artificiality, immorality, and the non-music of the whole? Let us console ourselves that we have heard the extreme cry of a talent afflicted by our times" (Schumann, *Schriften,* 1:319–21; trans. Thomson, "Meyerbeer and Schumann," **p.** 228.) It is just this opinion that still characterizes much presupposition about Meyerbeer.

211. From part 1 of *Oper und Drama* (1851), a pseudohistory of opera, in which Wagner explained his perception of "the artwork of the future." Reference to this essentially meaningless clause is regarded as de rigueur in any exercise that seeks to prove its intellectual credentials, and it recurs with sad predictability. Even thoughtful new books like Michael Tanner's *Wagner* (London: Harper Collins, 1996) pay it lip service (p. 36), in spite of the fact that Wagner's prose is tendentious and the tone and style used in referring to Meyerbeer

so venomous and hysterical as to be uncomfortable to read even today. For example: "Meyerbeer . . . wanted a monstrous, piebald, historico-romantic, diabolico-religious, sacro-frivolous, mysterio-criminal, autyloco-sentimental dramatic hodgepodge, therein to find material for a curious chimeric music—a want which owing to the indomitable buckram of his musical temperament, could not be quite suitably applied." Max Brod, in "Some Comments on the Relationship between Wagner and Meyerbeer," adds that the "abuse and venom . . . which permeates all Wagner's references to Meyerbeer . . . almost amounts to a curse on his work (I nearly said a *Cherem* [a biblical curse])" (*Leo Baeck Institute Yearbook IX,* 1964, pp. 202–3).

212.   In his letter to Karl Klingemann on 10 December 1831 he spoke of the music as having "something for everyone. But there is no heart!" To his father on 19 December he emphasized that he was speaking "of morality" when referring to the Ballet of the Nuns: "I consider it ignoble. If the present epoch demands this style . . . I shall write oratorios" (Mendelssohn, *Letters,* ed. Selden Goth [New York: Pantheon, 1945], pp. 180–84.)

213.   See 10 May 1839.

214.   See April 1843 and June 1847.

215.   See 5 April 1843 and 19 October 1854.

216.   Berlioz wrote to Princess Sayn-Wittgenstein on 13 December 1859: ." . . Verdi is a true gentleman, very proud and unyielding, who knows how to put the little dogs and great donkeys in their place when they get out of hand: he is as far from Rossini's ranting, buffooning and joking . . . , as he is from the snake-like flexibility of Meyerbeer" (Humphrey Searle, *Hector Berlioz: A Selection from his Letters* [1966; reprint, New York, 1973], p. 163). How ironic that tact and diplomacy should be construed as something hypocritical. The situation was intensified by other observations, like that of the tenor Gustav Roger, who secured his greatest fame in creating the title role of *Le Prophète,* yet spoke of Meyerbeer's "egotistical, Machiavellian brain, his trick of saying the most biting things in the sweetest manner, his eyes full of tenderness, his lips pursed as for a kiss" (*Le carnet d'un ténor,* quoted by Charles Stuart in *The Decca Book of Opera* [London: Werner Laurie, 1956], p. 260). But for others Meyerbeer was "the simplest, the gentlest, the least annoying, the most ordinary man that one could hope to meet. When he spoke of himself, he was modest. When he made a judgment about his rivals . . . he was fair, without flattery and without jealousy. He liked and sought obscurity, just as others like and seek triumph and glory" (Albin Body, *Meyerbeer aux eaux de Spa* [Brussels: Veuve J. Rozez, 1885] ; translation by R. I. Letellier). The opposing reactions remain as puzzling as ever.

217.   Liszt's love for Meyerbeer's music resulted in many of his famous operatic transcriptions. *Le Prophète* stimulated more than any other opera: four separate "reminiscences" for the piano and the massive Fantasia and Fugue for the organ on the chorale "Ad nos, ad salutarem undam" (G. 259, 1850). He dedicated the latter to Meyerbeer, and stressed to the publisher Breitkopf & Härtel that this work would "acquit me, in all reverence and friendship, of a dedication to Meyerbeer, which has been my intention for a long time. . . . I would be delighted, therefore, if you would help me to fill that spot in the recognition which I have for Meyerbeer" (*Franz Liszts Briefe,* ed. La Mara [Leipzig: Breitkopf & Härtel, 1893], Letter 78; trans. Thomson, "Meyerbeer and His Contemporaries," p. 188).

218.   In Dresden in 1848 Liszt was the Schumanns' guest of honor at a reception where Wagner was also present: In the course of the evening, Liszt spoke highly of Meyerbeer at Mendelssohn's expense. Schumann lost his temper, told him to keep his mouth shut, and stormed out of the room (see Peter F. Ostwald, *Schumann: Music and Madness* [London: Gollancz, 1985], pp. 221–22).

219. The most perspicuous and comprehensive account of this topic is provided by Joan L. Thomson, "Giacomo Meyerbeer: The Jew and his Relationship with Richard Wagner," *Musica Judaica* 1 (1975/76): 54–86. For a fuller development of the subject (including Meyerbeer's dealings with Heine and Schumann) see idem, "Meyerbeer and his Contemporaries."

220. *BT,* 3:196.

221. See 22 April 1812.

222. See 1 January 1841.

223. See 3 August 1847. The whole question is given rigorous reappraisal by Daniel Goldhagen in *Hitler's Willing Executioners: Ordinary Germans and the Holocaust* (New York: Alfred A. Knopf, 1996). In chapter 1, "Recasting the View of Antisemitism: A Framework for Analysis" he observes: "In the middle ages and the early modern period, without question until the Enlightenment, German society was thoroughly antisemitic. That the Jews were fundamentally different and maleficent . . . was at the time an axiom of German and most of Christian culture. This evaluation of Jews was shared alike by elites and . . . by the common people. Why not assume that such deeply rooted cultural beliefs, that such basic guides to the social and moral order of the world, persist, unless it can be *shown* that they have changed or dissipated?" (p. 30).

224. See also the analysis of James J. Sheehan (*German History, 1770–1866* [Oxford: Oxford University Press, 1993], p. 790): ". . . Jews continued to be divided from their fellow countrymen, not only in the persistence of traditional anti-Jewish feeling—what one contemporary called 'the abyss of barbarism behind the veneer of civilization'—but also by the emergence of yet more poisonous notions of racial superiority. In the last decades of the nineteenth century, therefore, Jews remained what they had been since the 1780s, a test case for the power and limitations of social emancipation as ideal and reality." Goldhagen's study also underlines Meyerbeer's empirical perceptions: "That a thoroughgoing antipathy towards Jews was integral to the moral order of society explains not only why antisemitism has persisted for so long and has possessed such a great emotional charge but also why it has had its remarkably protean quality" (*Hitler's Willing Executioners,* p. 42). Only a thorough historical reexamination of the social and cultural evidence can lead to the abandonment of "the *assumption* that, by and large, Germans in the nineteenth and twentieth centuries were not antisemitic" and can "*demonstrate* how they freed themselves of their culture's previously ingrained antisemitism, if indeed they ever did" (p. 30).

225. Frederick Morton (*A Nervous Splendour: Vienna 1888/1889* [New York: Penguin, 1980], p. 74) gives a description of this dangerous new racist ideology: Schönerer was "the violent pan-Germanist politician" who glorified "a pre-capitalist, pre-bourgeois ideal: he worshipped the idea of Germania . . . ancient and pure," which, restored, "would reunite once more all true-blooded Teutonic tribes in Europe. . . . He would slay the dragon Jew, that capitalist demon of all subversive change." Schönerer helped to elect Karl Lueger, the anti-Semitic mayor of Vienna, in the 1890s.

226. Alfred Dreyfus (1859–1935) was the son of a rich Jewish manufacturer from Mühlhausen in Alsace. While on the general staff of the French Army, he was unjustly accused of delivering documents connected with the national defense to a foreign government (1893–94). He was court-martialed and deported for life. The subsequent attempts of his wife and friends to prove him the innocent victim of malicious prejudice and forgery plunged France into a turmoil of militarism and anti-Semitism. Only in 1906, when anti-Semitism had quieted down a little, did a civilian court reverse the verdict and Dreyfus was reinstated.

227. Chamberlain (1855–1927) was the son of an English admiral, but settled in Dresden (1885) and later moved to Bayreuth, (1908) where he married Eva, daughter of Richard Wagner. He wrote on music, Wagner, Kant, and philosophy, and was finally naturalized as a German (1916). He was a committed supporter of the dogmas of Aryan supremacy—indeed, one of its theorizers and spokesmen. The work that made him famous was *Die Grundlagen des neunzehnten Jahrhunderts* (Munich, 1899); translated by John Lees under the title *The Foundations of the Nineteenth Century* [London: John Lane, The Bodley Head, 1910]). It expounds two basic themes: the Teutons have been the creators and bearers of civilization, and the Jews are a negative racial force and a disrupting, degenerate influence in history. The book became a best-seller in Germany, passing through eight editions by 1909 and strongly influencing Hitler's racial theories expressed in *Mein Kampf.*

228. Having just emerged from the ghetto, the Jews, with their alien culture, were excluded from the fundamental roots of Western civilization that nourish the European mind below the level of consciousness. The Jews therefore could never produce any art at a level beyond the composer's conscious intentions. It must always lack true artistic profundity and sincerity. "Mendelssohn," wrote Wagner, "has shown us that a Jew can have the richest abundance of specific talents, be a man of the broadest and yet most refined culture, of the loftiest, most impeccable integrity, and yet not be able—not once, with the help of all these qualities—to produce in us that deep, heart-seizing, soul-searching experience we expect from art." Anything musical which Wagner disapproved of was ultimately ascribable to the Jews: the whole bel canto tradition was ascribed to "the voice of the effeminate Jew" (see chapter 2 of Marc Weiner's *Richard Wagner and the Anti-Semitic Imagination* [Lincoln: University of Nebraska Press, 1995], pp. 176–94). For an account of Wagner's disturbing racial theories, see Gutman, *Richard Wagner;* in his last opera, he says, "Wagner celebrated the Aryans as the globe's noblest race, their rule and exploitation . . . of lower breeds being justified by ethnologic superiority and thus by natural law" (p. 592).

229. See Brian Magee, *Aspects of Wagner* (London: Panther Books 1968). He draws disturbing analogies: "Wagner's anti-Semitism is strikingly similar in its personal origins to Hitler's. The worst period of deprivation and humiliation he ever had to suffer was the two and a half years during which he tried and failed to establish himself in Paris, which was then the world capital of opera, at the time when the roost was ruled by Meyerbeer, a Jew, and the next figure to him was Halévy, also a Jew. It came close to breaking his spirit. . . . Even in its duration the period of the humiliation was roughly the same as Hitler's in the [Viennese] dosshouse . . . in both of them the experience of being brought to the edge of starvation by society's total disregard of them seems to have activated a sense of persecution which bordered on paranoia, which cast 'the Jews' as the villains, and which became a mad hatred that never afterwards died" (p. 41).

230. Jewish dynamism was a source of envy and unease. "What could not be denied was that the emancipation of the European Jews and their emergence from the ghetto into the intellectual and artistic mainstream greatly accelerated changes which were coming anyway. . . . The Jewish musical tradition, for instance, was far older than anyone else's in Europe. . . . But Jewish musicians, except as converts, had played no part in European musical development. Hence the entry, in considerable numbers, of Jewish composers and performers on the musical scene in the middle decades of the nineteenth century was a phenomenon, and a closely observed one . . . the musical world was aware of their Jewishness and the influence they wielded, not just as composers, but as directors of orchestras, academies, opera houses, musical theatres. . . . Between 1860 and 1914, public resistance to

innovation grew, particularly in centres like Vienna. . . ." See Paul Johnson, *A History of the Jews* (London: Weidenfeld & Nicholson, 1987), pp. 408–9.

231. The series *Entartete Musik,* "degenerate music," is a collection of music suppressed by the Third Reich and recorded by the Decca company. The composers featured were all Jewish, and include works by Goldschmidt, Korngold and Zemlinsky, and operas by Braunfels *(Die Vögel),* Ullmann *(Der Kaiser von Atlantis),* and Schreker *(Die Gezeichneten).* One should note that both Mahler and Schoenberg, the precursors of these composers, and both Jews who rejected their religion but still suffered from anti-Semitism all their lives, wrote music expressive of their sense of personal and artistic isolation and its attendant neurosis. The harmonic, melodic, and structural boldness of the musical language of *Le Prophète* and *L'Étoile du Nord* ought perhaps to be understood in the same light. Certainly the reaction of Schumann and Wagner to the former opera speaks much of its power to startle and disturb: Theodor Uhlig, writing in the *Neue Zeitschrift für Musik,* was to call this unsettling element "Hebraic art-taste." Newman (*Life of Wagner,* 2:230–31) sees this as a possible starting point for Wagner's notorious article. See also Max Nordau, *Entartung* (Berlin: C. Duncker, 1896), for the origins of this racist aesthetical notion.

232. This stressed the importance of the use of German prayers and sermons, and introduced organ accompaniment for Jewish worship. Because of a petition from orthodox Jews, Friedrich Wilhelm III ordered the Beer Synagogue to be closed in 1816. See Thomson, "Giacomo Meyerbeer," 56.

233. In 1818 Friedrich Wilhelm III awarded Amalia Beer the Luisen Orden in recognition of her philanthropic work during the Wars of Independence.

234. He was involved in the creation of the network for the new railways in Prussia. He was also active in the financial markets, and contributed regular newspaper articles on current affairs, particularly in relation to the introduction of a paper currency.

235. He was a member of the Parisian lodge Les trois Ecossais. See 19 September 1847 and 4 February 1849 for payments of his annual membership fee.

236. See 29 June 1850 and 5 July 1851.

237. See Leopold Hirschberg, "Meyerbeer's religiöse Tonwerke," *Die Musik* 13 (May 1914): 146–54.

238. Otto Klemperer is one of the few Jewish musicians to have spoken openly of his admiration for Meyerbeer. Talking about his early career as an opera conductor, he observed: "Then I moved to *Martha* and *Cavalleria Rusticana,* and above all, Meyerbeer's *Les Huguenots.* Why isn't that performed today? The fourth act is incomparable." See P. Heyworth, ed., *Conversations with Klemperer* (London: Faber & Faber, 1973), p. 41. Max Brod and Hermann Klein are solitary voices in their sympathetic and penetrating assessments of Meyerbeer's art. See Brod, "Meyerbeer," in *Über die Schönheit hässlicher Bilder* (Vienna and Hamburg: Paul Zsolnay, 1913), pp. 181–86; Klein, "The Treasures of Meyerbeer [Part 1]," *Gramophone,* September 1925; and idem, "The Treasures of Meyerbeer [Part 2]," *Gramophone,* March 1932.

239. One has only to think of Leonard Bernstein, George Solti, Daniel Barenboim, and James Levine, not one of whom has recorded a note of Meyerbeer's music, preferring to keep to the safe high ground of uncontested repertory favorites.

240. For a succinct account of the reform, see chap. 5, sec. 3, "Prussia: Humiliation and Renewal," in Sheehan, *German History, 1770–1866,* pp. 291–310.

241. Many of Stein's ideas were inspired by the French Physiocrats and the teachings of Adam Smith. Peasants were liberated from serfdom, cities were granted self-administration,

the nobles and the bourgeoisie obtained equal rights in the ownership of land, Jews were given rights for the first time, freedom of association was authorized, and the army was reformed from top to bottom. See ibid., p. 296: "In the short run, reform—and especially military reform—enabled Prussia to survive as a great power. In the long run, the reformers' achievements, and perhaps even more the historiographical celebration of these achievements, helped to provide the basis for Prussia's claim to primacy in German Europe."

242. New freedom of movement was accompanied by new opportunities for education and economic improvement. Migration to the larger cities increased, the Jewish population of Berlin, for example, rising from 3,373 in 1816, to 9,595 in 1848, and 36,015 in 1871. However, emancipation did not remove all restrictions on Jews. Some states still limited their rights of settlement, while in most they were still banned from the army and the civil service. See ibid., p. 790. For a wider European perspective, see chap. 5 of Johnson, *History of the Jews*.

243. The transformation of Berlin had begun earlier: "Under the reign of the art-loving King Friedrich Wilhelm II (1786–97) Berlin was elevated to the rank of a metropolis of art. Here the salons, well-known to literary history, of the highly intelligent Jewesses Rahel Varnhagen and Henriette Herz occupied a prominent place, especially in the development of romanticism; while Meyerbeer's parental home, as described by Heinrich Heine, was frequented by men like Humboldt, Iffland, Reichardt, Zelter, B. A. Weber, Benda, and others, and chiefly devoted to the cultivation of music" (Istel, "Meyerbeer's Way to Mastership," p. 74). For a complete social history of the city, see Ronald Taylor, *Berlin and Its Culture* (New Haven: Yale University Press, 1997).

244. The Schleswig-Holstein controversy culminated in a Prussian victory over Denmark at the Battle of Düppel (18 April 1864).

245. The dispute with Austria, which culminated in the Prussian victory over Austria at the Battle of Königgrätz (2 July 1866), decided the leadership of the German-speaking nations.

246. The overwhelming defeat of France by Prussia and her German allies at the Battle of Sedan (September 1870) led to the destruction of Napoleon III's Second Empire, and the proclamation of King Wilhelm I as German kaiser at Versailles on 18 January 1871.

247. Misfortune seemed to hang over Europe's great liberal princes: the death of the progressive-minded Emperor Friedrich in March 1888 and the suicide of Crown Prince Rudolph at Mayerling in January 1889 left the Hohenzollern and Habsburg successions open to forces of nationalism and reaction.

248. See Giles MacDonogh, *Prussia: The Perversion of an Idea* (London: Sinclair-Stephenson, 1994). This book endeavors to explain how the "severe virtues" of the Prussian state were eroded by the imperial ideal, which promoted German nationalism and militarism with catastrophic consequences. He draws attention to Gerhard Leibholz, who shows that in its intellectual origins "the National Socialist movement originated in Austria and South Germany and absolutely not in Prussia" (p. 362).

249. This is how the composer is named on his birth certificate. The names "Jakob Liebmann" seem to have been added later.

250. See 2 January 1861.

251. See, for example, 25 August 1863.

252. See 19 January 1842, 1 January 1843, 12 January 1843, 14 March 1843, 18 March 1844, 30 September 1844, 15 January 1845, August 1845 (in honor of Queen Victoria), 24 April 1847, 8 May 1847 (programme), 28 May 1847, 8 July 1847 (ideas for future concerts), 15 November 1847, 16 November 1847 (contract), 9 April 1850, 18 April 1850

(programme), May 1850, 13 July 1850, 9 January 1851 (programme), 5 February 1851, 28 February 1851, 6 March 1851, 14 March 1851, 8 July 1851 (programme), 17 November 1851, 10 December 1851 (programme), 28 December 1851, 16 January 1852, 21 January 1852 (programme), 20 February 1852 (tableaux vivants), 22 March 1852, 31 March 1852 (programme), 20 April 1852 (programme for the emperor of Russia), 26 April 1853, 19 November 1854, 28 November 1854 (programme), 29 November 1854, 23 September 1856 (for various monarchs), 19 November 1856 (programme), 17 January 1857 (programme), 21 January 1857 (programme), 2 March 1857 (programme), 19 March 1857, 30 April 1858, January 1860, 18 February 1860 (the closer involvement of Queen Augusta of Prussia), 8 March 1860, 22 March 1860, 2 May 1861, 30 May 1861, 12 December 1861, 23 January 1862, 22 March 1862, 27 March 1862, 3 April 1862, 31 January 1863, 19 February 1863, 26 February 1863, 5 March 1863, 12 March 1863, 19 March 1863, 22 March 1863.

253. King Wilhelm I was full of foreboding. On 17 January 1871 he observed, "Tomorrow is the saddest day of my life. We are carrying the Kingdom of Prussia to the grave and you, Graf Bismarck, are responsible" (see McDonogh, *Prussia,* p. 63). Ironically, his son, Kaiser Wilhelm II, very much taken by the imperial idea and in fact the arbiter of resurgent nationalism and anti-Semitism, also loved Meyerbeer: his favorite opera was none other than *Les Huguenots*, which he is said to have seen at least fifty times (see John H. Kahan, "Reminiscences of Mahler and *Les Huguenots*" in the programme of the 1968 concert performance of *Les Huguenots* at the Albert Hall).

254. The abandonment of Meyerbeer was part of a wider, tacit rejection of much of the French nineteenth-century musical heritage, particularly the traditions associated with the Opéra and the Opéra Comique, which were gradually but inexorably eroded after 1870. Martin Cooper captures this change in the French psyche in his perception of the fate of the *opéra comique:* "The Revolution was still fermenting in the 1830's, its deepest moral effects were only beginning to be seen. But the Second Empire brought to the surface much that had hitherto remained hidden, and the War of 1870 and the Commune destroyed at least in Paris—and the *opéra comique* has been a specifically Parisian form from its beginnings— the last traces of a universally accepted moral code. With all barriers down, laughter loses its flavour and becomes half-hysterical and wholly trivial" (*Opéra Comique* [London: Martin Parrish, 1949], p. 71). The venerable traditions of both houses are effectively dead: one goes to the Opéra now to hear Wagner and Verdi, and to the Opéra Comique for Rossini and Richard Strauss. The attitude is embodied in the new Bastille Opéra, which opened with Mozart's *Marriage of Figaro.*

255. The big exceptions were, of course, Massenet, Saint-Saëns, and the operetta composers like Lecocq and Planquette. Otherwise one has only to think of Debussy, D'Indy, Duparc, Fauré, Franck, Ravel, and Satie. Some of them did write operas (usually only one), and imitated Wagner openly in their choice of Germanic-Celtic mythology and musical style: e.g. Reyer (*Sigurd*, 1884), Franck (*Hulda*, 1885), Chabrier (*Gwendoline*, 1886), Lalo (*Le Roi d'Ys*, 1888), D'Indy (*Fervaal*, 1897), Chausson (*Le Roi Arthus*, 1903). The symphony hall began to replace the opera house as the major attraction as increasing numbers of groups were formed to play different kinds of music: the Société Nationale de Musique (1871) to perform the works of new French composers; the Concert Colonne (1873) to cultivate a taste for symphonic music, and the Concerts Lamoureux (1882) to advance the cult of Wagner (see Theodore Zeldin, *A History of French Passions, 1848–1945* [Oxford: Clarendon Press, 1993], 2:488).

256. One has only to think of the words spoken at Meyerbeer's obsequies at the Gare du Nord. The eulogy of Beulé, *secrétaire perpetuel* of the Académie des Beaux-Arts, captured

the depth of feeling about the meaning of his life and work for France: "Ainsi deux nations seront penchées à la fois sur une seule tombe, héritières chacune d'un lot inégal: l'Allemagne sera gardienne du corps du maître illustre qui lui devait la vie, la France gardera la meilleure part de lui-même, ses chefs-d'oeuvre, que personne ne peut disputer à la scène française et qui sont inscrits sur une des pages les plus éclatantes de notre *Livre d'Or*" [Thus two nations will mourn at the same tomb at the same time, each one an inheritor, but of unequal portions: Germany, to whom he owed his life, will be the custodian of the body of the illustrious maestro; France, however, will keep watch over his masterpieces, which no one can deny us {i.e., the French nation}, and which are inscribed on one of the most glittering pages of our Book of Gold] (*Discours de M. Beulé . . . prononcé aux funerailles de M. Meyerbeer, le vendredi 6 mai 1864* [Paris: Institut Impérial de France, 1864], p. 3). And yet by 1926 the tone of dismissal and derision in a popular musical guide like L. Bethléem's *Les opéras, les opéras-comiques et les opérettes* ([Paris: Éditions de la "Revue des Lectures," 1926], pp. 352–70) makes for uncomfortable reading.

257. *Robert le Diable* is based on the medieval legends surrounding Robert Duke of Normandy, the father of William the Conqueror (see Edouard Fournier, ed., *Le mystère de Robert le Diable, mis en 2 parties avec transcription en vers modernes, en regard du texte du XIVe siècle* [Paris: E. Dentu, 1879]), while *Les Huguenots* is centered on the Massacre of St. Bartholomew's Eve (24 August 1572), the most dramatic and notorious incident of the French wars of religion (the story was adapted by Scribe from Prosper Merimée's *Chronique du règne de Charles IX* [Paris, 1829]).

258. *Les Huguenots* had been performed 1,120 times at the Paris Opéra by 11 November 1936.

259. See Saint-Saëns's disillusioned outburst: "Oh *Huguenots*, who would have predicted it? Oh, *Prophète*, who would have believed that one day I would have to come to your composer's defence, since in his time, with his eminence, he dominated all the stages of Europe with a brilliant authority of which no one could foresee an end?" (*École buissonière: Notes et souvenirs* [Paris: Lafitte & Cie, 1913], pp. 277, 287; translated into English under the title *Musical Memories* [Boston: Small, Mayard, 1919]).

260. Zeldin, *A History of French Passions*, presents a complete overview of the periods concerned, looking at "Ambition, Love and Politics" (vol. 1) and "Intellect, Taste and Anxiety" (vol. 2) over ninety-three years of French history.

261. He was appointed commander of the Légion d'Honneur in 1849 after the première of *Le Prophète*.

262. See January 1846.

263. Jews were to be found at the very heart of Louis Napoleon's administration. "With Lumley at the Italian Opera, Rachel at the Comédie Française, the Rothschilds attending regularly as guests at the Élysée, and the Foulds as Louis Napoleon's bankers, people began to say that the President was in the pocket of the Jews, though violent anti-semitism did not arise in France until thirty years later." See Jasper Ridley, *Napoleon III and Eugénie* (London: Constable, 1979), pp. 245–46.

264. See 18 August 1857 and 29 October 1862.

265. For an account of this decisive event, which marks the move of Bismarck from the fringes to the center of power, see Sheehan, *German History, 1770–1866*, pp. 876–83. "To the liberal majority he [Bismarck] personified everything that was wrong with Prussia" (p. 880).

266. For a general survey of Meyerbeer's relations with his native city, see Heinz Becker, "Meyerbeer und seine Vaterstadt Berlin" in *Studien zur Musikgeschichte Berlins im frühen 19. Jahrhundert,* ed. Carl Dahlhaus (Regensburg: Bosse, 1980), pp. 429–50.

267. Cf. John H. Roberts: "[H]e always remained something of an outsider within the French musical Establishment. Berlioz and Wagner, remote from the centers of power, might imagine he controlled the Opéra, but in fact he was often unable to protect his own interests, let alone further the fortunes of others" ("Review of Heinz Becker's **Meyerbeer, Giacomo,**" *Nineteenth-Century Music,* Fall 1981, 160). See also Klaus Wolfgang Niemöller, "Meyerbeer und die Berliner Salons," in *Giacomo Meyerbeer-Musik als Welterfahrung,* ed. S. Döhring and J. Schläder (Munich: Ricordi, 1995), pp. 173–82.

268. See 31 August 1848.

269. See 21 September 1849.

270. See 16 to 19 June 1848.

271. See 5 March 1856.

272. See 22 to 34 November 1857.

273. See 23 June 1852.

274. See 18 July 1856.

275. See 4 July 1861.

276. See 5 July 1861.

277. See 11 May 1832.

278. See, for example, 4 May 1851.

279. The opening verse of *Festgedicht,* written for the première of *Le Prophète,* makes cruel reference to Meyerbeer's chronic alimentary complaint:

> Beeren-Meyer, Meyer-Beer!
> Welch ein Lärm, was ist die Mär?
> Willst du wirklich jetzt gebären
> Und den Heiland uns bescheren,
> Der verheissen, der versprochen?
> Kommst du wirklich in die Wochen?
> Die ersehnte Meisterstück
> Dreizehnjähriger Kolik,
> Kommt das Schmerzenskind am End',
> Das man "Jan van Leyden" nennt?

[Berries of the farmer, Farmer [Meyer] Berry [Beer]! / What a noise, what's the story? / Are you really going to give birth / And present us with the Saviour, / The promised, the preordained one? / Are you really coming this week? / The yearned-for masterpiece / This thirteen-year-old stomachache? / Is this child of woe they call "Jan van Leyden" / Appearing at last?]

This is even more tastelessly treated in the late poetic fragment *Zur Teleologie*:

> Ohren gab uns Gott die beiden,
> Um von Mozart, Gluck und Haydn
> Meisterstücke anzuhören—
> Gäb' es nur Tonkunst-Kolik
> Und Hämorrhoidal-Musik
> Von dem grossen Meyerbeer,
> Schon ein Ohr hinlänglich war.

[God gave us both our ears, / To listen to the masterpieces / Of Mozart, Gluck, and Haydn— / But if there's to be only tonal gripe / And hemorrhoidal music / By the great Meyerbeer, / Just one ear will do.]

280. See 6 January 1831.
281. See 26 September to 4 October 1851.
282. See 12 April, 11 and 29 June, 12 July, 25 August, 9 November 1861 and recurrent references in July, August, and September 1862.
283. See 24 September to 15 October 1841.
284. See 29 June to 25 August 1847.
285. See 19 June to 19 July 1848 and 15 August to 13 September 1849.
286. See 22 July 1848 to 30 August 1848.
287. See 24 August to 4 October 1851.
288. See 12 to 30 August 1853.
289. See December 1857 to March 1858.
290. See the period from 12 June to 9 September 1862, during which he moved from Wiesbaden to Schwalbach (16 June) and from there to Bad Ems (10 August).
291. Meyerbeer first went there in August 1828; his last visit was from 9 August to 15 September 1859.
292. See 22 August 1850.
293. See 29 July 1856 and 12 July 1857.
294. See 17 August 1852.
295. See 3 August 1851.
296. See 16 August 1856.
297. See 12 July 1857.
298. See 9 December 1827.
299. See 13 April 1829.
300. See 25 January 1831.
301. Gouin's illness and death dominate 1856: see 29 April, 6 May, 7 May, 13 June, 20 July, 21 August, 17 September, and finally 13 October.
302. See 21 February 1861.
303. His treatment at the hands of Dr. Herzberg particularly sets the teeth on edge: see 19 June and 30 November 1861, 9 April 1862, 22 April 1863.
304. See 25 May 1826.
305. See particularly Carl Baermann's account of his visits to Meyerbeer's home in Paris (14 December 1838 to 16 March 1839).
306. Cf. Zimmermann, *Giacomo Meyerbeer*, pp. 286–87.
307. See 20, 26–30 May 1846.
308. See 6 February 1839.
309. See 5 July and 1 September 1858, 1 January 1859, 11 June 1860.
310. See 20 May to 20 September 1846.
311. See 3 April 1860.
312. See the assumption of the role by Blanca (1 June 1846), Cornelie (4 May 1851), and Caecilie (25 November 1856).
313. See 27 December 1847; 15 January and 8 May 1848; 27 October 1855; 6 May, 9 June, 19 September, 19 August, 5 September 1856; 8 June and 5 July 1857; 12 July and 28 August 1858.
314. See 22 June 1846.
315. See 11 February 1863.
316. See 25 May 1851.
317. See 1 January 1858.
318. Mina Curtiss (*Bizet and His World,* p. 149) captures something of the lifelong

dilemma: "He was alone in Paris when he died. Louis Brandies [*recte:* Brandus], his business manager, stayed with him throughout his illness. Saturday, when he saw that Meyerbeer was growing seriously worse, Brandies suggested notifying Mme Meyerbeer. 'No, no,' Meyerbeer replied, 'it would be pointless. I am not that sick. Besides,' he added, 'it is impossible to be a universal man. You must be either a family man or a worker. I have been a worker. Do not notify my family.'"

319. See 1 June 1846.

320. See 5 July 1851. All three of Meyerbeer's daughters were to convert to Christianity.

321. See 28 May, 28 June, 31 October, 2 December 1856, and 18 March 1857.

322. See 13 July 1860, 2 April 1861 with the saga continuing through April, May and June 1861, and 10 July 1862.

323. See 12 April and 24 December 1861.

324. See 30 May 1858 and 11 September 1859.

325. See 27 December 1847 and 27 October 1855.

326. She spent the last years of her life in a hotel in Salzburg: "[A]fter a performance of *Everyman* . . . an ancient and venerable matron would descend from her widow's quarters, a small hotel room, and walk into the magnificent dining room, wearing a black silk dress and graceful high-heeled shoes. Her face was dark and weatherbeaten, mummy-like; it seemed to consist of nothing but lines and deep wrinkles. She would stride among the rows of people who would gaze upon the unusual guest with . . . curiosity. It was Meyerbeer's daughter, and she brought into the lively and frivolous present the cold breath a past long since part of history" (from the *Illustrierte Nachtausgabe* [Berlin], quoted in Becker and Becker, *Giacomo Meyerbeer: A Life in Letters,* pp. 178–79). In 1928 she gave an interview to Elsa Bienenfeld published in the *American Hebrew,* 2 November 1928, pp. 830, 878.

327. See 27 May 1851 and 27 January 1852.

328. See 22 March, 18 and 23 July, 16 October, 2, 3, and 4 November 1860.

329. He became famous for his portrait of Queen Luise of Prussia.

330. He is still remembered as one of Berlin's most dynamic citizens, and an exhibition devoted to his life and work was arranged at the Staatsbibliothek in 1997. See Jürgen Blunck, *Wilhelm Beer: Genius der Astronomie und Ökonomie, 1797–1850,* Staatsbibliothek zu Berlin: Preussischer Kulturbesitz (Wiesbaden: Dr. Ludwig Reichert Verlag, 1997).

331. See 27 March 1850.

332. See Henri Blaze de Bury, *Meyerbeer: Sa vie, ses œuvres et son temps* (Paris: Heugel & Cie, 1865) who captures the matriarchal spirit of this powerful woman: "[S]a mère était une femme forte, une Juive d'antique et superbe statue! Il la chérissait la vénérait . . . une vraie femme de la Bible. . . . Cette persévérance indomptable de caractère, cette fermeté de conviction, ce sens religieux, austère jusqu'à l'ascétisme dogmatique, qui s'est ouvert une si large voie dans certaines pages sublimes de *Robert le Diable,* des *Huguenots,* du *Prophète* surtout, de qui le grand artiste les eût-il tenus, sinon de la rare personne qui ne cesse jamais de mêler à sa tendresse pour ses enfants l'idée de Dieu, du Dieu d'Abraham et de Jacob!" [His mother was a strong woman, a Jewess of antique and superb stature. He cherished and venerated her . . . a true woman of the Bible. . . . From whom did the great artist get this indomitable character, this certainty of conviction, this sense of religion verging on ascetical dogmatism, which so powerfully characterize certain sublime pages of *Robert le Diable, Les Huguenots,* and especially *Le Prophète,* if not from this rare personality, who never ceased to infuse tenderness for her children with the idea of God, the God of Abraham and Jacob] (pp. 10–11).

333. See 26 June 1856. The paucity of diary entries and the prolonged stay at Spa suggest the depth of emotional exhaustion Meyerbeer suffered.

334. See 6 March 1856.

335. A good example of this was his way of coping with Wilhelm's mortal illness (7 March 1850).

336. See, for example, Gouin's role in early 1841: 1 and 20 January, 3, 15, and 16 February, 15, 19, 24, 25 and 26 March.

337. See 26 April 1846, 13 June, 4 July, 13 November, 11, 12, 15, 20, 29 December for the initiation of this devoted service.

338. Their friendship seems to have begun around 1 March 1837.

339. See 28 March 1847.

340. See 12 November 1847.

341. By 10 July 1856 this was already clear.

342. See 11 January 1831 for the beginning of this magnanimous association.

343. The friendship is fully described by Heinz Becker, "Vertrauliche Indiskretionen: Alexander von Humboldt und Giacomo Meyerbeer," *Jahrbuch Preussischer Kulturbesitz* 27 (1990): 477–513.

344. See 29 March 1813.

345. See 23 February 1856.

346. See 10 March 1848.

347. See Ronald Crichton, "Meyerbeer and *L'Étoile du Nord*," introduction to the Marco Polo recording of the opera (November 1997), p. 10, citing Johannes Weber.

348. It is once again Heine who is responsible for wide dissemination of such information. Writing to August Lewald in one of his *Vertraute Briefe*, he described coming across the composer one day "eating a sparse meal of dried cod." Reflecting on this, Heine observed: "[L]ike his outward appearance, Meyerbeer's pleasures are also essentially modest. It is only when he has guests that a good meal is served. . . . for others he is the essence of generosity."

349. See the crisis provoked by the death of his financial adviser, Bernheim, on 11 February 1858. Meyerbeer kept an eye on the stock market, and sometimes made investments himself, as illustrated in a letter to the London brokers Hermann Sillem & Co. of 25 November 1851, buying $5000 in American bonds (see Letter 84 in Becker and Becker, *Giacomo Meyerbeer: A Life in Letters*, pp. 136–37).

350. See, for example, 24 December 1861, and 10 July 1862 where Meyerbeer had to decide on allowances for his daughter Blanca and her errant husband, Emanuel Korff.

351. See 8 April 1861 where he selected the finest linen and literature for his wife.

352. See 30 September 1854.

353. See 20 May and 4 June 1862.

354. Tgb. "[N]ichts ist mir verhasster als das Andrängen an höhere Stände." See 15 June 1812 (*BT,* 1:181).

355. See 1 and 3 January 1856.

356. See 22 December 1859.

357. See 15 December 1847, 10 August 1851.

358. See 11 October 1847.

359. See 24 April 1854.

360. See 24 December 1846.

361. See 4 November 1851.

362. See 28 April 1861.

363. See 8 May 1848.

364. See 22 August 1849.

365. See, for example, 13 September 1849 (Meixner, an old man), 12 November 1849 (Gabrielle, a mentally disturbed girl), 3 November 1854 (victims of the flood in Silesia), 22 March 1855 and 22 March 1861 (Gustav Nicolai, bereaved father of the composer Otto), 11 January 1861 (Hauff, a blind violinist), 2 September 1861 (Rameau's grandson).

366. See 25 March 1851.

367. Verdi testified to this, speaking to Italo Pizzi: "One day he summarized for me the life of Meyerbeer—a friend of long standing—and praised the kind, rare quality of his soul and mind" (from *Interviews and Encounters with Verdi*, ed. Conati, p. 344).

368. The recurrence of these events was very much part of his latter years. See, for example, 19 February 1846 (Berlin), 29 December 1846 (the homage accorded him by the Viennese *Concordia*), 25 January 1847 (Vienna), 27 July 1849 (Paris), 1 August 1849 (Cologne), 29 August 1850 (Spa), 31 July 1851 (Spa), 24 October 1851 (Brussels), 12 July 1852 (Spa), 30 September 1854 (a banquet in Stuttgart), 26 July 1855 (Calais), 30 July 1855 (Spa), 29 January 1856 (Parma), 3 March 1856 (Florence), 11 March 1856 (Milan), 19 July 1856 (Aachen), 27 November 1857 (Nice), 9 August 1859 (Spa), 29 April 1862 (London), 27 May 1862 (Kissingen), 17 July 1862 (Schwalbach), 13 June 1863 (Schwalbach).

Register of Names

A

ABERT, Johann Joseph (1832–1915). German composer. Studied in Prague (1846–53). Played the double bass in the Stuttgart court orchestra, eventually conductor and leader of the Opera there (1867). Wrote several operas, and orchestral and chamber music. His son **Hermann** (1871–1927) was a music scholar. He wrote a short life of Meyerbeer (1918).

ACHARD, Louis-Amadée-Eugène (1814–75). French journalist, novelist, and dramatist.

ADAM, Adolphe-Charles (1803–56). French composer. Studied with Reicha and Boieldieu. *Le Chalet* (1834) established him as a master of the *opéra comique*; this was confirmed with *Le Postillion de Longjumeau* (1836). His fourteen ballets also made him a leading and innovative figure of the romantic dance, esp. with *Giselle* (1841). In 1847 he founded the Opéra National; it had to close the following year, bankrupting him, and obliging him to return to the Opéra Comique, e.g., with *Giralda* (1850) and *Si j'étais roi* (1852). Professor of composition at the Conservatoire. Wrote his reminiscences, *Souvenirs d'un Musicien* (Paris, 1857, 2 vols.).

AESCHYLUS (c. 525–c. 456 B.C.). Known as the father of Greek tragedy. The *Eumenides* is the third of the *Oresteia* trilogy. Meyerbeer never agreed to King Friedrich Wilhelm IV's request to set the choruses.

AGNESI, Luigi (1833–75). Belgian bass. Studied in Brussels and Paris with Duprez. Member of Merelli's Italian Company in Germany and Holland. Début in Paris (1864); London (1865). Famous as a Rossini singer.

AGOUADO, Alexandre, marques de las Marismas del Guadalquivir (1784–1842). Banker in Paris.

AIBLINGER, Johann Kaspar (1779–1867). Bavarian composer. Studied in Munich and Bergamo with Simon Mayr (1802). Vicenza (1803–11). *Maestro di capella* to the viceroy of Milan. Founded the Odéon (society for the training of choral music) with Abbé Trentino; engaged for the Italian opera in Munich (1819). Returned to Bergamo (1833) and made a fine collection of ancient classical music. Wrote many sacred compositions, an opera (*Rodrigo und Chimene*, Munich, 1821), and three ballets.

ALARY, Jules-Eugène-Abraham (1814–91). Italo-French composer. Settled in Paris (1838) as a successful voice teacher and composer of a number of operas (*Le tre Nozze*, 1851).

ALBERT, François-Decombe (1789–1865). French dancer and choreographer. Appeared at the Paris Opéra (1803), became *premier danseur* (1817–35) and choreographer (1829–42). Also worked in London, Naples, Vienna, and Brussels. Published *L'Art de da danse à la ville et à la cour* (Paris, 1834).

ALBERT FRANZ AUGUST KARL EMANUEL, the prince consort of England (1819–61). Prince of Saxe-Coburg-Gotha, husband of Queen Victoria (1840). He affirmed the constitutional role of the crown, and his interest in science and industry fostered the Great Exhibition (1851). He was an amateur composer and organist, and a devoted admirer of Mendelssohn and Meyerbeer.

ALBONI, Marietta (1823–94). Celebrated Italian contralto. Studied with Bertinotti. Début Bologna (1842). Covent Garden (1847). Appeared in London intermittently until 1858. Toured the United States (1853). Sang in operas and concerts until 1872. Meyerbeer wrote the Page's act 2 rondo in *Les Huguenots* for her (1848). One of the great altos of operatic history.

ALBRECHT, king of Saxony (b. 1828, r. 1873–1902). Son of King **Johann** (r. 1854–73).

ALBRECHT, prince of Prussia (1809–72). Fourth son of King Friedrich Wilhelm III and Queen Louise.

ALBRECHT FRIEDRICH RUDOLF, archduke of Austria (1817–95). General and Austrian chief of staff.

ALEXANDRA FEODOROWNA, empress of Russia. Daughter of King Friedrich Wilhelm III of Prussia and wife of Tsar Nicholas I.

ALEXANDRE, Jacob (1804–76). French organ builder. Established a firm of harmonium manufacturers that eventually introduced the "Alexandre" organ, a development of the so-called American organ (1874).

ALFIERI, Vittorio, count (1749–1803). Italian poet and dramatist. Inherited a vast fortune at an early age, traveled throughout Europe, and then turned his hand to writing, achieving success with his play *Cleopatra* (1775). He wrote over twenty tragedies, six comedies, and the *tramelogia Abele*, a mixture of opera and tragedy. He was the lover of the Countess of Albany and a precursor of the Risorgimento.

ALIZARD, Adolphe-Joseph-Louis (1814–50). French singer. Début Paris Opéra (1837). Brussels (1842–44), then again in Paris.

ALKAN, Henri-Charles-Valentin (1813–88). French composer and pianist. Child prodigy. Studied with Zimmermann. Visited London (1833), then returned to Paris, giving concerts and teaching in fashionable society. Wrote almost exclusively for the piano.

ALOYS, Franz Xavier, Graf von Rechberg (1766–1849). German diplomat. Represented Bavaria at the Congress of Vienna.

ALTMANN, Wilhelm (1862–1951). German music bibliographer. Studied philosophy and government in Marburg and Berlin. Librarian in Greifswald (1889–1900), then at the Prussian State Library (1900) where he became director of the Music Department (1915–27). Compiled a number of bibliographical works and made a copy of Meyerbeer's diaries.

ALTMÜLLER, Carl. German poet, author of the poem *Das Lied vom blinden Hessen,* which Meyerbeer set to music (1862).

ALTMÜLLER, Karoline. German coloratura soprano. From 1806 she was engaged in Munich. Later she appeared as an actress, and became famous in the title role of Schiller's *Die Jungfrau von Orleans*. She was engaged by the Hofburgtheater in Vienna (1837–38).

AMBROGIO. Italian bass. Engaged by the San Carlo in Naples (1822), and sang with David Fodor and Donzelli at the Italian Opera in Vienna (1823).

AMPÈRE, Dr. Jean-Jacques (1800–1864). French literary historian. Son of the physicist and a frequenter of the Récamier household. Traveled in Germany and visited Goethe. Later professor at the Sorbonne.

ANCELOT, Jacques-Arsène-Polycarpe (1794–1854). French playwright. Wrote dramas (*Louis XI, Fiesque*) and later also vaudevilles and comedies. Member of the Académie (1841).

ANDER, Aloys (1817–64). Bohemian tenor. Studied in Vienna. Début at the Vienna Court Opera (1845), where he was engaged until his premature death. First Viennese John of Leyden, Raoul, Lionel, Faust, and Lohengrin. His voice was lyrical rather than heroic.

ANDLAW-BIRSECK, Franz Xaver, Reichsfreiherr von (1799–1874). Baden minister resident in Munich (1838), Paris (1843), and then extraordinary ambassador in Vienna (1846–56).

ANDRASSY, Julius, count (1823–90). Hungarian statesman. He was prominent in the Hungarian struggle for independence (1848–49) after which he remained in exile until 1858. When the Dual Monarchy was formed in 1867, he was made prime minister of Hungary, and foreign minister of the Monarchy (1871–79).

ANDRÉ, Johann Anton (1775–1842). German composer, violinist, and pianist. Studied at the University of Jena, then took charge of his father's publishing business, acquiring all Mozart's musical remains and introducing lithographic processes (1779). He was a theorist, a teacher, and a composer of operas, symphonies, and songs.

ANDRÉ, Johann August (1817–87). Son of Johann Anton, succeeded to his father's business. His son **Jean-Baptiste** (1823–82), a pupil of Taubert and Dehn, lived in Berlin for years and wrote various pieces for piano and voice.

ANDRIAN ZU WERBURG, Ferdinand Leopold, Freiherr von (1835–1914). Austrian diplomat, husband of Caecilie Meyerbeer.

ANDRIAN ZU WERBURG, Leopold Ferdinand, Freiherr von (1875–1951). Austrian writer, director of the Burgtheater; Meyerbeer's grandson.

ANGELY, Louis (1787–1835). German comic playwright and actor. Worked as a theater director in Berlin. Creator of the local German farce, and wrote many adroit comedies, most of which were never published. Also a well-known restaurateur.

ANNA, princess of Prussia. Daughter of Prince Karl of Prussia. In 1853 she married Prince Friedrich of Hesse. Meyerbeer provided a *Fackeltanz* for the celebrations.

ANNE, Théodore. Music critic of the journal *La France*. Secretary of the Académie.

ANSCHÜTZ, Heinrich (1785–1865). Austrian actor. Famous for his appearances at the Burgtheater in Vienna from 1821. Previously played in various German cities. His intelligence and vocal powers made him outstanding in the older principal roles.

APOLLONI, Giuseppe (1822–89). Italian composer. Studied in Vicenza, but was forced to leave for Florence on political grounds (1848), returning in 1852. The most successful of his five operas, which follow Verdi's middle-period style, was *L'Ebreo* (1855). Also wrote orchestral and religious works.

APPONYI, Thérèse Nogarola. Famous Parisian socialite, "la divine Thérèse." Her salon was attended by the whole fashionable world of Paris. She was the wife of the revered Austrian diplomat, **Count Antoine Apponyi**, representative in Paris (1826–49).

ARAGO, François (1786–1853). French astronomer and physicist. His work on polarization, the measurement of the refraction of gases and speed of sound, and electromagnetic experiments were famous. A popular liberal figure, he was elected to the Provisional Government in 1848 as minister of war and the navy.

ARETIN, Johann Adam, Freiherr von (1796–1822). Bavarian diplomat. From 1817 he was *Bundesgesandter* in Frankfurt-am-Main.

ARETIN, Johann Christoph, Freiherr von (1773–1824). Bavarian civil servant. Librarian, then *Oberappelationsrat* in the judiciary (1811), representative in the Landtag. He was known for his book *Die Pläne Napoleons und seiner Gegner in Deutschland,* which was attacked by the Protestant party.

ARGOUT. See **D'ARGOUT.**

ARNDT, Bertha (née Nathorff). Widow of Jacob Arndt (Strelitz) in Berlin. Meyerbeer's housekeeper during the absences of Minna Meyerbeer.

ARNE, Michael (1741–86). English composer. Son of Thomas Arne. Composed *Cymon.* As composer and conductor he did not achieve the fame of his father.

ARNE, Thomas Augustine, (1710–78). English composer. Active at the Drury Lane Theatre, writing many operas and oratorios. Composed the alternative English anthem, "Rule Britannia."

ARNIM, Adolf Heinrich, Freiherr von (1803–68). Prussian politician. Minister of the interior (1842–45).

ARNIM, Bettina von (1785–1859). German writer. Sister of Clemens Brentano, and wife of Achim von Arnim. Famous for her friendship with Goethe, recorded in *Goethes Briefwechsel mit einem Kinde* (1835). As a writer she took an interest in social issues, politics, and the emancipation of women.

ARNSTEIN, Fanny von (1758–1818). Austrian socialite. Daughter of the Berlin banker, Daniel Hitzig. As wife of the banker Nathan von Arnstein she played a big role in Viennese society, hosting a salon that was comparable to Mme. Récamier's in Paris. She helped to establish the Gesellschaft für Musikfreunde.

ARRAGO, Étienne-Vincent (1803–92). French writer. Wrote many stage-worthy comedies and romances. Director of the Vaudeville. During the Restoration he lived in Belgium, but returned to Paris in 1865.

ARTARIA, Ferdinando (1781–1843). Italian publisher. Founded his firm in 1805 in Milan, and obtained the concession for music publishing in 1812. His business rapidly expanded into one of the leading houses of the time, printing the works of Boccherini, Asioli, Campagnoli, Orlandi, Rolla, Rossini, Donizetti, Bellini, Pacini, Mercadante, and Ricci.

ARTÔT, Désirée Montagney (1835–1907). Belgian mezzo-soprano, later soprano. Studied with Audran and Viardot. Opéra (1858); Germany and Italy as a mezzo, then emerged as a soprano in London (1859–66). Tchaikovsky proposed to her in Russia (1868), but she married the Spanish singer Mariano Padilla y Ramos.

ARTUS, Amédée (1822–92). French conductor and composer.

ASSANDRI, Laura (b. 1815). Italian soprano. Prima donna at the Italian Opera in Berlin until 1847.

ASSMAYER, Ignaz (1790–1862). Austrian composer. Studied with Michael Haydn, became organist in Salzburg (1808). Moved to Vienna (1815), studied with Eybler, appointed imperial organist (1825) and court conductor (1838). Wrote oratorios, fifteen masses, two requiems, sixty orchestral compositions.

AUBER, Daniel-François-Esprit (1782–1871). French composer. Studied with Cherubini. In 1823 he began a long and fruitful collaboration with Scribe, who provided him with thirty-eight libretti. After a brief Italianate period, he found his own unique style and established himself as Boieldieu's successor, e.g., in *Le Maçon* (1825) and *Fra Diavolo* (1830). He inaugurated the era of French *grand opéra* with *La Muette di Portici* (1828). After 1840 he developed a more lyrical and serious style (*Haydée*, 1847).

AUERBACH, Berthold (1812–82). German author. Studied at the universities of Tübingen, Munich, and Heidelberg. Imprisoned as a member of the Burschenschaft (1836). Abandoned theology for law, history, and philosophy. Translated the works of Spinoza (1841). Famous for his *Schwarzwälder Dorfgeschichten* (1843–54), which combined incipient realism with the romantic heritage and the idealism of the Junges Deutschland movement, and set the fashion for peasant literature.

AUERSPERG, Anton Alexander, Graf von (pseud. Anastasius Grüs). German poet.

AUGIER, Guillaume-Victor-Émile (1820–89). French dramatist. Rejected romantic extravagance, being himself rooted in the conventional morality of the middle classes. Wrote comedies about social and economic conflict, esp. *Le Gendre de Monsieur Poirier* (1854).

AUGUST, prince of Württemberg (1813–85). Member of the Prussian Army (1830), general (1858).

AUGUSTA (1811–90). Princess of Saxe-Weimar, married Prince Wilhelm of Prussia (1829), becoming queen of Prussia in 1861, and empress of Germany in 1871. She took a keen interest in music, was a warm friend of Meyerbeer, and was in constant contact with the composer about the Court Concerts during the Regency and first years of the accession.

AUMER, Jean-Pierre (1774–1833). French dancer and choreographer. Studied with Dauberval. Début Paris (1798). Aroused great interest with his first ballets at the Théâtre de la Porte-St-Martin (1804-06). Worked as ballet master in Cassel (1809–15), then in Vienna (1815–20), where he produced his biggest success, *Les Pages du Duc de Vandôme* (1820, music by Gyrowetz). Returned to Paris and the Opéra where he revived Dauberval's *La Fille mal gardée*, and created *La Somnambule* (1827) and *La Belle au bois dormant* (all with music by Hérold) and *Manon Lescaut* (1830, music by Halévy).

AZEGLIO, Massimo Taparelli, marchese d' (1798–1866). Italian novelist, painter and politician. He was a Piedmontese nobleman, and his work is permeated with an intense patriotism. He painted classical and historical subjects, and in 1828 began to write historical novels. He played a leading part in the political events of 1845–60, and became president of the Council of Piedmont (1849–52). His unfinished memoirs were published in 1867.

B

BABNIGG, Emma. German soprano. Sang in Breslau until 1855. Known as "the Silesian Nightingale."

BACH, Alexander. Austrian statesman.

BACH, August Wilhelm (1796–1869). German organist. Played in churches and in concerts, then became a teacher and director of the Royal Institute of Church Music in Berlin as Zelter's successor (1832). Member of the Akademie. Mendelssohn was his pupil in organ playing.

BACH, Carl Philipp Emanuel (1714–88). German composer, fifth son of J. S. Bach. Pupil of his father, he became domestic musician to Frederick the Great of Prussia until assuming a church post in Hamburg (1767). He was a noted keyboard player. His music departed from the style of his father and tended toward that of Haydn and Mozart.

BACH, Johann Christoph (1642–1703). German composer. Eldest son of Heinrich; an organist and composer of great prominence among the earlier Bachs. Organist at Eisenach (1665) and court musician (1700). C. P. E. Bach called him "a great and expressive composer."

BACH, Johann Michael (1648–94). Organist and town clerk of Gehren from 1673, also a maker of clavichords and violins. Composed motets and organ works. Father of Maria Barbara, first wife of Johann Sebastian.

BACH, Johann Sebastian (1685–1750). German composer. Attained high repute as an organist in his life, but his major standing as a composer came only with the posthumous nineteenth-century revival, as Meyerbeer's diary testifies. His works were all written as part of his official duties, including the two great passions, three hundred church cantatas, solo works for organ and clavichord, and various concertos, all demonstrating his prodigious contrapuntal skills.

BACHER, Joseph Adalbert. Doctor of jurisprudence, son of a wealthy banker, littérateur whose house was a meeting place for artists like Bauernfeld, Grillparzer and Castelli. Became the confidant of Meyerbeer, and dedicated his time after 1847 to the propagation of Meyerbeer's art. He was in constant correspondence with the composer and traveled indefatigably on behalf of his artistic interests.

BADER, J. Bavarian civil servant *(Oberst-Bergrat)*. He was in change of the fire-extinguishing services in Munich, and oversaw the improvement of the machinery. After the fire at the Munich Court Theatre, he gave an exhibition of new fire installations in theaters.

BADER, Karl Adam (1789–1870). German tenor. Cathedral organist at Bamberg (1807) before turning to the stage at Holbein's suggestion (1811). E. T. A. Hoffmann was his teacher in matters theoretical. Later he worked in Munich, Bremen, Hamburg, and Brunswick before becoming first tenor at the Berlin Court Opera (1845–49), where he was also régisseur. Later he became music director at the Hedwigskirche in Berlin. He was famous for his assumption of the heroic parts in Spontini's operas.

BAERMANN, Heinrich Joseph (1784–1847). Celebrated German instrumentalist, first clarinetist at the Munich Court Orchestra. He was a renowned performer and made extensive tours. Weber, Mendelssohn, and Meyerbeer were all his friends and wrote works for him. He himself composed concertos, fantasias, sonatas, and other chamber pieces for clarinet (about ninety works, of which thirty-eight were published).

BAERMANN, Karl (1782–1842). German instrumentalist, bassoonist in the Royal Orchestra in Berlin, brother of Heinrich.

BAERMANN, Carl, Sr. (1811–85). German musician. Son of Heinrich. Studied with his father, accompanied him on his tours, and succeeded him at the Munich Court Orchestra. Wrote a method for the clarinet.

BAERMANN, Carl, Jr. (1839–1913). German pianist and teacher. Studied with Liszt and Lachner. Teacher at the Munich Conservatoire. Emigrated to the United States (1881) and settled in Boston.

BALFE, Michael William (1808–70). Irish composer, singer, and violinist. Studied in Wexford and London with C. E. Horn, and further in Italy with Galli. Worked in London (*The Siege of Rochelle*, 1835), but failed to establish a national opera at the Lyceum and continued his career in Paris. He was later associated with the Harrison-Payne project for an English national opera. Traveled widely before settling in Hertfordshire. The most famous of his twenty-nine operas, *The Bohemian Girl* (1841), enjoyed great international success, and perfectly captures his fusion of Italo-French conventions with the English ballad style.

BALZAC, Honoré de (1799–1860). French novelist. His great collection of novels, known as *La Comédie humaine,* describes the lives of French men and women of every class. *Gambara* (1837) contains an enthusiastic discussion of *Robert le Diable.*

BAMBERG, Felix (1820–93). Prussian publicist and diplomat. Entered the Prussian Foreign Service (1851). Consul of the North German Confederation in Paris. Press officer at German headquarters (1870).

BANCK, Karl (1809–89). German composer of songs and music critic. Friend of Schumann, he worked for the *Neue Zeitschrift für Musik* and the *Dresdener Journal.*

BANTI, Brigida Giorgi (1757–1806). Italian soprano. Started as a street singer, and was discovered by De Vismes, director of the Opéra. Her wonderful voice and acting abilities made her a great favorite everywhere. She sang in Germany, Vienna, Venice, Florence. After marrying the dancer Banti (1779), she went to Rome and London, where she enjoyed particular triumph. She appeared in several operas by Paisiello, Zingarelli, Anfossi.

BARBAIA, Domenico (1778–1841). Italian impresario. Became director of the San Carlo and Teatro Nuovo in Naples (1809–40). Brought Rossini to Naples with a six-year contract (1815), rebuilt the devastated theater (1817), and obtained the concession of the Kärntnertor-Theater and Theater an der Wien in Vienna (1821–28), where he introduced Rossini and other Italian composers, and commissioned *Euryanthe* from Weber. Also directed the Teatro alla Scala and Canobbiana in Milan (1826–32). His special flair did much to confirm Rossini, Donizetti, Bellini, and others in their careers. Established the Italian tradition of *opera seria* with accompanied recitatives.

BARBIER, Jules-Paul (1825–1901) and **CARRÉ, Michel-Florentin** (1822–72). French librettists who worked in famous collaboration, providing texts for most of the leading French composers of the second half of the nineteenth century, including Meyerbeer, Massé, Thomas, Gounod, Bizet, and Offenbach. Texts derived from many authors, including Shakespeare, Dante, and Goethe, were altered to conventional and often sentimental versions of the originals.

BARBIERI, Carlo Emanuele di (1822–67). Italian composer. Pupil of Mercadante. Conducted in various Italian and German theaters; Rio di Janiero (1853); Vienna (1852–62). Director of the Budapest National Opera. Wrote five operas, German and Italian songs.

BARBIERI-NINI, Marianna (1820–87). Italian soprano. Studied with L. Barbieri, Pasta, and Vaccai. Début Milan (1840). An unfortunate appearance initially distracted from her great vocal gifts. Considered one of the finest dramatic sopranos of her time, and chosen by Verdi to create roles in *I due Foscari* (1844), *Macbeth* (1847) and *Il Corsaro* (1848). Retired in 1856 and taught.

BARBOT, Caroline (b. circa 1830). French soprano active in the 1860s.

BARBOT, Joseph-Théodore-Désiré (1824–97). French tenor. Studied with Garcia at the Paris Conservatoire. Husband of Caroline. Engaged by the Opéra (1848), created the title role in *Faust* (1859). Professor at the Paris Conservatoire in succession to Viardot (1875).

BARGIEL, Woldemar (1828–97). German composer. Half-brother of Clara Schumann. Studied with Dehn, Hauptmann, Moscheles, and Gade (1846–50). Taught and conducted in Rotterdam (1865–74), then returned to Berlin. Greatly admired by Schumann and Brahms. Wrote orchestral, chamber, and instrumental music, and songs.

BARRIÈRE, Théodore (1821–77). French playwright. Alone or in collaboration he wrote more than one hundred farces and serious plays during the Second Empire, with a particular vein of social satire, e.g., *Les Filles de marbre* (1853) and *Malheurs aux* *vaincus* (1865). *La Vie de Bohème* (1849) was one of his two most successful plays based on novels, the other being *Manon Lescaut* (1851).

BARTHÉLEMI, Adelaide Victoire (called Elina) (1819–38). French singer. Won first prize for singing at the Paris Conservatoire (1838).

BARTHÉLEMY, Auguste (1794–1876). French journalist and writer. Together with Méry, wrote satires against the Bourbons. Other works also show him as a political writer: *Napoléon en Egypte, La dupinade ou la révolution dupée, Les douze journées de la révolution.*

BASEVI, Abramo (1818–85). Italian composer and writer. His two operas were unsuccessful, so he turned to musical journalism, and founded the periodical *Harmonia.* Published a *Compendio della storia della musica* (1866) and other works.

BASILI, Francesco (1767–1850). Italian composer. Studied with Andrea Basili and Jannaconi. Conducted in various cities and produced fourteen operas and "dramatic oratorios" in Rome, Naples, Florence, Milan and Venice. Appointed to the faculty of the Milan Conservatoire (1827). *Maestro di capella* at St. Peter's in Rome (1837). Also wrote symphonies, sacred music, piano music, and songs.

BASSI, Carolina Manna (1781–1862). Italian contralto. Daughter of Giovanni Bassi, a comic bass. She appeared with her brother Nicola in a company, Raggazi Neapolitani, founded by her father (1789). She was one of the leading singers of her day, and created leading roles in operas by Meyerbeer *(Semiramide),* as well as in works by Rossini *(Bianca e Faliero),* Pacini, and Mercadante. She retired from the stage in 1828, but continued to sing in concerts.

BASSI, Nicola (1767–1825). Italian bass. Considered by Stendhal to be the best *basso buffo* of his day. Sang in Paris and Milan. Created Michele Gamautte in *Margherita d'Anjou.* Brother of Carolina Bassi.

BAST, Léon de. French journalist, active in Paris in the 1830s.

BATTA, Alexandre (1816–1902). Belgian cellist. Studied with Platel at the Brussels Conservatoire. Settled in Paris (1835). Successful concert tours on the continent. Wrote melodious pieces and arrangements for the cello.

BATTAILLE, Charles-Amable (1822–72). French bass. Studied in Paris with Manuel Garcia the younger. Début Opéra Comique (1848). He was a versatile actor with a capacity for florid singing and extensive range. Created many new roles for Adam, Halévy and Thomas, as well as Peter in *L'Étoile du Nord.* His career was interrupted by throat problems (1857), but he returned to the stage in 1860. Retired (1863) and taught at the Conservatoire. Published *Nouvelles Recherches sur la Phonation.*

BATTON, Désiré-Alexandre (1798–1855). French composer. Pupil of Cherubini; won the Prix de Rome (1816). Inspector for branch schools of the Conservatoire (1842), and teacher of vocal class at the Conservatoire (1849). Wrote four operas, notably *La Marquise de Brinvilliers* (1832), with Auber, Hérold, and others.

BAUDISSIN, Wolf Heinrich, Graf von (1789–1878). German writer working in Dresden. He was a civil servant who achieved a reputation as a translator. Contributed thirteen plays to the famous Schlegel-Tieck version of Shakespeare (1825–33). Produced modernized versions of Hartmann von Aue and translated Molière.

BÄUERLE, Adolf (1786–1859). Austrian author and journalist. Wrote over seventy plays in the style of the Viennese popular theater, and twenty novels dealing with Viennese life. Wrote three to four plays a year (1813–27), then restricted himself to journalism, editing the *Wiener Theaterzeitung* (1806–60). Developed the genre of the *Lokalstück*. He was a man of considerable influence, also famous for the collections he held regularly for victims of any disasters within the Austrian territories.

BAUERNFELD, Eduard von (1802–90). Austrian playwright. Most famous for his comedies, which depict the social life of Vienna with charm and verisimilitude, e.g., *Die Bekenntnisse* (1834). His diaries also provide perspectives on the period: *Aus Bauernfelds Tagebüchern I, 1819–1848*, ed. Carl Glossy (Vienna, 1895).

BAUMANN, Alexander (b. 1814). Austrian writer and composer of popular music.

BAUMANN, Friedrich (1763–1841). Austrian actor. Worked at the Vienna Burgtheater (1795–1822).

BAVARIA, king of. See **MAXIMILIAN II**.

BAVARIA, queen of. Karoline of Baden, second wife of Maximilian I.

BAWR, Alexander Sophie (known as baronesse de Champgrand) (1773–1860). French writer and composer. Pupil of Grétry. Married Count Claude-Henri de Saint-Simon. Wrote a history of music (1823), melodramas, comedies, and vaudevilles. Composed many popular romances.

BAYARD, Jean (1791–1853). French playwright. In collaboration with Scribe and others wrote over two hundred entertaining and witty plays, including *La Fille du Régiment* with Saint-Georges for Donizetti.

BAZIN, François-Emanuel-Joseph (1816–78). French composer. Studied with Berton and Halévy. Taught at the Paris Conservatoire from 1844. Succeeded Thomas as professor of composition. Wrote seven operas for the Opéra Comique.

BAZZINI, Antonio (1818–97). Italian violinist and composer. Studied the violin, encouraged by Paganini. Embarked on a series of successful tours through Italy, France, Belgium, Poland, England, and Germany (1837–63). Taught at the Milan Conservatoire

(1873), becoming director (1882). Composed the opera *Turanda* (1867), overtures (*Saul* and *King Lear*), violin pieces (esp. *La Ronde des Lutins*).

BEALE, Frederick. English music publisher and dealer.

BEAUMARCHAIS, Pierre-Augustin-Caron de (1732–99). French poet and playwright. Harp teacher of Louis XV's daughter. Became famous with *Le Barbier de Séville* (1771) and *Le Mariage de Figaro* (1781). The trenchant social analysis contained in these plays was to earn him the sobriquet "Stormy Petrel of the Revolution." He also published Voltaire's works and various memoirs.

BEAUMONT, Francis (1584–1616). English dramatist. Wrote over fifteen highly effective plays with John Fletcher.

BEAUREGARD, comte de. French writer. Editor of the *Gazette de France*.

BEAUVOIR, Roger de. See **BULLY, Eugène Roger**.

BECHER, Dr. Alfred Julius (1803–48). Austrian music critic and composer. Studied at Heidelberg, Berlin, and Göttingen. Traveled widely on the continent, then taught harmony at the Royal Academy of Music in London (1840). Settled in Vienna (1841). Contributed to the *Wiener Allgemeine Musikzeitung* and Frankl's *Sontagsblätter*. Wrote a biography of Jenny Lind (1846). Edited the revolutionary paper *Die Radikale* (1848), was court-martialed for his political activities and shot. Wrote a symphony, chamber music, and songs.

BECKER. Nanny of the Meyerbeer children.

BECKER, Constantin Julius (1811–59). German composer and author. Studied singing with Anecker and composition with Karl Becker. Edited the *Neue Zeitschrift für Musik* (1837–46). Settled in Dresden (1843), where he taught singing, composed, and wrote novels on musical subjects. Moved to Oberlössnitz (1846). Wrote a symphony, various vocal works, and several manuals, esp. *Männergesangschule* (1845).

BECKMANN, Friedrich (1803–66). Austrian actor and writer. Member of the Königstädter-Theater in Berlin (1824–46), then of the Burgtheater in Vienna. Wrote the Berlin farce *Eckensteher Nante,* in which he created the title role.

BEER, Amalia (1787–1854). Meyerbeer's mother, daughter of the Berlin banker Liepmann Meyer Wulff, married Jakob Herz Beer in 1788. Her home in Berlin was famous as a meeting place for artists and intellectuals. She was highly esteemed by the Prussian royal family and decorated for her civic services. Meyerbeer was devoted to her all his life, and in her devout Judaism, she was a major influence in his spiritual outlook.

BEER, Betty (née Meier) (1793–1850). Meyerbeer's sister-in-law. Granddaughter of Moses Mendelssohn, and hence a cousin of Felix Mendelssohn. She became the wife of Heinrich Beer (30 August 1818).

BEER, Doris (née Schlesinger) (1800–1859). Meyerbeer's sister-in-law. Wife of Wilhelm Beer (13 September 1818).

BEER, Elise (1821–80). Meyerbeer's niece, first daughter of Wilhelm Beer. Married the banker Alexander Oppenheim (1814–1905).

BEER, Georg Friedrich Amadeus (1825–96). Meyerbeer's nephew. First son of Wilhelm Beer. Married Alexandrine Rosen (1838–1904).

BEER, Heinrich (1794–1842). Meyerbeer's second brother. He stood in the shadow of his brothers' achievements, and was the source of concern to his family, particularly because of his excessive spending. He assembled a valuable collection of autograph scores. He married Betty Meier, a cousin of Felix Mendelssohn. The death of his son **Ludwig** (1821–30) at an early age may well account for something of his tragic sense of futility.

BEER, Jakob Herz (Juda Herz Beer) (1769–1825). Meyerbeer's father. His fortune was made from sugar refineries in Gorizia and Berlin. As a member of the Council of Elders of the Berlin Jewish Congregation, he played a major role in the Jewish Reform movement and in efforts directed at the emancipation of Jews in Prussia.

BEER, Julie Angelica (Jülchen) (1824–80). Meyerbeer's niece, second daughter of Wilhelm Beer. Married Samuel Arthur, Freiherr von Haber (1812–92).

BEER, Julius (1828–1913). Meyerbeer's nephew, second son of Wilhelm Beer. He become a musician and wrote some small stage works in Paris that were privately performed (1859 and 1861) and a grand opera, *Elisabeth de Hongrie* (Brussels, Monnaie, March 1871), which was indifferently received. Married **Regine Bischoffsheim** (1825–93).

BEER, Michael (1800–1833). German author. Meyerbeer's third and youngest brother. He achieved fame as a dramatist for his two works, *Der Paria* (1823) (which sought to draw attention to the social problems of the Jews using the symbolism of the Hindu untouchables), and *Struensee* (1829), based on the life and death of the reforming German doctor-politician.

BEER, Wilhelm (1797–1850). German banker, politician, and astronomer. Meyerbeer's second brother. He headed the Beer business concerns, was a representative in the German National Assembly (Frankfurt 1848). He attained particular renown as an astronomer: he established an observatory in the Beer residence in the Tiergarten in Berlin, and (with J. H. von Mädler) made studies of Mars and the Moon (1828–40); produced a detailed map of the Moon (1834–36).

BEETHOVEN, Ludwig van (1770–1827). German composer. Vastly extended the scope of the symphony, sonata, and string quartet, epitomizing the spirit of romantic heroism. Meyerbeer met him in 1815 when the young composer played in the first performance of the *Schlacht von Vittoria*. His universal appeal is attested to in Meyerbeer's diaries.

BEGAS, Karl. German painter. Commissioned by Friedrich Wilhelm IV to paint a series of prominent Prussians in royal service for the palace, Schloss Monbijou.

BEHREND, Friedrich Jacob, Kommerzienrat (1803–89). Prussian doctor. Instrumental in beginning the reform movement in Judaism, Genossenschaft für Reform in Judenthum (1846) as a countermove to the Gesellschaft zur Beforderung des Christenthums unter den Juden. Opposed strict adherence to orthodoxy.

BELGIOJOSO, Cristina, principessa di Trivulzio. Italian writer and socialite.

BELLETI, Giovanni Battista (1813–90). Italian baritone. Début Stockholm (1837), where he had great success with Jenny Lind in Meyerbeer and Donizetti roles. London (1848). Toured the United States with Lind and Benedict. One of the great baritones of the nineteenth century, esp. admired in Meyerbeer roles.

BELLERMANN, Johann Friedrich (1795–1874). German music scholar. Worked in Berlin. Dedicated himself to the study of ancient Greek music and its notation.

BELLINI, Vincenzo (1801–35). Italian composer. Studied with his father, and with Zingarelli in Naples. Had great success with *Il Pirata* (1827), *La Straniera* (1829), and *I Capuleti e i Montecchi* (1829). *La Sonnambula* (1831) and *Norma* (1831), with Pasta in the title roles, created furore. His long elegiac melodies distilled the essence of romantic melancholy. In 1833 he moved to Paris, where *I Puritani* (1835) was a triumph before his untimely death. *Norma,* in particular, was very influential on Meyerbeer.

BELLOC-GIORGI, Teresa (1786–1855). Italizan mezzo-soprano. Debut Turin (1801); Milan (1804–24). Devoted herself particularly to Rossini. Created roles for Mercadante, Pacini, and Rossini *(La Gazza ladra, L'Inganno felice)*.

BENDA, Georg (1722–95). Bohemian composer. Son and pupil of Hans Georg Benda. Chamber musician in Berlin (1742–49), then kapellmeister in Gotha. Studied in Italy (1765–66). Wrote fourteen singspiele (esp. *Der Dorfjahrmarkt*, 1775), and developed the novel idea of the music drama with spoken words, the music being carried by the orchestra alone. His *Ariadne auf Naxos* (1775) became famous as the principal work of the melodramatic genre and greatly impressed Mozart.

BENDEL, Franz (1833–74). German pianist. Studied with Prokesch and Liszt. Taught at Kullak's Academy in Berlin (1862). Composed extensively: symphonies, masses, piano concerto, chamber music, songs.

BENEDICT, Sir Julius (1804–85). German composer and conductor. He was a pupil of Weber, and a conductor in Vienna (1823), Naples (1825). Later settled in London (1836), where he took a leading role in the English musical scene and attained a great reputation as a musician in Europe and America, and as a composer of the opera *The Lily of Killarney* (1862).

BENEDIX, Roderich (1811–73). Saxon playwright. Most popular writer of German comedy since Kotzebue, combining homely provincialism with skill in character depiction.

BENELLI, G. B. Brother of the London impresario Giuseppe Augusto Benelli; theater agent in Bologna.

BENNETT, Sir William Sterndale (1816–75). English pianist, conductor, and composer. Educated at Cambridge, the Royal Academy of Music, and Leipzig, where he became an intimate of Mendelssohn and Schumann, who influenced him greatly. Gave a series of chamber concerts all over England (1843–56), conducted the Philharmonic Society (1856–66) and led the Leeds Music Festival (1858). Became professor of music at Cambridge (1856) and principal of the Royal Academy (1866). Wrote four piano concertos, orchestral, choral, chamber, and instrumental music.

BÉNOIST, François (1794–1878). French composer and organist. Studied Paris Conservatoire. Prix de Rome (1815). Professor of organ at the Paris Conservatoire (1819), *chef du chant* at the Opéra (1849). Wrote two operas and four ballets.

BENONI, Julius (b. 1833). Bohemian composer. Patronized by Countess Amelia von Taaffe and Prince Metternich. Appeared as a child prodigy; his operas were performed in the countess's palace. Later he studied economics and became an official in the Department of Economic Affairs.

BERG, Ottokar Franz (1833–86). Austrian playwright. Wrote 150 comedies, farces, parodies, and *Volksstücke*.

BERGSON, Michael (1820–98). Polish composer. Studied with Schneider in Dessau, and with Rungenhagen and Taubert in Berlin. Paris (1840), Italy (1846). Lived in Vienna, Berlin, and Leipzig. Professor of piano in the Geneva Conservatoire (1863); settled in London as a piano teacher. Wrote operas and piano music.

BERHAIN, Alexandre-Victor (1805–56). French journalist. Founded *Le Figaro* and *L'Europe littéraire*. Director of the Gymnase, Les Variétés, Les Nouveautés.

BÉRIOT, Charles-Auguste de (1802–70). Celebrated Belgian violinist. Studied with Viotti, début Paris (1821). Court violinist to the king of France and the king of the Netherlands. Concert tours throughout Europe (1830–35) with Maria Garcia-Malibran, whom he married in 1836. Professor of violin at the Brussels Conservatoire (1843–52). Wrote seven violin concertos, chamber music, and pedagogical works.

BERLIOZ, Hector-Louis (1803–69). French composer and music critic for several newspapers, especially the *Journal des Débats*. Had a general music training at the Paris Conservatoire and became an innovator in form and orchestration. Nearly all his works have a literary or extramusical association exploring the spirit of artistic freedom and the rapture of love. His relationship with Meyerbeer was friendly and based on a genuine mutual respect. Meyerbeer keenly attended performances of his major works:

Benvenuto Cellini, L'Enfance du Christ, La Damnation de Faust, the *Requiem,* and *Les Troyens à Carthage.*

BERRYER, Pierre-Antoine (1790–1868). French advocate. Member of the Chamber. Made his name as defense counsel in various political trials.

BERTHET, Armand (1820–74). French playwright.

BERTHOND, Samuel Henri (1804–91). French writer.

BERTIN, Louis-Marie-Armand (1801–54). French journalist, owner of the *Journal des Débats,* and a friend and supporter of Meyerbeer. There is a sympathetic portrait of him by Madame de Bawr in her *Souvenirs* (Paris, 1853), p. 229.

BERTIN, Louise-Angéline (1805–77). French composer, singer and pianist. Pupil of Fétis. Wrote the operas *Guy Mannering* (1827), *Faust* (1831), *La Esmeralda* (1833), and many small works, including *Six Ballades.*

BERTON, Henri-Montan (1767–1844). French composer. Self-taught with help from Sacchini. Music director at the Théâtre Italien (1807–9), chorus master at the Opéra. Professor at the Conservatoire, member of the Académie (1815). During the Revolution he turned to dramatic music. Wrote eighteen operas, producing in *Les Rigeurs du cloître* (1790) a pioneering example of the rescue opera. Renewed the *opéra comique,* developing local color and national genres with a concern for dramatic truth. *Aline, reine de Golconde* (1803) gave extra emphasis to the orchestra, and the chorus a more functional part in the drama.

BERTONI, Ferdinando Gioseffo (1725–1813). Italian composer. Studied with Martini and became organist at St. Mark's in Venice and *maestro di capella* at the Ospedale dei Mendicanti, and finally at St. Mark's. Composed a number of *opere serie* and achieved fame with his setting of Goldoni's *Le Pescatrici* (Venice, 1752) and *Quinto Fabio* (Milan, 1778). Worked in London (1779), Venice (1780), and London again (1781–83) before returning permanently to Venice. While unremarkable in style and form, his forty-nine operas enjoyed considerable popularity in their day.

BERWALD, Franz Adolf (1796–1868). Swedish composer, cousin of Johann Friedrich. Studied with his father. Berlin (1829), thereafter lived in Vienna, Paris. Music director of the University of Uppsala (1849). Taught in the Stockholm Academy (1864–67), Stockholm Conservatoire (1867). Wrote symphonies, operas, cantatas, concertos.

BERWALD, Johann Friedrich (1787–1861). Swedish violinist and composer. Child prodigy, studied with the Abbé Vogler. Gave concerts in Finland, Germany, Austria. Concertmaster in St. Petersburg (1808–12). Conducted the Royal Orchestra in Stockholm (1819). Wrote mainly stage music.

BESEKIRSKY. See **BEZEKIRSKY**.

BETHMANN, Heinrich (1774–1857). German actor. From 1794 worked at the Hoftheater in Berlin, usually in the role of the young lover. Director of the Konigstädter-Theater, later director of the theaters in Aachen and Magdeburg, and finally of a touring troupe in Saxony.

BETTINI, Alessandro (1825–98). Italian tenor. Sang in his home Novaro before appearing in Paris as Edgar in *Lucie de Lammermoor* (15 July 1846). Married the mezzo-soprano Zélia Trebelli. Their daughter Antoinette was also a singer, first under her own name, then as Antonia Dolores.

BETOURNÉ. French writer.

BEURMANN, Dr. Eduard (b. 1804). German advocate and writer. Used the initials "W.C." in the *Oberpostamtzeitung*. Published the *Telegraph* in Frankfurt (1837), which first appeared as the supplement of the *Frankfurter Börsenzeitung*, and was later edited by Gutzkow. Took over the direction of the *Journal de Francfort* (1837).

BEUTLER, Franz (1787–1852). Bavarian musician. Violinist and singing teacher at the Royal Opera in Berlin.

BEZEKIRSKY, Vassili (1835–1919). Russian violinist. Studied in Brussels with Léonard and Damcke. Toured throughout Europe, returned to Russia (1871). One of the best violin teachers of his day; taught at the Moscow Philharmonic School (1882). Wrote a violin concerto and edited the violin works of J. S. Bach.

BIANCHI, Eliodoro (1773–1848). Italian tenor. Sang at La Scala, Milan, for a long time, also in London, Paris, and Vienna. Several composers, including Rossini, wrote for him.

BIBIENA. See **GALLI-BIBIENA**.

BIGNARDI. Italian tenor.

BIRCH-PFEIFFER, Charlotte (1800–1868). German playwright. She adapted favorite novels for the stage: *Dorf und Stadt* (1847) is based on Auerbach's *Frau Professorin*, *Die Waise von Lowood* (1855) on Charlotte Brontë's *Jane Eyre*, *Die Grille* (1856) on George Sand's *Petite Fadette*. She had richness of invention, ardent imagination, and considerable dramatic power. Meyerbeer frequently turned to her for literary advice and assistance in modifying or expanding his operatic texts (*Vielka, Dinorah, L'Africaine*).

BISCHOFF, Ludwig Friedrich Christian (1794–1867). German writer. Teacher at Wesel (1823–49). Settled in Cologne where he founded and edited the *Rheinische Musikzeitung* (1850) and the *Niederrheinische Musikzeitung* (1853).

BISHOP, Sir Henry (1786–1855). English composer. Professor at Oxford and Edinburgh, director of the Philharmonic Concerts and professor at the Royal Institute of Music in

London. Music director to Queen Victoria. Wrote numbers of operas, ballets, and melo-dramas.

BISMARCK, Otto Eduard Leopold, Fürst von (1815–98). Prussian statesman. Delegate to the Saxon Provisional Landtag. Prime minister of Prussia (1862–90), founder and first chancellor *(Reichskanzler)* of the German Empire (1871–90). Unlike Humboldt, he was of a conservative tendency, opposed, for example, to the aspirations of Jewish emancipation, and the admission of Jews to official positions. Came into conflict *(Kulturkampf)* with the Catholic Church. But if he temporized in domestic affairs, he was at his greatest and most imaginative in foreign policy. After 1871 he built a system of important alliances and arranged a series of diplomatic actions to secure both the position of Germany and the peace of Europe.

BIXIO. French civil servant. President of the committee of investigation into the condition of French theaters.

BLANC, Adolphe-Edmond (1799–1850). French politician. Parliamentary deputy and secretary-general at the Ministry of Trade. Member of the commission that undersigned the contract for the administration of the Académie Royal with Véron. Under Molé and Guizot he was an official in the Ministry of the Interior.

BLANCHARD, Henri-Louis (1778–1858). French composer and music critic. Kapell-meister at the Théâtre des Variétés in Paris (1818–29).

BLANGINI, Giuseppe Marco Maria Felice (1781–1841). Italian composer. Child prodigy in Paris (1799), where he gave concerts and became popular as a composer of romances. Kapellmeister in Munich (1806). Succeeded Reichardt in Cassel in the service of Hieronymus of Westphalia (1809). After the collapse of the French régime, he went to Munich and then to Paris (1814), where he became superintendent of the king of France's private music, and professor of singing at the Conservatoire (until 1830). He wrote lyrical compositions of considerable naturalness and attractiveness, and was known as "the musical Anacreon" by the Italians: 30 operas, 4 masses, 170 nocturnes, 174 ro-mances.

BLANQUI, Louis-Auguste (1805–81). French politician. Studied law and medicine. Re-garded as the earliest French communist. Took part in the uprisings of 1830 and 1834. Under his direction the new provisional government was established in 1848.

BLASIS, Virginia (1807–38). French contralto. Achieved her first success in Piacenza. Sang in Paris (1827), then in London, Scotland, and Ireland before returning to Italy (1838).

BLAZE DE BURY, Ange-Henri (1813–88). French writer on music. First a diplomatic attaché, then journalist for the *Revue des deux Mondes* and *Le Ménestrel,* and biogra-pher of Meyerbeer (*Meyerbeer, sa vie, ses oeuvres et son temps* [Paris, 1865]).

BLONDEAU, Pierre-Auguste-Louis (1784–1865). French instrumentalist, composer, writer on music. Violist in the orchestra of the Paris Opéra.

BLONDIN. French acrobat. In 1811 he became director of a troupe of gymnastic artists in Vienna. Father of Charles Blondin who crossed Niagra Falls on a tightrope (1855–60).

BLUM, Karl (1786–1844). German composer and dramatist. Studied with Salieri in Vienna, visited France and Italy, and returned to Germany (1820), where he became court kapellmeister and later régisseur at the Royal Opera. Wrote many operas, operettas and comedies. Music teacher of the Princess Wilhelm.

BLUMAUER, Karl (1785–1840). German actor. He was celebrated in Iffland roles, and also worked as a producer and régisseur. After his retirement from the stage he wrote pedagogical books for the young.

BLUME, Heinrich (1788–1856). German singer and actor at the Royal Theatre in Berlin, where he created Caspar in Weber's *Der Freischütz* in 1821.

BLUMNER, Martin (1827–1901). German musician. Studied music with Dehn. Member of the Berlin Singakademie (1847), associate conductor (1853), chief conductor (1876). Composed oratorios, cantatas, a *Te Deum,* motets, and psalms.

BOAS, Eduard (1815–53). German dramatist.

BOCHSA, Robert-Nicolaus-Charles (1789–1856). French composer and harpist. Wrote eight operas for the Opéra Comique (1813–16), arranged numbers of works for the harp. Organized oratorio performances with Sir George Smart (1822). Professor of harp at the Academy of Music in London. Conductor at the Italian Opera, the King's Theatre (1822–32). Absconded with the English singer Mme. Bishop (1838) and undertook extended concert tours with her through Europe and America. Wrote a famous *Méthode pour la harpe* (London, 1816).

BOCK, Gustav (1813–63). German publisher and dealer in Berlin. See **BOTE & BOCK**.

BÖCKH, August (1785–1867). German music scholar. Studied at Halle, professor at the University of Berlin (1811), where he remained all his life. He edited the works of the Pindar with an introduction from which modern research into ancient Greek received a new impetus.

BOCKHOLZ-FALCONI, Anna (1820–79). German singer. Sang in London (1848), then Italy. Became a teacher in Paris.

BOGUSLAWSKY, Palon Heinrich Ludwig von (1789–1851). German astronomer. Director of the observatory in Breslau.

BOHRER, Anton. German violinist. Worked in Paris in the 1830s, and founded his own string quartet.

BOIELDIEU, François-Adrien (1775–1834). French composer. Studied in Rouen with Broche, later with Cherubini. Established himself as a master of *opéra comique* with *Le Calife de Bagdad* (1800) and *Jean de Paris* (1812). Worked in St. Petersburg (1804–12). Later he deepened his style and was receptive of romantic influences, triumphing with *La Dame blanche* (1825).

BOIGNE, Charles de. French journalist. Correspondent for the *Constitutionnel*.

BOISSELOT, Dominique-François-Xavier (1811–93). French composer. Studied in Barcelona and at the Paris Conservatoire. Married the daughter of Le Sueur. Won the Prix de Rome (1836). Inspector-general of music schools and theaters in Marseilles (1867). Enjoyed considerable success with *Ne touche pas la Reine* at the Opéra Comique (1847).

BOITO, Arrigo (1842–1918). Italian composer and librettist. Studied with Mazzucato, became friends with Faccio, went to Paris. Associated with the artistic reform movement Scapigliatura. His opera *Mefistofele* (1868) initially failed, but was later more successful (1875). Wrote the libretti for *La Giaconda, Otello,* and *Falstaff.* In words and music he was preoccupied with the conflicting attractions of virtue and evil.

BONARD. French lawyer working in London.

BONAWITZ, Johann Heinrich (1839–1917). German pianist and composer. Studied in Liège. New York (1872–73). Produced two operas in Philadelphia (including *The Bride of Messina*, 1874). Later lived in Vienna and London. Wrote operas, religious, orchestral, and piano music. Edited *Historische Klaviermusik*.

BONOLDI, Claudio (1783–1846). Italian tenor. Sang principally in Reggio and Milan, later at the Théâtre Italien in Paris. After retiring from the stage, he was a much-sought-after stage teacher in Milan.

BORDOGNI, Giovanni Marco (1789–1856). Italian tenor and teacher. Studied with Mayr. Début Milan (1813). Settled in Paris (1819). Professor of singing at the Conservatoire (1820). Retired from the stage (1833) and continued to teach privately. Pupils included Sontag, Cinti-Damoreau, and Mario.

BORGHI-MAMO, Adelaide (1826–1901). Italian contralto. Sang at the Théâtre Italien and the Opéra.

BÖRNE, Ludwig (Löb Baruch) (1786–1837). German writer. One of the leaders of the Junges Deutschland movement. Lived in Paris (1830) and published his outstanding *Briefe aus Paris* and *Neue Briefe aus Paris*.

BORNEMANN, Wilhelm (1767–1851). Prussian civil servant. Royal director general of the lottery in Berlin, member of the Zelter Choral Society.

BORNSTEDT, Adalbert von (1808–51). German journalist. Founded a German political-literary newspaper in Paris (1838). As a communist, his position was close to that of Karl Marx. He was obliged to leave France in 1845 on political grounds and moved to Brussels.

BÖRNSTEIN, Heinrich (1805–92). German journalist. Founder of *Vorwärts, Journal allemand de Paris*, and correspondent of the *Frankfurter Conversationsblatt* and the Viennese *Allgemeine Theaterzeitung*.

BOSIO, Angiolina (1830–59). Italian soprano. Studied in Milan and made her début there (1846). Appeared in Paris (1848), then toured North America. Sang regularly in London (1852), esp. in Verdi, and was chosen to sing Catherine in the London première of *L'Étoile du Nord* (1855). Engaged for St. Petersburg (1855–56) and died there suddenly, aged only twenty-nine.

BOTE & BOCK. German music publishing house founded by Eduard Bote and Gustav Bock (1838).

BOTT, Jean Joseph (1826–95). German violinist and conductor. Studied with his father, Hauptmann, and Spohr. Court conductor in Meiningen (1852–57) and Hanover (1865). Retired in 1878 and settled in New York (1885). Wrote two operas, orchestral and instrumental music.

BOTTÉ DE TOULMONT, Auguste (1797–1850). French cellist and writer on music. Correspondent for the *Revue musicale* (1827), librarian of the Conservatoire (1831). Wrote several musicological studies.

BÖTTICHER, Karl Friedrich (b. 1813). German singer. Tenor at the Royal Opera, Berlin (1836), then went to Hanover (1852).

BOUFFÉ, Hugues-Marie-Désiré (1800–1888). French actor.

BOULANGER, Ernest-Henri-Alexandre (1815–1900). French composer, son of a cello professor and the singer Marie-Julie Hallinger. Studied with Halévy and Le Sueur at the Paris Conservatoire. Wrote seven operas for the Opéra Comique, choruses for the Orphéonistes, and songs. Possessed a good tenor voice, and was professor of singing at the Conservatoire for twenty-two years. Married Princess Mychetsky. Father of Nadia and Lili.

BOULANGER, Marie-Julie (née Halligner) (1786–1850). French mezzo-soprano. Pupil of Garat. She was a famous soubrette at the Opéra Comique, where she worked as part of the ensemble (1811–35). Created the role of Lady Pamela in *Fra Diavolo* (1830).

BOURGEOIS, Auguste-Anicet (1806–71). French dramatist.

BOURGES, Jean-Maurice (1812–81). French music critic and composer. Correspondent for the *Revue et Gazette musicale de Paris*.

BOURSAULT-MALHERBE, Jean-François (1750–1842). French actor and playwright, author of several dramas and vaudevilles.

BOUSQUET, Georges (1818–54). French composer and critic. Conductor at the Opéra (1847–51), then at the Théâtre Italien. Wrote for the *Revue et Gazette musicale de Paris, Chronique musicale, Illustration, Commerces*.

BRACHVOGEL, Albert Emil (1824–78). German writer. Worked in various professions before becoming a writer. His two outstanding successes were fictions based on musical personalities; the tragedy *Narciss* (1856), about Rameau's nephew, and the novel *Friedmann Bach* (1858), about the son of J. S. Bach, which was reprinted many times.

BRAGA, Gaetano (1829–1907). Italian cellist and composer. Studied at the Naples Conservatoire, toured Europe and America as a cellist, and lived mostly in Paris and London. His *Leggenda valacca* attained great popularity. Composed several operas, sacred music, and a violoncello method.

BRAMBILLA, Teresa (1813–95). Italian soprano. Studied in Milan. Début 1831. Sang with success on several Italian and Spanish stages. She was popular in Paris, but returned to Italy (1847) where she created Gilda in *Rigoletto* (1851).

BRANDENSTEIN, Sophie von. See **EBERS, Sophie**.

BRANDES, Johann Christian (d. 1799). German actor. Appeared with the Schonemann Troupe in Lübeck (1757) and the Schuch Company. Wrote the comedy *Trau, schau, wem* and the melodrama *Ariadne auf Naxos,* set to music by Benda and Reichardt. Died poor and forgotten. His memoirs *Meine Lebensgeschichte* (1799–1800, 3 vols.) provide valuable materials for the history of the theater in the eighteenth century.

BRANDT, Georg Friedrich (b. 1773). German musician. Served the duke of Mecklenburg-Schwerin, then became a member of the Munich Court Orchestra (1806). Much admired bassoonist.

BRANDUS, Gemmy (1823–73). German music publisher and dealer. Took over Schlesinger's company in Paris (1846). Meyerbeer's business associate and confidante after the death of Louis Gouin.

BRANDUS, Louis (Ludwig) (1816–87). German music publisher and dealer. Obtained the book-marketing concession in Berlin.

BRASSIN, Louis (1840–84). French pianist. Studied with Moscheles in Leipzig. Toured with his brothers Leopold and Gerhard. Taught at the Stern Conservatoire in Berlin (1866), and Brussels (1869–79). Composed an operetta, piano concertos, and piano music, *École moderne de piano*.

BRAUN, Karl Anton Philipp (b. 1788). German oboist. Member of the Royal Orchestra in Copenhagen (1807). Undertook many concert tours, appearing in Munich in 1812.

BREITING, Hermann (1804–60). German tenor. Début in Würzburg (1826); Berlin (1827–29), later the Kärntnertor-Theater in Vienna, St. Petersburg and London. Had an extraordinarily powerful voice suited to heroic roles.

BRESSON, Charles, count (1798–1847). French ambassador in Berlin.

BRETZNER, Christoph Friedrich (1748–1807). German playwright. Ran a merchant business in Leipzig. Wrote numerous comedies and *Singspiele,* including *Belmonte und Constanze* (1781), from which Gottlieb Stephanie derived Mozart's *Die Entführung aus dem Serail*, and an arrangement of Lorenzo Da Ponte and Mozart's *Così fan tutte* as *Die Mädchen von Flandern* (1794).

BREXENDORFF, Mme. German singer.

BROCKHAUS, Heinrich (1804–74). German publisher.

BRODSKY, Adolf (1851–1929). Russian violinist. Studied in Vienna and Moscow, and succeeded Laub as professor. Toured extensively (1879–82); Leipzig Conservatoire (1883–91), founded the Brodsky Quartet. New York (1891–94); Manchester (1895), director of the Royal College of Music.

BRODT. Stage mechanic at the Paris Opéra in the 1830s.

BRÜGGEMANN, Theodor. German civil servant in the Ministry of Culture under Eichhorn. Uncle of Peter Cornelius.

BRUGNOLI (SAMENGO-), Amalia (c.1800). Italian dancer. Prima ballerina in Naples (1820). Went to London with her sister (1832). Developed a staccato technique in dancing *en pointe*.

BRÜHL, Karl, Graf von (1772–1837). German bureaucrat. General director of theaters in Berlin (1815–28).

BRUNSWICK, Léon-Lévy (1805–59). French writer. Wrote over one hundred comedies and vaudevilles, often containing very popular couplets. Wrote the libretto of *Le Postillion de Lonjumeau* for Adam (1836).

BUCHWIESER, Cathinka. Austrian singer. Daughter of the third kapellmeister at the Theater an der Wien in Vienna, where she was engaged as first soprano. She also worked with Milder at the Kärntnertor-Theater. Schubert dedicated some songs to her (1825).

BULL, Ole Bornemann (1810–80). Norwegian violinist and composer. Wrote two violin concertos and was an enthusiast of Norwegian folk music. Encouraged the young Grieg.

BULLY, Eugène-Auguste-Roger de (1806–66). French novelist and dramatist. With Saint-Georges he was to have redrafted the libretto of *Die drei Pintos*.

BÜLOW, Hans Guido, Freiherr von (1830–94). German pianist, conductor, and writer. Studied with Liszt in Weimar. In 1850 he went to Berlin, where he joined democratic groups and fell under the influence of Wagner's ideas. He married Liszt's daughter, Cosima, who later left him for Wagner.

BÜLOW, Heinrich, Freiherr von (1792–1846). Prussian politician. Minister of foreign affairs. Married Gabriele von Humboldt.

BULOZ, François (1803–77). French critic. Headed the *Revue de deux Mondes* from 1831. Acquired the collaboration of de Musset, George Sand, and Merimée.

BURCHARDT, Marie (d. 1870). German singer. Soloist in the Singakademie. Made guest appearances as a dramatic and coloratura singer in the Royal Opera in Berlin (1843).

BÜRGER, Gottfried August (1747–94). German poet. Professor at Göttingen. First great master of the German ballad (esp. *Lenore*, 1773).

BURGHERSH. See **WESTMORLAND**.

BURGUIS. French secretary of Amalia Beer and Meyerbeer.

BUSCH, Wilhelm (1832–1908). German cartoonist, painter, and writer working for the *Fliegende Blätter*.

BUSSCHOP, Jules-Auguste-Guillaume (1810–96). French composer. He was entirely self-taught and became successful as composer of motets, cantatas (*Le Drapeau belge*, 1834), a *Te Deum* and some instrumental music.

BUTEUX, Claude-François (1797–1870). French musician. Clarinetist at the Paris Opéra from 1825.

C

CABEL, Marie-Josephe (née Dreulette) (1827–85). Belgian coloratura soprano. Studied in Liège and Brussels, and at the Paris Conservatoire. Début 1849 at the Opéra Comique.

Her voice was supple and silvery, and she created bravura roles for Auber (*Manon Lescaut*, 1856), Meyerbeer (*Dinorah*, 1859), and Thomas (Philine in *Mignon*, 1866).

CADEAUX, Justin. French composer. Known for his operas *Colette* and *Les deux gentilhommes* (1844) (with words by Planard), both produced at the Opéra Comique.

CALDARA, Antonio (1670–1736). Italian composer. Pupil of Legrenzi. Lived in Rome, Milan, Bologna, Mantua, and Madrid. Settled in Vienna (1716) as assistant choirmaster to J. J. Fux. Wrote eighty-seven operas, thirty-two oratorios, and thirty masses.

CALZADO, Torivio (b. 1805). Director of the Théâtre Italien in the 1850s.

CAMBARDI (= CHAMBARD), Mathilde Jeanne (1828–61). French singer.

CAMBIASI, Pompeo. Italian civil servant. Provincial councillor in Como. Published a chronology of all opera and ballet performances at La Scala and the Teatro Cannobiana in Milan (1778–1872).

CAMOËNS, Luiz Vaz de (c. 1524–80). Portuguese poet. *Os Lusiadas* (1572), written during his trips to Goa and Macao, is the national epic of Portugal. It celebrates the ten-month voyage of Vasco da Gama that opened the seaway round Africa to India, and was used by Meyerbeer in the preparation of *L'Africaine*.

CAMPE, Julius (1792–1867). German publisher in Hamburg of Heine's works.

CAMPENHAUSEN, Ludolf (1803–90). German politician. Banker in Cologne. Elected as a liberal to the United Landtag (1847). For a short time minister president, then Prussian delegate *(Bevollmächtiger)* at the Frankfurt Parliament (1848).

CAMPITELLI, Luigi (b. 1780). Italian singer. A famous *basso buffo* who sang throughout Italy, and also in Lisbon.

CAMPORESI, Violante (1785–1839). Italian singer. Performed in Napoleon's private music. In 1817 took to the stage in England, then in Italy until 1830.

CANNABICH, Josephine (née Wowaleck) (b. 1781). German singer. Pupil of her father Nicholas Wowaleck. After an engagement in Frankfurt, she returned to Munich (1798), where she became a court singer in 1800, and prima donna of the Opera. Because of chest problems, she appeared only in straight theater after 1807.

CANNABICH, Karl Konrad (1771–1806). German composer. Worked as a violinist in Munich, becoming court kapellmeister. Also worked briefly as an opera conductor in Frankfurt, writing two operas as well as instrumental and vocal works. Married the singer Josephine Wowaleck.

CAPELLER, Nepomuk. Bohemian flautist and composer active in Munich. Worked on the improvement of the flute, adding a D key and making alternative arrangements of the keys.

CARAFA (DE COLOBRANO), Michele Enrico (1787–1872). Italian composer. After serving in Russia (1812) he devoted himself to music. Went to Naples, where he formed an enduring friendship with Rossini. French citizen from 1834. Member of the Académie des Beaux Arts. His operas were well-written but without melodic individuality, e.g., *Masaniello* (1827), *La Prison d'Edimbourg* (1833). Helped in the Paris revival of *Semiramide* (1860).

CARL FRIEDRICH, grand duke of Saxe-Weimar-Eisenach (b. 1783, r. 1828–53). Son of Carl August, patron of Goethe and Schiller.

CARL, Karl (Karl Andreas Bernbrunn) (1789–1854). Austrian dramatist and theater director. Manager of the Isarhortheater in Munich (1822–26), then of the Theater an der Wien in Vienna. In 1838 he bought the Theater in der Leopoldstadt, which he demolished and replaced with the Carl-Theater (1847). He directed the latter until his death. He was also an actor and writer of farces, being particularly famous on stage as the popular comic character Staberl. His successful company included Nestroy, and he performed many of the latter's plays.

CARLO III, duke of Parma and Piacenza (b. 1823, r. 1849–54). Penultimate duke of this territory, eventually assassinated.

CAROLATH, Heinrich Karl Wilhelm, Fürst von (1783–1864). Prussian general of cavalry.

CARRÉ, Michel. See under **BARBIER, Jules**.

CARUS, Dr. Karl (1789–1869). German doctor and natural philosopher. Director of the medical academy in Dresden.

CARVALHO, Léon (1825–97). French impresario. Studied at the Paris Conservatoire, singer at the Opéra Comique (1851–55), where he met and married Marie Miolan (1853). Director of the Théâtre Lyrique (1856–58), Opéra Comique (1876–87). In 1887 the theater burned down and 131 people were killed. After being imprisoned for negligence, he was reinstated on appeal (1891).

CASPERS, Louis-Henri-Jean (1825–1906). French composer. Studied at the Paris Conservatoire. Produced stage works at the Théâtre Lyrique, Opéra Comique, Bouffes-Parisiens, and Porte-St-Martin. Also wrote a cantata, instrumental works, and songs. Abandoned composition to run the family business (1861).

CASTELLAN, Jeanne-Anais (b. 1819). French soprano. Studied with Cinti-Damoreau, Bordogni and Nourrit. Début Varese (1837). Appeared in Italy, Austria, United States

(1843–44), St. Petersburg (1844–46) and London (1844–53). Principal singer at the Théâtre Italien from 1848. Created Berthe in *Le Prophète*.

CASTELLI, Ignaz Franz (1781–1862). Austrian writer. Court dramatist at the Kärntnertor-Theater in Vienna, where he wrote libretti and translated opera texts into German (including *Les Huguenots*). Also edited the *Allgemeiner musikalischer Anzeiger*.

CASTIL-BLAZE, François (1784–1857). French writer and composer. His chief work was *De l'opéra en France* (1850, 2 vols.), which discusses the suitability of words for music, and the components of opera. It attacks managers, critics, and translators, although he was himself a critic for the *Journal des Débats* (1822–32) and a distinguished translator. He did not hesitate to adapt needlessly, even to inserting whole numbers of his own (esp. in his notorious adaptation of *Der Freischütz* as *Robin des Bois*, 1824). Father of the critic Henri Blaze de Bury.

CATALANI, Angelica (1780–1849). Italian soprano. Studied with her father, Antonio, and P. Morandi. Début Venice (1797). Milan (1801), London (1806), manager of the Théâtre Italien in Paris (1814–17). Sang extensively in eastern Europe (1820–21). Retired and opened a singing school near Florence (1821). One of the highest paid of prima donnas.

CATEL, Charles-Simon (1773–1830). French composer and theorist. Studied in Paris with Gossec. Professor of theory at the newly founded Conservatoire (1795), member of the Académie (1815). His works for the Opéra reflect the mood of the empire and emergent romanticism and contributed to the evolving Grand Opéra (*Sémiramis*, 1802; *Les Bayadères* 1810). Also successful as a composer of *opéra comique*, in which ideas from Méhul are combined with *opera buffa* (*L'Auberge de Bagères*, 1807; *Les Aubergistes de qualité*, 1812). Best known for his *Traité d'harmonie* (1802).

CATRUFO, Giuseppe (1771–1851). Italian composer. From 1810 active in Paris as a singing teacher and opera composer, also writing piano and violin works. Settled in London (1835).

CERF, Carl Friedrich (Hirsch) (1782–1845). German impresario. Director of the Königstädter-Theater in Berlin.

CERFBERR, Maximilian-Charles-Alphonse (1817–83). French journalist. Administrator of the Théâtre du Gymnase Dramatique.

CERRITO, Fanny (1817–1909). Italian dancer. Studied with Perrot, Blasis, and Saint-Léon. Début in Naples (1832). Toured Europe triumphantly: Vienna (1836), Milan (1838), London (1840), Paris (1847), St. Petersburg (1855), Moscow (1856). She had great strength and brio, and became one of the great dancers of the romantic ballet.

CESARIS, Vincenzo da. A Roman who met Weber in Gotha and introduced him to the world of Italian opera, providing him with much stimulus and advice.

CHAMPEIN, Stanislas (1753–1830). French composer. Studied with Reccicio and Chavet in Paris (1770) where he wrote sacred music and twenty-two operas (–1792), including *Le nouveau Don Quichotte* (1789). Held a government position (1793–1804), continuing to compose but without success. Also director of *Le France Juge: Revue de la littérature, de la musique, des beaux arts* in Paris. Spent the last years of his life in poverty; a pension arranged by Boieldieu and Scribe came through only eighteen months before his death.

CHARTON-DEMEUR, Anne (1824–92). French soprano. Studied with Bizot. Début Bordeaux; London (1842–52). Sang in the first London performances of many French works. Later closely associated with Berlioz, creating roles in *Beatrice et Bénédict* and *Les Troyens à Carthage*. Sang in the Berlioz Festival (1870).

CHATEAUBRIAND, François-René, vicomte de (1768–1848). French writer and statesman. Apologist for the established order and the Catholic faith. His prose tales *Atala* (1801) and *René* (1802) capture the passion, idealism, and melancholy of his romantic vision. Ambassador in Berlin.

CHAVET, Abbé (= CHAVÉE, Honoré). French critic who worked for the *France musicale*.

CHÉLARD, Hippolyte-André-Jean-Baptiste (1789–1861). French composer. Pupil of Fétis, Gossec and Dourien (1808), at the Paris Conservatoire; Prix de Rome (1822). Opéra orchestra violinist (1826); Munich (1826). Conducted German opera in London (1832–33). Returned to Munich, where he produced his most important work, *Der Hermannschlacht* (1835), which took account of the conventions of German romantic opera. Kapellmeister in Augsburg (1836), in Weimar (1840). Lived in Paris (1852–54). Friend and supporter of Berlioz, whose music his own resembles.

CHÉRI, Rose (orig. Rose-Marie Ciszos) (1824–61). French actress.

CHERUBINI, Maria Luigi Carlo Zenobio Salvatore (1760–1842). Italian composer. Studied in Florence, Bologna and Milan. Wrote 13 Italian operas before settling in Paris in 1788. He joined the newly formed Conservatoire (1795) and eventually became director (1821–41). *Démophon* (1788) initiated his mature style and made him a pioneer of both *opéra comique* and *grand opéra* in more imaginative handling of the orchestra and ensemble, more dramatic motivation, and the development of strong character types. *Lodoïska* (1791) elaborated the rescue opera, which he brought to a high point in *Les deux Journées* (1800). It idealized the simple life and humble characters who embody qualities of the highest virtue. The passionately tragic *Médée* (1797) and the grandiose *Les Abencérages* (1813) were milestones in the emergence of *grand opéra*. In later years he turned from opera to sacred music.

CHEVÉ, Émile-Joseph-Maurice (1804–64). French physician. Became a zealous advocate of Pierre Galin's method of musical instruction. Collaborated with his wife Nanine Paris in a *Methode élémentaire de musique vocale* (Paris, 1844), attacking the method of the Paris Conservatoire. Published a long series of essays and articles causing acrimonious polemic for years.

CHÉZY, Helmine von (1783–1856). German poetess. Achieved modest fame as a lyricist, but is best known as the librettist of Weber's *Euryanthe* (1823). Meyerbeer's support of her in her poverty and blindness is an example of his many acts of disinterested kindness.

CHOLLET, Jean-Baptiste-Marie (1798–1892). Celebrated French tenor at the Opéra Comique. Creator of the title roles in *Fra Diavolo* (1830), *Zampa* (1831), and *Le Postillion de Longjumeau* (1836).

CHOPIN, Frédéric-François (1810–49). Polish composer. Master of romantic piano music, innovative in harmony, form, and melody. Lived in Paris after 1830. Chopin was deeply affected by *Robert le Diable*: the *Ballade* no.2 in F (op. 38) was inspired by Alice's "Va, dit elle" in act 1, and he wrote a *Grand Duo* for cello and piano on themes from the opera. Meyerbeer was a great admirer of Chopin's music, and a pallbearer at his funeral in 1849.

CHORLEY, Henry Fothergill (1808–72). English music critic and essayist. He was active as a dramatist, translator, art critic, poet, novelist, and journalist. From 1831 to 1868 he was music critic of the London *Athenaeum*. Traveled extensively, met celebrities, was intolerant of new musical ideas, particularly those of Wagner. Wrote *Music and Manners in France and Germany* (1844, 3 vols.), *Thirty Years' Musical Recollections* (1862, 2 vols.).

CHORON, Alexandre-Étienne (1771–1834). French music theorist and editor. Member of the Académie (1811). Director of the Paris Opéra (1816). Reopened the Conservatoire as the École Royale de Chant et de Déclamation, and established the Institution de Musique Classique et Religieuse (1817–30). Wrote and translated many works of musical theory.

CHRISTINA. See **ISABEL II**, queen of Spain.

CIBINI, Katherine von (née Kozeluch) (1790–1858). Austrian pianist. Lady-in-waiting to the empress of Austria.

CICÉRI, Pierre-Luc-Charles (1782–1868). French painter and stage designer. Pupil of Bellangé. Provided his first decor for the Opéra in 1809, moved to Cassel, returned to Paris (1813), and worked at the Théâtre des Tuileries, the Odéon, Nouveautés, and the Opéra, where his association with Louis Daguerre was epoch-making. His stage designs for *La Muette de Portici, Guillaume Tell, Robert le Diable,* and *La Juive* in particular were revolutionary in their power of conception and realization, with new accuracy in historical detail, grandeur of pictorial effect, three-dimensional scenery, and panoramic effects. His four pupils, Despléchins, Diéterle, Séchan, and Feuchères, developed his work further in the years 1833–48.

CIMAROSA, Domenico (1749–1801). Italian composer. Studied in Naples, where he produced his first operas. Active in both Naples and Rome until 1787, becoming Paisiello's great rival. From 1787 to 1791 he directed the opera in St. Petersburg. Succeeded Salieri as court kapellmeister in Vienna, where he wrote his most famous work, *Il Matrimonio segreto* (1792). *Maestro di capella* to the king of Naples (1792). His talent lay in comic opera, and he is the forefather of Rossini.

CINTI-DAMOREAU, Laure (née Montalant) (1801–63). French soprano. Studied with Bordogni and Catalani. Début Théâtre Italien (1815); Opéra (1826–28, 1831–35) where she created roles in operas by Rossini, Auber, and Meyerbeer (Isabelle in *Robert le Diable*). Opéra Comique (1837–43) where she created further roles by Auber. Toured the United States (1843–44). Professor at the Conservatoire (1833–56). Wrote a *Méthode de Chant* (1849).

CLAIRVILLE (= Louis François Nicolaie) (1811–79). French actor and writer. Wrote many vaudevilles in collaboration with the brothers Coignard, Blum, Siraudin, and others. Inaugurated a series of popular comic revues at the Théâtre Ambigu-Comique (1836). Wrote and collaborated on over 600 pieces, 450 of which were published. His best known libretti were for Lecocq and Planquette.

CLAPISSON, Antonin-Louis (1808–66). French composer. Studied in Bordeaux and Paris with Habeneck. Violinist in the orchestra of the Opéra. Member of the Académie (1854) and professor at the Conservatoire. Had early success with the comic opera *La Figurante* (1838), which was followed by a long succession of works that caught the taste of the Parisian public, esp. *Gibby la Cornemeuse* (1846).

CLEMENTI, Muzio (1752–1832). Italian pianist and composer. A virtuoso who lived in England after 1766, conducting the Italian opera and big concerts in London. Undertook many extended concert tours to Paris, Vienna, St. Petersburg, Rome, and Berlin. Here he lived at the home of the Beers and briefly instructed the young Meyerbeer. After 1810 dedicated himself principally to his music business and piano factory.

CLERC, Albert (b. 1804). French writer. Editor of the Parisian *Charivari* until 1848.

COCCIA, Carlo (1782–1873). Italian composer. Studied with Paisiello. Music teacher (1801). Accompanist in the private orchestra of Joseph Napoleon (1806–8). Venice (1809–17). Wrote thirty-seven operas (1808–33). Developed the *opera semiseria* and gave the chorus a more functional role. *Clotilda* (Venice, 1815), *Maria Stuarda* (London, 1827) and *Caterina di Guise* (Milan, 1833) were successful. Kapellmeister in Lisbon (1820–23). Went to London as conductor of the Italian Opera (1827). Returned to Italy (1828), where he became *maestro di capella* at the cathedral in Novara (1836), and director of the music academy in Turin (1836–40).

COCHE, Victor-Jean-Baptiste (1806–81). French flautist. Pupil of Tulon. One of the first to introduce the Bohm flute into France.

COIGNARD, Théodore (1806–72) and **Jean-Hippolyte** (1807–82). French playwrights. Together they wrote over two hundred vaudevilles and comedies.

COLBRAN, Isabella Angela (1785–1845). Italian contralto. Studied with Marinelli and Crescentini. Sang on the great stages of Europe. Rossini, whom she married in 1822, wrote several of his most famous roles for her, e.g., in *Otello, Ricciardo e Zoraide, La Donna del lago, Semiramide*.

COLLIN D'HARLEVILLE, Jean-François (1755–1806). French poet. Wrote a series of very successful character comedies.

COLMAN, George (1762–1836). English playwright. Directed the Haymarket Theatre. Wrote numerous operas, dramas, comedies, farces (among them *John Bull*, 1805) with much success.

COMMER, Franz (1813–87). German composer. Music director in Berlin (1844). Choirmaster at St. Hedwig's, Berlin (1845).

CONCONE, Giuseppe (1801–61). Italian vocal specialist. Lived in Paris as a singing teacher (1832–48). Wrote operas, vocal scenes, songs, a collection of famous *solfeggi* in five vols.

COOK, Thomas Simpson (1782–1848). Irish composer and singing teacher. Studied with his father and Giordani. Conducted in Dublin. Later a singer (tenor) and conductor at Drury Lane and professor at the Royal Academy in London. Wrote two singing treatises, twenty operas, overtures, songs, piano pieces.

COOPER, James Fenimore (1789–1851). American novelist. Wrote thirty-three romances of frontier life and historical adventure, esp. stories of the sea and American Indians, like *The Last of the Mohicans* (1826) and *The Red Rover* (1827).

CORALLI, Jean (1779–1854). French dancer and choreographer. Studied at the Paris Opéra Ballet School (1802), début (1802). Worked in Vienna, Milan, Lisbon, Marseilles, Paris. Belonged to the ensemble of the Opéra (1831–48), where he created some of the most famous ballets of the time (incl. *Giselle,* 1841, and *La Péri,* 1843).

CORMON, Eugène (1810–1903). French dramatist.

CORNEILLE, Pierre (1606–84). French playwright. Great exponent of the French classical tragedy, which, almost single-handedly, he welded into a new dramatic art form, e.g., *Le Cid* (1636). His dramas explore the conflict between love and honor.

CORNELIUS, Peter, Ritter von (1783–1867). German artist. Historical painter summoned to Berlin by Friedrich Wilhelm IV (1841). Uncle of the composer.

CORNELIUS, Peter (1824–74). German composer. Nephew of the famous painter. Studied with Dehn (1845–52), then joined Liszt in Weimar. Followed Wagner to Vienna

(1859) and Munich (1865), where he became professor at the Royal Music School. Wrote operas and songs, esp. *Der Barbier von Bagdad* (1858).

COSTA, Sir Michael (1808–84). Italian, then British, composer and conductor. Became the music director of the new Royal Italian Opera at Covent Garden (1847–69), where his discipline resulted in high standards.

COSTE, Jacques (1798–1859). French journalist. Founded the *Journal du Temps* (1830), and signed the protest by journalists against Polignac's cabinet and its press legislation (26 July 1830), which led to the outbreak of the July Revolution.

COSTENOBLE, Karl Ludwig (1769–1837). German actor and writer. Worked as an actor at the Hofburgtheater in Vienna (1818), later wrote numerous comedies that were collectively published in 1830.

CRAMER, Johann Baptist (1771–1858). German pianist, composer, and music publisher. Brought to London as a child. Studied with his father, Clementi, and Abel. Began to travel as a concert pianist (1788). Later taught in Munich and Paris (1832–45), finally returning to London. His greatest work is the piano method *Grosse Praktische Pianoforte Schule* (1815, in five parts), which became famous in piano teaching. Many editions by famous pianists followed. Also wrote 7 piano concertos, 105 piano sonatas, chamber and instrumental music. In 1824 established a publishing house, J. B. Cramer & Co., with R. Addison and T. F. Beale.

CRÉMIEUX, Isaac-Adolphe (1796–1880). French lawyer. Member of the Provisional Government (1848), minister of justice (1870–71). Founded the Alliance Israelite Universelle (1860).

CRESCENTINI, Girolamo (1762–1846). Italian male mezzo-soprano. Début Padua (1782). After successful appearances in Italy, he sang in Lisbon for several years, became singing teacher to the imperial family in Vienna (1805), and sang in Paris at Napoleon's request (1806–12). Taught at the Naples Conservatoire, where Isabella Colbran was one of his pupils.

CREVEL DE CHARLEMAGNE, Louis-Ernest-Napoléon (1806–82). French writer and translator. Known for his biography of Benedetto Marcello.

CRIVELLI, Gaetano (1768–1836). Italian tenor. Début Brescia (1794) and appeared in Verona, Palermo, Venice, Naples, Milan (1805), Paris (1811), London (1817), where he sang in the first performances of several Mozart works there. Returned to Italy where he created Adriano in *Il Crociato in Egitto* (Venice, 1824), a role that became his favorite, and that he sang at his farewell (1831).

CROSNIER, Louis-François (1792–1867). French intendant. Director of the Théâtre de la Porte-St-Martin (1834–45) and of the Opéra Comique (1852–56).

CRUVELLI, Sofie (1824–1907). German soprano. Studied in Paris with Piermarini, then with Bordogni and Lamperti. Début Venice (1847). One of the best Verdi sopranos of the mid-nineteenth century. Théâtre Italien (1851–53), Opéra (1854–56) with a salary of 100,000 fr. Sang Valentine, Rachel, Giulia, created Hélène in *Les Vêpres siciliennes*.

CRUX, Anton. German dancer. *Premier danseur* in Mannheim under Lauchery. In 1778 he was persuaded by the Elector Karl Theodor to transfer to Munich where he became royal ballet master.

CURSCHMANN, Karl Friedrich (1804–41). German composer. Originally a law student, then studied with Hauptmann and Spohr. Wrote songs of a poetic quality: eighty-eight lieder, nine duets, and trios, 2 vols. (1871). Also noted as a singer; gave concerts in Germany.

CUSTINE, Adolphe de, marquis (1793–1857). French writer Held a famous salon in Paris attended by Chopin, Victor Hugo, and esp. Balzac. Heine and Mme. Merlin were also among his friends. Meyerbeer set his poem "La folle de St Joseph" to music (1837) and Schlesinger published it in the same year.

CUVILLON, Jean-Baptiste-Philemon (1809–1900). French musician. Violinist and professor at the Paris Conservatoire.

CZARTORYSKI, Adam Jerzy, prince (1770–1861). Polish statesman. Hero of the Polish nationalist cause. Elected head of government after the Revolution of 1830. After the suppression of the uprising, he escaped to Paris where he afterwards resided until his death, a generous benefactor to poor Polish expatriates.

CZARTORYSKI, Constantin, prince (1773–1860). Polish nobleman. Lived in Vienna after 1832.

CZERNY, Carl (1791–1857). Austrian pianist and composer. Studied with his father, Beethoven, Clementi, and Hummel. Traveled to Leipzig (1836), Paris and London (1837) and Italy (1846). Otherwise lived in Vienna, where he taught many celebrated pupils and wrote famous instructional études and exercises used by generations of pianists all over the world. Prolific composer who wrote concertos, symphonies, overtures, chamber music, and sacred works.

D

DABADIE, Henri-Bernard (1797–1853). French baritone. Studied at the Paris Conservatoire. Début at the Opéra (1819), where he sang until 1835, creating roles in operas by Rossini *(Guillaume Tell)* and Auber *(La Muette de Portici)*. After retiring from the Opéra, he still appeared occasionally in Italy.

DACHRÖDEN, Ludwig Caesar von (d. 1882). German official. Intendant and chamberlain to Grand Duke Georg of Mecklenburg-Strelitz.

DACOSTA, Isaak (called France) (1778–1866). French instrumentalist. One of the most famous clarinetists of his time. From 1820 worked in the orchestra of the Paris Opéra.

D'AGOULT, Marie-Catherine-Sophie (née Flavigny), comtesse (1805–76). French writer. Using the pseud. "Daniel Stern" she contributed articles to Girardin's newspaper *La Presse*. Famous for relationship with Liszt (1833–44). Mother of Cosima Wagner.

DALAYRAC, Nicolas (1753–1809). French composer. Studied law and served the count d'Artois while studying music with Langlé and Grétry. Then devoted his energies to the theater, writing fifty-six operas and composing patriotic music in the Revolutionary and Napoleonic periods. During his lifetime his operas enjoyed great popularity. *Deux Mots, ou Une Nuit dans la forêt* (1806) was his last big success, performed at the Opéra Comique until 1828.

DAMCKE, Berthold (1812–75). German conductor. Pupil of Schmitt and Ries at Frankfurt. Conductor of the Potsdam Philharmonic Society and Choral Union for Operatic Music (1839–40). Active in St. Petersburg (1845), Brussels (1855), Paris (1859). Friend of Berlioz. Composed oratorios, part songs, piano pieces.

DAMERON, Pauline-Eulalie (1825–90). French singer. She made her début in *Robert le Diable* (1846), and was a member of the Opéra ensemble until 1861.

DAMOREAU. See **CINTI-DAMOREAU**

DANJOU, Jean-Louis-Felix (1812–66). French organist. Researcher and critic for the *Revue et Gazette musicale de Paris*.

DANTAN, Jean-Pierre (1800–1869). French sculptor. Created busts of Meyerbeer, Donizetti, Halévy, Spontini, and Nourrit.

D'ARGOUT (1782–1858). French civil servant. Directed the Ministry of Commerce and Public Works, which supported all the theaters from 1831. Governor of the Bank of France (1836).

DARTOIS, Armand (1788–1867). French playwright. Wrote c. 200 works in collaboration, esp. with Théaulon.

DAUSSOIGNE-MÉHUL, Louis-Joseph (1790–1875). French composer. Nephew and foster son of Méhul. Pupil of Catel and Méhul at the Conservatoire, won the Prix de Rome (1809). Wrote four operas, but was discouraged by a lack of success. Became director of the Liège Conservatoire (1827–62), was an associate of the Royal Academy in Brussels, and wrote a cantata and choral symphony.

DAUTRESME, August-Lucien (1826–92). French composer. Studied at the Royal College in Rouen, then the École Polytechnique (1846). Graduated as a naval officer, but left the sea for a business career in Elboeuf. Resumed music, studying with Jean Amadée

Méreaux, then at the Paris Conservatoire and with Meyerbeer. A dispute with Carvalho led to a prison sentence. On release he wrote music articles for the *Paris Magazine*. Took up the liberal cause in 1848. Elected to the National Assembly of the Third Republic (1876), and minister of commerce (1888). Wrote madrigals, melodies, and choruses for the *Orphéons*.

DAVELOUIS. Director of the casino in Spa during the 1850s.

DAVID, Félicien-César (1810–76). French composer. Studied at the Paris Conservatoire (1830). Joined the Saint-Simonists, traveled in the Near East. Returned to France and composed two symphonies (esp. *Le Désert*), twenty-four string quartets, two nonets, romances, piano works, operas (esp. *La Perle de Brésil*, 1851).

DAVID, Giovanni (1790–1864). Italian tenor. Studied with his father, Giacomo. Début Siena (1808). Milan (1814). Rossini wrote roles for him in *Il Turco in Italia*, *Otello*, *Ermione*, *La Donna del lago*, *Zelmire*. Also created roles for Pacini, Mayr, Donizetti. London (1829). Sang until 1839, then managed the St. Petersburg Opera. At its peak his singing aroused great admiration, his voice being full-toned, flexible, and of wide range.

DAVID, Pierre-Jean (1789–1856). French sculptor, known as David d'Angers. Influenced by Ingres and Canova in Rome. He executed the pediment of the Panthéon in Paris (1835–37). Prolific sculptor of portraits and medallions.

DAVISON, James William (1813–85). English critic. Editor of the *Musical World* (1844), published by his brother, William Duncan. From 1846–79 wrote for the *Times* as well as the *Saturday Review* and the *Pall Mall Gazette*.

DAVONS. French critic. Wrote for the *Patrie* and the *Assemblé nationale*.

DE BEGNIS, Giuseppe (1793–1849). Italian bass. Début Modena (1813). Became the leading buffo of his day: created Dandini in *La Cenerentola* (1817). Sang on various Italian stages until 1819, then in Paris and London (1821–27), before returning to Italy. Directed the opera in Dublin (1834–37).

DECKER, Constantin (b. 1810). German pianist and composer.

DEDOYARD, Henri. Belgian donkey-guide in the resort of Spa during the 1850s.

DEFFÈS, Pierre-Louis (1819–1900). French composer. Studied in Toulouse and at the Paris Conservatoire. Won the Prix de Rome (1847). Had contacts in Ems, where a number of his works were performed in the 1860s. Became head of the Conservatoire in Toulouse. None of his twenty works remained in the repertory (*L'Anneau d'argent*, 1855; *Le Café du Roi*, 1861; *Jessica*, 1898).

DEHN, Siegfried Wilhelm (1799–1858). German music theorist. Adopted music as his profession after losing his fortune (1829). Appointed music librarian of the Royal Library in Berlin through Meyerbeer's influence (1842); then royal professor (1849). Profound theorist and teacher of Anton Rubinstein, Theodor Kullak, Glinka, Kiel.

DEINHARDSTEIN, Johann Ludwig (1794–1859). Austrian playwright. Vice director of the Vienna Hofburgtheater and censor (1832–41).

DÉJAZET, Virginie (1798–1875). French actress. From 1834 she appeared at Théâtre du Palais Royal in Paris, and in 1859 took over the Théâtre des Folies-Nouvelles, which she renamed the Théâtre Déjazet.

DELACROIX, Ferdinand-Victor-Eugène (1798–1863). French painter. He was one of the great figures in nineteenth-century French art, and one of the most accomplished colorists of all time in his brilliant canvases of historical and dramatic scenes. Took great interest in politics, literature, and music. Kept a famous journal.

DELAFIELD, Edward. English impresario. Director of the Royal Italian Opera, Covent Garden in London (1847–51).

DELAROCHE, Paul-Hippolyte (1796–1856). French painter, popular for his historical scenes and portraits.

DELAVIGNE, Germain (1790–1868). French writer and librettist. Collaborated with Scribe on the libretto of *Robert le Diable*.

DELDEVEZ, Édouard-Marie-Ernest (1817–97). French composer and conductor. Studied at the Paris Conservatoire with Habeneck, Halévy, and Berton. Assistant conductor at the Opéra, and of the Conservatoire concerts (1859). Professor of orchestral classes at the Conservatoire (1874). Composed five ballets, two operas, three symphonies, chamber music, and songs. Wrote several learned monographs.

DELIBES, Léo-Clement-Philibert (1836–91). French composer. Studied with Tariot and Adam, whose work much influenced him. Composed a long series of operettas, and worked as chorus master at the Théâtre Lyrique, before moving to the Opéra as accompanist and chorus master under Massé. Won great fame with his two ballets and then his *opéras comiques*, esp. *Lakmé* (1883), influenced by David and Bizet.

DELIGNY. Official assistant to the director of the Paris Opéra.

DELLE SEDIE, Enrico (1822–1907). Italian baritone. Studied with Galeffi and Paersanola. Sang all over Europe with great success, and taught at the Paris Conservatoire (1867–71), then privately with his wife, Margherita Tizzoni.

DELMAR, Baron von (1780–1858). French socialite. Son of a Jewish Berlin banker, Salomon Moses Levy, and a millionaire. His Paris home was frequented by Liszt, Chopin, Rossini, Kalkbrenner. Heine discusses him in the ninth canto of *Lutezia*.

DELORD, Taxile (1815–77). French writer. Director of *Le Charivari* in Paris (1842–58). Member of the National Assembly (1871).

DEMERIE (Glossop-Demerie), Mme. French soprano. Sang in the Paris and London performances of *Robert le Diable* in the 1830s.

DEMIDOFF, Anatoli, prince (1813–70). Member of the Parisian Academy of Sciences.

DE MUNCK (= DEMUNCK), François (1815–54). French musician. Cellist in the orchestra of the Opéra, later professor in the Brussels Conservatoire.

DENNERY, Adolphe-Eugène-Philippe (1811–99). French playwright who alone and in collaboration wrote two hundred plays with E. Cormon, N. Dartois, E. Grangé, P. Dumanoir, A. Bourgeois, Clairville, A. Decourielle, L. Thiboust, F. Dugué. He favored romantic situations, bold colors, and scenic effect.

DEROY, Bernhard Erasmus, count (1743–1812). Bavarian general. Helped to reorganize the Bavarian Army. Fell in Russia, where he was commanding a Bavarian division.

DESCHAMPS, Anne-Louis-Frédéric (called **Émile**) (1791–1871). French writer. Prominent romantic poet. With Victor Hugo founded the newspaper *La Muse française* (1824). Translated Goethe, Schiller, Shakespeare, as well as writing poetry and libretti. Took an active part in the versification of both *Les Huguenots* (acknowledged) and *Le Prophète* (secretly), providing additional material or reworking Scribe's original text, as required by Meyerbeer.

DESLANDES, Raymond (1825–90). French dramatist.

DESNOYER, Auguste-Boucher, baron (1779–1857). French copper engraver, famous for his work on Raphael.

DESNOYER, Louis-François-Charles. French critic of *Le Siècle*.

DESSAUER. See **LEOPOLD** of Anhalt-Dessau.

DESSAUER, Joseph (1798–1876). Bohemian composer. Studied with Tomaschek in Prague. Wrote several romantic operas, esp. *Ein Besuch in Saint Cyr* (Dresden, 1839). Admired as a song writer by Liszt and Berlioz, and was a friend of Chopin. Also wrote overtures, string quartets, and piano pieces.

DEVÉRIA, Achille (1800–1857). French painter and lithographer. Designed several title pages for Meyerbeer's romances.

DEVRIENT, Eduard Philipp (1801–77). German baritone, actor, writer. Studied with Zelter. Sang in Berlin (1819–22), in other German and Austrian cities (1822–34). Lost his voice in 1834. Became an actor and producer in Dresden (1834–46), Karlsruhe

(1856–70). Wrote the libretto of *Hans Heiling* and other work for and on the theater (*Geschichte der deutschen Schauspielkunst*). Close friend of Mendelssohn; assisted in the Bach revival.

DEVRIENT, Emil (1808–72). German actor. From 1831 he was engaged by the Dresden Court Theatre.

DE WITT, Theodor (1823–55). German composer and editor. Liszt enabled him to study in Berlin with Dehn. Edited the first four volumes of Palestrina for Breitkopf & Härtel before his premature death. Composed a piano sonata and vocal pieces.

DICKENS, Charles (1812–70). English writer. His novels (e.g., *David Copperfield,* 1850) are famous for their variety of characters, depth of humanity, and attacks on abuses in society. He captured the popular imagination of his time, and was held in high critical esteem. Meyerbeer met him during his visits to London, and obtained his autograph for Cornelie Meyerbeer (1862).

DIEFFENBACH, Johann Friedrich (1794–1847). German doctor. Professor and director of the surgery clinic in Berlin.

DIELITZ, Emilie. German soprano from Berlin. Pupil of Bordogni. Undertook several artistic journeys to Italy. Worked in the Königstädter-Theater in Berlin after 1848.

DIÉMER, Louis (1843–1919). French pianist. Studied with Marmontel, Thomas, and Bazin. Played in the Alard, Pasdeloup, and Conservatoire concerts. Piano professor at the Conservatoire (1887). Famous for his series of historical recitals in which in specialized in early music, which he also edited.

DIESTERWEG, Adolf (1790–1866). German pedagogue. Primary school teacher, director of the Seminar for City Schools in Berlin (1832).

DIETRICHSTEIN, Moritz, count (1775–1864). Austrian civil servant. Intendant of the Court Theatre in Vienna (1821), director of the Court Library (1826), *Oberstkämmerer* (1845). Father of Thalberg.

DIETSCH, Pierre-Louis-Philippe (1808–65). French composer and conductor. Studied with Reicha. *Maître de chapelle* at St. Eustache, later at St. Madeleine. Played the double bass at the Théâtre Italien and the Opéra. Chorus master at the Opéra (1840), then conductor (1860–63). Composed sacred music and operas, including *Le Vaisseau fantôme* (1842), written to Wagner's original sketch of *Der fliegende Holländer*. Conducted the three notorious performances of *Tannhäuser* at the Opéra (1861).

DINGELSTEDT, Franz, Freiherr von (1814–81). German impresario, writer, and dramaturge. Intendant of the Court and National theaters in Munich, of the Grand Ducal Theatre in Weimar (1857), and then of the Court Opera and Hofburg Theater in Vienna. Made a baron in 1867.

DITTERSDORF, Karl Ditters von (1739–99). Austrian composer. Famous as a violinist. Kapellmeister to the prince-bishop of Breslau, Count Schaffgotsch, who built an opera house for his works. *Der Doktor und Apotheker* (1786) is one of the best German comic operas of the eighteenth century. *Hieronymus Knicker* (Vienna, 1789) was his second most popular opera, given on every German stage until 1810 and frequently revived afterwards.

DÖBBELIN, Caroline Maximiliane (1758–1828). German actress. She was the only daughter of the director Carl Theophil Döbbelin. Début (1762), after which she became the darling of the Berlin stage. Worsening eyesight forced her to withdraw from acting for many years, and eventually to retire (1815).

DOBRÉ, Marie-Rosalie-Claire (b. 1818). French singer. Won first prize at the Paris Conservatoire (1838). Engaged at the Paris Opéra (1840–47), then worked in Brussels before returning to Paris (1855).

DOBRZYNSKI, Ignacy Felix (1807–67). Polish composer, pianist, and conductor. Worked in Warsaw. Concert tour of Germany (1845–47).

DÖHLER, Theodor (1814–56). Italian pianist. Studied in Naples with Benedict, and in Vienna with Czerny and Sechter. Pianist to the duke of Lucca (1831). Embarked on a brilliant series of tours to Germany, Italy, France, Holland, England, Denmark, and Russia (1836–46). Ennobled (1846). Settled in Florence (1848). Wrote an opera and many piano pieces.

DONIZETTI, Gaetano Domenico Maria (1797–1848). Italian composer. Pupil of Mayr. Professor of counterpoint at the Royal Conservatory in Naples. Paris (1838–47), kapellmeister to the Austrian court (1842). The last years of his life were clouded by mental illness. Master of tragic romantic opera (*Lucia di Lammermoor*, 1835) and *opera buffa* (*L'Elisir d'amore*, 1832). He was also triumphant in French *grand opéra* (*La Favorite*, 1840) and *opéra comique* (*La Fille du Régiment*, 1840).

DONNER, Johann Jacob Christian (1799–1875). German classical philologist.

DONZELLI, Domenico (1790–1873). Italian tenor. Studied in Bergamo with Bianchi. Début there (1808). Had increasing success throughout Italy, creating roles in *Torvaldo e Dorliska* and *L'Inganno felice* and became Rossini's friend. His voice grew heavier (1821) and he was one of the first tenors to sing high notes with full voice. London (1829–30). Created roles for Pacini, Halévy, Bellini, Mercadante and Donizetti. He was an expressive and dramatic artist.

DOPPLER, Albert Franz (1821–83). Hungarian composer and conductor. Studied with his father, and played the flute in the Pest orchestra. Settled in Vienna (1858) as ballet conductor at the Court Orchestra, and taught flute at the Vienna Conservatoire (1865). He wrote six operas and fifteen ballets.

DOPPLER, Karl (1825–1900). Hungarian composer and conductor. Like his father and brother, he became an excellent flautist, and gave concerts in all the major cities of Europe. Kapellmeister in Stuttgart (1865–98). He wrote an opera and pieces for the flute.

DÖRING, Georg Christian Wilhelm (1784–1833). German writer, musician, and privy councillor. Dramaturge at the Cassel Court Theatre, then oboist in Frankfurt until he took over the periodical *Iris*. Editor of the Nuremberg *Correspondenten*, then *Legationsrat* to the duke of Meiningen. Wrote the libretto for Spohr's *Der Berggeist*.

DÖRING, Theodor (b. 1803). German actor. Worked in Dresden, Mannheim, Hanover, Stuttgart. From 1845 he was a member of the Berlin Court Theatre.

DORN, Heinrich Ludwig Egmont (1804–92). German composer. Studied with Berger, Zelter, Klein. Kapellmeister in the Königsberg Theatre (1828). Teacher in Leipzig (of Schumann) (1829). Music director in Riga (1831–42). Kapellmeister in Cologne (1843), where he founded the Rheinische Musikschule. Kapellmeister at the Royal Opera in Berlin (1849–69) at Meyerbeer's recommendation.

D'ORTIGUE, Joseph-Louis (1802–66). French music critic. Founded and edited the journal *La Maîtrise*. Wrote for the *Gazette musicale*, *France musicale*, *Revue de Musique ancienne et moderne*, *Le Ménestral*. Also published studies like *De la Guerre des dilettanti, ou de la Révolution opérée par Monsieur Rossini dans l'opéra français* (1829) and *Le Balcon de l'Opéra* (1833).

DORUS-GRAS, Julie-Aimée-Josephine (née Vansteenkiste) (1805–96). Belgian soprano. Studied at the Paris Conservatoire with Henri and Blangini, Paer, and Bordogni. Début Brussels (1826). Paris Opéra (1826), where she succeeded Cinti-Damoreau as prima donna (1835). London (1839, 1847, 1849). Created Alice and Marguerite de Valois. Famous Elvira in *La Muette de Portici*: sang in the performance that touched off the revolt in the Low Countries (September 1830).

DOUCET, Charles-Camille (1812–95). French playwright. Served in the privy cabinet of the king of France (1846). Director of the theaters of Paris (1835). Wrote several comedies.

DOUX, Émile (1798–1876). French opera director. From 1835 he headed a French troupe in Lisbon; he also took it on tours.

DRAGONETTI, Domenico (1762–1846). Italian contrabassist. Member of the orchestra at the Royal Opera in London (1794).

DRASCHKE (= DRAESEKE), Felix August Bernhard (1835–1913). German composer. Friend of Liszt and Wagner, and an ardent disciple of the German nationalist school. Taught at the Lausanne Conservatoire (1864–74). Prolific composer.

DREYSCHOCK, Alexander (1818–69). Bohemian pianist. Studied with Tomaschek, and acquired a technique regarded as rivaling Liszt's. Appeared in public at the age of eight, and toured Germany, Russia, Holland, Belgium, France, England, Austria, and America. Called to St. Petersburg as professor in the newly founded St. Petersburg (1862). Went to Italy (1868) where he died. His facility cast a glamour over all his appearances. Wrote an opera, orchestral and chamber music, and 140 piano pieces.

DROUET, Louis-François-Philippe (1792–1873). French flautist and composer. Studied at the Paris Conservatoire, played at the Opéra at age seven. Teacher to King Louis of Holland (1807–11); flautist to Napoleon and Louis XVIII. London (1818), then undertook a long concert tour of Europe. Kapellmeister in Coburg (1836). Visited America (1854), then lived in Gotha and Frankfurt. Wrote 150 works for the flute (ten concertos). The French popular air "Partant pour la Syrie" was taken by him at Queen Hortense's dictation.

DUCHESNE (= DUCHENE). French music critic, and secretary to Edmond Blanc.

DUESBERG (= DUISBERG), Joseph. German historian, journalist, and littérateur living in Paris. His services were employed by Meyerbeer in translating the German alterations and additions to *Dinorah* and *L'Africaine* into French.

DUFAURE, Jules-Armand-Stanislas (1798–1881). French lawyer and politician. Served as minister of the interior (1848–49, 1871–73), minister of justice (1875), and minister president (1877–79).

DUFRESNE, Alfred (1822–63). French composer. Studied with Halévy at the Paris Conservatoire. Wrote one-act operettas for the Théâtre Lyrique and the Bouffes-Parisiens; also wrote songs.

DULCKEN, Violanda (b. 1810). Bavarian singer. Took the prize at the Paris Conservatoire in 1830 and 1831.

DULKEN, Johann Ludwig (b. 1761). German instrument maker. Established as the court *mech. Klaviermacher* by the Elector Karl Theodor (1781). He manufactured outstanding pianos with specialized registers for bassoon, harp, etc., that incorporated the tremolo invented by Frederici in Gera.

DULKEN, Louise (née David) (1811–50). French musician. Sister of Ferdinand David. Studied with Schwarencka. London (1828), where she had brilliant success as a pianist and teacher. Queen Victoria was one of her pupils.

DULKEN, Sophie (b. 1781). German pianist and composer. Daughter of the musician Ludwig A. Le Brun and the singer Franziska Danzi. Studied with Knecht, Streicher, and Schlett in Munich, becoming one of the foremost pianists of her time. Her few compositions were not published.

DUMANOIR, Philippe-François-Pinel (1806–65). French playwright. He wrote more than two hundred works, often in collaboration: dramas and comedies, often in verse. Scribe and Dennery were his favored collaborators. With the latter he wrote *Don César de Bazan* (Th. Porte-St-Martin, 1844) for Lemaître. He wrote much for the actress Déjazet, esp. the comedy *Les Premières armes de Richelieu* (Palais-Royal, 1839).

DUMAS, Alexandre *(père)* (1802–70). French novelist and playwright. He was very influential in the emergence of French romantic drama, revolutionizing historical theater with *Henri III et sa Cour* (1829). Began writing historical novels after 1839, e.g., *Le Comte de Monte-Cristo* (1844–45). Provided Meyerbeer with the libretto of *Les Brigands* (1832), but relations between him and the composer were never easy. His *Charles VII chez ses grands Vassaux* (1831) served as model for Donizetti's *Gemma di Vergy* (1834).

DUMAS, Alexandre *(fils)* (1824–95). French author. Illegitimate son of Alexandre *(père)*. Theorized about art, morals, politics, and religion in both his fiction and plays, esp. in *La Dame aux camélias* (novel 1848, then as a play 1852), which in its depiction of the love of a son of a noble family for a courtesan has attained the status of a modern myth (particularly in Piave's and Verdi's operatic adaptation, *La Traviata*, 1853).

DUNKER, Alexander. German publisher.

DUPATY, Emanuel-Mercier. French playwright. Distinguished himself in the navy, becoming a hydrographical engineer. He wrote several small comedies and vaudevilles, esp. for Dalayrac.

DUPEUTY, Charles-Désiré (1798–1865). French dramatist. Specialized in historical plays, and also parodies of romantic dramas by Hugo and Dumas *pére*.

DUPIN, André-Marie *(aîné)* (1783–1865). French lawyer and statesman. After the July Revolution, he was a member of the Council of Ministers, president of the Chamber of Deputies, and a member of the Académie. Later procurator-general and senator.

DUPIN, Jules-Henri (1791–1887). French dramatist.

DUPONCHEL, Charles-Edmond (1795–1868). French architect, painter, and impresario. He was first a stage director and then intendant of the Paris Opéra (1835–40, 1847–49), an architect and scene painter of great originality and importance in the history of the theater. He took over the direction of the Opéra jointly with Nestor Roqueplan (1847), a matter of some significance for Meyerbeer who had withheld *Le Prophète* from production during Pillet's term of office.

DUPORT, Louis-Antoine (1781–1853). French dancer, choreographer and ballet master. One of the most famous dancers of the age. He enjoyed great success at the Paris Opéra (1797–1808), even rivaling Vestris in his *légèreté* and pirouettes. Fled to Vienna (1808) and worked in St. Petersburg in the ballets of Didelot (1812). Returned to Vienna, where he choreographed many ballets at the Kärntnertor-Theater, and eventually codirected the theater with Barbaia (1821–36). Retired to Paris.

DUPORT, Paul. French ballet master. Worked at the Paris Opéra, then in St. Petersburg and the Imperial Hoftheater in Vienna. Created pantomime ballets like *Figaro* and *Acis and Galatea*.

DUPORT, Mme. (née Neuman). Wife of Paul. She became prima ballerina at the Hoftheater in Vienna; from 1813 she was known as Mme. Duport when she appeared jointly with her husband.

DUPRATO, Jules-Laurent (1827–92). French composer. Won the Conservatoire prize for several years' study in Italy and Germany. On his return to Paris he composed several successful small comic operas.

DUPREZ (-VANDENHEUVEL), Caroline (1832–75). French soprano *leggiero*. Daughter of the celebrated tenor, Gilbert. Studied with her father. Possessed a light, high voice, and was chosen by Meyerbeer to create Catherine in *L'Étoile du Nord* (1854).

DUPREZ, Gilbert-Louis (1806–96). French singer. Studied with Choron. Début Odéon (1825). Went to Italy for further study and sang there (1829–35), creating Edgardo (*Lucia di Lammermoor*) in Naples. Returned to Paris and succeeded Nourrit as principal tenor at the Opéra (1837–49), creating Benvenuto Cellini, Polyeucte *(Les Martyrs)* and Fernand *(La Favorite)*. Professor of voice at the Paris Conservatoire (1842–50), then founded his own school (1853), where his pupils included Battu, Miolan-Carvalho, Nantier-Didier, and Alboni. Wrote two important books on vocal method and his memoirs, *Souvenirs d'un chanteur* (1880).

DURANTE, Francesco (1684–1755). Italian church composer and teacher. Studied in Rome with Pitoni at the Conservatorio di San' Onofrio. Taught in Rome most of his life. With Alessandro Scarlatti and Leo, founder and representative of the Neapolitan School of composition. Devoted himself exclusively to church music. His many pupils dominated the European lyric stage in the later eighteenth century.

DUSCH, Alexander von (1789–1876). German politician and musician. He was a lawyer and eventually the foreign minister for Baden. Also known as a gifted musical dilettante, he was a cellist and member of Harmonischer Verein, and wrote several treatises on music for the *Allgemeine musikalische Zeitung,* the *Cäcilia,* and the *Morgenblatt für gebildete Stände,* using the pseudonym "The Unknown Man."

DUVAL, Alexandre-Vincent-Pineu (1767–1842). French playwright, actor and director. Apart from numerous plays, also wrote libretti, e.g., *Joseph en Egypte* (1807, for Méhul), where he emerged as an opponent of romanticism.

DUVERGER, Alexandre. Father-in-law of the tenor Nourrit; régisseur at the Opéra Comique, then a theater agent.

DUVERGIER DE HAURANNE, Prosper (1798–1881). French political writer. Member of the National Assembly (1848–51).

DUVERNOY, Antoine-François-Frédéric (1800–1874). French musician. First horn player at the Opéra (1831–64).

DUVEYRIER, Anne-Honoré-Joseph. See **MÉLESVILLE**.

E

EBERS, Martin (Moses Heymann Ephraim) (1781–1826). Meyerbeer's uncle, married to Henriette ("Jette") Liepmann Meyer Wulff (1779–1852), Amalie Beer's youngest sister.

EBERS, Moritz (Meier Moses Ephraim) (1802–37). Son of Martin Ebers (Moses Heine Ephraim) and Henriette Liepmann Meyer Wulff, Meyerbeer's first cousin.

EBERS, Paul Wilhelm (Wulff Veitel Ephraim) (1795–1865). Son of Victor Ebers and Seraphine Liepmann Meyer Wulff, Meyerbeer's first cousin.

EBERS, Sophie (1811–91). Daughter of Martin Ebers and Henriette Liepmann Meyer Wulff, Meyerbeer's first cousin. In 1849 she married a second time, to **Adolf Freiherr von Brandenstein** (1805–88).

EBERS, Victor (Veitel Heymann Ephraim) (1776–1848). German banker and uncle of Meyerbeer. Member of the Börsen-Committé of the Börsenkorporation. Married Amalie Beer's sister, Seraphine (Sarchen) Liepmann Meyer Wulff (1774–1832).

EBERTY, Anna (1821–1906). Sister of Felix Eberty, Meyerbeer's niece.

EBERTY, Babette (née Mosson) (1788–1831). Sister of Minna Meyerbeer. Married Hermann Eberty (1784–1856) and was mother of Felix, Anna, and Mathilde Eberty.

EBERTY, Felix (1812–84). German lawyer and writer. Professor of law at Breslau (1854). Meyerbeer's first cousin once removed, and nephew. Son of Hermann Eberty, who married Babette Mosson, sister of Minna Meyerbeer. Wrote a *Geschichte des preussischen Staates seit 1815* (1867–73) and his reminiscences, *Lebenserinnerungen eines alten Berliners* (1878).

EBERTY, Mathilde (1813–29). Sister of Felix Eberty, Meyerbeer's niece.

ECCARD, Johannes (1553–1611). German composer. Pupil of Orlandus Lassus (1571–74), director of Fugger's private orchestra in Augsburg (1577), chief conductor of the Prussian chapel in Königsberg (1604), and finally court musician to the elector in Berlin (1608). An important composer of sacred music.

ECK, Jacob (1804–49). Swiss piano maker. Together with Lefevre, he built much-admired grand pianos at his workshop in Cologne. Returned to Zürich (1844) after bankruptcy.

ECKERT, Karl Anton Florian (1820–79). German composer and conductor. Child prodigy. Studied with Rungenhagen and Mendelssohn. Went to the United States with Henriette Sontag; then conducted at the Italian Opera in Paris (1852). Music director of the Vienna Opera (1853), Stuttgart (1860–67), Baden-Baden (1867–69). Succeeded Dorn as director of the Berlin Opera. Wrote four operas, oratorios, cello concerto, popular songs.

EDER, Josephine (b. 1816). Austrian soprano. Sang at the Cassel Court Theatre (1843), and later in Vienna.

EHLERT, Louis (1825–84). German composer. Pupil of Schumann and Mendelssohn in Leipzig; Vienna, then Berlin (1850–63) as teacher and critic. Visited Italy. Settled in Wiesbaden. The *Frühlings-Symphonie* was one of his most famous compositions.

EHRENBERG, Dr. Christian Gottfried (1795–1876). Prussian doctor. Professor of medicine. Traveled in Asia with Alexander von Humboldt.

EHRLICH, Alfred Heinrich (1822–99). Austrian pianist and writer on music. Pupil of Henselt, Thalberg, and Sechter. Lived in Hanover as court pianist, then in Wiesbaden (1855–57), London, Frankfurt, Berlin. Piano teacher at the Stern Conservatory (1864–77, 1886–98). Critic of the *Berliner Tageblatt.*

EICHENDORFF, Joseph, Freiherr von (1788–1857). German poet. Leading figure in the romantic movement and prominent Catholic apologist. Famous for his lyric poetry, his novel *Ahnung und Gegenwart* (1815), and his novella *Aus dem Leben eines Taugenichts* (1826).

EISENHOFER, Franz Xaver (1783–1855). German composer of lieder. Director of studies in Würzburg.

EITNER, Robert (1832–1905). German musicologist. Studied with Brosig, settled in Berlin as a teacher (1853), and gave concerts of his own compositions. Established a piano school (1863) and published a manual (1871). Devoted himself to researching the music of the sixteenth and seventeenth centuries.

ELISABETH LUDOVIKA, queen of Prussia (1801–73). Daughter of Maximilian I of Bavaria. Wife of Friedrich Wilhelm IV (1823).

ELLA, John (1802–88). English writer on music. Studied violin and harmony at the Royal College of Music, with Fétis in Paris (1827). Returned to London, played in theater orchestras. Founded the Musical Union (1845) for morning concerts of chamber music; director until 1880. Also Music Winter Evenings (1850–59). Wrote analytical programme notes; contributed to the *Morning Post,* the *Musical World,* and the *Athenaeum;* also wrote a *Personal Memoir of Meyerbeer* (1868).

ERL, Joseph (1811–74). Austrian singer. Sang at the Josefstädter-Theater in Vienna, then engaged at the Königstädter-Theater in Berlin (1836) and the Court Opera in Vienna (1838). Later sang in Paris and London.

ELSSLER, Fanny (1810–84). Famous Austrian dancer of the romantic ballet who developed the character dance. She studied in Vienna and joined the Kärntnertor-Theater (1818). Appeared in Naples (1825), Berlin (1830), London (1833), Paris (1834). Her meteoric career took her as far as Havana. She had great success everywhere, esp. in Moscow, before retiring in 1851 and returning to Vienna in 1855. Dramatic projection was her great contribution to the romantic ballet.

ENDLICHER, Stephan Ladislaus (1804–49). Austrian academic. Director of the Botanical Gardens in Vienna.

ENGEL, Carl (1818–82). German music scholar. Pupil of Enckhausen, Hummel, and Lobe. Lived in Hamburg, Warsaw, and Berlin, then went to Manchester (1846) and London (1850). Researched the history of musical instruments and the music of the non-European peoples.

ENGEL, David Hermann (1816–77). German composer and organist. Studied in Breslau. Organist in Berlin (1848) and teacher at the cathedral school in Merseburg (1848). Wrote a comic opera, *Prinz Carneval* (1852). Published *Beitrag zur Geschichte des Orgelbauwesens* (1855).

ENGEL, Johann Jacob (1741–1802). German academic. Professor at the Joachimsthaler Gymnasium in Berlin, teacher of the future Friedrich Wilhelm IV, then chief director of the Berlin Theatre. Also wrote stage works. His writing *Über die musikalische Malerei* (Paris, 1781) was dedicated to Reichardt. His theory was that true musical painting, the musical presentation of external, actual events and circumstances, can only happen with the help of words, and hence can be fully realized only through vocal music.

ERARD, Pierre (1796–1855). French piano manufacturer.

ERHARD, Dr. Daniel Johann Benjamin (1766–1827). German doctor. Began life as a wiredrawer, established his own piano factory in Nuremberg at the end of the century, then studied medicine. After a spell in Munich, he settled in Berlin as *Obermedizinalrat* and was frequently consulted by the Beer family. He published political, theological, and medical writings.

ERKEL, Ferenc (1810–93). Hungarian composer, conductor, and pianist. Studied in Poszony with Klein. Settled in Buda as the director of the Hungarian Theatre Company (1835–74). Composed *Hunyadi László* (1844) and *Bánk Bán* (1861), which incorporated Hungarian elements into the operatic conventions, with fluent and original structures and penetrating characterizations. These works founded the Hungarian national opera.

ERNST I, duke of Saxe-Coburg-Gotha (b. 1784, r. 1826–44). Father of Ernst and Albert.

ERNST II, duke of Saxe-Coberg-Gotha (b. 1818, r. 1844–93). Brother of Prince Albert, the prince consort, and a reputable composer of operas.

ERNST AUGUST, king of Hanover (b. 1771, r. 1837–51), the duke of Cumberland, and the most notorious of Queen Victoria's "wicked uncles." He was a capable administrator and popular with his subjects.

ESCUDIER, Léon (Jacques-Victor) (1821–81) and **Marie-Pierre-Pascal-Yves** (1819–80). French music publishers and writers. Established the musical journal *La France musicale* (1838). Léon collaborated on several other newspapers and edited the journal *Le Pays* (1850–58).

ESSLAIR, Ferdinand (1772–1840). Austrian actor. Worked in Salzburg (1795) and then on South German stages in Stuttgart, Mannheim, Karlsruhe, Munich (Hoftheater, 1820). Famed for his great stature and voice, which were particularly suited to heroic roles.

ESTERHÁZY, Paul Anton, Fürst von (1786–1866). Hungarian aristocrat, and imperial diplomat.

ÉTIENNE, Charles-Guillaume (1778–1845). French writer. Wrote many comedies and libretti *(Cendrillon, Joconde)* as well as a history of the French theater. Precursor of political liberalism.

EUGÉNIE (Eugénia Maria de Montijo de Guzman, comtesse de Téba) (1826–1920). Empress of the French (1853–70). She married Napoleon III in 1853, and was a devoted admirer of Meyerbeer.

EUNIKE, Friedrich (1764–1844). German singer. Premier tenor at the Royal Theatre in Berlin (1796–1823).

F

FALCON, Maria Cornelie (1812–97). French soprano. Member of the Paris Opéra (1832–37), but lost her voice and had to retire. Created Rachel *(La Juive)* and Valentine *(Les Huguenots)*. Her voice was full and resonant, and like Nourrit, she had exceptional dramatic talent. Her inspirational artistic personality became synonymous with the dramatic soprano roles in which she achieved an unapproachable style and success.

FARINELLI, Giuseppe (1769–1836). Italian composer. Studied in Este and Venice. *Maestro di capella* at the cathedral and theater in Trieste. As an opera composer he looked to the Neapolitan school. He was a follower of Cimarosa, and wrote twenty *opere serie* and thirty-eight *opere buffe*. He remained popular until the advent of Rossini, e.g., *Teresa e Claudio* (1801), *Chi la dura la vince* (1803), *I riti d'Efeso* (1803).

FASCH, Karl Friedrich Christian (1736–1800). German composer. Worked with Benda, harpsichordist to Frederick the Great. Taught music and composed contrapuntal pieces of great ingenuity and complexity. Organized a choral society, which led to the foundation of the famous Singakademie in Berlin (1790). He was still greatly admired in the early nineteenth century.

FASSMANN, Auguste von (1814–74). German mezzo-soprano. Sang at the Munich Court Opera, before being engaged for Berlin (1837). Retired in 1844 because of a decline in her vocal powers.

FAUBEL, Joseph (b. 1801). Clarinetist in the Munich Court Orchestra.

FAUCHER, Léon (1803–54). French politician. Delegate (1846) and later minister of the interior.

FAURE, Jean-Baptiste (1830–1914). Celebrated French baritone. Studied at the Paris Conservatoire. Début Opéra Comique (1852); sang there 1861–69, 1872–78, creating Hoël in *Dinorah*. Opéra (1861), where he created Nelusko, Posa, and Hamlet. Sang in London frequently until 1877.

FAVART, Charles-Simon (1710–92). French dramatist. Son of a pastry cook, he married an actress and became director of the Opéra Comique. He wrote numerous light comic operas that mark the transition from the *comédie à vaudevilles* (with popular airs) to the *comédie en ariettes* (with specially composed tunes).

FERDINAND-PHILIPPE-LOUIS, duke of Orléans (1810–42). Eldest son of King Louis-Philippe, and last holder of the title. He was killed accidentally long before his father's death.

FERRARI, Serafino Amadeo de. Italian composer of the *opera buffa Pipelè* (Venice, 1855), which enjoyed international fame and was particularly popular in Italy until the early twentieth century.

FERRARIS, Amalia (1830–1904). Italian dancer. Studied with Blasis, début Turin (1844). London (1849), Paris (1856), Russia (1858). Admired for her great technique. Created many new roles. Retired in 1868.

FESCA, Alexander Ernst (1820–49). German pianist and composer. Studied with his father and Taubert. Successful as a concert pianist (1839). Chamber musician to Prince Fürstenberg. Settled in Brunswick (1842). Wrote two operas, chamber music, and songs, some of which became popular.

FESTA, Francesca (1778–1835). Italian soprano. Sister of the violinist Giuseppe Festa. Studied Naples and Milan. Début Naples (1799). She had initial success in Italy (Milan 1805, 1814, 1816–17, 1819, 1824), creating Fiorilla in *Il Turco in Italia* and roles in operas by Mosca, Pavesi, and Paer. Sang at the Paris Odéon (1809–11), but returned to Italy, where she appeared on all the big stages. Later sang in Munich (1821) and, as Festa-Maffei, she joined the Italian Opera in St. Petersburg (1829).

FÉTIS, François-Joseph (1784–1871). Belgian music theorist and critic. Founded the *Révue musicale* in Paris. He was commissioned by Minna Meyerbeer to arrange a performing edition of *L'Africaine*. Famous for his *Biographie universelle des musiciens et bibliographie générale de la musique* (Paris, 1833–44, 8 vols.; 2d ed., 1860–65; supp. 2 vols., 1878–80, ed. A. Pougin), which was unprecedented in scope and often still remains a prime source of information.

FEUILLET, Octave (1822–91). French dramatist. Wrote first for the Vaudeville, then specialized in proverbs and comedies.

FICHTNER, Karl (1805–73). Austrian actor. He worked at the Burgtheater (1824–65).

FIELD, John (1782–1837). Irish pianist and composer. Pupil of Clementi. Traveled with him to Paris and ·St. Petersburg (1802). Appeared with great success in London (1832). After long concert tours all over Europe, he returned to Moscow where he died. Wrote five piano concertos and solo piano music, esp. his series of nocturnes, which were very influential on Chopin.

FIORAVANTI, Valentino (1764–1837). Italian composer. Studied in Rome with Jannaconi. Prolific composer of seventy-seven operas. Visited Naples and Paris (1807), where he enjoyed great success with his comic works. Overshadowed by Rossini in this genre, he succeeded his teacher as *maestro di capella* in St. Peter's (1816), and then wrote church music. His greatest success was the *opera buffa Le Cantatrici villane* (Naples, 1799), which was produced all over Europe and Russia, and found particular favor in Germany. *I Virtuosi ambulante* (Paris, 1807) was his second greatest success.

FIORENTINO DELLA ROVERE, Pier-Angelo (1806–64). Italo-French critic. Wrote for the *Constitutionnel, Corsaire, Moniteur Universel*, later for *La France*. Favored an ironic mixture of anecdote and biography to actual criticism. An outspoken opponent of Meyerbeer.

FIRMIAN, Karl Max, count. German aristocrat. *Reichshofrat.*

FISCHER, Prof. Karl von (d. 1820). German architect. Built the Court and National Theaters in Munich. Married the Munich singer Antonie Pleyerl.

FISCHHOF, Joseph (1804–57). Austrian musician. Studied with Halm in Vienna, became a private teacher with growing success until appointed teacher at the Conservatoire of the Gesellschaft für Musikfreunde (1833). Composed many piano pieces. Also collected musical manuscripts and materials for a Beethoven biography (presented to the Berlin State Library after his death).

FITZJAMES, Louise (b. 1809). French dancer. Danced at the Opéra (1832–46), where her most significant achievement was the Abbess in *Robert le Diable*, a part she took over from Marie Taglioni after only 6 performances and danced 232 times. She also assumed Taglioni's part in *Le Dieu et la Bayadère*, and participated in the première of Adam's *La jolie Fille de Gand* (1842).

FITZJAMES, Nathalie (b. 1819). French dancer and singer, sister of the above.

FLAD (= FLADT), Anton (b. 1775). German oboist. From 1790 worked in the Munich Court Orchestra, and enjoyed great success on his concert tours. He was offered a position by the prince of Weimar (1798).

FLAHAUT DE LA BILLARDERIE, Joseph, comte de (1785–1870). French general and diplomat. Natural son of Tallyrand and aide-de-camp to Napoleon. He had a son by Queen Hortense, the duc de Morny.

FLÉCHEUX, Louise Marie (1813–42). French singer. Worked at he Paris Opéra (1835–41). Created the role of Urbain in *Les Huguenots* in place of Dorus-Gras, who had originally been intended, but took over Cinti-Damoreau's role as Marguerite de Valois.

FLERX, Josephine (née Lang) (b. 1791). German actress. Daughter of the court musician Martin Lang and the famous actress Marianne Boudet. After 1807 she was a member of the Munich Court Theatre. Her singing and acting were very popular.

FLORIAMO, Francesco (1800–1888). Italian musician and historian. Studied at the Naples Conservatoire, and was librarian there (1826–51). Bellini's closest friend. Wrote extensively. His principal work is *Cenno storico sulla scuola musicale di Napoli* (Naples, 1869–71, 2 vols.).

FLOTOW, Friedrich, Freiherr von (1812–83). German composer of light romantic operas, esp. *Alessandro Stradella* (1844) and *Martha* (1847). Studied with Reicha and lived in Paris before becoming kapellmeister to the grand duke of Mecklenburg (1855–63). His style subtly combined German sentimentality with a French elegance.

FODOR, Enrichetta. German soprano. Daughter of Josephine Fodor. Prima donna at the Berlin Königstädter-Theater (1846–49), then at the Friedrich-Wilhelmstädtisches Theater.

FODOR-MAINVIELLE, Joséphine (1789–1870). French soprano. Daughter of the violinist Joseph Fodor, and wife of the actor Mainvielle (1812). Début St. Petersburg (1808), London (1816–18) where she had great success in Mozart and Rossini. Appeared in Paris, Naples, and Vienna (1824–25), where she sang *Semiramide* sixty times. She suddenly lost her voice (9 December 1825), retired to Naples, tried two comebacks (1828 and 1831), and finally retired to Fontainebleau.

FORMES, Karl Johann (1815–89). German bass. Début Cologne (1841). Sang in Vienna (1845), where he created Plunket in *Martha* (1847). London Drury Lane (1849), Covent Garden (1852–57). American tour (1857). Married the American soprano Pauline Gravewood and established a singing school in San Francisco.

FORMES, Theodor (1826–74). German tenor. Début Ofen (1846). Vienna (1848); Berlin (1851–66). Toured America with his brother, the bass Karl. Died insane.

FÖRSTER, Friedrich Christoph (1791–1868). German poet, theologian, and philosopher. Editor of the *Berliner Konversationsblatt*, publisher of the *Neue Berliner Monatschrift*.

FORTIS, Leone (1824–98). Italian writer, journalist, and dramatist. Part of an artistic circle around the *Rivista Euganea* and the Café Pedrocchi in Padua.

FOULD, Achille (1800–1867). French financier and politician. Elected to the Chamber of Deputies (1842). Four times minister of finance during the presidency of Louis Napoleon, then again later (1861–67). Stabilized the country's finances.

FRANCHOMME, Auguste-Joseph (1808–84). French cellist. Studied at the Paris Conservatoire with Levasseur. Played the cello in various Parisian opera houses, including the Théâtre Italien. Appointed teacher at the Conservatoire (1846). He was an intimate friend of Chopin. Arranged evenings of chamber music with Hallé and Alard. Wrote for the cello.

FRANCK, César-Auguste (1822–90). Belgian composer and organist. Studied in Liège with Daussoigne, in Paris with Reicha and at the Conservatoire. Settled in Paris (1843), where he became organist at Ste.-Clotilde and organ teacher at the Conservatoire. Here he taught a whole generation of composers who eventually formed a school of French instrumental music. His own compositions were characterized by contrapuntal lucidity, harmonic fullness, and chromatic procedures derived from Bach.

FRANCK, Dr. Hermann (1802–55). German writer. Friend of Schumann, Wagner, and Heine.

FRANK, Eduard (1817–93). German composer, pianist, pedagogue. Studied with Mendelssohn, and was friend of Schumann. Enjoyed renown as a piano teacher. Cologne (1851–56), Bern (1859–67), Berlin (1867–78). Wrote two piano concertos, two violin concertos, chamber music, piano music.

FRANZ JOSEPH, emperor of Austria (b. 1830, r. 1848–1916). Succeeded his uncle Ferdinand I aged only 18 in the wake of the revolts in Vienna, Prague, Hungary, and Lombardy. Presided over the inauguration of the dual monarchy of Austria-Hungary (1867), and despite defeats by France and Prussia, resisted the forces of nationalism, maintaining the diverse Habsburg lands as a single political entity. His reign marked a period of great cultural and scientific efflorescence.

FRANZ KARL, archduke of Austria (1802–78), son of Emperor Francis I.

FRÄNZL, Ferdinand (1770–1833). German violinist and composer. Studied with his father Ignaz, with Richter and Pleyel in Strasbourg, and Mattei at Bologna. Entered the Mannheim Orchestra (1782), toured with his father (1785). Appointed conductor of the Munich Court Opera (1806) while continuing his tours. Retired to Mannheim (1826). Had a great reputation as a violinist and was also a prolific composer: six violin concertos, a double concerto for two violins, six operas, nine string quartets, symphonies, overtures, songs.

FRASCHINI, Gaetano (1816–87). Italian tenor. Studied with Moretti. Début Pavia (1837). La Scala (1840); Naples (1841–48); London (1847, 1868), then various Italian stages, Vienna, Madrid, Paris. Admired by Verdi, and created many of his tenor roles (in *Attila*, *Alzira*, *Il Corsaro*, *La Battaglia di Legnano*, *Stiffelio*, *Un Ballo in maschera*).

FREIMÜLLER. German singer at the Dresden Court Opera (1837).

FREYTAG, Gustav (1816–95). German poet and writer. Together with Julius Schmidt, he took over the direction of the periodical *Die Grenzboten* (1848).

FREZZOLINI, Erminea (1818–84). Italian soprano. Studied with her father. Début Florence (1838), London (1850). Created Viclinda (*I Lombardi,* 1843) and the title role in *Giovanna d'Arco* (1845). Successful on the various Italian stages, enjoyed great triumph at the Italian Opera in Paris (1853). Retired (1860), returned to the stage (1863–68).

FRIEDRICH II, king of Prussia (1712–86). In campaigns of 1740–41 and 1744–45 he won new territories for Prussia. An episode from one of these campaigns provided the subject for *Ein Feldlager in Schlesien.*

FRIEDRICH AUGUST II, king of Saxony (b. 1797, r. 1836–54). Died accidentally by falling from a carriage.

FRIEDRICH WILHELM III, king of Prussia (b. 1770, r. 1797–1840). His reign witnessed Napoleon's victory over Prussia and his entry into Berlin (1806). Napoleon was responsible for lifting the restrictive laws that still applied to the Jews, something upheld by the reforms subsequently initiated in Prussia under the direction of Baron von Stein. The king is further remembered for having founded the university and reorganized the theaters. Berlin became known as "Athens on the Spree."

FRIEDRICH WILHELM IV, king of Prussia (b. 1795, r. 1840–61). Considered a "romantic ruler." His hatred of democratic constitutions prevented him from accepting the crown of a united Germany from the Frankfurt Parliament (1849). He became insane (1857), and his brother Wilhelm acted as regent (1858–61). His special interest in the arts was reflected in his consistent support for Meyerbeer, and appointment of him to the post of *Generalmusikdirector* and director of the court music.

FRÖHLICH, Joseph (1780–1862). German composer and music critic. He was professor of aesthetics and pedagogy at the University of Würzburg and wrote many articles on music (for the *Allgemeine musikalische Zeitung*), as well as an instrumental manual. He was to have been elected to the Harmonischer Verein.

FROMMANN, Alwine (d. 1875). German correspondent of Wagner. Sister of a Jena bookseller who had been a friend of Goethe, she was reader to Princess Augusta of Prussia; poor but independent, she was highly respected by the princess. After hearing *Der fliegende Holländer*, she felt a new age had dawned for German opera, and remained devoted to Wagner personally and to his cause all her life, trying always to exercise a certain amount of influence on his behalf at court.

FRY, William Henry (1813–64). American composer. Pupil of Meignen. His opera *Leonora* (Philadelphia, 1845) was the first publicly performed grand opera by an American. Went to Europe as music columnist of the *New York Tribune*. Lectured in New York (1852–53). Wrote four symphonies, four operas, cantatas and songs.

FUMAGALLI, Adolfo (1828–56). Italian pianist. Studied at the Milan Conservatoire. Toured Italy, France, Belgium: known as "the Paganini of the piano" before his early death. Composed about a hundred elegant and effective piano pieces.

G

GABRIELLI, Caterina (1730–96). Italian soprano. Studied in Rome and Naples. Début Venice (1754). Created a number of roles in Gluck's Italian operas (1755–60), also appeared in Vienna, Parma, Lisbon, London (1775) and St. Petersburg. Returned to Venice (1777). Her wonderful voice and beauty involved her intrigues with royalty and nobility all over Europe.

GABRIELLI, Giovanni (1557–1612). Italian composer. Pupil of his uncle **Andrea** (1520–86), whom he succeeded as chief organist at St. Mark's, Venice. Stands at the head of the Venetian school, his role as a composer and teacher being epoch-making. Works include *Sacred Symphonies* and other church music.

GABRIELSKI, Johann Wilhelm (1791–1846) and **Julius** (1806–78). German musicians. Both brothers were flautists in the Royal Orchestra in Berlin.

GADE, Niels Wilhelm (1817–90). Danish composer and founder of the modern Scandinavian school of composition. Wrote in the manner of Schumann and Mendelssohn, but nonetheless infused elements of Danish folk song into his music. Worked in Leipzig until 1848. Founded the Copenhagen Conservatoire (1866). Wrote eight symphonies, overtures, a concerto, cantatas, chamber and instrumental music, vocal music.

GÄHRICH, Wenzel (1794–1864). Bohemian violinist and composer. From 1845 he conducted the ballet at the Royal Opera House in Berlin. He wrote entr'acte music for plays and vaudevilles, and later ballet music for Paul Taglioni and Hoguet.

GAIL, Jean-François (1795–1845). French philologist and historian. Wrote about art and music for several journals. Published *Reflexions sur le goût musical en France* (1832).

GAILLARD, Carl (1813–51). German poet and editor of the *Berliner musikalische Zeitung* (1844–47). Also a codirector of the music shop Challier & Co.

GALITZIN, Nicolas Borissovitch, prince (1794–1866). Russian aristocrat and musician. Maintained relations with Beethoven, who dedicated various works to him. He was a fine cellist and founded a Philharmonic Society in St. Petersburg (1820).

GALLI, Filippo (1783–1853). Italian tenor, later bass. Début Naples (1801), and for ten years one of the leading Italian singers. When illness affected his voice he became one of the greatest basses of the day. Created roles by Rossini *(L'Inganno felice, La Gazza ladra, Maometto II)* and Donizetti *(Anna Bolena)*. Enjoyed triumphs in Italy, Spain, France, England, America, and Mexico. Taught singing at the Paris Conservatoire (1842–48).

GALLI-BIBIENA. Italian family of scene designers and architects of the baroque era, esp. **Fernando** (1656–1743) and **Francesco** (1659–1737). Fernando was one of Louis XIV's stage mechanists, and was then engaged in Parma and Bologna. Then went with his brother to Vienna, where they were responsible for court fêtes and theatrical performances. Francesco also worked in Bologna, and designed theaters there, and in Vienna, Verona, and Nancy. They were the first to exploit diagonal perspective.

GALLI-MARIE, Célestine (1840–1905). French mezzo-soprano. Studied with her father. Début Strasbourg (1859). Engaged in France, Belgium, and Italy. Paris Opéra Comique (1862–85), where she created Mignon (1866) and Carmen (1875). London (1886).

GAMBATI BROTHERS. Italian musicians. They were trumpeters at the King's Theatre in London, where their artistic reputation was controversial.

GÄNSBACHER, Johann Baptist (1778–1844). German musician. Fellow student with Meyerbeer at the Abbé Vogler's in Darmstadt, and a member of the Harmonischer Verein. Served in the war of 1813, led a roving life, and later became director of music at St. Stephen's Cathedral in Vienna (1823). Wrote some 216 works (religious, orchestral, instrumental, songs).

GANZ, Leopold Alexander (1810–69). German musician. Concertmaster, violinist, and violist in the Royal Orchestra, Berlin.

GARAUDÉ, Alexis-Albert-Gauthier (1821–54). French pianist. Accompanist at the Opéra Comique. Made many arrangements, including one of *L'Étoile du Nord*.

GARCIA, Manuel Patricio Rodriguez (1805–1906). Spanish baritone and teacher. Studied with his father. Début New York (1825). Vocal difficulties forced him to abandon the stage. Taught singing with great success in Paris from 1829, then at the Royal Academy of Music in London (1848–95). First to undertake a scientific study of voice production; invented the laryngoscope. Taught many distinguished singers. Father of the legendary artists Maria Malibran and Pauline Garcia-Viardot. Wrote his memoirs and treatises on singing.

GARDONI, Italo (1821–82). Italian tenor. Studied with De Cesari. Début Viadana (1840). Sang at the Opéra and Théâtre Italien, and later in London, Vienna, St. Petersburg and Madrid. In London he created the tenor role in Verdi's *I Masnadieri* (1847) and returned there regularly until 1874.

GAREIS, Gottlieb (d. 1859). German violist. Member of the Royal Orchestra in Berlin.

GARRICK, David (1717–79). English actor and poet. Obtained the Drury Lane Theatre (1747). Undertook numerous guest appearances outside England, becoming famous in the revivified Shakespearean dramas, which he arranged in his own way for the stage. His comedies were published (1768–98, 3 vols.).

GARRIGUES, Malvina. See SCHNORR VON CAROLSFELD, Malwina.

GASTINEL, Léon-Gustav-Cyprien (1823–1906). French composer. Studied with Halévy; won the Prix de Rome. Wrote several successful operas (1852–96), as well as ballets, oratorios, masses, orchestral and chamber compositions.

GATHY, August (1800–1858). German writer and translator. Lived in Paris from 1841. Friend of Heine.

GAUTIER, H. French lawyer regularly employed by Meyerbeer.

GAUTIER, Jean-François-Eugène (1822–78). French musician. Pupil of Habeneck and Halévy at the Paris Conservatoire. Became third conductor at the Théâtre Italien (1848). Professor of harmony at the Conservatoire, and professor of history (1872). Wrote fourteen comic operas, an oratorio, a cantata, and other religious pieces.

GAUTIER, Théophile (1811–1872). French poet, journalist, and novelist. Theorist of romanticism, and principal author of the scenario for *Giselle* (1841). Editor of articles for *La Presse* in Paris. The Parnassian creed he evolved had much to do with refining of the techniques of art.

GAY, Delphine (1804–55). French writer. Daughter of the writer Sophie Gay. She wrote poems, novels and plays. Under the pseudonym "Vicomte de Launay" she published her *Lettres parisiennes* (1836–39), which became very popular. Married the writer Émile de Girardin.

GAZZANIGA, Giuseppe (1743–1818). Italian composer. Studied in Naples with Popora and Piccinni. Wrote many operas for the Italian stage, but esp. *opere buffe,* in which his racy style made him a minor forerunner of Rossini. Best known for his *Don Giovanni Tenorio* (1786), which both in libretto (by Bertati) and music was of great influence on Da Ponte and Mozart. Became *maestro di capella* at the Cathedral of Crema (1791), after which he wrote only church music.

GEBEL, Franz Xaver (1787–1843). German composer. Pupil of Vogler and Albrechtsberger. From 1810 worked as kapellmeister in the Leopoldstädter-Theater in Vienna, later in Pest, Lemberg, and finally Moscow (1817), where he became a fashionable piano teacher. Wrote several operas, symphonies, and chamber music.

GEHRER, Joseph (d. 1846). Austrian singer at the Kärntnertor-Theater. in Vienna. Engaged by the Berlin Court Opera (1842–44), later in Vienna and Pest.

GELDER, JULIAN VAN. See **JULIAN.**

GENÉE, Richard (1823–95). German conductor, librettist, and composer. Conducted in theaters in Reval, Riga, Cologne, Düsseldorf, Mainz, Schwerin, Prague, and finally Vienna (1868–78). Wrote operettas and brilliant and witty librettos, esp. for Johann Strauss, Suppé, and Millöcker, often in collaboration with F. Zell.

GENERALI, Pietro (1773–1832). Italian composer. Studied in Rome and Naples. Achieved great success with *Pamela* (1804) and was in great demand in Italy and Vienna; wrote operas for stages in Germany, England, France, Poland, and Russia. Directed the Santa Cruz Theatre in Barcelona (1817–21). Returned to Naples, then settled in Novara as *maestro di capella* (1827). His music had a brilliance that won him great popularity, his orchestral effects anticipating Rossini. However, he lacked Rossini's unique individuality, and was soon eclipsed by the younger man.

GENTIL *(le Père Gentil).* French archivist or *conservateur du matérial de L'Opéra.*

GEORG, king of Hanover (1819–78, r. 1851–66). The only son of Ernst August, he lost his sight in childhood. He fell foul of Bismarck's ambitions to join Prussia and the Prussian Rhineland. Hanover was seized when Georg took Austria's side in the 1866 war.

GEORG, prince of Prussia (1826–1902). Prussian officer. Published several dramas under a pseudonym. Was a gifted pianist and showed great interest in music.

GEORG FRIEDRICH KARL JOSEPH, grand duke of Mecklenburg-Strelitz (b. 1779, r. 1816–60).

GÉRALDY, Jean-Antoine-Just. French singer and composer.

GÉRARD. Editor of articles for the journal *La Presse.*

GERN, Johann Georg (1757–1830). German singer. Bass at the Berlin Court and National Theaters.

GERNSHEIM, Friedrich (1839–1916). German composer. Studied with Rosenhain, Moscheles, and Hauptmann. Paris (1855–61), professor at the Cologne Conservatoire (1865–74), Rotterdam (1874–80), Stern Conservatoire in Berlin (1890–97). Wrote orchestral, chamber, and instrumental works, songs, and choral music.

GESSNER, Salomon (1730–88). Swiss poet and painter. His fame rests on his rhythmic prose work *Idyllen* (1756, 1772), which was inspired by Theocritus and combined pastoral themes with rococo sentiment, idealizing nature and promoting serenity through virtue. *Der Tod Abels* (1758) was inspired by Klopstock.

GEVAERT, François-Auguste (1828–1908). Belgian composer. Studied with his uncle and at the Ghent Conservatoire. Won the Belgian Prix de Rome (1847). Settled in Paris, where he composed *Georgette* (1853) and *Le Billet de Marguerite* (1854), and consolidated his reputation with *Quentin Durward* at the Opéra Comique (1858). During the 1860s he abandoned composition for musicology, esp. research into seventeenth- and eighteenth-century operas and cantatas. Became music director at the Paris Opéra (1867) before succeeding Fétis as director of the Brussels Conservatoire (1871) and becoming administrator of the Théâtre de la Monnaie. Author of treatises on orchestration and music history, as well as editor of early vocal music. Was particularly gifted as a composer of lighter *opéra bouffe*.

GEYER, Flodoard (1811–72). German musician and music writer. Founder and leader of an academic men's choral society, critic for the *Spenerscher Zeitung, Neue Berliner Musikzeitung, Deutscher Reichanzeiger*. Later taught theory at the Stern Conservatoire.

GHYS, Joseph (1801–48). Belgian violinist. Pupil of Lafont at the Brussels Conservatoire. Taught in Amiens and Nantes. In 1832 he began concert tours in France, Belgium, Germany, Austria and Northern Europe. Wrote music for the violin.

GIOIA, Gaetano (1758–1826). Italian dancer and choreographer. Studied with Traffieri. Début in Rome (1787). Choreographed 221 ballets. Admired Viganò, and was himself a great mime, known as "the Sophocles of the dance." Worked in Venice (1790), Milan (1793–94), Naples (1795), and Vienna (1800–1801). He wrote most of the music for his ballets himself. Among his most admired work was *Das Urteil des Paris* (Vienna, 1801) and *Cesare in Egitto* (Milan, 1815).

GIRARD, Narcisse (1797–1860). French musician. Professor of violin at the Paris Conservatoire, and conductor at the Paris Opéra. Died while conducting *Les Huguenots* (16 January 1861).

GIRARDIN, Émile de (1806–81). French politician, writer, and publisher, notably of the Parisian newspaper *La Presse,* which he founded to challenge the hegemony of Armand Bertin's *Journal des Débats*. Married the writer Delphine Gay.

GIRAUD, Giovanni (1776–1834). Italian poet and dramatist. Active in Rome, London, Paris, Florence, and again Rome. Worked in the shadow of Goldoni, but produced diverse cultural works, influenced by the *comédie larmoyante* and romantic realism.

GIULINI, Antonio (1833–65). Italian singer. Studied with Cellini; début Fermo. For a few years a celebrated tenor in Milan, London (1857–65), Berlin, Vienna, and St. Petersburg. Died shortly after showing symptoms of mental instability.

GLÄSER, Franz (1798–1861). Bohemian composer. Studied in Prague with Pixis. Conducted in Vienna (1817–30), then in Berlin, before becoming music director in Copenhagen (1842). He wrote over fifty works for the stage, esp. *Des Adlers Horst* (1832), once in most German repertories. He also set two texts in Danish by Hans Christian Andersen.

GLINKA, Mikhail Ivanovich (1804–57). Russian composer, founder of the Russian national school. Studied casually, then with Dehn in Berlin. Traveled much in Europe. Imperial kapellmeister. The historical *A Life for the Tsar* (1836) and fairy tale *Russlan and Ludmilla* (1842) set the trend for the future development of Russian opera. Meyerbeer was very generous in his treatment of Glinka, even though Glinka had disparaged him as a charlatan.

GLÖGGL, Franz (1796–1872). Austrian music dealer and publisher, esp. of the *Neue Wiener Musikzeitung* (1850–62).

GLÖGGL, Franz Xaver (1764–1839). Austrian musician. Music director and kapellmeister in Linz, and director of the theater there. He founded the Linz Music School (1797) and was owner of a music business. He edited the *Musikalische Zeitung für die oesterreichischen Staaten* (1812–13).

GLOVER, William Howard (1819–75). English composer and conductor. Joined the orchestra of the Lyceum Theatre at the age of fifteen, studied with William Wagstaff, and then on the continent. Traveled with Braham, and formed an opera company in Manchester and Liverpool. Conducted in London, and worked as critic on the *Morning Post* (1850–65). Went to New York (1868) and conducted at Niblo's Garden until his death. Wrote operas and operettas.

GLUCK, Christoph Willibald (1714–87). German composer. Studied with Sammartini in Milan (1741–45); London (1745); traveled widely, Vienna (1759), Paris (1773–79), finally settling in Vienna. His operatic reforms (expounded in the famous preface to *Alceste*, 1767) sought to curb the formality and virtuosity of eighteenth-century *opera seria*, stressing the subordination of music to dramatic needs. His operas were very popular in nineteenth-century Germany. Meyerbeer was particularly influenced by his use of recitative.

GNECCO, Francesco (1796–1810). Italian composer. *Maestro di capella* at the cathedral in Savona. Wrote many operas, texts as well as music, the most famous being *La Prova d'un opera seria*.

GODDARD, Arabella (1836–1922). English pianist. Studied with Kalkbrenner in Paris at the age of six. First public concert at the age of 14 in London. Studied for three years with J. W. Davison (whom she married in 1859), then toured Germany and Italy (1854–55) and later the United States, Australia, and India (1873–76). She wrote some piano works and a ballad.

GOETHE, Johann Wolfgang von (1749–1832). German poet, dramatist, and novelist. His understanding of literature, art, science, and philosophy made him a universal man. Zelter first drew Meyerbeer to Goethe's attention; the latter saw the young composer as a natural choice for the composition of *Faust* because of his sojourn in Italy, which meant that "his German nature [was] combined with an Italian perspective." He also recommended Michael Beer's *Der Paria* to Eckermann for review.

GOETHE, Walter von (1818–85). German composer. Nephew of the poet, and later chamberlain in Weimar. His opera was produced there in 1864.

GOLD, Leonhard (b. 1818). Russian violin virtuoso. First violinist in the theater orchestra at Odessa.

GOLDBECK, Robert (1839–1908). German pianist and conductor. Studied in Paris. New York (1857–67). Founded the conservatory in Boston (1867); Chicago (1868); St. Louis (1873–78). Returned there (1903). Wrote textbooks of harmony (1890) and music education (1903).

GOLDONI, Carlo (1707–93). Italian dramatist. Wrote a successful tragedy, *Belisario* (1732), but discovered his gift for comedy. Settled in Venice (1740), where he wrote 250 plays in Italian, French and the Venetian dialect over the next twenty years. He was influenced by Molière and the *commedia dell'arte,* and also by direct observation of daily life. In 1762 he went to Paris to write for the Italian Theatre, and was attached to the French court until the Revolution. His best known plays are *La Locandiera* (1753), *I Rusteghi* (1760), and *Le Baruffe chiozzotte* (1762). He published his *Mémoires* (1787).

GOLDSCHMIDT, Benny. Banker in London.

GOLDSCHMIDT, Siegmund (1815–77). Bohemian pianist. Played in private concerts in Berlin (1843).

GOLINELLI, Giovanni (d. 1884). Italian mime and choreographer. Worked at the Vienna Court Opera (1839–59); appointed ballet régisseur in 1855. Ballet master in Hamburg (1860–61), Theater an der Wien (1861–63), Munich (1864–69). Wrote *Manon Lescaut* (1852) and *Don Quixote* (1855), both with music by Strebinger.

GOLLMICK, Karl (1796–1866). German composer and theorist. Studied with his father Karl. Settled in Frankfurt as a French teacher and chorus master. Wrote for the piano. Translated French and Italian opera libretti into German.

GOLTZ, August Friedrich von der (1765–1832). Prussian minister of foreign affairs. In 1810, with Hardenberg, Prussian representative at the Congress of Erfurt. Then Prussian ambassador in Munich and later *Oberhofmarschall* and Prussian delegate at the Bundestag.

GOMIS, José Melchior (1791–1836). Spanish composer. Director of military music in Madrid and Valencia for twenty-one years. At Rossini's recommendation, he went to Paris (1823), then to London (1826), where he taught. His *Méthode et solfège de chant* was highly regarded by Rossini and Boieldieu. His comic opera *Le Revenant* (1833) was more successful than *Le Diable à Séville* (1831).

GORIA, Alexander-Édouard (1823–60). French musician. Popular piano teacher in Paris. Wrote salon pieces and opera fantasias.

GOSSEC, François-Joseph (1734–1829). French composer. Studied with Vanderbelen, helped by Rameau and Stamitz. His *opéras comiques* (e.g., *Les Pêcheurs,* 1766) were unsuccessful, partly because of his rivalry with Grétry. Then wrote for the Opéra (e.g., *Sabinus* 1773) and faced rivalry with Gluck, whom he supported in the controversy with Piccinni. Became second director of the Paris Opéra (1780), which he resigned as the result of the Revolution. Wrote music for the Revolutionary activities with original ranges of orchestral sonorities that were influential on Méhul and Spontini.

GOTHA, duke of. See **ERNST II**.

GOTTSCHALL, Rudolf von (1823–1909). German dramatist. Reflected a revolutionary spirit in his early plays, although his most successful piece was a comedy in Scribe's manner, *Pitt und Fox* (1854).

GOUIN, Louis (1780–1856). French civil servant. He was an administrative director of the Parisian postal services, Meyerbeer's most trusted confidant and agent in Paris.

GOUNOD, Charles-François (1818–93). French composer. Studied with his mother, then with Halévy, Le Sueur, Paer; won the second Prix de Rome. His first opera was *Sappho* (1851), which, while not successful, provided evidence of his superior talent, as Meyerbeer recognized. His most famous works embodied the new form of *opéra lyrique* (*Faust,* 1859, and *Roméo et Juliette,* 1867). Director of the Paris Orphéon.

GOUVY, Louis-Théodore (1819–98). French composer. Studied law at Metz, then music, and presented a concert of his works in Paris (1847). Traveled frequently to Germany, where his compositions were favorably received. Wrote over two hundred works, including an opera, seven symphonies, quantities of chamber music, and piano pieces.

GOZZI, Carlo (1720–1806). Italian playwright. Celebrated author of comedies and, in later years, of dramatic tales. *Turandot* (1762) became popular in Germany and the subject of several operas.

GRAHN, Lucile (1819–1907). Danish dancer. Studied with Bournonville, début aged only seven, and created many roles for him. Appeared in Paris (1838), St. Petersburg (1843), and London (1845). Retired as a dancer (1856), and taught in Leipzig (1858–61) and Munich (1869–75), where she helped Wagner. Left her fortune to the city of Munich.

GRANGÉ, Pierre Eugène (1810–87). French dramatist.

GRAUN, Carl Heinrich (1704–59). German composer and tenor. Musical director to Frederick the Great (1740). Influenced by Lotti in Dresden; later visited Italy. Wrote Italian and German operas, chamber music, and church music. The cantata *Der Tod Jesu* was particularly successful and enduring.

GRAZIANI, Francesco (1828–1901). Italian baritone. Studied with Cellini. Début Ascoli Piceno (1851). Paris (1853–61), the United States (1854), London (1855–80), St. Petersburg (1862). He possessed one of the most beautiful and mellow voices of the last century, but apparently little artistry, and was ineffective in his acting. A friend of Mazzini, he zealously supported the cause of Italian unification.

GRELL, Eduard August (1800–1886). German organist and composer. Studied organ with his father and theory with Zelter. At seventeen he became a member of the Singakademie, and was thereafter connected with it for fifty-nine years, becoming director (1853–76). His view was that only vocal music was true art, and consequently he wrote almost exclusively for voice. Compositions include a sixteen-part *Missa Solemnis*, an oratorio, and other church music.

GRÉTRY, André-Ernest-Modeste (1741–1813). Belgian composer. Studied in Rome, then settled in France (1787). One of the key figures in the history of *opéra comique*, he combined Italianate comedy and melody with French clarity and declamation. Wrote sixty-eight stage works, notably *Zémire et Azor* (1771) and *Richard Cœur-de-Lion* (1784). His work is characterized by a dramatically truthful treatment of the human situation and an early use of leading motive. His contribution was essential to the evolution of the genre.

GREY, Charles, second earl Grey (1764–1845). English politician. Whig member of Parliament (1786), foreign minister (1806). The Whig cabinet of 1830 tried for parliamentary reform, which led to a crisis and his retirement. He was nonetheless again made prime minister (May 1832) and was able to carry through his reforms.

GRIEPENKERL, Wolfgang Robert (1810–68). German writer. Lecturer at the Caroleinium Braunschweig für Kunstgeschichte (1839). Correspondent for the *Neue Zeitschrift für Musik*. Published *Die Oper der Gegenwart* (1847).

GRIEVE, John Henderson (1770–1845). English artist. One of the most important stage designers of his time. With his sons **Thomas** and **William**, created famous scenery for Covent Garden.

GRILLPARZER, Franz (1791–1872). Austrian dramatist (*Sappho*, 1818). Playwright at the Burgtheater (1818–23). Retired early from the stage (1838), and became the director of the archives in Vienna until his retirement. His plays explore the conflict between the will and the power to act, e.g., *Des Meeres und der Liebe Wellen* (1831), *Der Traum ein Leben* (1834). He enjoyed a friendly relationship with Meyerbeer and was present at the première of *Les Huguenots*. Wrote his reminiscences.

GRIMM, Karl (1819–88). German cellist. First cellist at the Wiesbaden Opera for fifty years. Composed many cello pieces, some of which became popular.

GRIMM, Karl Konstantin Louis (1820–82). German musician. Harpist in the Royal Orchestra in Berlin. Enjoyed a considerable reputation as a soloist. Wrote various pieces for the harp.

GRISAR, Albert (1808–69). French composer. Studied with Reicha. After writing a number of works in Paris in collaboration with Flotow and Boieldieu, studied further with Mercadante in Naples, before returning and creating another eleven light comic operas (esp. *Les Porcherons,* 1850; *Bonsoir, M. Pantalon,* 1851; and *Le Chien du Jardinier,* 1855). He had a gift for elegant, lively comedy, and anticipated aspects of Offenbach, Hervé, and Lecocq.

GRISI, Carlotta (1819–99). Celebrated Italian ballerina. Studied with Guillet in Milan. Joined La Scala as a dancer (1829). While touring Italy she met Perrot in 1833. She thereafter danced in Paris, achieving her breakthrough in the divertissement in *La Favorite* (1840) and creating the title role in *Giselle* (1841). Worked in London (1842–51) as well as in Vienna, Milan, Munich, St. Petersburg. Retired to Switzerland in 1853. One of the greatest dancers of the romantic ballet. Cousin of the soprano Giulia Grisi.

GRISI, Giulia (1811–69). Celebrated Italian soprano. Studied in Bologna and Milan, début Bologna (1828). Milan (1831–32), where she created Adalgisa in *Norma*; Paris (1832–46), where she created Elvira *(I Puritani)* and Norena *(Don Pasquale);* London (1834–61). She was both beautiful and gifted, and idealized by the public for her rich flexible voice and dramatic abilities. Her partnerships with the tenors Rubini and Mario became legendary, especially with the latter in *Les Huguenots*. Cousin of the dancer Carlotta Grisi.

GROPIUS, Carl Wilhelm. Theater and décor artist in Berlin.

GRÜNBAUM, Caroline (1814–68). German soprano. Daughter of Johann Christoph Grünbaum. Début in *Die Schweizerfamilie* (1828). Berlin (1832), where she created Anna in *Hans Heiling*. Retired in 1844.

GRÜNBAUM, Johann Christoph (1785–1870). German tenor. Début Regensburg (1804), Prague (1808–16), Vienna (1816–32), then Berlin, where he was active as a teacher and translator of libretti. He prepared the German version of *Dinorah* and several of Meyerbeer's songs.

GRÜNBAUM, Therese (1791–1876). Austrian soprano. Daughter of Wenzel Müller, with whom she also studied. Début as a child. Moved to Prague (1807) and sang in the first German *Don Giovanni*. Concert tours to Vienna, Munich, and Berlin. Then moved to Vienna where she became prima donna of the Court Opera (Kärntnertor-Theater) (1816–28), and created Eglantine in *Euryanthe* (1823). Berlin (1828–30), where she opened a singing school. Meyerbeer composed an aria with orchestra for her "Perchè muni tiranni" (Genoa, 3 October 1816).

GRÜNEISEN, Charles L. English critic. Editor of the *Morning Chronicle*. Meyerbeer used him as a type of agent for his interests in London. In 1848 he published a *Memoir of Meyerbeer, with Notices . . . of his Celebrated Operas*.

GUASCO, Carlo (1813–76). Italian tenor. Début La Scala (1837). Created the leading roles in *I Lombardi*, *Ernani*, and *Attila*.

GUBITZ, Anton. German writer and poet.

GUBITZ, Friedrich Wilhelm (1786–1870). German writer. Editor of the newspaper *Der Gesellschafter*, theater critic of the *Vossische Zeitung*.

GUERBER, Samuel. Banker in Florence.

GUERON DE RANVILLE, Martial Come Perpetuo Magliore, count (b. 1787). President of the courts in Caen. Minister of education and culture (1829). Signed the July Ordinance (1830), arrested on the flight to Tours, held prisoner in Han.

GUERRA, Antonio Alessandro (1806–46). Italian dancer and choreographer. Worked in Naples. Went to Paris (1837), where he choreographed various ballets, including *Robert le Diable* (1839).

GUEYMARD, Louis (1822–80). French tenor. Début Lyons (1845). Paris Opéra (1848–60). Sang the repertory of Nourrit and Duprez. Created Jonas in *Le Prophète*, as well as roles for Verdi (Henri in *Les Vêpres siciliennes* and Don Carlos) and Gounod. Verdi commented on his fine voice.

GUGLIELMI, Pietro Alessandro (1728–1804). Italian composer. Studied with his father and Durante. His first comic opera was produced in Naples (1757) and he wrote 24 operas over the next ten years, which were produced all over Europe and became very popular (*La Sposa infidele*, Venice, 1767). Spent five years in London (1767–72). Appointed *maestro di capella* at St. Peter's (1793) and turned to church music. Wrote 103 operas in all. His *opere serie* had a certain originality in use of chorus and orchestra in extended finales, but he had a natural feeling for *opera buffa*, a sense of the absurd, and a gift for ingenious effect.

GUGLIELMI, Pietro Carlo (1763–1817). Italian composer. Son of Pietro Alessandro. Studied in Naples. Went to Spain (1793), then lived in Naples, Florence, Rome, and

London (1809). He returned to Italy and was appointed *maestro di capella* in Massa di Carrara (1810). Wrote some forty operas, oratorios, and cantatas.

GUHR, Karl Wilhelm Ferdinand (1787–1848). German musician and composer. He became music director at the Nuremberg Theatre, then worked in Wiesbaden and Cassel before becoming conductor of opera at Frankfurt-am-Main and director of the museum there. Apart from concertos for violin and piano, he also wrote several operas, including *Deodata,* which was well received in Nuremberg.

GUIDI, Giovanni Gualberto (1817–83). Florentine music publisher of the first pocket scores *(Guglielmo Tell, Gli Ugonotti, Roberto il Diavolo).*

GUIZOT, François-Pierre-Guillaume (1787–1874). French politician and historian. Professor at the Sorbonne. Under Louis-Philippe he was minister of public education and foreign minister (1840). His rigidly conservative policies helped to bring about the revolution of 1848. Later president of the Académie des Sciences (1854).

GUNGL, Joseph (1810–89). Hungarian composer and conductor. Oboist in an Austrian artillery regiment, then bandmaster. Traveled with his band all over Germany. Wrote a number of marches and dances that became popular. Established his own orchestra in Berlin (1843). His concerts in the Summer Gardens provided a meeting place for diplomats and members of the elegant world. American tour (1849). Later lived in Munich and Frankfurt.

GUTZKOW, Karl Ferdinand (1811–78). German writer. Member of the Junges Deutschland movement, whose ideas on freedom impregnated all his writings, although his reputation rests on the books published after the 1848 revolutions, esp. *Die Ritter vom Geiste* (1850–51), which initiated the modern social novel in Germany. Lived in Berlin, Stuttgart, Heidelberg, Munich, Rome, Hamburg, and Paris. For a while he was dramaturge at the Dresden Court Theatre and then secretary-general of the Schillerstiftung in Weimar.

GYE, Frederick (1809–78). English impresario. Manager of Covent Garden (1849–77). Introduced many operas to London, esp. by Verdi and Wagner, as well as some of the greatest singers of the day like Patti, Lucca, Tamberlik, Faure, Maurel, and Alboni.

GYROWETZ, Adalbert (1763–1850). Bohemian composer. Enjoyed successes in Vienna, Naples, and Paris. Visited London before returning to Vienna where he became kapellmeister at the Imperial Court Theatre. *Agnes Sorel* (1806) and *Der Augenarzt* (1811) became popular among his thirty operas, *Singspiele,* and melodramas. He was admired by Mozart, Beethoven, and Haydn, whose style he sought to cultivate in his own work. *Il finto Stanislao* (1818) used the Romani text later set by Verdi; *Hans Sachs in vorgeruckten Alter* (1834) was on the same subject used by Wagner in *Die Meistersinger.* Meyerbeer provided him with a pension of 100 thalers in his old age.

H

HAACKE, Ida, Gräfin von. German noblewoman, lady-in-waiting to Princess, later Queen, Augusta of Prussia.

HABENECK, François-Antoine (1781–1849). French musician. Studied with his father, then with Baillot. Director (1821–24), then kapellmeister (1824–48) at the Opéra. Professor of violin at the Conservatoire (1825). Founder of the Société des Concerts des Conservatoire (1828). Major influence in French music because of the range of his programmes and his championing of Beethoven.

HABER, Jülchen von. See **BEER, Julie Angelica**.

HABER, Luidel von. German banker.

HACKLÄNDER, Friedrich Wilhelm, Ritter von (1816–77). German novelist and civil servant. He worked for a merchant before becoming a soldier, and then returning to business. He began to write, making use of his experiences as a soldier. Privy councillor and secretary to the crown prince of Württemberg in Stuttgart (1843). He was a war correspondent in North Italy (1849, 1859), and was ennobled by Austria (1861). Later director of buildings and gardens in Stuttgart (1859–64). Then lived as a man of letters on the Starnberger See. Wrote novels, comedies, and an autobiography. Produced his own opera, *Soldatenleben* (Stuttgart, 1848).

HAEHNEL, Amalie (1807–49). Austrian singer. A concert singer until her stage début as Rosina in Vienna (1829). From 1830 she was employed at the Königstädter-Theater in Berlin, then at the Royal Opera, where she eventually became *Kammersängerin*. She retired in 1845 and lived in Vienna.

HAHN, Theodor (1809–65). German composer and singing teacher. Went to Paris in 1838 in order to study the singing methods of Bordogni, Lablache, and Mainzer. He was financed by a grant from the king of Prussia, almost certainly at Meyerbeer's recommendation.

HAINL, François (1807–73). French cellist and conductor. Studied at the Paris Conservatoire. Went to Lyons to conduct theater music (1841–63), then at the Paris Opéra (1863–72). Published the valuable *De la Musique à Lyon depuis 1713 jusqu'à 1852*.

HAITZINGER, Anton (1796–1869). Austrian tenor. Studied in Vienna with Wölkert, Mozzati, and Salieri. Début Vienna (1821). Created Adolar *(Euryanthe)*. London (1833), opposite Schröder-Devrient. Associated with the theater in Karlsruhe (1828–50) where he established a singing school and wrote a handbook on singing. Made guest appearances in Paris, London, St. Petersburg, and Prague. Admired for his musicianship and intelligence.

HALÉVY, Jacques-Fromenthal-Elie (1799–1862). French composer. Studied with Berton, Méhul and Cherubini. After initial failure, he achieved fame in 1835 when he showed himself master of *grand opéra* with *La Juive* and of *opéra comique* with *L'Éclair*. Taught at the Paris Conservatoire (1827): Gounod, Massé, and Bizet among his pupils. *Guido et Ginevra* (1838) and *La Reine de Chypre* (1841) show great originality of harmony and orchestration, while *Les Mousquetaires de la Reine* (1846) and *Le Val d'Andorre* (1848) achieved wide popularity in the lighter vein.

HALÉVY, Ludovic (Léon) (1833–1908). French author and dramatist. Collaborated with Meilhac writing libretti for Offenbach, Bizet, Delibes, and others.

HALLÉ, Charles (orig. Karl Halle) (1819–95). German pianist and conductor. Lived in Paris as piano teacher (1836). Went to London (1848), where he worked as a conductor and later founded his own orchestra in Manchester.

HALLER, Dr. Karl Ludwig von (1768–1854). German journalist.

HALM, Friedrich (1806–71) (pseud. of E. F. J. von Münch-Bellinghausen). Austrian playwright. Educated in Vienna, he wrote for the Burgtheater, and developed an artistic relationship with the actress Julie Rettich. His plays surpassed even Grillparzer's in popularity and were once favorites in all German theaters, exploiting the tastes brought into vogue by the Junges Deutschland movement. His work embodies the advantages of privilege and financial security, and pays tribute to an ideal of beauty (*Griseldis,* 1835; *Wildfeuer,* 1842; *Der Sohn des Wildniss,* 1842; *Der Fechter von Ravenna,* 1854).

HAMMER-PURGSTALL, Joseph, Freiherr von (1774–1856). Austrian orientalist. *K.K. Hofrat.* President of the newly founded Academy of Sciences in Vienna (1847–49).

HANDEL, George Frideric (orig. Georg Friedrich Händel) (1685–1759). German, later English, composer. Cosmopolitan master of the baroque, together with his exact contemporary, J. S. Bach. For the most part wrote in the Italianate style, esp. in his forty-six operas. Invented the English biblical oratorio and wrote thirty-two, as well as cantatas, sacred music, *concerti grossi,* and other orchestral, instrumental, and vocal music. Meyerbeer's great admiration of Händel was based particularly upon regular experience of his oratorios.

HANOVER, king of. See **ERNST AUGUST GEORG**.

HANSLICK, Eduard (1825–1904). Viennese music critic. From 1846 he wrote for the *Wiener Musikzeitung*, then the *Wiener Zeitung, Die Presse,* and the *Neue freie Presse*. Professor of music and aesthetics at the University of Vienna (1861). Achieved fame through his book *Vom Musikalisch-Schönen* (Leipzig, 1854).

HANSSENS, Charles-Louis (1802–71). Belgian cellist, conductor, and composer. Became assistant conductor at the National Theatre in Amsterdam (1822), then cellist and assistant conductor at the Brussels Theatre, and professor of harmony at the Brussels

Conservatoire (1827). Directed French opera in The Hague, Paris, Ghent, and finally became conductor at the Théâtre de la Monnaie in Brussels (1848–69). He wrote eight operas, and considerable amounts of orchestral, religious, and choral music.

HANSTEIN. *Reisemarschall* and chamberlain of the duke of Gotha, and intendant of the Gotha Theatre.

HARLAS, Hélène (1785–1818). German singer. Soprano at the Court Opera in Munich, and companion of Heinrich Baermann. Meyerbeer wrote his cantata for soprano, clarinet, and chorus, *Gli Amori di Teolinda* (1816), for them.

HARPER, Thomas (1787–1853). English instrumentalist. Trumpet virtuoso and first trumpeter at the Theatre Royal, Drury Lane.

HÄRTEL, Gottfried Christoph (1763–1827). German publisher (with Breitkopf) of the *Allgemeine musikalische Zeitung* and of the German version of *Le Prophète*.

HÄSER, Charlotte (1784–1871). German soprano. Studied with her father, Johann Georg. Appointed to Dresden, then taken by Paer to Paris; Théâtre Italien (1803–6). Left for Italy where she triumphed (1806–12), singing trouser roles and competing with Crescentini and Velluti. She was one of the first German singers to make an international reputation—"la divina Tedesca." After further success in Germany she married the lawyer Giuseppe Vera and retired to Rome.

HÄSER, Christian Wilhelm (1781–1867). German bass. Brother of the celebrated Charlotte. Worked in Dresden, Leipzig, Prague, Breslau, and Vienna (1813), before acquiring a lifelong position at the Stuttgart Hoftheater. He was famous for his trills and coloratura, as well as his phenomenal range and fine acting. He translated Buonavoglio's *La Scelta dello Sposo* into German.

HASLINGER, Karl (1816–68). Austrian publisher and composer. Studied with Czerny. Brilliant pianist. Published works by Beethoven and Liszt, and the Strauss waltzes. In 1875 his firm was bought by Schlesinger of Berlin (subsequently R. & W. Lienau).

HASSELT (-BARTH), Anna Maria Wilhelmina van (1813–81). Dutch singer. Appeared at the Hofoper in Vienna (1838). Achieved great success in Berlin as Isabelle and Valentine. Her achievements were compared with those of Schröder-Devrient.

HAUCK, Carl. German musician. Royal chamber musician and violinist at the Opera in Berlin (1821).

HAUPTMANN, Moritz (1792–1868). German theorist and composer. Studied with Scholz and Morlacchi in Dresden, then with Spohr in Gotha (1811). Music teacher in Russia. Returned to Cassel as violinist (1820). Cantor of the Thomasschule and professor of composition at the Leipzig Conservatory (1842). Renowned as a teacher of violin and composition (David, Joachim, Bülow, Jadassohn, Sullivan). A master of classical form, composed sixty works, and theoretical treatises.

HAUSER, Miska (1822–87). Bohemian violinist and composer. Studied with Kreutzer. Child prodigy. Played in America and Australia (1853–58) with sensational success. Abandoned the public stage in 1874. Wrote operetta and numerous violin pieces, as well as an account of his travels.

HAYDN, Franz Joseph (1732–1809). Austrian composer. His enormous output includes 104 symphonies and 76 string quartets. He perfected the classical sonata form whereby European music departed finally from the old contrapuntal style derived from polyphonic chroral music. The oratorios *The Creation* (1798) and *The Seasons* (1801) are among his finest achievements. Meyerbeer attended performances of Haydn's music throughout his life.

HEBBEL, Christian Friedrich (1813–63). German dramatist. Describes conflict between the individual striving for self-expression and a general order that he or she either fatefully disturbs or rejuvenates, e.g., *Judith* (1840) and *Genoveva* (1843).

HÉDOUIN, Pierre (1789–1868). French advocate, writer on music, librettist, and composer. Vice-president of the Société Philharmonique of Boulogne.

HEINE, Carl (1810–65). German banker in Hamburg. Cousin of the poet Heinrich Heine.

HEINE, Heinrich (1797–1856). German writer. One of the principal poets of the romantic era who settled in Paris. His lyric poetry combines vivid natural imagery with a mixture of sentiment and irony, while his prose shows a penetrating awareness of the problems of the day coupled with an acerbic wit. Initially a friend of Meyerbeer, he later turned against him and attacked him in both his later poetry and musical writings, especially in the *Augsburger allgemeine Zeitung*.

HEINE, Mathilde-Crescence-Eugénie (née Mirat) (1815–83). Wife of Heinrich Heine, (1841). She negotiated with Meyerbeer about the suppression of some of Heine's late satirical poems.

HEINE, Salomon (1767–1844). German banker in Hamburg. Uncle of the poet.

HEINEFETTER (STÖCKL-), Clara (1816–57). German soprano. Début Vienna. Went to Berlin (1837) and also undertook engagements in Mannheim. London Covent Garden (1842) with a German company, the first London Valentine in *Les Huguenots*. Died insane.

HEINEFETTER, Sabine (1809–72). German soprano. Sister of Clara. Studied with Spohr and Tadolini. Début Frankfurt (1825). Sang at the Théâtre Italien. Returned to Germany (1829). Appeared with great success in Berlin and Milan.

HEINEMEYER, Ernst Wilhelm (1827–69). Famous German flautist. Studied with his father Christian. Went to Russia (1847), played in the Imperial Orchestra in St. Petersburg. Retired to Hanover (1859), Vienna (1866). Wrote several flute concertos.

HELD, Jacob (b. 1770). German musician. Studied with Danzi. Undertook many concert tours as a violinist. Worked in Munich as a court musician and music teacher.

HÉLÈNE, princess of Russia (1807–73). Daughter of Paul of Württemberg, married Prince Michael, brother of Tsar Alexander I (1824). Very active in the musical life of St. Petersburg. Founded the Imperial Russian Music Society with Rubinstein and Stassov (1859).

HELL, Theodor. See **WINKLER, Karl**.

HELLER, Stephen (1813–88). German pianist and composer. Studied with Brauer and Halm. Began to tour Austria and Germany, but remained in Augsburg (1828). Went to Paris (1838), where he became friendly with Berlioz, Chopin, and Liszt, and lived as a piano teacher for the rest of his life. Visited London (1849, 1862). Wrote several hundreds of piano pieces arranged in 158 opus numbers.

HELLMESBERGER, Joseph (1828–93). Austrian musician. Solo violinist in the Court Opera Orchestra. Leader and conductor of the orchestra of the *Gesellschaft der Musikfreunde* in Vienna.

HENDRICHS, Hermann (b. 1809). German actor. Assumed heroic roles in Berlin from 1844. *Struensee* contained one of his best parts.

HENNEBERG, Johann Baptiste (1768–1822). Austrian musician. Kapellmeister at Schikaneder's theaters (1790–1803). Later worked as organist and opera director for Prince Nicholaus von Esterházy, then as imperial court organist. Wrote several small operas. *Die Waldmänner* (Hamburg, 1787) was one of his most successful works.

HENNING, Karl Wilhelm (1784–1867). German violinist. Conductor of the Royal Orchestra in Berlin.

HENSEL, Fanny Cäcilia (née Mendelssohn) (1805–47). German pianist and composer, sister of Felix Mendelssohn. She received an excellent musical education in her own home. Married the painter W. Hensel (1829), but remained very close to her brother, who constantly asked her advice in musical matters. Her sudden death was a great shock to him, and he died himself a few months later. She published a number of songs.

HEQUET, Charles-Joseph-Gustav (pseud. Léon Durocher) (1803–65). French music critic and composer. Wrote for *L'Illustration* (1830–60).

HERING, Karl (1819–89). German violinist. Member of the Royal Orchestra (1846), later royal music director.

HERMANN, Johann David (1760–1846). German pianist and music teacher of Queen Marie-Antoinette.

HÉROLD, Louis-Joseph-Ferdinand (1791–1833). French composer. Studied with his father, Méhul, Catel, and Adam. Master of *opéra comique* in the manner of Boieldieu, attempting greater depths of romantic feeling, esp. in *Zampa* (1831) and *Le Pré aux clercs* (1832). Also chorus master at the Opéra Comique (1824–27) and then at the Opéra.

HERTEL, Peter Ludwig (1817–99). German composer. He worked at the Berlin Court Opera, composing ballets for Paul Taglioni (esp. *Satanella,* 1852; *The Adventures of Flick and Flock,* 1858; *La Fille mal gardée,* 1864).

HERZ, Henri (1803–88). German pianist. Studied at the Paris Conservatoire (1816). Became a fashionable teacher and composer. Toured Germany with violinist Lafont (1831). Professor at the Conservatoire (1842). Toured the United States, Mexico, and the West Indies (1845–51). Became a successful piano manufacturer. Wrote over two hundred piano compositions.

HERZ, Henrik (1797–1870). Danish dramatist. *Konig Renés Tochter* (1845) appeared in German translation (1846).

HERZ, Joseph. Meyerbeer's financial adviser.

HERZBERG, Dr. Joseph (1799–1871). German doctor. From 1844 worked at Jewish Hospital in Berlin. Later made *Geheimer Sanitätsrat.*

HESSE, Adolph Friedrich (1808–63). German organist. Made several concerts tours in Paris and London (1844). His father was an organ builder and his first teacher; he was later advised by Hummel and Spohr. Church organist in Breslau. Visited Paris for the inauguration of the new organ at St. Eustache. His virtuoso handling of the pedals evoked admiration. Gave organ demonstrations (1851). Returned to Breslau, where he enjoyed a great reputation not only as an organist, but also as conductor of the Breslau Symphony Orchestra. Published a *Practical Organist.* His complete works were brought out by Steggall.

HESSE, prince of. Married Princess Anne of Prussia.

HETSCH, Louis (1806–72). German musician. Music director in Heidelberg until 1846, then in Vienna.

HEUGEL, Jacques-Léopold (1811–83). French music publisher. In 1839 he acquired the firm Meissonnier (established 1812), and changed it to Heugel & Cie. Published the famous Paris Conservatoire methods, works of celebrated composers, the important weekly *Le Ménestrel* (1835–1940).

HEYSE, Paul (1830–1914). German writer. Studied in Berlin and Bonn, traveled in Italy, settled in Munich, and devoted his life to writing verse tragedies, *Novellen,* and poems. His was an ideal of beauty detached from everyday realities.

HILLER, Ferdinand (1811–85). German composer and conductor. Active in Leipzig (Gewandhaus Concerts), Dresden, Düsseldorf, and Cologne (Gürzenich Concerts). Maintained a regular correspondence with Meyerbeer. From 1828 to 1835 he lived in Paris, appearing in concerts with Baillot and directing Choron's Music Institute for a while.

HILLER, Johann Adam (1728–1804). German composer. Studied in Dresden, kapell-meister in Leipzig. More than any other composer he founded the *Singspiel,* incorpo-rating songs and concert pieces into the plays performed by the Leipzig theater com-pany. The best known are *Der Teufel ist los* (1766) and *Die Jagd* (1770).

HIMMEL, Friedrich Heinrich (1765–1814). German composer. He was a protégé of Friedrich Wilhelm II and a pupil of Naumann before moving to Italy. Succeeded Reichardt as kapellmeister in Berlin (1795). He wrote *opere serie,* but German works brought him to prominence. His *Singspiele,* particularly *Fanchon* (1804), are forerun-ners of Weber's *Der Freischütz.* His work shows the influence of Hiller and Weisse.

HITTDORF, Jacob Ignaz (1817–71). German architect. Rebuilt the Théâtre Favart and the new Théâtre de l'Ambigue comique in Paris.

HITZIG, Julius Eduard (1780–1849). German writer and director of the Berlin Kammer-gericht.

HOFFMANN, E. T. A. (1776–1822). German novelist, essayist, and composer, one of the central figures of literary romanticism; his writings and to some extent his music ex-erted influence on generations of authors and musicians (e.g., Schumann). Studied music with the organist Podbielski, acquiring great proficiency, serving as music director in Bamberg (1808–12) and conducting in Leipzig and Dresden (1813–14), before settling in Berlin (1814), where he remained. He was an important pioneer of the German ro-mantic opera, esp. in *Undine* (Berlin, 1816).

HOGARTH, George (1783–1870). Scottish writer on music. Practiced law in Edinburgh, then settled in London (1830). Wrote articles for the *Harmonicon* and reviews for the *Morning Chronicle.* His daughter married Charles Dickens in 1836, and when the latter became editor of the *Daily News,* he began writing for this and other papers. Secretary of the Philharmonic Society (1850–64). Published several books.

HOGUET, Michael-François (1793–1871). French dancer, choreographer, and ballet master. Studied with Coulon. Went to Berlin as *premier danseur* (1817) and stayed there until his retirement (1856), becoming second choreographer, director of the Bal-let School, and ballet master. Choreographed numbers of ballets, esp. *Der Geburtstag* (1833) and *Aladin* (1854).

HOLBEIN, Franz Ignaz von (1779–1855). Austrian actor and theater poet. Director of the Hofburg Theater and the Court Opera in Vienna (1849).

HOLDING. Theatrical agent in Vienna.

HOLLAND, the king of. See **WILLEM III**.

HOLTEI, Karl von (1798–1880). German dramatist, actor, theater manager. Director of the Königstädter-Theater in Berlin, then of the theaters in Breslau, Darmstadt, and Riga. Adapted French vaudevilles for the German stage. Known for his play *Lorbeer und Bettelstab* (1840) and his autobiography *Vierzig Jahre* (1843–50). Many of his poems became *Volkslieder*.

HOLZMÜLLER, Eduard (b. circa 1806). German singer at the Königstädter-Theater in Berlin (1830–36), then in Hanover.

HOPPE, Franz (1810–49). German actor. Began as a singer, then followed an acting career in Hamburg, Brunswick, and finally Berlin at the Royal Theater (1844).

HORMAYR, Joseph, Freiherr von (1781–1848). Austrian historian.

HORN, A. L. Ernst (1774–1848). German civil servant. Professor and health official in Berlin.

HORZALKA, Johann (1778–1860). Austrian painter and composer.

HOVEN. See **VESQUE VON PÜTLINGEN**.

HUGO, Carl (Carl Hugo Bernstein)(1808–77). German-Hungarian writer. Went to Paris to produce his new play *Bankár es Báro* (Banker and baron), which had already enjoyed success in Hungary and Germany.

HUGO, Victor (1802–85). French writer. In the prologue to his drama *Cromwell* (1827) he provided the manifesto of the romantic movement. This was consolidated by the appearance of his novel *Notre Dame de Paris* (1831). Was obliged to live in exile in Jersey and Guernsey (1852–70), but later returned to Paris.

HULLAH, John Pyke (1812–84). English composer and organist. Pupil of Horsley and Crivelli. As a composer he was self-taught; church organist at Croydon. Made several trips to Paris to study the vocal teaching methods of Wilhelm. Established the Singing School for Schoolmasters at Exeter Hall (1841). Taught singing at various colleges in London (1844–74). Inspector of training schools (1872). Wrote theoretical works, made collections of vocal music.

HÜLSEN, Botho von (1815–86). German theater director. Took over the directorship of the Royal Theatre in Berlin on the retirement of Theodor von Küstner (1851), and held this post for thirty-five years. His fervent and autocratic leadership saw the introduction of many theatrical innovations and the maintenance of a classical repertoire. In 1867 he also assumed control of the Royal Theatres in Hanover, Cassel, and Wiesbaden.

HUMANN, Adolph (1794–1853). German musician. First bassoonist of the Royal Orchestra in Berlin.

HUMBOLDT, Alexander, Freiherr von (1769–1859). German naturalist. His scientific work *Kosmos* (1845–62) describes his worldwide journeys, discoveries, and experiments, and is a physical description of the universe and a history of science. He actively supported the emancipation of the Jews in Prussia, and was very close to Meyerbeer and his family, especially Amalia Beer.

HUMBOLDT, Wilhelm, Freiherr von (1767–1835). German politician. Prussian minister of state. As leader of the Prussian Ministry of Culture and Public Education he founded the Berlin University and reformed Prussia's educational system (1809). He helped negotiate Austrian entrance into the alliance against Napoleon (1813) and the first Treaty of Paris (1814). Ambassador to Britain (1817). Like his brother Alexander, he was in favor of Jewish emancipation.

HUMMEL, Johann Nepomuk (1778–1837). Austrian pianist and composer. Studied with Mozart, Clementi, Albrechtsberger, Haydn, and Salieri. Haydn's deputy in Prince Esterházy's service (1804–11), then kapellmeister in Stuttgart (1811), and finally in Weimar (1819). Undertook extensive concert tours to Russia, France, Holland, Belgium, and England. Wrote 124 opus numbers: nine operas, seven piano concertos, and chamber music, including the Septet in D Minor. Also an *Anweisung zum Pianofortespiel* (1828).

HURTEAUX, Auguste-Hyacinthe (b. 1808). Belgian bass. Début (1830) in the title role of Rossini's *Moïse*.

I

IFFLAND, August Wilhelm (1759–1814). German playwright. He was an actor of considerable talent, and became director of the National Theater in Mannheim (1785–92), and subsequently at the Royal Theatre in Berlin. During the same period he was also director of the Opera House. His sixty-five plays popularized the *comédie larmoyante* in Germany and enjoyed great success. The best of them (*Die Jäger*, 1785; *Die Hagestolzen*, 1793) show a fine sense of the stage, and introduce a variety of characters and middle-class settings that vividly portray their age. *Ausgewählte Werke* (1859, 6 vols.).

ILLAIRE, Emil Ernst, *Kabinetsrat*. Official of the court chamberlain under both Friedrich Wilhelm III and Friedrich Wilhelm IV.

IMMERMANN, Karl Leberecht (1796–1840). German writer. Served in the campaign against Napoleon (1813), studied in the University of Halle, entered the Prussian civil service, becoming a judge in Magdeburg and Düsseldorf. He wrote several derivative plays, novels, and poetry. His later works won him considerable reputation and sought to exploit fantasy and realism simultaneously.

INGRES, Jean-Auguste-Dominique (1780–1867). French painter. He was a superb draftsman, noted for the refined sensuality of his nudes. He also painted portraits and historical scenes.

ISABELLA II, Maria Luise, queen of Spain (1830–1904, r. 1833–68). Her disputed succession caused the Carlist Wars. It was her political interference rather than her notorious immorality that led to her deposition.

ISOUARD, Nicolò (1775–1818). Maltese composer. Organist in Malta, then had a highly successful career in Paris. His operas show melodic gifts and solid workmanship, esp. *Cendrillon* (1810). *Jean et Colin* (1814) was one of his best-known works.

J

JACOB (= LACROIX), Paul (1806–84). German writer and cultural historian. Published works of older poets and wrote historical romances.

JACOBI, Karl Gustav Jacob (1804–51). German mathematician.

JACOBSEN, Dr. Hermann. German doctor. Fought for the political equality of the Jews in Prussia in the debates of 1847.

JAEGER, Dr. German oculist consulted by Meyerbeer.

JAEGER, Franz (1796–1852). German singer. Tenor at the Königstädter-Theater in Berlin.

JÄHNS, Friedrich Wilhelm (1809–88). German vocal pedagogue and writer on music. Studied singing with Grell. In 1854 founded a singing society, which he conducted until 1870. Successful as a voice teacher in Berlin, with over a hundred pupils. Compiled a celebrated thematic catalog, *C. M. von Weber in seinen Werken* (1871).

JANIN, Jules (1804–74). French writer and critic. Novelist of the *frénétique* school or *roman noir*, e.g., *L'Âne mort et la Femme guillotinée* (1829). Published criticism, such as *Histoire de la Littérature dramatique* (1853–56, 6 vols.). Member of the Académie (1870).

JANSA, Leopold (1795–1875). Bohemian composer and violinist. Studied in Vienna and taught the violin there. Director of university music. Dismissed on political grounds (1849) and remained in England for several years as a teacher. Returned to Vienna after the amnesty of 1868. He was esteemed as a violinist and wrote much violin music (including four concertos).

JASMIN (Jacques Boé) (1798–1864). Gascon poet from Agen, called "le Perruquier poète." His work was written in the local patois, "las Papillotos."

JERRMANN, Eduard (1798–1859). Austrian actor. Chief régisseur at the Theater an der Wien, director of the Theater in der Josephstadt (1847).

JOACHIM, Joseph (1831–1907). German violinist. Studied at the age of ten at the Vienna Conservatoire. Appeared in Leipzig (1843), studied with Ferdinand David. Concertmaster in Weimar (1849–54); Hanover (1854); director of the Hochschule für ausübende Tonkunst in Berlin (1868). Internationally renowned as a teacher, and also pursued a career as a performing virtuoso, being particularly popular in England, where he received various academic honors. His playing was famous for its dignity and flawless technique. He was determined to interpret works authentically, and was also esteemed as a chamber musician, founding the Joachim Quartet (1869). He composed virtuoso pieces for the violin (including two concertos).

JOANNE. French journalist. Editor of the journal *L'Illustration*. A relation of Louis Viardot.

JOHAN, king of Saxony (b. 1801, r. 1854–73). He succeeded his brother, Friedrich August II, who was killed in an accident.

JOHN, Karl Wilhelm (1821–75). Prussian pianist. Meyerbeer recommended his acceptance by the Paris Conservatoire, where he became a pupil of Kalkbrenner and Halévy. Returned to Berlin only in 1863.

JOLY, Antenor. Owner and editor of the *Vert-Vert*. Director of the Théâtre de la Renaissance (1838).

JOMELLI, Niccolò (1714–74). Italian compoer. Pupil of Leo. Worked in Naples, Rome, Bologna, and Venice, where he produced *Merope* (1741) and became director of the Conservatorio degli Incurabili (1743). Went to Vienna, where he was a warm friend of Metastasio (1749). *Maestro di capella* at St. Peter's (1751–53) and kapellmeister in Stuttgart (1753–69). Returned to Naples (1769). He was known as "the Italian Gluck," adopting elements of the German style during his stay in Stuttgart, emphasizing instrumental accompaniment and more solid harmonic substance, as well as pioneering the crescendo. Wrote over fifty operas and church music, esp. the famous *Miserere* for two voices.

JONCIÈRES, Victorin de (1839–1903). French composer. Student of art, then turned to music. Studied with Elwart, then with Leborne at the Paris Conservatoire. He was a devoted admirer of Wagner, and after 1871 music critic of *La Liberté*. Wrote six operas (esp. *Dimitri* and *Johann von Lothringen*) and several large orchestral works.

JOSEPHY, Siegfried Julius (1782–1856). German bookseller, owner of the Haude and Spenersche Buchhandlung.

JOUY, Victor-Joseph-Étienne (1764–1846). French writer. Initially an officer, then a librarian at the Louvre. Created the libretti for *La Vestale, Fernand Cortez,* and *Guillaume Tell.* His works were published (1823–28, 27 vols.). Wrote a very successful series of articles for the *Gazette de France.* In spite of his desire to work with Meyerbeer, the composer discouraged it, wishing to avoid invidious comparison with Jouy's accomplishments with Spontini and Rossini.

JULIAN VAN GELDER, Esther Eliza (b. 1819). French soprano. Sang on various French stages and also in London and Barcelona.

JULLIAT. French writer, associate of the widowed Mathilde Heine.

JULLIEN, Louis-Antoine (1812–60). French musician. One of the great virtuoso conductors of the nineteenth century, famous for his huge and flamboyantly directed promenade concerts in London, which did much to popularize music "for the masses" in the 1840s.

JÜNGER, Johann Friedrich (1759–97). German dramatist.

JÜNGKEN, Johann Christian (1794–1875). Prussian doctor. Professor of surgery and oculist at the Berlin Charité (1834–68).

K

KALISCH, David (1820–72). German writer. Invented the Berlin *Lokalstück* (like *Berlin bei Nacht, Berlin, wie es weint und lacht*), contained in his collections *Berliner Volkbühne* (1864, 4 vols.) and *Lustige Werke* (1870, 5 vols.). Founded the humorous and satirical Berlin weekly *Kladderadatsch* (1848).

KALKBRENNER, Christian (1755–1806). German composer. Kapellmeister to the king of Prussia (1788), then in the service of Prince Heinrich of Rheinsberg (1790–96). Later lived in Naples, eventually becoming chorus master and singing teacher at the Opéra in Paris. Wrote several operas and instrumental works, as well as the study *Kurze Abriss der Geschichte der Tonkunst,* revised as *Histoire de la musique* (1802).

KALKBRENNER, Friedrich Wilhelm Michael (1785–1849). German pianist and composer. Pupil of Albrechtsberger. Virtuoso who lived in London (1814–23) as part of Clementi's circle. He undertook tours to Vienna and Berlin, then settled in Paris, where he was part owner of the Pleyel Piano Company.

KALLIWODA, Johannes Wenzeslaus (1801–66). Bohemian composer. Studied at the Prague Conservatoire with Pixis (1811–17), then played in the Prague Orchestra (1817–23). Became kapellmeister of the prince von Furstenberg in Donaueschingen (1823), where he spent thirty years. Retired to Karlsruhe. Enjoyed a considerable reputation.

KANDLER, Franz Sales (1792–1831). Austrian writer on music. Sang in the Court Choir in Vienna as a boy, then studied with Albrechtsberger, Salieri, and Gyrowetz. Became an imperial draftsman, and worked as a navy clerk in Venice and Naples (1815–28). He studied Italian music, and wrote books on Hasse (1820) and Palestrina (1834), as well as *Cenni storico-critici sulle vicende e lo stato attuale della musica in Italia* (1836).

KARL, crown prince of Sweden (1826–72). Son of Oscar I and Josephine von Leuchtenberg; became regent (1857), and then king (1859) as **Karl XV.**

KARL, prince of Prussia (Friedrich Karl Alexander) (1801–83). Third son of Friedrich Wilhelm III, and a friend and patron of Meyerbeer, who was a regular visitor at his home in Glienecke.

KARL ALEXANDER, grand duke of Weimar (b. 1818, r. 1853–1901). He was an intellectual who reestablished Weimar as the German cultural capital.

KARL AUGUST, grand duke of Weimar (b. 1757, r. 1758–1828). He made Weimar the intellectual and artistic capital of Germany, with Goethe, Schiller, and others attending his court. He patronized the University of Jena and encouraged the theater and fine arts.

KARL FRIEDRICH, grand duke of Weimar (b. 1783, r. 1828–53).

KARL FRIEDRICH ALEXANDER, crown prince of Württemberg (1823–91). Became king as Karl I (1851).

KARL THEODOR MAXIMILIAN AUGUST, prince of Bavaria (1805–75). Second son of King Max Joseph.

KAROLYI, Aloys (1825–89). Austrian diplomat. Failed to win Prussian support for Austria against Napoleon III in 1858, or to prevent the breakdown between Austria and Prussia that led to the war of 1866. Austrian delegate to the Congress of Berlin (1878), and finally ambassador in London (1878–88).

KARR, Alphonse (1808–90). French writer. Published a satirical periodical, *Les Gnêpes* (1839–76). Collaborated on the newspaper *La Patrie* (1845).

KASKEL, Karl, Freiherr von. Dresden banker. Probably the grandson of the banker, wine dealer, and Saxon court agent Jakob Kaskel (d. 1788). Swedish consul in Dresden, and friend of Meyerbeer.

KASTNER, Johann Georg (1810–67). Alsatian composer and theorist. Studied under Berton and Reicha. Enormously erudite. Pursued the study of acoustics and formulated a theory of the cosmic unity of the arts. Member of the Institut, officer of the Legion of Honor. Created several volumes of *Livres-Partitions*, symphony cantatas illustrating musico-historical subjects.

KÄTHY, Dr. German dramaturge.

KEAN, Edmund (1787–1833). English actor. Director and actor in the Drury Lane Theatre (1814), and attained particular fame as protagonist in the principal Shakespearean plays, appearing with great success in Scotland, Ireland, North America, and Paris.

KEISER, Reinhard (1674–1739). German composer. Chief representative of the early Hamburg opera. Studied in Leipzig. Kapellmeister in Brunswick (1693). Followed Kusser to Hamburg (1695) where he began an association with the librettist Postel, and wrote over seventy operas (e.g., *Störtebecker and Jödge Michel*, 1701). In 1703 he took over the direction of the Theater am Gänsemarkt, and settled in Hamburg permanently (1724). He exerted an enormous influence both in his compositions and standards of performance. He was responsive to Lully and Scarlatti in vocal writing, but developed the German art of enriching the orchestral accompaniment, writing virtuoso parts for solo instruments.

KÉLER-BÉLA (orig. Albert von Keler) (1820–82). Hungarian violinist, conductor, and composer. Studied with Sechter in Vienna, played the violin at the Theater an der Wien, and composed dance music. Conducted the Gungl Orchestra in Berlin (1854), succeeded Lanner in Vienna (1855), then directed an army band (1856–63), finally the Spa Orchestra in Wiesbaden (1863–73). Composed dances and light music, esp. the *Hoffnungssterne Waltz* and the *Lustspiel Ouverture*.

KELLERMANN, Christian (1815–66). Danish cellist. Studied with Merck in Vienna, made several concert tours. Soloist in the Royal Orchestra in Copenhagen (1847). Wrote works for the solo cello.

KEMBLE, Charles (1775–1854). English actor and writer. Worked at the Drury Lane and Haymarket Theatres and jointly ran Covent Garden with his brother. He was a leading actor for twenty-five years, but his light voice meant that he largely played young men (esp. Romeo) in comedy and romance. Wrote many comedies, translated opera libretti, and did much to nurture German music in England. Father of the famous actress Fanny Kemble.

KEMBLE, Fanny (= Frances Anne) (1809–93). English actress. Daughter of Charles. She was beautiful and accomplished, and first appeared with her father (1829). She played comedy and tragedy equally well, and had many great roles in her repertoire. Later went to America, where she enjoyed great success.

KETTEN, Henri (1848–83). Hungarian pianist. Studied at the Paris Conservatoire with Halévy. Wrote several piano pieces in the salon style, suitable for teaching.

KIEL, Friedrich (1821–85). German teacher and composer. Studied with his father and with Kummer in Coburg. Leader of the ducal orchestra (1840). Moved to Berlin and studied with Dehn (1842–44). Elected to the Prussian Academy of Fine Arts (1865), taught at the Stern Conservatoire, then at the Hochschule für Musik. He was a prolific composer, his most successful work being a *Requiem* (Berlin, 1862; numerous performances in Germany).

KIENLEN, Johann Christoph (1784–1830). German composer. Studied with Cherubini and Schnyder von Wartensee. City music director in Ulm, then royal Bavarian music director. Went to Vienna (1811), where he became the kapellmeister of Freiherr von Zinicq in Baden and Pressburg. In Berlin he became chorus *répétiteur* at the Berlin Theater (1817). Returned to Ulm (1827) and found a position with Prince Radziwill in Posen (1828). Achieved a reputation as a composer of lieder.

KIESEWETTER, Raphael Georg, Edler von Wiesenbrunn (1773–1850). Austrian privy councillor. Famous for his collection of old music. Collaborated on the *Allgemeine Zeitung*.

KINDERMANN, August (1817–91). German bass-baritone. Sang in Berlin (1836) and Leipzig (1839–46) before moving to Munich (1846–91), where he enjoyed great popularity. Created Titurel in *Parsifal* (1876).

KINKEL, Johanna (née Mockel) (1810–58). German composer. Studied in Berlin with Karl Böhmer. Married the poet Gottfried Kinkel (1843). Wrote the *Vogel-Cantate*, the operetta *Otto der Schütz,* and the song "The Soldier's Farewell"; also a piano manual.

KLAGE, Karl (1788–1850). German pianist and guitarist. Royal music director, and joint owner of a publishing and music business. He was well known for his piano arrangements of classical works for four-hands.

KLEIN, Bernhard (1793–1832). German composer. Studied with Cherubini in Paris (1813). Returned to Cologne as director of the cathedral. Settled in Berlin (1818). Taught at the Royal Institute for Church Music (1820). Praised for his contrapuntal craftsmanship in sacred works—"the Berlin Palestrina." Wrote operas, oratorios, cantatas, religious music.

KLEIN, Dr. Julius Leopold. (1810–76). German literary historian, dramatist and a theater critic in Berlin. Author of a history of drama (*Geschichte des Dramas*, 1865–76, 13 vols.) and plays on historical and contemporary social issues.

KLENGEL, August Alexander (1783–1852). German pianist and composer. Pupil of Clementi. Lived in St. Petersburg, Paris, Italy, Dresden, and London (1815–16) before becoming organist at the court in Dresden.

KLESHEIM, Anton, Freiherr von (1812–84). Austrian folk poet.

KLINGENBERG, Friedrich Wilhelm (1809–88). German music teacher. Director of the music academy at Breslau (1830–37), then of the Peterkirche in Görlitz (1840–85).

KLITZSCH, Karl Emanuel (1812–89). German musician. Self-taught. Taught at Zwickau, where he founded and conducted the Music Society. Wrote for the *Neue Zeitschrift für Musik*. Composed under the name Emanuel Kronach.

KLOPSTOCK, Friedrich Gottlieb (1724–1803). German poet. Famous for his epic on the life of Christ, the *Messias* (1748–73), which is a lyrical expression of almost religious faith in language, unparalleled in German literature for its poetic and emotive power. His odes treat principally of religion, nature, friendship, love, and politics, and express intensely personal feelings in elevated, neoclassical diction. He represents at once the culmination of the verbal art of the baroque and the harbinger of the Sturm und Drang.

KNOWLES, James Sheridan (1784–1862). Irish actor and playwright. Specialized in tragedies like *Wat Tyler* (1825).

KOCH, Heinrich Christoph (1749–1816). German theorist. Studied with Göpfert at Weimar, played the violin in Rudolstadt (1768), and then became leader of the chamber music there (1777). He wrote books on composition, harmony, modulation, and esp. the *Musikalisches Lexikon* (1802, 1865). Also wrote for periodicals, music for wind band, and cantatas.

KOCH, Siegfried Gotthelf (1754–1831). German actor. Went to the Vienna Burgtheater at Kotzebue's recommendation (1798) where he became a darling of the public.

KOLB, Gustav (1798–1865). German journalist. Editor of the *Allgemeine Zeitung*.

KOLBE, Oskar (1836–78). German theorist and composer. Studied with Grell and Löschmann in Berlin, taught at the Stern Conservatory (1859–75). Wrote textbooks on general bass and harmony, composed orchestral works, piano works, songs.

KOLOWRAT, Franz Anton, Graf von (1778–1861). Austrian politician. Minister of state for the interior in Vienna (1825–48). Although not a liberal, he supported the development of Czech culture. As an opponent of Metternich, he received much liberal support, and after 1835 effectively undermined Metternich's influence.

KONI, Fedor Alekseevitch (1809–79). Russian librettist and theater critic. Editor of the newspaper *Repertuar i Panteon Teatrov* (1847).

KONTSKI, Antoine (1817–99). Polish pianist. Studied with John Field. Paris (1851); Berlin (1853); St. Petersburg (1854–87); United States (1883). World tour (1896–98). Wrote salon and virtuoso pieces for the piano; concerto, overtures, operettas.

KOPISCH, August (1799–1853). German artist and poet. Studied art in Dresden, damaged his hand, went to Italy for five years (1823) and discovered the Blue Grotto of Capri. He met A. von Platen and the future King Friedrich Wilhelm IV. In 1828 he returned to Germany, living in Berlin and Potsdam. The king commissioned *Die Schlösser und Gärten zu Potsdam*, published posthumously in 1854. Translated Dante and also wrote humorous fairy and elfin poetry.

KOREFF, David Ferdinand (1783–1851). German doctor and writer. Friend of Chamisso, E. T. A. Hoffmann, Novalis. Professor of medicine at the University of Berlin (1816). Translated Tibullus and wrote libretti and poetry. Later worked in Paris as a physician and confidant of society ladies.

KORFF, Emanuel Karl Heinrich von, Freiherr Schmysingk (1826–1903). German officer. Married Blanca Meyerbeer in 1857. He was later promoted to major general, and became a personal friend of the German emperor, Wilhelm II.

KORFF, Friedrich ("Fritz") von, Freiherr Schmysingk (1858–98). Meyerbeer's grandson.

KOSSAK, Ernest (1814–80). German philologist, writer on music.

KÖSTER, Hans (1818–1900). German dramatist.

KOTZEBUE, August Friedrich Ferdinand von (1761–1819). German playwright. Some of his two hundred plays enjoyed great popularity in the first half of the nineteenth century. The drama *Menschenhass und Reue* (1789) achieved a worldwide fame for at least twenty-five years, its sentimentalized Sturm und Drang themes and effects exercising a great influence, as did *Die deutschen Kleinstädter* (1803), a comedy of small-town life. Assassinated by a radical student, Carl Sand, in 1819 for political reasons. *Dramatische Werke* (1867–, 10 vols.).

KOTZOLT, Heinrich (1814–81). German singer. Sang first bass in the Domchor, becoming conductor (1860) and royal *Musikdirektor* (1866).

KRAFT, Nicolaus (1778–1853). Hungarian cellist. As a child undertook concert tours with his father, later worked with Duport and as a soloist in the orchestra of the Court Opera Orchestra in Vienna (1809). Member of the Schuppanzigh Quartet.

KREBS, Karl August (1804–80). German composer. Kapellmeister at the Vienna Court Opera (1826); Hamburg Court Opera (1827); Dresden Court Opera (1850–72). Wrote two operas. Many of his songs attained great popularity.

KREUTZER, Konradin (1780–1849). German composer. Studied privately. Read law at Freiburg. Stuttgart (1812); Vienna (1822–24); kapellmeister at the Kärntnertor-Theater in Vienna; Cologne (1840–46); Vienna (1846–49); settled in Riga. Wrote light operas fusing the traditions of the eighteenth-century *Singspiel* with German romanticism, esp. *Das Nachtlager von Grenada* (1834).

KREUTZER, Léon (1817–68). French composer and music critic. Studied with Fleche and Benoist. Wrote for the *Revue et Gazette musicale*, *Revue contemporaine*, *Le Quo-*

tidienne, *L'Union*. Published *Essai sur l'Art lyrique au Théâtre* (1845). Composed a prelude to *The Tempest*, string quartets, piano sonatas, and a treatise on modulation.

KREUTZER, Rodolphe (1766–1831). French violinist and composer. Studied with his father and Stamitz. Appointed first violinist in the Chapelle du Roi (1782) and first violin at the Théâtre Italien (1790). Teacher of violin at the Conservatoire (1791). He made a triumphant concert tour through Italy, Germany, and Holland and succeeded Rode as first violinist at the Opéra, becoming first conductor there (1817–26). Wrote forty-three operas (notably *Lodoiska*, Paris, 1791), nineteen violin concertos, much chamber and instrumental music, and *40 Études ou Caprices* for solo violin (published in countless editions). Joint author with Rode and Baillot of the violin method used at the Conservatoire.

KRIEHUBER, Joseph (1801–76). Viennese painter and lithographer.

KROLL, Franz (1820–77). German musician. Studied with Liszt. Worked in Berlin as a music teacher (1849). Edited the *Well-Tempered Clavier* for the Bach Gesellschaft, and Mozart piano works.

KRUG, Dietrich (1821–80). German pianist and teacher. Studied with Melchert and J. Schmidt. Taught in Hamburg. Wrote studies for the piano and published a teaching method.

KRÜGER, Franz (1797–1857). Prussian court painter from 1825 (known as Pferde-Krüger), famous for his depictions of grand ceremonial state occasions and official portraits (including two of Meyerbeer, 1843).

KUCHENMEISTER. See **RUDERSDORFF**.

KÜCKEN, Friedrich Wilhelm (1810–82). German composer. Studied with Lührss and Aron in Schwerin. Played in the duke's orchestra before going to Berlin to study with Birnbach (1832) and Sechter in Vienna (1841–43). Conducted festivals of male choruses in Switzerland. Court kapellmeister in Stuttgart (1851–61). Wrote operas, chamber music, and songs.

KÜHNEL, Ambrosius (1770–1813). German music publisher. Founded the Bureau de Musique with Franz Anton Hoffmeister (1800). After Kühnel's death, the publishing house was taken over by Carl Friedrich Peters (1813).

KULLAK, Theodor (1818–82). German pianist and teacher. Studied with Dehn and Czerny. Court pianist to the king of Prussia (1846). Founded the Berlin conservatoire with Julius Stern and Bernhard Marx (1850) and his own school, the Neue Alexander Tonkunst (1855). Music teacher to the princes and princesses of Prussia.

KUND (= KUNTH), Karl Sigismund (1788–1850). German botanist. Vice-director of the Botanical Gardens in Berlin. Arranged and presented the plants collected in America by Humboldt and Bonpland.

KUPELWIESER, Joseph (1781–1866). Austrian writer. Secretary of the Kärntnertor-Theater. Librettist of Schubert's *Fierrabras*. Brother of the painter Leopold Kupelwieser, and a friend of Schiller.

KURANDA, Ignaz (1812–84). German journalist. He founded *Die Grenzboden* in Brussels (1841), but was forced to leave. His paper was confiscated in Germany. He moved to Leipzig (1842) and then to Berlin, and continued directing his paper until 1848, when he moved to Vienna and established the *Ostdeutschen Post*.

KURPINSKI, Karol Kasimir (1785–1857). Polish composer. Studied with his father and became a violinist at a Warsaw theater (1810). Court kapellmeister and director of opera in Warsaw (1825–42), as well as a teacher at his own schools of singing and drama. Wrote twenty-four operas and Polish dances. Played an important part in Warsaw's concert life and the development of Polish opera.

KURZBÖCK (= KURZBECK), Magdalene (1767–1845). Austrian pianist. Studied with Clementi and Haydn. Praised by Mozart and Reichardt for her playing.

KÜSTNER, Karl Theodor von (1784–1864). German official. Intendant at the theaters in Leipzig (1817–28), Darmstadt (1830–32), and Munich (1833–42). Intendant-General of the Royal Theaters in Berlin (1842–51). Relations between him and Meyerbeer were strained and eventually led to the composer resigning as *Generalmusikdirector*.

L

LABARRE, Théodore-François-Joseph (1805–70). French musician. Composer of romances and five ballets (notably *La Révolte au sérail*, 1833). Harpist and conductor at the Opéra Comique (1847), kapellmeister to Napoleon III (1851), and professor of harp at the Conservatoire (1867).

LABAT, Eugène (1797–1867). French dramatist and archivist. Wrote some plays in collaboration with Charles Desnoyer.

LABICHE, Eugène (1815–88). French dramatist. Wrote 173 plays, often in collaboration.

LABLACHE, Luigi (1794–1858). Italian bass. Studied in Naples with Valente. Début Naples (1812). Palermo (1813–17), Milan (1817–24), Vienna (1824–30), London (1830–52), Paris (1830–51). A highly influential singer in the history of opera with a vast repertoire. Created roles by Donizetti, Bellini, Mercadante, Pacini, Vaccai, Mosca, Balfe. Possessed a magnificent voice and presence.

LABORDE, Jean-Benjamin de (1734–94). French musician. Studied violin with Dauvergne and composition with Rameau. Chamberlain to Louis XV. Wrote thirty-two comic operas and songs, the musicological study *Essai sur la musique ancienne et moderne* (1780, 4 vols.). Died on the guillotine.

LABORDE, Rosine (1824–70). French coloratura soprano at the Paris Opéra.

LACHNER, Franz (1803–90). German composer. Studied in Vienna and conducted there and in Mannheim before becoming music director of the Court Opera in Munich (1836) and *Generalmusikdirektor* (1852–65). Three of his four operas were produced there (esp. *Catarina Cornaro*, 1841). Also wrote eight symphonies; religious, choral, chamber, and instrumental music; and songs. Wrote recitatives for Cherubini's *Médée*.

LACOSTE, Eugène (1818–1907). French artist.

LADENBERG, Adalbert von (1798–1855). Prussian statesman. Minister of culture (1848–50).

LAFARGUE, Gustave (d. 1876). French journalist and theater administrator.

LAFONT, Charles-Philippe (1781–1839). French violin virtuoso. Studied with Kreutzer and Rode. Toured Europe (1801–8) and succeeded Rode in St. Petersburg. Returned to Paris as soloist to Louis XVIII (1815). Killed in an accident while on tour with Henri Herz. Wrote many works for the violin (incl. seven concertos), two hundred romances, and two operas.

LAFONT, Marcelin (1800–1838). French singer. Début Paris Opéra (1823). Engaged in Marseilles (1826–27).

LAGRANGE, Anna Caroline de (1824–1905). French soprano. Studied with Bordogni, then with Mandanici and Lamperti in Italy. Début Piacenza (1842). Sang in Paris, Vienna, New York (1855–58), and Milan (1861). Noted for her brilliant and florid singing.

LAGRUN, Mme. German soprano active in the 1850s.

LAMARTINE, Alphonse de (1790–1869). French poet. His early romantic verse was darkly melancholic in the Byronic manner. Wrote little poetry after 1839. Member of the Provisional Government (1848). Minister of foreign affairs (1851).

LAMPERTI, Francesco (1811–92). Italian singing teacher. Studied at the Milan Conservatoire. With Masini directed the Teatro Filodrammatico at Lodi. Students came to him from all over Europe. Professor of singing at the Milan Conservatoire (1850–75). He was a friend of Pasta and Rubini and based his method on the old Italian school. Wrote vocal studies and a treatise on singing.

LANDESMAN, Heinrich (pseud. Hieronymus Lonn) (1821–1902). Austrian writer. Had to leave Vienna in 1846 for political reasons, went to Berlin. Wrote for *Europa*. Returned to Vienna in 1849 after the fall of Metternich.

LANGE, Dr. Berlin critic, active in the 1840s.

LANGENSCHWARZ, Maximilian (1806–67). German writer known for his newspaper *Improvisator.* Lived in Paris from 1837.

LANGHANS, Karl Ferdinand (1781–1869). German architect.

LANGLÉ, Joseph-Adolphe-Ferdinand (pseud. M.-A.-F. "Egilio" Langlois) (1798–1867). French writer. Began his literary career as a journalist, then became a funeral director. One of his later literary works recounted the return of the remains of Napoleon from St. Helena. Wrote the play *Murillo,* for which Meyerbeer wrote some incidental music.

LANIUS, Christian. German singer. Worked as a singer, actor and theater director in Bavaria. Created the title role in *Jephthas Gelübde.*

LANNER, Joseph (1801–43). Austrian composer. Self-taught violinist and composer. Joined Pamer's dance orchestra when he was twelve. Formed a quartet with Johann Strauss Sr. (1818). The group grew in size and by 1824 had become a full orchestra, performing in coffeehouses and taverns, and at balls. Famous for his innovative dance music. Composed 207 popular pieces.

LANNOY, Heinrich Eduard, Freiherr von (1787–1853). Austrian composer. Studied in Graz and Paris. In 1813 he went to Vienna, where he promoted the Gesellschaft der Musikfreunde and directed the Viennese *concerts spirituels* (1824–48). He was a member of the executive board of the Vienna Conservatoire (1830–35), and was a friend of Liszt. Wrote several operas as well as orchestral and chamber music.

LAPELOUZE, Valentin. French journalist and newspaper editor, owner of the *Courier français.*

LA ROCHE (= LAROCHE), Karl (1794–1884). Austrian actor. Worked at the Burgtheater.

LA ROCHEFOUCAULD, François Sosthène, vicomte de. French civil servant, efficient and accommodating in securing Rossini's contract with the Departement des Beaux-Arts and Maison du Roi, which provided the artistic and financial basis of the composer's Parisian career (1824). Also helpful to Meyerbeer, both with *Il Crociato in Egitto* and *Robert le Diable.*

LASSELLE, Ferdinand (1825–64). German writer. Lived in Paris, Düsseldorf, and Berlin. Fell under the influence of Karl Marx, and became active in establishing social democracy in Germany.

LASSEN, Eduard (1830–1904). Belgian composer and conductor. Studied in the Brussels Conservatoire, won the Belgian Prix de Rome (1851). Toured Germany and Italy. Went to Weimar, where Liszt produced his opera *Landgraf Ludwigs Brautfahrt* (1857). Court music director in Weimar (1860–95). Composed ballets, symphonies, incidental music.

LASSUS, Roland de (Orlandus Lassus) (1532–94). Flemish composer. Trained in Mons. Choirmaster in Rome, Antwerp, Munich. Wrote madrigals and religious music, carrying polyphony to a high point.

LATOUR, Jean (1766–1840). French musician. Court pianist to the Prince of Wales (later George IV). Through his compositions and arrangements he was able to cofound the music partnership of Chappel & Co., later establishing his own business. Returned to Paris (1830).

LAUB, Ferdinand (1832–75). German violinist and conductor. Studied at the Prague Conservatoire and then in Vienna (1847). Toured Germany, Paris, London. Concertmaster in Weimar (1853), leader of the Court Orchestra in Berlin (1855). Taught at the Stern Conservatoire (1855–57); Vienna (1862–65). Toured Russia, then became professor of violin at the Moscow Conservatoire (1866). Wrote an opera, published two collections of Czech melodies. Spent his last years in Karlsbad and the Tyrol.

LAUBE, Heinrich (1806–84). German writer and journalist. Edited the *Zeitung für die elegante Welt*. In 1839 he traveled to France and Algeria. Artistic director of the Hofburg Theater in Vienna (1849–67), director of the Leipzig Theater (1869–70) and then the Vienna Stadttheater (1872–80). Wrote plays and novels, his greatest success being *Graf Essex* (1856). His *Erinnerungen* (in *Gesammelte Werke in 50 Bänden*, Leipzig, n.d.) contains a striking description of Meyerbeer.

LAUSKA, Franz (1764–1825). German pianist and composer. Studied in Vienna with Albrechtsberger. Chamber musician in Munich, taught in Copenhagen (1794–98) and settled in Berlin (1798). Piano teacher at the Prussian court and included Meyerbeer among his pupils. Wrote twenty-four sonatas.

LAUTERS. Soprano active in Paris in the 1850s.

LAVALETTE, Antoine-Marie-Chamans, comte (1769–1830). French statesman. Arrested after the fall of Napoleon, and sentenced to death (1815). He was rescued from prison by his wife, Emilie Louise de Beauharnais.

LAVATER, Johann Caspar (1741–1801). Swiss writer and Protestant pastor who developed the thesis that the human face is the mirror of the soul (*Physiognomische Fragmente*, 1775–78, 5 vols.).

LEBORNE, Aimé-Ambroise-Simon (1797–1866). French musician. Studied with Berton and Cherubini. Theoretician and composer, he succeeded Reicha as teacher of counterpoint at the Conservatoire (1836). Was also librarian and copyist at the Paris Opéra (1829–66). Wrote three operas.

LEBRUN, Carl August (1792–1842). German dramatist.

LEBRUN, Louis-Sébastien (1764–1829). French composer and tenor. *Maître de chant* at the Opéra. Wrote sixteen operas, notably *Marcelin* (1800) and *Le Rossignol* (1809), also religious music and romances.

LEBRUN, Rosine (b. 1783). French singer.

LE COUPPEY, Félicien. French musician. Professor of piano and theory at the Paris Conservatoire.

LEDEBUR, Karl, major (1806–72). Prussian cavalry officer. Published *Tonkünstlerlexikon Berlins von den ältesten Zeiten bis auf die Gegenwart* (1860–61) and essays on German court music.

LEDRU-ROLLIN, Alexandre-Auguste (1807–74). French lawyer and politician. Coordinated the far Left (1841). Minister of the interior (1848). From 1849 to 1870 he lived in England for political reasons.

LEDUC, Alphonse (1804–68). French musician. Bassoon, flute, and guitar virtuoso. Played in the orchestra of the Paris Opéra. Music publisher from 1841.

LEFÉBURE-WÉLY, Louis-James-Alfred (1817–69). French organist and composer. Pupil of his father, studied at the Paris Conservatoire (1832) with Benoist, Laurent, Zimmermann, Berton, Halévy. Organist at St. Madeleine (1847–58), St. Sulpice. Wrote operas, cantatas, three masses, symphonies, chamber music, salon music, études.

LEGOUVÉ, Ernest-Wilfred (1807–1903). French playwright. Collaborated with Scribe, esp. on *Adrienne Lecouvreur* (1849). Wrote his reminiscences of Scribe and the French theater (1874, 1893).

LEGRAND, Peter (1778–1840). German instrumentalist. Worked in the Munich Court Orchestra (1795); undertook several concert tours to Vienna, Strasbourg, Frankfurt, and Nancy.

LEHMANN, Heinrich (1814–82). German painter. Pupil of Ingres. Professor at the École des Beaux Arts in Paris. Lived with his brother Rudolf. Nephews of the banker Auguste Leo.

LEHMANN, Rudolf (1819–1905). French painter who worked in Paris.

LEHWESS, Dr. Heinrich. German physician and *Hofrat*.

LEIBROCK, Joseph Adolf (1808–86). German musician. Studied in Berlin. Cellist and harpist in the Court Orchestra at Brunswick. Wrote songs, cello and piano music, incidental music to *Die Räuber*.

LEININGEN-NEUDENAU, August, Graf von. German officer. Lawyer in Baden (1827). Intendant of court music and theaters (1832–39).

LEMBERT, Joseph (Wenzel Temler) (1780–1851). Bohemian actor and poet. Worked in Stettin, Leipzig, Dresden, and after 1807, at the Court Theatre in Stuttgart, also frequently appearing in guest roles. Went to the Hofburgtheater in Vienna (1817). Wrote a number of successful plays and stories.

LENORMAND, Mme. Niece and adopted daughter of Mme. Récamier. Published *Souvenirs et correspondence tirés des papiers de Mme Récamier* (1859).

LEO, Auguste. German banker from Hamburg who settled in Paris. Relative of the composer Ferdinand Hiller. The collapse of his banking business is referred to by Heine in his poem *Lutezia* (section 57).

LÉONARD, Hubert (1819–90). Belgian violinist and pedagogue. Pupil of Rouma and Habeneck. Extended European tour (1844). Succeeded Bériot as violin professor at the Brussels Conservatoire. Settled in Paris (1867).

LÉOPOLD I, king of the Belgians (b. 1790, r. 1831–65). Son of Duke Franz of Saxe-Coburg-Gotha. Widower of Charlotte Princess of Wales. An outstanding patron of science and education, highly influential in diplomacy.

LEOPOLD I, prince of Anhalt-Dessau (1676–1747). German soldier. Known as "the old Dessauer," he was field marshal to Friedrich Wilhelm I. Introduced marching in step to the Prussian Army, so initiating the military march.

LEOPOLDO II, grand duke of Tuscany (b. 1797, r. 1824–59). Popular liberal ruler, obliged to flee when Tuscany was invaded by Sardinia (1859).

LÉPAULLE, François-Gabriel (1804–86). French artist. Exhibited his work regularly between 1824 and 1876, but was active principally during the July Monarchy. Duponchel charged him with the creation of the costumes for *Robert le Diable,* and his painting of the act 5 trio (1834) became famous.

LERMINIER, Jean-Louis (1803–57). French writer. Editor of the *Globe.*

LEROY, Léon (d. 1887). French music critic and theater administrator.

LESCHETIZSKY, Theodor (1830–1915). Polish pianist. Pupil of Czerny and Sechter. Began teaching in Vienna when he was fifteen. From 1852 professor at the St. Petersburg Conservatoire. In 1868 he returned to Vienna, teaching and making occasional concert tours. Pupils came to him from all over the world (the most famous being Paderewski). Wrote an opera, chamber and piano music.

LESLIE, Henry David (1822–96). English conductor and composer. Studied with Charles Lucas. Cellist in the Sacred Harmonic Society, conductor (1853–61). With Heming founded an *a capella* singing society (1855). Composed operas, oratorios, and cantatas.

LESPINASSE (= ESPINASSE), Fort-Arthur (1815–82). French singer. Member of the Opéra (1848–51).

LESSING, Gotthold Ephraim (1729–81). German writer. His works embody the spirit of German neoclassicism. *Nathan der Weise* (1779) put into poetic form the principles of religious tolerance that he fought for in his controversialist writings.

LE SUEUR, Jean-François (1760–1837). French composer. Studied in the Abbeville and Amiens choir schools. Initially director of music at various cathedrals of France, eventually Notre Dame (1786). Kapellmeister to Napoleon I (1804). Professor of composition at the Conservatoire. Caught the mood of the Revolutionary times in his development of the rescue opera (*La Caverne*, 1793) and the reconciliation of elements from *opera seria*, *opera buffa*, and *opéra comique*. His greatest success was *Ossian, ou Les Bardes* (1804), which broke new ground in its formal and conceptual features and vast design. Teacher of Gounod, Thomas, and esp. Berlioz.

LETELLIER, Theodore (d. 1878). Belgian theater director.

LETRONNE, Jean-Antoine (1787–1848). French scholar. Professor of history and archaeology. General custodian of the Archives in Paris (1840).

LEUVEN, Alphonse de (comte de Ribbing) (1800–1884). French dramatist. Wrote 170 plays and libretti alone or in collaboration with Brunswick, Pittaud de Forges, and Planard. Director of the Opéra Comique (1862–74) with De Ritt (–1870) and then Du Locle. Member of the Légion d'Honneur (1847) and then an officer (1870).

LEVASSEUR, Nicolas-Prosper (1791–1871). Celebrated French bass. Studied with Garat. Début Paris at the Opéra (1813). London (1815–17, 1832), Milan (1819–28). Principal bass at the Théâtre Italien and the Opéra (1828–53). Created Bertram in *Robert le Diable*, Marcel in *Les Huguenots*, Zacharie in *Le Prophète*. Retired in 1853, and taught at the Conservatoire until 1870.

LEWALD, Fanny (1811–89). German author. Born Jewish, she later became Lutheran, and was influenced by the Junges Deutschland movement. Began to write at the age of thirty, particularly about social problems and marriage, e.g., *Clementine* (1842), *Jenny* (1843). Married Adolphe Stahr. Also wrote travel books.

LEWALD, (Johann) August (1793–1872). German writer on music. Founded and edited the journal *Europe, Chronik der gebildeten Welt* (1835). Artistic director of the Stuttgart Court Theatre (1848).

LEWANDOWSKI, Louis (1821–1904). German scholar. Studied at the Academy of Music in Berlin, became music director of the Berlin Synagogue (1841) and a voice teacher. Arranged traditional Jewish music for use in the synagogue, using the techniques of German romanticism and so often distorting the patterns of the originals.

LICHNOWSKY, Eduard, Fürst von (1789–1845). Patron of Beethoven. His grandson **Felix** (1814–48) was a member of the Frankfurt National Assembly.

LICHTENSTEIN, Karl August, baron von (1767–1845). German composer and theater director. Studied with Forkel. Intendant of Court theaters in Dessau, Vienna, Bamberg, and Berlin (1823–). Composed eleven operas.

LICHTENTHAL, Peter (Pietro) (1780–1853). German composer, journalist, and doctor. Worked in Milan, composing and arranging many ballets for La Scala (1818–20), and writing for the *Allgemeine musikalische Zeitung* in Leipzig. His most important work was the *Dizionario e bibliografia della musica* (Milan 1826, 4 vols.).

LIEBIG, Karl (1808–72). German conductor. Oboist in the Alexander Grenadier Regiment in Berlin. Organized the Berlin Symphonie-Kapelle, which attained a high level of performance. The orchestra elected another leader in 1867.

LILLO, George (1693–1739). English playwright, author of the drama *George Barnwell* (1731). Little is known of his life; he was perhaps a jeweller of Flemish descent. His introduction of middle-class domestic elements into tragedy was innovative and influential in European drama.

LILLO, Giuseppe (1814–63). Italian composer. Studied at the Naples Conservatoire with Zingarelli. Became teacher of harmony there (1849), and later of counterpoint and composition. Retired because of mental illness (1861). Wrote operas (*L'Osteria d'Anjudar*, 1840), symphonies, instrumental and church music.

LIMNANDER, Armand-Marie-Ghislain de Nieuwenhowe (1814–92). Belgian composer. Studied in Freiburg with Lambillotte and in Brussels with Fétis. Became choral director in Malines (1835) and settled in Paris (1845). Wrote the grand opera *Le Maître-chanteur* (1853), and three *opéras comiques,* as well as orchestral works, chamber works, and church music.

LIND, Jenny (1820–87). Swedish singer. One of the most celebrated sopranos of the nineteenth century, "the Swedish Nightingale." Studied in Stockholm with I. Berg, and later in Paris with M. Garcia Jun. Her first major triumph was in 1844 in Meyerbeer's *Ein Feldlager in Schlesien* and again in *Vielka* in Vienna in 1846. Her first London appearance was at Her Majesty's Theatre in 1847 as Alice in *Robert le Diable*. She abandoned the stage in 1849 for a concert career. Her voice was pure, brilliant, and powerful.

LINDBLAD, Otto (Jonas) (1809–64). Swedish composer. Pupil of Zelter. Chiefly known for his ensemble music; formed a vocal and instrumental trio. Conducted opera and oratorio. Established a music school in Stockholm.

LINDLEY, Robert (1776–1855). English instrumentalist and composer. Worked as cellist at the Royal Theatre.

LINDNER, Ernst Otto Timotheus (1820–67). German journalist. Collaborated on the *Vossische Zeitung*, and conducted the Bach-Verein. Wrote *Meyerbeers "Prophet" als Kunstwerk beurteilt* (1850).

LINDNER, Friedrich Ludwig (1772–1845). German writer. Friend of Heine.

LINDPAINTNER, Peter Joseph von (1791–1856). German composer. Studied with Winter. Musical director of the opera in Munich (1812). From 1819 until his death he conducted the Court Orchestra in Stuttgart, which he made famous. Wrote twenty-eight operas, notably *Der Vampyr* (1828), three ballets, five melodramas, five oratorios, symphonies, incidental music.

LIPINSKI, Carl (1790–1861). Polish violinist and composer. He was a brilliant performer, a pupil of Paganini, and a friend of Schumann and Liszt. Settled in Dresden (1839) as concertmaster of the Dresden Court Orchestra.

LIPPARINI, Caterina. Italian singer, perhaps the same as Matilde Lipparini, who sang in Rossini's *Matilda di Shabran* in 1821.

LISZT, Franz (1811–86). Hungarian composer and pianist. He was prolific as a composer (symphonic poems, concertos, piano music) and was one of the greatest of piano virtuosi, evolving new techniques and harmonic innovations. After a glittering career as a traveling soloist, he became kapellmeister in Weimar (1842). Always friendly to Meyerbeer, he wrote many reminiscences on themes from his operas (one on *Les Huguenots*, two on *Robert le Diable*, two on *L'Africaine*, and three on *Le Prophète*, including the huge organ fantasia and fugue "Ad nos, ad salutarem undam," as well as making piano arrangements of the song "Le Moine" and the *Schiller Festmarsch*.

LITOLFF, Henry Charles (1818–91). Anglo-French composer. pianist, and publisher. Studied with Moscheles. Début London (1832). Became an itinerant virtuoso: France, Poland, Germany, Holland. Settled in Brunswick (1848). Began publishing. Prolific composer, including a funeral march for Meyerbeer.

LOBKOWITZ, Franz Joseph Maximilian Ferdinand, Fürst von (1772–1816). Austrian nobleman and patron of the arts. Beethoven dedicated to him the string quartets op.18 and 74, the Symphonies nos. 3, 5, and 6, the Triple Concerto, and the song cycle *An die ferne Geliebte*.

LOCKROY, Joseph-Philippe-Simon (1803–91). French playwright. Was first an actor (Odéon and Comédie Français). Began collaborating with Scribe (1827). From 1840 devoted himself to writing, producing dramas, comedies, vaudevilles, and libretti.

LOEWE, Karl Gottfried (1796–1869). German composer. Studied at the Francke Institute in Halle. Music director at St. Jacobus and teacher at the Gymnasium in Stettin (1820–66). Traveled widely and won great renown as a composer of ballads (368), which he also performed in public. His seventeen oratorios were much less successful. Also wrote symphonies, overtures, chamber and instrumental works.

LOEWE (LÖWE), Ludwig (1795–1871). Austrian actor. Worked at the Burgtheater.

LOEWE-WEIMARS (LOEVE-VEIMARS), François-Adolphe (1800–1854). French writer. Cofounder of the *Revue de Paris*, collaborated on the *Revue Encyclopédique*, the *Figaro*, the *Revue des deux Mondes*, and the *Temps*. Published the works of E. T. A. Hoffmann in a French edition (20 vols.). Speculated on assuming the directorship of the Opéra, and was Véron's first choice as his successor. Thiers was prepared to support him in this as a feared opponent, while Duponchel paid him 100,000 fr. to secure the position for himself (cf. Véron, *Mémoires* [Paris, 1856], 3:132).

LORTZING, Gustav Albert (1801–51). German composer, conductor and singer. Studied in Berlin. Kapellmeister at Leipzig (1844–45), Vienna (1846). Returned to Berlin as conductor in a small theater (1850). Wrote enduringly popular romantic comic operas, esp. *Zar und Zimmermann* (1837) and *Der Wildschütz* (1842), also the magic opera *Undine* (1845).

LOTTI, Antonio (1667–1740). Italian composer and organist. Studied with Legrenzi in Venice. Worked at St. Mark's Cathedral (1687–), becoming *maestro di capella* (1736). Wrote much church music and was renowned as a teacher.

LOUIS FERDINAND, prince of Prussia (1772–1806). Nephew of Frederick the Great and an accomplished amateur musician. Met Beethoven and showed great interest in his music. Published a body of chamber music.

LOUIS NAPOLEON. See **NAPOLEON III**.

LOUIS-PHILIPPE, king of France (1773–1850, r. 1830–48). The so-called Bourgeois King inherited the situation resulting from the Revolution of 1830, which had overthrown the reactionary regime of Charles X. Under his "July Monarchy" the upper bourgeoisie prospered, but discontent grew when his government failed to make liberal reforms, and foreign policy ended in failure. He further became more and more repressive because of dissent caused by agricultural and industrial depression, and was eventually overthrown by the Revolution of 1848.

LOUISE, princess (b. 1848). Daughter of Queen Victoria and Prince Albert. Married Douglas Sutherland Campbell, ninth duke of Argyll.

LÖWE, Johanna Sophie (1815–66). German soprano. Studied with Ciccimara; début in Vienna (1832). Berlin (1836) where her appearance as Isabelle in *Robert le Diable* was so successful that she was engaged for the company. Nominated *Kammersängerin* (1838). London, Paris, and Italy (1840–45). In 1848 she married Prince Friedrich von Lichtenstein.

LUBBERT, Émile-Timothé (1794–1859). French musician. Director of the Académie Royal de Musique (1827), then took over the Théâtre Italien, returning to the Opéra, where he oversaw the birth of French grand opera in the revolutionary works of Auber and Rossini (1828–29), and built up a superb company of artists (Nourrit, Levasseur, Cinti-Damoreau, Dorus-Gras, Taglioni). Later went to Egypt as kapellmeister to Mehmet Ali.

LUBIN, Napoléon-Antoine-Eugène-Léon de St (1805–50). French musician. Concertmaster at the Königstädter-Theater in Berlin.

LUCAS, Hippolyte. French actor and writer.

LUCCA, Pauline (1841–1908). Austrian soprano. Studied in Vienna, début (1859). Engaged for the Berlin Court Opera (1861–72) at Meyerbeer's recommendation. She studied several roles with him, had particular success as Sélika both in London and Berlin (1865). London (1863), the United States (1872–74), Vienna (1874–89).

LUCCHESINI, marquis. Intendant of the Saxon Court Theaters.

LUDERITZ, Karl Friedrich (1803–84). German copper engraver.

LUDWIG I, grand duke of Hesse-Darmstadt (b. 1753, r. 1806–30).

LUDWIG II, grand duke of Hesse-Darmstadt (b. 1777, r. 1830–48).

LUDWIG III, grand duke of Hesse-Darmstadt (b. 1806, r. 1848–77).

LUDWIG I, king of Bavaria (1786–1868, r. 1825–48). He was a great patron of the arts and had Munich rebuilt as a neoclassical city. The reputation of Munich as a center of the arts dates from his reign. He alienated his subjects by reactionary measures and his liaison with the dancer Lola Montez, and was obliged to abdicate in the Revolution of 1848.

LUDWIG, Otto (1813–65). German playwright and writer. Studied music and then turned to drama as the result of illness and adverse criticism. Lived in Leipzig and Dresden (1842–44), then Eisfeld. Made his name with *Der Ebförster* and *Die Makkabaer*, published in his *Dramatische Werke* (1853). Analyzed literary techniques, explored the borders between normality and pathology (*Zwischen Hölle und Erde*). A representative of poetic realism, he tried to achieve a balance between stylized idealism and naturalistic realism.

LUMLEY, Benjamin (orig. **Lévy**) (1811–75). English impresario. A lawyer by profession, he became manager of Her Majesty's Theatre (1842–52). Reopened this theater (1856–59). Also director of the Théâtre Italien (1850–51). He was instrumental in bringing many singers to London, notably Jenny Lind.

LÜTTICHAU, August, Freiherr von (1786–1863). German official. Intendant-general of the Dresden Court Theatre (1824-62).

LUTZ, Matthäus (1807–53). Austrian medical doctor and singer. Member of the Court Orchestra in Vienna (1834).

LUTZER, Jenny (1816–77). Austrian singer. Famous coloratura soprano at the Vienna Court Opera. Wife of Franz von Dingelstedt.

LUX, Friedrich (1820–95). German composer. Studied with Schneider at Dessau, and remained there ten years as music director. Conducted at the City Theatre in Mainz (1851–77). Wrote operas, oratorios, chamber music, songs.

LVOV, Alexey Feodorovich (1798–1870). Russian composer. Major general and adjutant to Tsar Nicholas I. Director of the Imperial Court Chapel in St. Petersburg (1837–61). Wrote the imperial national anthem *Boge Tsarja krani* (1833). Edited a collection of services for the Orthodox ecclesiastical year. Traveled in Europe as a concert violinist (1840). Established orchestral concerts in St. Petersburg. Wrote in the Italian mode; three operas, violin works (including a concerto).

LYSER, Johann Peter (1803–70). German poet and painter, deaf from 1820. He was in contact with Meyerbeer to gain biographical details about Weber and their studies with Vogler. He published a review of *Les Huguenots* (1838) and a brochure on Meyerbeer.

M

MABILLE, Auguste. French ballet master. Choreographed the Skaters' Ballet in *Le Prophète*.

MACDONALD, Étienne, duc de Tarent (1765–1840). French soldier. Freed east Switzerland, and won the Battle of Wagram (1809). Defeated at Katzbach (1813) in the Russian campaign. Louis XVIII raised him to the nobility.

MACFARREN, Sir George Alexander (1813–87). English composer and teacher. Studied with his father and at the Royal Academy of Music, where he became a professor (1834). Professor of music at Cambridge (1875), and principal of the Royal Academy of Music (1876). Composed operas, oratorios, cantatas, sacred works, and pedagogical works.

MACREADY, William Sheridan (1793–1873). English actor. Appeared at Covent Garden and Drury Lane, where he won renown for his interpretation of Shakespeare. Later appeared as guest artist in North America and Paris.

MACMAHON, Edmé-Patrice-Maurice, comte de, duc de Magenta (1808–93). French monarchist statesman, marshal of France, and finally president (1873–79).

MÄDLER, Johann Heinrich von (1794–1874). German astronomer. Encouraged Wilhelm Beer to build an observatory on the roof of the Beer villa in the Tiergarten, and together with him published a big lunar map.

MAESEN, Leontine de (1835–1906). French soprano.

MAIER, Jakob (1739–84). German dramatist.

MAILLART, Louis-Aimé (1817–71). French composer. Studied with Leborne and Halévy. Between 1847–64 he wrote six operas for Paris, esp. *Les Dragons de Villars* (1856), which subsequently became very popular in Germany.

MAINZER, Joseph, abbé (1801–51). German musician. Achieved repute through his books on singing methods (*Singschule*, 1831; *Méthode de chant pour les enfants*, 1835). Lived in Paris as a music journalist. Founded singing schools in London and Manchester. Produced *Mainzer's Musical Times* (1844).

MALANOTTE (-MONTRESOR), Adelaide (1785–1832). Italian contralto. Début Verona (1806). Won great fame by creating the title role in Rossini's *Tancredi* (1813). Sang with much success all over Italy, but was forced to retire prematurely because of ill-health (1821).

MALCOLM, Sir John (1796–1833). English officer and colonial official. Administrator of conquered territory in India (1818). Governor of Bombay (1827). Wrote extensively about his experiences in Persia and India.

MALIBRAN, Maria Felicia (née Garcia) (1808–36). Celebrated soprano, daughter of Manuel Garcia and sister of Pauline Viardot-Garcia. Studied with her father. After her début in London (1825), she sang in New York (1826), Paris and London (1827–32), Italy (1832–35), London (1836). Married François Eugène Malibran (1826) and then the violinist Charles de Bériot (1836). Both in her life and art she embodied the romantic spirit of freedom and impassioned exploration, and was an inspiration to composers, writers and performers.

MALTITZ, Gotthilf August, Freiherr von (1794–1837). German dramatist. Served in the Wars of Liberation, and was then a forestry supervisor. Began writing plays (*Schwur und Rache,* 1826) and was soon in trouble with the censorship. He was obliged to leave Prussia, and went to Hamburg, Paris, and finally Dresden (1831) where he settled.

MANGOLD, Karl Armand (1813–89). German musician. Brother of Wilhelm Mangold, the kapellmeister in Darmstadt. Studied in Paris with Bordogni, Berton, Neukomm (1836–39). Director of music in Darmstadt (1848).

MANNA, Ruggiero (1808–64). Italian musician. Kapellmeister, composer, impresario, régisseur in Cremona. Made a reputation as a composer of church music. Son of the contralto Carolina Bassi.

MANNS, Sir August Friedrich (1825–1907). German conductor. Studied with Urban in Elbing. Played in a regimental band in Danzig, violinist in Gungl's orchestra in Berlin, conducted at Kroll's Garden (1849–51). Bandmaster in Königsberg and Cologne. Assistant conductor at the Crystal Palace in London (1854), then chief conductor. Inaugurated the Saturday Concerts (1856), which he directed for forty-five seasons. Also conducted the Triennial Handel Festivals, Promenade Concerts, and the Glasgow Choral Union.

MANTEUFFEL, Edwin von (1809–85). Prussian field marshal. He supported Wilhelm I's army reforms, and fought in the Austro-Prussian and Franco-Prussian Wars. In 1879 he became governor of Alsace-Lorraine, where his policy of conciliating the pro-French population met with little success.

MANTIUS, Eduard (1806–74). German tenor. Début 1830; professor of singing in Berlin (1857).

MARCELLO, Benedetto (1686–1739). Italian composer. Studied with Gasparini and Lotti. Had a political career. His masterpiece is the settings of Giustiniani's paraphrases of the first fifty psalms (*Estro poetico-armonico: Parafrasi sopra i cinquanti primi salmi*, Venice, 1724–26).

MARCHAND, Henri (b. 1774). French violinist and composer. Brother of the famous singer Marguerite Danai. Studied violin and composition with Leopold Mozart. Entered the service of the prince of Thurn und Taxis in Regensburg. Appeared publicly in Hamburg (1798). Eventually he settled in Paris.

MARCHESI, Luigi Lodovico (1754–1829). Italian male soprano. Début Rome (1773). Regarded as the greatest singer in Italy (1780). Sang in Munich, Vienna, St. Petersburg (1785), and London (1788), where he caused a sensation. In Venice he was involved in rivalry with Luisa Toldi. Sang at the opening of the Teatro Nuovo in Trieste (1801) and continued to appear in Milan until 1806.

MARCHESI DE CASTRONE, Salvatore (1822–1908). Italian baritone and teacher. Studied in Palermo and Milan with Lamperti and Fontana. Compelled to leave Italy after the events of 1848. Début New York. Returned to study with Garcia. Married Mathilde Graumann (1852), held teaching posts with her in Vienna, Cologne (1865–68), and Vienna again (1869–78). Settled in Paris. Translated French and German libretti into Italian.

MARCHISIO, Barbara (1833–1919). Italian contralto. Studied with Fabbrica in Turin, début Madrid (1856). Sang all over Europe with success. Paris (1860), London (1862). Her sister **Carlotta** (1835–72), a soprano, often appeared with her. Rossini wrote the *Petite Messe solenelle* for them. She later became a teacher, of Raisa and Del Monte among others.

MARHEINEKE, Philipp Konrad (1780–1846). German Protestant theologian in Berlin.

MARIA ANNA, empress of Austria, wife of Emperor Ferdinand I.

MARIO, Giovanni, marchese di Candia (1810–83). Celebrated Italian tenor. Studied with Bordogni and Ponchard. Début Paris as Robert le Diable (1838). London, Her Majesty's

(1839–46), Covent Garden (1847–67). Married Giulia Grisi (1844). His voice was considered one of the most beautiful ever heard, and was combined with elegance and style, a handsome appearance and great acting ability, making him an idol of the age. Meyerbeer personally coached him for his début, and later wrote a special Prayer for him in *Robert le Diable*.

MARKULL, Friedrich Wilhelm (1816–87). German composer and music director. First organist at the Marienkirche in Danzig. His opera *König von Zion* (1848) is textually related to *Le Prophète* in its treatment of the Anabaptist story.

MARLIANI, Marco Aurelio (1805–49). Italian composer. Studied philosophy, then had lessons with Rossini in Paris where he moved in 1830. Wrote several operas under his teacher's influence, esp. *La Xacarilla* and the ballet *La Gypsy* with Ambroise Thomas (both 1839). Returned to Italy and died in the revolutionary struggles of 1848–49.

MARMIER, Xavier (1809–92). French writer and journalist. Founded the *Nouvelle Revue germanique* (1829), contributed to the *Revue des deux Mondes*. Wrote a biography of Michael Beer (1834), and published translations of *Der Paria* (1834) and *Struensee* (1835), all in the former journal.

MAROT, Clément (1496–1544). French poet, notable for the elegant lightness, wit, and unaffected grace of his style. He was persecuted on religious grounds. His works include the *Epîtres*, *Elégies*, *Epigrammes*, and *The Psalter of the Huguenots* (1541–43), a translation of thirty psalms.

MARPURG, Friedrich Wilhelm (1718–95). German composer and theoretician. Director of the royal lottery. Wrote about the treatment of fugues (1753–54, 2 vols.).

MARRA (orig. **HACK**), **Marie von** (1822–76). Austrian soprano at the Vienna Court Opera, then St. Petersburg, Riga, Königsberg, Triumphed in *L'Étoile du Nord* in Amsterdam.

MARSCHNER, Heinrich August (1795–1861). German composer. Studied law, then music with Schicht in Leipzig. Teacher in Pressburg (1817), then worked in Dresden with Weber and Morlacchi (1821). Kapellmeister in Leipzig (1826), then Hanover (1831) for twenty-eight years. He stands between Weber and Wagner in the unfolding of German romantic opera, esp. with *Der Vampyr* (1828), *Der Templar und die Jüdin* (1829), and *Hans Heiling* (1831).

MARTINI, Giambattista (known as **Padre Martini**) (1706–84). Italian composer, theorist, and historian. Became *maestro di capella* at the church of San Francesco in Bologna (1725) and composed masses and oratorios. He won especial renown as a teacher (Gluck, Mozart, Grétry, Jommelli, Mattei) and member of the academies in Bologna and Rome.

MARX, Adolf Bernhard (1795–1866). German theorist and writer. Studied law at Halle and music with Türk and Zelter. Founded the *Berliner allgemeine musikalische Zeitung* with the publisher Schlesinger (1824–30). Took a doctorate at Marburg (1827) and lectured at the University of Berlin; music director of the scholastic choir there (1832). With Kullak and Stern, founded the Berlin Conservatoire (1850). Retired to devote himself to musical matters (1856). Had little success with his compositions, but his musical theory and aesthetics are still valuable.

MARX, Pauline (b. 1819). German soprano. Pupil of Bordogni. Sang in Dresden; Berlin (1843–51).

MASSET. Collaborator of the Parisian publisher Troupenas.

MASSOL, Jean-Étienne-Auguste (1802–87). French singer. Won first prize at the Conservatoire (1825). Sang baritone as member of the ensemble at the Paris Opéra (1825–58). Created De Nevers in *Les Huguenots*, as well as roles by Rossini, Donizetti, Halévy, and Auber. London (1846–51).

MASSON, Auguste-Michel-Benoit-Gaudichor (1800–1883). French dramatist and novelist.

MASSON, Pauline-Louise-Ferdinande (1816–84). French mezzo soprano. Prizewinner at the Paris Conservatoire. Début in *La Favorite* with great success (1847).

MASSOW, Ludwig Joachim Valentin. Privy councillor, director general of public gardens in Prussia.

MAURER, Ludwig Wilhelm (1789–1878). German musician. Violinist and conductor in Hanover, conductor of the French Opera in St. Petersburg (1833). Inspector-general of the imperial Russian orchestras (1841).

MAURICE, Charles. French journalist. Publisher of the *Courier des Théâtres*.

MAXIMILIAN I, king of Bavaria (b. 1756, r. 1805–25). With his talented minister Montgelas, he shaped a united and prosperous kingdom with perhaps the most liberal constitution in Germany. His alliance with Napoleon, forged because of his distrust of Austria, gained him new lands and royal status.

MAXIMILIAN II, king of Bavaria (b. 1811, r. 1848–64). Eldest son of Ludwig I.

MAYER, Charles (1799–1862). German pianist and composer. Lived in St. Petersburg (1819–45); undertook a big European tour, after which he settled in Dresden.

MAYR, Simone Giovanni [Johannes Simon] (1763–1845). Bavarian composer. Pupil of Bertoni. Moved to Bergamo, where he wrote many operas in the Italian style that enjoyed great popularity, e.g., *Medea in Corinto* (Naples, 1813). Famed for his orchestral technique, esp. the virtuosity of his wind writing and development of the brass instruments. He introduced orchestral numbers depicting natural phenomena, and did much in achieving greater continuity between numbers. Teacher of Donizetti.

MAYSEDER, Joseph (1789–1863). Austrian violinist and composer. Studied with Suche and Wranitsky. Became solo violinist in the Court Orchestra (1820) and chamber violinist to the emperor (1835). Although he never toured, he enjoyed a great reputation as a virtuoso, also as a teacher. Wrote five violin concertos and much chamber music.

MAZAS, Jacques-Féréol (1782–1849). French violinist. Pupil of Baillot. Won first prize for violin playing (1805) and in the following year toured throughout Europe. Later was soloist at the Théâtre Royal in Paris and director of the musical academy in Cambrai (1837–41).

MAZILIER, Joseph (1801–68). French dancer, choreographer, and ballet master. Début Paris (1822). Joined the Opéra and was an admired character dancer; ballet master (1839). Choreographed many ballets, including *Le Diable à quatre* (1845), *Pasquita* (1846), *Le Corsaire* (1856), and *Marco Spada* (1857).

MAZZUCATO, Alberto (1813–77). Italian violinist, composer, and writer on music. Studied with Bresciano in Padua. Wrote seven operas until overshadowed by Verdi. Concertmaster of the orchestra at La Scala, Milan (1859–69), and for several years editor of the influential *Gazetta Musicale*. Also published a *Trattato d'estetica musicale*.

MECHETTI, Carl (1811–47). Son of the music dealer Pietro (Carlo) Mechetti in Vienna.

MÉHUL, Étienne-Nicolas (1763–1817). French composer. Studied with a local organist and in Paris with Edelmann. He was encouraged by Gluck to write for the stage and provided patriotic music (both French Revolutionary and Napoleonic). He was appointed to the Institut National de Musique (1793) and became director of the Conservatoire (1794). He wrote in a simple Gluckian style, and took great care in providing each of his works with a particular and vivid atmosphere and setting achieved through a highly imaginative and romantic perception of orchestral color (e.g., his Ossianic opera *Uthal*, 1806). His dramatic use of the orchestra and of motive had, through Weber's admiration of him, a significant influence on German romantic opera. The chivalric *Ariodant* (1799) anticipates *Euryanthe* in several ways. The *opéra comique Joseph* (1807) reveals all his melodic grace as well as his feeling for atmosphere and situation.

MEIFRED, Joseph-Jean-Pierre-Émile (1791–1867). French musician. Horn virtuoso and professor at the Paris Conservatoire.

MEILHAC, Henri (1831–97). French dramatist. Wrote libretti in a famous collaboration with Ludovic Halévy for Bizet, but esp. for Offenbach and the operetta. They satirized contemporary society, frequently parodying old myths, treating of human foibles and shortcomings.

MEINHOLD, Johannes Wilhelm (1797–1851). German novelist. He was a private tutor, schoolmaster, and finally pastor. He became famous for his novel *Maria Schweidler, die Bernsteinhexe* (1838) about the witch trials of the seventeenth century. He enjoyed the patronage of the king, and in later years inclined to Catholicism.

MELANOTTI. See **MALANOTTE**.

MÉLESVILLE (pseud. of **Anne-Honoré-Joseph Duveyrier**) (1787–1865). French playwright and librettist. Author of over three hundred stage works (comedies, vaudevilles, libretti), many in collaboration with his brother Charles and Scribe, including operas for Auber, Adam, and Offenbach. Most famous was his text for Hérold's *Zampa* (entirely his own work), while Lortzing adapted *Zar und Zimmermann* from one of his plays.

MEMBRÉE, Edmond (1820–82). French composer. Studied at the Paris Conservatoire with Alkan, Carafa and Zimmermann. Wrote songs and ballads, later four operas (1857–79).

MENDELSSOHN, Alexander (1798–1871). German banker. *Kommerzienrat,* leader of the family banking house.

MENDELSSOHN, Joseph (1770–1848). German banker, son of Moses Mendelssohn.

MENDELSSOHN-BARTHOLDY, Fanny Cäcilia. See **HENSEL**.

MENDELSSOHN-BARTHOLDY, Jacob Ludwig Felix (1809–47). German romantic composer. Studied at home with his mother, then with Zelter, Hennings, and Mme. Bigot before entering the Singakademie. Wrote brilliantly in nearly every genre except opera. With Robert Schumann, he was an inflexible and relentless opponent of Meyerbeer. This tension was not only aesthetic, but also based on long-standing tensions between the two dynamic Jewish families, and the fact that the Mendelssohns embraced Lutheranism while the Beers did not.

MENGAL, Martin-Joseph (1784–1851). Belgian horn player, composer, and conductor. Studied with his father, played in Paris orchestras, director of the Ghent municipal theater, conductor in Antwerp, director of the Ghent Conservatoire (1835). Wrote sacred and chamber works.

MEQUILLET, Sophie. French soprano active in the Paris Opéra in the 1840s.

MERCIER, Louis-Sébastien (1740–1814). French playwright and journalist. He was an early rebel against classical and aristocratic taste. Author of domestic dramas in prose characterized by sentimentality, moralizing, and a pretentious style, in which he pleaded for social equality (*Le Déserteur*, 1770). In his preromantic historical dramas he preached a revolt against classical drama and its unities (*Childéric Ier*, 1774). Also wrote a *Tableau de Paris* (1781) combining topography with social observations and anecdotes.

MERELLI, Bartolomeo (1794–1879). Italian impresario and librettist. Studied law, and later music with Mayr. Wrote early libretti for Donizetti. Managed seasons in Varese, Como, Cremona (1830–35); director of La Scala (1836–46). Encouraged Verdi to write *Nabucco*. Directed the Kärntnertor-Theater in Vienna jointly with Carlo Balochino

(1836–48). Returned to Vienna (1853–55), La Scala (1861–63). Also wrote libretti for Mayr, Vaccai, Morlacchi. One of the great theater managers of the nineteenth century.

MÉRIMÉE, Prosper (1803–70). French lawyer and poet. Traveled in Spain (1830), and held posts under the ministries of the navy, commerce, and the interior. Inspector of historical monuments in France (1833) and a senator (1853). He wrote novels and short stories, archaeological and historical dissertations, and travel stories. His *Chronique du règne de Charles IX* (1829) was the source of Planard's *Le Pré aux clercs* and also to some extent of Scribe's *Les Huguenots*, and his *Carmen* (1845) the inspiration for Meilhac and Halévy's libretto. His later years were clouded by ill-health and melancholy. He was a friend of the Empress Eugénie's mother from his youth.

MERLE, Jean-Toussaint (1785–1852). French journalist and writer. Director of the Théâtre de la Porte-St-Martin (1822–26). Wrote many plays for the Vaudeville.

MERLIN, Maria de los Mercedes de Jaruco, countess. Parisian socialite. Wife of the state councillor, Merlin de Douai (1754–1838), who had been ennobled by Napoleon.

MERRUAU, Charles. French journalist. Collaborated on the *Temps* and the *Constitutionnel*. Secretary-general at the Ministry of Education (1840).

MÉRY, François-Joseph-Pierre-Agnes (1798–1866). French writer and librettist. Together with Barthélemy published the weekly paper *Némesis*. Remembered for collaborating with Du Locle on the libretto of Verdi's *Don Carlos*.

METHFESSEL, Albert Gottlieb (1785–1869). German musician. Court kapellmeister in Brunswick (1832–42). Composer of songs.

METTERNICH, Clemens Lothar Wenzel, Fürst von (1773–1859). Austrian chancellor. Coordinator of the Congress of Vienna, and architect of the balance of power that influenced European politics for a century (1815–1914). Dominated the affairs of Austria (1815–48), establishing an autocratic regime (cf. Karlsbad Decrees, 1819) increasingly repressive of dissent as his actual power waned under the influence of count von Kolowat (from 1835 onwards).

METZGER, Karl Theodor (b. 1774). German flautist. Worked at the court in Munich (1793). Traveled to Mannheim, Frankfurt, Mainz, Prague, Vienna, Leipzig, Milan, and Switzerland, where he enjoyed great success.

MEYENDORFF, Peter, Freiherr von (1796–1863). Russian diplomat. Ambassador in Berlin (1839), then in Vienna (1850–54).

MEYERBEER, Alfred (31 October 1828–13 April 1829). Meyerbeer's second child and only son, who died in infancy.

MEYERBEER, Blanca (1830–96). Meyerbeer's third child and second daughter. Married Emanuel von Korff, Freiherr Schmysingk.

MEYERBEER, Caecilie (1837–1931). Meyerbeer's fourth child and third daughter. Married Ferdinand Leopold, Freiherr von Andrian zu Werburg.

MEYERBEER, Cornelie (1842–1922). Meyerbeer's fourth daughter and last child. Married the court painter Karl Ludwig Richter.

MEYERBEER, Eugénie (16 August–9 December 1827). Meyerbeer's firstborn, who died after a few months.

MEYERBEER, Minna (née Mosson) (1804–86). Meyerbeer's first cousin, whom he married in 1826.

MICHELET, Jules (1798–1874). French historian and author. Professor at the Sorbonne (1832) and at the Collège de France (1838), a post he lost (1851) by his refusal to swear allegiance to Napoleon III. Wrote *Histoire de France* and *Histoire de la Révolution française*, literary works noted for their lyricism *(La Montagne, L'Oiseau),* and a diary *(Journal).*

MILANOLLO, Maria (1832–48) and **Theresa** (1827–1904). Italian violin virtuosi.

MILDE, Mme. German soprano active in Weimar in the 1850s.

MILDER (-HAUPTMANN), Pauline Anna (1785–1838). Austrian soprano. Studied with Tomaselli and Salieri. Début at the Vienna Court Opera (1803). Created Leonore in *Fidelio* (1805). Berlin (1812) and engaged there (1816–31), but left after a quarrel with Spontini. Admired in Gluck. Her voice was powerful and she was praised for her clarity and simplicity.

MILLENET, F. A. German grammar school teacher in Gotha and functionary at the court of the duke of Saxe-Coburg-Gotha (1840).

MILLER, Julius (1782–1851). German composer and singer. Active on several German stages. Worked for the grand duke of Hesse, and later assumed the direction of the theater at Dessau. Wrote several operas and other vocal compositions.

MILTITZ, Carl Borromäus von (1780–1845). German music journalist and composer. Dresden correspondent of the *Allgemeine musikalische Zeitung*.

MIOLAN-CARVALHO, Marie (1827–95). French soprano. Studied with Duprez, début Brest (1849). Paris Opéra (1849–55), Théâtre Lyrique (1856–67), where she created several Gounod roles, including Marguerite; London (1859–64, 1871–72), the first London Dinorah; Berlin, St. Petersburg. Married the impresario Carvalho.

MIRA. Bookkeeper at the Opéra.

MITTERMAIER (= MITTERMAYER), Georg (b. 1783). German singer. Court Opera in Munich (1805). His phenomenal range allowed him to sing all the male roles in *Don Giovanni*. Later he was much in demand as a singing teacher. Created the role of Abdon in *Jephthas Gelübde*.

MOLIÈRE (Jean-Baptiste Poquelin) (1622–73). French playwright. In the provinces he acquired experience as a comic writer, mostly in the style of the old farces. As theater manager in Paris, he fully realized his potential: *Les Précieuses ridicules* (1659) was followed every year by one of his comic masterpieces until his death (*Le Malade imaginaire,* 1673). His plays satirize departures from the norm of rational social behavior.

MOLIQUE, Wilhelm Bernhard (1802–69). German composer and violinist. Studied with his father and Rovelli in Munich where he succeeded his teacher as concertmaster of the Court Orchestra. Worked as music director and first violinist in Stuttgart (1826). He won fame with extended tours to Holland, Russia, England, and France. Lived in London (1849–66) before returning to Germany. Wrote six violin concertos, eight string quartets, and other chamber and instrumental music.

MONASTERIO, Jesús (1836–1903). Spanish violinist and teacher. Début in Madrid (1845) as an infant prodigy. Studied with Bériot and Fétis. Professor of violin at the Madrid Conservatoire (1857); director (1894–97). Conducted the Sociedad de Conciertos (1869–76) and helped to develop a taste for classical music in Spain. Wrote a number of violin pieces.

MONCK MASON, Thomas. Director of the King's Theatre in London (1831). The appointment of this Irish amateur was a source of some amazement, since he was entirely unknown in theater circles in London. He was responsible for the first authentic staging of *Robert le Diable* in London (11 June 1832).

MONGINI, Pietro (1828–74). Italian tenor. Leading tenor in London in the 1860s and 1870s. Created Radamès in Cairo (1871). Notable as Manrico, Arnold, and John of Leyden.

MONNAIS, Guillaume-Edouard-Désiré (1798–1868). French writer and journalist. Editor of the *Revue et Gazette musicale* and theater editor of the *Courier français*. Codirector of the Opéra (1839); commissioner of theaters and conservatoires (1840).

MONNIER, Albert (Étienne?) (d. 1850). French translator.

MONTALIVET, Marthe-Camille-Bachasson, comte de (1801–85). French politician. Minister of education (1831–32), then interim president. He administered the Royal Civil List. Later minister of the interior (1837–39). Also wrote for *Revue de Paris*.

MONTGELAS, Maximilian (1759–1838). Bavarian minister of the interior. He was devoted to the reform of agriculture. Noted for his anticlerical (esp. anti-Jesuit) tendencies, for which he was often attacked. Encouraged Bavarian support of Napoleon in the war against Austria (1805), as the consequence of which Bavaria was granted royal status. Elevated to the nobility (1810).

MONTI, Vincenzo (1754–1827). Italian poet. Professor of rhetoric in Pavia (1804) and "Poet of the Kingdom of Italy," honoring Napoleon in his writings. Also wrote opera libretti, esp. for Federici, Weigl, Perilli, and Minoja.

MORALT, Joseph (1775–1836). German violinist. Concertmaster of the Court Orchestra in Munich. Also achieved considerable fame with his quartet (the other members being his brother **Johann Baptist, Philipp,** and **Georg**). He was particularly devoted to the string quartets of Haydn.

MORANDI, Rose (née Moralli) (1782–1824). Italian singer. Married the composer and organist Giovanni Morandi. She was one of the finest mezzo sopranos of her time and sang with great success at La Scala.

MOREL, Auguste-François (1809–81). French composer and critic. Worked in Paris (1836–50), then in Marseilles as director of the Conservatoire (1852). Composed a grand opera, *Le Jugement de Dieu* (1860); much chamber music; two symphonies; and overtures. Also wrote for *Vert-Vert, Messanger de Chambre, Journal de Paris, Monde musical, Revue et Gazette de Théâtre.*

MORETO Y CABANA, Augustín (1618–69). Spanish priest and court dramatist. He derived his plots from predecessors, but gave them a new style and elegance. He influenced Molière and anticipated the eighteenth century. He published a volume of dramas in 1654 and two more in 1676.

MORI, Gosselin. French contralto. Sister of the violinist and composer Francesco Mori. Engaged at the Paris Opéra (1832). Was to have sung the role of Catherine de Medici in *Les Huguenots.* Later went to Italy, singing in Siena, Spoleto, Vicenza, Verona, and Mantua.

MORLACCHI, Francesco (1784–1841). Italian composer. Studied with Mazzetti, Zingarelli and Mattei. Worked in Rome and Milan. Became kapellmeister in Dresden (1810) where he improved standards, and established a fine ensemble. Showed great competence in the treatment of voices, especially in comic situations (e.g., *Il nuovo Barbiere di Siviglia*, Dresden, 1816), and latter some enterprise in handling the orchestra (e.g., in *Tebaldo e Isolina*, Dresden, 1820). He was the last important Italian composer to work as kapellmeister in a German theater and the closure of the Italian Opera in Dresden (1832) signaled the end of Italian operatic supremacy in Germany.

MORNY, Charles-August-Louis-Joseph, marquis de (1811–65). French politician. Natural son of Hortense of Holland and Count Flahault. Served as a soldier (1832–38), and worked as a businessman. Elected a deputy (1842, 1849), then minister of the interior under Louis Napoleon (1851–56); he organized the coup d'état. President of the Legislature (1854–65). Briefly ambassador in St. Petersburg (1857–58).

MORTIER DE FONTAINE, Henri-Louis-Stanislas (1816–83). French pianist.

MORTIER DE FONTAINE, Marie-Josine (née Vanderferren) (b. 1814). Dutch singer.

MOSCA, Giuseppe (1772–1839). Italian composer. Studied with Fenaroli. *Répétiteur* at the Théâtre Italien in Paris (1803–9). Traveled throughout Italy producing his various operas. *Maestro di capella* in Palermo (1817–21). Eventually became director of music in Messina (1823). Wrote forty-four operas, ballets, and other theatrical pieces.

MOSCHELES, Ignaz (1794–1870). Bohemian pianist and composer. Studied in Prague with Dionys Weber, then with Albrechtsberger and Salieri in Vienna. Lived in Vienna as a virtuoso and teacher before embarking on a concert tour, and settling in London (1821). Mendelssohn asked him to join the staff of the Leipzig Conservatoire (1846), where he taught many pupils. Meyerbeer first met him in 1813. He playing was energetic and brilliant, with an emotional absorption to balance the virtuosity. Wrote eight piano concertos, a *Grand Sextour*, a *Grand Septour*, many chamber and instrumental works (142 opus numbers). Translated Schindler's biography of Beethoven.

MOSCHELES, Lottchen (née Embden) (1805–89). Wife of the pianist. Wrote *Aus Moscheles' Leben* (Leipzig, 1872).

MOSEL, Ignaz Franz, Edler von (1772–1844). Austrian composer and theorist. Made arrangements of Handel's oratorios, and wrote various articles on the theory and history of music in different magazines. He became vice-director of the Court Theaters in Vienna (1820) and later custodian of the Court Library. Wrote three operas and published three collections of songs, and published *Versuch einer Ästhetik des dramatischen Tonsatzes* (1813; reprint, ed. E. Schmitz, Munich, 1910) in which several of Wagner's theories are preempted, and which also exercised a hitherto unperceived influence on Meyerbeer's art.

MOSENTHAL, Salomon Hermann, Ritter von (1821–77). Austrian playwright. His *Volksschauspiel Deborah* (1849) was long popular. Also provided libretti for Nicolai (*Die lustigen Weiber von Windsor*, 1848) and Goldmark (*Die Königin von Saba*, 1875).

MÖSER, August (1825–59). German violinist. Died while touring the United States.

MÖSER, Karl (1774–1851). German musician, Concertmaster of the Royal Orchestra in Berlin.

MOSSON, Adolph. Brother of Minna Meyerbeer; the composer's cousin and brother-in-law.

MOSSON, Babette (1788–1831). Meyerbeer's first cousin and sister-in-law. The first daughter of Joseph Mosson and Johanna Liepmann Meyer Wulff; sister of Minna Mosson. Married **Hermann Julius Eberty** (1784–1856), father of Felix, Mathilde, and Anna.

MOSSON, Johanna (1770–1847). Meyerbeer's aunt and mother-in-law; the first daughter of Liepmann Meyer Wulff. Married **Joseph Mosson** (1768–1834), producing a son, Adolph, and two daughters, Babette and Minna.

MOSSON, Minna. See **MEYERBEER, Minna**.

MOTTE, Karl August de la. Intendant of the Munich Theatre (1810–20).

MOZART, Wolfgang Amadeus (1756–91). Austrian composer, a universal genius of music. His facility and polish, fecundity of thought, gift of melody, control of form, and richness of harmony contributed to his excelling in every musical genre. Meyerbeer's love and admiration for Mozart are consistently attested to throughout his life.

MUCK, Aloys (b. 1761). German singer. Bass in a traveling troupe, and then appointed to the Munich Court Theater (1789). He was outstanding in German opera as well as being a fine actor.

MUFFAT, Georg (1653–1704). Alsatian organist and composer. Entered the service of the archbishop of Salzburg (1678). Studied in Italy with Corelli, with Lully in Paris. Kapellmeister to the bishop of Passau (1690). Developed the German *concerto grosso,* wrote organ works and sonatas.

MÜHLBACH, Luise. See **MUNDT, Klara**.

MÜLLER, Adolph (1801–86). Austrian composer. Kapellmeister and resident composer at the Theater an der Wien (1828). Achieved great success with his comic singspiele and parodies. Wrote the music for Nestroy's *Robert der Teuxel.*

MÜLLER, August (1810–67). German musician. Contrabassist and concertmaster in Darmstadt.

MÜLLER, Iwan (1786–1854). Estonian clarinetist and instrument maker. He invented the clarinet with thirteen keys and the *Altclarinet* (to supersede the basset horn). Went to Paris in 1809, where he opened his workshop and won popularity for his improved clarinet, in spite of initial opposition. Became professor at the Conservatoire. Court musician in Bückeburg in the last years of his life. Wrote chamber music and a clarinet method.

MÜLLER, Karl Friedrich (b. 1788). German composer, pianist, music teacher, and writer. Worked in Potsdam. Known for his study *Spontini und Rellstab* (1833).

MÜLLER, Karl Friedrich (also known as **Franz**) (1806–76). German writer on music. Became a government councillor in Weimar. Was closely associated with the growing Wagner movement, and published a number of pamphlets on Wagner's operas (1853–69), the last three at the request of King Ludwig II of Bavaria.

MÜLLER QUARTET. The first quartet to undertake regional concert tours: **Karl** (1797–1873), concertmaster; **Gustav** (1799–1855), violist; **Theodor** (1802–75), cellist; **Georg** (1808–55), conductor. All were born in Brunswick and belonged to the orchestra there. Tours included all the German cities, Vienna, Paris (1833), Copenhagen (1839), St. Petersburg (1845), Holland (1852).

MÜLLER, Wenzel (1767–1835). Austrian composer. Studied with Dittersdorf. Conducted in provincial theater orchestras. Director of the Prague Opera (1808–13); then at the Leopoldstadter-Theater in Vienna. Wrote an enormous amount of stage music (c. 250 works). His *Singspiele* were very popular in their day, esp. *Die Schwestern von Prag* (1794) and *Die Teufelsmühle am Wienerberg* (1799).

MÜNCH-BELLINGHAUSEN, Joachim, Graf (1786–1866). Austrian statesman.

MÜNCHHAUSEN, Septimus August Ferdinand Christian von (1798–1858). Theatre intendant.

MUNDT, Theodor (1808–61). German writer. Member of the Junges Deutschland movement, a journalist, professor of literary history in Breslau (1848), then in Berlin (1850). Wrote much on contemporary affairs and literature. His wife **Klara Müller** (née **Mühlbach**) was also a writer and critic.

MUNK, L. Prussian civil servant. Secretary to the intendant of the Royal Theaters.

MURAT, Anna Annunciata, later Caroline, ex-queen of Naples (1782–1839). Sister of Napoleon. After Murat's death, she lived in Trieste as Countess Lipona.

MURGER, Henry (1822–61). French writer. Led a life of privation and adventure, described in his novel *Scènes de la Vie de Bohème* (1846). This became famous in the dramatization he made with Barrière, which is the basis of the operas by Leoncavallo and Puccini. He wrote other, less successful novels and plays.

MUSARD, Philippe (1793–1859). French composer. Known as "the King of Quadrilles." Directed the balls at the Théâtre des Variétés (1830), then at the Opéra and the Opéra Comique. His orchestra of seventy members won great acclaim, and his waltzes and galops became immensely popular.

MUSÄUS, Johann Karl August (1735–87). German writer. Tutor to the pages in Weimar, then a grammar school teacher. Made his reputation with the collection *Volksmärchen der Deutschen* (1782–86, 5 vols.), and also wrote novels, tales, and *Straussfedern*.

MUSSET, Alfred-Louis-Charles de (1810–57). French playwright, poet, and novelist. Most original in the theater. In *Lorenzaccio* (1834) he created one of greatest of romantic dramas. Noted for his fantasy, elegance, lyricism, and psychological insight. e.g., *Contes d'Espagne* (1829).

N

NADAR (pseud. of **Félix Tournachon**) (1820–1910). French photographer whose portraits of famous figures in Paris from the late 1850s onwards provide an iconography of the times. His drawings, sketches, and writings are full of social observation.

NAGLER, Karl Ferdinand Friedrich von (1770–1846). German officer. Vice-postmaster-general, member of the Prussian foreign service.

NAPOLEON I (Napoléon Bonaparte, 1769–1821). Military leader, first consul (1799–1804), and emperor of the French (1804–15). He was one of the great conquerors of history, displaying a genius for military tactics and civil administration. The legend that portrayed him as a champion of liberalism and nationalism grew during the nineteenth century, and helped his nephew to secure power. Meyerbeer, like Heine, had great admiration for him.

NAPOLEON II (Napoléon Franz Joseph Karl, duke of Reichstadt, 1811–32). The only son of Napoleon I and Marie Louise of Austria. Lived at the Austrian court from 1814. Loyal Bonapartists proclaimed him Napoleon II in Paris on 28 June 1815, but he was formally deposed five days later. Created duke of Reichstadt (1818).

NAPOLEON III (Louis Napoléon Bonaparte, 1808–73). Emperor of the French (1852–70). He was carried to the presidency by virtue of his name, becoming president of the Second Republic (1850). He effected a coup on 2 December 1851 that was followed by a plebiscite in which all opposition had been safely silenced. The Second Empire was declared a year later. His dictatorship, modeled after 1859 on liberal reforms, brought prosperity: banking, industry, and agriculture were encouraged, Paris was boldly replanned by Haussmann, and the arts flourished. He intervened to restore the papacy (1849), while military campaigns in the Crimea and Lombardy increased French influence. Unrest grew after the ill-fated Mexican expedition; the Franco-Prussian War led to total defeat and deposition.

NAPOLEON, Prince (Napoléon Joseph Charles Paul Bonaparte, "Plon-Plon," 1822–91). Son of Jerome Napoleon by his second marriage, cousin of Napoleon III. After the death of the prince imperial (1879) became the head of the Bonaparte family.

NAU, Maria Dolores Benedette Giuseppina (1818–91). French singer. Pupil of Cinti-Damoreau. Début as the Page in *Les Huguenots*. Sang as a coloratura soprano in Paris, Brussels, London, and America.

NAUDIN, Emilio (1823–90). Italian tenor. Studied in Parma and Milan with Giacomo Panizza. Début Cremona (1843). Sang widely in Italy; London (1858, 1863–72); Théâtre Italien (1862); Moscow (1877). Created Vasco da Gama in *L'Africaine* (1865).

NAUMANN, Emil (1827–88). German composer and writer, grandson of Johann Gottfried. Studied Leipzig Conservatoire and Bonn University. Music director of the Court Church in Berlin (1856), for which he composed motets and psalms. Treatise *Die Einführung des Psalmengesanges in die evangelische Kirche* (1856).

NAUMANN, Johann Gottfried (1741–1801). German composer. Representative of Italian opera in Germany. Studied in Dresden, then with Tartini and Martini. Chamber musician in Dresden (1763, 1776). Kapellmeister in Stockholm. Wrote twenty-four operas, eleven oratorios, four masses. With Hasse and Graun, one of the last composers of the Neapolitan School in Germany. His Scandinavian operas reflected French influences and are closer to Gluck. He showed enterprise in orchestration and anticipates romantic opera. The operas for Berlin and Dresden were more Italiante. His most successful work was *La Dama soldata* (Dresden, 1791).

NEANDER, John August Wilhelm, bishop (1789–1850). German cleric. Professor of church history in Berlin.

NEGRINI, Carlo (1826–65). Italian tenor. Studied in Milan, and made his début there (1847). Created roles for Verdi (*Simone Boccanegra*, 1857) and Petrella (*Jone*, 1858).

NEHRLICH, Christian Gottfried (1802–68). German music teacher. Founded a singing institute in Leipzig (1839) that was later transferred to Berlin (1849).

NEIDHARDT, August Heinrich (1793–1861). German composer and conductor. Royal professor, founder and director of the Berlin Domchor.

NERUDA, Wilma Maria Francisca (Lady Hallé) (1839–1911). Bohemian violinist. Studied with Jansa, and played in public in Vienna (1846) with her sister, the pianist **Amelie**. Toured widely with her father and brother, appeared in Paris (1864) and married Ludwig Norman. Settled in London (1869), and played at the Crystal Palace. Later she married Sir Charles Hallé (1888) and toured the world with him, until he died (1895). After 1900 she settled in Berlin. She was regarded as one of the greatest virtuosi of her instrument, and was widely honored by royalty.

NESSELRODE, Karl Robert, count (1780–1862). Russian politician. Served as foreign minister (1822–56) and chancellor (1844). He was advisor to Alexander I and cooperated closely with Nicholas I. A conservative supporter of legitimacy and the status quo, he worked with Metternich, suppressed the Hungarian revolt (1848), opposed Polish nationalism, and promoted Pan-Slavism and Asian expansion, but later failed to prevent the Crimean War.

NESTROY, Johann Nepomuk (1801–62). Viennese playwright. Studied at the University of Vienna, became a comic actor. Witty and cynical satirist famous for his farces. First followed Raimund in the Viennese *Zauberspiel* (*Der bose Geist Lumpazivagabundus* 1833), then wrote comedies with a realistic Viennese setting (*Das Mädl aus der Vorstadt,* 1841; *Ein Jux will er sich machen,* 1842). He was aggressively satirical, attacked empty convention, and later developed a positive didactic purpose of solid virtue.

NETHERLANDS, the king of. See WILLEM III.

NETZER, Joseph (1808–64). Austrian composer. Kapellmeister at the Stadttheater in Leipzig, then after 1845 for a short time at the Theater an der Wien in Vienna.

NEUKOMM, Sigismund, Ritter von (1778–1858). Austrian composer and conductor. Pupil of Michael Haydn in Salzburg, then of Joseph Haydn in Vienna (1798). Traveled to Stockholm, St. Petersburg, and Paris, where he became pianist to Talleyrand and Louis XVIII ennobled him (1816). Went to Brazil and became music director to the emperor, then again to Talleyrand (1826). He traveled for many years, finally residing in Paris and London (where he was particularly popular). Wrote ten German operas, orchestral works, chamber works, piano music, organ works, and over two hundred songs, as well as an autobiography, *Esquisses biographiques de Sigismond Neukomm* (Paris, 1859).

NEUMANN, Louise. Austrian actress. Daughter of the actor Carl Neumann. Worked at the Burgtheater in Vienna.

NEUNER, Karl (1778–1830). Bavarian musician. Violinist at the Munich Court Orchestra. Wrote church music and many ballets and pantomimes for the Munich stage which proved very popular.

NICHOLAS I, emperor of Russia (b. 1796, r. 1825–1855). Married Charlotte Alexandra, daughter of Friedrich Wilhelm III of Prussia. Upheld absolute despotism with military power, increasing Russia's territories in wars with Persia and Turkey, integrating Poland as a Russian province, developing Pan-Slavism, supporting the status quo in 1848–49, tightening the alliance with Prussia, and, by his territorial ambitions on Turkey, precipitating the Crimean War.

NICOLAI, Gustav (b. 1795). German music critic. Chief correspondent of the *Berliner musikalische Zeitung*. Wrote several libretti for oratorios, and prepared arrangements of Spontini's opera texts.

NICOLAI, Otto (1810–49). German composer. Studied with Zelter. Held various posts in Italy and worked in Vienna at the Court Opera, winning a reputation as a fine conductor. Moved to Berlin as director of the Domchor and the Royal Opera, at Meyerbeer's recommendation (1848). He was sensitive to the voice and had special feeling for orchestral color. In his masterpiece, *Die lustigen Weiber von Windsor* (1849), he enriched the tradition of German comic opera with Italian elegance and fluency.

NICOLINI (orig. **Nicolas**), **Ernest** (1834–98). French tenor. Studied at the Paris Conservatoire; début (1857). Sang in Italy, Paris (1862–70), London (1866, 1872–84). Appeared opposite Patti, and married her in 1886.

NICOLINI, Giuseppe (1762–1842). Italian composer. Wrote numerous comic operas, but after being installed as kapellmeister in Piacenza concentrated on church music.

NICOLÒ. See **ISOUARD, Nicolò.**

NIEMANN, Albert (1831–1917). German tenor. Studied with Rusch and Duprez. Début Dessau (1851). Sang in Stuttgart, Königsberg, Stettin, and Hanover before going to Berlin (1866–88). Chosen by Wagner to sing Tannhäuser in Paris (1861), Bayreuth (1876), London (1882), New York (1886–88).

NILSSON, Christine (1843–1921). Swedish soprano. Studied in Stockholm and Paris. Début Paris (1864), London (1867–81), New York (1870–74). Sang at the opening of the Metropolitan (1883). Her voice was sweet and brilliant, and she had great charm and beauty.

NISSEN, Georg Nikolaus (1761–1826). Danish councillor of state. He married Mozart's widow (1809) and collected materials for a biography of Mozart, published by Constanze after his death as *Biographie W. A. Mozarts nach Originalbriefen* (Leipzig, 1828).

NORBLIN. French cellist, played in the orchestra of the Paris Opéra in the 1830s.

NORDRAAK, Rikard (1842–66). Norwegian composer of the national anthem *Ja, vi elsker.* Studied with Kiel and Kullak in Berlin, a close friend of Grieg. Died prematurely, aged only twenty-three. Wrote songs and piano music.

NOTA, Alberto (1775–1847). Italian advocate and writer. Wrote comedies in the style of Goldoni, esp. *Il Progettista* and *La Fiera.*

NOURRIT, Adolphe (1802–39). Celebrated French tenor. Studied with Garcia. Début at the Opéra (1821). Studied further with Rossini (1824), whom he in turn advised on French style. Created several Rossini roles, esp. Arnold in *Guillaume Tell* (1829), as well as Masaniello in *La Muette de Portici* (1828), Eléazar in *La Juive* (1835), Robert *(Robert le Diable),* and Raoul *(Les Huguenots).* When Duprez was engaged as principal tenor at the Opéra (1837), he toured Belgium and France, and studied further with Donizetti, but committed suicide in Naples. He was a highly intelligent and creative artist, one of the most influential figures of the romantic movement, a singer, actor, writer (including the scenario of the ballet *La Sylphide*), composer, and teacher. His voice had charm, subtlety, expressiveness, and flexibility, and he was much admired by composers and other performers. Raised the artistic standards of the Opéra and of Paris itself.

NOURRIT, Auguste (1808–53). French tenor. Brother of Adolphe. Directed theaters in Amsterdam, the Hague, and Brussels. Later taught singing.

NOVELLO, Clara (1818–1908). English soprano. Fourth daughter of Vincent Novello. Studied in London, Paris, and Milan. Spent several years on the concert platform before making her stage début (1841). Sang in London (1843) and widely in Italy.

NOZZARI, Andrea (1775–1832). Italian tenor. Sang in Naples (1812–25), where he was also soloist in the Capella di Corte. Created nine roles for Rossini (in *Elisabetta, Otello, Armida, Ermione, Ricciardo e Zoraide, La Donna del lago, Mosè, Maometto II, Zelmira*).

O

OBIN. French bass. Sang at the Opéra in the 1850s.

OCHSENHEIMER, Dr. Ferdinand (1767–1822). German actor. Appeared with the Quand and Seconda Troupes in Dresden, Leipzig, and Prague, then at the Vienna Hoftheater (1807), where he worked until his death. Attained great success in so-called *kalte Rolle* in plays of intrigue.

ODILON-BARROT, Camille-Hyacinthe (1791–1873). French politician. One of the founders of the July Monarchy. He hindered the proclamation of the Republic in 1830, and was a bitter opponent of Guizot. In December 1848 he became minister president and minister of justice.

OEHLENSCHLÄGER, Adam Gottlob (1779–1850). Danish poet and dramatist. Was an early disciple of romanticism; his poem *Guldenhornene* is seen as introducing a new era in Danish literature. Went to Weimar and met Goethe and Schiller, and wrote a series of Northern tragedies. Went on to Paris and Rome, before returning to Denmark where he became professor of aesthetics at Copenhagen. In 1829 he was honored as "poetic King of Scandinavia." Revived many old Scandinavian romances and sagas.

OETTINGER, Eduard Maria (1802–72). German writer and journalist. Wrote many novels, poems, and bibliographical works, including *Rossini, komischer Roman* (Leipzig, 1845).

OFFENBACH, Jacques (orig. Jacob Eberst) (1819–80). German, then French, composer. Chief exponent of French operetta. Studied at the Paris Conservatoire (1833). Played the cello in the orchestra of Opéra Comique (1837) and began writing light music for the stage. Conductor at the Théâtre Français (1850), then rented the Théâtre Marigny in the Champs Elysées and opened it as the Bouffes-Parisiens (1855), which became the mecca of French operetta. His works satirized contemporary politics and society, often by means of parodying the classics, as in *Orphée aux enfers* (1858).

OLDENBURG, duke of. See **PAUL FRIEDRICH AUGUST** and **PETER NIKOLAUS FRIEDRICH**.

OLFERS, Ignaz von (1793–1872). Prussian diplomat. Director of the Royal Museum in Berlin (1839).

OLIVIER, Caroline. French actress and singer. Appeared at the Vaudeville and the Théâtre des Variétés. Lived with Heine at the rue Cadet (January–July 1838).

OLLIVIER, Émile (1825–1913). French politician. First married to Blandine, daughter of Liszt and Marie d'Agoult.

ONSLOW, André-Georges-Louis (1784–1853). French musician. Studied with Dussek, Cramer, and Reicha. Wrote some comic operas, but had greater effect with his chamber music. Lived in Paris for a few months every year, enjoying a good reputation, and eventually was elected as Cherubini's successor at the Académie (1842).

OPPENFELDT, Georg Moritz von. Son of Mendel Oppenheim and Henriette Itzig. Married Minette Ebers, Meyerbeer's cousin (1817). Ennobled (1827).

ORTIGUE. See **D'ORTIGUE**.

ORTOLAN, Eugène (1824–91). French composer. Studied law, entered the Ministry of Foreign Affairs while studying music privately with Halévy. Secretary to the Société des Compositeurs de Musique, where he used his position to protect the foreign rights of composers. Produced operettas at the Bouffes-Parisiens.

OSBORNE, George Alexander (1806–93). Irish pianist. Studied in Paris with Pixis, Kalkbrenner, and Fétis. Famous as a virtuoso and teacher. Also composed salon pieces and duets for violin and piano. Moved to London (1843).

OSCAR, prince of Sweden (1829–1907). Third son of Oscar I, king as **Oscar II** (1872) in succession to his brother Karl XV.

OTTO, Ernst Julius (1804–77). German choral conductor and composer. Studied in Dresden and was a teacher there. Appointed cantor at the Kreuzkirche (1830), and held the position for forty-five years. His choir became one of the most famous in Germany, and he also conducted other choral societies. His best works are the male choruses in his collection *Ernst und Scherz* (including "Gesellenfahrten"). Wrote operas, oratorios, songs for solo voice, instrumental pieces.

OTWAY, Thomas (1652–85). English poet and actor. Wrote many dramatically effective tragedies (esp. *Don Carlos*, *The Orphan* and *Venice Preserv'd*), published by Thornton (1813, 3 vols.).

P

PACCHIEROTTI, Gasparo (1740–1821). Italian male contralto. Sang at the opening of La Scala, after which his fame spread throughout Europe (esp. London, 1778, where he triumphed). Had a long and brilliant career, and retired after singing at the opening of La Fenice (16 May 1792).

PACINI, Antonio (1778–1866). French music publisher and composer.

PACINI, Émilien (1811–98). Son of Antonio Pacini, he helped run the publishing house. He was also a librettist, collaborating with Scribe and Vernoy Saint-Georges, as well as translating German and Italian operas like *Der Freischütz, Luisa Miller* and *Il Trovatore.*

PACINI, Giovanni (1796–1867). Italian composer. Studied with Marchesi and Furlanetto. His first real success was *Adelaide e Comingio* (Milan, 1817). Went to Rome (1820) and wrote in an easy Rossinian manner. Music director of the San Carlo in Naples (1825). He was very successful, and especially famous for his energetic melodies, but was threatened by the growing reputation of Donizetti and Bellini. Founded a music school at Viareggia. After the death of Bellini and the retirement of Rossini, he made a comeback with his masterpiece *Saffo* (Naples, 1840), composed in a new, more careful and dramatic style. Continued writing successful works (e.g., *Maria Tudor*, Palermo, 1843) until eclipsed by Verdi. He improved on his harmony and orchestration and helped to unify aria, ensemble and chorus in the years before Verdi. Also wrote oratorios, church music, and chamber compositions, as well as musical essays and textbooks, and an entertaining autobiography, *Le mie memorie artistiche* (1865).

PACINI, Louis (1776–1837). Italian singer. Important *basso buffo*, and later professor of singing at the conservatoire in Viareggia.

PAER, Ferdinando (1771–1839). Italian composer. Studied with Fortunanti and Ghiretti. *Maestro di capella* to the court of Parma (1792). While in Vienna (1797–1802) his style became fuller and more various, probably influenced by Mozart. He was appointed court kapellmeister in Dresden (1802–7) before going to Paris as *maître de chapelle* to Napoleon, then becoming conductor at the Opéra-Comique and the Italian Opera (1812–27). He was elected to the Institut and made conductor of the Royal Chamber Music (1832). Some of his forty-three operas enjoyed great success: *Sargino* (Dresden, 1803), *Leonore, ossia L'Amore conjugale* (Dresden, 1804), *Agnese* (Parma, 1809), and *Le Maître de chapelle* (Paris, 1821) which long remained in the repertoire of the Opéra Comique.

PAGANINI, Niccolò (1782–1840). Italian violinist. Studied with Ghiretti and Rolla. Became legendary as a virtuoso. Court violinist at Lucca (1808), then toured Italy until 1827, securing his international reputation and fortune by his European tour: Vienna (1828), Berlin (1829), Paris and London (1831). His technique and mystique fascinated the musicians of his day, Meyerbeer among them; he followed Paganini around Italy and helped him socially both in Berlin and Paris.

PAISIELLO, Giovanni (1740–1816). Italian composer. Studied in Naples. Wrote over a hundred operas, mainly *opere buffe*, which were performed throughout Italy and established him as a rival to Piccinni, and later Cimarosa and Guglielmi. From 1776 to 1784 he was kapellmeister and inspector of the two Italian Operas in St. Petersburg. *La Serva padrona* (1781) was written there. Returned to Italy in 1784, where he became *maestro di capella* to Ferdinand IV and wrote *L'Amor constrastato* (or *La Molinara*), which became one of his most popular works, together with *Nina* (both 1789). He sided with Napoleon in 1799, and went to Paris after the Bourbon Restoration, but died in poverty in Naples. He helped to shape *opera buffa* into a more satisfying emotional and dramatic genre, and with Cimarosa, represents the high point of its development before Mozart.

PALFFY, Ferdinand, Graf von Erdöd. Austrian aristocrat and impresario. Took over the direction of both the Kärntnertor-Theater and the Theater an der Wien (1813), developing the latter into a significant institution, and directing it until Barbaia's lease (1821).

PALIANTI, Louis. French stage designer and régisseur at the Paris Opéra. Edited a famous collection of *mises en scène* from the Parisian theaters (1865).

PALLERINI, Antonia (1790–1870). Italian dancer. Member of a well-known family of dancers. Appeared under Gioia at La Scala, Milan, and subsequently created all the leading ballerina roles in Viganò's ballets from *Prometeo* (1813) to *Didone* (1821). She was known as the "prima ballerina seria assoluta" and "la più gloriosa delle attrici italiane d'ogni genere" (Ritorni).

PALM-SPATZER, Mme. German soprano at the Royal Court Opera in Berlin in the 1840s.

PALMERSTON, John Henry Temple, third viscount (1784–1865). British statesman. Foreign secretary (1830–41, 1846–51), prime minister (1855–58, 1859–65). Supported liberal movements abroad, opposed French and Russian expansion in the Eastern Question, brought the Crimean War to its conclusion.

PANNY, Joseph (1794–1838). Austrian violinist and composer. Founded a school of music in Mainz.

PANOFKA, Heinrich (1807–87). Bohemian singer, teacher, and music critic. Studied as a violinist in Vienna. Concerts in Munich Berlin (1829). Settled in Paris (1834) and founded the Académie du Chant with Bordogni there (1842). London (1844–52). Famous singing teacher. Assistant to Lumley. Settled in Florence (1866). Correspondent for the Leipzig *Allgemeine musikalische Zeitung* and *Berliner musikalische Zeitung*.

PANSERON, Auguste-Mathieu (1795–1859). French singing teacher. Studied at the Paris Conservatoire with Gossec, Levasseur, and Berton; Prix de Rome (1813); further study in Italy and Vienna. Returned to Paris (1818) and taught singing, first at the Opéra Comique, then at the Conservatoire, becoming professor of singing (1836). Wrote romances and church music, as well as instructive works on singing.

PAPPENHEIMER, Israel Hirsch (d. 1837). Leader of the Jewish community in Munich, and an ardent campaigner for Jewish emancipation in Bavaria.

PARISH-ALVARS, Elias (1808–49). English harp virtuoso. Studied harp with Bochsa. Gave concerts in Germany (1831–36). While in Leipzig he associated with Mendelssohn. Settled in Vienna (1847). His harp compositions were popular in his lifetime.

PARMA, duke of. See **CARLO III**.

PARIS, Claude-Joseph (1801–66). French composer. Won the Prix de Rome (1825–26). Was later professor of piano at the boarding school of the Sacré Coeur and the College of Saint-Barbe. Conductor at the Théâtre du Panthéon.

PASCAL, André Prosper (known as **Dammien**) (1829–64). French singer, member of the ensemble at the Paris Opéra.

PASDELOUP, Jules-Étienne (1819–87). French conductor. Studied at the Paris Conservatoire with Laurent and Zimmermann. Taught piano there (1847–50). Founded the Société des Jeunes Artistes du Conservatoire, which later gave popular concerts in the Cirque d'Hiver. Taught vocal ensemble at the Conservatoire (1855–68). His concerts gradually lost ground in competition with the Colonne and Lamoureux, and ceased in 1884.

PASTA, Giuditta (1797–1865). Italian soprano. Studied with Lotti and Asioli; début in Brescia (1815). Her fame dates from 1821 in Paris, when her beautiful voice, dramatic interpretation, and poignancy created a sensation. She became an almost legendary figure, creating Anna Bolena, Norma, and Amina. Appeared regularly in London, Paris, and St. Petersburg until 1837.

PATTI, Adelina (1843–1919). Italian soprano. Studied with Strakosch, début New York (1859). London (1861) and sang 25 consecutive seasons there in thirty roles, the most highly paid singer of her day. She was essentially a coloratura soprano, but sang many lyric roles, and even dramatic ones. Her voice had great range, was even and flexible, and was beautiful and pure in tone.

PATTI, Carlotta (1835–89). Italian soprano, sister of Adelina. Confined her career to the concert platform.

PAUL FRIEDRICH AUGUST, grand duke of Oldenburg (d. 1853).

PAUMER, Friedrich von (1781–1873). German historian. University professor, member of the Frankfurt Parliament (1848). Later German ambassador to Paris.

PAVESI, Stefano (1779–1850). Italian composer. Studied in Naples with Piccinni, later with Gazzaniga. Wrote seventy operas. Director of the Vienna Court Opera (1826–30), *maestro di capella* in Crema. One of the most active and prolific composers before Rossini, with distinct melodic invention and expert handling of the orchestra. *Ser Marcantonio* (1810), a similar subject to *Don Pasquale*, was very successful, as was *Fanella, o La Muta di Portici* (1831).

PEARSON (known as **PIERSON**), **Henry Hugh** (1815–73). English composer. Educated at Cambridge. Went to Germany (1839). Studied with Tomaschek and Reissiger, entered Mendelssohn's circle in Leipzig. Professor of music at Edinburgh (1844) then returned to Germany, where he remained for the rest of his life. Married Caroline Leonhardt, who wrote the German libretti for his operas. (Changed his name to Pierson for reasons of pronunciation; used the pen name Edgar Mansfeldt.) Wrote operas, oratorios, incidental music. His style was submerged in that of Mendelssohn.

PEDRO I, Dom, D'Alcántara, duke of Braganza, emperor of Brazil (1798–1834, r. 1822–31). After the death of his father, also king of Portugal (1826), he left the regency to his brother Dom Miguel, with whom he later went to war.

PEDROTTI, Carlo (1817–93). Italian composer. Studied in Verona with Foroni. Italian Opera in Amsterdam (1841), Verona (1845–68) where he wrote chiefly *buffa* and *semiseria* operas, esp. *Fiorina* (1851) and *Tutti in maschera* (1869). Music director of the Teatro Regio in Turin (1868) which he developed into a major musical center. His operas are tuneful, light, and deftly constructed.

PELLEGRINI, Felix (1774–1832). Italian *basso buffo*. Worked as a principal singer in Naples (1803–18), then at the Italian Theatre in Paris, and also in London. Professor at the Paris Conservatoire (1829).

PELLEGRINI, Julius (1806–58). Italian bass. Début in Milan, and sang briefly in Italy (1829). Joined the Italian opera in Munich. When this was disbanded, he was taken over by the Royal Opera in Berlin, and was soon made a *Kammersänger*.

PENCO, Rosine. Italian soprano. Active in London in the 1850s.

PEREIRA, Henriette (Judith), baroness (née Arnstein) (1780–1859). She was the daughter of the Berlin couple Fanny and Nathan Arnstein. In 1802 she married **Aaron (Heinrich) Pereira**, a wealthy Dutch Jew of Portuguese descent. Meyerbeer made her acquaintance in 1813 during his stay in Vienna. She appears to have been vivacious and charming person, and a gifted pianist.

PERINET, Joachim (1763–1816). Austrian actor and director. Worked at the Leopoldstädter-Theater. Wrote over seventy libretti set by Seyfried, Kauer, and Wenzel Müller.

PERRIN, Émile Cesare (1814–85). French impresario. Succeeded Basset as director of the Opéra Comique (1848–57). Also director of the Opéra (1862). His period of management at the Opéra Comique saw the production of many new works by Adam, Auber, Halévy, Massé, and Thomas.

PERROT, Jules-Joseph (1810–92). French dancer, choreographer, and ballet master. Studied in Lyons, then with Vestris. Début Paris (1823). Soloist at the King's Theatre in London (1830) and appeared at the Paris Opéra, where he became Marie Taglioni's regular partner. Appeared in London, Naples, where he met Carlotta Grisi, becoming her ballet master, partner, and lover, and choreographed all her roles in Paris. Ballet master in London (1842–48) and St. Petersburg (1851–58), also working in Berlin,

Warsaw, Brussels, Lyons, and Paris. He was considered the greatest dancer of his time, and was one of the most dramatic and expressive choreographers of the romantic movement.

PERSIANI (-TACCHINARDI), Fanny (1812–67). Italian soprano. Pupil of her father, Nicola Tacchinardi. Début Leghorn (1832). Created Donizetti's Lucia (1835). London (1838–49). Helped to found the Royal Italian Opera, Covent Garden with the support and financial backing of her husband. She was a great favorite in Paris (1837–49). Her voice was brilliant and clear. Married the composer **Giuseppe PERSIANI** (1799–1869): both were well known in Paris as teachers.

PERTI, Jacopo Antonio (1661–1756). Italian composer. Studied with Padre Petronio Francheschini, and elected a member of the Accademia Filarmonica in Bologna (1681). Worked as an opera composer in Parma, before becoming maestro at San Pietro in Bologna (1690), and then at San Petronio (1696). Wrote twenty-four operas, nineteen oratorios, and other religious works.

PERUCCHINI, Dr. Giovanni Battista (1762–1870). Italian musician. Lived as a dilettante in Venice, writing ariettas and piano music.

PETER NIKOLAUS FRIEDRICH, grand duke of Oldenburg (1827–1900).

PETERS, Carl Friedrich (1779–1827). German publisher. Purchased Kühnel & Hoffmeister (1813) and developed the company's rich catalog, containing the first collected edition of Bach, and much Beethoven. Later acquired works by Weber, Spohr, Czerny, Chopin, Schumann, Wagner, Liszt, and Brahms. From 1868 classical works were published in the inexpensive and reliable "Edition Peters."

PETIPA, Marie Surovshchikova (1836–82). Russian dancer. Studied in St. Petersburg. Married Marius Petipa (1854), and entered the Bolshoi Theatre. Created many roles in her husband's ballets. Divorced (1869), and declined as a dancer.

PEZZI, Francesco. Italian critic. Editor of the *Gazetta di Milano*.

PFISTER, Julius (b. 1817). Hungarian singer, from 1844 at the Royal Opera Berlin.

PICCINNI, Louis-Alexandre (1779–1830). French musician. Accompanist at the Théâtre Feydeau and Opéra, then kapellmeister at the Théâtre Martin, also at the Opéra (1816); later singing teacher and conductor of concerts. Also wrote melodramas and ballets.

PICCOLOMINI, Marietta (1834–99). Italian soprano. Studied in Florence with Mazzarelli and Raimondi. Début there (1852). London (1856), the United States (1858). Married the Marchese della Fargia (1860) and retired from the stage. She was admired for her beauty and acting abilities, whereas her voice aroused much controversy.

PIERSON, Karoline (née Leonhardt) (1811–99). German writer of short stories and novels. Married J. P. Lyser (between 1836 and 1842), then Henry Hugh Pierson (see **PEARSON**), for whom she wrote libretti.

PILLET, Léon-François-Raymond (1803–68). French impresario. Director of the Opéra (1841–47). His policies were dominated by his liaison with the soprano Rosine Stoltz who influenced the engagements of new singers and caused great hostility. In spite of new works by Donizetti, his tenure of office marked a reversal in the prestige and influence of the Opéra.

PILLET-WILL, Michel-Frédéric, count. French banker and amateur musician. Hosted musical soirées with his wife, **Louise**.

PISARONI, Benedetta Rosamunda (1793–1872). Italian singer. Pupil of Vellutti. Changed from soprano to contralto. After early success in Italy, she sang in Paris, London, Cadiz, Trieste, and was engaged by La Scala on several occasions. She participated in the first performance of *Romilda e Costanza* (Padua, 26 December 1817).

PISCHEK, Johann Baptiste (1814–73). Bohemian singer. Appeared in Prague, Brünn, Pressburg, and Vienna before being engaged in Frankfurt, then Stuttgart.

PIXÉRÉCOURT, Guilbert-René-Charles (1773–1844). French playwright. Librettist of numerous comic operas and plays, father of the French *mélodrame* with its emphasis on moral subjects. Influenced the librettists of his time both by his own dramatic example and as director of the Opéra Comique (1822–27). His *mélodrames* used music to heighten dramatic tension, and were designed for popular appeal with stereotyped characters, innocent heroines, virtuous heroes, evil villains, etc. Donizetti's *Chiara e Serafina* and *Otto mesi in due ore*, as well as Meyerbeer's *Margherita d'Anjou* are based on his plays. He also had some bearing on later romantic drama (Dumas and Hugo), and hence on romantic opera in general.

PIXIS, Johann Peter (1788–1874). German pianist. Studied at home. Went to Munich (1809) and Paris (1825), where he established himself as a teacher and was greatly admired as a performer. Settled in Baden-Baden, where he continued to teach (1845). Wrote several operas, a piano concerto, much chamber and instrumental music for the piano (150 opus numbers). Together with Liszt, Chopin, Czerny, Thalberg, and Herz, he contributed to the famous *Hexaméron* based on the march from Bellini's *I Puritani* (Paris, 1835).

PLANARD, François-Antoine-Eugène de (1783–1853). French writer. Archivist of the Council of State (1806), and later executive secretary of the legislative section. Provided many libretti for Auber, Carafa, and Hérold (*Le Pré aux clercs*), all produced at the Opéra Comique. His daughter married Alphonse de Leuven.

PLEYEL, Camille (1788–1855). French pianist. Pupil of his father, Ignaz Joseph, had some success as a composer, but is chiefly remembered as a piano manufacturer.

PLUNKETT, Adeline (1824–1910). Belgian dancer. Studied in Paris with Barrez. Appeared in Trieste and London. Principal dancer at the Opéra (1845) where she created leading roles for Mabille, Coralli, and Mazilier.

POISE, Jean-Alexandre-Ferdinand (1828–92). French composer. Studied at the Paris Conservatoire with Adam and Zimmermann; Prix de Rome (1852). Composed a number of light operas for Paris.

POISSL, Johann Nepomuk, Freiherr von (1783–1865). German composer. Studied with Danzi and Vogler. His first real success was with the heroic drama *Ottaviano in Sicilia* (1812), consolidated in *Athalia* (1814) and *Der Wettkampf zu Olympia* (1815). Director of court music (1823) and of the Court Theatre in Munich (1825–32), but was forced to resign because of financial loss. Produced *Untersberg* (1829) and *Zaire* (1843). Died in poverty. He was an important transitional figure between Mozart and Weber, and was one of the first German composers to move away from Italian and French models in favor of continuously composed German opera. Weber praised his melodies. Wrote twelve operas, his own libretti as well as criticism and essays on theater organization.

POKORNY, Franz (1797–1850). Viennese impresario. Concessionaire of the Josephstadt-Theater (1837) before becoming director there (1844), and buying the Theater an der Wien (1845).

POLLEDRO, Giovanni Battista (1781–1853). Italian composer and violinist. Pupil of Pugnani. Worked in Turin, Bergamo and Moscow before undertaking extended concert tours. Became concertmaster of the Royal Orchestra in Turin (1816).

PONCHARD, Louis-Antoine-Eléonore (1787–1866). French singer. Pupil of Garat. Début at the Opéra Comique (1812), where he worked until 1837. Created the role of Georges Brown (*La Dame blanche*, 1825). From 1819 he was also a teacher at the Conservatoire.

PONCHARD, Marie-Sophie (née Collault) (1792–1873). French singer. Wife of Louis. Début Paris Opéra (1814), but soon joined the Opéra Comique (1818), where she was part of the ensemble until 1836. Took part in the premières of many works by Hérold and Auber. Created the Queen in *Les Pré aux clercs* (1832). First singer to be awarded the Légion d'Honneur.

PONSARD, François (1814–67). French lawyer and playwright. Wrote many revolutionary dramas and contemporary pieces replacing the romantic style of Victor Hugo and Alexandre Dumas with more realistic speech. Known for his "dramatic proverbs" and his tragedy *Lucrèce* (1843), as well as his topical satires *Ce qui plaît aux femmes* and *Le Honneur et l'Argent* (1853), which was a great success at the Odéon and ran until 1876.

PONTMARTIN, Armand, comte de (1811–90). French critic and novelist.

POULTIER, Placide-Alexandre-Guillaume (b. 1814). French tenor. A member of the ensemble of the Opéra from 1840. Later he sometimes sang in the provinces.

PRADHER, Mme. (née More) (b. 1800). French soprano. Belonged to the ensemble of the Opéra Comique for twenty-one years. Married the pianist Louis Barthélemy Pradher, who was also a teacher at the Conservatoire. Created the leading soprano roles in several of Auber's works (like *La Neige, Léocadie, Le Maçon, La Fiancée, Lestocq, Le Cheval de bronze*).

PRATTÉ, Anton Eduard (1799–1875). Bohemian harp virtuoso.

PRECHTLER, Otto (1813–81). Austrian poet. Wrote many dramas and operatic texts. Succeeded Grillparzer as the director of archives in the Ministry of Finance in Vienna.

PRÉVOST, Jean-Marie-Michel-Hippolyte (pseud. P. Crocius). Music critic.

PRÉVOST, Mme. French soprano. Member of the ensemble at the Opéra Comique in the 1830s. Created the role of Zerline in *Fra Diavolo* (1830) and Madeleine in *Le Postillion de Longjumeau* (1836).

PROCH, Heinrich (1809–78). Austrian musician. Conductor at the Josephstadt-Theater in Vienna (1837), kapellmeister of the Viennese Court Opera (1840–70). Also famous as a voice teacher (e.g., of Materna and Tietjens), and as a composer of songs.

PROKESCH VON OSTEN, Anton, Graf (1795–1876). Austrian diplomat. Ambassador to Athens (1834–49), Berlin (1849–52), Paris (as *Bundespräsidialgesandter*) (1853–54), Berlin.

PRUDENT, Émile-Beunie (1817–63). French pianist and composer. Studied at the Paris Conservatoire with Laurent and Zimmermann. Toured as a pianist in France, Belgium, England, and Germany. Settled in Paris and was highly regarded as a piano teacher. Wrote a number of piano works.

PRUME, François (1816–49). Belgian violin virtuoso.

PRUTZ, Robert Edward (1816–72). German writer and literary historian. His liberal political views meant that he was not allowed to proceed to his *Habilitation* in Jena and Halle. His lectures on the history of the German theater were published in 1847. In early 1849, after the revolution, he was nominated as professor of literary history at Halle.

PÜCKLER-MUSKAU, Hermann Ludwig Heinrich, Fürst von (1785–1871). German author associated with Junges Deutschland. Wrote the enormously popular *Briefe eines Verstorbenen* (1830–32) and books of travel. Famous for the landscaping of his huge estates.

PUGNI, Cesare (1805–70). Italian composer. Studied with Rolla and Asioli. Worked in Paris (1830–43), London (1843–50), St. Petersburg (1850–70). Wrote and arranged some three hundred ballet scores for Jules Perrot, Arthur Saint-Léon, Paul Taglioni, and Marius Petipa, esp. *Esmeralda* (1844) and *Le Fille du Pharaon* (1864).

PUTLITZ, Gustav Heinrich Gans, Edler Herr zu (1821–90). Prussian civil servant and playwright. Resigned from the service (1848), and then became theater director in Schwerin (1863–67) and Karlsruhe (1873–89). Wrote several comedies, some of them successful at the time (*Lustspiele*, 1850–51).

Q

QUAGLIO, Domenico (1787–1837). Italian artist. Scene painter at the Munich Theatre. Later he devoted himself to architectural painting, decorating the Sebalduskirche in Nuremberg and the Freiburg Minster. Also took part in the restoration and embellishment of Hohenschwangau.

QUETELET, Lambert-Adolph-Jacob (1796–1874). Belgian astronomer. Director of the Observatoire Royal in Brussels, founder of modern social statistics.

R

RACHEL, Elisa (orig. **Felix**) (1820–58). French actress. From 1840 to 1855 she worked at the Théâtre Français in Paris, where she was unrivaled in classical roles. She had immense success in *Adrienne Lecouvreur* (1849), written for her by Scribe and Legouvé. Toured, London, Brussels, Berlin, St. Petersburg.

RACINE, Jean (1639–99). French dramatist. He was a great master of tragic pathos, developing on Corneille's achievement in the depiction of a consuming dominant passion, e.g., *Phèdre* (1677).

RADECKE, Robert (1830–1911). German conductor and composer. Studied at the Leipzig Conservatoire, held various posts, then choral conductor and teacher in Berlin. Director of the Court Opera (1871–87), teacher at the Institute of Church Music (1892–1907). Wrote orchestral and vocal music.

RADETZKY, Johann Joseph, Graf Radetzky von Radetz (1766–1858). Austrian field marshal. Won victories over the Sardinian armies at Custozza (1848) and Novara (1849), restoring the Lombardo-Venetian territories to Austrian rule. His popularity was celebrated in the famous march by Johann Strauss Sr.

RADZIWELL, Anton Heinrich, Fürst von (1775–1833). Polish-Prussian aristocrat and musician. He was governor of Posen, a singer, composer, and patron of the arts (including Chopin). Composed the incidental music to Goethe's *Faust* (publ. 1835), the *Complainte de Maria Stuart* with cello and piano; French *Romances*, and various duets and quartets.

RADZIWELL, Bogoslav, Fürst von (1809–73). Polish-Prussian aristocrat. Head of administration for charitable organizations in Prussia. Member of the royal household (1845).

RADZIWELL, Wilhelm, Fürst von (1797–1870). Polish-Prussian aristocrat. General of infantry (1846).

RAFF, Joseph Joachim (1822–82). German composer and pianist. Assistant and secretary to Liszt in Weimar (1850–56). Collaborated on the *Caecilia, Neue Zeitschrift für Musik*. Achieved fame as a composer of symphonies (esp. no. 5 *Leonore*) and piano concertos. Made piano arrangements of many of Meyerbeer's works, and was chosen by Meyerbeer to teach the piano to Cornelie Meyerbeer.

RAIMUND, Ferdinand (1790–1836). Austrian actor and playwright in Vienna. He inherited the traditional Viennese *Zauberspiel*, a dramatic fairy tale with music and allegorical figures centering around simple comic characters. He wrote his plays for production in the theater where he performed. His best plays (*Der Alpenkönig und der Menschenfeind*, 1828; *Der Verschwender*, 1834) are characterized by humor tinged with melancholy, and teach a moral of self-sufficiency.

RAMLER, Carl Wilhelm (1725–98). German poet. His lyrics were published in 1772.

RAUCH, Christian Daniel (1777–1857). German sculptor. Studied in Rome (1804). Executed the tomb of Queen Louise (1811–15), as well as statues of Blücher, Dürer, Goethe, Schiller, Schleiermacher, and Frederick the Great (his masterpiece).

RAUMER, Friedrich von (1781–1873). German historian. A university lecturer, he became member of the Frankfurt Parliament (1848) and later German ambassador in Paris.

RAUPACH, Ernst Benjamin (1784–1852). German playwright. Wrote historical dramas, but most famously the sentimental melodrama *Der Müller und sein Kind* (1835).

REBER, Napoléon-Henri (1807–80). French composer. Studied with Reicha and Le Sueur at the Paris Conservatoire. Professor of harmony (1861); inspector of branch conservatoires (1871). Wrote one ballet, four operas, chamber music, songs, *Traité d'harmonie* (1862).

RÉCAMIER, Jeanne-Françoise-Julie-Adelaide (1777–1849). Famous Parisian socialite who presided over a glittering and influential salon. Married the banker Jacques Récamier.

RECIO, Marie-Geneviève. French soprano from Paris. Mistress and subsequently second wife of Hector Berlioz.

REDERN, Friedrich Wilhelm, Graf von (1802–83). German court official and musician. Studied with Zelter and Bernhard Anselm Weber (1830–42). Associated from 1826 with the directorship of the Royal Theatres, becoming intendant-general of the Royal Theatres in Berlin (1830), and later director of the music at court; the Domchor and military music also came under his jurisdiction.

REEVE, William (1757–1815). English composer. Organist in Devon, then moved to a post in London where he wrote pantomimes and stage music. Also appeared as a singer and actor.

REEVES, John Sims (1818–1900). English tenor. Studied with his father, and made his début as a baritone (1838). Studied further in London and Paris with Bordogni, Milan with Mazzucato. La Scala (1846), London (1847), His Majesty's from 1848. The later part of his career was devoted to oratorio.

REGLI, Francesco (1802–66). Italian writer on music. Founder and editor of the theater journal *Il Pirata* (1835) and compiler of a *Dizionario biografico dei più celebri poeti ed artisti melodrammatici che fiorirono in Italia dal 1800 al 1860* (Turin, 1860).

REHFUSS, Philip Joseph von (1779–1843). German writer and editor.

REICHA, Anton (1770–1836). Bohemian composer, violinist and teacher. Flautist in Bonn (1788), teacher in Hamburg, Paris, Vienna (1801–8), where he knew Beethoven, Haydn, Albrechtsberger, and Salieri. Returned to Paris, where he gained a reputation as a teacher (Liszt and Gounod), theorist, and instrumental composer. He succeeded Méhul as professor of counterpoint at the Conservatoire, and to Boieldieu's chair at the Institut (1833). His four sets of six woodwind quintets are among his best works.

REICHARDT, Johann Friedrich (1752–1814). German composer and writer on music. Studied with Richter and Veichtner, then studied philosophy at Königsberg and Leipzig. Court conductor in Berlin (1775–94). Founded the *concerts spirituels* for the performance of new works. Lived in Altona (1797), Giebichstein, Cassel (where he was court conductor, 1806) then in Vienna, before returning to Giebichstein. Composed numerous German and Italian operas; orchestral, chamber, and instrumental music; and over sixty songs. Edited various musical periodicals and published several books.

REIMANN. Prussian privy councillor. Tutor to the Royal Prussian children, visitor to the Beer household, and a friend of Amalia Beer.

REINA, Domenico (1797–1843). Italian tenor. Studied Milan, début there (1829). La Scala (1831–36), where he created roles by Bellini *(La Straniera)*, Donizetti *(Gemma di Vergy)*, and Pacini *(Maria Tudor)*. Admired by Bellini, and performed in the first performances of several Rossini operas in London (1832).

REINECKE, Carl Heinrich Carsten (1824–1910). German pianist and composer. Studied with his father. Court pianist to King Christian VIII, spent some years in Paris, teacher at the Cologne Conservatoire (1851), music director at Barmen, Breslau, director of the Gewandhaus Concerts in Leipzig, as well as teaching piano and composition at the Conservatoire Made annual concert tours, and composed extensively, with refined workmanship.

REISSIGER, Karl Gottlieb (1798–1859). German composer. Studied with Winter in Munich (1822). Succeeded Marschner as music director of the Royal Opera in Dresden, Weber as court kapellmeister, and Morlacchi at the Italian Opera. Vigorous supporter of Beethoven, Weber, Wagner. Prolific composer, notably of the opera *Die Felsenmühle zu Etalières* (Dresden, 1831).

REISSMANN, August (1825–1903). German writer on music. Studied with various masters; lived with Liszt in Weimar (1850–52) and developed a literary style; then in Halle, and finally in Berlin (1866–75), where he lectured in the history of music at the Stern Conservatoire. Wrote extensively.

REITER, Ernst (1814–75). German composer. Conductor of the Basle Gesangverein.

RELLSTAB, Heinrich Friedrich Ludwig (1799–1860). German poet and writer. Editor and music critic for the *Vossische Zeitung* in Berlin (1826). Wrote satirical pamphlets, biographies, opera and concert criticisms. Initially hostile to Meyerbeer, he later became his Berlin collaborator, translating the libretto of *Ein Feldlager in Schlesien* into German from Scribe's original French, as well as providing the composer with other texts for cantatas, songs, and alterations to libretti.

REMÉNYI, Eduard (1830–98). Hungarian violinist. Studied Vienna Conservatoire (1842–45). Banished for participating in the Hungarian Revolution (1848), he traveled in America. Returned to Europe (1853), became solo violinist to Queen Victoria (1854) and then to the emperor of Austria (1860). European tour (1865), world tour (1886). He had a prodigious and passionate technique. Composed various pieces and made many arrangements.

REMORINI, Ranieri (1783–1873). Italian bass, famous in Rossini roles.

RÉMUSAT, Charles-François de (1797–1875). French jurist, historian, and philosopher. Deputy under Louis-Philippe; minister of the interior (1840).

RENNER, Marie Johanna (1775–1824). German actress. Pupil of Marchand. Also studied music with Leopold Mozart. Married Franz von Holbein. Worked in Mannheim, Munich, and Würzburg, and later in Prague with great success. She excelled in light comic roles.

RETTICH, Julie (née Gley) (1809–66). Austrian actress. Worked at the Burgtheater in Vienna.

REYER, Ernest (1823–1909). French composer and critic. Largely self-taught. While he made a reputation with three early operas, his most famous work was *Sigurd* (1884), which shows considerable independence of thought. Defended Wagner and Berlioz eloquently.

REYNOLDS, John Hamilton (1796–1852). English writer and close friend of Keats. Wrote novels and verse tales, and had a gift for parody and comic verse.

REYNOLDSON. Representative of the management of the Drury Lane Theatre in London.

REZIO, Marie-Geneviève. See **RECIO**.

RICCI, Frederico (1809–77) and **Luigi** (1805–59). Italian composers. Both studied in Naples. Frederico composed nineteen operas (two with his brother); St. Petersburg (1853); Paris (1869); Conegliaro (1876). Luigi composed thirty operas; Trieste (1836); Prague (1844); died there insane.

RICHARDS, Henry Brinley (1817–85). British composer and pianist. Studied at the Royal Academy of Music and won the King's Scholarship (1835). Resided in London, highly esteemed as a concert pianist and teacher. Wrote the popular hymn "God Bless the Prince of Wales."

RICHTER, Gustav (1823–84). German court painter. Married Cornelie Meyerbeer.

RICHTER, Hans (1876–1955). Meyerbeer's grandson. Son of Cornelie Meyerbeer.

RICHTER, Joseph (1749–1813). Austrian journalist and author of plays, stories, and poetry. Best known as the pseudonymous author of the "Eipeldauer letters," which appeared from 1785 until his death; they were a commentary on the Viennese scene and exercise in satirical journalism. After Richter's death the series was continued by others, most notably A. Bäuerle.

RICORDI, Tito (1811–88). Italian music publisher. Succeeded to his father's business. Established the *Gazetta musicale* (1848), one of the most important Italian musical journals. Under his administration the business became the largest music publishing firm in Italy. He was on intimate terms with Verdi, and together they made a fortune. Eventually published all the Italian editions of Meyerbeer's scores.

RIEHL, Wilhelm Heinrich von (1823–97). German writer on music. Studied in Munich, where he became professor of political economy, and also lectured on music history. Published the valuable compendium *Musikalische Charakterköpfe* (1853–61, 3 vols.) and two vols. of original songs.

RIEM, Friedrich Wilhelm (1779–1857). German organist at the Thomasschule in Leipzig (1814), and director of the Bremen Singakademie (1822).

RIES, Ferdinand (1784–1838). German composer and pianist. Pupil of Beethoven. Obtained a good post in London (1813). Later went to Godesburg and Frankfurt-am-Main. Became civic director of music in Aachen (1834) and director of the Cäcilienverein in Frankfurt.

RIES, Hubert (1802–86). German musician. Brother of Ferdinand. Studied with Spohr and Hauptmann. Violinist and concertmaster of the Royal Orchestra in Berlin (1836). Teacher at the Royal Theateristrumentalschule (1851). Published manuals of instruction, duets, exercises, two concertos.

RIGHINI, Vincenzo (1756–1812). Italian composer. Studied with Bernacchi and Padre Martini. Début as a tenor in Parma (1775). Conductor of the Opera Buffa in Vienna (1780), kapellmeister in Mainz (1788–92), then kapellmeister of the Court Opera in Berlin (1793–). Wrote twenty operas, including *Gerusalemme liberata* (Berlin, 1803), and vocal exercises.

RISSE, Carl. German singer. Engaged at the Dresden Court Theatre (1823–28, 1829–55).

RISTORI, Adelaide (1822–1906). Italian actress. Began touring with her troupe after 1855, winning accolades before a French audience. Traveled widely in Europe as well as in America and Australia (1866, 1875, 1884–85). Wrote *Memoirs and Artistic Studies* (trans. 1907).

RITT, Eugène (1817–98). French impresario. Joint director of the Opéra Comique with Alphonse de Leuven (1862–70).

ROCHETTE, Raoul. French archaeologist. *Sécretaire perpetuel* of the Académie des Beaux Arts.

ROCK, Carl Ludwig (1790–1869). Fraternity brother of A. von Dusch.

RÖCKEL, Joseph August (1783–1870). Austrian conductor and composer. Directed his own touring German opera group. Father of the writer on music August Röckel (1814–76).

RODE, Jacques-Pierre-François (1774–1830). French violinist. Pupil of Fauvel and Viotti in Paris. Toured Holland and Germany, appeared in London, and was appointed professor of violin at the newly opened Paris Conservatoire. Personal violinist to Napoleon (1800) and Tsar Alexander I (1803–8). Lived for a time in Berlin (1814). Wrote thirteen violin concertos, twenty-four caprices, and a violin method.

RODENBERG, Julius (orig. Levy) (1831–1914). German writer. Journalist in Berlin (1862). Wrote novels, verse romances, travelogues (on England, France, Italy).

RODRIGUES, Edouard. Banker in Paris.

ROGER, Gustave-Hippolyte (1815–79). French tenor. Studied in Paris with Martin. His début was at the Opéra Comique (1838), and he went to the Opéra in 1848. A celebrated and popular singer, he created Jean de Leyde in *Le Prophète*, as well as numerous roles in operas by Halévy, Auber, and Thomas. His high intelligence and artistry won him a wide circle of friends among the composers and authors of his day, like Meyerbeer, Gounod, and Alexandre Dumas *(fils)*.

ROHLEDER, Friedrich Traugott. German minister of religion. Lutheran pastor at Lähn in Silesia. Published *Musikalische Liturgie in der evangelisch-protestantischen Kirche* (1831).

ROMANI, Felice (1788–1865). Italian librettist. Lectured at the Liceo in Genoa, but abandoned law for literature, becoming foremost theater poet of his time. Worked at La Scala and directed the *Gazetta Ufficiale Piomontese* (1834–48), as well as occasionally editing the *Messagero Torinese* with Brofferio. Wrote over a hundred works for Mayr, Winter, Vaccai, Rossini, Donizetti, Bellini, Pacini, Ricci. He provided *Margherita d'Anjou* (1820) and *L'Esule di Granata* (1821) for Meyerbeer.

ROMANI, Pietro (1791–1877). Italian composer and conductor. Studied with Fenaroli. Conductor at the Teatro della Pergola in Florence, and taught at the Istituto Musicale. Wrote two operas and ballet music.

ROMBERG, Anton (b. 1777). Austrian instrumentalist. A bassoon virtuoso like his father, **Anton**. His brother **Bernard** was a famous cellist.

RONCONI, Giorgio (1810–90). Italian baritone. Studied with his father, the tenor Domenico. Début Pavia (1831). Sang in Italy (1832–42), creating several roles for Donizetti. Covent Garden (1847–66). One of the great singers of the age.

RONCONI, Sebastiano (1814–1900). Italian baritone. Third son of the famous tenor Domenico. Studied with his father. Début Lucca (1836). Appeared as guest artist in Berlin (1847). Sang the same roles as his brother Giorgio, who was more famous. Sang for some thirty-five years in Europe and America, then taught singing in Milan.

RONNEBURGER, W. German violinist in the Royal Orchestra in Berlin.

RONZI (-DE BEGNIS), Giuseppina (1800–1853). Italian soprano. Studied with Garat. Début Florence (1815). Married the bass Giuseppe de Begnis, and attained her greatest success after returning to Italy from Paris and London (1830). She appeared in all the big houses. Created the leading roles in five Donizetti operas *(Fausta, Sancia di Castiglia, Maria Stuarda, Gemme di Vergy, Roberto Devereux)*. Retired on the death of her husband.

ROQUEPLAN, Louis-Victor (1804–70). French journalist and impresario. Correspondent for the *Constitutionnel*. Editor of *Le Figaro* in Paris, director of the Théâtre des Variétés, director of the Opéra with Duponchel (1847–54), and then of the Opéra Comique (1857–60).

ROSENHAIN, Jacob (1813–94). German pianist and composer. Studied with Schmitt in Mannheim, Schnyder von Wartensee in Frankfurt. Went to Paris and London (1837), and continued to travel until 1870, when he settled as teacher in Baden-Baden. Wrote three operas, three symphonies, three string quartets, four piano trios, piano works.

ROSSI, Countess. See **SONTAG, Henriette**.

ROSSI, Gaetano (1774–1855). Italian librettist. Worked in Venice and Verona, and wrote over 120 libretti for Carafa, Coccia, Donizetti, Mayr, Mercadante, Nocolai, Pacini, Rossini, and Meyerbeer (*Romilda e Costanza, Emma di Resburgo, Il Crociato in Egitto* and the uncompleted *Almanzor*). His plots were taken from classical and historical drama, introduced many romantic themes into opera, and contributed to the loosening of set forms characteristic of early-nineteenth-century opera.

ROSSINI, Gioacchino Antonio (1792–1868). Italian composer. Studied in Bologna. His masterpiece of *opera buffa* was *Il Barbiere di Siviglia* (1816), and he set decisive standards and models for the *opera seria* of Italian romanticism during his time in Naples (1815–20). In 1823 he became director of the Théâtre Italien in Paris, and invited Meyerbeer to Paris to produce *Il Crociato* in the following year. He was appointed director of royal music two years later. His French revisions of *Maometto II* and *Mosè in Egitto*, and particularly *Guillaume Tell* (1829), helped to establish the style and fame of French *grand opéra*.

ROTA, Giuseppe (1822–65). Italian dancer, choreographer and ballet master. Started as a self-taught choreographer in Turin. Went on to Milan and Vienna, where he enjoyed great success with his spectacular *azione mimo-danzante*.

ROTHSCHILD, James Meyer de (1792–1866). Parisian head of the famous banking family. He was a personal friend of Meyerbeer and present at the première of *Les Huguenots*.

ROTHSCHILD, Salomon. German banker, founder of the banking dynasty in Frankfurt. Went to Vienna in 1821, where his success ousted the families Arnstein, Eskeles, Sina, and Geymüller from their preeminence.

RÖTTSCHER, Dr. Heinrich Theodor. (1803–71). German writer. Professor and influential critic for the *Spenersche Zeitung*.

ROUGET DE L'ISLE, Claude-Joseph (1760–1836). French composer of the *Marseillaise* (1792). Not a revolutionary, he was imprisoned for not taking the oath against the crown. Went to Paris after Robespierre's downfall, and composed other national military hymns. Published *Chants français* (1825) and several opera libretti.

ROUNAT, Charles de la. Director of the Odéon in Paris.

ROUSSEAU, Jean-Jacques (1712–78). French writer. One of the great universal geniuses of eighteenth-century French literature. Also an occasional composer; in the "Guerre des Bouffons" he was a devotee of the Italians. Published his *Lettre sur la musique française* (1742), wrote several articles on music for Diderot's encyclopedia, which were published as his own *Dictionnaire de la musique* (Geneva, 1767). His *Le Devin du village* (1752) initiated the French *opéra comique* and was very successful, remaining in the repertory for seventy-five years. The later years of his life were devoted to more personal works like the *Confessions* (1765–70), misleading on fact but revelatory of his psychology. His insistence on the complexity of the human soul and a lyrical evocation of nature make him a harbinger of romanticism.

ROUSSEAU, Johann Baptiste (1802–67). German journalist. Editor of the *Frankfurter Oberpostamtzeitung* (1829). During the 1840s he was without a permanent position; Vienna (1845); Cologne (1863). In 1844 he turned to Meyerbeer several times requesting help.

ROWE, Nicholas (1674–1718). English dramatist. Undersecretary of state. Wrote numerous tragedies, among them *Jane Shore* (1714). Published an important edition of Shakespeare.

ROYER, Alphonse (1803–75). French writer and translator. Worked in collaboration with Gustave Vaez, most famously in the libretto for Donizetti's *La Favorite* (1840) and the translation of Verdi's *I Lombardi* (1847).

ROYER-COLLAD, Hippolyte. Editor of *L'Europe littéraire*, member of the Commission of the Ministry of the Interior for the Opéra.

RUBINI, Giovanni Battista (1794–1854). Celebrated Italian tenor. Studied in Bergamo and Naples. Début Pavia (1814), Naples (1816–29), Paris (1831–43), London (1831–43), St. Petersburg (1843–44). He influenced Italian romanticism through his vocal gifts, and won great success in the operas of Rossini, Donizetti, and Bellini. Toured widely, winning fame and fortune and the admiration of many composers. His powerful, flexible voice was complemented by his intense, dramatic performance.

RUBINSTEIN, Anton Grigorievich (1829–94). Russian composer and legendary pianist. Studied in Russia with Villoing and in Berlin with Dehn. Composed several operas (esp. *The Demon,* 1875), five piano concertos, six symphonies, oratorios, and much chamber and instrumental music, in the German romantic rather than the Russian nationalist style. Founded the Russian Musical Society (1859) and the St. Petersburg Conservatoire (1862). His brother **Nikolay Grigorievich** (1835–81), a pianist of similar virtuosity, and also a powerful force in Russian music and education, founded the Moscow Conservatoire (1864).

RUDERSDORFF-KUCHENMEISTER, Helmine (1822–82). German dramatic soprano. Pupil of Bordogni in Paris and of de Micherout in Milan. Sang in Germany (1840–54), then London (1854–65). Engaged for the Boston Jubilee (1869), she settled there, becoming renowned as a teacher. Her son Richard Mansfield (1857–1907) was a famous actor.

RUHL VON LILIENSTERN, Joseph Jacob (1780–1847). Prussian general.

RUMFORD, Benjamin Thompson, count (1753–1814). American engineer. Laid out the English Garden in Munich and imported the potato into Bavaria. Became a privy councillor and personal adjutant to Prince Karl Theodor of Bavaria (1784). Conducted various experiments in England (1799).

RUMMEL, Christian (1787–1849). German musician. He was a fine performer on the piano, violin, and clarinet. Municipal conductor in Wiesbaden (1815–41). Published a clarinet concerto and two quintets.

RUNGENHAGEN, Prof. Karl Friedrich (1778–1851). German musician. Pupil of Benda. Succeeded Zelter as director of the Berlin Singakademie and teacher in the School of Composition.

RUSSELL, Lord John, first earl Russell (1792–1878). British Whig statesman. A liberal reformer, he supported the Catholic Emancipation Act (1829) and was largely responsible for the Reform Act of 1832. He brought in other reforms as home secretary (1835–39), and was prime minister (1846–52 and 1865–66).

S

SACHS, Dr. Michael (1808–64). Jewish scholar. Rabbi in Prague (1836) and in Berlin (1844).

SAINT-GEORGES, Jules Henri Vernoy de (1799–1875). French writer. After Scribe, the most gifted and fertile French librettist. Wrote vaudevilles, ballets, and over eighty texts for Hérold, Halévy, Donizetti *(La Fille du régiment),* Flotow *(Martha),* Bizet *(La jolie Fille de Perth),* and others. He was elected president of the Société des Auteurs Dramatiques six times.

SAINT-LÉON, Arthur (1821–70). French dancer, choreographer, ballet master, and teacher. Studied with his father, who was ballet master in Tuscany and Stuttgart. Début as a violinist in Stuttgart (1834). Studied further in Paris with Albert. Toured widely (1841–51), including London, where he appeared with Fanny Cerrito, whom he married. Appointed teacher at the Opéra, where he also created many divertissements in operas. Succeeded Perrot as ballet master in St. Petersburg (1859–61); also ballet master at the Opéra (1863–70).

SAINT-MARC-GIRARDIN, François-Auguste (1801–73). French writer and politician. Professor of history at the Sorbonne (1831), member of the Académie (1844), member of the National Assembly (1871). Wrote articles for the *Journal des Débats* and the *Revue de Paris.*

SAINT-PRIEST, Alexis-Guignard, comte de (1805–51). French diplomat.

SAINT-SAËNS, Camille (1835–1921). French composer. Studied with Maledon and Halévy. Made an early mark as a child prodigy pianist. Wrote thirteen operas that showed little dramatic flair. *Samson et Dalila* (1877) revealed a sense of characterization and created a consistent emotional world.

SALIERI, Antonio (1750–1825). Italian composer. Studied in Venice with Gassmann, who became his patron and took him to Vienna. Conducted at the Burgtheater and succeeded Gassmann as court composer (1774), and eventually kapellmeister (1788–1824). Produced Italian and French operas under the influence of Gluck, and enjoyed great renown as a teacher. He was a master of the Italian method of composition, harmony, and counterpoint. Wrote thirty-nine operas, religious music, various instrumental works.

SALOMON, Rudolph Heinrich (b. 1825). German tenor. Début 1844. Vienna (1847). From 1850 sang at the Royal Opera in Berlin.

SALOMON, Siegfried (1816–99). German composer. Studied with J. P. Hartman in Copenhagen and worked there many years. Then settled in Russia (1859), and finally in Stockholm (1879).

SALVINI, Tommaso (1830–1915). Italian actor. Gained a reputation as a member of Ristori's company. In Paris he played in Racine and in London he attained immense popularity in Shakespeare. Although he also acted in comedies (esp. Goldoni), he won fame mainly as a tragedian. His role in the 1848 revolutionary wars added to his popularity. Retired in 1884.

SAND, George (Amandine Aurore Lucie, baronne de Dudevent, née Dupin) (1804–76). French writer. Her novels won her great renown, and her position as an influential figure in French romanticism was confirmed by her general interest in all the arts. She asserted women's rights to love and independence, considered social and political questions, and wrote about the pastoral life. Her *François le Champi* (1847–48) is from this later rustic period. She was closely associated with Alfred de Musset and Chopin, and a devoted admirer of Meyerbeer, whom she famously addressed in the eleventh letter of her *Lettres d'un Voyageur* (1837).

SANDEAU, Léonard-Silvain-Julien (1811–83). French writer and dramatist. Wrote for the *Revue de Paris* (1837–44) and *La Mode* (1844–45). Collaborated on four plays.

SANTINI, Vincenzo-Felice (d. 1836). Italian buffo singer in Munich.

SAPHIR, Moritz Gottlieb (1795–1858). Austrian writer. With Bäuerle edited the *Theaterzeitung* (1835), and later the newspaper *Der Humorist*. His witty but superficial conversational pieces began appearing in 1832.

SARDOU, Victorien (1831–1908). French playwright, one of the most successful of the nineteenth century. Like Scribe, whose techniques he copied, he was a brilliant theatrical craftsman. He wrote comedies of manners, melodramas, and historical plays full of striking dramatic effects, but characterized by vulgarity of feeling—most famously in *La Tosca* (1887).

SASS, Dr. Friedrich. German author of *Berlin in seiner neusten Zeit und Entwicklung* (Leipzig, 1849).

SASS, Marie-Constance (1834–1907). Studied with Gevaert, Ugalde, Lamperti. Début Venice (1852). She made her Paris début at the Théâtre Lyrique (1859), and went to the Opéra a year later. There she sang Elisabeth in *Tannhäuser* (1861), created Sélika in *L'Africaine* (1865), and Elisabeth de Valois in *Don Carlos* (1867), and became very famous. Later went to Italy (La Scala, 1869–70). Married the bass Castelmary, retired from the stage (1877), and taught singing. Died in great poverty.

SAUVAGE, Thomas-Maria-François (1794–1877). French writer. Author of many vaudevilles. For Meyerbeer he prepared the scenario for *La Nymphe du Danube* (1827). He had previously made the French version of *Margherita d'Anjou,* which was performed on 11 March 1826 at the Odéon, where he was director at the time.

SAVIGNY, Friedrich Karl von (1779–1861). Prussian civil servant. Lawyer, professor of the University of Berlin. Minister for the revision of legislation.

SAVOYE, Henri-Charles-Joseph. French journalist. Worked in Paris for the periodical *Panorama de l'Allemagne* and the *Allgemeine Zeitung für neue Kunst und Literatur in Paris.* He was a naturalized French citizen, professor at the Collège Louis le Grand, and delegate of the French Republic in Frankfurt (1848).

SAX, Antoine-Joseph-Adolphe (1814–94). One of the most important instrument makers of his time. At his workshop in Paris he developed the bass clarinet, cylinder trumpet, saxophone, and various other brass instruments.

SAXONY, king of. See **FRIEDRICH AUGUST**.

SAYN UND WITTGENSTEIN, Jeanne Elisabeth Carolyne, princess (née Iwanowska) (1819–87). Polish-Russian aristocrat. Liszt's longtime companion from 1847, when they met in Kiev.

SAYN UND WITTGENSTEIN, Wilhelm, Graf von Stollberg-Wernigerode (1770–1851). Minister of the royal household in Berlin.

SBIGOLI (d. 1822). Italian tenor who sang at the Pergola in Florence and the Argentina in Rome. Mentioned by Louis Spohr in his memoirs.

SCHACHNER, Rudolph Joseph (1821–96). German pianist and composer. Pupil of J. B. Cramer. After appearing in Paris, Leipzig, Berlin, and Munich, went to London (1853) as a teacher. Later moved to Vienna. Composed two piano concertos and a number of pieces for solo piano.

SCHADEN, Johann Nepomuk Adolf von (b. 1791). Bavarian soldier and writer. As a lieutenant he fought in Greece. Then lived in Munich, Stuttgart, and Dresden, writing several books, among them *Lebensgemälde üppig gekrönter Frauen* (1821) in collaboration with J. von Voss.

SCHÄFER (= SCHEFFER), Ary (1795–1858). Dutch artist who lived in Paris.

SCHÄTZELL, Pauline von (b. 1812). German singer. Member of the Berlin Court Opera (1828–32).

SCHÄTZLER, Johann Lorenz, Freiherr von (1762–1826). German banker. Founded his own bank (1800); financial councillor and chairman of the Board of Trade because of his financial advances to Bavaria (1811); then deputy at the Assembly of the Estates (1819). Noted for his philanthropic work.

SCHEBEST, Anna (Agnes) (1813–69). Austrian mezzo-soprano. Studied in Dresden and sang there. Appeared as guest artist on all the big German stages from 1836. Her career ended in 1841 with her marriage to the theologian D. F. Strauss.

SCHECHNER-WAAGEN, Nanette (1806–1860). German singer. Soprano in Vienna (1825), Berlin (1827), Munich (1827).

SCHELBE, Johann Nepomuk (1789–1837). German singer, conductor, and composer. Studied with Weisse, Vogler, and Krebs. Worked in Vienna (1813–16). Founded the Cäcilienverein in Frankfurt (1818). His teaching methods were much admired.

SCHELLING, Friedrich Wilhelm Joseph von (1775–1854). German philosopher. Secretary-general of the Academy in Munich (1806) where he met Meyerbeer in 1812.

SCHEMENAUER, Joseph. Theater director in Augsburg.

SCHENCK, Eduard von (1788–1841). Bavarian statesman. Minister of the interior (1828–32). Wrote many plays and was a close friend of Michael Beer, whose collected works, life, and correspondence he published in 1835.

SCHENK, Johann Baptiste (1753–1836). Austrian composer. Studied with Wagenseil in Vienna. Wrote sacred music and operas. Beethoven took surreptitious lessons from him. His most popular work was *Der Dorfbarbier* (1796).

SCHICK, Friedrich (b. 1794). Prussian musician. Clarinetist, later oboist in the Kaiser Alexander Regiment, and music director.

SCHIKANEDER, Emanuel Johann (1751–1812). German impresario, singer, actor, and playwright. His early life was spent as a wandering musician. Reached Vienna where he became manager of the Kärntnertor-Theater (1786). Directed the theater at Regensburg before returning to Vienna to manage the small Theater auf der Wieden, for which he wrote *Die Zauberflöte* for Mozart (30 September 1791). Directed the new Theater an der Wien (1800–1806). Other composers who set his fifty-eight *Singspiele* were Schach, Süssmayr, Paisiello, Seyfried, Weigl, and Winter.

SCHILLER, Johann Christoph Friedrich von (1759–1805). German playwright, poet, and historian, the foremost dramatist of German classicism. The fundamental theme of his dramatic, aesthetic, and philosophical writing is a passionate concern for freedom. His idealistic plays enjoyed great popularity throughout the nineteenth century. Meyerbeer wrote music for the celebration of his centenary in Paris.

SCHILLING, Dr. Gustav (1803–81). German essayist, director of the Stoepel Music School in Stuttgart. Editor of the *Jahrbuch des deutschen Nationalvereins für Musik und ihre Wissenschaft* (1839–42) and publisher of an *Encyclopädie der gesammten musikalischen Wissenschaften* (1835–38, 6 vols.).

SCHIMON, Adolph (1820–87). Austrian composer and singing teacher. Studied at the Paris Conservatoire, studied the Italian method of singing in Florence. Worked at Her Majesty's Theatre in London (1850–52), then at the Italian Opera in Paris. Professor of singing at the Leipzig Conservatoire (1874–77) and in Munich (1877–86). Meyerbeer was probably helpful in having his study accepted by the Paris Conservatoire. Composed two operas, chamber music, and songs.

SCHINDELMEISSER, Ludwig (1811–64). German composer. Conducted opera in Salzburg, Innsbruck, Graz, Berlin, Budapest and Darmstadt. Wrote seven operas, oratorios, concertos, sonatas, songs, and the overture *Uriel Acosta*.

SCHINDLER, Anton Felix (1795–1864). German writer. Close friend of Beethoven, and wrote a famous biography of the composer (1840), based on invaluable conversation and sketchbooks. After his death, a vast amount of papers and personal notes on Beethoven passed to the Royal Library in Berlin.

SCHLADEBACH, Julius (1810–72). German physiologist and musician known for *Die Bildung der menschlichen Stimme zum Gesang* (1860). Wrote the critical essay *Meyerbeers Prophet (unter besonderer Berücksichtigung der Dresdener Aufführung)* (Dresden, 1850).

SCHLEGEL, August Wilhelm (1767–1845). German author and academic. Literary critic, historian, and theoretician. Leading figure of the romantic movement with his brother Friedrich. Professor in Bonn. Famous for his translation of Shakespeare with Tieck.

SCHLESINGER, Carl (1808–31). Son of the Berlin music publisher, Maurice Adolphe Schlesinger.

SCHLESINGER, Heinrich. Music publisher in Berlin.

SCHLESINGER, Liebmann Salomon (1792–1850). German bookseller. Married the widow of the Berlin engraver Julius Samuel Zülzer (1831) and later established his own book and art business.

SCHLESINGER, Maurice-Adolphe (Moritz) (1798–1871). Music publisher in Paris, where he brought out the piano music of Beethoven, Weber, and Hummel, and the vocal scores of the Mozart operas. Published the French version of *Margherita d'Anjou* as well as *Robert le Diable* and *Les Huguenots*. Founded the *Gazette musicale de Paris* (1834), which was amalgamated with the *Revue musicale* the following year. In 1846 he sold his firm to Gemmy & Louis Brandus and retired to Baden.

SCHLETT, Joseph (1763–1836). Bavarian musician, writer, and courtier. Studied singing and organ in Wesserburg, philosophy at the University of Ingolstadt. Was in change of training the pages at the Munich court. Published compositions and historical writings, especially Rousseau's letters relating to music.

SCHLICHTGEROLL, Adolf von (1765–1822). German scholar. General secretary of the Academy of Sciences and director of the Court Library in Munich. Published the *Nekrolog der Deutschen* (1790–1806, 28 vols.).

SCHLÖSSER, Louis (1800–1886). German composer. Pupil of Salieri, Spohr, Kreutzer at the Paris Conservatoire. Kapellmeister at Darmstadt. Wrote operas, symphonies, ballets, chamber music, songs.

SCHLOTTMANN, Louis (1826–1905). German pianist and composer. Studied with Taubert and Dehn. Gave successful concerts in London and elsewhere, and settled in Berlin as a teacher. Wrote orchestral, chamber and instrumental works and songs.

SCHMALZ, Amalie Auguste (1771–1848). German actress and singer in Berlin.

SCHMIDT, Dr. August (1808–91). Austrian musician and journalist. Editor of the *Allgemeine Wiener Musikzeitung* and the pocketbook *Orpheus*, writer on music and founder of the Wiener Männergesangverein.

SCHMIDT, Elise (b. 1824). German dramatist.

SCHMIDT, Gustav (1816–82). German conductor and composer. Conducted in Frankfurt, where he produced his operas *Prinz Eugen* (1845) and *Die Weiber von Weinsberg* (1858). Wrote songs, ballads, choruses.

SCHMITT, Aloys (1788–1866). German pianist and teacher. Son of a cantor; also studied with Andrée in Offenbach. Settled in Frankfurt (1816), where he remained except for a few years in Berlin and Hanover. He wrote four operas, two oratorios, church music, and piano works (concertos, instrumental and solo, as well as a method).

SCHNEIDER, Friedrich Johann (1786–1853). German composer and organist. Studied at Leipzig University, and with Ungher at Zittau. Organist of the Thomaskirche (1812), music director of the city theater (1817). Kapellmeister in Dessau (1821). The oratorio *Das Weltgericht* (1829) made him famous. Founded a celebrated school of music (1829–54). Wrote oratorios, masses, operas, symphonies, concertos, chamber music.

SCHNEIDER, Johann Julius (1805–85). German musician. Pupil of A. W. Bach and B. Klein, among others. Organist and cantor of the Friedrichsweder Church (1829), where he organized a choir (1852). Singing teacher at the Municipal Industrial School (1835–58). Teacher of organ, singing and composition at the Royal Institute for Church Music (1854). Royal music director and member of the Academy of Arts. Wrote mainly church music and choruses (over two hundred). His opera *Orlando* was first performed in Schwerin.

SCHNEIDER, Louis (1805–78). Prussian actor. Worked in the Royal Theater in Berlin. Also appeared in opera and wrote the music for many vaudevilles. Later regisseur at the Comic Opera, royal *Hofrat,* and reader to the king.

SCHNEIDER, Wilhelm (1781–1811). German musician. Pianist, organist, and composer in Berlin.

SCHNEITZHÖFFER, Jean-Madeleine (1785–1852). French musician. Professor of choral singing at the Conservatoire. Composed the first full-length romantic ballet, *La Sylphide* (1832).

SCHNORR VON CAROLSFELD, Ludwig (1836–65). German tenor, son of the painter Julius. Studied Dresden, Leipzig, and Karlsruhe, where he made his début (1853). Wiesbaden, Frankfurt, Mainz, Düsseldorf, and finally Munich (1860–65). Created Tristan.

SCHNORR VON CAROLSFELD, Malwina (née Garrigues) (1832–1904). Danish soprano, wife of Ludwig. Sang opposite her husband. Created Isolde. Sang in Hamburg and Karlsruhe, then taught.

SCHNYDER VON WARTENSEE, Xaver (1786–1868). German composer. Studied in Vienna with Kienlen. Teacher and writer on music in Frankfurt (1817). Composed vocal works and wrote for the *Cäcilie* and *Allgemeine Musikzeitung.*

SCHOBERLECHNER, Franz (1797–1843). Austrian pianist and composer. Studied with Hummel and E. A. Förster in Vienna. Toured Italy as a concert pianist (1814), writing two operas and becoming *maestro di capella* to the duchess of Lucca. Returned to Vienna (1820), where he wrote another opera. Toured Russia (1823), then Italy and Vienna, before settling in Florence (1831). Also wrote orchestral, chamber, and instrumental works (including a *Gran Fantasia sopra un tema nell'opera Margherita d'Anjou, del M. Meyerbeer* for piano [Leipzig, 1824]).

SCHOLZ, Bernard E. (1835–1916). German conductor and composer. Studied with Pauer and Dehn, taught in Munich. Kapellmeister in Hanover (1859–65), then led the Cherubini Society in Florence (1865–55) and the Breslau Orchestral Society (1871–82). Succeeded Raff as director of the Hoch Conservatoire in Frankfurt (1883–1908). Wrote operas (esp. *Der Trompeter von Säkkingen*, 1877), numerous orchestral, chamber and instrumental works.

SCHÖNBERGER-MARCONI, Marianne (1785–1882). Italian contralto. She possessed an extraordinarily wide range, and usually appeared in male roles (Tamino, Belmonte, Titus). Both Goethe and Weber praised her achievements. She married Lorenz Schönberger (1770–1847), the landscape and scene painter.

SCHÖNHOLZ, Ignaz von. Austrian journalist. Editor of the *Wiener allgemeine musikalische Zeitung* (1813), the continuation of the *Musikalische Zeitung für die oesterreichischen Staaten*.

SCHÖNLEIN, Prof. Johann Lukas (1793–1864). German doctor. Practiced in Berlin from 1839. Personal physician to the king, and the Meyerbeer family. Returned to his native Bamberg in 1859.

SCHOTT. The publishing company was founded by the three brothers **Johann Andreas** (1781–1840), **Johann Joseph** (1782–1855), and **Adam Joseph** (1794–1840). The son of the first, **Franz Philip** (1811–74), was also active in publishing.

SCHREIBER, Dr. Aloys Wilhelm (1763–1841). German poet and academic. Professor of aesthetics at the University of Heidelberg. Wrote lyrics and libretti.

SCHRÖDER-DEVRIENT, Wilhelmine (1804–60). Celebrated German soprano. Studied with her parents, then Mazatti. Debut Vienna (1821). Sang at the Dresden Court Opera (1823–68), where she created roles in Wagner's *Rienzi, Der fliegende Holländer*, and *Tannhäuser*. Her passionate acting compensated for certain vocal weaknesses.

SCHRÖTER, Christoph Gottlieb (1699–1782). German organist and theorist. Pupil of the Kreuzkirche, Dresden, and Lotti's music copyist. Traveled in Germany, Holland, England. Lectured on music at Jena University, organist at Linden and Nordhausen (1732). Wrote seven sets of church cantatas, orchestral and organ music.

SCHUBERT, Franz (1808–78). German composer and violinist. Son and pupil of Franz Anton Schubert. Joined the Royal Orchestra in Dresden (1823). Succeeded Lipinski as concertmaster (1861). Wrote numerous works for violin, esp. the famous *L'Abeille*.

SCHUCHT, Dr. Jean F. (1822–94). German music teacher and writer. Studied with Kassel and Wartensee at Frankfurt. Consultant for the *Neue Zeitschrift für Musik* in Leipzig (1868). Wrote *Meyerbeers Leben und Bildungsgang* (1869).

SCHULZ, Ferdinand (1821–97). German choral conductor and composer. Pupil of A. W. Bach and Dehn. Conducted the Cäcilienverein (1856). Wrote motets, chamber music, male choruses, piano music.

SCHULZ, Johann Abraham Peter (1747–1800). German composer and theorist. Princely kapellmeister in Rheinsberg (1780–87).

SCHULZE, Hedwig (1815–45). German singer at the Royal Court Opera in Berlin (1839–43), then engaged in Breslau.

SCHULZE, Dr. Johann (1786–1869). Prussian civil servant. Ministerial councillor (1818), director of the Department of Education (1849–59).

SCHUMANN, Robert Alexander (1810–56). German composer. Wrote most characteristically for the piano, but also expressively melancholy and tender songs, symphonies, and chamber works. Meyerbeer regarded Schumann as his most relentless opponent. Schumann's aversion to Meyerbeer dated from his notorious critique of *Les Huguenots* (1837), a polemic that fostered an almost traditional critical dismissal of the composer and has done great damage to Meyerbeer's reputation out of all proportion to its intrinsic critical worth. Meyerbeer was able to keep an open mind about Schumann's art. Like Mendelssohn, Schumann was fundamentally antagonistic to the dramatic expression of opera as art form.

SCHÜTZ, Heinrich (1585–1672). German composer. Standing at the parting of the ways between Palestrina and Bach, he was of central importance to German art in his application of the grand Italian choral style and the dramatico-monodic style of Monteverdi to the development of semidramatic church music; also the composer of the first German opera, *Daphne* (1627).

SCHWÄGERCHEN, Friedrich (b. 1775). German academic. Prof. of natural history at the University of Leipzig (1815)

SCHWANTHALER, Ludwig von (1802–48). German sculptor. Professor at the Munich Academy.

SCHWARZ, Carl Wilhelm Emanuel (1768–1838). German actor. Worked at the Stuttgart Court Theatre (1809) and in the same year moved to the Burgtheater in Vienna. He undertook several artistic tours, appearing as a guest actor in Berlin, Dresden, and Hamburg.

SCRIBE, Augustin-Eugène (1791–1861). French writer. After 1816 his productions became so popular that he established a kind of theater workshop, using numerous *collaborateurs* under his supervision. Alone and in collaboration, he produced over four hundred stage works: plays, vaudevilles, comedies, and dramas, and some one hundred libretti for the most famous composers of the time, most particularly Auber (thirty-eight) and Meyerbeer (six). He gave *opéra comique* a new strength and *grand opéra* a new style, direction, and prestige. He inherited the historical awareness of Jouy's libretti for Spontini, utilized the potential for elaborate staging, and was a master of novel effects. He thoroughly reworked all his sources, whether historical or literary, and frequently dealt with the clash of religious and political allegiances and orthodoxies. He gave grand opera a definitive form and exercised a potent influence on all librettists who came after him.

SCUDO, Pietro (Pierre Paul) (1806–64). French music critic. Played the clarinet in military bands, before turning to journalism and becoming a critic for the influential *Revue des deux Mondes*. Writer of considerable talent and reactionary views. Published his collected reviews. Died insane.

SECHTER, Simon (1788–1867). Austrian composer and teacher. Studied with Kozeluh and Hartmann. Organ instructor in the Institute for the Blind in Vienna (1810). Active as court organist, eventually professor of harmony and composition at the Vienna Conservatoire (1851). The excellence of his teaching won him a great reputation and he numbered many famous musicians among his pupils (like Thalberg, Henselt, Vieuxtemps). He was a master of counterpoint and wrote much church music.

SEDLNITSKY VON CHOLTIZ, Joseph, Graf von (1778–1855). Austrian civil servant. President of police and chief of censorship until 1848. Close confidant of Metternich, he provoked much dissatisfaction, even hatred, and was undoubtedly a contributory factor to the outbreak of revolution in Austria.

SEELIGMAN, Arnold E. Court banker in Munich. He was held in great respect and in 1815, in recognition for over forty years of service, he and his descendants were raised to the minor nobility with name of Freiherr von Eichthal.

SEGHERS, François-Jean-Baptiste (1801–81). Belgian violinist. Studied in Brussels with Genesse and at the Paris Conservatoire with Baillot. Founded the Société Sainte Cécile (1848) in Brussels and conducted it until 1854. His concerts of orchestral and choral works were famous, but declined after his death and were later dissolved.

SEIDELMANN, Eugen (1806–64). German musician. From 1830 kapellmeister in Breslau.

SEIDLER, Caroline (née Wranitzki) (c. 1790–1872). Singer at the Berlin Court Opera.

SEMET, Théophile-Aimé-Émile (1824–88). French composer. Studied with Halévy. Drummer at the Opéra. Wrote songs and four operas.

SEMLER, Franz Xaver (1772–1875). Violist and royal chamber musician in Berlin.

SEMPER, Gottfried (1803–79). German architect. Professor of the Bauakademie in Dresden (1834).

SENDTNER (= SENDNER), Jakob Ignaz (1784–1833). Bavarian journalist. Directed the *Münchener politische Zeitung*, the *Oberdeutsche allgemeine Literatur-Zeitung* (1810), and the *Gesellschaftsblatt für gebildete Stände* (1811-15). Later a university professor in Munich.

SENFF, Barthold Wilhelm (1815–1900). German publisher. Began printing *Signale für die musikalische Welt* in 1842, one of the most important German musical periodicals of the nineteenth century. Hans von Bülow was a contributor. Established his music publishing business in 1847.

SERDA, Jacques-Émile (1804–63). French singer. Engaged by the Opéra (1835). Created St. Bris in *Les Huguenots*.

SERVAIS, Adrien-François (1807–66). Belgian cellist. Studied at the Brussels Conservatoire, played in a theater orchestra there. Famous performer all over Europe, esp. in Russia. Professor at the Brussels Conservatoire (1848).

SESSI, Maria Teresa. Italian soprano. No relation to the famous Roman singers. She was trained in Vienna and Italy, made her début in Parma, and appeared in Vienna, London, Paris, Poland, Russia, and Italy (1805–37).

SEVESTE, Jules-Henri (d. 1854). French impresario. Director of the Théâtre Lyrique (1852–54). Also wrote some vaudevilles and libretti.

SEYFRIED, Ignaz Xaver, Ritter von (1776–1841). Austrian composer. Close friend of Mozart and took lessons from him, as well as from Kozeluh, Haydn, and Albrechtsberger. Conducted at Schikaneder's theater in Vienna, then at the new Theater an der Wien at its opening (1801–27). A prolific composer, some *Singspiele* were very successful, esp. *Die Ochsenmühle* (1823), based on Haydn's music. Wrote melodramas, ballets, oratorios, motets, symphonies, and quartets. Edited theoretical works by Beethoven and Albrechtsberger.

SHAKESPEARE, William (1564–1616). English playwright, poet, and actor, the greatest of English writers and a universal genius. His poetry and plays have a unique density and richness of language, and treat recurrent themes of love, ecstasy and despair, lust, ambition, implacable time and mutability, separation, betrayal, fame, and death. His perennial appeal is attested to by the number of his plays Meyerbeer attended all over Europe throughout his life.

SHERIDAN, Richard Brinsley Butler (1751–1816). Irish writer and parliamentary orator. Joint owner of the Drury Lane Theatre. Received high civil positions under Fox and Pitt and wrote many comedies, notably the masterpieces *The Rivals* (1775) and *The School for Scandal* (1777).

SILCHER, Friedrich (1789–1860). German composer. Studied with his father and the organist Auerleben. Lived in Stuttgart, then in Tübingen (1817) as music director at the

University. He was an influential promoter of German popular singing, and published several collections of German folk songs, among which he included his own. His song *Lorelei* (a setting of Heine's poem) became so popular as to be thought a folk song.

SILLEM, Hermann. Banker in London; financial broker for Meyerbeer.

SINA, Georg Simon (1782–1856). Viennese wholesale merchant later elevated to the minor nobility for his public services. Financially superseded by the Rothschilds.

SINGER, Edmund (1830–1912). Hungarian violinist. Studied Budapest, Paris Conservatoire. Concertmaster in Weimar (1853–61); professor at the Stuttgart Conservatoire. Wrote a number of attractive violin pieces and cadenzas for the Beethoven and Brahms concertos. He edited études by Rode, Kreutzer, and others. With M. Seifiz compiled the *Grosse theoretisch-praktische Violinschule* (1884, 2 vols.).

SIRAUDIN, Paul (1812–83). French dramatist. Among the most inexhaustible providers for the Parisian stage. Collaborated with many authors in all dramatic forms.

SIVORI, Ernesto Camillo (1815–94). Italian violinist. Child prodigy, pupil of Paganini and Costa. Caused a sensation in London and Paris (1827). At the age of sixteen embarked on a grand concert tour through Austria, Germany, Russia; later North and South America (1846–50). His playing was of incredible virtuosity and modeled on Paganini. Composed two violin concertos, fantasias on operas, characteristic pieces.

SKROUP, Franz (Frantisek) (1801–62). German composer and conductor. Studied law in Prague and sang in a chorus. Became kapellmeister in the Bohemian Theatre in Prague (1827–57). Staged several Wagner operas for the first time, was an outstanding member of the nationalist movement, and wrote a number of operas to Czech libretti. In 1860 he directed the German opera troupe in Rotterdam for two seasons. Also wrote chamber music and songs, one of which, *Kde domov muj,* became the Czech national anthem.

SMART, Sir George (1776–1867). English organist and conductor. Chorister at the Royal Chapel. Knighted in 1811. Original member of the Philharmonic Society and conducted its concerts (1813–44). Edited and published various collections of music.

SOBOLEWSKI, Eduard de (1808–72). German, later American, composer. Pupil of Weber in Dresden. Opera conductor in Königsberg and Bremen. In 1859 he emigrated to the United States, where he organized a symphony orchestra in St. Louis.

SOLGER, Reinhard (1817–66). German writer. Emigrated to America (1848). In Germany known for his novel *Anton in Amerika* (1862).

SOLIVA, Carlo E. (1792–1853). Italian composer. Studied at the Milan Conservatoire. Wrote several operas from 1816, before becoming professor of singing at the Warsaw Conservatoire (1821). Kapellmeister in St. Petersburg (1832) and professor of singing at the Imperial Theatre School. Returned to Italy (1841) and eventually settled in Paris.

SÖMMERING, Samuel Thomas von (1755–1830). German doctor and scientist. Professor of anatomy. Worked in Cassel, Mainz, Frankfurt, and Munich. From 1805 he was a member of the Munich Academy and royal physician. Returned to Frankfurt (1820). Also concerned himself with other scientific matters and constructed the electric telegraph (1809).

SONTAG, Henriette (1806–54). German soprano. Studied Prague, début there (1821). Pursued a brilliant career in the 1820s. Created the title role in *Euryanthe* (1823). Married Count Rossi. Returned to the stage after 1848. Her execution was said to have surpassed that of any other singer of her time, and her clear, bright voice was used with taste and charm.

SOR, Fernando (1778–1839). Spanish composer and guitarist. Studied at the school of the monastery of Monserrat. Wrote an opera, *Telemaco nella isola di Calypso* (1797). Distinguished himself in Napoleon's army, later fleeing to Paris (1813). Met Cherubini and Méhul, who encouraged him to appear as a guitarist. Produced two ballets, *Cendrillon* (1823) and *Le Sicilien* (1827). Went to London and Russia (1825). Settled in Paris (1828). While his opera and ballets enjoyed little success, he wrote outstandingly for the guitar (he was called "the Beethoven of the guitar"), modeling his work on classical forms. Also wrote a guitar method.

SOUMET, Alexandre (1788–1843). French poet, librettist, and member of the Académie (1824). Wrote poems, epics, and verse dramas, e.g., *Saul* (1821), *Jeanne d'Arc* (1825), *Une Fête de Néron* (1830).

SPAZIER, Richard Otto (b. 1803). German writer. Lived in Paris as a journalist after he was obliged to leave Germany in 1833 for political reasons. Meyerbeer granted him monthly support of 500 fr.

SPECHT, Adolphe (d. 1874). French civil servant. Held a high post in the Parisian postal administration. Knight of the Légion d'Honneur. Contributed to the *Gazette de France* and the *Revue des deux Mondes*, and became director of the *Revue et Gazette musicale* (1840).

SPEYER, Wilhelm (1790–1878). German violinist and composer. Merchant in Frankfurt, where he helped to establish a great festival in 1838 and a Mozart Scholarship from the profits. He composed chamber music and numerous songs and choral works for men's voices, which won him great popularity, esp. "Der Trompeter" and "Die drei Liebchen."

SPEZIA, Mme. Italian soprano active in London and Milan in the 1850s, often in partnership with the tenor Giulini.

SPIEKER, Dr. Samuel Heinrich (1786–1858). German writer and royal librarian. Editor of the *Spenersche Zeitung*. Member of the Singakademie from 1807.

SPIESS, Christian Heinrich (1755–99). German playwright and novelist.

SPINA, Karl Anton. Companion of Diabelli.

SPINDLER, Karl (1796–1855). German actor, then novelist. He was a prolific writer who achieved success with his historical novels, like *Der Bastard* (1826), *Der Jude* (1827), and *Der Jesuit* (1829). Edited the pocketbook *Vergissmeinnicht*.

SPOHR, Louis (1784–1859). German composer and violinist. He was a major figure in the history of German romantic opera, esp. with *Faust* (1816) and *Jessonda* (1823). Music director at the Theater an der Wien and Frankfurt, then kapellmeister in Cassel from 1822. There he became *Generalmusikdirector* in 1847. Wrote extensively in all musical forms. He was a friend of Meyerbeer from the early Italian days. Wrote famous reminiscences (*Selbstbiographie* [Cassel, 1860–61]).

SPONTINI, Gaspare Luigi Pacifico (1774–1851). Italian composer. Studied in Naples. Took up Cimarosa's post in Naples (1800), before moving to Paris, where he made his name with *Milton* (1804) and began a collaboration with the librettist Étienne de Jouy. He selected features of Gluck, Cherubini, and Méhul, and put them to use in the operas written for Napoleon's Paris. They provided new models of structure and grandeur in operatic composition (*La Vestale,* 1807; *Fernand Cortez,* 1809; *Olympie,* 1819), and can be regarded as the founding works of French *grand opéra*. From 1820 to 1841 he was court composer and *Generalmusikdirector* to Friedrich Wilhelm III.

SPRINGER, Julius (1817–77). German publisher and city councillor.

STADLER, Maximilian (1748–1833). Austrian composer and organist. He was a Benedictine monk, and abbot of Lilienfeld (1786–96). Settled in Vienna (1796). He was a friend of Mozart. He took care of the manuscript of Mozart's *Requiem* when he died, and later defended the authenticity of the work (1825). He was a composer of oratorios, cantatas, church and organ music, and songs.

STAËL, Madame de (Anne Louise Germaine Necker, baronne de Staël-Holstein) (1766–1817). French woman of letters, who hosted one of the most brilliant political and intellectual salons of her time. Her most famous work was *De l'Allemagne* (1810). Because of her opposition to Napoleon, she lived mainly in exile.

STAINLEIN, Louis-Charles-Georges-Corneille, comte de (1819–67). Hungarian cellist and composer. In Germany and France he gave concerts of chamber music with Sivori, Ney, and others. Wrote chamber music and songs.

STAUDIGL, Joseph (1807–61). Famous Austria bass. Studied medicine, and then joined the chorus at the Vienna Court Opera. He established himself at the Theater an der Wien (1848–54). Sang in London (1841–43), Marcel in the first English *Les Huguenots* (1842), and Bertram in *Robert le Diable* (1847, with Jenny Lind). Sang widely in Europe.

STAWINSKY, Karl. German régisseur. Stage manager of the Royal Opera in Berlin.

STEGMEYER, Matthaeus (1771–1820). Viennese composer, writer and actor. His *Rochus Pumpernickel* (1809) was very popular.

STEIBELT, Daniel (1765–1823). German pianist and composer. Studied with Kirnberger. Gave concerts in Germany and Paris (1790), where he became a favorite teacher. Led an unsettled life of concert tours (Holland, London, Vienna). Achieved success in Paris as a composer of operas and ballets (1800–1808). Became kapellmeister at the court of Alexander I. Wrote operas, ballets, five piano concertos, much solo piano music, including his *Études,* op. 78 (1805), and a *Méthode de Piano*.

STEIGENTESCH, August Ernst, Freiherr von (1776–1826). German writer and soldier. Jouined the Austrian army (1789), eventually becoming adjutant general to Prince Schwarzenberg (1813). Military attaché at the Bundestag (1820). He became well-known through his comedies, poems, and stories, which were collected in his *Gesammelte Schriften* (1819, 15 vols.).

STENSCH (= STENZSCH), Karl (b. 1772). German actor. Trained by Schröder in Hamburg. Worked in Mannheim, and from 1799 at the Munich Hoftheater, where he usually assumed the principal male lead or lover.

STENSCH (= STENZSCH), Rosine (née Le Brun) (b. 1785). German singer-actress. Pupil of Franz Danzi and Streicher. Appeared in German opera as well as in straight theater, later court actress in Munich. Wife of the actor Karl Stensch. Their daughter married Peter von Lindpaintner in 1822.

STEPHAN, archduke of Austria (1817–67). Civil governor of Bohemia (1843–47). *Statthalter,* then *Palatin,* of Hungary. Retired in 1848.

STERN, Julius (1820–83). German conductor and teacher. Meyerbeer's recommendation to Friedrich Wilhelm IV secured him the means to study in Paris. On his return to Berlin, together with Kullak and A. B. Marx, he founded the Berlin Conservatoire (Sternsches Konservatorium) (1850).

STIEBER, Wilhelm (1818–82). Prussian civil servant. He was a lawyer and official in the police commission in Berlin; later, a member of the secret police and chief of Bismarck's secret service. It is conceivable that Wilhelm Beer provided him with information from artistic circles.

STIEGLITZ, Dr. Johann (Israel) (1767–1840). Personal physician to the king of Hanover (1802), considered one of Germany's most prominent doctors.

STIFTER, Adalbert (1805–68). Austrian poet and writer. Private tutor and school councillor in Upper Austria. He was deeply disturbed by the Revolution of 1848, and settled in Linz, where he became an official in the Ministry of Education. His unhappiness and illness terminated in suicide. Famous for his short fiction (*Studien* and *Bunte Steine*) and novels, esp. his bildungsroman *Die Nachsommer* (1857), which reflects his humanism, love of traditional values, and belief in the greatness of life.

STIGELLI, Giorgio (Georg Stiegele) (1815–68). German tenor. Made extensive concert tours in Europe, and appeared in America (1864–65). Composed many songs, including the popular "Die schönsten Augen."

STOEPEL, Dr. Franz David Christoph (1794–1836). German music pedagogue. Established music schools in Berlin, Potsdam, Erfurt, Frankfurt-an-der-Oder, and Paris, after the example of Logiers. They were not successful. Translated Cherubini's *Cours du Contrepoint*.

STOLL, Joseph Ludwig (1778–1815). German dramatist.

STOLLBERG-WERNIGERODE, Anton, Graf von (1785–1854). German civil servant. Lieutenant-general and Prussian minister.

STOLTZ, Rosine (Victorine Nöb) (1815–1903). French mezzo-soprano, member of the Opéra (1837–47), where she created several leading roles in Donizetti's works *(Les Martyrs, La Favorite, Dom Sébastien)*. She was praised for her intelligence, power of expression, and dramatic abilities, but her voice was found lacking in training. Her liaison with Léon Pillet gave her great, and often negative, influence at the Opéra during his directorship.

STORCH, Anton (1813–88). Austrian composer. Director of the Wiener Männergesangs-verein. Conductor at the Carl- and Josefstadt-Theaters, where he produced several of his operettas.

STRAUSS, Johann *(Vater)* (1804–49). Austrian violinist, conductor, and composer. He played in a quartet formed by Joseph Lanner, together with whom he founded the Viennese waltz tradition, a development from Schubert. He toured extensively with his own orchestra, and played in London during Queen Victoria's coronation festivities (1838). He composed numerous waltzes including the *Lorelei-Rheinklänge*, as well as the *Radetsky March* (1848) in honor of the field marshal. As a composer he was eclipsed by his son.

STRAUSS, Johann *(Sohn)* (1825–99). Austrian composer, violinist and conductor. Flouted his fathers wishes and appeared as a young conductor and composer (1844). He toured with his orchestra, visiting St. Petersburg every year, London (1869), and the United States (1872). He wrote some 365 waltzes, polkas, galops, and marches, the best known becoming a symbol of the old romantic Vienna (*The Blue Danube*, 1867). Also wrote thirteen operettas, notably *Die Fledermaus* (1874) and *Der Zigeunerbaron* (1885). Along with Suppé, he established the golden age of Viennese operetta.

STRODTMANN, Adolf (1829–79). German writer and publisher. Issued Heine's works in twenty-one volumes.

SUE, Eugène (1804–57). French author. Prolific writer of novels about the Parisian underworld, like *Les Mystères de Paris* (1842–43) and *Le Juif errant* (1844–45).

SULZER, Salomon (1804–90). Austrian music scholar. Studied with Seyfried. Cantor of the Jewish community in Vienna (1825), professor of singing at the Conservatoire (1844–47). Received the gold medal for arts and science, the Order of Franz Joseph (1868).

SUPPÉ, Franz von (Francesco Ezechiele Ermenegildo Suppe Demelli) (1819–95). Austrian composer. Studied with Ferrari and Cigala, then with Seyfried and Sechter. Conductor at the Josephstadt-Theater (1840–45) and Theater an der Wien (1845–62). From 1865, inspired by Offenbach, he began a long series of works that gave the Viennese operetta its classic form (esp. *Die schöne Galathea* [1865], *Fatinitza* [1876], and *Boccaccio* [1879]). He had the gift of melodic charm and deft characterization.

T

TAAFFE, Eduard Franz Josef, Graf von (1833–95). Eleventh viscount Taaffe and baron of Ballymore in the Irish peerage. Austrian statesman. His father was minister of justice under Ferdinand I, and he became minister of the interior (1867), chief minister (1869–70), and then prime minister of the "no-party" government under Franz Joseph (1879–93). He tried to conciliate the Slavs and force the German Austrians to live in unity with the other national groups.

TACCHINARDI, Niccolò (1772–1859). Italian tenor. Début Leghorn and Pisa (1804). Appeared with great success on many Italian stages, Paris Odéon (1818). Later appointed singer to the grand duke of Tuscany (1822). Undertook several concert tours to Spain, retired in 1831 and became a renowned teacher in Florence, among others of his daughter Fanny Persiani and Frezzolini.

TADOLINI, Eugenia (née Savonari) (1809–72). Italian singer. Studied with Favi and Grilli. Début Parma (1829). Paris (1830) with her husband Giovanni Tadolini. After her return to Italy (1834), she was regarded as one of the principal singers of the day, famed for her powers of improvisation.

TAGLIAFICO (orig. Dieudonné), **Joseph** (1821–1900). French bass-baritone of French descent. Studied in Paris with Lablache, début there (1844). Sang at Covent Garden every season until 1876. Stage manager (1877–82). Also sang regularly in Russia, France, and the United States. Music critic of *Le Ménestrel*.

TÄGLICHSBECK, Thomas (1799–1867). German composer and conductor. Kapellmeister to the prince of Hohenzollern-Hechingen (1827). After 1848 he worked in Löwenberg, Dresden, and Baden-Baden. One of his symphonies was performed at the Paris Conservatoire concerts (1836).

TAGLIONI, Filippo (1777–1871). Italian dancer, father of Marie and Paul. Ballet master and choreographer at the Opéra. Danced in Livorno, Florence, and Venice before going to Paris in 1799, where he studied with Coulon. Appointed dancer and ballet master in Stockholm (1803). Also worked in Cassel, Vienna, Munich, Milan, Turin, Stuttgart, Berlin, St. Petersburg, Warsaw, and Paris. Retired to Como. His artistry reached its peak in Paris, where he created the romantic ballet in *Robert le Diable* (1831) and *La Sylphide* (1832). He was admired as the father of a new style of gracious lightness, his ballets having a chaste purity and mystic quality.

TAGLIONI, Marie (1804–84). Italian dancer. Prima ballerina of the Paris Opéra (1827–32). Created the Abbess in *Robert le Diable* and the title role in *La Sylphide*. Later danced in Milan, Turin, Berlin, London, and St. Petersburg, where she was enormously popular (1837–42). Famous teacher and inspectress at the Opéra, where she initiated the system of examinations that still continues. She assisted in creating a new style, transforming dance on points into a poetry of physical etherealness.

TAGLIONI, Paul (Paulo) (1808–84). German dancer and choreographer. Brother of Marie. Début Stuttgart (1824). Settled in Berlin, where he became ballet master at the Royal Opera House (1839–83) and enjoyed great popularity. Mounted over forty ballets. Also worked at Her Majesty's Theatre in London (1847–57).

TAMBERLIK, Enrico (1820–89). Celebrated Italian tenor. Studied in Naples, Bologna, Milan. Début Rome (1837); Covent Garden (1850) and regularly until 1864; St. Petersburg (1850–63), Paris (1858–77). Possessed a strong, ringing voice (one of the first singers to use *ut de poitrine*). Sang lyrically and dramatically, with taste, and was noted for his good looks and acting ability.

TAMBURINI, Antonio (1800–1876). Italian baritone. Studied with Boni and Osidi. Début Cento (1818); Milan (1822, 1827–30), Naples (1824, 1828–32), London (1832–51), Paris (1832–54). His voice was rich and even, and he possessed a great coloratura technique and comic ability. He was a very handsome man and popular artist, and frequently appeared with Lablache. Created ten roles for Donizetti (incl. Malatesta in *Don Pasquale*) and three for Bellini (incl. Sir Richard in *I Puritani*), and was famous in roles by Mozart and Rossini.

TAUBERT, Karl Gottfried Wilhelm (1811–91). German composer. Pupil of Neidhardt. Taught music in Berlin. Assistant conductor of the Court Orchestra (1831); court kapellmeister (1845–70). Composer of operas, e.g., *Der Kirmes* (1832), over three hundred songs.

TAUWITZ, Eduard (1812–94). German composer. Kapellmeister in Vilna (1839), Riga (1840), Breslau (1843), Prague (1846–63). Wrote over a thousand compositions, including operas, chamber music, and songs.

TAUX, Alois. Austrian composer. First director of the Dommusik-Verein and the Mozarteum, founded in 1841 in Salzburg.

TAYLOR, Isidore-Justin-Severin, baron (1789–1879). French artist and civil servant. He was a copper engraver and lithographer. Became a royal commissioner of the Comédie Français, and then general inspector of fine arts.

TAYLOR, Tom (1817–80). English playwright. From the 1840s to the 1870s he supplied the theaters with a range of burlesques, farces, comedies, and historical plays, many of them adaptations. They made him one of the most famous of British Victorian dramatists. He was house writer to important London theaters like the Olympic and the Haymarket. Also a Fellow of Trinity College, Cambridge, and editor of *Punch*.

TEICHMANN, Johann Valentin (1791–1860). Prussian official. Secretary to the intendant-general of Royal Theatres in Berlin.

TEMPELTEY, Kurt Ernst Eduard (1832–1919). German dramatist.

THACKERAY, William Makepeace (1811–63). English novelist famous for *Vanity Fair* (1847–48) with its epic survey of society and satire of the futility of upper-class life. Contributed to *Fraser's Magazine* and *Punch*, and took over direction of the *Cornhill Magazine* (1860).

THALBERG, Sigismond (1812–71). Swiss pianist. Son of Prince Moritz Dietrichstein. Studied with Hummel and Sechter. Toured Germany. Settled in Paris (1835) as one of the most admired of virtuosi. In 1843 he married the widow of the painter Boucher. Eventually settled in Florence. Wrote several reminiscences on themes from Meyerbeer's operas.

THÉAULON DE LAMBERT, Marie-Emanuel-Guillaume-Marguerite (1787–1841). French dramatist and librettist.

THERESE, queen of Bavaria (1792–1854). Born princess of Sachsen-Hildburghausen.

THIERRY, Amadée (1797–1873). French historian and littérateur. Clerk of petitions in the Council of State (1838) and member of the Académie.

THOMAS, Charles-Louis-Ambroise (1811–96). French composer. Won the Prix de Rome (1832). He made major contributions to *opéra comique* (*Le Caïd*, 1849), *grand opéra* (*Hamlet*, 1868), and *opéra lyrique* (*Mignon*, 1866). Succeeded Spontini at the Académie des Beaux Arts (1852). Professor of composition at the Paris Conservatoire (1856), and then director (1871).

THOMAS, John (1826–1913). Welsh harpist. Entered the Royal Academy at fourteen. Studied the harp with Chatterton, and succeeded him as harpist to the queen (1872). Leader of the Eisteddfod festivals. Gave a series of concerts of Welsh music in London (1862–). Wrote two harp concertos, dramatic cantatas, collected Welsh melodies.

THOMAS À KEMPIS (Thomas Hemerkem) (1379–1471). Catholic spiritual writer, famous for *De Imitatione Christi*.

THÜMMEL, Moritz August von (1738–1817). German writer. Worked for the duchy of Coburg (1761–83), becoming a minister of state. Wrote comic stories in the mode of Wieland.

TIBALDI, Costanza (b. 1806). Italian singer. Daughter of the famous tenor Carlo Tibaldi. Studied with Bemnelli. Engaged by the Italian Opera in Dresden. Successor to Sontag at the Königstädter-Theater in Berlin (1827). Sang in London and Paris, where after a fiasco she retired. Admired in men's roles.

TICHATSCHEK, Joseph Aloys (1807–86). Celebrated Bohemian tenor. Member of the Dresden Court Opera (1838–72), where he created the title roles in *Rienzi* and *Tannhäuser*. He also sang Robert, Raoul, and John of Leyden. Meyerbeer wrote a special polonaise and arioso for him in *L'Étoile du Nord*. He was admired for his impassioned delivery, brilliant tone, and heroic presence.

TICHY, Kommerzienrat von. Austrian official in Vienna.

TIECK, Ludwig (1773–1853). German romantic poet, novelist, and dramatist. Part of the early romantic school at Jena, he lived as a man of letters in Dresden, Frankfurt-an-der-Oder, and Berlin. Helped to bridge the gap between the Enlightenment and romanticism. Collected medieval lyrics and translated Shakespeare, and was an important literary critic.

TIETJENS, Therese Johanna Alexandra (1831–77). Austrian singer. Studied in Hamburg and Vienna. Début in Hamburg (1848), member of the Vienna Court Opera (1856–58), then sang in London until her death. Her voice was powerful, rich, pure, and very flexible, and she was regarded as unsurpassed in her best roles.

TILLY, Johann Tserklaes, Graf (1559–1632). General of the Catholic League during the Thirty Years' War, in which he won several major battles before his defeat and death.

TITL, Anton Emil (1809–82). Austrian composer and conductor. Became kapellmeister at the Burgtheater in Vienna (1860). Wrote two operas, incidental music, a mass for eight voices, overtures and violin pieces, esp. the famous *Serenade*.

TOCHTERMANN, Philipp Jacob (1774–1833). German singer. Pupil of Danzi. Engaged in Munich (1799), becoming the leading tenor in German opera. Famous for his assumption of Simeon in *Joseph* and heroic roles. Later he worked as régisseur and director of the Munich Court Opera.

TOLBECQUE, Auguste-Joseph (1801–69). Belgian violinist. Worked at the Opéra from 1824.

TOLBECQUE, Jean-Baptiste-Joseph (1797–1869). Belgian violinist. Pupil of Kreutzer and Reicha. Played the violin at the Théâtre Italien, and became a successful conductor of the music for the court balls under Louis-Philippe. Wrote much dance music (waltzes, galops, quadrilles, including *Trois galops et valses sur des motifs de Robert le Diable*). In 1851 he staged his ballet *Vert-Vert* (in collaboration with Deldevez) at the Paris Opéra.

TÖLKEN, Ernst Heinrich (b. 1785). German scholar. Professor in Berlin (1816), secretary of the Academy of Arts, director of the collection of antique coins at the museum, and editor of the *Berliner Kunstblatt* (1828–29).

TOLLMANN, Johann (1775–1829). Violinist and music director in Basel.

TOLSTOY, Leo, count (1828–1910). Russian novelist and moral philosopher. Wrote the masterpieces *War and Peace* (1866–69) and *Anna Karenina* (1875–77). He was unsurpassed in his depiction of whole movements in European society and his analysis of man as a social being. Meyerbeer met him in Schwalbach in 1858.

TOMASCHEK, Johann Wenzel (Vaclav) (1774–1850). Bohemian composer of songs, symphonies, chamber and piano works.

TÖPFER, Friedrich (1790–1844). German cellist.

TÖPFER, Karl Friedrich Gustav (1792–1871). German playwright. He ran away from home to become an actor, studied at Göttingen University (1820–22), then settled in Hamburg where he contributed to various periodicals. He wrote a series of popular comedies, and some fiction. *Lustspiele* (1830–51, 7 vols.).

TÖRRING-CRONSFELD, Josef August, Graf von (1753–1826). Bavarian politician and writer. From 1773 worked for the Bavarian civil service. President of the Staatsrat, *Reichsrat,* minister of state (1817). He was a writer in his leisure time, and a chief representative of the *Ritterstück,* e.g., *Kaspar der Thorringer* and *Agnes Bernauerin.*

TOSI, Adelaide (1797–1859). Italian singer. Début at La Scala, Milan (1821). Performed widely in Italy, Madrid, and London.

TRAXEL, August (d. 1839). German journalist. Paris correspondence of the *Dresdener Abendzeitung.*

TREBELLI, Zélia (orig. Gloria Carolin Gillebert) (1834–92). French mezzo-soprano. Studied with Wartel. Début Madrid (1859). Appeared in Germany, London (1862, 1868–71, 1881–82, 1888), New York (1884). Admired in *travesti* roles. Married the tenor Alessandro Bettini.

TREITSCHKE, Georg Friedrich (1776–1842). German impresario and writer. He was the régisseur and theater poet of the Vienna Court Opera, and also directed the Theater an der Wien. He reworked the text of *Fidelio* for the 1814 revival.

TRENTO, Vittorio (1761–1833). Italian musician and impresario. Accompanist at various Venetian theaters, then an opera director in Amsterdam and Lisbon. Also wrote operas and ballet. Returned to Italy (1818).

TROUPENAS, Eugène (1799–1850). French publisher. First studied mathematics. Published many of Auber's operas.

TRUHN, Friedrich Hieronymus (1811–86). German composer and writer. Collaborated on the *Neue Zeitschrift für Musik*, later writing articles for the *Neue Berliner Musikzeitung* and the *Hamburger Korrespondent*.

TSCHIRSCH, Friedrich Wilhelm (1818–92). German musician. Pupil of the Royal Institute of Church Music in Berlin, music director at Liegnitz (1843–52), court conductor at Gera. Visited the United States (1869), where he produced many of his famous men's choruses. Also wrote salon pieces.

TUCZEK, Leopoldine Margarete. German soprano in Berlin, where she created Vielka in *Ein Feldlager in Schlesien*.

TULON, Jean Louis (1786–1865). French instrumentalist. Flautist in the orchestra of the Paris Opéra (1813).

TURCAS, Joseph-François-Chrysosthome (1788–1841). French military intendant. Son-in-law of Cherubini.

TUSCANY, grand duke of. See **LEOPOLDO II**.

U

UGALDE, Delphine (1829–1910). French soprano. Studied in Paris with Moreau-Santini. Début Opéra Comique (1848); sang there until 1853, then 1870–71; Théâtre Lyrique (1854–60). Her graceful virtuoso technique enabled her to create various roles by Massé, Thomas, and Adam.

UHLAND, Ludwig (1787–1862). German poet. Wrote ballads and romantic poetry with folk affinities. Also developed a deep interest in German medieval literature and legend. Leader of the Swabian school of romantic literature.

UMLAUFF, Ignaz (1746–96). Austrian composer, conductor and violist. Appointed kapellmeister of the newly opened National-Singspiel at the Burgtheater by Josef II and wrote the archetypical *Die Bergknappen* (1778) for the opening night. He was one of the founders of the Viennese *Singspiel,* which combined folk music with elements of Italian opera and the local theater tradition, and was able to mix humor with a strong sense of drama.

UMLAUFF, Michael (1781–1842). Austrian composer, conductor, and violinist. Son of Ignaz. Studied with his father and Weigl. Kapellmeister at the various Viennese Court Theaters. Composed three *Singspiele* and several ballets. Conducted the première of Beethoven's Ninth Symphony and the revival of *Fidelio* (1814).

UNGHER-SABATIER, Caroline (1803–77). Austrian mezzo-soprano. Studied in Vienna. Début there (1821). Sang in the first performance of Beethoven's *Missa Solemnis* and Ninth Symphony. Created many roles in operas by Donizetti, Bellini, Mercadante (1825–38). Sang in Prague, Vienna, Dresden (1839). Married the writer François Sabatier (1841). Continued to sing in concerts. Composed many songs.

URHAN, Chrétien (1790–1845). French musician. Solo violinist and violist in the orchestra of the Paris Opéra. Drew attention by playing the viola d'amore at historical concerts. Meyerbeer wrote the viola obbligato accompaniment to "Plus blanche" in act 1 of *Les Huguenots* for him.

V

VACCAI, Nicola (1790–1848). Italian composer and singer. Studied with Jannaconi and Paisiello. Produced his first opera in Naples (1815), experienced two failures in Venice, and then became a singing teacher. His *Giulietta e Romeo* (Milan, 1825) was a great success, and he went to Paris as a teacher and London as a composer. Returned to Italy (1836) and wrote further operas, which were appreciated for their understanding of the voice and melodic manner. Became professor of composition at the Milan Conservatoire. The penultimate scene of his *Giulietta* became famous as a substitute for the last scene in Bellini's *I Capuleti e i Montecchi*. His *Metodo practico di canto italiano per camera* (1833) is still respected.

VAERST, Friedrich Christian Eugen, Freiherr von (pseud. of Lelly) (1792–1855). German littérateur and director of the Breslau Stadttheater (1840–47).

VAEZ, Jean-Nicola-Gustave (1812–62). French writer and translator. Collaborated with Royer on Donizetti's *La Favorite* and the translation of Verdi's *I Lombardi* as *Jérusalem*.

VALENTIN, Nanette. French socialite. A native of Hamburg and sister-in-law of the banker Leo. The Valentin household in Paris was famous for its elegant balls and receptions, which were frequented by many famous artists and celebrities like Börne, Heine, and Humboldt. Although not highly educated, she was intelligent and witty.

VALLOTTI, Francesco Antonio (1697–1780). Italian theorist and composer. He was a Franciscan friar and a pupil of Calegari in Padua. He was *maestro di capella* at the Church of San Antonio (1728), and one of the foremost organists of his time. Published various works; his system is explained in *Le vera idea delle musicali numeriche signature* by L. A. Sabbatini, who was his pupil with the Abbé Vogler.

VANDERBURCH, Louis-Émile (1794–1862). French playwright. Worked in regular collaborations with other dramatists.

VAN GELDER, JULIAN. See **JULIAN**.

VARESI, Felice (1813–89). Italian baritone. Début in Varese (1834). Became a leading Verdi singer, and created Macbeth, Rigoletto, and Germont. London (1864).

VARNEY, Pierre-Joseph-Alphonse (1811–79). French composer. Studied with Reicha. Theater conductor in New Orleans (1840–50). Returned to Paris (1851). Composed a song to a poem by Roget de L'Isle, "Mourir pour la patrie," which became popular during the Paris Revolution of 1848. Father of the operetta composer Louis Varney.

VARNHAGEN VON ENSE, Karl August (1785–1858). Prussian diplomat and writer. Married **Rahel Levin,** the literary hostess (1814); their apartment in Berlin became the center of social and literary life. His literary works were overshadowed by his correspondence and diaries (1861–70, 14 vols.).

VATRY, Count. French deputy.

VAUDEMONT, Princess. Parisian socialite.

VAUTHROT, François-Eugène. French musician who arranged the piano version of *L'Africaine.*

VELLUTI, Giovanni Battista (1780–1861). The last great Italian castrato. Studied with Calpi and Mattei. Début Forlì (1800). Worked in Rome, Naples, Milan, Venice, Vienna, Munich, and London. Rossini wrote Arsace in *Aureliano in Palmira* (1813) for him. Created the title role of Armando in *Il Crociato in Egitto* (Venice, 1824). Appeared in this role in London (1825) opposite Malibran and Caradori. Directed the King's Theatre (1826) and returned to London (1829) for a series of concerts. His voice was said to be sweet and full, smoothly produced, but of little emotional range.

VENEDEY, Jacob (1805–71). German publicist. Editor of the *Bund der Geächteten* in Frankfurt. Member of the Frankfurt Parliament (1848), and lecturer in Zürich (1853).

VENZANO, Luigi (1814–78). Italian composer. Played the cello in the Carlo Felice Theatre in Genoa, taught at the Conservatoire there. Published many songs, esp. the *Valzer cantabile;* also, a ballet, an operetta, piano pieces, and vocal exercises.

VERDI, Giuseppe (1813–1901). The greatest Italian opera composer of the second half of the nineteenth century. He reinvested traditional Italian operatic models with his own unique mastery of vocal, orchestral, and dramatic resources. The triumphal progress of his operas is charted in Meyerbeer's diaries. He captured Italy's nationalistic yearnings with *Nabucco* (1842) and the youthful lyricism of *Ernani* (1844). The period of his greatest international successes began with *Rigoletto* (1851) and *Il Trovatore* (1853). *Les Vêpres siciliennes* was composed for Paris (1855) in the light of Meyerbeer's example. The two composers admired each other and were on friendly terms.

VÉRON, Dr. Louis-Désiré (1798–1867). French physician, impresario, and journalist. Manager of the Paris Opéra (1830–35), consolidating its position as the most successful and influential house in Europe. He founded the *Revue de Paris* (1829) and became the owner of *Le Constitutionnel* (1844). He published his *Mémoires d'un Bourgeois de Paris* (1853–55, 6 vols.).

VERROUST, Louis-Stanislas-Xavier (1814–63). French instrumentalist. Oboe virtuoso and first oboist at the Opéra. Professor at the Paris Conservatoire.

VERTPRÉ, Jenny (Françoise Fanny Vausgien) (1797–1865). French actress. Engaged at the Gymnase (1825–35), and also toured overseas.

VESPERMANN, Katherina (b. 1802). German singer from Munich. Pupil of Winter. Engaged by the Munich Court Opera, later by the Italian Opera in Paris. Retired prematurely because of illness. Married to the actor Vespermann.

VESQUE VON PÜTTLINGEN, Johann (pseud. J. Hoven) (1803–83). Austrian civil servant and composer. Head of the Department of Foreign Affairs in Vienna. Wrote five operas.

VESTRIS, Auguste (1760–1842). French dancer and teacher. Studied with his famous father, **Gaetano**. Soloist at the Paris Opéra (1776). Appeared with his father in London (1781). His extraordinary *élévation* and dazzling virtuosity made him the most famous dancer in Europe. Fled to London (1789), but returned to the Opéra, where he danced until 1816. He later became one of the most famous teachers of his day, counting Didelot, Perrot, Bournonville, and Marie Taglioni among his pupils.

VIARDOT, Louis (d. 1883). Director of the Théâtre Italien, then from 1841 impresario for his wife, Pauline Viardot-Garcia.

VIARDOT-GARCIA, Pauline (1821–1910). Celebrated mezzo-soprano, daughter of Manuel Garcia; one of the greatest and most influential singers in operatic history. Début in London (1839). Toured in Russia, Germany, and England. Returned to Paris in 1848. Because of her great intelligence and ability, Meyerbeer entrusted the creation of Fidès in *Le Prophète* to her; she sang the role more than two hundred times. Her assumption of Valentine was also very famous and in the tradition of her great dramatic interpretations.

VICTORIA, queen of the United Kingdom of Great Britain and Ireland (1819–1901). She loved opera, and command performances were a regular feature at Covent Garden and Windsor Castle. A devoted admirer of Meyerbeer's music, she regularly attended his operas, even sketching Mario in the role of John of Leyden.

VICTORIA, Tomás Luis de (Vittoria) (1549–1611). Spanish composer. With Palestrina, the greatest representative of the Roman polyphonic school.

VIEL-CASTREL, Louis de Salviac, baron (1800–1887). French politician. Director of the Ministry of Foreign Affairs (1849–51).

VIERLING, Georg (1820–1901). German organist and composer. Pupil of his father, Rinck, and Marx. Occupied various posts in Germany before settling in Berlin where he founded and conducted the Bach-Verein. Member of the Academy (1882). Wrote cantatas, orchestral and chamber works.

VIEUXTEMPS, Henri (1820–81). Belgian violinist and composer. Studied with his father, Bériot, Sechter, and Reicha. Undertook a European tour, composing music all the while. Professor at the St. Petersburg Conservatoire for five seasons. Then resumed touring (1853–). Professor at the Brussels Conservatoire (1871–73). Composed several violin concertos.

VIGANÒ, Salvatore (1769–1821). Italian ballet master. Son and pupil of Onorato Viganò. Also studied music with Boccherini and wrote many ballets, often with his own music. Regarded as the first ballet master of Italy. Also worked at the Kärntnertor-Theater in Vienna (1793–98, 1803–6), stimulating Beethoven to write *Die Geschöpfe des Prometheus* (1801) for his troupe.

VIGNY, Alfred-Victor, comte de (1797–1863). French romantic writer. His works explore the theme of the misfit who bears his loneliness with dignity, esp. the drama *Chatterton* (1835). The poet is a godlike outsider. His drama *La Maréchale d'Ancre* (1831) was adapted by Prati as the libretto *La Marescialla d'Ancre* for Alessandro Nini (1839).

VILBACH, Alphonse-Charles-Renaud de (1829–84). French composer. Studied with Lemoine and Halévy at the Paris Conservatoire, won the Prix de Rome (1844). Organist at St. Eugène's in Paris (1856). Wrote two operas, piano pieces, opera transcriptions, and a piano method.

VILLAIN DE SAINT-HILAIRE, Amable. French librettist. With Duport wrote an opera for Prévost (*Cosimo*) and, with Léon Pillet, *La Diadeste* for Godefroid.

VILLARET. French tenor, active at the Paris Opéra (1863–77).

VITET, Ludovic (1802–73). French writer and politician. Councillor, member of the Académie (1845), the Legislative Assembly (1849), and the National Assembly (1871).

VIVIER, Eugène-Léon (1817–1900). French horn virtuoso. Learned the violin, then the horn. Moved to Paris and was successful because of his connection with the French court. He was an eccentric and could play two notes simultaneously. Published pamphlets on music and theater, and an autobiography (largely fictitious), *La Vie et les Aventures d'un Corniste* (Paris, 1900).

VOGEL, Charles-Louis-Adolphe (1808–92). French violinist and composer. Studied at the Paris Conservatoire with Kreutzer and Reicha. Won popularity with "Les trois couleurs" during the July Revolution of 1830. Wrote a series of successful operas (1831–85), notably *Le Siège de Leyde* (The Hague, 1847), as well as symphonies, chamber music, sacred works, songs, and piano works.

VOGEL (= VOGL), Johann Michael (1768–1840). Austrian singer. Baritone at the Vienna Court Opera (1794–1822). He was particularly famous as a lieder singer; a friend and promoter of Franz Schubert.

VOGLER, Georg Joseph, abbé (1749–1814). German composer, theorist, pianist, and organist. Mastered the organ at an early age. Studied law and theology in Würzburg and Bamberg. Went to Mannheim and won the favor of the elector (1771). Studied in Bologna with Padre Martini and in Padua with Padre Vallotti. Director of the Court Orchestra in Darmstadt. Went to Rome, took holy orders (1773), and received several papal honors. He returned to Mannheim as court chaplain and second kapellmeister (1775) and founded the Mannheimer Tonschule for teaching his own method of composition. He followed the Electoral Court to Munich (1780), and then traveled to France, Spain, Portugal, England, and Denmark. He became court conductor in Stockholm (1786), where he worked intermittently until 1799, in between traveling to Russia, Poland, Greece, and the Near East. After brief sojourns in Copenhagen, Berlin, Prague, Vienna, and Munich, he settled in Darmstadt (1807) as court conductor to Grand Duke Ludwig of Hesse-Darmstadt. There he lived quietly and securely until his death. He established another *Tonschule,* finding his most congenial work in teaching. Teacher of Danzi, Weber, and Meyerbeer, as well as Gänsbacher, Stöchel, Winter, and Krauss. Wrote seven operas that had little success (esp. *Samori* for Vienna, 1804), ballets, sacred works (incl. a *Requiem,* his masterpiece), instrumental works, and many theoretical works, both in German (collected as *Mannheimer Tonschule*) and in Swedish (theory of harmony, piano and organ methods, through-bass).

VOGT, Gustav (1781–1870). French oboist and composer. Studied at the Paris Conservatoire. First oboist at the Opéra Comique, then at the Opéra (1814–34). Taught at the Conservatoire. Wrote four oboe concertos, duos for two oboes, music for military band.

VOLKERT, Franz (1767–1845). Austrian composer and organist. Active as an organist; became kapellmeister at the Leopoldstädter-Theater in Vienna (from 1821) where he produced over one hundred comic operas, *Singspiele,* melodramas, and farces, many of which enjoyed success. Also wrote church music, chamber music, and organ pieces.

VOLLWEILER, Karl (1813–48). German musician. Pupil of his father, Georg Vollweiler. Worked for several years as music teacher in St. Petersburg, then in Heidelberg. Wrote piano works.

W

WACHTEL, Theodor (1823–93). German tenor. Studied in Hamburg and Vienna with Eckardt. Début Hamburg (1847), Schwerin (1848–51), Berlin (1863–68), London (1862–

65), and the United States (1871–76). First London Vasco da Gama. Sang the title role in *Le Postillon de Lonjumeau* more than a thousand times.

WAGENER, Joachim Heinrich Wilhelm, Konsul. Berlin merchant. Bestowed on Friedrich Wilhelm IV his private collection of 262 paintings by Berlin and Düsseldorf painters, the foundation of the Berlin National Gallery.

WAGNER, Albert (1799–1874). German tenor and director. Brother of Richard Wagner, and father of the singer Johanna. Worked in Würzburg and Bamberg. Stage manager in Berlin.

WAGNER, Carl Jacob (1772–1822). German conductor and composer in Darmstadt.

WAGNER, Johanna (Jachmann-Wagner) (1826–94). Famous German soprano, niece of Richard Wagner. Created Elisabeth in *Tannhäuser* (1845). Appointed a *Kammersängerin* in Berlin (1853). Lost her singing voice for several years (1861), but performed as tragic actress.

WAGNER, Minna (née Planer) (1809–66). First wife of Richard Wagner.

WAGNER, Wilhelm Richard (1813–83). Brought the German romantic opera to its high point. He originally admired Meyerbeer's music and sought his protection. Meyerbeer provided financial support and references, and brought his influence to bear in having *Der fliegende Holländer* accepted for performance in Berlin. But Wagner turned against him (perhaps because Meyerbeer refused his further requests for money), and Wagner bitterly attacked him on aesthetic and racial grounds (in *Das Kunstwerk der Zukunft, Oper und Drama,* and *Das Judentum in der Musik*), all of which have had the most enduringly negative effects on Meyerbeer's artistic and personal reputation. The concept of the *Gesamtkunstwerk* was already fully achieved in French *grand opéra*, while even aspects of the Wagnerian music drama, ostensibly a rival concept to Meyerbeer's art, contains elements already developed in *grand opéra* (like the uses of leitmotif, arioso, melodic mosaic, or *ligne brisée* in the achievement of more continuous musical textures).

WAILLY, Léon de (1804–63). French writer and critic. Collaborated with Auguste Barbier on the libretto of Berlioz's *Benvenuto Cellini* (1838).

WALLACE, Vincent (1812–65). Irish composer. Studied with his father, W. S. Conran and Haydn Corri. Played in the Dublin Theatre Royal, then emigrated to Tasmania and became a traveling violin virtuoso. His many adventures took him to Mexico City and New York before he returned to England. The most famous of his six operas was *Maritana* (1845), which reflects French and Italian conventions and has a feeling for local color; it long enjoyed an international reputation.

WALLENSTEIN, Albrecht Wenzel Eusebius, Herzog von Friedland (1583–1634). German general. One of the major figures in the Thirty Years' War. Assassinated.

WALLERSTEIN, Anton (1813–92). German violinist and composer. Played in public as a child. Joined the Dresden Court Orchestra (1829–32), then worked in Hanover (1832–41). Wrote over three hundred dance compositions, violin pieces, and songs.

WALTER, Ignaz (1759–1822). German composer, singer, and impresario. Worked at the Burgtheater in Vienna and as part of the Grossmann Troupe in Hanover, eventually taking over its direction, and appearing with it in Frankfort-am-Main and Regensburg. He wrote many *Singspiele* and instrumental works.

WAPPERS, Gustav, baron (1803–74). Belgian artist. Director of the Academy in Antwerp (1840–53).

WAROT, Victor (1834–1906). Belgian tenor. Studied with his father and Alary. Début Paris (1858). Opéra (1861–68), Brussels (1868–74). Taught at the Paris Conservatoire (1888).

WARTEL, Pierre-François (1806–82). French tenor. Studied with Nourrit and Banderalli. Member of the ensemble of the Paris Opéra. Début as a *comprimario* (1831). Created Don Gasparo in *La Favorite* (1840). In 1843 he undertook concerts in Berlin and Vienna. In Berlin he gave a song recital. After leaving the stage, he taught in Paris—Christine Nilsson and Trebelli, among others.

WATZDORF, Bernhard von (1804–70). German civil servant. *Oberappelationsgerichtsrat* in Dresden. Minister of state in Saxe-Weimar (1843–69).

WEBER, Bernhard Anselm (1766–1821). German composer, conductor, and pianist. No relation to C. M. von Weber. Studied with Vogler. Conducted at Hanover (1787), then toured with Vogler. Became joint director of the Berlin National Theatre (1792), later first director (1796). Illness reduced his activity (1818), and he relinquished the post to Spontini (1820). Wrote operas, *Singspiele,* and melodramas. Was briefly Meyerbeer's teacher in composition.

WEBER, Carl Maria von (1786–1826). German composer, pianist, and conductor. The founding father of German romantic opera *(Der Freischütz, Euryanthe, Oberon)* was Meyerbeer's fellow pupil with the Abbé Vogler in Darmstadt (1811–12). The chivalric, folk, and fairy themes of his operas, as well as their melodic, orchestral and dramatic language, exercised a decisive influence on his successors. He was kapellmeister in Breslau (1804), Prague (1813–16), and Dresden (1816–26). Meyerbeer's stay in Italy and the success of his Italian operas caused a certain estrangement between the friends, in spite of Weber's friendly efforts in having *Emma di Resburgo* performed. After his premature death, Weber's family entrusted the completion of the sketches for the comic opera *Die drei Pintos* to Meyerbeer, a commitment he was unable to fulfill because of the rudimentary nature of the material. Gustav Mahler later used additions and other music by Weber, as well as composing some of the pieces himself (1888).

WEBER, Caroline (née Brandt) (1794–1852). Wife of Carl Maria von Weber. She engaged in long and ultimately fruitless negotiations with Meyerbeer over the completion of Weber's unfinished opera, *Die drei Pintos.*

WEBER, Gottfried (1779–1839). German composer and music theorist. Studied law at Heidelberg and Göttingen. Published the *Cäcilia, Zeitschrift für die musikalische Welt*, was one of the members of the *Harmonischer Verein*, and founded the Mannheim Conservatoire. Wrote the influential *Versuch einer geordneten Theorie der Tonsetzkunst* (1817–21; 3d ed. in 4 vols., 1830–32; pub. in English in Boston [1846] and London [1851]). Worked as a jurist and ducal district attorney of the state of Hesse (1832). Wrote religious music, chamber music, and part-songs.

WEBER, Johannes (1818–1902). French writer and Meyerbeer's Parisian secretary and biographer. Studied theology and music. Musical correspondent for the *Temps* (1861–95). Published his reminiscences of Meyerbeer (1898).

WEBER, Max Maria von (b. 1818). Son of the composer. Became an engineer, *K.K. Hofrat.* Wrote a famous biography of his father (Eng. translation, 2 vols., 1865). The younger son, **Alexander** (1825–44), became a painter.

WEHL, Feodor (1821–90). German dramatist.

WEICHSELBAUM. See **WEIXELBAUM.**

WEIGL, Joseph (1766–1846). Austrian composer. A godson of Haydn, he studied with Salieri and Albrechtsberger. Assistant conductor to Salieri at the Vienna Court Theatre (1790–1823). Wrote fourteen Italian and nineteen German operas, notably *La Principessa d'Amalfi* (1793) and *Die Schweizerfamilie* (1809). The latter was performed all over Europe until 1900. After 1825 he turned exclusively to church music.

WEIGL, Karl Christian Lebrecht (b. 1769). Saxon privy councillor. Worked in Dresden as a doctor.

WEIHRAUCH, August (1818–83). German dramatist.

WEILL, Alexander (Abraham) (1811–99). German journalist. Worked for Louis Blanc's *Revue de Progrès, La Presse*, and the *Gazette de France* (1848). Paris correspondent of the *Zeitung für die elegante Welt.* Met Meyerbeer in Frankfurt in 1837, where he was editing *Iris.* The connection was consolidated in Paris through their mutual friendship with Heine. Meyerbeer paid for Weil's lodgings in the rue du Croissant for two years, and Weil was able to render him services in the French press. He become one of Meyerbeer's confidants, even offering at one stage to become his secretary. Wrote several interesting biographical reminiscences, esp. the introduction to Meyerbeer's letters in his *Briefe hervorrangender verstorbener Männer Deutschlands an Alexander Weil* (Zürich, 1889).

WEIMAR, grand duke of. See **CARL FRIEDRICH**.

WEINMÜLLER (= WEINMILLER), Carl Friedrich (1764–1828). Austrian bass. One of the best dramatic singers in Vienna (1764–1828). He was the first Rocco in Beethoven's *Fidelio* (1814) and was in contact with Schubert.

WEISS, Gottfried (b. 1820). German singer.

WEISS, Julius (1814–55). German violinist. Published instructive works for the violin, musical criticism.

WEISSENTHURN, Johanna Franul von (1773–1845). German writer and actress. Worked at the Burgtheater in Vienna (1789–1842) and wrote many plays, particularly the popular sentimental family drama *(Familienrührstück)*.

WEITZMANN, Karl Friedrich (1808–80). German theorist and composer. Studied the violin with Henning, Klein, Spohr, and Hauptmann. Concertmaster in Riga (1832–34), Reval (1834–36), St. Petersburg (1836–46), London (1846–48), then settled in Berlin as a teacher of composition. He was an ardent disciple of Liszt and Wagner. An original thinker in harmonic theories, he made an investigation of the modulatory functions of the whole-tone scale and interested in Liszt in its use. Published many theoretical works, Wrote operas, piano works.

WEIXELBAUM, Georg (b. 1780). German tenor and violinist. Studied with Krebs in Stuttgart. Court singer in Munich (1805). Later worked in Darmstadt, Karlsruhe, and Mannheim, also as a composer.

WELLINGTON, duke of (Arthur Wellesley) (1769–1852). English soldier and statesman. Defeated Napoleon at Waterloo, and was prime minister (1828–30).

WENZEL, Ernst Ferdinand (1808–80). German pianist and writer on music. Studied philosophy, and music with Friedrich Wieck, a fellow pupil and friend of Schumann, and of Mendelssohn. Contributed to the *Neue Zeitschrift für Musik*. Taught piano at the Leipzig Conservatoire from its inception (1843) until his death.

WERNER, Zacharias (1768–1823). German writer and cleric. Became a Catholic (1811) and a priest in Aschaffenburg (1814) before going to Vienna, where he became famous as a preacher. As a poet and dramatist he was a prominent member of the romantic school.

WERTHER, Karl Ludwig (1809–61). German dramatist.

WERTHER, Wilhelm (1772–1859). Prussian civil servant. Royal privy councillor and Prussian ambassador in Paris (1824–37). Friend of Humboldt. After his return to Berlin, he became minister of foreign affairs.

WESSENBERG, Johann Philipp, Freiherr von West-Ampringen (1773–1858). Austrian official. Worked in the Austrian civil service from 1797 in Frankfurt, Berlin, Munich (1811). Concluded the treaty with Great Britain (1813). In later years headed the Gesamtministerium and the Department of Foreign Affairs.

WESTENHOLZ, Friedrich (1778–1840). German instrumentalist. Oboist of the Royal Orchestra in Berlin.

WESTMORLAND, countess of (Lady Priscilla Wellesley, countess of Mornington). With her husband, an ardent lover of music, and close friend of Meyerbeer.

WESTMORLAND, eleventh earl of (John Fane, Lord Burghersh) (1784–1859). English diplomat and musician. Studied music in Lisbon with Marcos Portugal (1809–12). Founded the Royal Academy of Music in London (1822). Served in the British Army in Spain and Egypt, became a general (1854). British Resident in Florence (1824–30), ambassador in Berlin (1841–51) and then in Vienna until 1854. He was a composer in his own right, *inter alia* of seven Italian operas (three produced in Florence), church music, a symphony, and piano music. A devoted friend of Meyerbeer.

WESTMORLAND, earl of (Francis Henry William Fane, Lord Burghersh) (1825–91). Son of the above, succeeded as twelfth earl.

WESTPHALEN, Christine (1758–1840). German poet. Her poems enjoyed great popularity. Andreas Romberg set some of them to music (1810).

WETTE, Wilhelm de (1780–1849). German Protestant theologian, professor in Heidelberg, Berlin, and Basel.

WHITAKER, J. (1776–1847). English composer of some fourteen stage works.

WICHMANN, Hermann (1824–1905). German composer. Son of the sculptor Ludwig. After a long sojourn in Italy, he returned to Bielefeld as conductor of the Musikverein (1857), and later settled in Berlin.

WICHMANN, Ludwig Wilhelm (1786–1859). German sculptor.

WIEBEKING, Karl Friedrich von (1762–1805). Bavarian privy councillor. Head of water, bridge, and street building, and much honored for his services.

WIECK, Friedrich (1785–1873). German music teacher. Father of Clara Schumann and Marie Wieck.

WIECK, Marie (1832–1916). German pianist. Daughter of Friedrich, sister of Clara. Début aged eleven. Court pianist to the prince of Hohenzollern (1856). Toured Germany, England, Scandinavia. Settled in Dresden as a teacher of piano and singing; professor

(1914). Published piano pieces and songs; reminiscences, entitled *Aus dem Kreise Wieck-Schumann* (1912).

WIELHORSKY, Joseph, count (1817–92). Russian musician, composer, pianist, and cellist. Studied in Berlin at the university and with Taubert. Brother of the cellist Matvey.

WIELHORSKY, Matvey Jurgevich, count (1794–1866). Russian cellist. His salon played an important role in the musical life of St. Petersburg.

WIEPRECHT, Wilhelm Friedrich (1802–72). Prussian military music director and composer. Meyerbeer set great store by his ability and expertise, and consulted him frequently in matters of military music. He further entrusted the orchestral arrangements of his *Fackeltänze* to him.

WIEST, Franz (1814–47). Austrian journalist and critic. Editor of *Das Rheinland* in Mainz (1839–42). Returned to Vienna (1843).

WIHL, Ludwig (1806–82). German writer. Lived in Paris (1837–38). and then in Hamburg, where he worked on the *Telegraph für Deutschland* together with Gutzkow. He belonged to Heine's circle.

WILDAUER, Mathilde. Austrian actress. Folk actress and singer of popular songs in Vienna. *K.K. Hofschauspielerin.*

WILHELM I, king of Württemberg (b. 1781, r. 1816–64). Meyerbeer dedicated the score of *Le Pardon de Ploërmel* to him.

WILHELM, Princess. See **AUGUSTA**, princess of Prussia.

WILHELM FRIEDRICH LUDWIG, prince of Prussia (1797–1888). Second son of Friedrich Wilhelm III. Became prince regent (1858), king of Prussia (1861), and emperor of Germany (1871). His reign saw the rise of Germany as a world power. Although often in disagreement with his prime minister, Bismarck, he usually followed the latter's policies. He and his wife were devoted supporters of Meyerbeer.

WILHELM, Guillaume Louis (Bocquillon) (1781–1842). French teacher. Music pedagogue at the Lycée Napoléon, general director of musical education in the primary schools of Paris, arranging singing instruction in all of them. Also established the workers' choral unions, the *orphéons*. Developed the method of *enseignement mutuel* and the principles of choral education.

WILLEM III, king of the Netherlands (b. 1817, r. 1849–90).

WILLISEN, Wilhelm, Freiherr von (1790–1879). Prussian general and military writer.

WILLMERS, Heinrich Rudolf (1821–78). German pianist. Studied with Hummel and Schneider. Toured Germany and Austria, and was acclaimed in Paris and London (1846–47). Wrote several brilliant piano solos.

WILSING, Daniel Friedrich Eduard (1809–93). German composer. Organist in Wesel (1829–34), then moved to Berlin. Composed an oratorio, *Jesus Christ* (1889); a *De Profundis;* piano sonatas; and songs.

WINKLER, Karl Gottlieb Theodor (1775–1856). German man of letters. Russian and Saxon court councillor, writer, deputy director of the Dresden Court Theatre, publisher of the Dresden *Abendzeitung*. His theater writing (e.g., the German translation of *Oberon*) appeared under the pseudonym "Theodor Hell." A close friend of Meyerbeer, his dealings with the composer were increased by his assumption of the guardianship of the children of C. M. von Weber.

WINTER, Peter von (1754–1825). German composer. Studied briefly with Vogler, whom he later disowned. Musical director in Mannheim and moved with the court to Munich (1778); kapellmeister (1798). Traveled widely to Naples, Venice, Paris (1791–1806). Composed forty operas based on Italian and French conventions; his most original work is in his *Singspiele,* notably *Das unterbrochene Opferfest* (1796), which contains romantic features and was performed throughout Germany. Also composed symphonies, concertos, chamber music, and sacred music.

WINTERHALTER, Franz Xaver (1805–73). German painter and lithographer. Court painter to Grand Duke Leopold of Baden, then to Queen Marie Amélie in Paris (1834). Painted many royal portraits, and became the fashionable artist of the day. Some of his work is in Versailles and in the British Royal Collection.

WITT, Johann (called von Doring) (1800–1863). Writer and adventurer who occasionally lived in Berlin.

WITTING, Karl (1823–1907). German violinist and composer. Studied in Paris with A. Reichel. Returned to Germany (1855) and lived in Berlin, Hamburg, and Glogau, and finally settled in Dresden (1865) as a teacher. Published a cello sonata and instructive pieces for the violin, as well as violin methods and a history of violin playing.

WOHLBRÜCK, Johann Gottfried (1770–1822). German actor and director working in Munich. Wrote the libretto for *Wirt und Gast.*

WOLFF. See **BEER, Wilhelm**. His original name, which he kept until 1818.

WOLFF, Édouard (1816–80). Polish pianist and composer. Studied at Warsaw with Zawadski and Elsner, with Würfel in Vienna. Settled in Paris (1835), an esteemed teacher and friend of Chopin. Imitated him in piano music (350 opus numbers); piano concerto, thirty duos with Bériot, eight more with Vieuxtemps. His sister Regina was the mother of Wieniawski.

WOLFSSOHN, Aron (1754–1835). German pedagogue. He was professor and director of the Wilhelmschule in Breslau. In 1807 he went to Berlin to tutor the Beer brothers. Published a Hebrew reader for the young in 1790. Later wrote several works on religious themes, and helped to publish the journal *Meassef*.

WOLZOGEN, Karoline von (née von Lengefeld) (1763–1847). German writer, sister-in-law of Schiller. *Schillers Leben* (1830, 2 vols.) is considered her chief work.

WORMS DE ROMILLY. French banker. Headed a large banking house in Paris which enjoyed particular prestige during the reign of Charles X. Later he was president of the Jewish Consistory in Paris.

WRANITSKY, Anton (1761–1820). Austrian composer. Brother of Paul and conductor at the Kärntnertor-Theater in Vienna.

WRANITSKY, Paul (1756–1808). Austrian composer. He was highly regarded in Vienna and held various court appointments. Haydn and Beethoven admired him as a conductor. He knew Mozart and belonged to the same Freemasons lodge. Wrote ten stage works, notably *Oberon, König der Elfen* (1789), the first important *Zauberoper* (fairy opera), which was performed throughout Germany and inspired Schikaneder to write *Der Zauberflöte*.

WULFF, Liepmann Meyer (1745–1812). Prussian banker, Meyerbeer's maternal grandfather. Manager of the Prussian postal delivery service, general concessionaire of the Prussian state lottery. Father of four daughters: Johanna [Mosson], Amalia [Beer], Seraphine [Ebers], and Henriette [Ebers].

Z

ZABEL, Albert Heinrich (1830–1910). German harpist and composer. Studied in Berlin. Toured Germany, Russia, England, America with Gungl's orchestra. Solo harpist at Royal Opera House Berlin (1848–51), Imperial Ballet at St. Petersburg (from 1854). Joined St. Petersburg Conservatoire (1862). Composed works for the harp, and wrote a harp method.

ZAHN, Wilhelm (b. 1800). German archaeologist. Professor of the Academy of Arts in Berlin. Leader of the excavations in Pompeii (1830).

ZELTER, Carl Friedrich (1758–1832). German composer. Close friend of Goethe. Director of the Berlin Singakademie (1800). Founded the Royal Institute for Sacred Music in Berlin (1822). Composer of songs and religious music, and teacher of Meyerbeer.

ZERR, Anna (b. 1822). Austrian singer. Pupil of Bordogni. Worked in Vienna from 1846. Later appointed a *Kammersängerin*.

ZEUNE, Johann August (1778–1853). German teacher. Professor of geography and pedagogy of the blind.

ZEUNER, Karl Traugott (1775–1841). German pianist and composer. Studied with Türk and Clementi. Gave concerts and taught in Paris, Vienna, St. Petersburg, and Dresden.

ZIEGLER, Friedrich Wilhelm (1760–1827). Austrian writer and actor. Appeared at the Vienna Hofburgtheater (1783), where he was a favorite of the Emperor Joseph II. His stage works (published in 13 vols.) were seen on all German stages and rated with those of Kotzebue and Iffland in popularity.

ZIMMERMANN, Mme. Berlin violinist, singer and teacher.

ZIMMERMANN, Pierre-Joseph-Guillaume (1785–1853). French composer and piano teacher. Studied at the Paris Conservatoire (1798) under Cherubini and Boieldieu. Professor at the Conservatoire (1816–48). Pupils included Alkan, Thomas, Franck. Wrote operas, piano works, and a complete method for the piano *(Encyclopédie du Pianiste)*.

ZINGARELLI, Niccolò Antonio (1752–1837). Italian composer. Studied in Naples with Fenaroli, Speranza, Anfossi, and Sacchini. His greatest triumphs were in Milan, where he wrote popular works at great speed. *Maestro di capella* in Milan, Loreto, and Rome (1804–11), where he composed comic operas. After being Napoleon's prisoner, he became director of the Royal Conservatoire in Naples (1812), and maestro at the cathedral kapellmeister (1816). He was the last great composer of *opera seria*, mostly on mythological subjects. He was a skillful orchestrator, and his tragic heroines were especially well drawn, as in *Giulietta e Romeo* (1796), his best-known work.

ZOTTMAYER, Ludwig. German bass. Sang at the Munich Opera, and created King Mark in *Tristan und Isolde.*

ZSCHIESCHE, August (1800–1876). German singer. Chorister at the Royal Court Theatre in Berlin, then sang as bass in Pest. Arrived as Wächter's successor at the Königstädter-Theater in Berlin (1826), soon moving to the Royal Theatre, where he worked until 1861. He was famous for his wide range.

ZSCHOKKE, Heinrich (1771–1848). German writer. Led a varied life as an actor, student, and pastor before settling in Switzerland, where he was involved in politics. He was a prolific writer in various genres. Known for his dramas and novels, esp. *Aballino, der grosse bandit* (1794). Also edited journals. He wrote a number of historical works and a popular devotional book, *Stunden der Andacht* (1809–16). *Schriften* (1825–28, 40 vols.).

ZUCHELLI (= ZUCCOLI), Carlo (1793–1879). Italian bass.

ZULEHNER, Georg Karl (1770–1841). German publisher and conductor. Taught composition in Mainz, where he was also member of the Academy of Science and Arts. Known especially as an arranger of operas and oratorios for piano.

Part I:
The Early Years and Italy
(1791–1826)

Meyer Beer aged 11 years. Oil Painting by Friedrich Georg Weitsch (1802). (Staatliches Institut für Musikforschung Preussicher Kulturbesitz, Berlin.)

Section 1
1791–1812

1791

[Birth on 5 September 1791[1] in Tasdorf, near Berlin, of Meyer Beer,[2] son of Juda (Jakob) Herz Beer* and Amalia (née Meyer Wulff)*, into a rich bourgeois family of the Jewish community in Berlin.[3] He was a child prodigy, a piano virtuoso who showed an astonishing skill at improvisation. He began his musical studies in Berlin with Lauska*, a pupil of Clementi*. Later that year, on 25 December, Eugène Augustin Scribe* was born in Paris, in a silk shop called the Chat Noir.]

1794

[Birth of Heinrich (Henoch) Beer*.]

1797

[Birth of Wilhelm (Wolff) Beer* on 4 January. He was to become a famous astronomer.[4]]

1800

[Birth of Michael Beer* on 19 August. He was to attain a certain fame as a dramatist in his short life, especially with the dramas *Klytämnestra* (1819), *Der Paria* (1823),[5] and *Struensee* (1829).[6] On 14 October Meyerbeer performed in a public concert, playing Mozart's Concerto in D Minor, K. 466, and variations by his teacher Lauska.[7]]

1810

[On 26 March Meyerbeer's first stage composition was produced at the Court Opera in Berlin: the ballet divertissement *Der Fischer und das Milchmädchen,* *oder Viel Lärm um einen Kuss (Le passage de la rivière, ou la femme jalouse)*, with scenario by I. E. Lauchery).[8] On 1 June Meyerbeer arrived in Darmstadt, accompanied by his personal tutor, Dr. Aron Wolfssohn*, to pursue his musical studies with the Abbé Georg Joseph Vogler*.[9] Carl Maria von Weber*, ten years his senior, was a fellow pupil and friend.[10] On 30 December, Meyerbeer, Weber, Gottfried Weber*, Johann Baptist Gänsbacher, and Alexander Dusch* founded a private musical association, the Harmonischer Verein.]

1811

[Meyerbeer's oratorio *Gott und Natur* was performed on 8 May in a concert at the Royal National Theatre in Berlin by the Singakademie.[11] The first of Meyerbeer's diaries, describing his life in Darmstadt, has been lost.[12]]

1812

April 1812

By the beginning of January it was already decided that Vogler and I should go to Munich. I therefore postponed starting the diary from day to day because I really wanted to begin it with the journey. The only problem was that this journey was also put off for a thousand reasons until 8 March (Sunday) when we at last left Darmstadt. We arrived in Würzburg on the evening of the ninth. Unfortunately I had to stay there for five weeks, because Vogler wished to hold three organ concerts that I very much wanted to attend.[13] The first concert was given only after five weeks. I had to be in Munich soon to try to stage a new opera, *Jephthas Gelübde* (which I completed on 6 April in Würzburg), so I decided to leave before Vogler.

The most interesting acquaintances that I made in Würzburg this time were: the landlady of the house where I lodged (Marktgasse no. 168, 2nd District), the widow of the banker Getschenberger, and her son Ludwig; Stempelmeister Marks (formerly a court tenor) and his son; Sturm, who has started to compose; Reichel, a court musician and brother-in-law of Professor Fröhlich; Liskmann; and, above all, the well-known theatrical poet and manager of the Würzburg Theatre, Franz von Holbein*, for whom I had a letter from the actor Blumauer* in Darmstadt. He most gallantly allowed me free entry to the theater and made available a box in the pit for me. On my leaving he asked me to send any new opera that I should complete to his theater, where he would immediately have it performed.

The Würzburg Theatre, however, is as yet in difficult circumstances (which is most understandable when one learns that Holbein undertook the enterprise only two months ago). None of the actors is above average, with the exception of Madame Renner*, who is quite outstanding in naive roles and who has long been acknowledged a supreme actress in this genre. If she had a little less individuality, even Madame [Unzel-?]mann would have to defer to her. Herr von Holbein is also a very gifted actor, except that his duties as director hardly allow him to tread the boards. In the Opera only Herr Bader* is noteworthy; nature has bestowed on him one of the most charming and resonant tenor voices I have ever heard. Unfortunately, he is lacking all musical and theatrical training. Madame Möller is tolerable. I saw there the following plays for the first time: *Alisbertha, Kriegerin der Indianer* [?], a chivalric drama in three acts by Theodor Hell*; *Der Urlaub* and *Der Verräter,*[14] two neat little plays by Holbein; *Die Proberollen*, a comedy in one act,[15] *Scherz und Ernst*, a musical quodlibet[16] in two acts; *Der Augenarzt,*[17] an opera in three acts by Holbein and Gyrowetz*; and *Die Dorfsängerinnen,*[18] an opera in two acts by Fioravanti*.

Among the other remarkable things I observed in Würzburg were the art collections of the two Patres [religious?], Bonavita and Blanc. That of the first brother, which he made himself from almost every imaginable material (plant seeds, animal wool, flowers, but no stones), is particularly noteworthy. What pleased me most were the depictions of the Rhine waterfall at Schaffhausen, a fire, and an eruption of Vesuvius.

Sunday 12 April. Early this morning we left Würzburg and arrived in Bamberg at six o'clock in the afternoon. Since I made this journey last year and wrote about it in my diary, I will say nothing about it now. In the evening at dinnertime we received a visit from Dr. Feist, a friend of Professor Wolfssohn. He is a charming young man (of the Jewish religion) and has a most prepossessing appearance.

Monday 13 April. Today we visited an institution for the terminally ill; the superintendant (a Catholic priest) is an acquaintance of the professor . The scrupulous cleanliness of every part of the establishment struck me very positively. Afterwards we went to the abbey on the Michaelsberg, a royal building that is now used as a general hospital. From the so-called viewing-room, one is able to enjoy a delightful perspective.[19] Our fellow guests at the table d'hôte today were the equerry to the king of Bavaria,[20] Oberst Stierle, the Bavarian Lieutenant von Stader, and a lottery inspector (the last two both acquaintances of the professor). After lunch the doctor fetched us for a walk to the little village of Bug. The route there is exceptionally romantic. In Bug we found several other guests, among them the present music director, E. T. A. Hoffmann*,[21] formerly Prussian war counselor (see last year's diary). Dr. Feist introduced me to him, and since, as he said, my name has been known to him for some time now, a lively musical discussion was soon underway. After an hour we went back to Bamberg over the hills, which again presented us with wonderful vistas.

Tuesday 14 April. At seven o'clock in the morning we set out for Nuremberg, where we arrived at six-thirty in the evening. For an account of the journey from

Bamberg to Nuremberg, as well as for Nuremberg itself, see last year's diary. We lodged in Bitterholz.

Wednesday 15 April. We walked in the city a little, and then went to Bestelmeier's famous art shop, where we lingered for a couple of hours. After lunch we went to Fürth[22] in order to see the charming Madame Königswarth (see my previous diary). She received us in the most friendly and cordial way, but when she heard that in a few hours I wanted to return to Nuremberg to see *Die Zauberin Sidonia,*[23] she was somewhat piqued. I was very sorry, but the opportunity of getting to know a strange theater is too important for me, even if it does mean forgoing the most delightful company. After a few hours I did indeed travel back to Nuremberg to the theater. The building is small, but fairly elegant. The décor is pretty, but in a wretched condition. The actors have a good sense of ensemble. I did not know the names of any of the actors who impressed me (nor of those who did not, for that matter). The visit on the whole was definitely worth our while.

Thursday 16 April. Called on Music Director Guhr* (see the previous diary) whom I did not find at home because he was rehearsing Méhul's* *Joseph*[24] in the theater. I looked him up there and arranged to visit him tomorrow, when we will play several of our compositions together. Afterwards I traveled to Fürth to see Madame Königswarth, and improvised on a theme from Gyrowetz's opera *Der Augenarzt* [see example 1]

Example 1. Theme from Gyrowetz's *Der Augenarzt*

and a few hours afterwards returned to Nuremberg in order to hear Méhul's wonderful opera *Joseph.* The orchestra played rather untidily, but with considerable energy in the powerful passages. On stage everything unfolded very precisely. Herr Bonhac as Joseph seemed the best to me. His tenor voice has timbre and considerable resonance. His acting (even if sometimes artificial) is always lively and entertaining. Moreover, he bears a passing resemblance[25] to Eunike. The arrangement of the table in act 3 surprised me most agreeably: all the vessels placed on it (vases, bowls, and drinking utensils) were transparent.

Friday 17 April. Visited Music Director Guhr. He played me the introduction and opening allegro of his new symphony. I found many brilliant features[26] in it, particularly very original modulations; one, however, from the *grave* of the symphony, is identical to a modulation in Spontini's* overture to *Die Vestalin*.[27] The whole is characterized by an eccentric youthfulness—exaggerated length, a confused structure, overladened instrumentation. His overture to *Deodata*[28] pleased me much more, even though it too has nearly all the negative characteristics just described. It nevertheless contains some really striking effects. What particularly struck me was a passage where the horns consistently play in fifths and octaves, and one is at a loss to know whether a major or minor resolution will result until the bassoon eventually enters in the major third. This passage is very impressive. The idea itself, though, is not new: Zelter* has already used it in his motet *Der Mensch lebt und besteht*. I then played him the overture to my opera *Jephthas Gelübde* and several choruses (no. 1 and no. 8) from my oratorio *Gott und Natur*.[29] Afterwards I returned to Fürth, where I spent a really pleasant social evening, and enjoyed a friendly supper with Herr von K. Today I also saw gold leaf beaten for the first time. I improvised on a theme from Weigl's* *Die Schweizerfamilie*[30] [see example 2].

Example 2. Theme from Weigl's *Die Schweizerfamilie*

Letter from Herr von Dusch in Mannheim.

Saturday 18 April. Called on Dr. Hechheimer, a jovially disposed septuagenarian, and also on Madame Heilbronn (sister of Madame Königswarth), a charming and intelligent woman. Intense toothache prevented me from making more visits this morning. At midday we dined with Herr Königswarth. After lunch I traveled to Nuremberg to take leave of Music Director Guhr and to return his score of Cherubini's* *Elisa*,[31] which he had lent me. Yesterday we amused ourselves as composers, today as pianists. He played me a *Capriccio* by Hummel* very beautifully, so much so that it could have been taken for a masterpiece if it were not so fragmentary, so long, and often rather eccentric. He particularly excels in passages that present the unusual combination of originality, flow, and brilliance. Moreover, since this piece is exceptionally heavy and so demands an excellent pianistic technique, I definitely want to buy it in Augsburg. Afterwards I played him the first allegro of my *Sonata in E-flat*.[32] Lastly, he shared some observations with me about a pianist whose name he unfortunately *forgot!*, who, according to his story, must surely be the first among all living pianists. Among other things, he played me a charming variation written by this mystery pianist that he knew by heart, and that, if it is played quickly and fluently, resembles a carillon. Afterwards I went to Bestelmeier's art shop to buy a pretty cage so that I can present Fanny Königswarth with her favorite bird (a canary). I bought it for twelve gulden. I then returned to Fürth, where I was invited today for a big tea party. There I quite unexpectedly found my old friend and playmate of my youth, Herr von Lämmel from Prague, with whom I used to share my innocent childhood games in Berlin ten years ago. We had heard nothing of each other in the interim, so our joy at this unexpected reunion[33] was all the greater. He was accompanied by his uncle, Herr von Lämmelsfeld. It was a lively gathering and lasted until midnight. I played J. B. Cramer's* *Variations* and improvised, both rather badly. I also made the acquaintance of the local chief of police (a charming young man), who invited me to call on him tomorrow afternoon.

Sunday 19 April. A warm farewell to Herr von Lämmel, who is returning to Prague, and who gave us a letter for Augsburg.

Monday 20 April. At six o'clock in the morning we departed and arrived at nine o'clock in Schwalbach, where we lingered a few hours in order to inspect the wire and needle factories there. Afterwards we traveled to Ellingen (which is less than halfway between Nuremberg and Augsburg) where we stayed overnight. The road from Nuremberg to Ellingen is amazingly gravelly, and the views very monotonous.

Tuesday 21 April. This morning at five o'clock we left Ellingen. From here on the view becomes more interesting all the time. The region is very built up, and one can see eight to nine villages at any one time. At midday we lunched at Donauwörth, and we stayed overnight at Mertingen, four hours from Augsburg.

Wednesday 22 April. We departed from Mertingen at six o'clock in the morning, and arrived in Augsburg at nine. I changed and went to deliver my letters of recommendation. I had seven of them, all to businessmen: two to Herren J. and G. W. von Halder (one from Schwendel in Frankfurt and one from Father), two for Herr von Schätzler* (one from Winkler in Leipzig and one from Schwendel), one to Herren Erzberger and Schmidt (from Schwägerchen* in Leipzig), one for Herr Johann Elias Meissner (ditto), one for Herr J. G. Süsskind (from Winkler). I first delivered those for Halder and Süsskind. I did not find Meissner at home. At midday I had lunch at the table d'hôte.[34] Some young women[35] there wounded me to the depths of my soul, spoiling my mood and cheerfulness for the rest of the day. When will I learn to accept peacefully what I have so long known to be inevitable?[36]

After lunch I went with the professor to Kriegshaber, a small village half an hour from Augsburg[37] where he had spent some of the early years of his boyhood. He found none of his acquaintances there, only houses he once knew well, but now occupied by strangers. Such occasions cause a flow of emotion even for the most dispassionate; so how much more so for me, whose depression paved the way for all kinds of sad intimations. Sick in body and soul, I returned to spend the rest of the evening languishing in dreary inactivity.

Thursday 23 April. Today I delivered my other letters of recommendation. All the recipients promised me letters for Italy, apart from Herr Meissner, who does not have acquaintances there. At Finanzrat Schätzler's I met only his manager, Bauer (Schätzler himself was ill); I arranged to write to him from Munich when I eventually need the Italian letters.[38] I came to the same agreement with Herr von Halder. Afterwards I went with the professor to the banker Seeligmann: we had a letter of recommendation for him from Herr von Lämmel. He received us like all the other merchant class—courteously, but coldly and obviously bored.[39] At our request he gave us a letter for his father in Munich.

Afterwards we saw the most remarkable hydraulic system: water is jetted upwards from its source, feet into the air, and, falling down with redoubled force, is channeled through other pipes to run under the whole city; in the event of fire, one need only open valves, which are to be found in each street, to have access to a full supply of water. After lunch we saw the city hall, which on account of its regularity, size, and beauty is recognized as one of Germany's best.[40] The famous Golden Hall did not have the imposing appearance I had expected, since it was hung with pictures that are being stored here temporarily. We inspected this collection of paintings, but were so rushed by Cicero[41] that I unfortunately could hardly take in anything. On returning we saw the three famous fountains decorated by statues of Augustus, Hercules, and Mercury (after old Roman originals).[42] The one of Augustus particularly pleased me because of its wonderful drapery and (what may perhaps sound strange) its outstretched hand, which in my opinion combines great dignity with peace.

Friday 24 April. Wrote to Father in Berlin. Afterwards we went to the cathedral,[43] notable for the many side chapels it contains (I counted twenty-four) and several beautiful paintings, among which the *Resurrection* by Mettenleiter[44] and the *Ascension* by Christoph Schwarz[45] (I believe) are very appealing. The light in the latter picture creates a special impression, in that the rays emanating from the Christ floating upwards radiate out and partially illumine the people standing below. Afterwards I visited the Ulrichskirche,[46] with its audaciously constructed dome, the tomb of St. Afra, the first Christian in Augsburg (A.D. 300).[47] We opened the tomb and found the skeleton still well preserved. The teeth were the loveliest I have ever seen.[48] The relic is covered in an apparently costly garment decorated in precious stones and other treasures, no doubt presents from the pious ladies of Augsburg. Before lunch we went to the Liebert Hall[49] with its adjoining rooms (a series of thirteen). The hall itself (white and filled with golden moldings and carvings, illumined by sixty-five wall brackets and chandeliers) is very imposing, but would be even more so if the windows were not so small. The building contains thirteen other front rooms, which take two minutes to traverse (at a moderate walking pace).

Called on the music publisher Gombart,[50] with whom I had earlier corresponded: a hearty, affectionate reception. I played Cramer's *Variations*. He asked me to provide him with a list of my compositions.

In the evening I attended the theater, where they mangled Mozart's *Don Juan*[51] so awfully that I left after act 1. Madame Röhl from the Breslau Theatre sang Donna Anna as guest artist. This fine singer (I have heard her much praised already) exceeded my expectations. What a pity that such a pearl should find herself in such a lamentable setting.

Saturday 25 April. At ten o'clock in the morning we left Augsburg for Munich. Our hotel in Augsburg, Die Goldene Traube,[52] was quite acceptable, and not too expensive. We arrived in Munich at nine o'clock in the evening. The route there is monotonous and unattractive. We are lodging in Der Goldener Hahn[53] (chez Albert): also good and not too dear.

Sunday 26 April. Walked through the city, which is not particularly large, but very beautiful, regularly laid out, and densely populated. I took good old Wohlbrück* by surprise: he was appointed a court actor here three months ago. Promenade in the Court Gardens. After lunch Wohlbrück took me to a wind band (a group who meet to practice). In the evening I attended the theater,[54] where they performed *Klara von Hoheneichen*[55] to a bad press. There was hardly an actor who was above average. The house itself with its four tiers of boxes seems antiquated and far too small for the Munich public. I wrote to Mother, and received letters from Wolff,[56] Bauscher in Frankfurt, and Mother and Kühnel* in Leipzig.

Monday 27 April. Answered Kühnel's letter, as well as writing to Herr von Dusch in Mannheim.

After lunch I had a long promenade in the English Garden, Count Rumford's* wonderfully extended park, where quite by chance I came upon the famous violinist Madame Larcher[57] from Paris, whom I have often met in Darmstadt. In the evening I attended a concert given by a violinist called Mazas* from the Paris Conservatoire. He plays as one would expect of any average student of the Conservatoire—purely and with color, but wildly and affectedly. The hall is small, but very brilliantly and pleasantly decorated. The lighting seemed a little excessive, which may well be because the chandeliers were hung too low. The orchestra performed the symphonies and overtures such as I had never before heard them: energy, precision, ensemble, crescendo, and pianissimo, everything at the highest level of accomplishment. This evening I encountered several acquaintances from other places: both the Schönbergers*,[58] the flautist Metzger*, Madame Larcher, and the singer Lohmeier, all of whom I have met in Darmstadt, and the banker Strassburger, whose acquaintance I made last year in Switzerland.[59] Schönberger introduced Baron Poissl* to me; he is a composer of Italian operas, and would appear to be a charming young man.

Tuesday 28 April. With Baron Poissl I visited my countryman, the clarinetist Baermann*.[60] There I found three letters from Herr von Weber and my mother. Afterwards, with the professor, I delivered a letter to the banker Marks. In the afternoon I walked in the English Garden with Poissl, Baermann, and the bassoonist Brandt.* In the evening to the theater, where they performed Iffland's* *Die Aussteuer,* which all the critics have found bad;[61] even Wohlbrück was not his usual outstanding self.[62]

Wednesday 29 April. At nine o'clock I attended the rehearsal of the Court Concert that was to take place in the evening: the famous violinist Polledro* played a concerto and variations of his own composition. After Rode* I have never heard such an accomplished performer. He has, moreover, invented his own genre. One cannot deny his composition at least the merit of attractiveness. There I made the acquaintance of the oboist Fladt*, the cellist Legrand*, and the concertmaster Moralt*. Afterwards I presented my letter of recommendation to Legationsrätin von Fladt, who invited me to tea tomorrow. On returning to my rooms I made the acquaintance of Polledro. After lunch I delivered my letter to the old banker Seeligmann*. In the evening I went to the theater to see *Die Jungfrau von Orleans.*[63] As usual, the actors were pathetic, apart from Demoiselle Altmutter*, who played the Maid and revealed a talent that promises much for the future. The décor was worthy of the famous Quaglio*.

Thursday 30 April. Various visits. Today I moved into private lodgings in the Max Joseph Platz, no. 20. In the evening to tea at Frau von Fladt's, where I played Vogler's *Variations on the Seraphiner March* with an addition that I composed early this morning. There I met Geheimrat von Aretin*, Herr von Lieberkind and his wife, Legationsrat von Fladt, and a certain Herr von Tauber.

May 1812

Friday 1 May. Early this morning I played through Baron von Poissl's Mass with him; it is written in a very dignified style. Some of the small changes that I proposed appeared to please[64] him greatly. Visit from Eduard Seeligmann, whom I knew in Hamburg. Afterwards I went to the rehearsal of *Die Sängerinnen auf dem Lande* [*Le Cantatrici villane*]. In the afternoon I called on Wohlbrück. In the evening to the theater, where they performed Fioravanti's opera fairly well. The principal singer, Madame Harlas* (formerly Frau von Geiger), has a wonderful, vibrant voice and great agility. Only her intonation is occasionally impure. The second singer, Madame Neumann, was not at all bad. The tenor, Herr Weichselbaum*, has an attractive (but weak) voice and method. In any case he appears more suited to singing romances than to dramatic roles. All the others were at least tolerable.

Saturday 2 May. Called on the banker Herr Pappenheimer*, but he was not at home. For the rest of the morning I practiced Vogler's *Seraphiner March* and Cramer's *Variations* with a different cadenza. At midday I had a wonderful meal with the old Seeligmann. After lunch I attended the rehearsal of Baron Poissl's Mass, which went badly. There I met the oboist Braun*[65] from the Copenhagen orchestra. Afterwards I went with Legrand, Baermann, Braun, and Poissl to the wind band in the gardens, and then to Baermann's, where we all supped[66] with great enjoyment with his lover and companion, Madame Harlas.

Sunday 3 May. Visit from Baron Poissl. I went with him and Wohlbrück to the Court Chapel, where his Mass was performed. In spite of the bad rehearsal yesterday, the performance today was successful. (There I found the young composer Konradin Kreutzer*, whom I knew in Darmstadt.) On the whole it created a very pleasant impression, but I mean only pleasant. Great intentions or effects are totally lacking (there is not a single striking moment). In the afternoon I went to Wohlbrück's, where I made the acquaintance of the actor Röhl, husband of the famous singer. Very pleasant walk with Wohlbrück and Röhl over the hills to Bogenhause,[67] from which one can look down on the meadows. In the evening I went to the theater to see Kotzebue's*[68] *Minnesänger*,[69] Stoll's *Scherz und Ernst*,[70] and Crux's* pantomime, *Der Maler Teniers*. The two plays were given badly, as usual, but the pantomime was really well composed, the several tableaux vivants being especially well arranged. The dancing, however, was only mediocre.

Monday 4 May. Attended a rehearsal of Winter's opera *Calypso*[71] in the foyer of the theater. Here I met Winter himself. He is tall and just as heavy: his whole figure is clumsy. Hair, totally white, hangs around his head like shafts of light, while his eyes are staring and slightly squinted. His very long nose is always full of snuff, which usually runs down to his lips. He appears so awkward as to be genuinely sinister, but is in fact really courteous and friendly: he invited me to come on Friday to hear something from his new cantata *Die vier Tageszeiten*.[72]

Tuesday 5 May. Called on Frau von Fladt who played me her sonatas. One cannot deny this lady a considerable degree of originality in her compositions; this nonetheless occasionally degenerates into baroque gestures because of a lack of education. Afterwards I went to Madame Dulken* (wife of the well-known instrument-maker) who is the first among women pianists here. This charming brunette is graced with a dainty little figure and really decorous, modest behavior. She played some extremely difficult variations by a certain Marchand* (the brother-in-law of Danzi) very precisely and with great expression. I played her the first allegro of my new *Sonata in E-flat* and Vogler's *Variations on the Seraphiner March*. It was a joy for me to notice that my playing impressed her.

After lunch I paid Wohlbrück a long visit. In the evening to the theater, where they performed *Der gutherzige Polterer*.[73] Wohlbrück played the title role marvelously, in some parts particularly so, but I missed the polished ensemble work that I so admired in this outstanding artist in Darmstadt. Madame Flerx* was very good as Adelaide. The group as a whole was not as bad as usual, even though they had started very poorly with *Leichtsinn und gutes Herz*.[74]

Wednesday 6 May. Called on Wohlbrück. On my return home I received visits from Eduard Seeligmann, Baron Poissl, Brandt and the young Braun. I had to improvise twice, on Joseph's first romance and the concluding ensemble from Méhul's *Joseph*.[75] Afterwards I called on the banker Strassburger, whom I had met in Switzerland. At midday Poissl and I dined with Eduard Seeligmann in Michael's Restaurant; after lunch we traveled to Nymphenburg,[76] the famous pleasure palace about an hour from Munich. Neither the garden nor the palace lived up to my expectations. Everything was very ordinary until we reached the queen's violet dressing room, which I think is very tastefully appointed.

Thursday 7 May. Poissl and I breakfasted with Seeligmann, who had invited me over so that Count Rechberg could hear me play. The latter was actually prevented from coming, but I played all the same: the *Variations on the Seraphiner March*, as well as improvising on Benjamin's Romance from Méhul's *Joseph* and the end of no. 3 [see example 3].

Afterwards I went to the Court Chapel, where they performed a Mass by Lindpaintner*, one of Winter's pupils. I cannot assess its worth because I was constantly distracted by ceaseless chattering. There I met the famous composer and Westphalian music director, Blangini*.

At midday I attended a big lunch given by the banker Pappenheimer. The most interesting people I met there were the famous dike builder Geheimrat von Wiebeking*

Example 3. Theme from Méhul's *Joseph*

and the famous necrologist von Schlichtegroll*. I played Cramer's *Variations* with a newly arranged cadenza that I had composed earlier in the day. After lunch I went with Wohlbrück to the intendant of the theater, De la Motte*, to whom he wished to introduce me. However, we did not find him at home, and went on to Seeligmann's box to hear Winter's opera *Calypso*. The music is, as in all Winter's new compositions, simply blithe reminiscence of his earlier works. The opera was, moreover, badly mounted[77] in every possible respect. Letter from Niechsgale.

Friday 8 May. Called on Winter. I played him (because he cannot play the piano at all) several pieces from his French opera *Castor et Pollux*[78] and some choruses from his new cantata, *Die vier Tageszeiten*. The latter were very well worked out. After lunch I went to Baermann, where I found Polledro. Both of them came to my rooms because Polledro wanted to hear me. I played Cramer's *Variations* with a new variation that I had composed early today, and improvised on a theme from *La Molinara* ("Nel cor più non mi sento")[79] [see example 4].

Nel cor più   non   mi   sen - to

Example 4. Theme from Paisiello's *La Molinara*

Afterwards I went to the theater, where for the first time they performed a comedy, *Der Dichter und Schauspieler*[80] by Lembert*, based on Dupaty's* libretto, and Benda's* *Ariadne*. Letters from Gottfried Weber and Dusch in Mannheim, and from Father in Berlin.

Saturday 9 May. Visit from Poissl. With the professor called on Oberkirchenrat Schmidt, to whom we had to deliver a letter from Professor Michaelis in Tübingen.

Called on Wohlbrück. Serious and important discussion about the local performance of my *Jephtha*. After lunch visited Baermann. I spent the rest of the afternoon completely reworking Himmel's *Variations* [see example 5], and on practicing this.

Example 5. Theme of Himmel's *Variations*

Sunday 10 May. Practiced the new *Variations*. Visits from Braun, Poissl, and Baermann. I went to the Court Chapel, where they performed a mediocre Mass in F major by Winter. (The *Kyrie* in F major begins with two horns.) The *Credo* with appeggiated bass is really lovely; pity that the conclusion is so operatic. At midday I was invited to dine with old Seeligmann. There I met Geheimrat von Kröner, Medizinalrat Krafft, and Herr von Bader*. The latter invited me to call on him. After lunch I played the *Variations* I practiced yesterday and improvised on a theme of Haydn*[81] [see example 6]:

Example 6. Theme by Haydn [Mozart?]

In the evening I went to the theater, in Seeligmann's box. They performed *Der Wasserträger*[82] with fairly good ensemble. Letters from Kley and Mother. Wrote congratulatory letters to Father[83] and to Mother.

Monday 11 May. Practiced. Attended the rehearsal of Polledro's concert. Afterwards I called on the Prussian ambassador, Count Golz*, to whom I had to deliver a letter. He received me very courteously, and offered to mediate should I want to play at court. I declined, however. Visited Wohlbrück. Practiced in the afternoon. At five o'clock I presented a letter (from Prince Hatzfeld) to the Austrian ambassador, Baron von Wessenberg*, who also received me very graciously. Afterwards I delivered two letters to the Russian ambassador, Prince Bariatinsky. He was entertaining a large gathering who had just finished supper. He introduced me to the wife of the minister Montgelas,[84] whose acquaintance is very important to me at the moment. At his request I played a little on his very beautiful Viennese grand piano. However, the moment I wanted to start, coffee was brought in. Now I have always hated nothing more than playing to the accompaniment of rattling cups. I had also been put out beforehand by a few trivialities; I therefore played very badly (a few of the E-flat variations). If these people had had even a spark of musical knowledge, I fear that this performance could have done me great harm. In the evening I went to Polledro's concert: he played divinely, and the appreciation of the public was considerable. He was applauded, even before he began, also between each variation, and in triple measure at the end. He performed his own concerto, the same one I had recently heard him play, which begins with very attractive melodies [see examples 7 and 8],

Example 7. First theme from Polledro's Violin Concerto in G Major

Example 8. Second theme from Polledro's Violin Concerto in G Major

followed by variations on themes from *La Molinara* and *Una Cosa Rara*.[85]

Tuesday 12 May. Practiced my concert. Visit from Herr H. Pappenheimer and the violoncellist Legrand. I played him my new *Sonata in E-flat* and improvised on three notes that he provided for me (E, D, G) to my complete satisfaction. In the afternoon visits to Wohlbrück, Baermann (whom I did not find at home, and so went on to Madame Harlas), and Frau von Fladt. Afterwards Braun called on me. I played him my *Variations in E-flat Major.* I practiced for my concert and the Steibelt* *Études* all evening.

Wednesday 13 May. Practiced very diligently. Called on Baermann. At midday we lunched with Seeligmann. Towards six o'clock Simon Seeligmann took me to meet his mother-in-law, Madame Meyer. I found her to be a talented, delightful woman. She has two daughters, one of whom has a wonderfully lovable and quiet charm (if I might say so). I played the Cramer *Variations.* In the evening I was at Baermann's, who was entertaining: Polledro played three trios[86] and a potpourri wonderfully. We supped there astoundingly well, and I stayed until nearly midnight.

Thursday 14 May. Practiced very diligently. I hope that Polledro will have a favorable effect on my playing. Visits from Poissl and Braun. I played the former Jephtha's recitative in act 3. He advised me to shorten the repetition of the Chorus of Maidens which seems like a good idea. Afterwards I took Wohlbrück to the local theater singer, Madame Neumann (née Hegemann). I found her and her husband very friendly, kind people. I played the *Variations in D Major.* Afterwards I called on the singer Margarethe Lang,[87] whom I had met in Frankfurt, but she was not at home. Practiced all afternoon. Letters from Madame Königswarth in Fürth, and Herr Reiner in Würzburg. In the evening I attended the theater, where they revived a charming little comedy, *Der Dichter und Schauspieler*, together with a very ordinary little ballet, *Der verliebte Maler.*[88]

Friday 15 May. Practiced. Wrote a note[89] to Poissl. Called on Madame Dülken. There I made the acquaintance of the actor Stensch* and his wife [Rosine]* (Madame Dulken's sister). I played the *Variations in F Major*, but not as well as usually, and repeated at her request my new *Sonata in E-flat,* which I performed to my satisfaction. In the afternoon I went walking with Wöhlbrück in the gardens. On our return I met Demoiselle Altmutter. In the evening I went to the theater for *Die Schweizerfamilie.* Margarethe Lang from the Frankfurt Theater sang Emmeline much better than in Frankfurt—indeed, almost tolerably well. There I also met Herr Hunsch, a composer, and, they say, a very good contrapuntalist. Up to now he has been studying composition with Winter.

Saturday 16 May. Practiced. Drew up various points for a critique of Poissl's Mass. Attended the rehearsal of an orchestral concert. Walked in the afternoon, and practiced in the evening.

Sunday 17 May. Visit from Konradin Kreutzer. He played me his little opera *Feodore*,[90] which contains some lovely pieces. The only problem is that everything is on too big a scale for such a small subject.[91] At midday I dined with the banker Herr Pappenheimer. In the evening I attended the orchestral concert, where I quite fortuitously bumped into Concertmaster Mangold* from Darmstadt. I have had to refuse three invitations for tomorrow (from Kapellmeister Winter, the banker Strassburger, and Marks), because I have already accepted one from Legationsrat von Fladt. Polledro played wonderfully today, but nonetheless not as beautifully as usual.

Monday 18 May. Called on Fräulein von Schmalz*, with whom I practiced a duet from Righini's* *Der Zauberwald*[92] that she wants to sing this evening at Baron Miltiz's, where I am also invited. Afterwards I went to Frau von Fladt's to make up a party for Schloss Schleissheim, a three-hour journey away, in order to see the picture gallery there. Oberst Epp and his wife, and Herr von Schaden* and his wife and sister, were also with the party. We had to rush through this wonderful gallery, and I hope to see it again at greater leisure. In the evening I was again at Baron Miltiz's, where some of the aristocracy[93] had gathered to hear Polledro and me. I played the *Variations in E-flat Major*, and a new piece made up of a small polonaise in F major by me, concluded by Steibelt's *Étude* in F minor with a new coda that I composed. In the interests of brevity I will in future call this piece *Divertimento*.[94]

Tuesday 19 May. Called on Herr von Bader, Madame Pappenheim, and Concertmaster Moralt. At midday I was invited to dine at Prince Bariatinsky's. Since I knew hardly any of the diplomats and other guests who were there, and conversation turned[95] on subjects quite unknown to me, I felt incredibly isolated and miserable, until after lunch when the prince asked me to play (the *Variations in F Major*), and all gathered around me. As I was returning home, Concertmaster Mangold saw me; today he was having supper at Stallmeister Thiel's, and he invited me to come up. I made the acquaintance of the Stallmeister and his wife, a really charming couple.

Wednesday 20 May. Attended the rehearsal of *Das unterbrochene Opferfest*.[96] Afterwards, with Poissl, I called on Winter, where I played through the remaining choruses from *Die vier Tageszeiten*. At midday I dined with Baermann, who held a small farewell party for Herr Braun (who is leaving for Berlin today). I gave him three letters for C. M. von Weber, C. W. Henning, and Mother. In the evening I went to the Vorstadt-Theater, where they performed a wretched *Ritterschauspiel*, *Der Sturm von Boxberg*,[97] which all the critics have censured. Letter from Father.

Thursday 21 May. Visit from Poissl; I showed him my *Fugue in A Minor*. Visit from Herr Dorville,[98] whom I met in Offenbach. He brought two friends with him who wanted to hear me play: the postmaster Herr von Vetter and Professor Schlett*, a contrapuntalist and teacher of page boys; he resembles Dr. Erhard* in external appearance and behavior. I played the *Variations in F Major* and improvised on the theme "Ich war wenn ich erwachte" from *Das Opferfest* that Dorville proposed to me [see example 9].

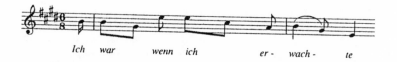

Example 9. Theme from Winter's *Das unterbrochene Opferfest*

Afterwards I took Concertmaster Mangold to Winter at his country house. In the afternoon I played Poissl act 1 of *Jephtha*, and wrote a letter to Father. In the evening I attended the theater, where they performed *Das Opferfest* for Gretchen Lang's benefit (she sang Myrrha very badly). Madame Schönberger sang Murney particularly well, although today no one achieved excellence. The opera is very much enlivened[99] by the ballet, which is usually omitted in all other theaters, even though the dances are very well composed.

Friday 22 May. Visit from Poissl to whom I played nos. 7 and 9 of *Jephtha*. Afterwards I accompanied him to Baron Hautguer who, among the local nobility,[100] has the reputation of being a very competent musician. Afterwards to Madame Dulken whom I did not, however, find at home. At midday I dined with the banker Strassburger where I met the intendant of theaters, De la Motte. On my return home I quite unexpectedly found Demoiselle Friedrike Sommer from Darmstadt, who is passing through on her way to Vienna. In the evening I went to the theater, where they performed Kotzebue's *Wirrwarr*.[101]

Saturday 23 May. Composed a rondo theme for Baermann.[102] Visit from a piano teacher, Triebel. I improvised. Afterwards visits from Poissl, Baermann, Brandt. I played my *Sonata in E-flat* and the *Divertimento*, then several choruses (nos. 1, 6, 8, 12, 13) from my oratorio *Gott und Natur*. In the evening I went to the Vorstadt-Theater, where Johann Schenck's* opera *Der Dorfbarbier*[103] was performed rather comically.

Sunday 24 May. Rehearsal of Ferdinand Paer's heroic-comic opera *Sargines*.[104] Played the rest of *Jephtha* to Baron Poissl. Called on Fräulein Schmalz and Frau von Fladt (the latter was not at home). In the afternoon I traveled with Demoiselle

Sommer and the professor to Nymphenburg in order to see the great fountains playing. In the evening to the theater, where Kotzebue's *Landjunker in der Residenz*[105] was performed. Stensch as the Landjunker was really excellent today. He used a whole series of small, characteristic gestures in his acting that (without caricature) most resourcefully expressed the awkwardness and timidity of this character; for example, when he observes the card game that interests him (with his head propped on the table between his hands), when he first visits his aunt (and stumbles on the threshold), when he watches the intermezzo (and constantly slips off his stool), etc.

Monday 25 May. I delivered my letter to Count Pappenheim, adjutant to the king, but did not find him at home. Called on Madame Mayer, but she was also out. Bade farewell to the good Sommer, who is traveling to her friend Madame Hauf in Glanzgow near Brünn. In the evening to the theater for *Sargines*. Gretchen Lang was Sophie and Madame Schönberger sang the young Sargines as guest artist. The first sang well by all critical accounts; the latter, however, very beautifully, only with too much embellishment, unfortunately. Both were called out. The burning village in the battle created a marvelous effect. The battle itself, as with all *combati* at the Munich Theatre, was outstanding. Today I handed the intendant, De La Motte, a letter from Demoiselle Schmalz. This turned out to be an unpleasant qui pro quo, since in her letter Demoiselle Schmalz wrote that I have a commission from the court to write an opera.

Tuesday 26 May. Visits from Baermann and Poissl, who brought his brother and the Prussian Kammerherr von Wilknitz with him. Both of them wanted to hear me. I played the *Variations in D Major*, and improvised on three suggested notes: C, E, G. In the evening I attended the theater, where, on the eve of the king's birthday, the whole house had been illuminated. This indeed was initially very impressive, but it spoiled the performance in many respects, the décor seeming especially dull as a consequence. Today they performed Kotzebue's *Feuerprobe*,[106] and, for the first time, *Herz und Verstand*[107] (based on the French *L'amour et la raison*), with an allegorical divertissement to conclude with.

Wednesday 27 May. Practiced. Visit from Brandt; he played me the bassoon concerto that C. M. von Weber has composed for him.[108] Called on the intendant of music, Count von Seefeld; I had a letter for him from Berlin. Rehearsal of *Die Entführung*[109] in which Mme. Schönberger is appearing for the last time tomorrow.[110] There I handed a letter of recommendation I had from Mannheim to the music director, Fränzl*, who has only just returned from an artistic journey. In the evening the professor told me that because Vogler is staying away so long, and this absence is doing my opera the greatest damage, he wants to travel to Nuremberg tomorrow to have a serious discussion with him. Since Vogler is giving an organ recital there on Saturday, I would like to utilize this opportunity and join him on this short journey.

Thursday 28 May. Practiced. Visits from Poissl, Baermann, Brandt, and Reuter, who all joined me to watch the Corpus Christi procession which takes place today. The procession lasted two and a half hours and was made up of five thousand to six thousand people: all artisans with their banners, schoolchildren with their teachers, the court singers with the kapellmeister (all in choir dress, with Winter looking like an upright bear), the clergy, many deacons, and eventually the king and the princes with the whole court. When the procession had ended, I called on Seeligmann and then went on to Baron Hautguer's,[111] where I was invited to lunch; I could not stay, however, since my departure had already been fixed for one o'clock. There I played my new *Rondo in G Major* for the first time, partially to my satisfaction. I met Herr Dulken* there at last. His wife was also present, as were Count Merci and several other very pleasant people.

At two o'clock in the afternoon we left for Nuremberg. We did not take the route via Augsburg (as on the previous occasion), but via Ingolstadt which shortens the journey by ten hours. At eight o'clock we arrived in Pfaffenhofen, a neat little town (twelve hours from Munich) where we stayed overnight. N.B. Our landlord's father, the merchant Link from Allersberg, is traveling with us.

Friday 29 May. At four-thirty in the morning we left Pfaffenhofen and arrived in Ingolstadt at midday. There we met with two ladies, relations of Gottfried Weber. At twelve o'clock we set out again, but did not take our usual route via Eichstätt, but went through Beilngries and Berching. This route is indeed shorter, the only problem being that the road[112] there is being resurfaced and we were terribly jostled. The route is through the former bishopric of Eichstätt, a wonderfully fertile stretch of land. From a tower in Ingolstadt one is supposed to be able to make out 140 villages in a single panorama. We saw the former Eichstätt mountain and hunting castle of Hirschfeld,[113] a very big building that is now for sale at four thousand gulden. At seven o'clock we arrived in Berching, where we stayed overnight at Das Ross,[114] a good and very comfortable hotel.

Saturday 30 May. We left Berching at four-thirty in the morning, and arrived in Nuremberg at one o'clock. We established ourselves at Der Goldene Radsbrunnen[115] (good and not too expensive), where every room was fully booked on account of the organ recital. After lunch I went to Papa Vogler, who was not a little surprised to find me here. Afterwards we adjourned to his concert in the Wörther Church. Today he played inimitably well, especially nos. 1, 3, 4 and 7 of his recital: 1. *Seraphiner March;* 2. *Adagio;* 3. *Hottentottenlied;* 4. Chorale "Wie schön leuchtet"; 5. Flute Concerto; 6. *Chinesisches Lied;* 7. Handel's "Hallelujah" (with a new descant) [see example 10];

Example 10. Vogler's descant for Handel's Hallelujah Chorus in *Messiah*

8. *Hirtenwonne*. In the evening I supped with Vogler and Guhr in Das Rote Ross.[116]

Sunday 31 May. Walked to Erlangen with Vogler and Guhr. (I met Dr. Brei again.) There we inspected three organs, the one in the French church appealing most to me, even though it is not appropriate for concerts, since it has only one manual and only twelve to fourteen stops. The stops that it does possess, however, are very good. At midday we dined excellently in Wallfisch. In the afternoon a walk in the very beautiful Welsescher Garden. On our return to Wallfisch I had Guhr dictate to me another three variations by an unknown pianist. N.B. I have promised to buy Vogler's *Deutsche Messe* for Guhr. We arrived home at nine-thirty in the evening.

June 1812

Monday 1 June. Return to Munich. We could not leave as early as we had hoped, and in any case still had permission to stay on our passports. Visit from the younger merchant Kramer. Departure at ten o'clock. At two we arrived in Allersberg where we called on Herr Link. At four we traveled further and arrived in Berching at 8 where we again slept at Das Weisse Ross.

Tuesday 2 June. We left at five o'clock in the morning and arrived in Ingolstadt at noon. At three we set off again and arrived in Pfaffenhofen at eight o'clock, where we stayed overnight. Since I traveled this route only three days ago, I have nothing further to observe.

Wednesday 3 June. We departed at six o'clock and arrived in Munich at one o'clock. There I found two letters waiting for me, from Father and Mother. In the afternoon I called on Baron Poissl. In the evening I practiced.

Thursday 4 June. Today being the last in the Octave of Corpus Christi, a Mass in C major by Winter was performed in the Court Chapel (the *Kyrie* has an oboe solo). The *Gloria* and *Credo* especially pleased me, particularly the latter, in which the bass constantly traverses the scale. Winter introduced me to the composer Lindpaintner from Augsburg, one of his pupils. He is very handsome and appears to be a really charming young man, but I spoke far too little with him to form a definite opinion (at least for today). He told me that in November he wants to travel to Italy and compose an opera for Milan. In the evening to the Vorstadt-Theater, where *Kaspar der Thorringer*[117] was lamentably performed.

Friday 5 June. I attended the rehearsal of the opera *Macdonald* (which is called *Der Turm von Neustadt* in Berlin).[118] Afterwards I visited Seeligmann and asked for his intercession at court. In the evening to Dalayrac's delightful opera *Macdonald*. Cannabich* has added a new section to the finale (of act 1) that is very effective and brilliant for the singers.[119] Baermann's habit of stating the obvious irritated me so much that for today I can write nothing about the opera, even though I have so much to say about it *in petto*. Letters from Vogler in Nuremberg and Carl Maria von Weber.

Saturday 6 June. Letter from Brandt. Note from Baermann, which only increased my irritation. I do indeed feel that I should take the proposed first steps, but I simply cannot bring myself to overcome my opposition to it. How much I wish I had a stern taskmaster right now who would take me by the ears, if necessary, and force me to act.[120] At midday I dined with Seeligmann *en famille*. His son Arnold from Augsburg was also there. In the evening I went to the Vorstadt-Theater, where they performed an extremely vulgar comedy by Joseph Richter*, *Die Zimmerherren in Wien*, for his benefit.

Sunday 7 June. Visited Wohlbrück. With Poissl, I called on Madame Dulken. I played the *Variations in E-flat Major* very well, but the *Rondo in G Major* very badly. Dined with Seeligmann at midday. There I met Finanzrat von Karly from Augsburg and Herr von Geiger. After lunch I played the *Variations in F Major* and improvised on a theme from *La Molinara* ("Nel cor più non mi sento"). In the evening to the theater, where they performed Frau [Johanna Franul] von Weissenthurn's insipid creation, *Adelheid von Burgau*.[121] Madame Cannabich*, who very seldom acts, played Adelheid.

Monday 8 June. Note from Kammerherr von Wilknitz. My irritable mood, which has persisted since Friday, kept me at home all morning even though, unfortunately, I did absolutely nothing. In the afternoon I walked with Poissl and Wohlbrück in the English Garden. In the evening I practiced a little, and wrote a letter to Carl Maria von Weber in Berlin.

Tuesday 9 June. Visit from Music Director Fränzl. I played the *Variations in E-flat Major*. Afterwards I called on Kammerherr von Wilknitz, but I did not find him at home. Called on Poissl. Practiced a little in the afternoon, and sketched out a choral fugue for Poissl's psalm setting. Worked a little on the vocal score of *Gott und Natur*. In the evening I attended the theater, where Mercier's* *Essig-händler*[122] and Kotzebue's *Die Zerstreuten*[123] were performed.

Wednesday 10 June. Various visits. Practiced. Called on Wohlbrück for a conference about the finale of the new opera, *Wirt und Gast*.[124]

Thursday 11 June. Letter from Vogler in Augsburg. Dinner *en famille* with Pappenheim. After lunch I played the *Divertimento* and improvised on three suggested notes: A-flat, C, B. Practiced. Called on Wohlbrück to confer about the finale of the new opera.

Friday 12 June. Practiced. Passed the morning, like all the previous fourteen days, without doing anything. Called on Wohlbrück to confer about the finale of the new opera. In the evening to the theater, where they performed Himmel's* *Singspiel Fanchon*[125] very badly. Muck* as Tapezier was funny enough. He sang the aria "Die spottet meines Herzens Triebe" more beautifully than I have ever heard it, all in an extraordinary *sotto voce,* as if lost in reflection and choice. His arm movements at the words "Fanchon, Adele, Adele, Fanchon" had great comic effect: Fanchon with the right hand, gesture to the right, Adele with the left hand, gesture to the left, Adele with the right hand, gesture left, Fanchon with the left hand, gesture right.

Saturday 13 June. Called on Wohlbrück to confer about the finale of the new opera. Passed the morning and afternoon again quite uselessly.

Sunday 14 June. Received act 1 of the new opera *Wirt und Gast* from Wohlbrück. Wrote a long letter to Mother about the state of the local theater and my opera. Afterwards went to the theater, where I saw the most delightful ballet by Crux, *Der Mechanicus*. Reconciliation with Baermann.

Monday 15 June. Practiced. I was on my way to Madame Dulken when I met Vogler, who arrived in Munich yesterday evening. In the afternoon visited Wohlbrück. In the evening there was a big gathering at Baermann's; I even had my piano brought over. Polledro played two of his trios, not as well as usual, but he concluded divinely with his *Variations in G*. I played my *Rondo in G Major* and the *Variations in F Major* to my complete satisfaction. The audience (all of them artists) were very enthusiastic, and I consequently found myself in a genial mood that inspired me all evening. At midnight, in the midst of the happy merrymaking, Poissl called me into an empty room and asked me, as an enduring remembrance of our friendship, henceforth, from this joyful moment on, to use the familiar form of address in our dealings with each other. I share this wish with all my heart, and only the disparity in our respective social standings (he is a baron and chamberlain to the king) prevents me from agreeing and telling him so, because such circumstances could easily be surmised as importunity, and nothing is more distasteful to me than pushing for higher social status. I hope the friendship of this good man and fine artist will accompany me through life as the fondest of remembrances.[126] Today I met the Hofbaumeister Fischer* and his wife the singer, as well as the court musicians Held* and Capeller*.

Tuesday 16 June. Called on Vogler and explained to him the circumstances surrounding my new opera. He said he would come round this evening so that we could agree on the steps that need to be taken. Several visits. Vogler came in the evening and we decided that tomorrow he will travel to Nymphenburg to the queen in order to speak to her about my opera, and should it be possible, to arrange that I should play in the Court Concert tomorrow. The latter is almost an impossibility, because the programme has already been fixed, and they have no appropriate instrument there. But it is almost out of the question to play without prior reference to the intendant of music, Count Seefeld.

Wednesday 17 June. At nine o'clock I traveled with Vogler to Nymphenburg. Vogler had himself announced to the queen. He was, however, too early and had to wait until twelve o'clock. He spoke to the queen about my opera, and about my wish to play in her Court Concert. When the king is there she never decides these things alone, and said she would confer with him. In the meantime I traveled back to the city in order to be correctly attired should the king wish to hear me this evening. On my return to Nymphenburg the king had already sent invitations to Vogler and me for the concert today. Fränzl played a violin concerto and Capeller a flute concerto, Mme. Röhl sang an aria, and Mme. Harlas and Brizzi a duet. The noise, however, was so great (with everyone talking, and later cards being played at twelve tables) that I could hardly hear a thing. When I came to play at last, things were much quieter. I performed the *Rondo in G Major*. When I had finished, the queen came over, complimented me kindly on my playing, and questioned me on my compositions. I made the most of the opportunity to tell her about my opera, and asked for permission to present it to her. She took it all well, so that at least some progress has been made for my opera. Since the musicians are always treated to a meal at every Court Concert, I attended a very jolly supper,[127] and arrived back in Munich only at one o'clock in the morning.

Thursday 18 June. Called on the intendant of music, Count Seefeld, in order to excuse myself, since it is very unusual to play at Court without his arranging it. He received me with extraordinary friendliness, complimented me very much on my playing yesterday, and was not in the least annoyed, as the musicians had led me to believe last night. Called on Vogler. At midday I dined with Vogler at Frau Fladt's. There I met Countess Függer, Oberappellationsrat Christoph von Aretin*, and his sister. After lunch I played the *Variations in E-flat Major*. In the evening I attended the theater, where they performed Weigl's* little opera *Die Verwandlung* and a ballet, *Der Ball*.[128]

Friday 19 June. Rehearsal of Méhul's *Joseph*. There I made the acquaintance of the ballet master, Crux. Vogler came to see me. Then I practiced all afternoon. In the evening attended the theater, where *Joseph* was performed quite outstandingly. Tochtermann* as Simeon was particularly good.

Saturday 20 June. Practiced a reworking of the *Divertimento* nearly all day, then played it in the evening at Fränzl's for a big musical gathering, but not very well, I fear. It went much better with the *Rondo in G Major*, which I had to perform by popular demand.

Sunday 21 June. Because I arrived home from last night's supper very late, I slept in and was in no fit state for any serious activity. Walked with Poissl in the Hofgarten. Afterwards I visited Madame Dulken. Since the professor was not in his rooms,[129] I invited Poissl to dine with me. We had a very merry lunch. In the afternoon Vogler called on me. We decided to compile a programme about the opera for the queen. The professor wanted to undertake this task. In the evening I had intended to go to the theater, but at the door I met Winter, and we became involved in a discussion about art that lasted so long that the theater was already emptying by the time we concluded.

Monday 22 June. I went with Vogler to hear him play on the newly built organ with three manuals in the Peterskirche. In the afternoon called on Wohlbrück. There I found Röhl, who is leaving tomorrow morning: he has been engaged by the Augsburg-Strassburg Company. On my arrival home, I was surprised by a visit from Dr. Erhardt of Berlin. Almost at the same time, Vogler brought round Herr and Frau Fladt, who wanted to hear me perform. I played them the *Sonata in E-flat*. When they left, I played Dr. Erhardt the overture and act 3 from my new opera. In the evening I went to the Vorstadt-Theater, where they performed *Die Proberollen*[130] and *Erbschaft*.[131]

Tuesday 23 June. Called on Vogler. First orchestral rehearsal of *Octavian*. Made the acquaintance of Weichselbaum (through Mittermaier*). Called on Madame Pappenheim. In the afternoon Vogler brought me Lanius* so that I could hear his voice. I believe he could sing Jephtha very well. Poissl and Brandt came to see me. Farewell visit from Madame Fränzl, who is leaving for Frankfurt.

Wednesday 24 June. Called on Vogler. Went with Reiner to the Michaelskirche, where Mozart's Mass in C major[132] was performed. The *Credo* with its rushing violin figures is very powerful. Afterwards I attended the second orchestral rehearsal of Poissl's opera. Called on Dr. Erhardt, but he was not at home. At midday I was invited to dine with the wind band where about twenty people, most of them artists, had assembled. In the afternoon with Vogler I went through act 1 of *Jephtha*. Called on Wohlbrück, but he was not in. To the theater in the evening, where Johann Hutt's *Das war ich*[133] and the ballet *Der Ball* were performed.

Thursday 25 June. Several visits; practiced.

Friday 26 June. Visit from Vogler. We went through acts 2 and 3 of *Jephtha* together. We decided to shorten the chorus "Vater, wir schauen" a little, and to have Sulima's entrance in act 3 preceded by a few bars of chorus. At midday I was invited to dine at Herr Pappenheim's, where I met Hofbauintendant Gärtner. After lunch Pappenheim declaimed Bürger's* "Lied vom braven Mann," while Vogler improvised on it outstandingly. (Tomorrow Herr and Frau Pappenheim are leaving for Bad Gastein.) In the evening I went to the theater, where they performed Weigl's opera *Das Waisenhaus*[134] very badly. I felt so bored[135] today and I had no interest in music at all.

Saturday 27 June. Now that I have finished the outline of my opera that I want to present to the queen, at eleven o'clock I traveled with Vogler to Nymphenburg. Even though the queen had just arisen, she received us at once. I presented the outline of the opera to her, but she immediately asked whether I had the score with me. In my embarrassment I told her that the copy was not yet ready, and that the outline was only provisional. Then I spoke quite frankly and told her of my wish to see my opera performed on her stage.

At midday I was invited to dine at Prince Bariatinsky's. Today was much more agreeable than the first occasion, because virtually everyone present were artists. I met Baron von Gomberg there; he foolishly sees himself becoming a composer. At five o'clock I went to the first stage rehearsal of Poissl's *Octavian*, but could not stay long, because Dr. Erhardt had invited me to supper and he is leaving tomorrow.

Sunday 28 June. Note to Intendant de la Motte requesting an interview.[136] Visit from Poissl. Called on Wohlbrück and Madame Meyer, accompanied to the latter by Vogler. In the afternoon I went to the intendant in order to inform him, as head[137] of theaters, of the step I took yesterday in going to the queen. He accepted this very well and assured me that he would do everything possible for my opera, but made it clear that it cannot be produced before October, since Demoiselle

Häser* will be arriving in fourteen days and there will be performances of Italian opera for two months *de suite*.

Wrote a big letter to Mother (explanations, accounts of both my interviews with the queen; Dr. Erhard). Afterwards I went to the Vorstadt-Theater, where they performed a bad (but, for all that, fairly effective) tragedy by Ziegler*, *Jolantha, Königin von Jerusalem*.[138]

Monday 29 June. Wrote a letter of congratulations to Winter on the occasion of his name day. Afterwards I went with Vogler to the Peterskirche where the feast day of St. Peter and St. Paul was celebrated with a solemn service. They performed a bad setting of the Mass in C minor by Himmel (dedicated to the elector of Mainz). In place of the gradual, the offertory and the recessional Vogler played an andante, the first allegro of a flute concerto, and a fugue on the organ, but not as beautifully as he usually does. Visits from Herrn Weichselbaum and Brandt. At midday I was invited to Winter's for a big lunch that his wife had arranged in honor of his name day. In the evening, at the Vorstadt-Theater, I saw a couple of acts of Ziegler's *Das Gastrecht*.[139]

Tuesday 30 June. Called on Vogler. Brought my neglected diary up to date. Sketched no. 3 of the new opera *Wirt und Gast*. Attended the dress rehearsal of *Ottaviano*. It all went so badly that I am fearful for tomorrow's performance.

July 1812

Wednesday 1 July. Several visits. In the afternoon I went to Poissl to keep him company until the start of his opera, knowing as I do how painful a composer can find the last hours before the first performance of his work. After I left Poissl, I went straight to the theater to see the première of his Italian opera *Ottaviano in Sicilia*. The success far surpassed his expectations and even my best wishes. Every item, from the overture to the closing chorus, was applauded, and he was eventually called out with the principal singers. The performance was the most accomplished I have seen in a long time. The three main characters were superbly sang by Brizzi, Mesdames Harlas and Weichselbaum, while the orchestra, quite unprecedentedly, played with heavenly ensemble. The music, considered as an Italian opera, is a masterpiece: apart from the magic of the Italian style of singing, which he has made his own, he has also assimilated the brilliant orchestration and powerful harmonic handling of the choruses from the Italians. After the performance I went on stage with all his friends to congratulate him.

Thursday 2 July. Completed a critique of Poissl's opera and gave it to Wohlbrück, who wants to send it to the morning paper accompanied by several other notices.[140] Began a revision of my *Jephtha*. In the evening went to the Vorstadt-

Theater where I saw the act 1 of Karl Ditters von Dittersdorf's* *Singspiel Das rote Käppchen.*[141]

Friday 3 July. Devoted the day to revising my *Jephtha.* I reached act 3.

Saturday 4 July. In the morning, from six until ten o'clock, I completed the revision of act 3. Visit from Poissl. Called on Vogler. Practiced a little in the afternoon. In the evening I was invited to a gathering at Frau von Fladt's. There for the first time I heard a quartet recital by the Brothers Moralt.* Even though their great reputation led me to expect much, they exceeded my highest expectations. There I also met Geheimrätin von Wiebeking and her daughter Fanny,[142] two very charming ladies; I really appreciate their invitation to call on them. Today I played the *Variations in F Major.*

Sunday 5 July. Called on Vogler. Practiced. Called on Madame Dulken. In the afternoon Baermann and Poissl came to see me. Went to the theater, where *Ottaviano* was performed for the second time, with as much success as on the first.

Monday 6 July. Went with Vogler to Oberhofprediger Schmidt to promote my opera to him. Then we traveled to Nymphenburg, where I presented the full score of my opera to the queen, and begged her to arrange a performance. She does not appear to have complete confidence in me, since she questioned me about all my activities, where my works had been performed, etc. The audience nevertheless lasted as long the previous one; indeed, she was far more cheerful and talkative.

In the afternoon I attended a colloquium that Vogler delivered to several organists about the reconstruction of the organ of the Neuminster in Würzburg. In the evening I was invited to a very merry farewell party that was given for Polledro, who is leaving early tomorrow morning.

Tuesday 7 July. Called on Oberhofprediger Schmidt to pass on the libretto[143] of my opera. Called on Intendant de la Motte: I likewise presented the text of my opera to him, and informed him of yesterday's audience with the queen. Attended the rehearsal of Nicolò Isouard's* *Aschenbrödel.*[144] In the afternoon I again saw the intendant: he told me that he had spoken with the queen and had asked her if she would like to pass on my score; she said that she first wanted to play through it herself on the piano. Called on Vogler in the Michaelskirche. In the evening to the theater, where Kotzebue's *Üble Laune*[145] was performed.

Wednesday 8 July. Today I received from the intendant an open-ended ticket granting free access to the Court Theatre. Visit from Brandt. In his company I noted down several good ideas for a bassoon concerto.[146] Sketched the first chorus of act 2 of my new opera, *Wirt und Gast*. Walked to the wind band with Wohlbrück and Lindemann. In the evening attended the theater, where Nicolò's opera *Aschenbrödel* was performed fairly well.

Thursday 9 July. Called on Vogler. Visit from the old minister and *Oberkammerherr,* Count Rechberg. I played (1) the *Variations in E-flat Major*; in the fantasia section I counterpointed a new theme [see example 11],

Example 11. A new theme by Meyerbeer for the fantasia section of his (lost) *Variations in E-flat Major* for piano

which I finally united with the principal theme, and (2) the *Divertimento*. Visit from Baermann, who brought me several phrases he had written down, and out of which he would like to create a clarinet quartet.[147] In the afternoon heard a second lecture from Vogler. In the evening went to the Vorstadt-Theater, where they performed Stegmayer's quodlibet *Rochus Pumpernickel.*

Friday 10 July. Sketched the duet, no. 7 of the new opera. Visit from Baermann. In his company I noted down themes for his quartet. Went to the theater in the evening, where *Wilhelm Tell*[148] was performed, with Stensch as Tell.

Saturday 11 July. Visit from Baermann. I completed the first part of the first allegro of his Quartet. Letter from Mother. At midday I was invited to dine with the wind band, which is made up solely of musicians. After lunch I bought a porcelain *déjeuner*[149] as a present for Baermann (nineteen florins), who celebrates his birthday tomorrow. Then in the Vorstadt-Theater I saw a couple of acts of Weissenthurn's play *Der Wald bei Hermannstadt,*[150] which was performed with a reasonable sense of ensemble. After supper I wrote a congratulatory note to Baermann that I want to send to him early tomorrow morning together with the *déjeuner* set.

Sunday 12 July. Visit from Baermann (his name day is not until the fifteenth of July).[151] With him I called on Geheimrat von Wiebeking. Unfortunately we did not find Fräulein Fanny at home. In the afternoon I practiced. In the evening to the theater, where they performed Schiller's *Kabale und Liebe.*[152] The famous Esslair* from Mannheim played Ferdinand outstandingly, although he was somewhat hindered by his enormous physique.

Monday 13 July. Called on Wohlbrück, Vogler, then Frau von Fladt who was not at home. Visit from Baermann. I completed the *allegro* of his Quartet right up to the last passage. After lunch I went to Professor Sendtner*; I had to give him a letter from Dusch. In the evening to the Vorstadt-Theater, where they performed a musical quodlibet, *Der Eipeldauer in Wien.*[153]

Tuesday 14 July. Visits from Baermann and Poissl. Called on Vogler. He came with me to the famous Sömmering*, whom I had consulted about my eyes. Afterwards to Frau and Herr Arnold Seeligmann from Augsburg, who are in Munich at the moment and wanted to make my acquaintance. I played the *Variations in E-flat* and the *Rondo in G Major.* In the evening I went to the theater to see *Wilhelm Tell.* Esslair played Tell, outstandingly at times. Between acts 3 and 4 I went backstage, where Poissl introduced the actor to me. After the performance I dined with Baermann and Poissl in Der Hahn[154] since the latter is going away tomorrow for some time. Today Demoiselle Häser arrived.

Wednesday 15 July. Note from Frau von Geiger. Accompanied Poissl to the post coach. Visit from Herr Hunsch: I played him nos. 8 and 13 from my oratorio *Gott und Natur.* Visit from Baermann. At midday I was invited to dine at Geheimrat von Wiebeking's. After lunch his daughter Fanny played us some variations by C. M. von Weber very sweetly. She really has acquired a very charming manner.[155] Afterwards I went with Baermann to the wind band for a while, and from there to Winter, who showed me a wonderful *Salve Regina* by my harmonic grandfather, Francesco Antonio Vallotti* (who taught Vogler theory). Then I went with Baermann to Madame Harlas who had arranged a little supper[156] in honor of his name day. We had a very happy time and parted only at two o'clock in the morning. There I met the director of the Aschaffenburger Theater, Herr Schemenauer*.

Thursday 16 July. Called on Vogler. Attended the rehearsal of *Deodata.* Practiced. Several visits. In the evening went to the performance of Bernhard Anselm Weber's* opera *Deodata.*[157] I sadly recalled today the outstanding performance of this work in Berlin, since this local one, or today's at any rate, was bad by all critical accounts. Practiced C. M. von Weber's *Momento capriccioso.*[158]

Friday 17 July. Called on Wohlbrück, Madame Dulken and Baermann. Visit from Dorville. I improvised on an old Italian song he proposed [see example 12].

At midday I was invited to a big dinner at Frau von Meyer's (Seeligmann's daughter). There I met Frau von Kobler, her daughter Sophie, Herr von Wolff, and Frau von Vetter. On my return home I dropped in at the theater, where I saw a few scenes of Kotzebue's play *Falsche Scham.*[159] Esslair played Captain Erlach. Practiced the *Momento capriccioso.*

Example 12. Theme of an old Italian song

Saturday 18 July. Practiced the *Momento capriccioso*. Visit from Baermann. Called on Wohlbrück. Letter from Mother. Music Director Fränzl came to see me. Practiced again.

Sunday 19 July. Called on Vogler. Visit from Herr von Vetter. He brought Herr von Wolff and two other friends whose names I have forgotten. They all wanted to hear me perform. Wohlbrück also arrived, bringing Herr Lindemann and Lindpaintner with him, so that eight people in all were crammed into my small room. I played the *Variations in F Major* and then the *Rondo in G Major* at Lindpaintner's request. Wrote a letter to Mother. Went to see Wohlbrück. In the evening I was invited to tea and supper at Oberhofprediger Schmidt's, and left only at one o'clock in the morning.

Monday 20 July. Called on Vogler. Wrote a letter of recommendation for Esslair to Mother. Visit from Baermann. Dorville came to see me, and introduced me to one of his friends, Herr Krafft from Offenbach. I improvised twice, firstly on an original theme [see example 13],

Example 13. An original theme by Meyerbeer

and secondly on one provided, namely Joseph's romance from Méhul's opera. Practiced in the afternoon. Called on the Wiebekings. I returned to the city with a fellow countryman, Bacherer,[160] and went to the theater for Törring's *Agnes Bernauer,*[161] which was performed for Esslair's benefit. Between acts 4 and 5 I went backstage in order to give Esslair his letter of recommendation and to take my leave of him, since he is departing tomorrow.

Tuesday 21 July. Practiced. Sketched the aria no. 10 in *Wirt und Gast.* Visits. In the evening to the Vorstadt-Theater, where they performed *Die Wiener in Eipeldau,* the continuation of *Der Eipeldauer in Wien.*

Wednesday 22 July. Worked on the finale. Practiced. Letter from Carl Maria von Weber. Called on Wohlbrück. In the evening to the Vorstadt-Theater, where they performed *Die Waldmänner,* an opera by Schikaneder* with music by Kapell-meister Henneberg*. Subject[162] and music are equally trivial and bad.

Thursday 23 July. Worked on the finale. Practiced a little. Called on Vogler. Passed the afternoon uselessly, as is so often the case with me in Munich. From tomor-row I want to tackle seriously many outstanding tasks; I also want to improvise daily on three notes or on a given theme, as I used to do in Darmstadt. Went to the theater, where I saw Schiller's *Die Jungfrau von Orleans.* Improvised on the three notes G, D, A.

Friday 24 July. Arranged the chorale "Wer nur den lieben Gott lässt walten" for four voices. I did this at Vogler's wish since this arrangement has been requested of him by the Reformed Community in Basle. Visit from the Abbé Seiler, a pia-nist from Hungary. I do not want to judge him on his playing today, since my instrument appeared to be tuned too low for him. Visit from Brandt. Went to Vogler. With him I called on Frau von Fladt. Practiced. Went to the show-riding school of Herr Guillaume, which I previously saw in Würzburg. It belongs to the best of its kind. On returning home, I briefly attended *Die Jungfrau von Orleans,* and saw the closing scene.

Saturday 25 July. Called on Wohlbrück. Wrote a letter to Poissl in Kamms.[163] To-day Wohlbrück completed the libretto[164] of my new opera *Wirt und Gast, oder Aus Scherz Ernst,* and I want to study it carefully. Sketched the trio no. 11. To the Vorstadt-Theater, where they performed an elegant little comedy in one act by Castelli*, *Domestikenstreiche,*[165] and Dalayrac's opera *Die beiden Savoyarden.*[166]

Sunday 26 July. Visits from Winter with his youngest pupil, and then from Baer-mann. At the request of both I improvised on a theme provided by Winter [see example 14] and then played my *Variations in E-flat Major.* At midday I was in-vited to a dinner at Winter's that he had arranged for his wife's name day.[167] A young woman who has been very good to me was also there, but today she was

Example 14. An original theme by Winter

remarkably cold and withdrawn.[168] This rather soured the otherwise very merry lunch, and I hurried away after the meal and went to the Vorstadt-Theater, where they performed the famous opera by Perinet* and Wenzel Müller*, *Evacatel und Schnudt.*[169]

Monday 27 July. Visits from Winter and Vogler, Baermann and Wohlbrück. The first told me many interesting things about voice training; for example, he urges his pupils to practice scales[170] in order to articulate with resonance and to learn pure intonation.[171] After lunch I went to Wohlbrück. Then I called on Geheimrat von Wiebeking, who is traveling to Lindau tomorrow with his family. I played the *Rondo in G Major* and, with Fanny, pieces for four hands by C. M. von Weber. Afterwards I went walking a little with Bacherer.

Tuesday 28 July. I received a letter of recommendation from Frau von Wiebeking for Fräulein Kurzböck* in Vienna. Attended the rehearsal of Gyrowetz's *Der Augenarzt.* Sketched the closing chorus of *Wirt und Gast.* In the evening attended *Der Augenarzt.* The performance was only average. Mademoiselle Flerx as the blind girl was, however, very good.

Wednesday 29 July. Sketched the trio no. 10 of *Wirt und Gast.* At midday I was invited with Vogler to Frau von Fladt's. After lunch I played her the choruses from my oratorio *Gott und die Natur.* Called on Wohlbrück. In the evening I went to the show by the tightrope-walker Blondin*, but found nothing of particular interest.

Thursday 30 July. Finished the trio no.10. In the afternoon I was startled by a visit from my friend Gänsbacher from Prague, who is traveling with Count Firmian to Salzburg,[172] and took me by surprise here. In the evening to the theater, where they performed a big pantomime, *Harlekins Hochzeit*, by Schlotthauer, with delightful music by Neuner*.

Friday 31 July. Went with Gänsbacher to Vogler. He played me the first half of his *Requiem*, a big, wonderful work. I performed half of my oratorio for him. After lunch I introduced him to Winter and Lindpaintner, and in the evening we went to see Blondin.

August 1812

Saturday 1 August. Visit from Winter. Gänsbacher played Vogler the whole of his *Requiem*. Unpleasant letters (about Gottfried Weber) from Wolff and Father. In the afternoon I traveled with Gänsbacher and the professor to Nymphenburg, in order to show the former the gardens, and to go with the latter to Oberhofprediger Schmidt to ask him to remind the queen about my opera. On our return we spent a few moments in the Vorstadt-Theater, where they performed Kotzebue's *Don Raimundo*.[173]

Sunday 2 August. I played Gänsbacher the second half of my oratorio. Sent off a letter of congratulations to Grandfather, and another letter to Father (about my journey to Vienna). When I had finished writing, I saw act 2 of *Der Augenarzt*. Letter from Poissl.

Monday 3 August. Gänsbacher played me his Trio, and I showed him my Italian *ariettes*.[174] Afterwards we attended the rehearsal of Häser's concert. In the afternoon Gänsbacher played me half of his new Mass in D, and I showed him the overture to my *Jephtha*. In the evening we went to Häser's concert, which took place in the theater and was crowded. The following is the programme of this very full concert: Part I—(1) overture *Beherrscher der Geister*[175] by Herr von Weber; (2) an aria by Cimarosa*, sung by Demoiselle Häser; (3) a clarinet concerto by C. M. von Weber, played by Baermann;[176] Part II—(4) an aria by Zingarelli*, sung by Demoiselle Häser; (5) a violin concerto by Fränzl; (6) a duet by Farinelli*, sung by Brizzi and Demoiselle Häser; (7) the overture to *Anacreon*[177] by Cherubini.

Häser, however, hardly lived up to the expectations of the public. As far as I am concerned, I found her middle notes outstanding, but her high register too sharp. She sings very simply, but also monotonously. Furthermore, she is so nervous that she certainly cannot employ all the means[178] at her disposal. In the evening I had supper[179] with Baermann.

Tuesday 4 August. Vogler played Gänsbacher the reworking of his responsories and half of the Mass in D. Afterwards I took him to Madame Dulken, who performed several things for him most charmingly. In the afternoon I accompanied him to Frau von Fladt who played him a quartet she has composed. In the evening to the theater, where they performed Steigentesch's* *Verstand und Herz* and Kotzebue's *Die Quäker*[180] and *Die Feuerprobe*.

Wednesday 5 August. Today Gänsbacher played Vogler and me the whole of his Mass in D. Visit from Poissl, who has just returned from his journey. At midday I had Poissl and Gänsbacher to lunch with me. I played Gänsbacher my *Rondo in*

G Major. After lunch Wohlbrück called, and later Winter. He advised me, in the event of my composing an Italian opera, to use the poetry of Socraffi[181] since this librettist has an astonishing power of invention[182] in new forms. He lives in Padua or Venice. (Brizzi, with whom I later discussed this opinion, tells me that he lives in Padua.)[183] Afterwards we went to the Peterskirche, where Vogler played the organ for Gänsbacher. He improvised outstandingly for two hours. There I also met the piano teacher, Hubert. At seven-thirty I took Gänsbacher to a rehearsal of *Ottaviano:* we heard act 3.

Thursday 6 August. At eight o'clock in the morning I went with Gänsbacher to Winter, who wanted to play us several of his compositions. We heard the *Kyrie, Gloria,* and *Credo* from his big *Mass for Two Orchestras,* and act 1 of his opera *Colmal and Colma.*[184] The Mass contains much work and creates a considerable impression. The layout of the *Credo*, however, seems to me to have several similarities with that of Jomelli's*, where the articles of faith are all sung by solo voices while the chorus repeatedly comes in with the word "credo," each time a tone higher. I had to leave at eleven o'clock, because Music Director Fränzl told me that he would be calling on me about this time to hear act 1 of my opera *Jephtha*. He did indeed come and appeared to be as satisfied with the composition as I could wish. In the afternoon I played the same act to Gänsbacher, which pleased[185] him very much up to the canon—which he thinks is too complicated; he also finds the vocal writing in the choruses rather too heavy. Afterwards we went to the third performance of *Ottaviano*.

Friday 7 August. Vogler brought Frau von Fladt and Gänsbacher to me and played them the new Mass and eighteen responsories. This took all morning. In the afternoon, with Gänsbacher, I called on Brizzi, but he was not at home. We then went to Winter, who played us his *Requiem*. Even though the opening tutti begins in C minor, the chorus enters with the word "requiem" in C major, a lovely effect. He handles the *Dies Irae* with considerable originality, not at all stormily, as in most other settings, but like a narrative, since, as he says, no event is taking place, but only the prophecy of things to come. At six o'clock we went to the theater, where for the first time they performed Duval's* *Der Haustyran*, translated by Iffland.[186]

Saturday 8 August. I played Gänsbacher act 2 of my opera *Jephtha*. He made several enlightening observations, e.g., (1) that the words "Zum Tode geweiht" (Finale II) [see example 15], which are important for the action, lie too low (and therefore risk not being heard); (2) there should be a more powerful cadence on the words "Ich schwör's" (Finale II); (3) he feels that the fusion of the three themes in the trio no. 12 is too turgid. Called on Frau Oberhofprediger Schmidt. At midday I dined with dear Gänsbacher at Baermann's, for the last time. This afternoon

Example 15. From the act 2 finale of *Jephthas Gelübde*

he has to travel to the Tyrol, to his parents, and on 18 September he will have to be back in Salzburg with Count Firmian. I hope to see him again at the end of this year, since we have decided to travel to Italy together. This thought alone gives me the strength to cope with the sadness of parting from this true friend. In the evening to the Vorstadt-Theater, where, for the first time, they performed a charming little comedy in two acts from the French, *Die beiden Grenadiere*,[187] as well as a comedy in one act by Costenoble*, *Die neue Zauberflöte*.[188]

Sunday 9 August. Called on Vogler. Passed the whole day in idleness, unfortunately. In the evening to the theater, where they performed a neat little play in one act by Holbein called *Das Wiedersehen*,[189] and then a pantomime, *Die Begebenheiten Harlekins im Erzgebirge*. Called on Poissl, who is ill.

Monday 10 August. Called on Poissl. Attended the rehearsal of Herr Mayseder's* concert. (He is a concertmaster and first violinist from Vienna.) He draws beautiful sounds from his instrument and masters the greatest difficulties with ease; his playing is, however, a little monotonous. What amazed me[190] most was a run of three octaves through broken thirds that *in alt* (in the third octave) becomes chromatic. I cannot remember ever having heard the violin played like this. Made several calls in the afternoon. In the evening to Herr Mayseder's concert, which was held in the theater. It was not very full, but the applause was so extraordinarily enthusiastic that one could have supposed a claque had been hired for the occasion. The content of the programme: Part I-(1) a Haydn symphony; (2) a violin concerto composed and played by Mayseder (this composition is among the most unusual concert music I have heard in a long time, even though there are occasional flashes of genius);[191] (3) a scene from *Zayre* (with chorus) by Winter, sung by Madame Harlas; Part II—(4) an oboe concerto played by Herr Fladt; (5) a trio from *Horaziern*[192] by Cimarosa, sung by Brizzi, Mittermaier and Madame Harlas; (6) variations composed and played by Herr Mayseder; (7) a symphony by Mozart.

On my return home, Fränzl gave me the very pleasant news that the queen has sent him the score of my opera for his inspection.

Tuesday 11 August. Wrote a letter to Father (telling him that the queen has sent the score to Fränzl, about my new opera, questions about Grandfather's health, about the ballet in *Jephtha*). Called on Oberhofprediger Schmidt in order to thank him for his mediation with the queen. Called on Vogler and Poissl, both of whom were not at home. Went to Wohlbrück. To the theater, where *Caesario*[193] was performed rather well. This play has some very funny situations: more the pity that it is so full of trivialities. In any case, I have seen it far better performed in Darmstadt and Frankfurt.

Wednesday 12 August. Visit from Wohlbrück. Called on Madame Pappenheim. Bad toothache meant that I had to spend the rest of the day lying on the sofa, and also that I could not sleep at night.

Thursday 13 August. On waking I found my cheeks badly swollen, and the pain still intense. This meant another day like yesterday. Visit from Fränzl, who wanted to play through the opera. Poissl came to see me. Letter to Dusch (about social events, testimonials, operas, Gänsbacher).

Friday 14 August. Even though the swelling has reduced a little, I am still suffering pain. Today is my twenty-first birthday.[194] Letters from Father and Mother. Received a charming present from the professor (a signet). Visits from Wohlbrück and Baermann. Wrote a note to Fränzl.

Saturday 15 August. Letter from Father containing permission for me to travel to Vienna. The swelling has reduced, but I still have to keep to my room and could not accomplish anything. I began a letter to J.[195]

Sunday 16 August. My indisposition has ended, but I still kept to my room. At midday my friends Wohlbrück and Poissl dined with me, a very happy occasion. In the afternoon a visit from Legrand. I completed my letter to J., and wrote to Father. Afterwards to the theater, where Grétry's *Richard Löwenherz*[196] was very badly performed.

Monday 17 August. Visit from Poissl. We played through the new duet in his *Merope*,[197] which is lovely. I proposed some alterations, which he accepted. In the afternoon Wohlbrück came to me. He read the dialogue and I played the music of our new opera, *Wirt und Gast,* in order to see how long it would take to perform. It lasted one and a half hours.

Tuesday 18 August. Visit from the oboist Fladt, who asked me to compose an oboe concerto for him. I promised to do it if I do not travel to Vienna. Baermann came, and with him I played through several scenes of my opera *Jephthas Gelübde,* in which Harlas will feature, to see if they suit her voice. I altered a few small details. Visit from Vogler. Wrote a note to Music Director Fränzl. In the afternoon I walked with Wohlbrück in the English Garden. In the evening to the theater, where they performed Kotzebue's *Die Unvermählte*[198] remarkably badly.

Wednesday 19 August. Letter from Father. Visit from Director Fränzl. We played through act 2 of my opera at the piano. Went walking in the afternoon. In the evening in the Vorstadt-Theater I saw an act of the old opera *Das neue Sontagkind*[199] by Wenzel Müller. Afterwards I went to Herr Pappenheim's, since I was invited to a supper[200] he gave in honor of the poetess Christiane Westphalen* from Hamburg. The gathering was both numerous and brilliant. Verses were declaimed and there was music-making. I played the *Variations in D* partially to my satisfaction. I also met Schelling*.

Thursday 20 August. Attended to several small details in my papers. Called on Vogler. In the afternoon to the museum, where I spent several hours acquainting myself with the Italian repertoire. In the evening to the theater, where *Egmont*[201] was performed scandalously: among other things, the five acts had been conflated into three.

Friday 21 August. Called on Poissl. Since he was running short of time, I scored the closing chorus of *Merope* for him. Afterwards I went to Director Fränzl and brought him home with me in order to play him act 3 of my opera. In the afternoon I composed a new piano piece (an arrangement of an étude by Steibelt). In the evening to the Vorstadt-Theater, where Johanna von Weissenthurn's *Der Wald bei Hermannstadt* was performed really well.

Saturday 22 August. Called on Kabinetprediger Schmidt, Wohlbrück, Vogler, and finally Baermann. Attended the rehearsal of the opera *Merope*. Went to Poissl; he showed me the theme of the overture to *Merope*, but was very disappointed on hearing it. In a quarter of an hour I composed the first half; he liked it so much that he wants to retain it. To the rehearsal of Weigl's *Korsar*. In the evening, at nine o'clock, Poissl came to see me. I completed his overture (including the orchestration), working at it uninterruptedly until midnight.[202]

Sunday 23 August. Note to Poissl. At five o'clock in the morning I left by coach with the professor on an excursion to Salzburg. We stayed overnight at Kirchzur. The scenery up to this point is very ordinary with the exception of the town of Wasserburg-am-Inn, which has a very picturesque setting.

Monday 24 August. At five o'clock in the morning we left Kirchzur and arrived at six in the evening in Salzburg.[203] The landscape remains boring until just before

Salzburg. But Salzburg itself, surrounded as it is by mountains, with the Salza flowing through it, presents a wonderful picture. We lodged at the inn Zum Schiff,[204] quite acceptable and not too dear. Today there was theater in the open air (because of fireworks), all in the gardens of Mirabell,[205] the summer residence of the crown prince.[206] The Schauplatz was crowded, and was very attractive, which made the bad performance of the play *Die Feldmühle, oder Wer hat die Braut?*, a comedy in two acts by Joseph Richter, all the worse. Afterwards there was a delightful fireworks display by Herr Vidacowich, culminating in a pattern depicting a basket with cascading forget-me-nots.

Tuesday 25 August. Walked in and around Salzburg in order to see the sights. The lovely cathedral[207] has six organs, all of which are played on certain festivities (although one wonders how they are synchronized). St. Peter's Monastery:[208] the rock on which the cemetery stands has been completely quarried by the monks, a vast undertaking.[209] It must have taken tremendous time and patience to complete it. Deep in the caves are several cells that are still preserved, where the monks fled during the invasion of the Huns. Alas, they were all found and massacred. Then we went to the Summer and Winter Riding Schools, the first open and decorated with boxes carved in stone, the latter covered, both of them spacious and well built. Then there is the New Gate, actually a rock tunneled through 100 to 150 feet (during the reign of the penultimate archbishop, Sigismund).[210] It is a bold idea until one learns that the rock consists of white sandstone. Leopoldskron[211] (half an hour from Salzburg), a lovely castle, belongs to Count Firmian. Apart from an unimportant collection of copper engravings and natural history, there is a very big series of portraits of the famous artists (which the cognoscenti say is unique). Even a Jew is to be found among them: Benjamin Horeb, from Arabia. Wrote a long letter to Mother (consoled her, and refused the gift).[212]

Wednesday 26 August. At six o'clock in the morning we left for Hallein (four hours from Salzburg) and arrived there at eight. Die Post is a good inn. We traveled on immediately to Golling (one hour).[213] From there it takes another three-quarters of an hour to reach the famous Schwarzenberg Waterfall. The waterfall has several sections, the loveliest being the second, just before the source. Here the water flows behind a round jutting rock, another fine perspective. Return journey to Golling, and from there to Hallein[214] where we had lunch. Afterwards we went to the salt mines, about an hour away.[215] (The professor stayed at home because of toothache.) We met people even up the mountain. We went down three shafts to three hundred fathoms (here calculated at eight feet to a fathom) under the earth. The descent differs here from the usual practice in other mines. One positions oneself on two smooth perches one foot apart, holds onto a rope hanging close by, and glides down with amazing speed. The unbelievably huge illumined caverns (containing, as I saw, two hundred thousand buckets) are astonishingly lovely: they are filled with water in order to extract the salt from the rocks in the earth. Finally we sat in a truck (holding ten people), which is propelled by the miners with such speed that we traversed one thousand fathoms in fourteen minutes.

Thursday 27 August. At five o'clock in the morning we left Hallein and arrived in Berchtesgarden[216] at seven. This region is extremely picturesque. In Berchtesgarden we lodged at Das Leithaus[217] and had breakfast. Afterwards we voyaged across Lake Bartholomä [the Königsee][218] to a pleasure palace where the king of Bavaria is actually hunting right now. Returned to Berchtesgarden on foot because of the professor's toothache, and in the company of a building director from Salzburg and his wife. Reached Salzburg in thunder and rain. There has been a military confrontation[219] to the east (one hour from Salzburg).[220]

Friday 28 August. At five o'clock in the morning we left Salzburg and arrived in the evening in Zur, where we stayed overnight.

Saturday 29 August. At six in the morning we departed from Zur and arrived in Munich at midday. There I was confronted with the terrible news that my poor grandfather, Liepmann Meyer Wulff, had died on 16 August after long suffering.[221] My God! Poor Mother! I fear for her health. With this sad news I will close my diary for some time. Why go on mulling over the same old feelings of grief?

September, October, November, December 1812

At the end of the year I am taking up my pen again to recount at least a summary of the past four months.

In September Demoiselle Häser sang Nasolini's *Merope* in the Italian Opera (Poissl newly composed all the singers' parts, with the exception of Häser's). Häser more than made up in this opera for any shortcomings in her concert.[222] She sang and declaimed very well, at first somewhat monotonously, and later too slowly. And although she does not make the slightest attempt to act convincingly, she nonetheless always knows how to establish her presence on the stage appropriately. All her movements are noble, although once again extremely monotonous. She was received with tremendous applause. I still, however, feel myself confirmed in the opinions I reached after her concert. I subsequently came to know her rather well and established a good relationship with her. I will most likely meet her again in Rome, since she is to marry a rich procurator there, called Veri, and will leave the stage. She also sang Roratia in the Italian opera *Gli Orazi ed i Curiazi* by Cimarosa. She was followed by the famous dancer Duport* from Paris with his pupil Demoiselle Neumann*, who delighted us greatly in the ballet *Venus und Adonis* (twice) and *Pigmalion*,[223] both by him, and in several dances[224] from Crux's ballet *Der Ball*. He was called out on every occasion. His pirouettes especially demonstrate the highest degree of perfection.

At the beginning of October Prince Friedrich of Gotha came to Munich. I met him at Winter's, and soon found myself in his favor in a big way. Every week I had to dine with him three to four times, and make music with him just as often. He is very good, but a weak man. Thanks to this acquaintanceship I have obtained the best recommendations for Italy so far, and very much hope that they will stand me in good stead in the future. I also established a very good relationship with his chamberlain, Baron Erthal, and with his music master, a Roman called Vincenzo de Cesaris*.

During these months they performed a newly rehearsed version of Mozart's charming opera *Die Mädchen von Flandern* (Bretzner's* arrangement of *Cosi fan tutte*). Sadly, it was virtually empty by the second performance.[225] On 10 October the new Vorstadt-Theater in Isator opened with the melodrama *Salomons Urteil*.[226] The house is built along the lines of the Odéon in Paris and has a very friendly aspect. In retrospect, the production of the melodrama—in regard to décor, costumes, and everything else one associates with theatrical pomp—was among the most brilliant I have ever seen on stage. On 12 October, for the first time, Kapellmeister Bernhard Anselm Weber's small opera *Die Wette* was performed here: it failed completely, but was given badly, according to all the critics.[227]

In November Pierre Rode came, played at court, and gave a concert. I heard him on both occasions, as well as privately at a gathering at Fränzl's, and again at Madame Dulken's. His beautiful tone is the same as it was ten years ago; on that occasion, however, I found greater passion and warmth in his playing. It has been replaced by a dubious correctness that left me quite cold. At court he played a new Concerto in D[228] [see example 16].

Example 16. Theme from Rode's Violin Concerto in D Major

The reception and opinions were very much divided.

I can also not forget a French tightrope walker (with his family) called Ravel.

He had the impudent audacity to call himself "L'incomparable" on the billboard. But, truth to tell, I have to concede that his achievements really were incomparable, and that he quite surpasses Furioso[229] (whom I also know).

At last, on 23 December (a Wednesday), my opera *Jephthas Gelübde* was produced for the first time. The rehearsals had began on 18 November, but were interrupted several times. The opera was performed three times. Deliberate and accidental hindrances of every sort intruded, and even on 20 December I was not certain whether the opera would be given on the twenty-third. Anxiety, annoyance, and vexation of every sort bothered me in these six weeks. I was nevertheless rewarded by an almost perfect performance. Apart from Jephtha (played very mediocrely by Lanius), I had reason to be satisfied with everyone. All the pieces apart from no. 1, no. 8, and no. 11 were applauded. Harlas surpassed herself. I wrote two new scenes (completely tailored to her individuality), which she sang to perfection. At the end she was called out tumultuously. I also wrote a new scene and cavatina for Weichselbaum; he sang the latter with particular charm. His acting was more natural than usual. The ballet master, Crux, in the space of ten days purposefully and effectively arranged the many ballets that are integral to the action. The orchestra was simply dynamic[230] in all the ensembles[231] and decisive moments.[232] In individual passages, however, their performance was not polished. *Jephtha* was repeated on 29 December, then put away for the while because Harlas has left for Vienna.[233]

On 31 December I played in a concert that the orchestra held for the benefit of wounded Bavarian soldiers. For this occasion I reworked the *Variations in E-flat Major* and added a big fantasia. For twelve days and twelve nights I practiced like a madman, but the results rewarded my efforts. Tumultuous and repeated applause, mixed with wild cries of "bravo" (I could even say shouting), accompanied me when I returned to the hall after the orchestra had finished playing. The queen (most unusually) herself applauded. On the same evening there was a big supper[234] at Strassburger's to which I was also invited. When I entered the room the whole gathering burst into applause, everyone came up to me, embracing and kissing me. It was, in short, a wonderful evening for me. Two days later I went to the queen to take my leave of her. She overwhelmed me with compliments about *Jephtha* and my playing on the evening before, and gave me a letter for the viceroy in Milan.[235] On the following day (Sunday, 3 January 1813) at midday I left Munich. Two hours earlier I was summoned by Countess Taxis (the queen's chief lady-in-waiting), who, on behalf of the queen, presented me with a ring (a jacinth[236] encircled with diamonds), a token, as she put it, of the pleasure that the queen has derived from my opera and my playing. An hour later I left Munich with the professor.

I am flooded by memories of every kind when I think of my nine-month stay in Munich, the pleasant ones far outweighing anything unhappy. Munich will always remain remarkable for me (beyond even the delightful social contacts I made), because it was there that my first opera was staged, there that my musical appprenticeship ended (when I left Vogler),[237] and finally because it is the first place where I won serious artistic regard. I pray that 1813 will fare as well as 1812 has ended.[238]

NOTES

1. On 6 *Elul* 5551 by the Jewish calendar.

2. He was no doubt called after his maternal great-grandfather, Meyer Wulff Tausk (d. 1759). The name "Liebmann" [*sic*] was never used by the composer, even though it formed part of his maternal grandfather's name, Liepmann Meyer Wulff. The name "Jakob" was first used on 1 February 1819, when he signed the official oath formula for the acquisition of Prussian civic rights, an opportunity for the assumption of his father's first name (which, since the emancipation of 1812, had been changed to "Jakob" from the distinctly Semitic "Juda"). After his father's death, from 19 May 1826, he systematically used his father's first name, but out of gratitude for his first great artistic successes in Italy, in the Italianized form of "Giacomo." See Heinz Becker, *Giacomo Meyerbeer in Selbstzeugnissen und Bild dokumenten* (Reinbek: Rowohlt, 1980), p. 14.

3. A family tree tracing the family Beer/Meyerbeer and its ancestors in Berlin (1675–) was compiled by Meyerbeer's great-great grandson, Reinhold Becker, as an appendix to the Berlin exhibition catalog by Heinz and Gudrun Becker, *Meyerbeer: Weltbürger der Musik* (Wiesbaden: Dr Ludwig Reichert Verlag, 1991). A succinct introduction to the Beer family and Judaism in early-nineteenth-century Berlin is provided by Heinz Becker in the chapter "Das Haus Beer" in *Giacomo Meyerbeer*, pp. 9–21); the bibliography on genealogy and family (p. 152) is crucial. A lengthier discussion of the topics, and especially Herz Beer's role in the Jewish Reform movement, can be found in Heinz Becker's introduction to *BT* (1:31–32) and in the chapter "Meyerbeer the Jew" in Joan Lewis Thomson's "Meyerbeer and His Contemporaries" (diss., Columbia University, 1972), pp. 245–74.

4. Together with J. F. Mädler, he published a large map of the moon (1837).

5. A one-act play in support of Jewish emancipation. Goethe's advocacy was to secure it a performance at Weimar (1824).

6. The subject is the conspiracy by which the German dictator Count F. J. Struensee was overthrown in Copenhagen in January 1772, and subsequently executed for treason. Meyerbeer was to provide the incidental music (1846).

7. Spohr's *Selbstbiographie* (1860) contains a vignette of Meyerbeer as a boy prodigy. Writing of his visit to Berlin in 1804 he says: "I still remember another Music-party—it was at the house of the Banker *Beer*—where I heard for the first time, the now so celebrated *Meyerbeer*, play in his parental house, then but a boy of thirteen years of age. The talented lad already then excited so much attention by his accomplished execution on the piano-forte, that his relatives and admirers regarded him with the greatest pride. It is related, that, one of them, on returning from a Lecture on popular Astronomy, exclaimed full of joy to the boy's parents, 'Only think! our *Beer* has already been placed among the Constellations! The Professor showed us a constellation which in honour of him is called 'the little *Beer*!' [This pun on the *idem sonans* of the word 'Beer' with 'Bär' anglice 'Bear', being almost as obvious in English as the German, will readily be understood by the reader. *Trans.*]" (*Louis Spohr's Autobiography* [London: Longman, Green, Longman, Roberts & Green, 1865], 1:80).

8. See Reiner Zimmermann, *Giacomo Meyerbeer* (Berlin: Henschel Verlag, 1991), pp. 25–27.

9. Vogler's role in Meyerbeer's musical development was fundamental, and his originality as a theorist, performer, and teacher very considerable indeed. "Vogler must be regarded as one of the key figures of European music history. He was the first who systematically treated music in an analytical and historical manner and he is considered the spiritual father of comparative musicology. He was of great importance to the development of the German music drama, owing to his influence on the musical aesthetics of the romantic movement and his theories of instrumentation and harmony. His theoretical writings are among the most important of the period, and his work as a pedagogue can hardly be overestimated. He was the teacher of Weber and Meyerbeer, both of whom he influenced greatly" (Niels Jørgensen in his introduction to Vogler's *Gustav Adolf och Ebba Brahe* [New York: MRF Records, 1979], p. ii).

10. Weber's fondness for Meyerbeer comes across clearly in his diaries. On 23 January 1811 he wrote: "He is my true, dear friend. The separation from him hurts me, and only the hope of seeing him again soon comforts me."

11. See Edgar Istel, "Meyerbeer's Way to Mastership: Employment of the Modern Leading-Motive before Wagner's Birth," *Musical Quarterly* 12 (January 1926): 81–83 for a detailed description. Carl Maria von Weber, writing in a Berlin newspaper, commented on its "glowing life, genuine loveliness, and above all the perfect power of burning genius."

12. Among the works essayed in Darmstadt are the fragments of two operas, *Abu Hassan* (1810) and *Der Admiral, oder Der verlorene Prozess* (1811). See Georg Richard Kruse, "Meyerbeers Jugendopern," *Zeitschrift für Musikwissenschaft* 1 (1918–19): 399–400.

13. Würzburg was Vogler's birthplace. His organ recitals were famous, and wherever he went he solicited interest in his system of organ construction and exhibited a portable organ called the "orchestrion."

14. *Der Verräter*, comedy in one act (first performed in Vienna, 1810; in Berlin, 1811) [Richel 69].

15. Farce in one act, also by Holbein (first performance in Vienna, 1807; Berlin, 1815) [Richel 69].

16. A quodlibet (Lat., "what pleases") is a comic polyphonic potpourri of popular songs. It was a kind of musical game played in the sixteenth, seventeenth, and eighteenth centuries, involving extempore juxtapositioning of different melodies (like the three dances in the act 1 finale of Mozart's *Don Giovanni*). In the nineteenth century, in German theaters, it came to mean a confection made up of the favorite pieces of many composers, and interpolated into plays, especially at the Theater an der Wien.

17. Text by J. E. Veith (after a French libretto for Lebrun, *Les Aveugles de Franconville* by Crouzette and Chateauvieux); Vienna, Kärntnertor-Theater, 1 October 1811. This was one of Gyrowetz's most successful works, given ninety-three times in Vienna (until 1813) and all over Germany. The Würzburg performance took place on 3 April 1812. According to Holbein, writing in *Theater* 2 (1812), the libretto was plagiarized from his own play *Die beiden Blinde* (Alfred Loewenberg, *Annals of Opera, 1597–1940*, 2nd ed., revised and corrected [Cambridge: Cambridge University Press, 1955; reprint, as one vol., New York: Rowman and Littlefield, 1970], col. 522).

18. *Le Cantatrici villane* (G. Palomba; Naples, Teatro dei Fiorentini, January 1799). Not only was this Fioravanti's greatest success, but it was one of the most popular *opere buffe* of the nineteenth century, given in German, Spanish, Danish, Russian, and Polish. It

enjoyed particular popularity in Germany, being revived many times into the latter years of the century (Dresden, 1877; Hamburg, 1880; Berlin, 1890), even into the twentieth century (Gladbach, 1930; Erfurt, 1931). Loewenberg does not list the Würzburg performance (cf. *Annals of Opera,* col. 542).

19. The *Tagebuch* [= Tgb] reads *vue.*

20. The art-loving Maximilian I, who had been elevated to royal status in 1806 in Napoleon's restructuring of the Holy Roman Empire. The elector was rewarded for his pro-French stance.

21. Hoffmann directed the Bamberg Theatre Company from 1808 to 1813.

22. Fürth is a town (now industrialized) adjoining Nuremberg.

23. Drama in four acts by Heinrich Zschokke (first performed in Berlin, 1796; in Darmstadt, 1811; published 1798) [Richel 167]. The author is more famous for his *Räuberroman* (robber novel) *Aballino, der grosse bandit* (1793).

24. This *drame mêlé de chants* (A. Duval; Paris, Opéra Comique, 17 February 1807) is Méhul's chief work, illustrating all his severely beautiful melodic gifts and feeling for atmosphere and situation (recreating a "biblical" atmosphere with an all-male cast). It was performed throughout the nineteenth century in all the major European languages, and was revived often in Paris (1851, 1866, 1899, 1910). It attained great popularity in Germany and Switzerland, where it held the stage into the twentieth century (Berlin, 1909; Basle, 1912), and is still retained in the Peters Catalogue. This opera was one of Weber's favorite works and influenced him considerably.

25. Tgb. *fausse resemblance.*

26. Tgb. *traits de génie.*

27. *La Vestale* (Étienne de Jouy; Paris, Opéra, 16 December 1807), monumentally neoclassical in the line of Gluck and Cherubini, established Spontini as one of the leading composers of the day, famous for his grasp of large-scale dramatic effect. This work has been regarded as the cornerstone of French *grand opéra,* and was performed 216 times in Paris (rev. 1854, 1909) and across Europe in all the major languages. It retained its popularity in the first half of the century, and was revived frequently in the twentieth century, especially for Rosa Ponselle (New York, 1925) and Maria Callas (Milan, 1954).

28. The opera *Deodorata* (with text by Kotzebue) had been written for Nuremberg, where it enjoyed a warm reception (*BT*, 1:614). It is properly a *Schauspiel mit Gesang,* a four-act drama [Richel 84]. The first musical setting was by Bernhard Anselm Weber (Berlin Königliches Schauspielhaus, 1810).

29. This was Meyerbeer's first large-scale work, an oratorio for solo voices and chorus, with text by Alois Schreiber, first performed on 8 May 1811 in Berlin. It was well received, his only success in the field of German music. Even then the critic of the *Allgemeine musikalische Zeitung* 13 (1811): 570 commented on the composer's search for new forms and original effects. It remains unpublished.

30. *Die Schweizerfamilie,* opera in three acts (I. F. Castelli; Vienna, Kärntnertor-Theater, 14 March 1809), was Weigl's most famous work, given on every German stage throughout the nineteenth century, as well as being performed in Italian, French, English, Danish, Polish, Russian, Swedish, Hungarian, and Czech.

31. *Éliza, ou La Voyage au Mont-Bernard, comédie* in two acts (V. Révéroni Saint-Cyr; Paris, Théâtre Feydeau, 13 December 1794). The opera was a harbinger of the romantic preoccupation with sublime nature: the Alpine setting plays an important part in the action, as does the use of natural forces (an avalanche).

32. Meyerbeer's early instrumental works remain either largely lost, or still unpublished.

33. Tgb. *rencontre.*

34. The common table for guests at a hotel.

35. Tgb. *gracien.*

36. This incident is almost certainly a reference to anti-Semitism. See Meyerbeer's extended letter of September 1818 (quoted below) to his brother Michael for a discussion of this issue fundamental to Meyerbeer's perception of himself both as man and artist. Also see 1 January 1841 and 3 August 1847.

37. Today this is a district of the city itself.

38. Meyerbeer's intention to travel to Italy clearly predates his meeting with Salieri in Vienna (1813) quite considerably, and had little, if anything, to do with disappointment in his career as concert pianist.

39. Tgb. *ennuyant.*

40. The Augsburg Rathaus was built between 1615 and 1620 by Elias Holl (1573–1646), a native of the city, and is an important example of Italianate influences in German Renaissance architecture. It is perhaps the most important Renaissance building in Germany.

41. Prof. Wolfssohn.

42. The Augustus Fountain was built by Huber Gerhard (1540–1620), the Mercury and Hercules Fountains by Adrian de Vries (1560–1627), Dutch pupils of Giovanni di Bologna. Both artists are representatives of mannerism.

43. The cathedral, erected between 994 and 1065 in the style of the Ravenna Basilica, was originally a Romanesque pillared basilica with a flat roof and three naves. It has four altars by Holbein the Elder, famous eleventh-century bronze doors, and five windows that have the oldest stained glass with figurines in the world.

44. Johann Michael Mettenleiter (b. 1765) was initially noted for his battle scenes before becoming engraver to the Bavarian court (1790).

45. Christoph Schwarz (1550–97).

46. The Cathedral of St. Ulrich and St. Afra (1474) is the last late-Gothic church built in Central Europe. Beside it is the 69 m high Perlach Tower, a well-known landmark.

47. St. Afra (d. 290) died in the persecution of Diocletian and was venerated in Augsburg from the Middle Ages.

48. Meyerbeer's vivid perception of the grotesque is clearly in evidence, even early in his career.

49. The Schätzlerpalais, which contains a famous rococo hall.

50. Gombart & Co. had published C. M. von Weber's *Momento capriccioso,* which was dedicated to Meyerbeer.

51. Mozart's *Il Dissoluto punito, o sia Il Don Giovanni, drama giocoso* in two acts (Lorenzo da Ponte; Prague, 29 October 1787), had already established itself as one of the most popular operas ever written. It was in the repertoire of even the smallest houses.

52. "The Golden Grapes."

53. "The Golden Cock."

54. The Munich Residenztheater was built by François Cuvilliés (1695–1768) between 1750 and 1753.

55. *Ritterschauspiel* or chivalric drama in four acts by Christian Heinrich Spiess (published 1790; first performed in Berlin, 1791; in Vienna, 1796) [Richel 142]. Spiess was famous for his supernatural *Schauerroman* (horror or Gothic novel) *Das Petermännchen* (1791).

56. Wilhelm Beer.

57. Mme. Larcher was a French violinist who first performed in Munich on 28 December 1811. She was popular for her expressive playing.

58. The singer Marianne Marconi married Lorenz Schönberger (1770-1847), a landscape painter.

59. In 1811 Meyerbeer had attended a music festival in Schaffhausen with C. M. von Weber.

60. Heinrich Baermann had been on a joint concert tour with Weber. On 28 March 1812 he left Potsdam to return to Munich.

61. The observation no doubt concerns the production. Iffland's sixty-five plays enjoyed a popularity in their day that far exceeded that of either Goethe or Schiller. Their appeal to the contemporary middle-class tastes and values (sentimentality, a moralizing tendency, and the optimism of inevitable happy endings) not only conveys a realistic picture of the age, but secured them a special public affection.

62. Opinions about Wohlbrück's acting abilities were divided in Munich. See *BT,* 1:616 for a selection of reviews.

63. Johann Friedrich Schiller's verse play on Joan of Arc, subtitled *Eine romantische Tragödie* (Leipzig, 18 September 1801). Schiller was particularly attached to this play. It makes greater use of pageantry and music than any other of his works.

64. Tgb. *goutieren.*

65. Braun appeared in Munich on 12 April 1812. There he enjoyed great success playing his oboe concerto and variations.

66. Tgb. *soupierten.*

67. A suburb of Munich.

68. Kotzebue's prolific output and skills as a dramatist and librettist (his ability to create tension and surprise, his witty and effective dialogue and appeal to the sentimentality of the age) assured him tremendous popularity in the early decades of the nineteenth century. In the five months from January to May 1812, for example, Meyerbeer attended productions of no fewer than twelve of his plays, and in the seven months from January to July 1813 in Vienna, a further five.

69. Actually *Der arme Minnesänger,* comedy in one act (first published in Berlin, 1811). This Munich performance antedates the Berlin one listed in Richel [84] by a year.

70. Comedy in one act from the French (first performed in Weimar, 1803; published 1804) [Richel 146].

71. *La Grotta di Calypso,* opera in two acts (Lorenzo da Ponte; London, Royal Theatre, 31 May 1803). This was the first opera Winter wrote for London and it was very successful there, with Elizabeth Billington. It was first performed in Munich on 17 April 1807.

72. This cantata was first performed in Munich on 23 December 1811; the choruses and fugues were praised for their clarity.

73. Comedy in three acts by Iffland, a translation of Goldoni (first performance in Berlin, 1811) [Richel 73].

74. Comedy in one act by Friedrich Gustav Hagemann (published in 1791; first performance in Berlin, 1793) [Richel 57].

75. The tenor aria "Champs paternels."

76. Schloss Nymphenburg, with its sumptuously decorated interior, is the largest baroque castle in Germany, and was also built by François Cuvilliés. It was presented by the Prince Elector Ferdinand Maria to his consort on the birth of Max Emanuel (1679).

77. Tgb. *montiert.*

78. In 1806 Winter tried to win over the French public for a second time with his five-act *tragédie lyrique*, *Castor et Pollux* (Bernard, revised by Morel; Paris, Opéra 19 August 1806). It was a failure and, disheartened, he henceforth devoted his energies to writing for Munich.

79. *La Molinara, ossia L'Amor contrastato*, opera in two acts (Giovanni Palomba; Teatro dei Fiorentini, Naples, summer 1788), was one of Paisiello's most popular works. The theme "Nel cor più non mi sento" inspired many sets of variations, e.g., Beethoven (WoO 69; also "Quant'è più bello," WoO 70), Paganini and Velluti (see 3 January 1818). The opera was also the origin of the cycle of poems *Die schöne Müllerin* by Wilhelm Müller, used by Schubert for his song cycle (1823).

80. *Der Dichter und Schauspieler, oder Das Lustspiel im Lustspiel*, comedy in three acts from the French (1812) (first performance in Berlin, 1814) [Richel 97].

81. This melody, the serenade "Liebes Mädchen hör mich zu," was erroneously ascribed to Haydn, but is presumed to be by Mozart. See *BT*, 1:619.

82. *Les deux Journées, comédie lyrique* in three acts (Jean-Nicholas Bouilly; Paris: Théâtre Feydeau, 16 January 1800), is an outstanding example of rescue opera. Beethoven regarded the libretto as the best of any contemporary work, and the opera was also admired by Weber. It is Cherubini's most important creation and was given in Paris until 1842. It was even more popular in Germany, where it was performed throughout the nineteenth century (in H. G. Schmieder's translation as *Der Wasserträger*).

83. Herz Beer's birthday fell on 16 May (Jewish calendar) in 1812. Weber composed a celebratory chorus for the occasion.

84. Wife of the Bavarian minister Maximilian von Montgelas*, who was responsible for Bavaria's alliance with Napoleon and oversaw many reforms, believing that only French influence had made possible the modernization of government in Germany.

85. Opera in two acts by Martin y Soler (Lorenzo da Ponte; Vienna, Burgtheater, 17 November 1786). Famous for its citation in the Supper Scene of *Don Giovanni*.

86. Op. 2, 4, and 9.

87. Daughter of the Munich violinist Theobald Lang. Meyerbeer came to know her through C. M. von Weber who had a romantic relationship with her in Stuttgart. See John Warrack, *Carl Maria von Weber* (Cambridge: Cambridge University Press, 1968), p. 69.

88. Properly *Der Maler Tenniers*, pantomime by Anton Crux.

89. Tgb. *billet*.

90. Kreutzer's opera was the setting of a text by Kotzebue. The success of its production in Stuttgart in 1811 led to Kreutzer's appointment as court conductor in succession to Danzi, a post he occupied from 1812 to 1816. The work illustrated his light, popular style with appealing melodies.

91. Tgb. *sujet*.

92. Righini's most important work, properly consisting of two two-act operas, *Gerusalemme liberata, ossia Armida al Campo* and *La Selva incantata* (A. de' Filistri da Caramondani, after Tasso). This was one of the last Italian works to be produced at the Berlin Court Opera, 17 January 1803. Revived there in 1811.

93. Tgb. *noblesse*.

94. Unpublished.

95. Tgb. *roulierte*.

96. This two-act opera (F. X. Huber; Vienna, Kärntnertor-Theater, 14 June 1796), Winter's most famous work, was influenced by the French rescue opera. It "was about the most successful German opera between *Zauberflöte* (1791) and *Freischütz* (1821)"

(Loewenberg, *Annals of Opera,* col. 526), and was performed in Germany throughout the nineteenth century. Last revived in Leipzig (1917).

97. Chivalric drama by Maier.

98. Apparently Peter Friedrich D'Orville, a merchant from Offenbach, and uncle of Goethe's friend, Lili Schönemann (see *BT,* 1:620).

99. Tgb. *reliviert.*

100. Tgb. *noblesse.*

101. *Der Wirrwarr, oder Der Muthwillige,* farce in five acts (Kotzebue; Berlin, König- liches Schauspielhaus 1801; published in 1803) [Richel 89]. It was translated into English as *The Confusion, or The Wag* (1842).

102. This presumably refers to the rondo finale *(Allegro scherzando)* of the Quintet in E-flat major for clarinet, two violins, viola, and violoncello that Meyerbeer wrote for Baermann. It was completed in Vienna (1813) and performed in that year by Baermann on his name day. The work was believed lost until traced by the clarinetist Dieter Klöcker, who found it in the possession of Baermann's descendants. Also see 9, 11, and 13 July 1812.

103. With this opera (P. and J. Weidmann; Vienna, Burgtheater, 30 October 1796) Schenk made a successful contribution to the creation of an indigenous Viennese *Singspiel.* It was much admired by Weber and Lortzing, and became the composer's most popular work, appearing on every German stage throughout the nineteenth century. It was revived in Breslau and Prague (1898) and Berlin (1929).

104. *Sargino, ossia L'Allievo dell'amore* (G. M. Foppa; Dresden, 26 May 1803) was one of the composer's most successful works, was widely performed (in German, Swedish, Danish, Polish, and Russian) until the 1830s, and last given in Riga, 1843.

105. Actually *Das Intermezzo, oder Der Landjunker zum ersten Mal in der Residenz,* comedy in five acts (Kotzebue; Berlin, Königliches Schauspielhaus, 1808) [Richel 86].

106. *Die Feuerprobe,* comedy in one act (Kotzebue; Berlin, Königliches Schauspielhaus, 1809). This Munich performance antedates the Berlin production listed by Richel [85] by a year.

107. *Verstand und Herz,* comedy in one act by August Ernst von Steigentesch (first performed in Weimar, 1807; in Berlin, 1809; published 1808) [Richel 143].

108. Concerto in F major for bassoon and orchestra, J. 127 (1811, rev. 1822).

109. *Die Entführung aus dem Serail, Singspiel* in two acts (Gottlob Stephanie, an al- tered version of Christoph Friedrich Bretzner's libretto for André's *Belmont und Constanze* [1781], in turn adapted from one of various English or Italian plays on the subject of escape from Turkish captivity; Vienna, Burgtheater, 16 July 1782). This was Mozart's first major German opera, and his first great success, given in Vienna thirty-four times until the Na- tional-Singspiel ended on 4 February 1788. It spread all over Germany in the 1780s, and throughout Europe in the decades that followed. It never, however, achieved the ubiquity of *Le Nozze di Figaro* and *Don Giovanni.*

110. As Belmonte, the hero of *Die Entführung aus dem Serail,* in one of her famous assumptions of male roles.

111. This is perhaps a reference to Baron Hoggier from Wolfsberg on Lake Constance, mentioned by C. M. von Weber in his report on the Swiss music festival in Schaffhausen in 1811 *(BT,* 1:620).

112. Tgb. *chaussée.*

113. The castle is called Hirschfeld after the counts of Hirschberg, who were bailiffs of the bishopric of Eichstätt (founded by St. Boniface in 745) until 1291.

114. "The Steed."

115. "The Golden Waterwheel."

116. "The Red Horse."

117. *Ritterschauspiel* in five acts by Josef August, Graf von Törring-Cronsfeld* (published and first performed in Munich, 1785; in Berlin, 1788). The performance Meyerbeer attended antedates Richel's listed Munich production by three years [149]. The subject of this play is taken from Bavarian history, which Törring treated from a loyal dynastic point of view.

118. Dalayrac's three-act *opéra comique, Léhéman, ou La Tour de Neustadt* (J. P. Marsollier; Paris, Opéra Comique, 12 December 1801), was translated into German as *Macdonald* by C. M. Heigel for the Munich production. It was more successful in Germany than in France; in Germany it became another of the rescue operas so popular at the time (last revived in Weimar, 1830), and was also given in Swedish, Polish, Dutch, and Russian until 1824.

119. Cannabich was married to the singer Josephine Wowaleck and probably wrote this virtuoso finale for her.

120. Wolfssohn had not returned to Munich.

121. Drama in four acts (published 1810, first performed in Berlin in the same year). This performance attended by Meyerbeer in Munich antedates that listed by Richel [158] by ten years.

122. *Der Schubkarren des Essighändlers*, comedy in three acts, is a translation by Moritz Brahm of a play by Louis Sébastian Mercier (1775) (first performed in Vienna, 1775; in Leipzig, 1817) [Richel 23].

123. Farce in one act (Berlin, Königliches Schauspielhaus, 1809) [Richel 89].

124. The first mention of Meyerbeer's second opera, which was thus started even before his first was produced.

125. *Fanchon, das Leiermädchen, Singspiel* in three acts (A. von Kotzebue, derived from a French vaudeville by J. M. Pain and J. N. Bouilly; Berlin, Court Opera, 25 May 1804), possessed a charm and simplicity that made it one of the most popular works of the first half of the nineteenth century in Germany (rev. Königsberg, 1855, 1909). Also given in Dutch, Danish, Polish, and Swedish until 1827.

126. Meyerbeer's doubts would appear to have been borne out, since no further developments were to take place in this association, which seems to have petered out after Meyerbeer's departure from Munich. No record of any further communication between the two composers has survived, even though Poissl was to die a year after Meyerbeer in 1865 and Meyerbeer was a loyal friend and assiduous correspondent (as with Baermann, for example).

127. Tgb. *souper*.

128. Ballet by Anton Crux.

129. Wolfssohn had returned to Munich by now.

130. Comedy in one act by Franz von Holbein.

131. *Die Erbschaft*, comedy in one act from the Italian by Kotzebue (first performed in Dresden, 1807; and in Berlin, Königliches Schauspielhaus, 1808) [Richel 85].

132. Mass no. 11 in C (the *Credo Mass*), K. 257 (1776).

133. Comedy in one act (first performance in Vienna, 1807) [Richel 73].

134. Opera in two acts (G. F. Treitschke; Vienna, Kärntnertor-Theater, 4 October 1808). This was one of Weigl's most popular works, given throughout Germany and revived in Prague (1826).

135. Tgb. *ennuierte*.

136. Tgb. *entrevue.*

137. Tgb. *chef.*

138. Tragedy in four acts (first performed in Berlin and Vienna, 1797; published 1799) [Richel 166].

139. Drama in five acts (first performed in Vienna, 1798; published 1800). This performance attended by Meyerbeer antedates the date of the first Munich production listed by Richel by four years [166].

140. The review appeared in the *Morgenblatt für gebildete Stände,* no.167 (13 July 1812): 668.

141. *Singspiel* in two acts (text by Dittersdorf himself after *Giannina e Bernadone* by Livigni), one of the composer's more popular works, frequently performed in Germany well into the nineteenth century (rev. Munich, 1868; Dessau, 1899).

142. One of C. M. von Weber's favorite piano pupils.

143. Tgb. *Poesie.*

144. *Cendrillon,* opera in three acts (text by C. G. Étienne after Perrault; Paris, Opéra Comique, 22 February 1810). One of Isouard's most successful works, surviving through the nineteenth century, and last revived in Germany at Mannheim in 1872 and in Paris in 1896. After 1820 it was displaced in most countries by Rossini's *La Cenerentola* (1817).

145. Drama in four acts (Berlin, Königliches Schauspielhaus, 1797) [Richel 88]. Translated as *The Peevish Man* (1799).

146. Meyerbeer's *Musikalischer Nachlass* contained sketches for a bassoon concerto.

147. This would become Baermann's Clarinet Quintet in E-flat Major, op. 23. The adagio of this work was long thought to have been by Richard Wagner. Dieter Klöcker was able to trace the original manuscript to the National Museum in Prague.

148. Schiller's play (Weimar, 17 March 1804) on the William Tell legend, the nucleus drawn from Ägidius Tschudi's *Chronikon Helveticum.* Except for a short allegory, *Der Huldigung der Künste,* this was his last completed stage work.

149. A breakfast service made up of cup, saucer, and plate.

150. Drama in four acts from the French (first performed in Vienna, 1807; in Berlin, 1808; published 1810). This performance in Munich attended by Meyerbeer antedates that listed by Richel by four years [159].

151. The Feast of St. Henry (Henry II, Holy Roman Emperor who died in 1024). In the revision of the Roman Calendar his feast day was moved to 13 July (1971).

152. *Ein bürgerliches Trauerspiel* (Frankfurt-am-Main, 13 April 1784), dealing with unhappy lovers separated by class in the context of a despotic state. The original title, *Luise Millerin,* was changed at the suggestion of Iffland early in 1784. It is one of Schiller's most realistic and tautly constructed plays.

153. Musical quodlibet by Anton Eberl.

154. "The Cock."

155. Tgb. *manier.*

156. Tgb. *souper.*

157. See above, 17 April 1812.

158. Op. 12.

159. Drama in four acts (first performed in Hamburg, 1795, in Vienna, Burgtheater, 1796; first published in 1798) [Richel 85]. Translated as *False Shame* (1799).

160. I.e., Bacher. This is the first mention of Dr. Joseph Adalbert Bacher, the Viennese journalist who later (1847) became such a devoted friend of Meyerbeer.

161. Actually *Agnes Bernauerin,* tragedy in five acts (published and first performed in

Munich, 1780; in Berlin and Vienna, 1781) [Richel 149]. The famous protagonist is drawn from Bavarian history: her tragic love and death have made her the subject of numerous literary works, folk ballads, plays, epics, and operas.

162. Tgb. *sujet*.

163. Chamm in the Oberpfalz.

164. Tgb. *Poesie*.

165. Comedy in one act from the French (first performance in Vienna, 1804; and in Berlin, 1817) [Richel 27].

166. *Les deux petits Savoyards*, *opéra comique* in two acts by Nicolas Dalayrac (B. J. Marsollier; Paris, Comédie-Italienne, 14 January 1789). One of the composer's greatest successes, given in Paris until 1847. Even more popular in Germany, where it was given throughout the nineteenth century; last revived in Karlsruhe (1894, 1902).

167. The Feast of St. Joachim and St. Anne is on 26 July.

168. Wilhelm Altmann identifies her as Fanny von Wiebeking.

169. Properly *Prinzessin Evakathel und Prinz Schnudi*, a *Karikaturoper*.

170. Tgb. *scala*.

171. Winter, whose early works lacked vocal lyricism, was advised by Salieri to study the voice intensively in Italy. He went in 1791 and wrote both serious and comic operas for Naples and Venice (1791–94), so extending his knowledge and understanding of vocal matters that he opened a singing school in Munich (1805).

172. Gänsbacher became part of the household of Count Karl Max Firmian, a *Reichshofrat*. In the years 1806–13 he accompanied the family to Bohemia and on many other journeys (see *BT,* 1:624).

173. *Dom Raimundo de Colibrados*, comedy in four acts, from a play by Holberg (Berlin, Königliches Schauspielhaus, 1802) [Richel 85 has *Don Ranundo*].

174. The *Sei Canzonette italiane* and *Douze Ariettes italiennes* are songs to texts by Pietro Metastasio that were composed under Vogler's supervision in Darmstadt (December 1810). In style they look back to the Italian musical tradition of the eighteenth century, and provide another instance of the Italian influence already beginning to affect Meyerbeer's development as a composer.

175. During 1811 Weber had established himself as a traveling virtuoso. While in Munich he revised the overture to an earlier opera, *Rübezahl*, which had been written in 1804, and then was lost. He reworked the overture as a concert piece, *Der Beherrscher der Geister* (J. 122), particularly noted for its brilliant orchestral writing, and conducted it in London in 1826 just before the première of *Oberon*, also a fairy opera.

176. During his thirteen concert tours over the years Baermann constantly introduced his audiences to the pieces for clarinet and orchestra that C. M. von Weber had written expressly for him during 1811: the concertino for clarinet and orchestra in C minor (J. 109), and the two concertos, no. 1 in F minor (J. 114) and no. 2 in E-flat major (J. 118).

177. Cherubini's two-act *opéra-ballet*, *Anacréon, ou L'Amour fugitive* (R. Mendouze; Paris, Opéra, 4 October 1803), was a failure, but the overture established itself as a popular concert piece, even into the twentieth century.

178. Tgb. *moyens deployren*.

179. Tgb. *soupiert*.

180. Drama in one act (first performed in Vienna, 1811, and in Berlin Königliches Schauspielhaus, 1812) [Richel 87].

181. I.e., Sografi. Antonio Simone Sografi was an Italian librettist known for his Italian version of Rousseau's *Pygmalion* (1770), set to music as *Pimmaglione* (by Giambattista

Cimadoro; Venice, Teatro San Samuele, 26 January 1790). Cherubini's one-act opera *Pimmaglione* (S. Vestris; Paris, Théâtre des Tuileries, 30 November 1809) was partly founded on this libretto.

182. Tgb. *force.*

183. Nevertheless, Meyerbeer's first, and principal, Italian librettist would be Gaetano Rossi.

184. Winter considered the three-act *Colmal und Colma* (text by M. von Collin after Ossian; Munich, 15 September 1809) his masterpiece. However, it had such a poor reception that he did not stage another opera in the city for another eleven years.

185. Tgb. *goutierte.*

186. Richel [28] ascribes the translation to Ignaz Franz Castelli: drama in three acts from the French (first Viennese performance, 1819; published 1829).

187. Comedy in two acts by G. Conds, from a French source.

188. Richel [32] calls it simply *Die Zauberflöte* (first performance in Hamburg, 1810).

189. Drama in one act (first performance in Vienna, 1807; in Berlin, 1808) [Richel 69].

190. Tgb. *frappierte.*

191. Tgb. *traits de génie.*

192. *Gli Orazi ed i Curiazi, opera seria* in three acts (A. S. Sografi; Venice, Teatro La Fenice, 26 December 1796), the most successful of Cimarosa's serious operas, with a wide European currency until its last revival in Vienna (1822).

193. Comedy in five acts by Pius Alexander Wolff (first performed in Berlin and Vienna, 1810; published 1823) [Richel 164].

194. Meyerbeer's birthday was still being celebrated according to the Jewish calendar: 6 *Ehul* fell on 14 August in 1812.

195. Perhaps "Jörgl," a diminutive for Gänsbacher, who had just left Munich (*BT,* 1:625).

196. *Richard Coeur-de-Lion, opéra comique* in three acts (J. M. Sedaine, after Lhéritier's thirteenth-century fable; Paris, Comédie-Italienne, 21 October 1784), is perhaps Grétry's masterpiece, famous for its use of recurring melody to unify both score and story. It was performed on French stages throughout the nineteenth century, and retained something its popularity into the twentieth (Paris, 1918; Liège, 1930; Brussels, 1933).

197. Nasolini's *Merope*, opera in three acts (M. Butturini; Venice, San Benedetto, 21 January 1796) was very successful in London (1802) and was performed for Napoleon (1811). It was chosen by Häser for her Munich appearance, but found to be thin and uninteresting. Poissl was commissioned to arrange some pieces and rewrite others, including a new duet for Häser and Harlas in act 1. He wrote ten new items, including the overture and closing chorus. Meyerbeer actively contributed to the composition. Loewenberg's reference to Mayr is clearly a confusion (*Annals of Opera,* col. 523).

198. Drama in four acts (first performed in Dresden in 1806, and in Vienna, Burgtheater, 1808) [Richel 89].

199. *Das Neusonntagskind, Singspiel* in two acts (C. Perinet, after P. Hafner's *Der Furchtsame;* Vienna, Theater in der Leopoldstadt, 10 October 1793), was very successful all over Austria and Germany. The 154th Viennese performance was in 1829. Revived in Berlin (1852) and Breslau (1862).

200. Tgb. *souper.*

201. Tragedy by five acts by Johann Wolfgang von Goethe (completed after much revision on 5 September 1787, and performed in Weimar in 1791). It reflects the transition from his early Sturm und Drang period to the classical perceptions he had formulated in Italy. The first performance was arranged by Schiller, with Iffland's acting abilities in mind.

202. The opera was reviewed in the *Allgemeine musikalische Zeitung* 39 (1812): 640. The scoring of the overture and the closing chorus are both attacked. See *BT,* 1:625–26.

203. At the Treaty of Schönbrunn (14 October 1809), as a result of the defeat at Wagram (9 July 1809), Austria was forced to sue for peace with France yet again, and was obliged to hand over Salzburg to Bavaria. The Tyrol had already been ceded to Bavaria in the Treaty of Pressburg (6 December 1805), after the defeat at Austerlitz (2 December 1805).

204. "To the Ship."

205. Schloss Mirabell (1606) was later converted to the baroque style and sumptuously furnished. The garden was laid out in about 1700, and retains much the same appearance to the present.

206. The reference is to the crown prince of Bavaria. It was actually one the residences of the prince-archbishops of Salzburg. The political power of the archbishop was broken by Napoleon, and never regained.

207. The Dom, with its façade of bright Salzburg marble, was begun in 1614, and is the purest example of an Italian monumental building north of the Alps. It has elaborate Renaissance stucco work.

208. Sankt Peterstift forms the west of the Kapitelplatz, and has famous wrought-iron gates leading to the churchyard.

209. The oldest cemetery in German-speaking lands.

210. The Sigismund Gate, or New Gate (Neutor) is a 136 m long tunnel through the Mönchsberg (1767).

211. This a rococo edifice with an attractive artificial lake (the Leopoldskroner Teich).

212. Meyerbeer's maternal grandfather was very ill. Meyerbeer's parents sent him a generous birthday gift of money, which he returned to them.

213. Crossing to the far side of the Salzach on leaving Hallein, the road continues south to Golling, with its attractive main street, castle, and church. It is best known for its waterfall; the lower cascade is approached by road and path.

214. Hallein is an ancient town which retains several streets from the seventeenth and eighteenth centuries. It is of importance for processing salt from the ancient Dürrnberg mines.

215. A road ascends steeply to Dürrnberg. A visit to the salt mines entails negotiating several underground galleries and slides.

216. Situated among the Berchtesgarden Alps, and known since 1100 for a monastery belonging to the Augustinian Canons. It is also famous for its saline springs.

217. "The Beacon."

218. The Königsee is of the most beautiful lakes of the Alps, surrounded by mountains 2,000 m in height.

219. Tgb. *glacis.*

220. There were already stirrings of opposition to Napoleonic rule. These would find full expression in the Wars of Liberation that erupted all over Europe in 1813 as the consequence of Napoleon's disastrous Russian campaign. The call to arms had already been made by Andreas Hofer, who was shot in 1810 for his initially successful attempts to expel the French and Bavarians from the Tyrol.

221. The *Morgenblatt für gebildete Stände* (26 October 1812) provided an obituary: "Hr Liepmann Meyer Wulff, ein sehr reiches Mitglied der hiesigen jüdischen Kolonie der früher in den Finanz-Geschäften des Staates bedeutend hülfreich war, ist gestorben, und er hat den Armen 500 Thaler vermacht" [Herr Liepmann Meyer Wullf, a very wealthy member of the local Jewish community, who has been significantly helpful in the financial af-

fairs of the state, has died, leaving 500 thalers to the poor]. Meyerbeer's wealth and civic-mindedness, as well as his name Meyer, were part of the inheritance and influence of his grandfather.

222.   Häser's benefit concert on 3 August 1812 was not the success all had expected. An unfortunate choice of music, and her shyness, had not impressed the public, but her appearance in *Merope* (1 September 1812) elicited applause and curtain calls.

223.   Both ballets were compiled from the music of famous composers like Haydn and Cherubini.

224.   Tgb. *pas.*

225.   Actually *Weibertreue, oder Die Mädchen sind von Flandern* (Leipzig, 1794). *Così fan tutte, o sia La Scuola degli amanti, opera buffa* in two acts (Lorenzo da Ponte; Vienna, Burgtheater, 26 January 1790) never established itself in repertory in the nineteenth century because of unease over the libretto, which was regarded as immoral and subjected to many different versions and attempts at improving it.

226.   *Le Jugement de Salomon,* a *mélodrame* by Adrian Quaisain (according to *BT,* 1:707). Altmann ascribes it to L.-C. Caigniez, and this is corroborated by Wicks [1595] (*mélodrame* in 3 acts; Paris, Théâtre de l'Ambigue-Comique, 28 niv. X).

227.   According to the *Allgemeine musikalische Zeitung* the performance took place on 11 October 1812. Becker puts the lack of success down to popular disappointment that a more significant work was not performed on a day of national importance (*BT,* 1:627).

228.   Violin Concerto no. 11, op. 23.

229.   Furioso was one of the most accomplished acrobats of his time, and undertook tours as far as Russia.

230.   Tgb. *gigantisch vortrefflich.*

231.   Tgb. *morceaux d'ensembles.*

232.   Tgb. *Hauptcoups.*

233.   The work was dismissed as being more oratorio than opera, heavy in erudition and scholastic exercises, but poor in melody. Reviews are reprinted in *BT,* 1:627–28. The best analysis and assessment of the work, with numerous musical examples, is provided by Edgar Istel in "Meyerbeer's Way to Mastership," 83–102. The score remains unpublished; a particularly fine copy of the autograph is held in the British Library.

234.   Tgb. *souper.*

235.   This, and the meeting with the prince of Gotha in October, makes it clear that Meyerbeer's intentions to visit Italy were already well developed.

236.   Translucent blue gem, a variety of zircon.

237.   Relations between Meyerbeer and Vogler appear to have become clouded in the last months of 1812. This probably accounts for the absence of any mention of Vogler's concert in the Church of St. Michael's in Munich (1 November 1812) to inaugurate the new organ.

238.   Meyerbeer left Munich and immediately traveled to Stuttgart. There is no evidence that he went to Berlin as asserted by Mendel (*Meyerbeer: Sein Leben und seine Werke* [Berlin: R. Lesser, 1869], p. 32) and Kapp (*Giacomo Meyerbeer* [Berlin: Schuster & Loeffler, 1920], p. 39).

Section 2
1813–1826

1813

January–February 1813

On 3 January I left Munich for Stuttgart, where my opera *Wirt und Gast*[1] was produced for the first time on Wednesday, 6 January, for the benefit of my friend the actor Schwarz*. I arrived one day before the performance, and was able to supervise two rehearsals, but could do nothing to help really, since in every respect it had been badly and hurriedly prepared. The production was judged as poor by all critical accounts, and the opera was received very tepidly.[2]

Thursday 18 February. Today I traveled from Mannheim by return coach[3] to Frankfurt. A young man called Rindskopf (a Jew from Frankfurt-am-Main) was my traveling companion. Since I have made the journey to Nuremberg so often, I will be very brief about the details of this trip. At the end of every day I will draw up an account of expenditure, but not my *menu plaisirs* as long as this remains under a gulden. The Neckar was so turbulent we could not cross it, and we had to travel via Heidelberg. We stayed the night in Darmstadt, where I called on no one, other than Mlle. Sommer.[4]

Account: in Mannheim lunch for me, 45 xr.;[5] ditto for the servant, 30 xr. *Summa,* 1 fl. 15 xr.

Friday 19 February. At eleven o'clock in the morning I arrived in Fürth, and instead of attending to the matter of my passport, I decided to rove about and went to Cullmann (his address had been given to me by his sister in Vienna, the widow of the Austrian commissariat officer Joseph Leopold Müller). In the evening to Mathilde, and then to the concert given by the clarinetist Hofman. I again lodged in Der Pariser Hof.

Account: in Darmstadt for night lodgings, etc., 1 fl. 54 xr.; ditto for the servant, 42 xr.; traveling expenses from Mannheim to Fürth, 11 fl. 30 xr.; tip for the coachman, 1 fl.; highway tariff,[6] 1 fl. 45 xr., 2 fl. 24 xr.; concert, 1 fl. 20 xr. *Summa,* 20 fl. 44 xr.

Saturday 20 February. The whole morning was taken up rushing around for my passport. I obtained it without the slightest difficulty. In the afternoon I called on Flersheim. Wrote a letter to Father in Berlin. In the evening to the theater, where they performed *Johanna von Montfaucon* rather badly. The theater has been re-decorated during the eleven months of my absence, and looks very attractive now.

Account: for the passport, 36 xr.; theater, 48 xr. *Summa,* 1 fl. 24 xr.

Sunday 21 February. Called on Cullmann. Wrote a second letter to Father, which I entrusted to Herr Flersheim for delivery. Dined with Herr Flersheim at midday. In the afternoon walked with him to Bonnheim, half an hour from Fürth, where we found a great number of people crowded into two halls. On this occasion I made the acquaintance of his sister-in-law, Mlle. Osten, who was one of the party; she is a charming and seemingly intelligent little woman, made even more inter-esting for me by her passing resemblance[7] to Mlle. Flerx. In the evening to the theater, where Dalayrac's elegant little opera *Macdonald* was performed (see my diary for 1812). From every point of view it was not given nearly as well as in Munich.[8] I found some of the orchestra even better than before, especially as they have been joined by an excellent first cellist and first contrabassist (also VC 3 and CB 3).

Account: theater, 48 xr.

Monday 22 February. Departed from Fürth at midday. Stayed overnight in Aschaffenburg, lodging in the public house. Very good and not as expensive as Das Fass.[9] I have every reason to be content, were it not for the unease about my parents in Berlin, which disturbs my every happy moment.[10]

Account: Louis for expenses, 12 fl. 15 xr. Lodgings in the public house for three and a half days, 13 fl.; lunch, 30 xr.; tip for the waiter, 24 xr.; highway tariff, 53 xr. *Summa,* 26 fl. 2 xr.

Tuesday 23 February. Left Aschaffenburg at five o'clock in the morning, and ar-rived in Würzburg at seven o'clock in the evening.

Account: night lodgings at Aschaffenburg, 2 fl.12 xr.; ditto for the servant, 48 xr.; transport from Fürth to Würzburg, 16 fl.; tips, 2 fl.; lunch for me and Louis, 1 fl. 36 xr. Highway tariff, 2 fl. *Summa,* 24 fl. 36 xr.

Wednesday 24 February. I was much more satisfied with the inn Der Kleebaum[11] than Der Adler,[12] at least from the point of view of economy. Visited the Getschenbergers (see diary for 1812).[13] These people received me so warmly and affectionately that I felt real sadness at leaving them after half an hour. When I arrived home, I found Professor Fröhlich (see diary for 1811 and 1812).[14] We chatted again for a couple of hours, agreeably and informatively. I promised to recommend him to Kapellmeister Glöggl* as a correspondent for Linz's musical paper[15] (should I ever reach Linz and make his acquaintance). In the afternoon at two o'clock I traveled by return coach to Nuremberg. We stayed overnight in Mainbernheim (twelve hours from Nuremberg). [Wrote] letters to Gottfried Weber in Mannheim and Herr Königswerther in Fürth.

Account: Louis for three days' expenses, 5 fl. 33 xr. In Würzburg for night lodgings and lunch, 2 fl. 9 xr.; ditto for Louis, 42 xr.; tips, 30 xr.; *chaussé,* 14 xr. *Summa,* 9 fl. 8 xr.

Thursday 25 February. Left Mainbernheim at four o'clock in the morning. In spite of this, I arrived in Nuremberg only at ten o'clock in the evening, since the roads were so unbelievably bad.

Account: customs tariff at Regensburg, 3 fl. In Mainbernheim for night lodgings, 2 fl.12 xr.; ditto for Louis, 30 xr.; lunch, 51 xr.; ditto for Louis, 36 xr. *Summa,* 7 fl. 10 xr.

Friday 26 February. Called on Fanny Königswerther (see diary, 1812).[16] She has faded somewhat in the year since we last saw each other, but has therefore become all the friendlier to me. She accepted my kisses and gave me a locket of her hair. Only Heaven knows how this friendship will develop, but I now feel absolutely nothing for her. What cooled me off completely was how she laughingly listened to and repeated[17] several very ambiguous jokes about her husband (initiated[18] by a certain Rat Toussaint, who had come over expressly to meet me). At four o'clock in the afternoon we parted and I went to the theater, where they performed the famous *Evactel und Schnudi* for the first time (for Herr Roland's benefit). Apart from Herr Roland, who played Schnudi very well, the actors did not satisfy me nearly as much as those in the Vorstadt-Theater in Munich.[19] They so drawl the verses that the rhymes are not sufficiently emphasized.[20] They also lack the Viennese dialect and humor that make the jokes so piquant. The public seemed never to have heard doggerel[21] before, and laughed at every couplet. Nevertheless, minority good taste eventually took the upper hand, and any applause beginning in the gods [upper tiers] was suppressed with loud hissing. The parody of the big Italian aria with chorus (sung by Schnudi) amused me as much as ever before. It really is a delightful play and does Wenzel Müller much honor.

Account: night lodgings, etc., 1 fl. 57 xr.; ditto Louis, 1 fl. 14 xr.; transport from Würzburg to Nuremberg, 9 fl.; trip for the coachman, 2 fl.; ditto in the inn, 36 xr.; Louis for expenses, 13 xr.; theater, 1 fl. 12 xr. *Summa,* 16 fl. 39 xr.

Saturday 27 February. Since I could not find a coach returning to Regensburg, I was obliged to hire a private vehicle for eighteen gulden. I left at ten o'clock in the morning and stayed the night in Hemau (sixteen to eighteen hours from Regensburg). Considering the ill-repute of the inns between Würzburg and Nuremberg, it was tolerable. The region between the two cities is barren and uniform.

Account: night lodgings, etc., in Nuremberg, 1 fl. 24 xr.; ditto for Louis, 30 xr.; tips 24 xr.; customs tariff, 4 xr. *Summa,* 2 fl. 28 xr.

Sunday 28 February. In Regensburg I wrote a letter to Father, ditto to Königswerther, enclosing the one to Father. I left Hemau at five in the morning, and arrived in Regensburg at four in the afternoon. I went to the theater (the composer Walter* is entrepreneur). The building is as big as that in Fürth and has a similar shape. They performed Kotzebue's comedy *Die Belagerung von Saragossa*[22] most tolerably; Herr Eugen as Feldkümmel is even quite waggish. What particularly pleased me was the voice that he assumed for this role, like that of a plump contralto. The house was filled to capacity. I went to the big box on the middle tier, where I made the acquaintance of the very pleasant wife of some professor, whose name I unfortunately never found out.

Account: night lodgings, etc., 1 fl. 58 xr.; ditto for Louis, 30 xr.; lunch, 32 xr.; ditto for Louis, 30 xr.; Louis for expenses, 18 xr.; theater, 1 fl.; transport from Nuremberg to Regensburg, 18 fl.; tip for the coachman, 1 fl. 36 xr. *Summa,* 24 fl. 24 xr.

March 1813

Monday 1 March. I received a letter of recommendation from Dr. Königswerther for Herr Sekstein, an associate[23] of his son-in-law, Wertheimer. I delivered this and obtained 100 fl. bills of exchange, for which I paid 87 fl. Afterwards I surprised Dorville (see diary, 1812)[24] who, in the last few months, has established a tobacco factory here with his brother. He gave me the happy news that Poissl (see 1812) arrived the day before yesterday, and is apparently still here. I must try to find my dear friend immediately. Dined at midday with Herr Sekstein, where I met his charming little wife. Spent the whole afternoon vainly searching for Poissl: he had returned to Chamm two days ago. In the evening to the theater, where *Der Dorfbarbier,* and Kotzebue's *Max Helfenstein,*[25] were performed. In the latter, I was particularly taken by Herr Stahl. He seems to me an excellent actor in roles for humorous young men, being blessed with a resonant voice, a pleasant face, and relative fluency. (In these respects he bears a passing resemblance[26] to Eunike.) In the evening I had supper[27] with Dorville *en famille,* where I met his wife, his brother, and his sister-in-law. The two women are very attractive, although of a somewhat provincial[28] appearance. I played the *Rondo in G Major.*

Account: theater, 36 xr.; customs tariff, 3 fl.; Louis for expenses, 12 xr. *Summa,* 3 fl. 48 xr.

Tuesday 2 March. Wrote to Poissl, inviting him to come to me in Straubing, ditto to Gottfried Weber. Dined at midday with Herr Sekstein. In the afternoon I tried to find a coach for Staubing, Linz, or Vienna, and as I could find nothing, I decided to travel by water, since the next mail boat sails for Vienna tomorrow. In the evening to the theater, where I saw *Das Ehepaar aus der Provinz*, a comedy by Jünger.[29] Herr Stahl in the role of the bridegroom from the provinces was very good. Afterwards I had tea at Dorville's, and then went on to Sekstein's (I played the *Variations in F*), where I met his son-in-law, Dr. Cannstein, and went with him to the masked ball in Das Kreuz,[30] which was extremely brilliant and friendly. I would have enjoyed myself very much had I not been tortured with unease about my parents in Berlin. Every day this thought haunts me before sleeping, in my dreams, and on waking. If only I were already in Vienna, where I hope to find news.

Account: theater, 36 xr.; *ball masqué*, 1 fl.; boots heeled, 1 fl. 30 xr. *Summa,* 3 fl. 6 xr.

Wednesday 3 March. At ten o'clock in the morning I set off by ship. I had only one other traveling companion, Herr Meurer, a watchmaker from Chauxdefond, near Neuchâtel. The cabin was very roomy and contained an iron brazier that was kept constantly heated. This mode of travel pleases me greatly, and moreover has advantages of economy, since the fifty-six miles from Regensburg to Vienna carry a road tariff[31] of 6 fl. per person. We spent the night in Straubing.

Account: two and a half days in the public house in Regensburg, 3 fl. 36 xr.; ditto for Louis, 2 fl. 30 xr.; provisions on the journey, 6 fl. 26 xr.; tips, 1 fl. *Summa,* 13 fl. 32 xr.

Thursday 4 March. Today we were joined by another traveling companion, Herr Bekker, a young merchant from Speyer. At six o'clock we embarked; as we came on board I was given the unpleasant news that my dog, Courage, had run off. We set sail at a rate of knots, and since there are tables in the cabin, I had marvelous leisure for working. Unease about my parents in Berlin so overpowered me, however, that I was incapable of any reflection. If only I could be relieved of this anxiety about the safety of my loved ones. Should I find letters from home on my arrival, the first needy person I meet will have 1 fl.[32] Today we reached Vilshofen. Because the weather is so unfriendly, with blizzards blowing, I spent the whole day in the cabin, and could hardly see the landscape.

Account: night lodgings for me and Louis, 1 fl. 59 xr.; to Louis for expenses, 16 xr. *Summa,* 2 fl. 18 xr.

Friday 5 March. We departed at five o'clock this morning. Because I had been disturbed all night by restless dreams about my parents, and also had to get up so early, I felt exhausted all day. Today we reached Engelhartszell, the Bavarian customs post. At midday we reached Passau and passed a few hours there. Wrote letters from Passau to Hermann Levi in Regensburg, and to my brother in Vienna.

Account: night lodgings for me and Louis, 1 fl. 2 xr.; tips, 40 xr.; bread/writing paper/breakfast rolls, 8 xr.; midday meal in Passau for me and Louis, 1 fl. 24 xr.; coffee, 40 xr.; barber, 12 xr.; postage stamps, 30 xr.; bookbinder for the passport, 4 xr. *Summa,* 4 fl. 18 xr.

Saturday 6 March. We left Engelhartzell at six o'clock in the morning, and towards midday reached Aschach, the first Austrian customs post. I was very thoroughly searched, but treated very courteously for all that. One is required to let the police stamp a visa in one's passport, and to tell them one's business in Vienna; their behavior was polite throughout. The customs held us up here for the whole day.

Account: night lodgings for me and Louis, etc., 36 xr.; for the customs, 1 fl.; in Aschach, 12 xr.; for a Prussian laborer to redeem his goods from the customs, 2 fl. *Summa,* 3 fl. 48 xr.

Sunday 7 March. Because the wind is blowing contrarily, we were unfortunately obliged to remain here the whole day. Fortunately, I am on very good terms with my traveling companions, so we have been able to endure our boredom *à trois.*

Account: a half-day stay in Aschach for me and Louis, 6 fl. 5 xr. *Summa,* 6 fl. 5 xr.

Monday 8 March. The contrary wind blew all day again, and we had to stay on here. Added to the tedium is my fearful anticipation of news from my parents: this worried me all day.

Account: customs tariffs, 9 xr.; expenses to Louis, 36 xr. *Summa,* 45 xr.

Tuesday 9 March. Today I again had to cope with boredom in Aschach, because the wind will still not die down. A man called Wangmüller from Passau (he seems an adventurer to me), who is commissioned to convey a loaded ship to Vienna, has, by his intrusiveness, disturbed the only pleasure that I have had here, peace. Walked to the castle of Count Harrach a quarter of an hour away.

Account: to Louis, 1 fl. 48 xr., for his night lodgings, 30 xr.; bill for 2 days in Aschach, 3 fl. 4 xr.; tips, 30 xr. *Summa,* 5 fl. 52 xr.

Wednesday 10 March. The elements at lasted smiled on us propitiously again, and we left Aschach. At ten o'clock we landed at Linz, where all passports were inspected. As I was disembarking, a young man came up to me asking my name, and, on hearing my answer, urgently asked me to accompany him to Kapellmeister Glöggl, since it appeared that someone very much wanted to speak with me. I went along with him, and as the door opened (how can I describe my amazement?) Vogler stepped out to greet me. He was just about to travel to Vienna, but learned of my arrival from the police. He immediately told me the news that *the grand duke of Hesse has appointed me court and chamber composer*. Since the grand duke supposed me, as well as Vogler, to be in Paris, the patent has been sent there.[33] He then introduced me to Kapellmeister Glöggl (the editor of the *Linzer musikalische Zeitung*), who seemed very pleased to meet me, and showed me an important article that he has published in his paper about my opera *Jephtha*. Afterwards I went to my lodgings, wrote a letter to Gottfried Weber in Mannheim, then dined with Glöggl, before traveling on. Our group has increased by several members. Among them only a Huron clergyman seemed to warrant observation. His body was small and dumpy, typical of a priest; his head, dark as a mulatto, suggested crudeness, wildness, and malice; indeed, he could well have furnished the subject for a portrait of a Huron bandit. He seemed a mixture of priestly cowardice and Huron wildness, such an unusual and original contrast that the character seemed perfect for representation.[34] We stayed overnight in Mauthausen.

Account: sugar, 56 xr., apples, 4 xr.; letters, 43 xr.; alms, 1 fl. *Summa,* 2 fl. 43 xr.

Thursday 11 March. We voyaged from Mauthausen to Stein-bei-Krems, where we stayed overnight. The inclement weather confined me to the cabin for the whole day.

Account: Louis for expenses, 50 xr.; night lodgings in Mauthausen, 1 fl. 38 xr; ditto for Louis, 1 fl. 30 xr. *Summa,* 3 fl. 58 xr.

Friday 12 March. We landed at two-thirty in the afternoon at Nussdorf (an hour from Vienna). Here we had to relinquish our passports (for which we were given a stamped receipt, which must be handed in at the police station tomorrow), and our luggage was inspected (for the third time since entering Austria). When all this was over, we took a cab[35] to Vienna. The city did not present a very brilliant picture from this perspective. We entered through the Schottentor and dismounted at the hotel Zum Erzherzog Karl[36] in the Kärntnerstrasse. I went immediately to Der Roten Igel[37] at Unter den Tuchladen (this being my brother Wilhelm's address), in order to ascertain whether he is still here, and was delighted to have confirmation of this. I did not find him in, however, and had to look him up at Baermann and Harlas's hotel. (Both are appearing as guest artists here with great success.) The joy of these three dearest people (not to mention my own!) at this reunion was something to behold. My brother had already rented a room for me, close to his own (for a 25 fl. bill of exchange). I also made the acquaintance of his traveling companion, Herr Lomnitz from Berlin, whom I had met earlier. In the evening we went to the Kärntnertor-Theater, where they performed an opera by Weigl, *Der Bergsturz*.[38] I was so excited[39] and fascinated by the new house and public that I cannot entrust myself with any critical reactions.

Saturday 12 March–Sunday 28 March.

During these sixteen days I was so distracted by delivering my letters, invitations, visits to famous composers, looking at the sights, and attending the theater that I was not able to keep my diary. I would at least like to keep a record of the names of the pieces (largely new to me) that I saw in the theaters of both the city and suburbs. There are actually five theaters, each specializing in a different genre (almost as in Paris, only here the genres are not quite so differentiated). Of the two theaters in the city, the Burg performs only plays, comedies and tragedies,[40] the Kärntnertor only operas and ballets.[41] The Theater an der Wien[42] gives both drama and opera, but aims particularly at so-called spectacle plays,[43] which are then mounted to perfection (with regard to décor, machinery, and costumes). The Leopoldstädter-Theater and Josephstädter-Theater are really popular playhouses, where comedians perform in the Austrian patois, and where, for the most part, local comedies, or parodies in doggerel, sometimes magic operas,[44] are performed.[45] The Kärntnertor-Theater is a building of five stories (inclusive of galleries), with each tier made up of boxes. The building overwhelms one, especially on first entering, because of its immense spaciousness; on closer inspection one finds that everything has a faded and used appearance. This is also the case with décor and costumes. Indeed, neglect is the principal failing of the current administration. I will remain silent about the artists, since I will have opportunity to speak of them in relation to individual performances; all I will say at the moment is that they have a finer troupe than any other opera stage I have yet seen. The orchestra is very much inferior to those of Munich and Frankfurt, and (if I rightly remember) even to that of Berlin. The complementation is completely disproportionate; for example, there are only twelve violins and yet four contrabasses (the latter having five strings!), which are played sitting down. One has the impression of a curtailment of timbre, and hears only a terrible racket in forte passages. The positioning is also bad, and the conducting (apart from Weigl's) sluggish. The timpani also deserve a negative mention, since they sound like old broken kettles. Spohr*[46] tells me that this is because the heads of the drumsticks are bare wood and not wrapped in cloth. The chorus, particularly the men, are on occasion (as in *Ferdinand Cortez* and *Der Bergsturz*) quite outstanding, often good, and always at least tolerable, better than in Munich. The first kapellmeister in this theater is Joseph Weigl, the second Gyrowetz, the third Umlauff*,[47] the Kapellmeisteradjunct Drechsel, and the Director of Orchestra Wranitsky*.[48] The theater production[49] rotates between Vogel, Weinmüller, and Saal. There is a resident ballet master, the famous Duport; the theater poet is Castelli. Prince Lobkowitz* is the entrepreneur of this and the Burgtheater. The seat prices are, at the moment, as follows: orchestral stalls,[50] 1 fl. 15 xr.; reserved seats in the orchestral stalls, 2 fl.; second orchestral stalls, 36 xr.; first tier of boxes, [?]; second tier, [?]; third tier, 45 xr.; fourth tier (gallery), [?].

The Theater an der Wien has one tier less than the Kärntnertor, and therefore seems much friendlier, as well as fresher and more brilliant than the latter. It was built by Schikaneder only a few years ago. Because this theater plays all genres, and magnificence and variety are a matter of policy, it does not consider the public quite so carefully with regard to individual casting of roles as do the Kärntnertor and the Burg. However, in every other arrangement it takes the greatest care and precision. The orchestra and chorus are less important than those of the Kärntnertor. The first kapellmeister is von Seyfried*, the second Buchwieser, the principal director of the orchestra for the last few weeks is the well-known Spohr (with the title of kapellmeister), the second von Blumenthal. The production manager rotates between the actors Grüner, Scholz, and Meyer. The theater inspector (who seems to me to be of great influence) is Treitschke*. Count Ferdinand Palffy* has the enterprise of this theater.[51] Seat prices are as follows: first orchestral stalls, 48 xr.; reserved seats, 1 fl. 12 xr.; and in this respect everything is so much cheaper than in the city. The Leopoldstädter-Theater and the Josephstädter-Theater are, as I observed earlier, popular theaters. There can be no question here of high artistic standards: one goes there to laugh. Nonetheless, the Leopoldstädter-Theater has much fine machinery and décor, an area in which the Josephstädter cannot compete, since it is so much smaller. Both have ballet, although it is not very significant. The first is under the direction of Herr Häusler (Ferdinand Kauer and Franz Volkert* are the music directors), while the latter is directed by Herr Joseph Huber (with Franz Roser as music director). The prices are 36 xr. for the first stall seats, and in this respect more expensive. I have not yet been able to visit the Burg-Theater. The following are the pieces I have seen during the past sixteen days.

In the Kärntnertor: Weigl's latest opera, *Der Bergsturz*; Dalayrac's *Die Savoyarden;* a ballet devised and danced by Duport, *Der ländliche Tag;* Mosel's* grand opera in four acts, *Salem;*[52] Gyrowetz's *Der Augenarzt;* Mozart's *Titus,*[53] in which Mme. Harlas sang Sextus and Mme. Schönberger Titus; and Cimarosa's *Gli Orazi ed i Curiazi* with Mme. Harlas as Curiazio. There was the first performance of *Fünf sind zwei*, an opera in one act based on Castelli's *Domestiken-streiche*, with music by ten Viennese composers. I further saw *Telemach*, a grand ballet in three acts devised and danced by Duport; Spontini's grand opera in three acts, *Ferdinand Cortez;* and [Gaetano] Gioia's* ballet *Der Schatz im Traume.*

In the Theater an der Wien: Kotzebue's *Die kluge Frau im Walde;*[54] Winter's *Das unterbrochene Opferfest.*

In the Leopoldstädter-Theater *Die drei Wunderrätsel, oder Die Zauberbrille*, a magic opera in 3 acts.[55]

In the Josephstädter-Theater the first performance of *Die Bedienten in Wien*, a comedy in three acts [by ?].

These are the concerts I have attended during this time: Nikolaus Kraft* the younger, violoncellist at Prince Lobkowitz's; Baermann and Harlas; Mme. Aurnheim (a theater singer); Louise Pascal, a harpist from Paris. The concerts are always

held in the hours of midday in a small ballroom. The locale is small (by my esti-
mation it holds no more than five hundred people). The hall looks cold and unfriendly. The daylight finally lends an unendurable air of ordinariness to the whole.
During these sixteen days my expenses came to 100 fl.

Sunday 28 March. In the morning I brought my diary, which has been in arrears,
up to date. Then I went to a concert given by the bassoonist Anton Romberg* (the
brother of my friend Bernard Romberg). Beethoven's powerful overture to the
tragedy *Coriolanus*[56] was followed by Romberg's Bassoon Concerto. I have never
heard a more beautiful tone elicited from the bassoon; he knows how to give an
air of unity to the biggest leaps and runs. His delivery lacks only light and shade,
and is on the whole too tame for me. After his recital, Harlas sang a lovely cavatina
from Nasolini's *Merope* [see example 17]

Example 17. Theme from Nasolini's *Merope*

just as superbly as during the last season in Munich.[57] This divine talent, here at
least, finds the reception it deserves. To conclude with, Romberg played some
variations by Kapellmeister Umlauff. Today I dined with Herr Leopold Herz. There
I met Salieri*: he is in his sixtieth year, is very small with a fine sharp face full of
satirical wrinkles; his small flashing eyes, full of movement, are his most striking
feature. Lavater* would have likened him to a shrew.[58] He was in any case very
genial and talkative; he had just heard the news from Paris that *Axur*[59] has been
given with outstanding success at the Odéon. I asked his permission to call on him,
which he granted most charmingly. After lunch the awful pianistic strummings of
two dilettantes (the daughters of Herr Herz) so upset my digestion that I quickly left
for home. Carl Maria von Weber is coming here tomorrow and Baermann is traveling to meet him.[60] I cannot do likewise because Weber has not answered my letter
extending him the hand of reconciliation.[61] I therefore feigned an indisposition in
the evening so as not to have to accompany him, and thus did not attend the theater.

Monday 29 March. I had just written a letter to Gottfried Weber, when the door
opened and Carl Maria von Weber walked in. The sight of my beloved friend
extinguished all resentment in my heart, and with a loud cry I flung myself into
his arms. We immediately went to look for Papa Vogler, but we did not find him

at home. Then we dined together at the *restaurateur* Jahn's, where I usually eat when not invited out. In the evening I attended the Kärntnertor-Theater, in order to see a little opera by Umlauff, called *Der Grenadier*. The subject[62] has been very skillfully planned, and the first scenes have an extraordinary tension; but thereafter it slackens off, and I particularly disliked knowing so far in advance that the Grenadier is really the girl's cousin. It seems to me that there would have been a very interesting scene if they had brought the trial onto the stage. Vogel told me afterwards that the libretto is by Babo. The music is very pretty, but far too heavy for such a lightly sketched story. It is strange how this music has affected me: often at the beginning of a scene it would displease me, but by the time it had ended I found myself pleasantly impressed. It seems to me (if I am to explore this reaction) that it is better understood as progressing rather than developing.[63] This little opera was acted and sung by Vogel*, Weinmüller*, and the two ladies Bondra with a perfection of ensemble the like of which I have never before seen or heard. Afterwards came a ballet that I already knew, so I went to the Burgtheater to see the last acts of *Sorgen ohne Noth*.[64] The theater has four storeys and is long but narrow, with wide low boxes, the whole having a depressed appearance. I can say nothing about the actors today, since I saw only a few acts.

Tuesday 30 March. Wrote and practiced in the morning. Visit from Carl Maria von Weber. At midday dined with Herr von Reyer. In the afternoon called on Harlas, who is ill, then went on to Baroness Arnstein.* Afterwards I attended the Theater an der Wien to see the last acts of Kotzebue's magic play *Die kluge Frau*, half of which I had earlier missed because of company. The splendor of the décor far surpassed the earlier performance.

Wednesday 31 March. Today I delivered a number of letters of recommendation (which I should have done earlier) to the Prussian ambassador (Wilhelm von Humboldt*),[65] Frau von Eskeles, Count Fries, Königstein, Mme. Uffenheimer, Baron Steigentesch (the well-known writer), Count Ferdinand Palffy (entrepreneur of the Theater an der Wien). The last three were not at home. All the others received me with friendliness, some even cordially. In the afternoon I went to Baermann, afterwards to C. M. von Weber, and then with both of them to the Theater an der Wien, where they performed Mozart's *Figaros Hochzeit*.[66] The production was very successful, on the whole. Demoiselle Buchweiser*, as Susanna, was particularly outstanding. Today I cashed the bills of exchange that I bought in Fürth from Königswerther, which in all amounted to 281 gulden in notes.

April 1813

Thursday 1 April. Account: Louis for expenses, 7 fl.; washerwomen, 7 fl.; alms, 5 fl.; piano tuner, 1 fl.

I spent almost the whole day viewing the big collections of natural history. In the afternoon I paid a sick call to Harlas. There I made the acquaintance of Therese Sessi*, who arrived here a while ago. (She is the cousin of the famous Mariane Sessi.) At midday I dined with C. M. von Weber at Jahn's and in the afternoon I went walking with him and Baermann. In the evening to the Kärntnertor-Theater, where they performed Spontini's *Die Vestalin*. I have to say that the production of this opera in Darmstadt appealed to me much more. Here they rushed the tempi so absurdly that the orchestra did not have the appropriate energy to convey the giant accentuation of this divine music, and the choruses were uncharacteristically weak. Only Siboni was really powerful on several occasions. I must refer to one alteration that seems particularly purposeful to me; they have some of the ensemble for the Vestals sung by the High Priestess alone, which improves on the otherwise hurried and pinched[67] effect of this passage when sung by all the sopranos [see example 18].

Example 18. Theme from Spontini's *La Vestale*

Account: to Wolff [= Wilhelm Beer] for expenses, 5 fl.

Friday 2 April. Called on Vogler. Practiced. Dined at midday with Frau von Eskeles. There I met the famous Italian poet, Herr von Carpani (author of *Die Uniform,*[68] etc.). A face exhausted by nervous twitching contrasted wonderfully with the Italianate fire of his speech. We sat next to each other at table and I learned many interesting things about Italian music from him. After lunch I accompanied C. M. von Weber home. (He too had dined at Frau von Eskeles's.) Here at last ensued the explanation of our misunderstanding, which has lasted for six months. We both had anxiously and assiduously steered clear of this explanation, thereby seeking to avoid unpleasant issues, and only a happy chance led us on to the subject, which could no longer be evaded. I had actually been reconciled with my friend in my inmost heart from the moment I saw him again. But thank heaven that the reconciliation has now taken place in all its forms.[69] We then went out to Baermann, and with him to the Kärntnertor-Theater, where they performed Boieldieu's* opera in two acts, *Johann von Paris*.[70] Since this opera has been mounted with extraordinary success[71] both in Paris and Vienna, I went with intense expectations. These expectations were not fulfilled. Boieldieu is known to me from *Der*

Kalif von Bagdad[72] and *Ma Tante Aurore*[73] as a composer who excels[74] at pleasant melodies, fluent phrasing,[75] and touches of Dalayracian naturalness. To my amazement I found no trace of these features in this opera. There is hardly any charming melody and the appropriate delicacy of touch for this slight and frivolous subject;[76] on the contrary, everything is dragged out, and the musical elements in the situations (which are always light[77] and friendly) affect a very serious and precious[78] tone. If, on the one hand, and to my great surprise, I missed those features of the Boieldieu I know so well, on the other I discovered new ones, unfamiliar to me: treasurable rhetorical command (especially in the trio no. 2), wonderful vocal writing (especially at the conclusion of the Troubadour's Romance), many really striking harmonic progressions, power, fire, and especially in the act 1 finale, many attractive figures (which pass between the singers and the orchestra), great liveliness in the handling of the voices, a striving, drive, and urgency that rises to something quite gripping towards the end of the act. I suppose, with hindsight, that my expectations were indeed surpassed. The pieces that afforded me greatest pleasure on today's hearing are the trio no. 2 and finale (in act 1), while in act 2 I especially liked the aria "Alles für Liebe und Ehre," the Troubadour's Romance no. 9 (with its genuine Spanish refrain), and the duet no. 12. I will discuss the subject and production after the next performance, since I have used up too much time and space for today. Suffice it to say that the orchestra played with the precision, power, and fire (especially in the act 1 finale) that one would always like them to have. Unfortunately, this will have to remain a *pia desiderata*. In the morning I called on my old pupil, Charlotte Mangold (see diary, 1811).

    Account: lent Wolff, 45 gulden; theater, 1 fl.15 xr. Gefr., 30 xr. *Summa,* 1 fl. 45 xr.

Saturday 3 April. Called on Vogler. Unfortunately I lazed about all morning instead of working. At midday I was invited to dine with the Prussian ambassador, Wilhelm Freiherr von Humboldt. To begin with, the meal was awkward,[79] like the one in Munich at Prince Bariatinsky's (see diary, 1812), although the conversation gradually became more general.[80] By the time I left, boredom[81] had gained the upper hand. I did make the acquaintance of the nephew[82] of the Prussian *Staatsrat* [Gottfried Johann Christoph] Kunth, who has been called to Paris by Alexander von Humboldt*, and the Prussian Count Henkel, who is going to the army[83] in Breslau.[84] The son of the famous Madame de Staël* was also there, but I did not find the opportunity of exchanging a word with him. He would appear to be just a very ordinary young French whippersnapper.[85] When I arrived home, I found letters from Mother and the Herr Professor [Wolfssohn] in Berlin, and from Herr Reuter in Munich. I wrote a letter to Mother and then went to Spontini's opera *Ferdinand Cortez.*[86] This seems to me very much inferior to *Die Vestalin.* While some of the material is vast and terrifically stirring, most of it is wild and bizarre. The divine flow of lyricism that permeates *Die Vestalin* is hardly discernible in

Cortez: at the moment I am not able to cite any music other than the aria "Abitre de ma destinée," the duet "L'airainsonne" [= act 3, duet no. 5, "Un espoir me reste"], the final chorus, and the hymn. However, this reproach is valid only if, in criticizing, one has *Die Vestalin* in mind. There are many glorious details: the whole introduction and the duet during which one hears the Indian March in the distance (in act 1); the duet between Telasco and Almazily, and thereafter between Cortez and Almazily; the following *morceau d'ensemble*, and the aria "Abitre de ma destinée" (in act 2); the chorus for thirteen tenors; the hymn and final chorus (in act 3)—all very impressive. What a pity that in *Cortez* Spontini has *sought* originality, and has believed himself to have found it in crude and relentlessly consecutive modulations and bizarre harmonies. And yet on occasion one finds the most unbelievable harmonic banalities: in the otherwise very lovely duet between Almazily and Cortez, for example, the bass sustains nothing other than the dominant and tonic for thirty to forty bars, which is really awful. In this opera Spontini also appears to have forgotten the negative lever[87] to all effectiveness, *contrast.* But in this respect the librettist may well have misled him since the subject . . . However, the conditions of my diary dictate that I should limit my opinions to fleeting observations, and not give way to full-blown reviews. And since *Cortez* is often performed here, there will be opportunity enough to discuss the lyricism of the subject on the next occasion.

   Account: to Louis for expenses, 1 fl. 7 xr.; beer money, 2 fl. *Summa,* 3 fl. 7 xr.

Sunday 4 April. Today the violinist Mayseder gave a concert (see diary, 1812).[88] I find him positively changed in all respects. His playing (which in any case had always pleased me) has acquired more aplomb, as has his composition (without effacing his geniality).

June 1813

Saturday 19 June. Letter from Baermann, from Father in Johannisbrunn in Bohemia, and another from Landshut in Silesia that had been delayed, from Mother and from Reimann* in Berlin. Called on Dr. Wolff. Worked on the general sketches for the Italian opera.[89] In the evening to the Leopoldstädter-Theater, where they performed *Ritter Diamantino* for the first time, and for the benefit of the singer Pfeifer; this is a big romantic opera in 4 acts by Perinet*, music by a local composer called Gebel*. Of all Perinet's bungling, all of it wretched, this seems to me to be the worst. It is utter nonsense,[90] and since it is unfortunately meant to be serious, proves to be unendurable. The music fits the poetry. And yet at the end of the performance the public called Perinet out!

Sunday 20 June. Called on Frau von Levinger. Went to Dornbach,[91] where I dined at Reyer's[92] and stayed on until theater time. Then I attended the Theater an der

Wien, where they gave the opera *Die Schwestern von Prag*.[93] Even though it was the fourth performance of the reprise, it was crowded. This is particularly because of the droll acting of the court actor Baumann* as the tailor's apprentice, and the singing of Herr Häser*, who, as the second sister, has an aria in falsetto. He parodies the usual roulades of the Italian singers with much elegance and agility.

Monday 21 June. Letter from Herr Fiedler in Prague. Called on Dr. Wolff. At three o'clock in the afternoon I went with Herr von Levinger to the criminal trial of the thief apprehended for stealing fifty Kronenthalers from me three months ago. Called Anton Giovanelli, he is the former hired servant of my brother. A cunning ploy in the examination by the judge led him to admit to the theft in my presence. In the evening to the Kärntnertor-Theater, where they performed *Die Schweizerfamilie*.

Tuesday 22 June. Letter from my father in Prague. To the criminal trial. Anton had lent the fifty thalers to a cabinetmaker who was summonsed and must pay back the money in fourteen days. Because he asked for an extension, I allowed him four weeks. On the street I met Moscheles* and with him called on Pixis*, but we did not find him at home. Then a visit to Sina*. Afterwards to the Theater an der Wien, where they performed *Die vornehmen Wirte*.[94] Today Dr. Wolff is traveling back to Berlin.

Wednesday 23 June. Practiced. Worked on the Italian opera.[95] To the Leopoldstädter-Theater, where they gave the three-act comedy, *Die Weinhändler von Grünzing, oder Der Kreutlerweiberpickering* [by ?], which contains some genuinely comic scenes.

Thursday 24 June. Practiced. Made some visits. In the afternoon called on Sina, where there was a quartet recital. Mayseder played one of his own compositions, which has some inspired traits, but on the whole struck me as too eccentric and fragmentary. In the evening to the Theater an der Wien, where, for the first time, they revived *Don Juan* with new décor, costumes, and cast.[96] I will reserve my judgment until the second performance.[97] Notes from Baroness Münk and Father.

Friday 25 June. Various visits. Practiced. Worked on the Italian opera. In the evening to the Burgtheater, where they performed the tragedy *Die Schuld*.[98]

Saturday 26 June. Made many calls, which took up the whole morning and made me so tired that by the afternoon I could do nothing. In the evening to the Josephstädter-Theater, where, for the first time, they performed a parody of Kotzebue's *Kluge Frau im Walde*, called *Die kuriose Frau im Walde*, as a musical quodlibet. It contains some comic scenes amidst a lot of platitudes. The public were mur-

muring the name of the anonymous author, apparently a Herr [Stephan] von Menner.

Sunday 27 June. Today I arose early at five o'clock in order to make up a party with Petersen, Veit,[99] and Moscheles to travel to the baths at Baden,[100] two post stations from Vienna. One can reach it in three hours. Baden is a friendly little town made almost entirely of new houses, since virtually all of it was burnt down two years ago. The park containing the pump house is very charmingly laid out. From the hill in the park, if one climbs up to the chapel, there is an enchanting perspective. The elegant society at the spa all promenade along the big avenue of this park between twelve and one, a really brilliant gathering[101] that delighted me. I called on Frau von Arnstein, Herr Reyer, Wüstenberger, and Liepmann. In the afternoon we traveled to Helenenthal. This valley is beautifully placed, and from the surrounding hills and mountains one can enjoy wonderful views. We stayed there until seven o'clock, then journeyed back to the town, and to the theater, where they performed *Aschenbrödel*—most tolerably for such a small theater. The house is fairly spacious and most tastefully constructed. Major Zichy[102] is the entrepreneur, and Künlen [Kienlen][103] (known for his composition of *Claudine von Villabella*)[104] the kapellmeister.

Monday 28 June. At seven o'clock in the morning we left Baden and traveled back to Vienna via Laxenburg.[105] We stopped at Laxenburg for a few hours in order to see the gardens of the Schloss and the Old Castle.[106] It is of the same kind[107] as those in Ludwigsburg and Napoleonshöhe, although here there are many more historical points of interest than in either of the others. At four o'clock we arrived back in Vienna. In the evening I went to the Kärntnertor-Theater, where they performed an Italian comic opera in two acts by Buonavoglia, *La Scelta dello Sposo*,[108] music by Guglielmi*.[109] This music has the charm of naturalness, so much so that neither the frivolous genre of the composition, nor the bad instrumentation, nor the boring *secco* recitatives could spoil it. The poet (a person who, in Italian operas anyway, one can usually disregard) has in this case devised several really lovely, and at the same time lyrical, situations: for example, the duet where the widow and the jealous lover dictate their reciprocal conditions; the *morceau d'ensemble* where the three offended lovers have decided not to give the widow any answer to her questions, and then when she comes into the room, each one takes up his favorite activity, one dancing, one singing, and the third fencing. The role of the Widow is the specialty[110] of Demoiselle Therese Sessi, which she also chose earlier for her local début and in which she is very popular. She sings with a wonderful facility and elegance, and also acts with agility.

Tuesday 29 June. Today is the Feast of Peter and Paul. Visit from Pixis. We went to his rooms, where he played me several brilliant sonatas of his own composition. He also gave me a presto, which he says he composed for me without even knowing me since he had already heard from my friends about the genre I usually play. It is fiendishly difficult, with chromatic runs in thirds and sixths and other such devilish stuff. I will have to study it. Worked on the general sketches of the Italian opera. Letter from Father in Teplitz. In the evening to the Burgtheater, where they performed Holbein's elegant little comedy *Der Verräter*; then for the first time *Die beiden Auvergnaten*,[111] a comedy by Kotzebue from his almanac of last year. It pleased, as indeed all sentimental pieces generally do in Vienna, even if it is only relatively enjoyable. To conclude with, they gave another first performance, a comedy in one act, *Lully and Quinault*, freely adapted from the French (in alexandrines) by Castelli.[112] I think it was a bad idea to rob this piece of its original charming music by Nicolò [Isouard]. As a comedy it was rather dull (in spite of the fine situations and Castelli's often very fetching verses). Its appeal was only average.

Wednesday 30 June. Practiced the *Presto*. Worked on the Italian opera. Visits. Letter from Vogler in Munich. To the Kärntnertor-Theater for *Johann von Paris*. Madame Grünbaum* sang the Princess of Navarre very beautifully, while her husband[113] sang Johann rather badly. The Troubadour's Romance had to be repeated today. I bumped into Rode in the theater, and we walked together for a long time on the walls.[114] He told me many interesting things about the state of music in Paris. Then to Geiger's, where I had supper.

July 1813

Thursday 1 July. Practiced the *Presto*. In the afternoon I was invited to coffee at Herr Pohlmann's. Then I went to the Prater with Veit and Kränker (who is from Hamburg), afterwards to De Noaily's Circus Gymnasticus, and finally to the Leopoldstädter-Theater, where they premiered Wenzel Müller's operetta in one act, *Der Windmüller und der Schlossgartner*.[115] The music very much surpassed even the smallest expectations suggested by the name of its author: it is full of song and lovely melodies that the other works of this composer hardly lead one to expect. I drew it to the attention of Herr von Schönholz*, the editor of the local musical paper, hoping that he will mention it. What a pity that it is so full of reminiscences. Afterwards they gave the third performance of a new pantomime by Hempel, *Die Unterhaltung in der Ukraine*,[116] in which Ragnoldi again comically parodied Duport's Russian *pas de deux*.

Friday 2 July. Riding lesson. Practiced the *Presto*. Worked on the Italian opera. Went with Baroness Münk to the instrument-maker Löscher to try out a new instrument. Then to the Leopoldstädter-Theater, where I saw the second performance of *Der Windmüller und der Schlossgärtner*.

Saturday 3 July. Visit from Herr von Schönholz. Practiced the *Presto.* With Baroness Münk went to see the Empress's Rooms.[117] To the Theater an der Wien, where they performed *Die Brandschatzung,*[118] a comedy in one act by Kotzebue. Herr Ochsenheimer* was excellent as Klippfisch. Then followed an Italian intermezzo composed by Herr Häser, *Pigmalion.*[119] The music is flat and ordinary, to say the least. To conclude with, *Pächter Robert*[120] from the French. Letter from Vogler.

Sunday 4 July. Practiced the *Presto.* Called on Frau von Levinger. Arranged the polonaise by Rode (from his Violin Concerto)[121] in order to play it at Rieker's, but because of the bad weather I did not go after all. To the Josephstädter-Theater for the first performance of *Herr von Schindel*[122] (a local farce[123] in three acts). It has very topical characteristics, but does not fail to please for all that, even if it does use the hackneyed theme of the young man from the provinces visiting the capital for the first time.

[During the second half of 1813 and early 1814 Meyerbeer was frequently ill.[124] On 12 October 1813 his setting of Psalm 23, *Gott ist mein Hirt,* for five soloists and chorus, was successfully performed in Berlin; it is understood to have been written to mark his brother Wilhelm Beer's voluntary enlistment in the First Silesian Hussars.[125]]

1814

[On 2 January Meyerbeer participated in the première of Beethoven's *Wellingtons Sieg (Die Schlacht bei Vittoria),* (op. 91), playing the timpani—but far too hesitantly in Beethoven's opinion.[126] A more sympathetic picture of Meyerbeer in this Vienna period is provided by Spohr in his *Selbstbiographie.*[127] On 15 April Meyerbeer's setting of E. M. Arndt's *Des Teutschen Vaterland* (for four male voices) was performed. On 6 May in Darmstadt Vogler died suddenly of a stroke. During May Meyerbeer completed the *Singspiel Das Brandenburger Tor* to a libretto by Salomon Veith.[128] On 25 September, King Friedrich Wilhelm III and Tsar Alexander I arrived in Vienna.[129] *Wirt und Gast* was performed in Vienna (Kärntnertor-Theater, 20 October) as *Die beiden Kalifen,* but without success, receiving only one performance.[130] Towards mid-November Meyerbeer, having failed to make his mark on the participants of the Congress of Vienna, left for Paris. En route he appeared in a concert in Munich (20 November) with great success.[131]

Meyerbeer's first impressions of Paris, the biggest city he had yet encountered, with over one million inhabitants, was of decisive importance for the rest of his life. The immediate effect was overwhelming, as he confided to Gottfried Weber in a letter of 5 January 1815, addressed to him in Mannheim: "The marvels of art and nature, and especially the theater, overpowered my being with such fervor, that I was overcome by a passion of the senses, and went from museum to museum, from library to library, from theater to theater, etc. with a restlessness that would do honor to the Wandering Jew."[132]]

1815

July 1815

Friday 1 July. I obtained Engel's* essay on musical painting[133] from the Imperial Library, read it, and wrote out excerpts. Worked on the Italian operetta.[134] In the evening walked in the boulevards, the most interesting of all theaters! Moreover, most theaters happened to be closed: only two on the Boulevard du Temple were open.

Saturday 2 July. Passed the day in much the same way as yesterday.

Sunday 3 July. Two days without a play is too much for a man of the theater like myself. I therefore betook myself to the Gaité,[135] in spite of all the dust and heat; they performed Guilbert de Pixérécourt's* melodrama, *Le Précipe, ou Les Forges de Norvège*.[136] It is based on *Fridolin* by Holbein.[137] Many of the changes are all to the good.

Monday 4 July. In the library I read Engel's essay and made notes from it.

Tuesday 5 July. In the library I read and made notes from Engel's outstanding essay on musical painting. I spent the rest of the day wandering around the streets, observing the many different groups, expressions, and movements that the current circumstances so stir up among the people. All these things so completely and urgently absorb my interest and attention that I have no time left for my studies and other affairs.

Wednesday 6 July. In the library I completed studying and summarizing Engel's essay, and began reading the other aesthetic matters contained in this volume. In the evening to the Théâtre de la Gaité for *Le Duc de Craon*, a melodrama by Duperche,[138] a very ordinary old French tale of chivalry. Afterwards *La Citerne*,[139] a melodrama by the inexhaustible Herr Pixérécourt, a tapestry of improbabilities and trivialities; one's interest is nonetheless sustained up to the last moment.

Thursday 7 July. Today a newspaper reported one of Bonaparte's doctors as having said of his return from Elba:[140] "Il est encore en état de faire des conceptions, mais il ne peut le suivre plus longtemps que pendant cinq minutes."[141] In these words I found a frightening analogy with my own situation. Indeed, for the last year I have not kept to any of my resolutions for more than a few moments. Even my energies for the small Italian operetta are slackening.[142] Since yesterday, however, the pianistic spirit has started to glow again, but how soon will it be before it is extinguished? What terrible prospects for someone already twenty-three years old! And could anyone else be more blessed by heaven in his outward circumstances, by his freedom, and by his independence, than I am? I fear that that which, for most other artists, would only be a misfortune in my case becomes a sin against the gifts of heaven. O God, give me the earnest intention to extricate myself from this harmful stupefaction, and grant me, loving Father, the will to action!

Friday 8 July. Looked for a French libretto in order to test my powers again, since I have lost all interest in the little Italian operetta.[143] Went with Herr Grossner to the Champs Élysées in order to see the bivouacs of the Prussian and English troops who arrived today.

Saturday 9 July. Played the piano, and composed a new movement. Spent from two until five o'clock on the boulevards to see Louis XVIII's entry.

Sunday 10 July. Today on the streets, quite fortuitously, I encountered a Berliner, Herr Jordan, whom I used to meet often in Vienna last year. He also did not participate in the last campaign, nor did he want to, since he is a bon vivant and an *indifferentist.* He was nonetheless not exempted this time, as his uniform made very obvious. How very much his appearance hurt and humiliated me! Indeed, what plausible excuse could I give for my exemption when neither age nor rank has been immune? The study of my art? How my conscience would punish me! This apathetic condition that so much encourages introspection, these fantasies of composition that go up in smoke between head and pen, this unsystematic reading that retains nothing because it wants to encompass all: does this pass for study?—No, the only advantage ensuing from my sojourn in Paris has resulted from my hearing so much new music (performed, on the one hand, by a different type of orchestra, for a different kind of public, on the other). This indeed is an advantage, but one that stands me in very little stead. I could not overcome the impression that this encounter left on me all day: new thorns for my bleeding heart!

In the evening to the Théâtre Français. They performed *Le vieux Célibataire, comédie en vers* by Collin d'Harville*.[144] The ways to artistic perfection are as many as those to blessedness: Iffland's *Hagestolzen*[145] is a very good play, so much so that Goethe said it established a new type of German comedy (something that I have not been very clear about so far; it seems to me to be more a character play). Collin d'Harville has given his *Hagestolzen* a principal role almost contrary to that of Iffland's, and has, notwithstanding, produced a very good piece of theater.—Then they performed Beaumarchais's* *Le Barbier de Séville.*[146] (I saw it today for the first time, a fact that I, as a man of the theater, can hardly believe.)

Monday 11 July. Finished taking notes from Engel's essay on musical painting and began reading the third part of Laborde's* *Essais.* In the evening to the Vaudeville.

Tuesday 12 July. Vegetated. At midday I dined for the first time in a long while with . . . [?]

November/December 1815

Thursday 30 November. The planned visit to London before my journey to Italy (unfortunately delayed for four weeks by dysentery) was at last put into action today: at ten o'clock my brother Wilhelm, my servant Anton, and I set out for Calais by diligence. Our travel companion was a Creole called Foyer, a captain in English service, a highly educated man of ripe judgment who, moreover, speaks very good German. The route we followed was very uninteresting, and we journeyed through the night.

Friday 1 December. Today we again traveled all day and night. Amiens and Boulogne are the only important places on the way to Calais, and we passed through both by night.

Saturday 2 December. We arrived in Calais at ten o'clock, and spent the day there. Today for the first time I saw a harbor and the sea, the latter impressing me more than I had ever expected.

Sunday 3 December. At two o'clock we left on the English ship *Elizabeth* for Dover. We sailed into contrary winds and had to pay the sea its usual tribute of seasickness. After a voyage of eight hours, we arrived in Dover at ten o'clock at night.

Monday 4 December. At ten in the morning we went to Customs House to have our effects inspected—which was soon done. This was not the case with the Alien Office, where we were very thoroughly examined and eventually given a paper that we have to present to the Alien Office in London. At two o'clock we left by post chaise. Heaven protect me from ever doing this again! Anything more arbitrary than the English postmaster [-general] in respect to the quantity and price of horses, not to mention the road taxes,[147] simply cannot be imagined. The journey from Dover to London cost us sixteen pounds sterling. The route is beautiful, the regions various and charming, each in its own particular way, in large measure because of the wonderful meadow grass, which is still green in December (to my great amazement). The two most important places one passes through are Rochester and Canterbury; the latter is apparently very beautiful, but I could not enjoy this because we traveled by night. We arrived in London at two o'clock in the morning.

Tuesday 5 December. Even though between us we possessed no more than two pounds sterling, I awoke in lighter spirits than for a long time, in a really relaxed frame of mind. We set out to find the banker B. A. Goldschmidt, for whom we had a letter of credit from Father. There I met a young man whom I had often seen in Paris (Emeric), who helped me pass the time until Mr. Goldschmidt arrived. The latter received us politely, but coldly, which struck me more than it would have if we had not just come from Paris, where kindness[148] and dignity[149] appear to be the heritage of the entire nation. He invited us for Sunday (which we declined), and gave us each fifty pounds sterling. Afterwards we went to Mr. Robert Bock, the son of my English teacher in Paris. His father had recommended that we should seek lodgings with his son in London, for two hundred fr. each, for fourteen days. We found Herr Bock to be a kind, polished man with almost French manners, and his wife, a charming little Englishwoman, also received us very kindly. We both proposed to move in today, and proceeded to do so. In the evening we went with Herr Bock to Covent Garden Theatre to see an old tragedy by Otway*, *The Orphan*, over 120 years old.[150] Since I have been learning English for only three months, and have read nothing other than *The Vicar of Wakefield*,[151] I had to spend the whole evening following the lines of the actors from the text to make any sense of the words and verses, and this in spite of the kindness of Herr Bock, who had explained the plot[152] to me. After the tragedy they performed a farce.

Wednesday 6 December. One has breakfast in this house only at ten, whereas we are used to having coffee as soon as we get up. They spend two hours at it, so that the morning is spoiled for any work, especially if one wants to see things. At midday very little is eaten—apart from meat washed down with beer, which I do not like drinking. We are living in narrow and cramped circumstances, and are nonetheless paying *au bout du compte*, as much as in a hotel. All I can say is that these unacceptable features are sufficiently compensated by the fact that we are living with a most educated and pleasant man, who is not only acquainted with all the sights and peculiarities of the city, but also draws our attention to everything; indeed, I believe that, with him, I can learn more about London in fourteen days than in six weeks on my own. Furthermore, in the morning he reads through all the plays that we are to see in the evening. Today we made a promenade through the city, and then through the parks. In the evening we went to the Covent Garden Theatre, where they performed a comedy by Sheridan*, *A Trip to Scarborough*.[153] Today I understood even less than I had of yesterday's tragedy, because of the rapidity of the dialogue.

Thursday 7 December. I devoted the whole morning to studying[154] Shakespeare's* *Richard II*[155] with my brother, since it is to be performed this evening at Drury Lane Theatre, with Kean as Richard. Afterwards came the first performance of a musical farce in two acts, *My Spouse and I*,[156] which was very successful. The Drury Lane orchestra is better than Covent Garden's, but nevertheless very wooden, stiff, and feeble in the strings. Only the trumpets were outstandingly good and powerful. One notices that they are accustomed to playing Handel's* music; he famously wrote very high notes for the trumpet, as well as providing them with many muted notes. The timpani also sound better than our German ones.

Friday 8 December. Walked in the city with Mr. Bock, traversing the elegant and most newly built part, the West End. In the evening we saw a new comedy in Covent Garden, *What's a Man of Fashion?*, by Reynolds*. Then came an opera, *Cymon*, which Garrick* wrote forty-five years ago, and which a contemporary composer, Dr. Arne,[157] set to music.[158] Everything one hears by this musician breathes naturalness, even if it is somewhat old-fashioned: it has good declamation, with especially close observation of caesuras. At least a half had been newly composed by Bishop* (who does this with all operas produced at Covent Garden, even the French ones—and then in a Punch-and-Judy manner). Even though the music he composed for *Cymon* is much better than his other work, the disparity of styles creates a jarring effect.

Saturday 9 December. Visited Westminster Abbey. My first viewing did not impress me as much as I had expected, because it is so overbuilt and neglected. In the evening to Covent Garden: *The Orphan*. I regard Miss O'Neil as the first *tragédienne* in Europe.

Sunday 10 December. With Mr. Bock, prepared *Othello*.

Monday 11 December. Called on Mr. Goldschmidt. St. Paul's Church. Drury Lane for *Othello*.[159] Today Kean* played Iago. As I entered the box I met Iwan Müller*, somewhat embarrassed, but otherwise just as in Paris.

Tuesday 12 December. Visited the Tower. In the evening to Sans Pareil, a small theater on the Strand: *Love in Mist*, a bad Scottish ballet with ear-splitting Scottish music. This was followed by a comic opera, *The Merchant's Daughter*.[160] Miss Scott not only sang and played the leading role, but is also the authoress of this and nearly all other pieces at this theater. The orchestra performed very badly. Afterwards a pantomime.

Wednesday 13 December. At midday dined with Goldschmidt. The gathering, made up solely of Germans, stayed until midnight. I strongly resisted playing the piano after lunch, maintaining that I had rheumatism in my arm. I now no longer dare to perform in company, since during my time in Paris this past year I have not practiced.

Thursday 14 December. To the London Museum, formerly the Liverpool Museum. In the evening to Drury Lane for the reprise of *The Merchant of Bruges,* an old play by Beaumont* with new music by Cook* (very little of it, actually);[161] it contains a neat little ensemble piece. Kean played the Merchant. I felt my opinion confirmed: he is a man of great talent, but a charlatan. Afterwards *My Spouse and I.* The music is common, and like all the other English operas I have heard, with the exception of *Cymon,* in the style of the Leopoldstädter-Theater.

Friday 15 December. To Müller in order to accompany him to meet some other pianists. [Ferdinand] Ries*, for whom I have a letter from Nieth, was not at home. To Klengel,* who has been here for a few months. He knows me from Berlin, where I met him at Clementi's. He performed variations on a gavotte by Vestris*, with a fugue and concerto. He plays with extraordinary accomplishment,[162] with a good *touche,* the piano always under his control, but coldly, not very tastefully, and because of his great *fini,* without the many new technicalities one would expect from his great fund[163] of pianistic experience. His variations were well thought out, difficult, and yet without brilliance. In the evening to Covent Garden to see *The Orphan* for the third time. Afterwards came *Brother and Sister,*[164] with music by Bishop and Reeve*, again typical of the Leopoldstädter genre. Miss Stephens had an aria of some effectiveness: a flute placed behind the scene provided an echo and played a lovely a capella cadenza with the voice.

Saturday 16 December. Alien Office. Since the Alien Office is very close to Westminster, I went there and then visited the two houses of Parliament. The Circus Theatre in Southwark: we saw a melodrama with singing.

Sunday 17 December. Arose early, then went to Müller, and with him to Ries. I took him a letter from Nieth. Cordial reception: he recognized my name, and played his Symphony, entirely in E-flat. One immediately realizes he is a pupil of Beethoven by the many violent extremes,[165] contrasted unpleasantly with an unaffected tameness.[166] The symphony is very regular in conception, but for this very reason it made very little impression on me. His Concerto in C-sharp Minor[167] is both difficult and brilliant. On the whole he plays very well, not with the *fini* that Klengel evinces in his performance, but with more fire and life. Moreover, in spite of the firmness of attack that is required in handling English pianos, he has a lightness and grace in many fast passages that, until now, I have always thought was characteristic only of the Viennese *touche.* His wife is pretty and charming, as though she had just been taken out of an ornament cabinet. From there, because Müller had forgotten Cramer's address, we went to Klengel's, where I accidentally heard that the Schönbergers are also here. We immediately called on them: what deep joy. She has been engaged by the Italian Opera for this year—

which means that I will be able to write the opera very easily. Then to Cramer whom we did not find at home. From there, through Hyde Park, to Kalkbrenner*, who also was not in. After supper I wanted to work, but they obliged me to go downstairs again and play silly waltzes all evening. Mr. Bock in fact robs us of half our time.

Monday 18 December. Venice Preserved,[168] a tragedy by Otway, more or less the same story as Manlius. Visit from Ries. Again did not find Cramer at home. Müller proposed inviting him to a meal. Called on Schönberger.

Tuesday 19 December. In the expectation of an answer from Müller, as to whether or not Cramer will accept the invitation to dinner (an answer I await with painful impatience), I went to Friedrich Kalkbrenner, who is regarded as the first among all French pianists, and for whom I have a letter. I reached him just as he was preparing to go out, and we therefore arranged that I should call on him again at four o'clock, since I could not accept his invitation to dinner. I found him to be refined, and charming, with all the French polish,[169] even though he is actually not French, but really the son of a fairly well known composer from Berlin, Christian Kalkbrenner* (the author of a history of music); as a boy of twelve or thirteen years he went with his father to Paris. When I arrived at four o'clock, he played me twelve piano studies and several variations. He is a more powerful version of Moscheles, and I say this because to possess ease, brilliance, and precision of attack, using an English piano, is a much greater feat than performing these things on the light Viennese instrument. Kalkbrenner's playing has given me the almost certain hope that, with a little study, I too will be able to perform everything on an English piano that I formerly did on a Viennese one, even my method of attack. It is only the negotiation[170] of staccato passages that I fear, since from neither from Ries, Kalkbrenner, nor Klengel did I hear anything approaching one. Even without this marvelous attack, Kalkbrenner is a very great pianist. Müller assures me that he is far less popular in London society than Klengel and Ries, and yet he has brought me just as much pleasure as these other two. With an instrument like the piano (which is inclined to be dry and lack lyricism), it seems to me that there can be no question of charlatanism when, through *jeu perlé*, fleet, elegant mannerisms, new piquant passage work, and stimulating, gracious effects, one seeks to make good the somewhat harsh contrasts of the instrument, what nature has denied by way of lyricism and tenderness. Every art must sacrifice to the Graces, so why not the pianist? Klengel's playing, as accomplished as it is, is a little monotonous, and I am convinced that Kalkbrenner would surpass him in concert. I want to buy his piano exercises. I stayed with him from four until seven. In the morning I had tried to deliver a letter from Mälzel to the music theorist Engelhard, but he was not at home.

Wednesday 20 December. Passed today rather uninterestingly, since Mr. Bock's negligence and procrastination have again robbed us of our time, as has been the case with nearly half of our stay here. This, the very bad lodgings and expenses of living with him, is the serious counterbalance to the charm of meeting with the local people, especially in the theaters, which, because of our completely isolated life here, would otherwise have been impossible. Further, in Mr. Bock we have found not only a journalist, but also a theater poet who has already written an opera for Drury Lane, and would gladly have given it to me to set to music if I had been staying here longer. But he is counting on my returning to England within a year. Then we will work together on an English opera for the summer theater, the Lyceum, which gives only operas, and where he appears to have much influence.

Thursday 21 December. I went with Mr. Bock to see the London Docks, an area[171] of warehouses. In the evening to Covent Garden, where they performed a comedy by Charles Kemble*, *Smiles and Tears*. It is cobbled together from two totally different French plays. Then *Cymon* was given, now conflated into two acts.[172]

Friday 22 December. Since I still have no answer from Müller about Cramer, I went round to see him. There I learned that Cramer had declined the invitation to dinner on Wednesday because he is due to go to the country. I begin to doubt whether I shall ever get to hear Cramer, so many attempts having so far come to nothing. However, I have decided to leave no stone unturned until I hear the man regarded as the first pianist of Europe. Afterwards I went to the British Museum. In the evening attended a very boring gathering at Dr. Derbyshire's. His wife played me Scottish dances, which I found uncomfortable on the ear, since nearly all the principal modulations are made up of two harsh triads played consecutively. Because the waltz is now so very popular in London, I improvised for a quarter of an hour on one waltz after another, all of which enraptured these *maroquins* ears.

Saturday 23 December. I stayed at home in the evening, feeling very unwell with a feverish attack, chest pains and rheumatism in all my limbs.

Sunday 24 December. Even though I felt unwell on getting up, I was up very early so that Müller could take me to Cramer. The only problem was that the lazy fellow was still in bed when I arrived, and it was another half hour before we set out, and I had given up all hope of meeting Cramer. Fortune, however, was on my side, and he received us. My heart was beating with excitement. Cramer is in his forties, a big, powerfully built man, with similarly imposing facial features, his fingers long and thin, but strong-boned. He left Germany at such a young age, and he hardly understands German anymore. We spoke in French, in which he expresses himself fluently. We spoke for half an hour, a conversation that largely focused[173] on the condition of the Philharmonic Society, of which he is a member.

Strangely enough, he is still a member even though he formed an opposing society of the same sort (they say out of pique that Ries has become a codirector of the Philharmonic Society). He was kind enough, of his own accord, to play us twelve pieces that he has dedicated to Madame Montgeron in Paris under the title *Utile dolce*.[174] I do not think I am exaggerating when I say that even on the heaviest Broadwood instrument he has a touch lighter than Hummel's on the Viennese piano, something he is so famous for. His equality of distribution, lightness, and diminuendo are beyond all praise. These three qualities bestow a new effect and elegance on even the most ordinary things. Even in the most difficult double stops this light touch and exquisiteness[175] do not change, something that gives his playing a unique color and impressiveness, even if totally different from that of Clementi's. On the other hand, this astonishing evenness of tone[176] results in a certain monotony, while the bending of the fingers, appropriate to this style, hinders strong, powerful playing: in every passage that he wants to play energetically, Cramer is inclined to bang and hammer a little. But this is merely a sunspot[177] that hardly diminishes his fame. Whoever is as accomplished in his genre as Cramer, is *eo ipso* the first pianist in the world, no matter what one thinks of the genre itself. He received me with such courtesy and obvious artistic sincerity that we passed four hours together, delightfully conversing on artistic matters. The time just rushed by, at least for me. Apart from these twelve pieces, he also played me a big sonata (called *L'Ultime*), and in conclusion, after we had breakfasted, and again without prompting, two fugues by [Johann] Sebastian Bach*. His rendition of the latter, however, did not fully satisfy me, because his manner of playing is quite inappropriate to the style required by this music; he played them somewhat affectedly, I thought.

Monday 25 December. Today is the first of the Christmas holidays. My cold and coughing have worsened a great deal.

Tuesday 26 December. Through the kindness of Dr. Derbyshire, we had the permission to see the inside of a battleship, the dry dock, and the marine arsenal [at Greenwich?]. In the evening to the Covent Garden Theatre, where they performed a pantomime, *Harlequin and Fortunis*.[178] This was preceded by the tragedy *George Barnwell*.[179]

Wednesday 27 December. I promised, by way of recompensing the poor Müller for all the trouble and loss of time it cost him to let me hear Cramer, to complete and score several clarinet pieces that he had begun. In spite of my limited time, I wanted to keep my promise, and so went to him today. Fortunately, however, I found several people there—in whose presence I could not work, of course. Among them was a Swedish composer[180] who is now giving piano lessons in London; Müller had earlier told me many praiseworthy things about him. He is called

Litander, and since he mentioned to me in conversation that he is also a pupil of the Abbé Vogler,[181] a camaraderie immediately drew us together. When he heard that I want to make a collection of national melodies,[182] he offered to acquire me a collection of old Swedish songs and dances from Gothenburg that will soon appear in print there. Afterwards I went with Müller to Cheapside, where Clementi has his big music shop and part of his instrument factory, so that we could see these enterprises. I do not know whether since leaving Berlin my tastes, or the English instrument-makers, have changed. Be it as it may, I now prefer Clementi's instrument, the Broadwood, although it used to be the contrary. I also bought the first volume of a collection of fugues for the piano, since I have made the firm resolve to again begin diligent and thorough piano practice. I also hope that hearing the London pianists (especially Cramer) will have had a really positive influence on my playing. In the evening, my last visit to Covent Garden where they performed an old tragedy by Rowe*, *Jane Shore*.[183]

Friday 29 December. I went through some English poems with Mr. Bock that I would like to set to music; they are full of caprice and feeling. At six o'clock in the evening we left for Dover by diligence.

Saturday 30 December. At nine this morning we arrived in Dover, but could find no mail boat leaving today; the next leaves only early tomorrow morning. In the evening to the theater for a drama by Colman*, *The Iron Chest*.[184] The production was very poor.

Sunday 31 December. At ten in the morning we set sail. At ten o'clock in the evening we eventually arrived in Calais, without seasickness, which we warded off by laughing over old stories. The year has rushed by: 365 days have flowed past without my having produced any important musical work: a year spent in Paris without coming closer to the special dream of my life: writing something for the Théâtre Feydeau. In my piano playing I have regressed by a year, rather than progressing. What remains to comfort me for such self-inflicted loss at the end of the year 1815?

1816

January 1816

Monday 1 January. What remains to me? These were the last words from my pen written in the last moments of 1815, elicited by the depression caused by wasted time. What remains to me? I am 24 years old, have talent, a very respectable fund of experience, good musical acquaintances, means, and such a gentle dependence on my parents that it amounts to independence. Is this nothing? When I think back on the past year, barren of productivity, or any outstanding industry, I could easily fall into depression. But a new year brings fresh hope, and I want to hope, by heaven and hell, I want to! And why should I not? If regret about the past, draining my spiritual powers like a vampire, could serve as a spur and goad to my positive instincts, which are so often paralyzed, then why should these two forces of regret and hope, so dynamic when they are united, not thoroughly eliminate the hydra of laziness and negligence from me?

At six o'clock in the evening we set out by diligence from Calais.

Tuesday 2 January. Spent both day and night on the road.

Wednesday 3 January. This afternoon at three o'clock we arrived in Paris. We immediately sent for our anxiously anticipated letters in order to learn whether our parents have given permission for Wilhelm to travel to Italy with me. We found their consent in the first letter, but what a blow to find this retracted in the second! I was also disappointed to find that my mother does not want to visit me in Italy, as had been agreed, but rather to see me beforehand in Prague, since Father's business does not allow him to make the extended journey to Italy. I cannot, however, go along with this; otherwise I will lose the best part of my Italian visit. In the evening to the Théâtre Feydeau for an elegant little opera in two acts, *Avis au public*,[185] by A[lexandre] Piccinni*, which I had seen once before. The performance was badly cast with many of the pieces omitted, but fortunately not the best one, a charming rondeau at the end of act 1. The rest of the music is mediocre. Afterwards came Grétry's *Le Sylvain*.[186] Even though I have already heard this opera twice, and am indeed an enthusiastic admirer of Grétry's fine intentions and genial melodies, I found no taste for this music, in spite of its fame in France. The pieces, even the woman's aria, seem too long, too tragic, too dry for the situations and the characters. Then came the third performance of the opera *Un mari pour étrennes*[187] by Bochsa*. This is the second new opera by this composer to be produced during my four-week absence from Paris, and the fourth in six months: unfruitful productivity, empty writing, mere chaff and theater routine. And to think that men like Bochsa and Catrufo* are the exclusive providers for the Feydeau, while Cherubini and Méhul sit by idly.[188] The subject[189] is attractive up to the development, but then becomes very commonplace. The music is in Bochsa's usual manner, but even more arid than in his other operas.

Thursday 4 January. Attended to the various matters necessary for my departure. In the evening to the Théâtre du Vaudeville.

Friday 5 January. Played the piano a little and composed a new passage. In the evening to the Théâtre de la Gaité. To finish, they performed *La Marquise de Cange*, a melodrama in three acts by Boirie and Léopold [Chandezon].[190] This melodrama has had an extraordinary success.[191] The stage performance corresponded completely with the impression I had on reading it. It has great theatrical effect, as well as a lyrical one, which means it would be suitable for an operatic arrangement. If it were possible, I would have it appropriately adapted.

Saturday 6 January. In order to give myself a little enthusiasm[192] for Italian, which I have neglected for several years now, I have taken on an Italian teacher, with whom I will study for two hours daily until I go to Italy. Called on Véron*, and played the piano there. In the evening to the Théâtre Favart, where they performed a comic opera by Simon Mayr*, *Il Fanatico per la musica*.[193] In spite of the really terrible omissions and cuts, it remains a charming little work. Catalani* developed her many-sided talent in this role, especially in the duet where she has her father practice scales.[194]

Sunday 7 January. Played the piano a little. Attended to some arrangements for the journey. In the evening to the Opéra. They performed Rousseau's* *Le Devin du village*.[195] The warmth and naturalness of this music overcomes all the meagreness of its old-fashioned style. I must buy the score, particularly because of the recitatives in which Rousseau endeavored to vary the usual forms of modulation, and really does relieve the monotony without clouding the clarity—as has happened in other more recent attempts. Then they gave *Aristippe*,[196] an opera by Rudolph Kreutzer*, and, in my opinion, his best music: lovely, often really fine comic declamation and warm, charming melodies. In this house everything is broader and nobler than at the Feydeau, more appropriate to this big opera house, with its particular voices and the numbers of its performers. Here music may smile, but not laugh; it must always play the *grand Seigneur*, even when joking. The evening concluded with the ballet *Télémaque*, music by Miller*.

[Soon after this, Meyerbeer traveled to Italy, where he would stay until 1826. It is here that Meyer Beer became Giacomo Meyerbeer, by eventually italianizing his father's adopted patronym, and definitively prefixing his own first name to his family name. Early in the year, in Verona, he was reunited with his friends, the clarinetist Heinrich Baermann and the soprano Hélène Harlas, who were on tour, and also made the acquaintance of the librettist Gaetano Rossi*, who lived in this city. As a consequence, he produced his dramatic monologue, *Gli Amori di Teolinda* (to a text by Rossi), written expressly for a benefit concert for Baermann and Harlas, on 18 March. From the end of March until the end of June, Amalia Beer's letters were directed to Meyerbeer in Rome, then in June and July to Naples.[197] From late July until late September he visited Sicily, where he collected thirty-eight folk melodies from Palermo, Syracuse, and Messina.[198] By early October he was in Genoa,[199] and later in the month in Venice.[200] By the end of the year we hear of him in Florence[201] and Rome.[202]]

1817

[At the beginning of January Meyerbeer accompanied his mother as far as Munich on her return journey to Germany.[203] By the end of January he had returned to Rome.[204] In March he visited Milan, and then left for Venice.[205] By now he had made important contacts with Pietro Lichtenthal* in Milan and Franz Sales Kandler* in Venice. On 29 April C. F. Peters* in Leipzig published his *Sieben geistliche Gesänge*.[206] The first written communication with Rossi dates from 8 May (a letter from Angelica on behalf of her husband), with an undertaking from Gaetano himself on 14 May to provide "un Melo-drama à piacere del Signore Giacomo Meyerbeer" [a melodrama at the wish of Signore Giacomo Meyerbeer]. The contract with the impresario Girolamo Mazzucato for *Romilda e Costanza* followed on 1 June.[207] On 19 July the première of Meyerbeer's first Italian opera, *Romilda e Costanza*, took place at the Nuovo Teatro in Padua.[208] This *melodrama semiserio in due atti* was successful.[209] The title role was created by Benedetta Rosamunda Pisaroni*.[210] Meyerbeer stayed in Venice until the end of August, and then moved to Milan for the rest of the year.]

1818

My diary was first started in 1811 in Darmstadt, then interrupted, continued in 1812 in Munich and not completed, begun anew in 1813 in Vienna and neglected after four months; attempted again in 1815 in Paris before being given up after two months, then tried for the last time in London at the end of the same year and abandoned after six weeks: perhaps I should doubt whether I have constancy enough to keep such a steady daily record. The closing year always leaves me sunk in despondency when I look back at the disproportion between the generous time given me and the poverty of my achievement, and yet I am always filled with courage and lively hopes of improvement at such moments. I then think that, by redoubled diligence, I will make good the lost time. It is just such a (perhaps delusory?) ecstasy that has again taken hold of me, so that in 1818 I will try once more, if I can be steadfast enough, to keep a regular diary.

Before I write down the first days of January, I want to record a few impressions about three lyrical works that have just appeared during the first days of the Carnevale in Milan: (1) *I due Valdomiri*, a new *opera seria*, libretto by Felice Romani*, music by Winter;[211] (2) *Icaro e Daedalo*, a big ballet by [Salvatore] Viganò*,[212] music mostly by Lichtenthal (both at La Scala); and (3) *Adelaide e Comingio*,[213] a sentimental opera by Rossi, with music by the young Giovanni Pacini*, son of the well-known *buffo**[214] (at the Teatro Rè).

Winter's opera failed, and rightly so, I think. It is feeble, monotonous, and without melodies, something the public here will not tolerate. One expects from the author of so many lovely overtures at least a good example, but even the one in question made hardly the slightest impression because the principal theme, while well developed, is too small and fragmentary for this colossal theater [see example 19].

Example 19. First theme from the overture to Winter's *I due Valdomiri*

The same is true of the second theme in A major, whose second half is enjambed with the first (a sin against the clarity of the exposition), being, moreover, woven into the first theme after the fourth bar. If I am not mistaken, this theme goes something like this [see example 20].

The introduction and the tenor's aria are insignificant, and elicited neither approval nor enthusiasm from the public. The duet between Tomino and Mico passed by just as coldly, but I found the beginning of the stretta brilliant and fiery [see example 21].

However, instead of letting this song flow on freely, he seeks to modulate it, doing so in stages, and eventually, on the entry of the tonic, has it carried strongly by the chorus; while this is logically thought through, in an Italian opera duet its effect is completely misplaced. The chorus of virgins, which precedes the prima donna's aria, is beautifully written for the voices, but in thought and style is modulated like a chorus by Gluck* [see example 22].

The prima donna's aria, which follows, comprises a romancelike andante (A minor, 2/4) accompanied by only the harp and occasional woodwind harmonies.

**Example 20. Second theme (a & b) from the
overture to Winter's *I due Valdomiri***

**Example 21. Theme of the stretta in the soprano-tenor
duet from Winter's *I due Valdomiri***

Example 22. Chorus of Virgins from Winter's *I due Valdomiri*

With a change of meter, the allegretto in A major then begins. If the aria had had two themes, this turning point would no doubt have pleased, but it was carried only by the lovely performance of Camporesi*. The subsequent trio did not make the slightest impression, apart from the middle tempo, which is obviously modulated after a piece in *Die Zauberflöte*[215] [see example 23].

Example 23. Theme from the trio in Winter's *I due Valdomiri*

The whole finale is monotonous and cold (and during fifteen to twenty minutes, the ear is never enlivened by a single striking theme). The stretta (if I am not mistaken, in E-flat major), with ostinato triplets in the violins, is very fervent and powerful, but again without any definite theme. No stronger or better impression remains with me about act 2. The accompaniment of the aria for the singer [Klara]

Metzger has a local color expressed in the strings, as mysterious and nocturnally eerie as the text itself: A-flat major, clarinets playing the principal line (at least in the ritornello), violoncelli in sixths, the bass in quavers, and the whole largely in three parts, this "emptiness" creating a marvelous effect [see example 24].

Example 24. Theme from the act 2 soprano aria in Winter's *I due Valdomiri*

The *terzettino* for the three soprano voices is one of the few pieces that made a define appeal: it is without accompaniment (a sort of *preghiera*), and only on the reprise of the theme do the horns provide a bass line. The narrow range of the harmony, which necessarily results from using three soprano voices, creates a wonderful impression. In the quintet that follows, nothing particularly struck me, other than the moment when the bells toll. In order to achieve an ostinato imitating the bells, the horns constantly play the following figure (the piece moves from E-flat major to resolve itself in C [see example 25]:

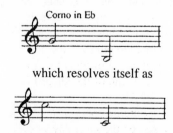

Example 25. Horn part (a & b) from act 2
terzettino **in Winter's *I due Valdomiri***

and the five vocal parts weave around this note in different harmonies). The following harmonies make an especially beautiful effect around this kind of pedal note [see example 26].

Example 26. Andante from the act 2 quintet in Winter's *I due Valdomiri*

Camporesi's big aria (which has considerable impact because of her performance) is in itself not important, apart from the lovely style, and this, in any case, is partly modeled on a scene from Nasolini's *Merope*, and partly on one from Carafa's* *Adele de Lusignano*[216] (especially the fact that the cabaletta begins in A flat major, but is sung in C major). The closing chorus is insignificant. Neither the composer nor the singers (Mesdames Camporesi, Schönberger, Metzger, and Sig. Bonoldi*) were called out after the first performance, although the friends of the management[217] redressed this affront on the second and third performances by applauding the composer.

The ballet *Icaro e Daedalo* is by the first among all Italian ballet masters, Salvatore Viganò, and also did not live up to expectations generated by the seven-month-long rehearsals. One found many ingenious[218] details, which is to be expected from such a great man, but in the end one missed his passion and rational guidance, which so distinguish, say, *Mirra*, especially in the variety of the groupings and general performance.[219] The whole seemed more like a sketch. The music is largely by my friend Lichtenthal from Milan. I arranged the last of the additional pieces used. The trombones and trumpets that depict the pushing of the nereids are placed on the stage, and come in suddenly on every fourth measure of the andante with a fanfare, so that however much the harmonies may roam, on every fourth bar they are obliged to return to the octave, fifth, or third of the keynote. This gives the melody an air of originality, as also the constantly recurring refrain [see example 27]. The theme of the allegro is also not bad [see example 28].

In the Teatro Rè, the last autumn opera (*Il Re Teodoro* by Paisiello) was performed until 30 December, and on the same day a new opera by the young Pacini (*Adelaide e Comingio*, a *semiseria*) was produced. It is popular, and was bound to please because of the number and charm of motives, except that if everything

Example 27. Fanfare from Lichtenthal's ballet *Icaro e Daedalo*

Example 28. Allegro from Lichtenthal's ballet *Icaro e Daedalo*

that the author stole or borrowed were to be removed, hardly anything original would be left. At the very beginning, the public applauded the principal theme of the overture [see example 29].

I do not like this melody, because it is made up of constant modulations, and so offers no adequate material to work with. The modulations in the development no longer hold attention when they have already been so misused in the exposition. Of pleasanter effect, and really original, is the passage in the act 2 aria of the prima donna [see example 30].

This opera concludes the series of new things to be seen in Milan. I still want

Example 29. First theme in the overture to Pacini's *Adelaide e Comingio*

**Example 30. Theme from the act 2 soprano aria in
Pacini's *Adelaide e Comingio***

to hear [Rosa] Morandi* in Cremona—given that I will write for her this coming
autumn in Trieste; the same applies to Velluti* (who is in Parma): I do not want
to correspond with him, but to hear and study him, something that is always useful and interesting for a composer of vocal music. Finally, I wanted to accompany my brother Michael, who is returning to Germany, as far as Trieste. We set
out on 31 December (1817), in the company of our Veronese friend, [Giovanni]

Failoni,[220] for Cremona, where we arrived the same evening, in time to hear *Elisabetta Regina d'Inghilterra*, an *opera seria* by Pavesi*. Since, however, we had the misfortune of finding that Morandi had become dangerously ill two days before, the opera was sung by a replacement,[221] and so we decided to go to Parma as soon as possible, on the morrow, and to return only when Morandi has recovered. I will therefore keep my review of the opera and the ballet, *Cesare in Egitto*,[222] until then.

January 1818

Thursday 1 January. We left Cremona by the post in order to reach Parma by the same evening. The shocking road, however, dashed our hopes. We had reached Casa Maggiore by sunset, and the bargeman no longer wanted to cross the Po at that stage. We therefore had to pass the first night of the year in this wretched town.

Friday 2 January. The tavern near the post where we lodged was bad and extremely expensive. Even though they forced another four horses on us, we still arrived in Parma only towards evening. The road, which is appalling in winter, furthermore offered no lovely views, while the heavy snow gave the landscape a monotonous appearance. (We lodged in Parma at Il Pavone;[223] supper at 4 fr., room for two at 4 fr., firewood very expensive.)

Saturday 3 January. We called on Velluti, who received us with extraordinary friendliness and affection, even though I have only spoken to him once before in my life (at Perucchini's* in Venice). He warned[224] us that he was very unwell and hardly able to sing. In the inn they had already told us that Mme. Belloc* had actually appeared in the opera, and that this, as well as the music, had not pleased Velluti at all. He sang us his variations on the theme "Nel cor non più mi sento," which he had written for the Academy in Venice when Catalani had sung her own version there. His are far more original and artistic, but would have little effect in concert. The big weakness in his voice is mostly in the intonation of reduced intervals, which comes through a great deal. We spent the rest of the day indoors because the weather is so bad.

In the evening we went to the theater. They performed *Balduino*, an *opera seria* in two acts by Peracchi, with music by Nicolini*. The latter wrote this opera two years ago (in the spring of 1816), with Velluti, Framezzani, and Mme. Zahré, for the theater in Lucca.[225] The opera did not succeed then, and has not proved popular. The beautiful choral work *Desirò and his 10 Apostles* that he wrote at the time, and the great success that Coccia* had enjoyed shortly before with his *Clotilde*,[226] tempted him to follow the same path and write nine individual choruses for the opera, of which only one can really be called good. I felt this because of its brevity and originality. It is for warriors who, in the stillness of the night, plan to attack the enemy camp. The chorus is entirely without orchestra, accompanied only by muffled drums behind the scene [see example 31].[227]

Example 31. Chorus from Nicolini's *Balduino*

[Meyerbeer returned to Venice where he remained for most of the year. From 11 September to 17 September 1818 he wrote an extended letter to his brother Michael in Berlin; the letter is really a form of epistolary diary, providing a chronicle of operatic life in Italy at the time, and affording valuable insights into Meyerbeer's character, opinions and activities.]

Dear Brother!

At last I am making up for my past neglect! In the three letters I have sent to you I have more than repented of my silence . . . Today's missive contains the final installment of my promise (made in the first letter), that is, to provide a fleeting survey of everything theatrical that has happened during your absence . . .

I will start with the first, or rather the last, Italian city, Trieste.[228] That Adolfo[229] chose Coccia rather than me, you already know from my earlier letter. He mounted his *Fayel* (the same subject as *Gabrielle di Vergy*), an opera he wrote last autumn for the small Theatre al Cocomero in Florence.[230] The lying Nachtstuhl[231] told us that only the staging had proved successful, so I was not a little surprised to hear that it had in fact provoked a furore in Florence. I have read through the score, and am of the opinion that it is Coccia's best opera. The first finale is a true masterpiece of lovely declamation, passionate expression and artistic, theatrical effect. If it were not for the fact that, out of common arrogance, he has stolen several small figures and turns from the *Vestalin* (which were placed in such unimportant places as to be entirely useless to him), the finale would place him among the great masters.

In Venice, shortly after your departure, Rossini's* *Otello*[232] was staged. The first act did not please at all, and is also very weak, with the exception of a very beautiful canonlike adagio in the finale, which he has transferred to *Otello* from an old farce, *Il Matrimonio per stravaganza* (written in Bologna).[233] In act 2 what appealed most is the stretta of a duet taken entirely from his *Torvaldo e Dorliska*,[234] the stretta of a trio copied nearly entirely from his *Gazza ladra*,[235] and twelve measures of a cabaletta from an otherwise awful aria by Festa*. This occurred in act 2, and the thinking part of the audience gave loud voice to its dissatisfaction with the unprecedented extent of the self-borrowing. The old theater habitués started talking about a fiasco, especially since one had heard that act 3 contains only three pieces, of which two (a romance and a prayer) are, moreover, very short. And yet these two small items not only saved the entire opera, but elicited such a furore, the like of which had not been seen for twenty years. The enthusiasm was so great, even after thirty performances, all of which were sold out, that considerable sums were paid to Tacchinardi* and Mme. Festa to perform *Otello* again this autumn for three consecutive months. This third act of *Otello* so firmly established Rossini's reputation in Venice that even a thousand follies[236] could not rob him of it. But this act is divinely beautiful, and what is so strange is that all the beauties it contains are blatantly un-Rossinian: outstanding, declaimed, even passionate recitative, mysterious accompaniments, lots of local *couleur*, and especially the antique style of romance in its highest perfection. And since we are talking about Rossini, we will interrupt the order of towns for a moment, and follow his unusual fortunes up to the present moment. You know that last autumn he brought out his *Armida*[237] in Naples, but perhaps you did not know that his *opera seria Adelaide di Borgondia*[238] was a complete fiasco at the Carnevale in Rome. Towards the end of Lent,[239] his new oratorio *Mosè in Egitto*[240] was staged in Naples. Reports are divided about its success. Those which speak of a great furore are counterbalanced by several which say that after the second performance the whole of act 3 was booed.[241] In the spring he went to his hometown of Pesaro to produce his *Gazza ladra* in the newly built theater there. You know that this was not very successful from my earlier letters. I like this opera very much: many pieces are very impressive indeed. Now he is writing an *opera seria* for Naples that will be produced at the beginning of October.[242] Perhaps he will also write for the carnival in Milan, but this is not certain. He is, moreover, engaged in serious negotiations about going to Paris in order to write for the French Grand Opera. The Italian Opera there has come under the administration of Catalani (which is like saying that one has put the fox in charge of the hens, and given the canary into the care of the cat). It has already sent agents to Italy to scrutinize the singers. To date they have robbed the poor Italians of three of their greatest subjects: *coiè* Mme. Lipparini*! Mme. Ronzi*! and De Begnis*! From the lips of these very agents I know that Rossini approached them on behalf of the Opéra. His terms[243] (which are apparently outrageously extravagant)[244] have already been sent to Paris. Should they be accepted, he will go to the French capital, and we will perhaps experience curious things.—But I must return to Venice.

In Holy Week Cavaliere Grizzo (whom you know from Baermann,[245] and whom the emperor recently made prince of Ponte-Lungo), at his own expense, with doubled orchestra and fivefold illumination of the Teatro San Benedetto, gave several concerts for the poor in which Handel's *Messiah*[246] and Haydn's *Stabat Mater*[247] were performed. These recitals were, according to the letter of the score, not bad at all, except that the spirit of the performers constantly contradicted that of the compositions (how could it be otherwise?), which hence seemed something of a travesty (in so far as we know the intentions of the composers through the traditions maintained in London, Vienna, and Berlin). The only truly enjoyable spectacle was the elegant ladies and gentlemen in the illuminated boxes, sitting there ravaged by boredom, and yet not daring either to speak or to groan, since a few days before the performance, Grizzo, with his usual courtesy, explained that these works are among the masterpieces of the human spirit; that those who did not appreciate them were donkeys; and that those who spoke during the music, as at the Italian opera, could only be regarded as uneducated peasants. The sole impressive feature was the new arrangement of the orchestra on the stage, as in an amphitheater (organized by me).

For the spring, the Facchini Company again took over the management[248] of the Teatro San Benedetto. They gave *L'Orbo che si vede*,[249] an old opera by Generali*, a fiasco; *Il Barbiere di Siviglia*[250] by Rossini, which was so-so; *Adelina,*[251] which pleased without provoking a furore; *Carlotta e Werther*[252] and *Arrighetto,*[253] both by Coccia, and both fiascos. Towards the end of the season the confused management took on an opera written by a young man called Vaccai* who has been in Venice for two years, wants to write everywhere, and cannot achieve anything because his theatrical début showed him to be a poor, wretched imitator of Rossini, lacking all spirit and character. Since then he has regarded any success by a stranger as theft of his laurels and an intrusion into his domain, and has accorded me the particular honor of hating me because of *Romilda*. He has done me damage with several individuals, but he is not capable of helping himself, because his talent is too weak: he is able to produce padding but no melodies. His opera is called *Il Boemondo*, to a text from the coffers of Merelli*.[254]

For the Carnevale, the cavaliere's company, which had been pregnant with a giant troupe, gave birth to a mouse: Mme. Brizzi and Mme. Fodor* from Paris, both as prima donnas; Mesico, Mme. Bonnini, the tenor Bolognesi; the composers Morlacchi* and Carafa*; the poets Peracchi and Romani. Only the ballet will be able to hold together this miserable opera company: four new French dancers; [Antonia] Pallerini* and [Nicola] Molinari as the first character dancers, the sublime Viganò as ballet master, and his two loveliest productions, *Otello*[255] and *La Vestale*.[256]

Facchini's Company will again appear in the San Benedetto. The company is made up of Mme. Angeloni, Pacini, Cusioni, and Remorini. I should have been the first maestro, but because of Trieste I could not take it on, so Trento* took my place; Pavesi as second conductor, and perhaps Coccia as the third.

Holy Week[257] in Padua was glittering beyond belief this year, and this whore, who is pursued only by the rogues and shunned by respectable people, so favored her worthy darling Mommolo [Girolamo] Mazzucato that at the end of the season he made a clear profit of 20,000 fr. after costs had been deducted. Note well, neither of the two operas has been successful: neither Rossini's *Elisabetta*,[258] nor *Atala*, just written by the young Pacini. The second of the two ballets was also whistled off, and only the first (which you know from Turin as *Quadeberga*) pleased at all. A chance development had brought all these people into the theater. Mazzucato had secured a prima donna, a Venetian dilettante called Angeloni, who has a charming voice and a precise method. Her status, both as a Venetian and a dilettante, secured her a large following: they wanted to suppress Mme. Bonini, who was playing the role of the Musico at the first performance, but she acquitted herself well on this occasion, and thereby won her own following, so that both groups filled the theater every evening with their supporters in order to provide their respective protégées with the appropriate applause. The tension nearly resulted in duels. Poor Venice: once taking sides in noble contests between Gabrielli* and Pacchierotti*, Marchesi* and Crescentini*, Banti* and Sylva—to what have you been reduced![259]

It is the same in Vicenza with Velluti, Bianchi*, and Pellegrini*, but with rather greater justification. Nachtstuhl and Pavesi had to come in order to supervise the changes to *Celanire*[260] that have so often been discussed. These have worked very well, they say. When the season is over, Velluti is going to Munich for two months.

In Brescia Coccia's *Evelina*[261] has come to nothing. The same is true of Mme. Schönberger and Mme. Cusioni; only Mme. Morandi gave a good account of herself. The ballet *Le Niobe*, mounted by Gioia himself, provoked a furore. On the whole all the festivals this year have worked out well, with the exception of Reggio, even though Generali himself produced his *Bacchanali*.[262] I have written about this spectacle in earlier letters, and will say no more now.

From Verona there is nothing particular to report. In Lent[263] Mme. Ronzi appeared with her husband;[264] in the spring Mme. Lipparini (later Mme. Amati), Sbigoli*, Bianchi, and Niccola. The operas were *Clothilda*, Paini's *Il Portantino*,[265] *Il Barbiere di Siviglia* (a furore), *La Gazza ladra*, *L'Italiana [in Algeri]*,[266] *Il Matrimonio segreto*.[267]

In Milan during Lent, just after your departure, Soliva's* new grand opera, *Giulia Sesta e Pompeo*, was received fairly coldly. The members of the Conservatoire called him out on the first evening, but after eight days the whole opera passed into oblivion. People have assured me that the first finale is a lovely composition.

The spring season (with a company made of Camporesi, David*, Ambrogi*, Pacini) opened with Winter's third and last opera. Because Kapellmeister Winter (as Wolff[268] very accurately observed) has as fine a scent for dross[269] as a hunting dog for game, and runs for ten miles when he knows where to find it: this time he picked up some real rubbish in the form of Rossi's *L'Etelinda*. *O che fiasco! che fiascone!! basta dire*[270] that after the third performance he returned in silence to Genoa, where his Clär'l[271] sang as prima donna in the spring, with some success. He has now gone back to Munich. At the same time as *L'Etelinda*, Viganò's new ballet *La Spada di Kenneth* was mounted. The subject is very monotonous and unclear (but of course; the management[272] chose it) and only a few details and a really lovely scene in act 3 (although somewhat similar to the Sleep Scene in the *Psammi*)[273] which was wonderfully acted by Mme. Pallerini and Molinari, and two delightful dances for Scottish *Montagnards* [Highlanders] prepared by the charming pupils of the dance school, secured the ballet a worthy, if not brilliant, success. The public, however, again demanded *Otello*, even though this work was performed all Lent. Only the wonderfully composed act 5 (in which Lichtenthal most aptly introduced Haydn's cantata, *Ariadne auf Naxos,*[274] with all its recitatives), the sublime miming of Pallerini and Molinari as Desdemona and Othello, and a décor lovely beyond words (presenting the illuminated Hall of the Signorina),[275] and, most especially, a sweet and original *furlana* (a popular dance from Trieste) performed by the pupils of the dance school in appropriate costumes, gradually established this as the public's favorite ballet, even though it had caused no stir at the first performance. People were even calling it Viganò's most charming composition. —But there was another triumph in store when Viganò, at the end of the spring season, mounted his last new ballet for La Scala, *La Vestale al campo scellerato*. La Scala had never before experienced such a furore. As long as the ballet held the stage, Viganò was called out every night; the huge theater was crammed every evening an hour before the angelus, and at the end of the season, the enthusiasm was so still so great, they were obliged to reengage the entire dance company, and to give the ballet for another month in the midst of the run of comedies. They made a tragedy from this ballet (*alla* Stadera), which was very popular; and when, one evening, Viganò entered a box at the Stadera to watch the drama, the public recognized him, called out "Look, the real author" *(Ecco il vero autore),* and applauded him. On the last evening *alla* Scala, genii appeared on the stage, read verses to Viganò and Pallerini, and crowned them both. The first scene of this ballet presents a wonderful tableau. It depicts the games in honor of the victorious consul. On the one side, one sees a ring with boxing games; on the other, discus throwing; and, in the middle, at the back of the immense *palco scenico*, seven chariots teamed with small Arabian horses, rushing to the finish line with great speed. One chariot breaks while in full course; another shows a horse taking fright and throwing the driver from the vehicle. A fist fighter falls to the ground dead—these, and many other such details, give the tableau, taken as a whole, unbelievable vivacity and variation.

But I must return to opera. After the leaden affair of Winter's *Etelinda*, the management had to think quickly in terms of repair,[276] and since Morlacchi was not yet ready, they presented Weigl's *Il Rivale di se stesso*.[277] In the last ten years, this opera has been revived three times and always proves popular—rightly, I think. I am really taken with this work. As with many others, I have experienced that when music is very complicated in its harmonic and periodic [recurring?][278] combinations, or when its effectiveness hinges on dramatic intention that is not made clear by too strong an instrumental coloring (as with much of Cherubini's work), such music leaves one cold on the first night, but with each subsequent performance it becomes more interesting and pleasing. But I have never had the experience that an opera which has seemed dry, common, or loosely constructed (indeed, has come across as very undramatic) has, on every subsequent evening, nonetheless seemed more gracious, elegant, beautifully phrased, and dramatic, so that eventually one has come to love it completely. But this is just what has happened to me with *Il Rivale di se stesso*. Weigl remains the greatest living German composer for the theater, whatever one might say, and I would like to reply to his many detractors (to which, as far as his character is concerned, I belong *de coeur et d'âme*)[279] with the same answer as given recently by the count of Artois to the young poet Cheaulon (when the latter criticized Étienne's* character and writings): "Vous avez beau dire, Monsieur, il pense mal, mais il écrit bien."[280] The management are engaged in negotiations with Weigl, to have him write the first new *opera seria* for the next season.

Towards the end of the season[281] Morlacchi produced his new opera, *Gianni di Parigi*,[282] which pleased without provoking a furore. Romani translated the libretto charmingly; all changes demanded by the musical numbers were well done, and occasionally most happily so. David sang Gianni elegantly[283] beyond words; Mme. Gallianis was really arch as the page; Pacini was endlessly droll as the host; Ambrogi sang the Senechal excellently, and also acted outstandingly in this role; Mme. Camporesi sang with her usual mastery,[284] which, nevertheless, can become very monotonous and boring. But what can one say about such a heavenly company giving their all for *Gianni di Parigi*? The chances of such a company being available for such an appropriate work is not likely to present itself again in years.

In the present autumn season the singers are Camporesi, the daughter of the ballet master Gioia, the tenor Scilotti (who withdrew after the first performance and was replaced by Rubini*), Remorini, and Ambrogi. The first opera (*Il finto Stanislao,* with book by Romani) was written by Gyrowetz, who had been called from Vienna expressly.[285] What a terrible fiasco! They tried to make up with Rossini's *Torvaldo e Dorliska*, which was very popular on the first evening, but thereafter went downhill steeply.[286] And who was to write the second new opera?—

the young Pacini! *cosa ti pare?*[287] Niccola, who wrote to me from Turin, was very funny about this: "ma niente paura, suo padre l'assisterà!"[288]

Everyone expected Fabris's ballet *La Morte di Pyrro* to be a big disaster: Fabris after Viganò! and after the unexpected furore of the *Vestale*! Only success proves the worth of Thümmel's* aphorism: "Wenn der grösste Mann der Welt stirbt, so kommt darüber kein Schweinestall in Unordnung."[289] The ballet had great appeal, and Fabris was called out. Pezzi, who is certainly not Fabris's friend, berated the public in his review. And I hereby close my theatrical review from Milan, which I have mentioned in greater detail than any other city, because Milan is far and away the most important city in Italy from a theatrical point of view.

To conclude with, I must mention a new comedy by Advocate Nota* (famous because of his *Atrabiliare,* which has never appealed to me). It is called *La Lusinghiera*, has been outstandingly successful, and has recently been performed over thirty times by the Compagnia Marchioni in the Teatro Rè. Charlotte Marchioni wins herself distinction in the role of the Lusinghiera. (It is the first time they have italianized the word *coquette* in this way.)[290] The subject is a variation on Goldoni's* *Locandiera scaltra*, but worked out much more forcefully in plot and character, somewhat caricatured, and satiric in the Gallic mode. For such a famous man, the prose does not have enough Italian *Schmalz*,[291] but is very tense and nervous, and even on occasion has the terrible *agro dolce frizzante*[292] (which Alfieri* so loves). In spite of the furore it has caused, I nevertheless (*mi comme mi*) prefer Goldoni's *Locandiera*. Indeed, over the past few months, I have developed a real passion for the friendly old fellow. During the many and heavy bouts of melancholy that I have suffered recently, and indeed am still experiencing, I have greedily sought out all distractions that do not exclude me from human contact. And since I passionately love the Venetian dialect, as you know, I have sometimes sought to refresh myself with those comedies of Goldoni that are written in this patois. They have more than entertained me; indeed, how often have they moved me to tears! Recently I have read everything by him I could find, and to date[293] I know 127 of his plays; even his worst ones have so much that is characteristic in them. I strongly advise you to acquire his works (not the new collections, but rather the good old Venetian one in forty-six volumes). You will not find anything directly translated, but an immeasurable fund of arrangements and imitations in modern format. I advise you to observe nothing of this to the *Kaschale*[294] who have fortunately long forgotten him.

In the realm of Italian literature (as far as I know), nothing of any consequence has appeared since your departure. Monti's* additions to Crusca have elicited a quantity of controversial writing both for and against him, but nothing rising above the sphere of grammatical analysis. A *cavaliere* from Cremona has published a really lovely, richly rhythmical imitation of the Psalms. Several of them (at least according to the title) are set in the choral style of the *maestri* Pavesi and Gazzaniga*. O God, the good Pavesi! The good Gazzaniga! Considerable attention has been elicited by a brilliantly written and truly interesting description of the barbarities suffered by the young and talented poet Panati (who was contracted a while ago to become theater poet of the Italian Opera in London), and who, on the voyage there, was captured by pirates and sold as a slave in Algeria.[295]

Otherwise, there is nothing but translations in the theaters and everywhere else. I have, nonetheless, collected a number of sonnets and odes for you that Morelli in Verona has composed for very ordinary occasions (like actors' benefits, name days, etc.).

After a pause of ten days I am taking up my pen again. A dream, a terrible dream, disturbed my moral and spiritual faculties to such an extent that only ten days after this awful night do I feel more composed. What a terrible nervous system I must have if it can be shattered by a bad dream—to the point where I felt myself on the edge of a breakdown. I can assure you that, with my depression, I feel like a man who has to carry a heavy load for which he feels he does not have the strength. I do not feel I have the energy to fight it, and so I try to endure it; but the burden is too heavy for my heart, for my spirit. It will weigh down on me ever more heavily until it crushes whatever is left of my weakened spirit.

I cannot prevent myself telling you, my dearest Michael, that my love for you since your departure has become a veritable passion. Since I have been alone, I can no longer doubt from whence my dissatisfaction, my anger, my depression, arise, whether from my circumstances, or from my daemon. Since then, I daily endure the moral whiplash more impatiently and resentfully; since then, I acknowledge what a burden and pain I must, on occasion, have been for you, and acknowledge my love in the meekness and patience with which you endured it. I swear to you that I love you doubly, and will until my last breath.

Perhaps you are asking why I am going into these disheartening details—since sharing them can be of no help to me, and only depresses you. I have to answer like this, in italics: *because I see the obvious similarities between us in body and soul, in character and inclinations.* I see all these dispositions similar to mine, and that you run as quickly into the arms of melancholy and sickness; you should therefore give much more weight to my depressing picture and warning. It means work and abstinence (in every respect). It further means caution in the choice of professional standing. Never forget what I forgot in choosing mine: the iron word *Richesse.*[296] From individual to individual, this word can be forgotten for a while (although not forever), but by the collective public never, since it requires only one who remembers to bring it into general consciousness again. Choose therefore from doctor, advocate, teacher, merchant, but turn your back on diplomacy and the theater (as a profession). Compose as Philomela sings—for yourself. Free yourself, once and for all, from the need to acknowledge spiritual equality and impartiality, and you will have lost nothing, but can only look forward.

I once more take up my pen, and rush to finish this report on the theaters so that this missive does not swell into the dimensions of a book.

In Florence during Lent they gave Generali's *Bacchanali* with Mme. Bertinotti, Malanotte*, and Bianchi. Both music and artists created a furore. In the spring Rossini's *Cenerentola*[297] was a complete fiasco. Mme. Gorgis lost her voice completely on the sixth evening, and did not find it again, and has had to give up singing in her twenty-eighth year. They brought in Mme. Bertinotti, who had created such a stir during Carnevale, but in the spring she was a fiasco.[298] They performed *Don Juan* and *Figaro* at the Teatro Nuovo. I have spoken of both in my earlier letter to Mother.

In the summer *alla* Pergola Coccia's *Clothilda* was very popular. The bass Botticelli (as Pio) created a stir. Then Trento's *Gli Assasini*,[299] good old music, but coldly received. At the same time in the small Teatro Santa Maria (with an orchestra and personnel that are pathetically poor) they gave Winter's *Sacrifizio interotto*.[300] A terrible fiasco! Then Paisiello's *La Molinara*,[301] somewhat better, and finally Mozart's *Zauberflöte*. Nowhere in the four corners of the world would be possible to find a similar musical disappointment. The public behaved with authentic Italian malice. Even though it was neither hissed nor whistled off, the whole opera was laughed at uproariously.[302]

This autumn the Pergola mounted Mosca's* *La Gioventù d'Enrico V*,[303] but it was disastrous, as was Cimarosa's *I Traci amanti*[304] at the Teatro Cocomero. Now they are preparing Pavesi's *Cherusci*[305] with Pinotti. At the Pergola they are rehearsing *La Gazza ladra*. Afterwards *Agnese*[306] will be given, and, to conclude with, a young composer from Vienna, Schoberlechner*, will venture his first work. I believe he is talented and theater-wise. If he succeeds, our musicianly ranks will be swollen by yet one more intriguer[307] and bad character.

In Naples, during the last Carnevale, Morlacchi's serious opera *Laodicea*[308] was successful, but a new opera by Carafa, *Binareccia*,[309] had little appeal. Pavesi's *Agatina (Cendrillon)*[310] and Rossini's *Cenerentola* both pleased. Barbaia*, who was in Paris, has signed on both Paer and Spontini for Naples. The general feeling is that the latter will go, and would rather pay his penalty of 100 louis d'or. Good for him if does, otherwise he will break the neck of his reputation (in my opinion, anyway).

In the spring, Colbran*, after a sojourn of seven years, finally left Naples, and Festa and Malanotte* have been secured in her place. Both, however, experienced a fiasco in their début in *Tancredi*, and what followed made up for it only a little. Next October a new company will make its début in Rossini's latest opera—indeed, the newly engaged Colbran, Nozzari*, David, the divine bass Porto from Paris, and Mme. Pisaroni; the latter has been engaged for twenty-two months at 30,000 fr.

Now you know everything that has taken place in musical Italy. I must add that Campitelli* has gone to Palermo, and has been a disaster there; Mme. Belloc is going to London for a year for a fee of 1500 louis d'or, and Galli*, who has caused a sensation in Barcelona, has been engaged for a year for the sum of 400 *pezzi*.

So now I will close this long theater report with the news that will perhaps interest you most, i.e., that yesterday, after much delay, and writing backwards and forwards, I signed the contract[311] for the second *opera seria* in the Carnevale in Turin. I have not sacrificed my convictions, but if I have to have a fiasco with a bad libretto, I would rather it were at a Cartello theater.

I entrust again and again to you, dear Brother, what I wrote to you in my second and third letters, about Mother's coming here. You know how important and vital this is for me . . . Adieu dear Brother.

[By mid-December, Amalia Beer was addressing her letters to Turin where Meyerbeer had gone to direct the rehearsals of his new opera *Semiramide*.]

1819

[The première of *Semiramide (dramma per musica in due atti)* took place on 3 February at the Teatro Regio in Turin,[312] with the contralto Carolina Bassi*[313] in the title role and Bonoldi singing the first tenor. The text was Gaetano Rossi's adaptation of Metastasio's libretto (1729).[314] This was followed by the première of *Emma di Resburgo (melodramma eroico in due atti)* on 26 June at the Teatro San Benedetto in Venice, with Rosa Morandi, Carolina Cortesi, and Luciano Bianchi.[315] The libretto was again by Gaetano Rossi.[316] During the winter of 1819–20 Meyerbeer remained largely in Milan and Venice.]

1820

[On 11 February *Emma di Resburgo* was produced in Berlin, in a German version as *Emma von Leicester*, directed by Weber. In June the composer was in Bologna for a revival of *Semiramide*. All track of his movements is lost until the première of *Margherite d'Anjou (melodramma semiserio in due atti),* which took place on 14 November at the Teatro alla Scala in Milan.[317] The libretto, by Felice Romani,[318] was based on Guilbert de Pixérécourt's *mélodrame-historique*.[319] The principal roles were created by Carolina Pellegrini, Rosa Mariani, Nicolas Prosper Levasseur*, and Nicola Bassi*.[320] On 15 December Meyerbeer signed a contract with Giovanni Paterni, the impresario of the Teatro Argentina in Rome, to write a new opera, entitled *Almanzore*. The libretto by Rossi was based on a play by Jean-Pierre Claris de Florianto, and the opera was to be performed in February 1821.[321]]

1821

[Meyerbeer spent the first months of the year in Rome, but *Almanzore* could not be produced: he became ill and there were problems in the theater (Carolina Bassi was also unwell).[322] By July he was in Venice, and by August settled in Milan and working with Romani on a new libretto, perhaps the redrafting of Rossi's text.[323]]

1822

[The première of *L'Esule di Granata (melodramma serio in due atti)* took place on 12 March at the Teatro alla Scala in Milan.[324] The libretto was by Felice Romani, and the principal roles were created by Luigi Lablache*, Benedetta Rosamunda Pisaroni,[325] and Adelaide Tosi. In August Meyerbeer was in Recoaro. He then traveled to Berlin to see his family.[326] Upon returning to Italy, he established himself in Venice for the rest of the year.]

1823

[Until May, Meyerbeer remained in Venice. From May until August he lived in Milan. He visited Recoaro from August to September, and Milan in October, before returning to Venice. The year was devoted to correspondence with Gaetano Rossi on the libretto of a new opera and the composition of its music.[327] In December he signed a contract with Giovanni Glossop, impresario of the San Carlo in Naples, for an opera scheduled for autumn 1824, again with a text by Rossi.[328]]

1824

[The première of *Il Crociato in Egitto (opera seria in due atti)* took place on 7 March at the Teatro alla Fenice in Venice.[329] The libretto, by Gaetano Rossi, was based on a French *mélodrame, Les Chevaliers de Malte*,[330] and the title role was created by the castrato, Giovanni Battista Velluti.[331] On 7 May the opera was staged at the Teatro della Pergola in Florence. Meyerbeer was invited to supervise the rehearsals of this work in Paris by Sothènes de la Rochefoucauld*, subintendant to Rossini, who had assumed the directorship of the Théâtre Italien on 30 July, together with Paer. By November Meyerbeer was in Trieste to direct the autumn production of his new opera.]

1825

[In January *Il Crociato in Egitto* was again triumphantly produced, this time in Trieste.[332] On 23 February Meyerbeer went to Paris, but he was back in Italy to oversee a production of *Il Crociato* in Padua early in July.[333] The English première of the opera took place at the King's Theatre in London on 29 June.[334] Meyerbeer arrived in Paris in late July to supervise rehearsals[335] for the French première that followed on 22 September at the Théâtre Italien.[336] The composer afterwards returned to Italy. On 27 October his father, Herz Beer, died in Berlin. Meyerbeer

MEYER~BEER

Giacomo Meyerbeer at the high point of his Italian career. Lithograph by Loche, the frontispiece in the Pacini vocal score of *Il Crociato in Egitto* (Paris, 1826).

did not attend the funeral, but returned to Berlin by 28 November to conclude a formal marriage contract with his cousin, Minna Mosson*.]

1826

[In February Meyerbeer was in Milan to direct the last rehearsals of *Il Crociato,* which was produced on 2 March. On 4 March he traveled back to Berlin via Augsburg (9 March). *Marguerite d'Anjou* was produced at Théâtre de l'Odéon in Paris on 11 March. This was a three-act adaptation by Thomas Sauvage* of the original Italian two-act version, with the music arranged by Pierre Crémont.[337] It seems unlikely that the composer was in attendance. On 28 May *Margherita d'Anjou* was revived at La Scala. Three days earlier, on 25 May, Meyerbeer had married his first cousin, Minna Mosson, in Berlin, and set out for Paris on the same day, with his bride, in order to begin work on a new operatic scenario, *La Nymphe du Danube.*[338] On 9 June he received the news of Carl Maria von Weber's death in London (5 June); Weber's heirs committed the sketches of his projected opera, *Die drei Pintos,* to Meyerbeer, with the commission to complete it.[339] *Il Crociato* was performed at the San Carlo in Naples on 30 September, and on 14 November, in both Munich (in German) and in Dresden (at the Italian Opera).[340]]

NOTES

1. *Wirt und Gast, oder aus Scherz Ernst,* Meyerbeer's second opera, was produced at the Stuttgart Court Theatre on 6 January 1813. It is described as "Lustspiel mit Gesang in 2 Aufzügen von Hofschauspieler Wohlbrück aus München, Musik von Meyerbeer, Tonkünstler aus Berlin." Edgar Istel gives the fullest account of the opera, with some musical examples, in "Meyerbeer's Way to Mastership: Employment of the Modern Leading-Motive before Wagner's Birth," *Musical Quarterly* 12 (January 1926): 102–7.

2. A small notice in the *Hamburgischer Unterhaltungsblatt* 20 (10 March 1813) nonetheless says that the opera "hat verdienten Beifall erhalten. Die Musik hat treffliche, ächt originelle Stellen, und der Text ist mit vielem Fleiße und grosser Theaterkenntniß bearbeitet" [The opera earned a deserved success. The music has striking, genuinely original passages, and the text has been diligently prepared, with great knowledge of the theater] (*BT,* 1:630).

3. Tgb. *retour chaise.*

4. Friedrike Sommer was a Darmstadt acquaintance. See 22 May 1812.

5. xr. = *Kronenthäler.*

6. Tgb. *chaussée.*

7. Tgb. *fausse resemblance.*

8. See 5 June 1812.

9. "The Hogshead."

10. Following on the defeat of Napoleon's *grande armée* in Russia (1812), a new struggle for liberation from France had begun. King Friedrich Wilhelm III of Prussia hesitantly agreed to war with France in February 1813. Public opinion greeted the news of the outbreak of the conflict with enthusiasm.

11. "The Clover Tree."

12. "The Eagle."

13. See early April 1812.

14. See early April 1812.

15. *Musikalische Zeitung für die oesterreichischen Staaten,* which emerged from the *Musikalische Notizen.*

16. See 16 April 1812.

17. Tgb. *replicierte.*

18. Tgb. *debutierte.*

19. See 26 July 1812.

20. Tgb. *carrikiert.*

21. Tgb. *Knittelverse.*

22. *Die Belagerung von Saragossa, oder Pächter Feldkümmels Hochzeitstag,* comedy in four acts (first produced in Berlin in 1810, and first published in 1811) [Richel 84].

23. Tgb. *associé.*

24. See 21 May 1812.

25. Comedy in two acts, first produced at the Königliches Schauspielhaus, Berlin, 1811, and published in the same year [Richel 87].

26. Tgb. *fausse resemblance.*

27. Tgb. *soupierte.*

28. Tgb. *Ffurthischen.*

29. Comedy in four acts (first performances in Vienna and Dresden, 1792) [Richel 76].

30. "The Cross."

31. Tgb. *Conventionsmünze.*

32. The increasing political tension, however, was to interrupt postal services between Prussia and Austria severely.

33. The patent from Grand Duke Ludwig of Hesse reads as follows: "Demnach Wir dem Kompositeur Mayer Beer das Prädikat als Hof- und Kammer Kompositeur gnädigst ertheilet haben; so ist sich darnach schuldigst zu achten und derselbe für Unsern Hof- und Kammer Kompositeur zu erkennen . . . Darmstadt. 12sten Febr: 1813. Ludewig [*sic*]" [Whereas we have graciously bestowed on the composer Meyer Beer the title of Court and Chamber Composer, it is therefore incumbent upon one to respect and acknowledge him as our Court and Chamber Composer . . . Darmstadt, 12 February 1813, Ludwig] (*BT,* 1:218).

34. Meyerbeer's vivid observation and sense of the grotesque are again in evidence. They would later find artistic expression in his famous characterizations of religious fanaticism and exoticism in his mature works (like *Le Prophète* and *L'Africaine*).

35. Tgb. *Fiaker.*

36. "At the Archduke Charles's."

37. "The Red Hedgehog."

38. Weigl's three-act opera (J. A. F. Reil, after a real incident, a landslide near Goldau in 1806) had just been premièred at the Kärntnerthor-Theater on 19 December 1812. It marked the end of the so-called grief-and-pain operas that Weigl had initiated with *Das Waisenhaus* (1808). See 23 November 1852.

39. Tgb. *échauffiert.*

40. In order to house the elaborate production of Cesti's *Il Pomo d'oro* for Emperor Leopold I's wedding celebrations, the architect Burnacini designed a theater in the main square of the Imperial Palace, the Hofburg (1667). In Joseph I's reign (1705-11), Giuseppe

Galli-Bibiena*, the chief theater architect, rebuilt it as the Burgtheater, which, in Maria Theresa's time, was refashioned as the Theater bei der Hofburg (1748). The house saw many important productions (including premières of works by Gluck [ten operas between 1754 and 1770], Mozart [*Die Entführung aus dem Serail, Le Nozze di Figaro, Così fan tutte*] and Cimarosa), but after the departure of Gluck for Paris (1773), it yielded its position as court opera to the Kärntnertor-Theater. It is now the Staatstheater, still used for spoken drama.

41. The Kärntnertor-Theater (1761) resulted from the demand for a theater for the ordinary people, and was originally built in 1708. By 1712 it had become the permanent home of German players and indigenous drama, but from 1790 was used for opera and operetta, and soon became the K.K. Hof-Operntheater. After Salieri's appointment as court conductor (1788), he produced many of his own works here. Barbaia was famously the director from 1821 to 1828, and commissioned Weber's *Euryanthe* (1823). The theater also saw the premières of Donizetti's *Linda di Chamounix* (1842), *Maria di Rohan* (1843), Flotow's *Martha* (1847), and the first Viennese productions of operas by Verdi and Wagner (*Lohengrin*, 1861). It was demolished to make way for the Court Opera on the new Ringstrasse (1869), now the Staatsoper.

42. The Theater an der Wien (1801) was built by Schikaneder, as a successor to his Theater auf der Wieden (1787). This house saw the premières of Beethoven's *Fidelio* (1805) and works by Lortzing (*Der Waffenschmied*, 1846), Strauss, Millöcker, and Léhar. Under the management of Barbaia (1820–21), several Rossini works were introduced to the Austrian capital, and it was the scene of Jenny Lind's Vienna triumphs (1846–47, especially in *Vielka*). The Vienna State Opera used this house (1945–54), and after renovation (1962), it became the official theater of the annual Vienna Festival.

43. Tgb. *Spektakelstücke.*

44. Tgb. *Zauberopern.*

45. For a succinct survey of the emergence of the Viennese popular drama, in which the ordinary people found their authentic cultural expression (especially in the character of Hanswurst), see Ernst Wangermann, *The Austrian Achievement, 1700–1800* (London: Thames and Hudson, 1973), pp. 51–53.

46. In 1812 Spohr gave a series of concerts in Vienna, and was received warmly both as composer and violinist. He was offered the position of concertmaster at the Theater an der Wien and held this post until 1815.

47. Michael Umlauff, son of the more famous Ignaz.

48. Anton Wranitsky, brother of the more famous Paul.

49. Tgb. *Regie.*

50. Tgb. *parterre.*

51. Palffy had taken over the direction of both the Theater an der Wien and the Kärntnertor-Theater at the same time (1813). He developed them into the viable and important institutions that Barbaia was to lease in 1821.

52. Lyric tragedy (Castelli; Vienna, Kärntnertor-Theater, 1812).

53. *La Clemenza di Tito, opera seria* in 2 acts (Metastasio, reduced and altered by C. Mazzolà; Prague, 6 September 1791) written in eighteen days to celebrate the coronation of Emperor Leopold II as king of Bohemia, remained a popular work all over Europe in the nineteenth century, despite Mozart's relative lack of interest in it.

54. *Die kluge Frau im Walde, oder Die stumme Ritter*, drama in five acts (first produced in Vienna, Burgtheater, 1799; published in 1801) [Richel 86].

55. By Franz Volkert, one of this prolific composer's forty-six stage works.

56. Op. 62 (1807). The overture was for the play *Coriolan,* by Heinrich Joseph von Collin.

57. See September 1812.

58. Johann Caspar Lavater's theories of physiognomy, as a sure key to psychological insight, had only recently been propounded (1775), and enjoyed great currency.

59. Salieri's *Tarare, tragédie lyrique* in three acts (P. A. Caron de Beaumarchais; Paris, Opéra, 8 June 1787) was his chief work, given in Paris 131 times until 1826. Even more successful was the Italian adaptation by Lorenzo da Ponte, *Axur, re d'Ormus* (Vienna, Burgtheater, 8 January 1788) for the wedding of Archduke Francis, which had an international career. It retained its popularity in Germany throughout the first half of the nineteenth century, and was revived in Stuttgart as late as 1863.

60. Weber came to Vienna to appear in a concert with Baermann and Harlas (25 April 1813) and to prepare for the performance of his opera *Abu Hassan* (28 May 1813).

61. The alienation would seem to have originated in some petty misunderstanding arising from character differences, rather than in some specific disagreement between the two composers.

62. Tgb. *sujet.*

63. Tgb. *er sich besser aufs fortführen als aufs anspinnen verstehet.*

64. *Sorgen ohne Noth und Noth ohne Sorgen,* comedy in five acts by Kotzebue (first performed in Berlin, 1809, and in Dresden, 1810) [Richel 88].

65. Humboldt was in Vienna to negotiate Austria's joining in the alliance of Russia and Prussia against France. Metternich* feared a French hegemony in Europe would be replaced by a Russian dominance, and tried to pursue a policy of armed neutrality. This failed because of Napoleon's intransigence, with the result that Austria entered the conflict on the side of the alliance in August 1813, decisively shifting the balance of military power in favor of the anti-French coalition.

66. *Le Nozze di Figaro, opera buffa* in four acts (Lorenzo da Ponte, based on Beaumarchais's comedy *La jolie Journée, ou Le Mariage de Figaro* [1785]; Vienna, Burgtheater, 1 May 1786) was already established as one of the most popular operas of the international repertoire.

67. Tgb. *mesquine.*

68. Giuseppe Carpani's Italian text for Weigl's two-act opera (Vienna, Kärntnertor-Theater, 15 February 1805) was translated into German by Georg Friedrich Treitschke.

69. A rift had developed between Meyerbeer and Weber, as revealed in Weber's letter to Gänsbacher of 2 April 1813, presumably written and despatched earlier on the same day, before the reconciliation in question. The letter also sheds some light on Meyerbeer's awkwardness with Vogler at the end of the Munich sojourn. "The situation with Beer is like this; I approached him with all the old love and affection and mentioned nothing, and nor has he as yet said a single word about the tension between us. It all appears just to be as it used to, but I have lost my pure trust in him. Baermann, and particularly Vogler, complain astonishingly about him, and his pride, unbelievable vanity, and touchiness are as great as ever, and will always put people off him." (Cited by I. Nohl, *Musikerbriefe* [Leipzig, 1867], p. 221; rpt. in *BT,* 1:225).

70. *Jean de Paris, opéra comique* in two acts (C. Godard d'Aucour de Saint-Just; Paris, Opéra Comique, 4 April 1812), was Boieldieu's first major work written after his return from Russia. The charm and vigor of this opera confirmed his international reputation. It was performed in Paris until 1862 (rev. 1893) and enjoyed particular popularity in Germany, where several versions were produced in the same year, two simultaneously in

Vienna: at the Kärntnertor-Theater on 28 August 1812 (trans. I. F. Castelli) and at the Theater an der Wien on 29 August 1812 (trans. J. von Seyfried). The last German revival was in Greifswald in 1931.

71. Tgb. *succès*.

72. *Le Calife de Bagdad, opéra comique* in one act (C. Godard d'Aucour de Saint-Just, after an oriental tale; Paris, Opéra Comique, 16 September 1800), was one the most successful works of Boieldieu's pre-Russian period. It was given in Paris until 1836, with reprises in 1851 and 1867. It enjoyed a wide European vogue, but particularly so in Germany, where it was regularly revived (Frankfurt, 1876; Breslau, 1890; Königsberg, 1939).

73. *Ma Tante Aurore, ou Le Roman impromptu, opéra comique* in two acts (C. de Longchamps; Paris, Opéra Comique, 13 January 1803), was given in Paris until 1836, and revived there in 1851, 1894, and 1921. It traveled as far afield as New Orleans (1810), Moscow (1822), and New York (1827). The melodic grace and elegant harmony of this work and *Le Calife* won Boieldieu his earliest major recognition.

74. Tgb. *excelliert*.

75. Tgb. *Tournüren*.

76. Tgb. *sujet*.

77. Tgb. *légèren*.

78. Tgb. *precieuse*.

79. Tgb. *pitoyable*.

80. See 11 May 1812.

81. Tgb. *ennuy*.

82. Tgb. *neveu*.

83. Tgb. *armée*.

84. Friedrich Wilhelm III had removed the seat of government to Breslau, the only provincial capital not under foreign control. On 13 March 1813 he issued his famous call *An mein Volk*, in which he encouraged those men not conscripted to volunteer for the *Jäger* battalions.

85. Tgb. *freluquet*.

86. *Fernand Cortez ou La Conquête du Mexique, tragédie lyrique* in three acts (J. A. Esménard and Étienne de Jouy, after Alexis Piron's tragedy [1744]; Paris, Opéra, 28 November 1809). This grand historical pageant was even more successful than *La Vestale*, receiving c. 250 performances in Paris by 1840. The first Viennese performance was on 26 May 1812 in I. F. Castelli's translation. In Berlin it enjoyed especial success, and was given there 161 times until 1894. Its popularity was maintained throughout the nineteenth century (with a New York performance in 1888), and there have been twentieth-century revivals (Prague, 1900; Milan, 1916; Florence, 1950; Milan, 1966; Italian Radio [Rome], 1974).

87. Tgb. *negativen Hebel*.

88. See 10 August 1812.

89. Meyerbeer had already begun planning a stage work in the Italian style. See below, 23 June 1813.

90. Tgb. *Nonsens*.

91. Today this is a suburb of Vienna.

92. A member of the firm Reyer & Schlick, which owned a sugar refinery in Wiener Neustadt. This means that it was probably a business call, since Herz Beer had commercial connections with them because of his own refining concerns in Gorizia (*BT*, 1:632).

93. Opera in two acts by Wenzel Müller (C. Perinet, based on P. Hafner's comedy *Die reisenden Comödianten* [1774]; Vienna, Leopoldstädter-Theater, 11 March 1794). This opera

was even more popular than the *Neusonntagskind*, and was performed on every German stage throughout the nineteenth century; it even reached New York (1859). It was revived as late as 1863 (Munich) and 1870 (Königsberg), and in the twentieth-century at Baden near Vienna (1935). Beethoven used the aria "Ich bin der Schneider Kakadu" for his Variations in G major, for piano, violin and cello, op. 121a (1824).

94. *Les Aubergistes de qualité, opéra comique* in three acts by Catel* (V. J. Étienne de Jouy; Paris, Opéra Comique, 17 June 1812), was given in Paris until 1825, and proved popular in Germany for a while in the translation by I. von Seyfried for the performance of 5 February 1813 at the Theater an der Wien. The work was revived in Vienna in 1831.

95. This is presumably a reference to *Quinto Fabio*, an *opera seria* by Zeno (previously set by Ferdinando Bertoni* [Milan, 1778]), which is later mentioned as being among Meyerbeer's sketches for 1813 (see 8 February 1831). It is unlikely to mean *Romilda e Costanza*: how would Meyerbeer have come by Gaetano Rossi's libretto at this stage, when the first recorded correspondence between them is on 8 May 1817 (*BT,* 1:323)? It could refer to the monodrama or dramatic cantata for soprano, clarinet, chorus, and orchestra *Gli Amori di Teolinda*, which Meyerbeer wrote for Harlas and Baermann (Verona, 18 March 1816), but this also has a text by Rossi. Whatever the actual work, it confirms the young composer's interest in the Italian style, and casts doubt on the legend that he turned to opera because of disillusionment with his pianistic skills after hearing Hummel play in Vienna, and subsequently went to Italy to study the human voice on Salieri's advice. This counsel had, in any case, already been given to Winter in 1791 (see 27 July 1812).

96. The first Viennese performance was at the Burgtheater on 7 May 1788.

97. Not recorded.

98. *Trauerspiel* in four acts by Adolf Müllner, who founded the genre of the *Schicksalstragödie* (tragedy of fate) with this play, first produced in Vienna in April 1813 and published in Leipzig (1816).

99. Johann Veit (1790–1854) was a grandson of Moses Mendelssohn.

100. Baden bei Wien is the largest sulfur spa in Austria. It is located at the point where the river Schwechat enters the plain of the Vienna basin, and famed for its excellent wines. At no. 4 Renngasse Mozart composed his *Ave verum Corpus*, while at no.10 Rathausgasse Beethoven composed the greater part of his ninth Symphony.

101. Tgb. *réunion.*

102. = Baron Zinicq.

103. = Kienlen*.

104. *Claudine von Villa Bella* (1774) is a play by Johann Wolfgang von Goethe, later revised as a *Singspiel* (1779). There are twenty-two settings of the text (including one by Schubert, 1815). Kienlen's dates from Munich, 9 September 1810, and is the most successful of his works.

105. Laxenburg is famous for its eighteenth-century mansions, the residences of important courtiers (like Prince Kaunitz and Countess Auersperg) and its church (1673–1726) by Matthias Steinl.

106. The Alte Schloss (c. 1381) was rebuilt by Ludovico Burnacini. The park was laid out in the English style and surrounded by a lake. It contains the mock-medieval castle Franzenburg (1796–1836), built for the Emperor Francis II.

107. Tgb. *genre.*

108. Luigi Buonavoglia also wrote *Di Locanda in Locanda* (1805) for Giovanni Simone Mayr. *La Scelta dello sposo* was produced by the bass Christian Wilhelm Häser in Vienna in a German translation under the title *Die Gattenwahl.*

109. Pietro Carlo Guglielmi, not to be confused with his more famous father, Pietro Alessandro.

110. Tgb. *Force-Rolle*.

111. Actually *Die beiden kleinen Auvergnaten*, comedy in one act (first produced in Darmstadt and Dresden, 1813) [Richel 84].

112. Richel 28.

113. Johann Christoff Grünbaum*.

114. The medieval walls of Vienna remained intact until their famous demolition, to make way for the modernization of Alt Wien (1857-63). The event was commemorated musically by Johann Strauss II's *Demolirer-Polka*, op. 269 (1863).

115. Usually *Der Schlossgartner und der Windmüller*. Text by Koller. This was the première.

116. *Singspiel* by Franz Volkert. The first performance had been at the Leopoldstädter-Theater on 24 June 1813.

117. Presumably Maria Theresa's rooms in the Schönbrünn Palace.

118. First produced at the Königliches Schauspielhaus, Berlin, 1805, and published in 1806 [Richel 84].

119. Intermezzo by C. W. Häser with text by C. Wilhelm.

120. Comic *Singspiel* by Louis-Sébastien Lebrun (I. von Seyfried, after Bernard-Valville).

121. No. 11 in D major.

122. Actually *Der Hausteufel*, a *Lokalposse* in three acts by J. Perinet.

123. Tgb. *Lokalposse*.

124. For the first sustained account of Meyerbeer's highly strung disposition with its psychosomatic symptoms, see his letter to Prof. Wolfssohn of 20 January 1814 (*BT,* 1:230–31).

125. *BT,* 1:230. Germany was freed from French rule by the victory of the coalition forces (Russia, Prussia, and Austria) at the Battle of Leipzig (16–19 October 1813). The three powers entered Paris on 31 March 1814.

126. Beethoven is supposed to have expressed himself to Tomaschek: "I was not at all satisfied with him; he struck the drum badly and was always behindhand, so that I had to give him a good dressing-down. There is nothing in him; he hasn't the courage to hit a blow at the right time." Cited in Alexander Wheelock Thayer, *The Life of Ludwig van Beethoven* (London: Centaur Press, 1960), 2:297.

127. "From the list of my Compositions, I find that I wrote that opera [*Faust*] in less than four months, from the end of May to the middle of September [1813]. I still remember with what enthusiasm and perseverance I worked upon it. As soon as I had completed some of the parts I hastened with them to *Meyerbeer*, who then resided in Vienna, and begged him to play them to me from the score, a thing in which he greatly excelled. I then undertook the vocal parts and executed them in their different characters and voices with great enthusiasm. When my voice was not sufficiently flexible for the purpose, I helped myself by whistling, in which I was well practiced. *Meyerbeer* took great interest in this work, which appears to have kept its ground up to the present time, as he during his direction of the Opera in Berlin put 'Faust' again upon the stage, and had it studied with the greatest care" (*Louis Spohr's Autobiography,* translated from the German [London: Longman, Green, Longman, Roberts & Green, 1865], 1:178).

128. This overtly patriotic work was written for Berlin to celebrate the triumphal entry of the Prussian troops into the capital after the French defeat. (On 11 April 1814 Napoleon

had been obliged to abdicate and retire to Elba.) Iffland was prepared to stage the work, as Amalia Beer's letter of 21 May 1814 indicates (*BT,* 1:235), but it was never performed. The première took place only on 5 September 1991 at the Schauspielhaus in Berlin, as part of the bicentennial celebrations of the composer's birth.

129.   The Congress of Vienna met in the nine months from September 1814 to June 1815. The map of Europe was redrawn and a new political order was created, largely under the aegis of the Austrian chancellor, Prince Clemens von Metternich. This reaffirmation of the status quo, based on the balancing of powers, by and large brought stability and tranquility to Europe for a century.

130.   The billboard read: "Im Theater nächst dem Kärnthnerthor / zum ersten Mahl / DIE BEYDEN KALIPHEN / Eine komische Oper in zwey Aufzügen von Wohlbrück. / Die Musik ist von Hrn. Meyerbeer." A selection of reviews is reprinted in *BT,* 1:637–40. The *Harmonicon* explained: "At this period no music but Italian had a chance of being listened to in the Austrian capital; it is not to be wondered at, therefore, that Meyerbeer's opera, written upon an opposite principle and very nearly in the same style with his *Daughter of Jephtha,* failed completely." The only other performances were in Prague (22 October 1815) and Dresden (22 February 1820, as *Alimelek*). Both these latter performances were conducted by Carl Maria von Weber, who admired the music, commenting on its "active, alert imagination, the well-nigh voluptuous melody, the correct declamation, the entire musical attitude," and singling out the instrumentation: "It is surprisingly combined, interwoven with great delicacy, and consequently demands almost the care of a quartet performance" (see Istel, "Meyerbeer's Way to Mastership," p. 107).

131.   See *BT,* 1:255.

132.   *BT,* 1:267.

133.   *Über die musikalische Malerei* (Paris, 1781) was dedicated to Reichardt. His theory is that true musical painting, the presentation of external, actual events and circumstances, can only happen with the help of words, and hence can be fully realized only through vocal music.

134.   Presumably *Quinto Fabio.*

135.   The essential reference for theatrical life in nineteenth-century Paris is Nicole Wild's *Dictionnaire des théâtres parisiens au xixe siècle: Les théâtres et la musique* (Paris: Aux Amateurs de Livres, 1989); see also Marvin Carlson, *The French Stage in the Nineteenth Century* (Metuchen, N.J.: Scarecrow Press, 1972).

136.   *Mélodrame* in three acts (Paris, Théâtre de la Gaîté, 30 October 1811) [Wicks 2384].

137.   Drama in two acts (first performance in Vienna, 1806; in Berlin, 1807) [Richel 69].

138.   *Le Duc de Craon, ou Le Ministre français, mélodrame* in three acts (with von Bilderbeck and Duboir; Paris, Théâtre de la Gaîté, 11 November 1814) [Wicks 819].

139.   *Mélodrame* in four acts (Paris, Théâtre de la Gaité, 14 January 1809) [Wicks 569].

140.   On 1 March 1815 Napoleon landed in southern France and rapidly resumed control of the country in the Hundred Days. He beat the Prussian army under Marshal Blücher at Ligny on 16 June, but was defeated by the united German and English forces under Blücher and the duke of Wellington at the Battle of Waterloo (18 June 1815). Napoleon was obliged to abdicate in favor of his son, Napoleon II, the duke of Reichstadt, and Louis XVIII returned to Paris in triumph on 7 July 1815.

141.   "He is still in a position to evolve new plans, but he has only five minutes to put them into practice."

142. Tgb. *relachieren*.

143. Meyerbeer's papers contained sketches for an opera entitled *Le Bachelier de Salamanque*, an adaptation of Scribe's *comédie in 1 acte, mêlée de vaudevilles* (with H. Dupin and G. Delavigne; Paris, Théâtre des Variétés, 18 January 1815) [Wicks 265]. This is remarkably prefigurative of the composer's future illustrious collaboration with the French playwright. See 7 July 1832.

144. Wicks [2955] lists only *Le Vieillard et les jeunes gens*, a verse *comédie* in five acts (Paris, Théâtre de la Rue Louvois [Comédie de l'Odéon], 4 June 1803), perhaps identical with *Le vieux Celibataire*.

145. *Die Hagestolzen*, a comedy in five acts by Iffland (first performed in Berlin and Vienna, 1792, and in March 1796 at the Weimar Court Theatre, with Iffland himself as guest artist) [Richel 73]. A wealthy bachelor finds happiness in marriage after much disillusionment.

146. Paris, Comédie Français, 1775. The scheming and resourceful barber Figaro, also the valet hero of *La folle Journée, ou Le Mariage de Figaro* (1784), is sympathetically presented in the context of a class-conscious critique.

147. Tgb. *Chaussée-Gebühren*.

148. Tgb. *prévenance*.

149. Tgb. *représentation*.

150. *The Orphan, or The Unhappy Marriage* (London: Dorset Garden Theatre, 1680). Otway's tragedy in blank verse proved a great success and was often revived.

151. Oliver Goldsmith's idyllic family novel (1766) had great effect, not least through the plain, detached style of the narrative, which was so different from the exclamatory manner of the contemporary novels of sentiment. It attained great popularity and was translated into many languages.

152. Tgb. *sujet*.

153. *A Trip to Scarborough* (London, Theatre Royal Drury Lane, 1777). Sheridan's musical play is a careful adaptation of Sir John Vanbrugh's (1664-1726) *The Relapse*, with all coarse language expunged for a more prudish stage.

154. Tgb. *proponieren*.

155. *King Richard II*, a historical tragedy probably both written and acted in 1595 with immediate success, the first quarto of 1595 being followed by two more in 1598. It is written entirely in verse and contains some of Shakespeare's most famous speeches.

156. One of J. Whitaker's fourteen stage works.

157. Michael Arne, son of the more famous Thomas.

158. *Cymon, a dramatic romance* (Garrick, based on Dryden's poem *Cymon and Iphigenia;* London, Drury Lane, 2 January 1767), was Arne's most successful work. Performed in Dublin (1771), Philadelphia and New York (1773), and Edinburgh (1783), and frequently revived in London. Meyerbeer attended the revival of 20 November 1815 in which the work had been reduced from five to three acts with additions by Bishop and interpolated airs by Stevenson, Braham, and Paer.

159. *Othello, The Moor of Venice*, a tragedy written by Shakespeare between 1602 and 1604, when it was performed before James I at Whitehall. It was first printed in quarto in 1622. The story was taken from Giambattista Giraldi Cinthio's *Hecatommithi* (1574).

160. Listed neither in Loewenberg, Clément and Larousse, nor Towers.

161. This title is listed neither among Beaumont's plays, nor among Cook's sixteen musical stage works.

162. Tgb. *fini*.

163. Tgb. *fonds.*

164. The première of this work.

165. Tgb. *Extravagancen.*

166. Tgb. *natürliche Zahmheit.*

167. Op. 55.

168. *Venice Preserv'd, or a Plot Discovered* (London, Dorset Garden Theatre, 1682), a tragedy in blank verse, with Betterson as Jaffeir and Mrs. Barry as Belvidera, was well received and remained popular throughout the eighteenth and early nineteenth centuries.

169. Tgb. *pli.*

170. Tgb. *conversation.*

171. Tgb. *quarré.*

172. The revival of 14 December 1815, which was given again in 1817, 1820, and 1827.

173. Tgb. *roulierte.*

174. *Dulce et utile, 6 petites études,* op. 55.

175. Tgb. *perlé.*

176. Tgb. *égalité.*

177. Tgb. *tache de soleil.*

178. Rather, *Harlequin and Faustus* (London, Covent Garden, 1793), a pantomime by Samuel Arnold (1740-1802). Clément and Larousse also mention a comic opera of this name by Galliard (Haymarket, 1816).

179. *The London Merchant, or the History of George Barnwell.* (London, Theatre Royal Drury Lane, 1731), prose tragedy in five acts by George Lillo. For the first time, everyday commercial life was made the theme of tragedy: an innocent young apprentice is seduced by a heartless courtesan, led into murder, and finally executed. It was very successful, and translated into French, German, and Dutch. Lillo's introduction of middle-class domestic tragedy exercised an influence far beyond England, affecting Lessing (*Miss Sara Sampson,* 1755) and Diderot (*Le Fils naturel,* 1757).

180. Tgb. *compositeur.*

181. Vogler spent the years 1786-92 in Stockholm in the service of King Gustav III, as conductor of the Royal Chapel.

182. This intention was partially fulfilled in Sicily (July–September 1816).

183. London, Theatre Royal Drury Lane, 1714.

184. *The Iron Chest* (London, Theatre Royal Drury Lane, 1796), with music by Stephen Storace, a dramatization of William Godwin's domestic Gothic novel, *Caleb Williams* (1794).

185. *Avis au Public, ou Le Physionomiste en défaut, opéra comique* in two acts (Déaugiers; Paris, Feydeau, 22 November 1806).

186. *Silvain,* opera in one act (J. F. Marmortel, based on Gessner's *Erast;* Paris, Comédie-Italienne, 19 February 1770). Given in Paris until 1827. Popular outside France for thirty years in German, Dutch, Russian, and Swedish.

187. Opera in one act (Théaulon and Armand Dartois; Paris, Opéra Comique, 1 January 1816).

188. Cherubini had written nothing since *Les Abencérages* (1813) and Méhul nothing since *Le Prince Troubadour* (1813). The latter was soon to come up with *La Journée aux Aventures* (1816), but Cherubini turned away from opera in his later years to give his attention to sacred music; his next opera would be his last, the unsuccessful *Ali Baba* (1833).

189. Tgb. *sujet.*

190. *La Marquise de Cange, ou Les trois Frères, mélodrame-historique* in three acts

(E. Cantiran de Boirie and Léopold Chandezon; Paris, Théâtre de la Gaîté, 18 November 1815) [Wicks 1858].

191. Tgb. *succès*.

192. Tgb. *élan*.

193. Opera in one act. First performed in Paris at the Théâtre Italien in 1815.

194. Tgb. *solfeggieren*.

195. This is Rousseau's most famous composition (Fontainebleau, 18 October 1752) in which he used simple melodies and accompaniments to express rustic virtue in contrast to aristocratic corruption. It was produced at the Opéra on 1 March 1753 and performed there four hundred times until 1829, and revived in Paris in 1912 and 1923. Productions took place right across Europe into the nineteenth century.

196. Text by P. F. Giraud and M. T. Leclerq; Paris, Opéra, 24 May 1808. It was successful in Paris until 1830; the one hundredth performance was on 5 June 1822.

197. The lost aria for a one-act German opera, *Robert und Elise*, was inscribed "Neapel, d. 20 Juni 1816," and carried the date "Palermo, d. 22 Juli 1816."

198. See Fritz Bose, *Meyerbeer: Sizilianische Volkslieder* (Berlin: Walter de Gruyter, 1970), esp. part A: "Die Quelle und ihre Entstehung" (pp. 5–13).

199. The aria with chorus and orchestra, "Perchè muni tiranni," written for Therese Grünbaum, is dated "Genua, 3. Oct. 1816." See the composer's discussion of his sketches from 1816 (8 February 1831). For Meyerbeer's recollections of this visit to Genoa, see 6 March 1856.

200. Spohr's *Selbstbiographie* provides more interesting glimpses of Meyerbeer in Italy, and helps to fix the chronology. On 20 October 1816 Meyerbeer was in Venice: "This morning, on going out, we had the wholly unexpected pleasure of meeting *Meyerbeer* and all his family. He is now returned from a tour through Sicily to meet his parents here, who have not seen him for five years: he will then turn back through Florence and Rome to Naples, where he will be present at the opening of the new theater of *St. Carlo*. It was a real enjoyment to be able once more to converse with a well-educated German artist on subjects of art. His brother gave me the gratifying information that my opera 'Faust' had been performed in Prague. On their journey through they were present at a rehearsal of it" (*Louis Spohr's Autobiography,* 1:238).

201. See Lillian Day, *Paganini of Genoa* (New York: The Macaulay Company, 1929). "Meyerbeer came to Italy and heard Paganini in Florence. It is said that he changed his plans to go to Naples ... in order to follow Paganini through Tuscany and that not until he had heard the violinist eighteen times could he tear himself away" (p. 66). Paganini played in towns like Arezzo, Pistoia, and Siena.

202. Spohr had also reached the Eternal City by now, where he found Meyerbeer's three brothers, Wilhelm, Heinrich, and Michael. During Advent, with all the theaters closed, the brothers would join Spohr in his lodgings, where they whiled away the winter evenings playing whist, all huddled together for warmth. On 23 December 1816 Spohr recorded the arrival of Meyerbeer and his mother. In Florence Meyerbeer had received a letter from C. M. von Weber, and communicated to Spohr the happy news that his opera *Faust* had already been performed twice in Prague with extraordinary success. On 27 December Spohr wrote: "Yesterday, at last the theaters were once more opened, after being closed six months. At the *Argentino* theater, the largest and handsomest, *Rossini's* 'Tancredi' was performed, at the theater *Valle*, a new *Opera buffa* by Signor *Pietro Romano*, called 'Il Quidproquo.' As 'Tancredi' is an old opera ... *Meyerbeer* easily persuaded me to go with him to the *Valle* theater, while my wife and the children, with Madame *Beer*, went to the *Argentino* theater"

(*Louis Spohr's Autobiography,* 1:314). And on 29 December: "Last evening I went with *Meyerbeer* to hear 'Tancredi' at the *Argentino* theater. I never witnessed a more wretched performance" (1:319).

203. As a farewell gesture Spohr wrote a *Canone finito a 4* for Meyerbeer that has the inscription "Zum Andenken von Ihrem Freunde und Verehrer . . . Rom, 4.1.1817."

204. See Day, *Paganini of Genoa,* pp. 100–104, for the following anecdote: "The Carnival of 1817 found Paganini in Rome . . . Rossini was indeed the spoilt child of Rome. [He was there for the première of *La Cenerentola* at the Teatro Valle on 25 January]. Round and impish he was the apotheosis of King Carnival. . . . 'Let's get Meyerbeer,' shouted Rossini, "and start something.'

"Meyerbeer, it will be remembered, was also an admirer of Paganini. 'Where our reason ends,' he said, 'there Paganini begins.'

"The three artists masqueraded as female beggars. Rossini permitted his too-large belly to attract solicitude for a delicate condition, while Paganini accentuated his gauntness by a long, straight skirt. Rossini had written a song *Carnevale, Carnevale,* and the group went from house to house and in and out of the cafés, strumming their guitars and singing. . . .

"Paganini made speeches in a falsetto voice and Meyerbeer passed the hat. Rossini was permitted to rest after the songs by virtue of his imminent motherhood.

"People remarked that they did not play at all badly, this robust son of a slaughter house inspector, the 'Jew banker to whom it occurred to compose operas' [Richard Wagner's words], and the gaunt Genovese, a decade older than his companions."

According to Andrew Everett, "Bewitched in a Magic Garden: Giacomo Meyerbeer in Italy," *Donizetti Society Journal* 6 (1988): 177, this event occurred in 1821 in the company of the future politician Massimo D'Azeglio. (At the time, Paganini was in Rome and conducted the première of Rossini's *Mathilde di Shabran* [24 February 1821].) D'Azeglio mentions the story as happening in 1821, but does not refer to Meyerbeer. See *Things I Remember (I miei ricordi)*, trans. E. R. Vincent (London and New York: Oxford University Press, 1966), pp. 235–36.

205. He took up residence in Venice with Herz Beer's business associate, Johann Georg Hartmann (*BT,* 1:322).

206. These four-part settings of poems by Friedrich Gottlob Klopstock* (1724-1803) *(Morgenlied, Dem Dreieinigen, Vorbereitung zum Gottesdienst, Danklied, Nach dem Abendmahl, Wach auf, mein Herz, Liebster Jesu, wir sind hier)* were dedicated to Gottfried Weber, and were first performed in the Museum Carl Stephanie in Mannheim in October 1812.

207. See *BT,* 1:324–26.

208. The best general introduction to Meyerbeer's Italian operas is by Philip Gossett, *Giacomo Meyerbeer: Excerpts from the Early Italian Operas (1817–1822)* (New York: Garland, 1991), pp. i–xiii. For *Romilda e Costanza,* see pp. ii–iii. A detailed introduction to the opera and its first performance is provided by Jeremy Commons and Don White in *A Hundred Years of Italian Opera, 1810–1820* (London: Opera Rara, 1988), pp. 152–64.

209. It was revived at the Teatro Carcano in March 1820, in Florence in the spring and summer of the same year. Outside Italy it was performed twice in 1822, in Copenhagen (in Danish) and in Munich. Three excerpts were published: the overture and a cavatina by Ricordi (Milan, 1818) and the quartet by Cipriani (n.d.).

210. By falling in love with Meyerbeer, which was unrequited, she nearly succeeded in sabotaging the first performance.

211. This opera is not listed in Loewenberg, while Clément and Larousse give it a

perfunctory sentence (Félix Clément and Pierre Larousse, *Dictionnaire des Opéras,* rev. Arthur Pougin [Paris, 1905; reprint, New York: Da Capo, 1969], 1:372; page numbers are to the reprint edition).

212. From 1813 until his death in 1821 Viganò was ballet master at La Scala, where he choreographed his most inspired works.

213. Pacini's fifteenth opera (Gaetano Rossi, after a comedy by G. A. Gualzetti; 30 December 1817) and first great success. Further performances followed in Rome, Florence, and Naples (1819), Munich (1820), Barcelona (1822), Madrid (1823), Oporto (1825), Bern (1830), and Mexico (1835).

214. Luigi Pacini, the first Geronio in *Il Turco in Italia* (1814).

215. *Zauberoper* in two acts by Wolfgang Amadeus Mozart (E. Schikaneder; Vienna, Theater auf der Wieden, 30 September 1791). The opera was a success from the start, and established itself as a permanent feature of the international repertory.

216. First produced in Naples at the San Carlo in 1817. The cavatina "Grazie vi rendo, amici" became famous, written "dans le style élégant et mélodieux qu'on retrouve plus tard dans les opéras du même maître" [in the elegant and melodious style that one finds later on in the operas of the same master] (Clément and Larousse, *Dictionnaire,* 1:8).

217. Tgb. *impresa.*

218. Tgb. *ingenieuse.*

219. Viganò worked slowly, methodically, and with difficulty, rehearsing relentlessly until he had achieved the desired effect. Stendhal emphasized his extraordinary patience, reporting how he began *Dedalo e Icaro* on 4 August 1817 and completed it on 25 December "by rehearsing from ten in the morning to six, and from ten at night to four in the morning" (*Rome, Naples et Florence,* quoted in Cyril W. Beaumont, *Complete Book of Ballets* [Garden City, N.Y : Garden City Publishing Co., 1938], p. 25).

220. See 8 January 1831.

221. Tgb. *supplement.*

222. Heroic-tragic mime-ballet in five acts (Naples, San Carlo, 1807; Expanded for Milan, La Scala, 18 August 1809). This was Gaetano Gioia's most famous ballet. Napoleon was present at the first performance, and it was much admired by Viganò for its blending of dance, drama, and music. It was revived at La Scala in 1815.

223. "The Peacock."

224. Tgb. *prävenierte.*

225. Clément and Larousse give the date as 1813 and the place as Venice (*Dictionnaire,* 1:111).

226. Coccia's most famous work (G. Rossi; Venice, San Benedetto, 8 June 1815), given in Italy until the 1860s and as far afield as Mexico (1832) and Odessa (1839).

227. This chorus made a deep impression on Meyerbeer, and later served as the model for the Coro dei Congiurati "Nel silenzio frà l'orror" in *Il Crociato in Egitto* (no. 13 in the Pacini vocal score).

228. Trieste occupied an ambiguous position as both Italian city and Dalmatian port.

229. Presumably the impresario of the Trieste Theatre.

230. *Il Fajello* was first produced at the Teatro degli Infuocati in autumn 1817, and then revived at the Teatro Nuovo in Trieste in 1818 as *Gabriella di Vergy.*

231. *Nachtstuhl* or "night soil." This derogatory term is the first instance of Meyerbeer use of nicknames, here applied perhaps to Lichtenthal.

232. *Otello, ossia Il Moro di Venezia, opera seria* in three acts by Rossini (Marchese Berio di Salsa, after Shakespeare's *Othello;* Naples, Fondo, 4 December 1816). One of

Rossini's most popular operas, it was produced all over Italy, and around the world (Trinidad, 1844; Rio di Janeiro, 1855; Valparaiso, 1868) throughout the nineteenth century, until overtaken by Verdi's opera (1887), after which it fell into oblivion.

233.   Actually *L'Equivico stravagante,* written in 1811 for the Teatro del Corso in Bologna.

234.   Opera in two acts by Rossini (C. Sterbini; Rome, Teatro Valle, 26 December 1815). It enjoyed an international career (Mexico, 1831; Algeria, 1842) until the early 1840s.

235.   *La Gazza ladra, opera semiseria* in two acts by Rossini (G. Gherardini, after a French *mélodrame, La Pie voleuse,* by J.-M.-T. Baudouin d'Aubigny and L.-C. Caigniez; Milan, La Scala, 31 May 1817). One of Rossini's more popular works, performed regularly in Italy for another forty years; its international career continued for the rest of the century (e.g., St. Petersburg, 1873; New York, 1883).

236.   Tgb. *spropositi.*

237.   *Opera seria* in three acts (Giovanni Schmidt, after Tasso; Naples, 11 November 1817). In spite of its considerable musical power, this proved to be one of Rossini's least successful mature operas, even in Italy. The German version by J. von Seyfried attained a modest success until the early 1830s.

238.   *Adelaide di Borgogna, ossia Ottone, re d'Italia, dramma* in two acts (Giovanni Schmidt; Rome, Teatro Argentina, 27 December 1817). Rossini's twenty-first opera had a few later stagings in Italy, but does not appear to have been heard elsewhere.

239.   Tgb. *Quaresima.*

240.   *Azione tragico-sacra* in three acts by Rossini (A. L. Tottola; Naples, San Carlo, 5 March 1818). This was to prove one of Rossini's most popular works during the nineteenth century, with performances all over the world (e.g., Havana, 1834; Rio di Janeiro, 1858; Sydney, 1873). It was frequently given in concert form as an oratorio, and revived into the twentieth century (Florence, 1935; Milan, 1937) even before the *ottocento* revivals of the 1950s.

241.   Tgb. *gelevàt.* The meaning of this word is unclear. Becker proposes the manifestation of disapproval, like whistling (*BT,* 1:661).

242.   *Ricciardo e Zoraide,* opera in two acts by Rossini (Marchese F. Berio, after the poem *Ricciardo* by N. Forteguerri; Naples, San Carlo, 3 December 1818). This was not among Rossini's most popular works, although it did enjoy a brief career in the 1820s.

243.   Tgb. *pretese.*

244.   Tgb. *oltre modo stravagante e forte.*

245.   Baermann was involved in a social misunderstanding with the cavaliere, who had invited him to play at a society function but advertised it in such a casual way as to cause offense to the artist, who stormed out of the gathering and, having lost his bearings, fell into a canal. The count complained to the police about him, resulting in Baermann's immediate departure from Venice. For a fuller account of the incident, see *BT,* 1:662.

246.   Oratorio in three parts, HWV 56 (words by Jennens, arranged from the Old and New Testaments; Dublin, 13 April 1742).

247.   *Stabat Mater* for soloists, chorus and orchestra in G minor, HobXXbis (1767).

248.   Tgb. *impresa.*

249.   First performed in Bologna 1812. "Ce petit ouvrage est charmant et obtenu le plus franc succès" [This small work is charming and obtained the most unequivocal success] (Clément and Larousse, *Dictionnaire,* 2:813).

250.   *Almaviva, ossia L'Inutile Precauzione, opera buffa* in two acts by Rossini (C. Sterbini, based on Beaumarchais's *Le Barbier de Séville;* Rome, Teatro Argentina, 20 February

1816). One of the most famous of all comic operas. Rossini's most popular and enduring work, still performed throughout the world.

251. Farce by Generali, first produced in Venice, 1810.

252. Opera by Coccia (Rome, 1816).

253. Opera by Coccia (Venice, 1814).

254. This opera is not listed in Clément and Larousse, Loewenberg, or Towers. Becker presumes it to be synonymous with *Il Lupo d'Ostenda, ossia L'Innocenza salvata della colpa* by Vaccai (Bartolomeo Merelli; Venice, San Benedetto, spring 1818) (*BT,* 1:662).

255. *Otello,* tragic ballet in five acts (choreography and scenario by Salvatore Viganò, music by various composers; Milan, La Scala, 6 February 1818). This was a spectacular production with much crowd work and superb sets by Alessandro Sanquirico.

256. Tragic ballet in five acts (choreography and scenario by Salvatore Viganò, music by various composers; Milan, La Scala, 9 June 1818). This was considered to be Viganò's masterpiece: "Salvatore Viganò has transcended all other forms of expression. His instinctive art has enabled him to discover the true nature of the dance: romantic above all" (Stendhal).

257. Tgb. *Santo.*

258. *Elisabetta, Regina di Inghilterra, opera seria* in two acts by Rossini (Giovanni Schmidt, after Federici's drama, based on Lee's play *The Recess;* Naples, San Carlo, 4 October 1815). The opera enjoyed currency through the 1820s and was performed as far afield as Mexico (1834), but did not attain great popularity. The last nineteenth-century performance was in Würzburg, 1841 (Alfred Loewenberg, *Annals of Opera, 1597–1940,* 2d ed., revised and corrected [Cambridge: Cambridge University Press, 1955; reprint, as one vol., New York: Rowman & Littlefield, 1970], col. 641). The overture, already borrowed from *Aureliano in Palmira* (1813), was famously reused by Rossini for *Il Barbiere di Siviglia.*

259. Meyerbeer is referring to the artistic rivalries between various legendary castrati and sopranos in Venice in the late eighteenth century.

260. First produced in Venice in 1815.

261. First performed in Milan in 1815.

262. *I Baccanti di Roma,* opera in two acts by Generali (Gaetano Rossi; Venice, La Fenice, 14 January 1816). The opera was performed across Europe in the 1820s, and given in Havana as late as 1840.

263. Tgb. *Quadragesima.*

264. Giuseppe de Begnis.

265. First produced in 1760 (Clément and Larousse, *Dictionnaire,* 2:890).

266. *L'Italiana in Algeri, opera buffa* in two acts (A. Anelli; Venice, San Benedetto, 22 May 1813). Rossini's first comic masterpiece, and a great success that rapidly spread around the world. It has consistently maintained its place in the repertory.

267. *Opera buffa* in two acts (G. Bertati, founded on *The Clandestine Marriage,* by G. Colman and D. Garrick; Vienna, Burgtheater, 7 February 1791). This was the first opera Cimarosa wrote on returning from Russia, and his most successful work. It is the only *opera buffa* between Mozart and Rossini still to be performed regularly.

268. Wilhelm Beer.

269. Tgb. *Nachtstühle.*

270. "What a fiasco! what a huge fiasco!! suffice it to say that . . ."

271. Klara Metzger (later Vespermann) was Winter's foster daughter.

272. Tgb. *impresa.*

273. *Psammi, Re d'Egitto*, ballet by Salvatore Viganò (Milan, 1817).

274. Hob XXVIb/2 (1790).

275. In the Palace of the Doges in Venice.

276. Tgb. *ripiego*.

277. Opera in two acts (L. Romanelli, from a play by F. J. W. Ziegler; Milan, La Scala, 18 April 1808). Also produced in Parma, Paris, Dresden, Vienna, and Lisbon (1820). The revival Meyerbeer mentions was on 18 April 1818.

278. Tgb. *periodologischen*.

279. "Heart and soul."

280. "You have spoken accurately, sir: he thinks badly but writes well." These words are curiously prophetic of Richard Wagner.

281. Tgb. *stagione*.

282. Opera in two acts (Felice Romani, after Saint-Just's French libretto for Boieldieu [1812]; Milan, La Scala, 30 May 1818). Also produced in Dresden, Naples, Vienna, Barcelona, Rome. Revived in Genoa (1836).

283. Tgb. *gracieus*.

284. Tgb. *maesteria*.

285. Opera in two acts (Milan, La Scala, 5 August 1818), the only opera Gyrowetz wrote for Italy. The libretto was used again twenty-two years later by Verdi.

286. Tgb. *parterre*.

287. "What do you think?"

288. "Not to worry, his father will help him!"

289. "When the greatest man in the world dies, no pigsty is thrown into disturbance!"

290. The Italian word *lusinghiero* means "flattering, alluring, tempting."

291. "Sentimentality."

292. "Fizzy, sweet, and sour."

293. Tgb. *questa ora*.

294. "So-called experts."

295. During the eighteenth century the activity of the Barbary pirates, centered principally at Algiers, Tunis, and Tripoli, declined as Europe developed. The Napoleonic Wars increased commercial and naval possibilities, but also brought French invasion in their wake. Any such piratical activity as continued into the nineteenth century received a decisive blow with the French conquest of Algeria in 1830. Until then, as this experience shows, the subject matter of operas like *Die Entführung aus dem Serail* and *L'Italiana in Algeri* remained disturbingly topical.

296. Yiddish for "anti-Semitism."

297. *La Cenerentola, ossia La Bontà in trionfo, opera buffa* in two acts (J. Ferretti, based on C. G. Étienne's French libretto for Isouard [1810]; Rome, Teatro Valle, 25 January 1813). One of Rossini's greatest successes, and an enduring mainstay of the comic repertoire all over the world.

298. Tgb. *ma gli toccò di far fiasco*.

299. *Quanti casi in un sol giorno, ossia Gli Assassini, opera buffa* in 1 act by Vittorio Trento (G. Artusi; Venice, La Fenice, 1818). Clément and Larousse incorrectly give 1819 (*Dictionnaire*, 2:921).

300. See 20 May 1812.

301. See 8 May 1812.

302. Tgb. *aux éclats*.

303. First performed in Palermo, 1817.

304. Opera in two acts (G. Palomba; Naples, Teatro Nuovo, 19 June 1793). It was successful in Italy, and given until 1818.

305. First performed in Venice, 1808.

306. *Agnese di Fitz-Henry*, opera in two acts by Paer (L. Buonavoglia, after Amelia Opie's tale *The Father and Daughter* [1801]; Ponte d'Altaro [near Parma], October 1809). Performed all over Italy, and internationally (e.g., Odessa, 1821; Mexico, 1832) until 1850, and known simply as *Agnese*.

307. Tgb. *cabaleur*.

308. Clément and Larousse incorrectly give 1825 (*Dictionnaire*, 2:639).

309. Actually *Berenice in Siria* (Clément and Larousse, *Dictionnaire*, 1:147).

310. First performed in Milan, 1814.

311. Tgb. *scrittura*.

312. See Gossett, *Giacomo Meyerbeer*, pp. iv–v; Commons and White in *A Hundred Years of Italian Opera, 1810–1820*, pp. 195–202, provide an account of the première.

313. Bassi's creation of Semiramide was far from routine, but a genuine act of friendship for Meyerbeer. This affection was to survive for many years, and Meyerbeer presented her with the manuscript of his opera. They were in frequent correspondence later in life, mainly in connection with her son, the composer Ruggero Manna. See entry for 22 March 1848.

314. The première was a triumph for composer and prima donna, yet the career of the opera was short-lived. Under the amended title, *Semiramide riconosciuta*, it was produced at the Teatro Communale in Bologna in June 1820, again with Bassi and Bonoldi. It was also given in Sinigaglia in the *fiera* (fair) of the same year, but there is no record of any other performance. Loewenberg does not even list it. Two excerpts—a duet and the final *Canzonetta con Variazioni*—were published by Ricordi (Milan, in 1821 and 1823, respectively).

315. See Gossett, *Giacomo Meyerbeer*, pp. v–vii; Commons and White, *A Hundred Years of Italian Opera, 1810–1820*, pp. 203–12. The opera was a brilliant success, and performed seventy-four times.

316. This was the work that established Meyerbeer's reputation throughout Italy and carried it into Germany. It was staged in Venice, Milan, Genoa, Florence, and Padua. In Italian it was further given in Dresden (29 January 1820) and Barcelona (31 January 1829); in German (as *Emma von Leicester*) in Vienna (Theater an der Wien, February 1821), Munich, Dresden, Frankfurt, Budapest (20 February 1821), and Brünn (20 February 1821), and as *Emma von Roxburgh* in Berlin (11 February 1820) and Stuttgart. It was even translated into Polish for Warsaw (6 April 1821). The vocal score was published (Berlin, 1820) and the overture enjoyed some popularity. Some nine excerpts were published by Ricordi (Milan, n.d.) and Falter e figlio (Munich, 1821).

317. See Gossett, *Giacomo Meyerbeer*, pp. vii–ix; Commons and White, *A Hundred Years of Italian Opera, 1820-1830* (London: Opera Rara, 1994), pp. 5–16.

318. Romani and Meyerbeer had already met, as is described by Emilia Branca in her biography of her husband, *Felice Romani ed i più riputati maestri di musica del suo tempo* (Turin, Florence, and Rome, 1882), pp. 259ff. While a young man Romani had traveled to Germany and had met a youthful student of music, Jacob Meyer Beer. They became friends and traveled together, Meyerbeer helping Romani with German, and Romani instructing Meyerbeer in Italian versification. In 1820 they met again: "The reunion was most cordial; they both made it a welcome duty to visit each other every day to discuss art and artists. The Genovese again began instructing the German in Italian literature, for which the latter had

a great passion; and meeting in an uncomfortable room, they passed the happiest moments over volumes of our classics, and as they studied lyric poetry, practised recitation. 'I am always thinking of great things and hope to achieve much,' said Meyerbeer; and he did, for he did not lack the boldness of those splendid minds who waste no time in opening up luminous paths for themselves." (Translated by Commons and White, *One Hundred Years of Italian Opera, 1820–1830*, p. 7). There is no surviving documentary evidence of any contact between composer and poet before work began on *Margherita d'Anjou*.

319. *Marguerite d'Anjou, mélodrame-historique* in three acts (Paris, Théâtre de la Gaîté; 11 January 1810), with music by Gerardin Lacour [Wicks 1783].

320. The opera was played fifteen times at La Scala. Like *Emma di Resburgo*, it was performed outside Italy. In Italian: Munich (February 1822), Dresden (20 March 1824), Barcelona (10 May 1825), London (12 January 1828), Madrid (14 March 1836) and Lisbon (22 October 1837). In German: Graz (26 March 1831), Prague (December 1831), Budapest (February 1832), Laibach (24 January 1833). In French: Paris (Odéon, 11 March 1826), Brussels (21 December 1826), Amsterdam (spring 1835), The Hague (22 October 1839). The vocal score of the Italian version was published by Schlesinger (Paris, 1826) and four excerpts by Ricordi.

321. *BT*, 1:426–27. Whether *Almanzore* was ever completed is not known. The fact that the name of the opera and the principal character of *L'Esule di Granata* are the same suggest that the latter work is a revision of the former.

322. It is possible that Donizetti's *Zoraide di Granata* (Rome, 28 January 1822) is an adaptation by Bartolommeo Merelli of the scenario of this abortive opera, perhaps undertaken to defray the outlay on scenery and costumes (see William Ashbrook, *Donizetti and his Operas* [Cambridge: Cambridge University Press, 1982], pp. 22–25, 287–88).

323. Statements by Emilia Branca that "the friends and collaborators were sorely tried" (Branca, *Felice Romani,* pp. 267–68), and comments in Romani's preface to the original libretto, point to serious problems in the gestation period. Cf. Gossett, *Giacomo Meyerbeer,* pp. ix–x.

324. See Gossett, *Giacomo Meyerbeer,* pp. ix–xi; Commons and White, *A Hundred Years of Italian Opera, 1820-1830*, pp. 54–66.

325. The opera was staged so late in the season that only nine performances could be given. Only one other subsequent performance has been traced: in Florence (September 1826), with Pisaroni again singing Almanzor. Five vocal excerpts were published by Ricordi (Milan, n.d.).

326. While in Berlin he met up with Weber again, and spent a day and much of the night in reminiscence with him. In a letter to Gottfried Weber, Carl Maria von Weber wrote: "Last Friday I had the joy of having Meyerbeer spend a whole day with me. It was a truly happy day—a reminder of the good old times in Mannheim. We did not part until midnight. Meyerbeer is going to Trieste to produce his *Crociato*. Next year he returns to Berlin where he will perhaps write a German opera. Heaven grant it! I have made many appeals to his conscience" (quoted in the *Illustrated London News,* 11 August 1855, p. 173). Also see John Warrack, *Carl Maria von Weber* (Cambridge: Cambridge University Press, 1968), p. 309. During this visit Meyerbeer tried unsuccessfully to secure a performance of *Das Brandenburger Tor* in Königsberg.

327. Rossi addressed seventy-five surviving letters to Meyerbeer between 28 November 1822 and 6 December 1823 (*BT*, 1:449–572). None of Meyerbeer's letters to Rossi have so far come to light.

328. The opera did not eventuate, but an extant text by Rossi, *Ines de Castro, o sia*

Pietro di Portogallo (*melodramma tragico* for the Teatro San Carlo, Naples, 1825), is most likely the projected work. See *BT,* 1:576–80.

329.   See Philip Gossett, ed., *Il Crociato in Egitto: A Facsimile Edition of a Manuscript of the Original Version,* 2 vols. (New York: Garland, 1979), 1:i–v. Don White, "Meyerbeer in Italy," introduction to the libretto of *Il Crociato in Egitto* (London: Opera Rara, 1992), pp. 13-70.

330.   *Les Chevaliers de Malte, ou L'Ambassade à Alger, mélodrame* in three acts (J.-A.-M. Monperlier, H. Albertin, and J.-B. Dubois; Lyons, Théâtre des Célestins, February 1813; Paris, Théâtre de la Gaîté, 4 November 1813) [Wicks 550]. See Mark Everist, "Meyerbeer's *Il Crociato in Egitto: Mélodrame,* Opera, Orientalism," *Cambridge Opera Journal* 8:3 (1996): 215–49, for an investigation of the origins of Rossi's libretto, French dramatic conceptions of the Orient in 1813, Italian ideas of the same subject in 1824, and an analysis of the Orientalist dimension in Meyerbeer's music.

331.   This opera was Meyerbeer's first definitive triumph and enjoyed a worldwide success, retaining its popularity even after the advent of Meyerbeer's great Parisian operas. It was given in every major and minor opera house in Italy over the next twelve years: Trieste, Parma, Padua, Genoa, Milan (both La Scala and the Cannobiana), Reggio, Modena, Sinigaglia, Brescia, Lugo, Naples, Bologna, Turin, Messina, Lucca, Verona, Ferrara, Mantua, Livorno, Palermo, Bergamo, Pavia, Siena, Rome. Outside Italy it was given in 1825 (London, Paris, Barcelona); 1826 (Pressburg, Munich, Dresden); 1827 (Cadiz, Oporto, Graz); 1828 (Budapest, Prague, Lisbon, Havana); 1829 (Vienna); 1831 (Rio de Janiero); 1832 (Berlin, Hamburg); 1835 (Bucharest); 1837 (Mexico); 1838 (Corfu); 1839 (Constantinople); 1841 (St. Petersburg); 1847 (Königsberg). Major revivals were in 1859 (Milan, La Scala) and 1860 (Paris, Théâtre Italien; Graz). It has also enjoyed modern revivals in London (Queen Elizabeth Hall, 28 March 1972), New York (Carnegie Hall, 28 March 1979), Montpellier (1990), and Ludwigsburg and Dresden (1991). The vocal score was published in Milan, Bonn, and Cologne (1824) and by Pacini in Paris (1826).

332.   The *Harmonicum,* June 1825, pp. 96–97, gives a vivid account of the success: "[O]f all living composers, Meyerbeer is the one who most happily combines the easy, flowing, and expressive melodies of Italy, with the severer beauties, the grander accompaniments, of the German school. . . . After the performance, the composer was met at the door of the house by an immense concourse of people, who came prepared with bands of music, and lighted torches, and accompanied him to his residence with tumultuous acclamations. He was then obliged to show himself from the balcony, amidst the roar of a thousand evvivas, the clang of trumpets, and the deafening roar of drums. . . ."

333.   Renée de Saussine (*Paganini* [London: Hutchinson, 1953] p. 90) observes that "it was Meyerbeer, who for the next few months accompanied the maestro [Paganini] wherever he went."

334.   Meyerbeer did not attend the London production, which featured Barbaia's Italian Troupe headed by Velluti and which paid close attention to Meyerbeer's details. The young Maria Malibran sang Felicia in what was her first season.

335.   The performance had been delayed at Meyerbeer's request so that he could personally supervise the proceedings. The *Harmonicum,* April 1825, p. 60, reported: "M. Rossini has been defeated in his design of bringing out M. Mayerbeer's opera *Il Crociato in Egitto,* in such a way as to endanger its safety. The composer himself lately arrived in this city, and immediately represented his case to the minister, who, handsomely ordered that . . . [he] should be allowed . . . to produce the work in his own manner."

336.   The cast included Ester Mombelli, Giuditta Pasta, Domenico Donzelli, and Nicholas

Levasseur. The *Harmonicum,* December 1825, p. 234, reported that "the opera of *Il Crociato* has obtained a brilliant and merited success." On 24 September King Friedrich Wilhelm III and his son attended the second performance.

337. It was performed thirty-six times. For a full account of the history of the French version and production of *Margherita d'Anjou,* see Mark Everist, "Giacomo Meyerbeer, the Théâtre Royal de l'Odéon, and Music Drama in Restoration Paris," *Nineteenth Century Music* 17:2 (fall 1993): 124–47. The French version was published in full score by Pacini (Paris, 1826).

338. It was intended to be a *pasticcio,* using music from the Italian operas. See Heinz Becker, "Eine Undine-Oper Meyerbeers für Paris," in *Festschrift Martin Ruhnke,* ed. Mitarbeiten des Instituts für Musikwissenschaft der Universität Erlangen-Nürnberg (Neuhausen-Stuttgart: Hännsler, 1968), pp. 31–44; Everist, "Giacomo Meyerbeer, the Théâtre de l'Odéon," pp. 137–46.

339. For a survey of the complicated history of Meyerbeer's relation to this work and with Weber's family, see Heinz Becker, "Meyerbeers Ergänzungsarbeit an Webers nachgelassener Oper *Die drei Pintos,*" *Die Musikforschung* 7 (1964): 300–312.

340. The castrato role of Armando was arranged for a contralto (Adelaide Schiasetti), and the tenor role of Adriano sung by Giovanni Battista Rubini. Once again the *Harmonicum,* 1827, p. 54, reported a success: "It was received with the most stormy applause."

Part II:
The Parisian Triumphs
(1827–1839)

Section 1
1827–1831

1827

January 1827

Monday January 1. At 3 to Scribe, then to Castil-Blaze* with the chorus.

3 January. At 10 to Sauvage.

5 January. At ten o'clock M. Sauvage.

6 January. At 3 to Scribe.

10 January. At 10 M. Sauvage.

12 January. Letter to Mme. Pasta*.

13 January. At 2:30 took Germain Delavigne* to Scribe.

20 January. [Wrote] to Mme. Biagioli. To de la Rochefoucauldt.

26 January. Cherubini.

27 January. To Boieldieu in the evening at 8.

29 January. Subscribed to *Le Siège de Corinthe*.[1]

February 1827

Thursday 1 February. At 10:30 to Delavigne. To Halévy*.

3 February. Invited to Fould's* ball. At 10 Sauvage.

11 February. Soirée at Countess Merlin's.[2]

15 February. [Sent] Specht* the duet from *L'Esule di Granata.*[3]

16 February. Today I wrote to Duport.

18 February. Robert le Diable.[4]

23 February. Soirée at Princess Vaudemont's.[5] Coda to the trio in *Margherita.*[6]

March 1827

Thursday 1 March. [In the handwriting of T. Sauvage] *Je m'engage à remettre à Monsieur Meyerbeer 'La Nymphe du Danube', poème et paroles chantées, le premier mars au plus tard. Si à cette époque je n'ai pas tenus ma promesse, M. Meyerbeer sera libre de porter le sujet, le titre et la musique déjà faite de cette ouvrage à tel auteur et tel théâtre qui lui conviendra.*[7] *T.S.*[8]

3 March. At 10 A. Schilling* came. At 11 to Schlesinger with two pieces from *Margherita.*

8 March. Today I hosted a dinner in the Café de Paris.[9] At nine o'clock to Germain Delavigne. At 1:30 took Leo* to Choron*.

16 March. At two o'clock took Pixérécourt to Versailles.

22 March. Scribe came at 3.

23 March. To Gouin*.

24 March. At 10:30 to Soumet.*

25 March. At 12 to Scribe.

26 March. At 11:30 to Scribe.

27 March. [Wrote] to Pixérécourt: Scribe would like to have a reading on Friday.

28 March. At ten o'clock to Scribe. At two o'clock Sauvage came.

April 1827

Tuesday 3 April. Today Sauvage delivered act 1.

6 April. At 11:30 to Soumet.

8 April. Today is Minna's birthday. To Germain Delavigne. To Soumet.

[On 12 April the libretto of *Robert le Diable* was submitted to the censors. On 16 April they returned their conclusions, authorizing the opera.][10]

22 April. Full score of *Crociato* for Vienna.

May 1827

Tuesday 1 May. Soumet. Passport.

3 May. Letter to Lubbert* about the score of *Crociato*.

5 May. At 12 sent the full score of *Crociato* to Lubbert.

[In a letter to Pixérécourt dated 20 May Meyerbeer wrote: *Je travaille sans relâche à notre Robert le diable et j'y suis bien avancé. Cependant je vous serai obligé de retarder d'un mois mon arrivée à Paris, c'est à dire d'y être le premier de novembre au lieu du premier d'octobre comme je me l'étais proposé. Ce retard arrive de ce que ma femma a mal calculé l'époque de son accouchement.*[11]]

21 May. Arrived this afternoon in Berlin

29 May. [Wrote] to Schwarz, Barbaia, Léon [de Wailly]*, Soumet, Holtei* (about Goethe).

June 1827

Sunday 3 June. Sent Zelter Lichtenthal's book.[12]

9 June. Between 1 and 2 to Mme. Milder*.

11 June. To Mme. Milder.

13 June. Visited Gubitz*.

16 June. [Wrote] to Rossi about *L'Esule di Granata*. To Milder, and sent the full score.

17 June. Today Schlesinger arrived.

18 June. Called on Milder and Schlegel.*

July 1827

Sunday 15 July. At 10 to Schlegel, having previously sent him Bürger's, Ramler's*, and Goethe's poems.

16 July. Sent Maurice Schlesinger *Margherita d'Anjou*.

31 July. Today received the full score of *Margherita d'Anjou* from Blum*.

August 1827

Friday 3 August. Wrote to Benelli*. [Sent] the copyist of the Königstädter-Theater the two pieces from the *Crociato* for Sontag.

16 August. Early today at seven o'clock God granted me a daughter [Eugénie].

[On 12 August Lubbert replaced Duplanty as director of the Paris Opéra.]

24 August. To Tibaldi*. Have the cavatina from the *Crociato* written out for Sontag.*

25 August. Today I dined with Mother, and sent Sontag the cavatina "O come rapida."[13]

[At the end of August Pixérécourt gave up the direction of the Opéra Comique.]

September 1827

Wednesday 5 September. Today is my birthday.[14]

[On 9 December Eugénie Meyerbeer died.]

1828

[Meyerbeer spent the year in Berlin. On 19 July there was a reprise of *Il Crociato in Egitto* in Paris at the Théâtre Italien with Mmes. Pisaroni and Blasis*. A letter of Maurice Schlesinger of 20 August is addressed to the composer in Spa,[15] and in early September he was in Liège for the Grétry celebrations.[16] It is not certain just when he left Spa,[17] but by autumn he was back in Berlin (as indicated by Wilhelm Beer's letter of 20 September)[18] to be with Minna at her latest confinement. On 31 October his son Alfred was born. Zelter further mentions Meyerbeer among those who congratulated him on his seventieth birthday (11 December), while on 14 December he observes, "To the Tiergarten to Madame Beer, then back to Meyerbeer, Unter den Linden no.26, up two steps."][19]

1829

[Notes for a letter to Michael Beer at the beginning of the Berlin *Taschenkalender* for 1829.]
To Michael. What permission do I need to send books through Frankfurt?[20] Bochsa is the opera director and my enemy.[21] When should I begin the changes in *L'Esule* that I am expected to deliver in March?[22] That Scribe has rejected the *Galgenmännlein*[23] and is writing a grand opera with devilry[24] in it for Auber[25] smacks of treachery. What if it meant that I would not receive this opera [*Robert*] . . . ? Scribe will now be against all splendor in *Robert* because of Auber.[26]

[Undated entry at the beginning of the 1829 *Tk* shows that Meyerbeer consulted the Berlin scene designer Gropius* about possibilities for the *mise en scène* of *Robert le Diable:*]
[Consulted] with Gropius about the gallery in three levels, Fata Morgana, the magnification of Bertram on stage. Sparks must shoot from Bertram's clothes. Transformation of the view of the landscape with the mountains into a hall. The white horse.

[The following undated notes relating to the projected opera *Angiolina*[27] were also written in Berlin.]
Plays to examine 1829—*Angiolina, ou L'Épouse du doge* (Nouveautés) *drame.*[28] Angiolina. A morning scene (conspiracy on Murano or Chiozzo. The trading hour on the Rialto (chorus of Jewish moneylenders, goldsmiths, Armenians, etc. Below the Rialto Angiolina and the gondoliers are conspiring on the canal. The people must sing in Venetian dialect. Cypriot women as dancers. The marriage of the Doge to the sea. Venetian folk melodies. Introduction: gondoliers sing verses of Tasso behind the scenes.

March/April 1829

Sunday 8 March. Today between 11 and 12 took [the guitarist] Dr. Sobbrenheimer to Paganini.[29]

13 April. Today my beloved son Alfred died, aged only five and a half months.

[This bereavement led to a cancellation of Meyerbeer's plans to travel to London for the performance of *L'Esule di Granata.* Instead he took Minna to Baden-Baden for a cure. Before leaving Berlin, the composer made the acquaintance of Heinrich Heine*. During spring the casting of *Robert le Diable* at the Opéra Comique had been fixed.][30]

23 April. Departure from Berlin.

26 April. Weimar-Eisenach.

28 April. Arrival in Frankfurt-am-Main.

17 May. Departure from Frankfurt.

18 May. Darmstadt.

19 May. Arrival in Baden-Baden.

2 June. Departure from Baden-Baden.

6 June. Traveled via Mannheim, arrival in Aachen.

22 June. Departure from Aachen, via Battire and Verviers, arrival in Spa.[31] Lodged with Valcain. Hired a piano.[32]

July 1829

6 July. [Wrote] to Rossi in Verona and sent him 250 fr. as half of the 500 fr. for the opera to be written [*Angiolina*].

31 July. To Brussels and Paris about *Angiolina.*[33]

August 1829

1 August. [Wrote] to Rossi. My decision will reach Verona on 10 September. Can it be performed until 10 March? Is it a long Carnival? My opera must be the last [of the season]. Who is the impresario? I must be invited. He must write to Micheroux so that I do not receive any letter. Have Bellini* and Pavesi been engaged? Who will be the first to write? Is he writing the libretti, and [if so] what are the *argomenti?* [Write] to Troppeani about Trieste: which singers have been definitively engaged?

18 August. Departure from Spa.

19 August. Arrival in Brussels.

23 August. Arrival in Paris.

26 August. Hôtel de l'Elysée, rue de Beaune.

September 1829

Tuesday 1 September. Read through *Robert* and wrote down my observations for Scribe.

2 September. Today [wrote] to the king of Bavaria.[34]

3 September. I want to arrive [to appear to have arrived?] today.[35] At 11:30 I met Scribe at Casimir [Delavigne]'s.[36] [Wrote] to Rossi: because of Minna's indisposition I arrived only today and therefore will be able to inform him of the results only in five to six days.

4 September. At the notary Corbin, Passage Varenne, deposited charitable contribution for the old widow Jeannet. Today at 2:30 [went] with him (concerning Casimir) to Scribe in Montalais (called for him [the notary] at Sèvres) and took the manuscript of *Robert* with me.

6 September. At 3 to Scribe in Montalais.

7 September. To Pixérécourt to ask him about the manuscript of *Robert,* and sent him the *Donaunymphe.*[37]

9 September. Wrote a note to Scribe, that he should bring the cavatina.[38]

12 September. The day before yesterday I moved to rue Le Peletier, no. 5. Scribe must make the changes by Monday. I must arrange in writing with Lubbert that *Robert* be given first in a benefit performance.[39]

14 September. Wrote out the content of "Der Gott und die Bajadere"[40] and "Der Heimkehr,"[41] and the rhythm of the Sicilian song.[42]

16 September. Completed "Der Gott und die Bajadere" and sent it to Scribe.

20 September. To Aiblinger*. Wrote to Rossi.[43]

23 September. At 12 I went to Scribe in the country.

25 September. Today Scribe departed.

[On 17 October the vicomte de la Rochefoucauld secured Meyerbeer's entrée to the Opera.[44] During the autumn the libretto of *Robert le Diable* passed from the Opéra Comique to the Opéra.]

November 1829

Wednesday 4 November. Received Rellstab's* critique of Paganini and his life story. Sent Fétis* [Nissen's*] life of Mozart.[45]

8 November. From 2 until 4 at Count Apponyi's,[46] and took *Oberon*[47] with me.

10 November. Hiller* came at 2.

23 November. To Breitkopf & Härtel*.

24 November. Looked through Louise Bertin's* music. "Der Sonntag Romanze."

26 November. Rouget de Lille*.

28 November. Today I moved to the Hôtel des Princes.[48]

December 1829

Wednesday 2 December. Soirée at Émile Deschamps's* at 7:30. [Wrote] to Germain [Delavigne]*, whether he could explain the "Chanson de la Reine Marguerite."[49]

2 December. Sent Germain the altered lines: "il nous regarde du haut des cieux" should not be the refrain of the romance.[50] To [Mme.] Apponyi about *Euryanthe*.[51] Corrected the romance.

13 December. Went through *Euryanthe*.[52] Asked [Mme.] Sontag whether she is coming to Apponyi.

14 December. Fetched *Euryanthe* [from Schlesinger]. [Wrote] to Laurent about the trio from *Margherita von Anjou*.

24 December. Wrote out Princess Aurélie's small essay for Casimir. [Wrote] to Thackeray*.[53]

[On 29 December Meyerbeer, together with Scribe and Germain Delavigne, signed a contract with the director of the Opéra, Lubbert, for *Robert le Diable, grand opéra en 5 actes et 7 tableaux.*][54]

30 December. Thackeray came at 4. Fetched Scribe at 11:30.

[Undated at the end of the *Taschenkalender.*]
Germain Delavigne should be invited.[55] They must leave me four months. Scribe is [now] against the poem, because Lubbert wants it, [and] on account of Auber.[56] Endeavored to find out just how far Rossini has been influential against me so that I can defend myself.[57] Is it because I have not yet finished with the Feydeau,[58] or because the poem is bad, or because the other opera will be ready earlier?

1830

[Meyerbeer passed the year in Paris. On 28 January he gave power of attorney to the theater agent, Jean-Noël Guyot, to administer any receipts due to him from performances of his operas at the Académie Royale de Musique. On 5 February the emperor of Brazil, Dom Pedro I, conferred on Meyerbeer the Order of the Southern Cross *(Imperial do Cruzeiro)* in recognition of the success of *Il Crociato in Egitto.*[59] On 5 March and 29 March, de la Rochefoucauld wrote to Scribe pressing him to deliver to Meyerbeer act 5 of *Robert le Diable* which he had promised by 17 January. On 22 April Meyerbeer was nominated to the Académie Royale des Beaux Arts de l'Institut de France. On 4 June Scribe and Maurice Schlesinger concluded an agreement for a song cycle that Meyerbeer was to set to music.[60] On 3 June de la Rochefoucauld had authorized Meyerbeer's absence from Paris for a month, but he was to return at the beginning of July to definitively fix the casting of *Robert le Diable.* Meyerbeer arrived in Spa on 16 June; he stayed at the Hôtel d'Orange and finished the composition of *Robert le Diable.*[61] On 15 July Blanca Meyerbeer was born in Baden-Baden, in Meyerbeer's absence.[62] On 21 July de la Rochefoucauld instructed Lubbert to begin study of the roles in *Robert* on 1 August, and to commence the production of décor and costumes. On 26 July Meyerbeer met Lubbert in conference: because of the delay in the *mise en scène* of Auber's new opera,[63] the rehearsals of *Robert* were postponed until 10 December. The July Revolution further disrupted the schedule.[64] On 15 November Lubbert delivered a report to the Commission de l'Opéra on *Robert le Diable.* On 27 November work began on the décor for the opera. In December Meyerbeer received two letters from Wilhelmine Schröder-Devrient concerning the possibilities of a contract with the Opéra for a role in the new opera.[65]]

1831

January 1831

Sunday 1 January. For many years now at the beginning of every new year I have been intending to record regularly my intentions, circumstances and experiences, just as I did earlier, in the years of my youth in Darmstadt, Munich and Vienna. Only my laziness in writing and my negligence have turned any such intentions to water, even though it would be really desirable to keep such a record. At the end of every year one should see how one has persevered in the will to action—in every respect. Time dulls the recollection of both pleasant and unpleasant memories and experiences alike, and eventually one forgets them completely; here, however, each little event should find its own special place of preservation: like the names and characteristics of acquaintances, or the description of my reactions to works of art and artists (costly materials for my projected work). All this would be most usefully recorded in a diary. In order to succeed in this aim, I would have to combat the two powerful enemies of this projected diary: laziness in writing, and negligence, and would have to agree that, in order to make the record easier, I will reduce things to their simplest expression.[66] This means succinct, short phrases without any ornament of style, and even if somewhat sloppily, to jot down the events of the previous day early on the next morning, while still in bed. May God grant his increase to this undertaking. The empty opposite page is intended for extra observations I want to remember, which will then remain separate from the body of the diary. It will also mean that later on there will be room in this free space to note any possibly altered observations on the diary entries themselves.

Today I awoke with many good resolutions. I want to use my time in an orderly and systematic way, to write and answer letters regularly, to adopt an equable frame of mind, to keep an accurate ledger of my expenses, but, most especially, to try to make my dear, precious Minna as happy as I am able, and always to be working on some musical project. If I had always done the latter, how many works would I have produced by now! Today my little daughter Blanca is five and a half months old. May God preserve her and her mother for one hundred years in health and happiness!

Sunday 2 January. Today was also almost completely taken up with the delivery of New Year's cards. I wanted to wish Liebman Schlesinger* well for the New Year in a letter, but just could not bring myself to do it. So much for the resolutions of 1 January! At midday we dined with Mother. In the evening we went to the Théâtre de l'Opéra Comique, where they performed *Josephine, ou Le Retour de Wagram*,[67] a one-act opera about Napoleon's divorce (very flatly handled, dramatically speaking). The music by Adam* is full of individual, pretty, and fresh ideas, but unduly influenced by Rossini and Auber,[68] with flashy but mundane orchestration. The whole, however, is so undeveloped and superficially put together, the forms so imitative, that one is never struck by a pleasantly original idea. There is, however, a very good theme in the overture, played on the valve trumpet [see example 32.].

Example 32. Trumpet theme from the overture to
Adam's *Josephine, ou Le Retour de Wagram*

I must say that I had expected more from Adam on the basis of the charming and original songs that he has composed for various productions at the Théâtre du Vaudeville, and also for his *semiseria* opera *Danilowa*.[69] Afterwards they performed a one-act opera, *La Langue musicale*,[70] with music by Halévy. I will reserve my opinion about this work and its composer until I have seen another production.

Monday 3 January. On my last visit to Paris (1826) I bought a collection of scores (about five hundred volumes) for the small price of 3000 fr. from the young Champein*. In my opinion it has proved an investment really worth twice that amount.

In the evening I went to the Opéra for a while in order to communicate to Lubbert the conditions that Mme. Devrient has stipulated for her engagement. He was not very happy to hear them. Then I went to the Feydeau, at Pixérécourt's request, in order to persuade Boursault* to secure the post of director for him. The only problem was that the former had already given this post to Merle* twenty-four hours before (even if only provisionally).

Tuesday 4 January. Called on Scribe in order to find out whether there is any foundation to the rumor that Véron (the editor of the[71] *Revue de Paris*) is to receive the directorship of the Opéra. He did not know, however. In the evening I attended a soirée at Lenormand's* where Léon de Wailly read his outstanding translation of *Hamlet*. Because I had heard him reading this often before, I actually accepted the invitation only in the hope of making the acquaintance of the long-famous Madame Récamier* (his aunt). Even though, on arriving, I had informed Lenormand of my wish to be introduced to her, he did not arrange it. I did, however, meet the young Ampère* (a doctor), whom I had known in Berlin.

Wednesday 5 January. Since I have not yet written my letter to Schlesinger, I had to abandon the intention. In this way I have lost the only appropriate opportunity of communicating with a man I have not written to before, and yet have often wanted to contact in this way. So much for the resolutions of 1 January! *Ad vocem* the resolutions! I granted myself an indult of eight days to begin the resolved activities again, because I had realized that they would not be put into immediate effect, but even this remission will be over in three days now, and the old laziness rules me again. At midday I dined with Spontini at Mother's. He appears to be very hopeful of nomination to the Institut on the election of a successor to Catel*. He told me that, apart from *Les Atheniennes* by Jouy*[72] and Châles (which he has had considerably altered), he has taken on another two *poëmes d'opéra* by Dumas*[73] and Alfred de Vigny*[74] with Soumet. In the evening I went with Koreff* to Guizot*, who receives every Wednesday. His salon was thronged by even more prominent people than when he was minister. That is much in his favor. At his request I brought Friedrich Raumer's* and Hormayer's* historical pocket-books for his perusal. I furthermore wanted to thank Madame Guizot for the interest she showed in the production of *Robert le Diable* during the time of her ministerial influence. There I also made the acquaintance of Saint-Marc Girardin*, deputy[75] to Guizot as professor of history, and an outstanding collaborator on *Le Journal des Débats*. He was very friendly with Wilhelm in Berlin, and also knows Michael.

Thursday 6 January. An important reason why I cannot progress with my work is because of the way I am having to divide up the morning, and lose so many of these precious early hours. I am awoken at six-thirty instead of six o'clock these days, write up my diary for half an hour, then get up and walk under the arcades until nine, since without this early movement I cannot hope for proper bowel motion nor adequate digestion of the roughage I am taking because of the decline in my stomach condition.[76] Visited the editorial staff of *Le Journal des Débats* in order to find out more about the future destiny the Opéra from Bertin, who is closely associated with Montalivet*. He knew nothing, however. In the evening, for the first time, to a soirée at Alphonse Cerfberr's*, who must have invited me at Scribe's behest. Cerfberr is one of the administrators of the Théâtre du Gymnase and is an astute man (he is a Jew). Since apart from Fould,* Rodrigues* and Worms* I know no Jews in Paris, it was very interesting for me to meet many of the Jewish notabilities of the city, like General Wolff, Advocate Crémieux* (counsel for Guernon de Ranville*) etc.

Friday 7 January. I believe it was Bloch, *chef d'orchestre du Théâtre des Nouveautés*, who told me about a year ago that Henri Lasouche (the clever author of the *Fragolette*, the article about camaraderie, etc.) had the intention of making a drama from Cooper's* *Corsaire rouge.*[77] But I heard of this more than half a year ago, so it would seem that he has given up the idea. I will therefore read the novel myself to see whether it could provide material for an opera. In the evening to the Gymnase, where they gave the fourth performance of a new vaudeville by Scribe, *La Famille Riquebourg,*[78] which has been very successful. It makes quite an impression, being outstandingly acted, and the details handled with all Scribe's usual skill. The total effect, however, is decidedly disturbing,[79] since three good people are made unhappy through no fault of their own, and the curtain falls on the prospect of a careworn future. Afterwards there was a two-act vaudeville by Scribe, Bayard* and Mélesville*, *Jeune et Vieille.*[80] In act 1 Jenny Vertpré* quite marvelously portrays a lively grisette who becomes an old, bigoted, miserly little mother in the second.

Saturday 8 January. Today the indult I granted myself comes to an end. From tomorrow productivity is de rigueur. Among the daily tasks I have set myself is the rereading of Marpurg*. I have nothing to observe about yesterday. Failoni[81] dined with us. In the evening I stayed at home and read the whole score of Paisiello's *La Serva padrona,*[82] which will soon be performed by Lablache[83] and Malibran*. It does not appear to be one of Paisiello's best creations.

Sunday 9 January. Called on Germain Delavigne. He has spoken to Lesourd,[84] and gives me reason for optimism about *Robert:* the fate of the Opéra will soon be decided, and then work will immediately begin on my opera. May Heaven grant it! I took the libretto of *Robert* to Duponchel*, but he was not in. Called on Alphonse Cerfbeer and Pixérécourt, who likewise were both out. At midday I dined with Leo. After lunch I went to the Théâtre des Nouveautés, where they performed *Le Fils de l'homme*, a one-act sketch[85] that depicts the attempt made by the poet Barthélemy to reach the duke of Reichsstadt* in Vienna in order to present him with his poem "Bonaparte en Égypte." Where will theatrical license find its limits? The most tender personal situations of living people of all kinds are brought onto the stage in their most secret details. In the Variétés they produced a *Madame Lavalette;*[86] at the Gymnase King Louis-Philippe* is brought on to the stage in the play *Souvenirs de Suisse,*[87] while in the various *Napoléon*s, and in *Robespierre,*[88] numbers of living people are depicted. The *censure dramatique* has no more fervent an opponent than I, but I am almost beginning to believe that he is necessary to a certain degree. Afterwards I saw three tableaux from a *vaudeville*

populaire en 5 tableaux called *Le Charpentier*[89] (nothing special), and then returned to Leo's, where there was a big social gathering. Fortunately, I missed my
nocturne "Mère grand,"[90] which Mmes. Dulken* and Louritz sang during my absence.

Monday 10 January. Today also passed by without my keeping to any of my resolutions. The only thing I have done regularly is to update my diary in bed on
awaking, and then, on getting up, to take my very strengthening morning walk.
At Moritz Schlesinger's I read a letter from Holtei in which he maintains that
both my romances are untranslatable as far as he is concerned, and he cannot
undertake this task! Visited Lubbert, where I also found Rossini and Duponchel.
On the way home Duponchel told me of some of his ideas for the *mise en scène*
of *Robert,* which seem very new and piquant to me.[91] We agreed[92] that I would
arrange a small dinner at which he, Scribe, Lubbert, and both Delavignes would
be present to develop his ideas. I also saw Valdes about the letter to Mme. Devrient.
At midday I dined at Crémieux's. He is a Jewish advocate from Nîmes where he
gained such a reputation that the impeached minister, Guernon de Ranville, chose
him as counsel for his defense in the famous trial. He now lives in Paris and has
taken over Odillon-Barrot's* practice.[93] I recognized his wife as an old acquaintance: she is the youngest sister of Eugenie Syllny, and I saw her at the home of
her aunt, Mme. Levy, years ago in Vienna. I enjoyed many happy hours in that
house. There were many interesting people at Crémieux's dinner: the deputies
Madier de Montjeau, Lassaignolles, General Jemeté, etc. I also made the very
interesting acquaintance of the two editors of *Le Temps,* Coste* and O'Reilly.[94]

Tuesday 11 January. Again I have to complain about a situation[95] that goes to
show just how little I have kept to the resolutions undertaken on 1 January. I arranged a rendezvous with [Alexander von] Humboldt[96] today, in order to describe
to him the situation of my opera so that he can inform the king about it on his
return to Berlin. I had, after all, more than two years ago promised the opera for
Berlin after its Paris production, and the king could unfavorably have noted the
delay of so many years (if indeed he remembers the matter at all). So then, the
closer the hour of the rendezvous with Humboldt approached, the more uncomfortable I felt about explaining the matter to him, and I therefore went *à dessein*
to him half an hour earlier than arranged in order not to find him at home! When I
returned home late from the theater, I discovered a charming note from him in
which he apologized for his absence, and proposed another *rendezvous* with me
for Friday. At the Opéra Comique the first performance of a three-act opera, *Les
deux Familles* by Planard, music by Labarre*,[97] a pupil of Boieldieu. This work
in every way reveals the hand of a gifted and clever musician (and more about it
after the second performance). It appears to have won considerable success inso-
far as one can judge anything here with the claque system in place.

Wednesday 12 January. I wanted to call on Lubbert in order to inquire about the results of the negotiations with Mme. Devrient, but I could not talk with him, because he had been suddenly taken ill with angina. I nonetheless met Duponchel, who, in his petulantly artistic enthusiasm, inadvertently revealed to me all the secrets of the present transactions taking place with the government about the change of direction at the Opéra.[98] In the evening to the Opéra, where I saw act 1 of the ballet *Manon Lescaut* by Scribe and Aumer*, with music by Halévy.[99] The music is a little sterile for the ballet. Actual thematic invention is very rare, and grace in the phrasing is often lacking. On the other hand the old French music of the baroque period (1720) is outstandingly recreated, interpreted, reworked, harmonized, and scored in the manner of the great majority of original songs and dances of this period. It testifies to an accomplished musical master. I was delighted by many of these old French melodies, and intend to write down some of them on the opposite page.

Thursday 13 January. Last year I presented the wife of the Austrian ambassador, Countess Apponyi, with my latest romances, and I do not want to omit doing so again this year, in spite of the coldness that has in the meantime come between us. I therefore wrote her an affectionate note and delivered it to her myself. Afterwards I called on Prince Craon. Unfortunately, his mother-in-law, Countess Ducayla, whom I most wanted to see, has not yet returned to Paris. Visited Armand Bertin* at *Le Journal des Débats*. Because he enjoys the greatest confidence with Minister Montalivet, I asked him to support[100] the engagement of Mme. Devrient, and also to give me his advice about my own situation. He suggested that I write to Lesourd, and promised to support me actively. In the evening I went with Minna to the Théâtre Italien for *La Gazza ladra*. Lablache, who is not quite suited to the role [of the Podestà], was outstanding and showed again just how many expedients[101] the true master has at the disposal of his art. Malibran had her stirring[102] moments. She was particularly fine in the duet with the tenor in act 2, and was superbly supported by David. Most effective was the variety of tempi she used in singing the cabaletta. I doubt whether this is indicated in the score; she took the opening very slowly [see example 33].

Friday 14 January. Visits. I once again did not find Humboldt at home, but later received a friendly letter from him in which he apologized and proposed a new time for tomorrow. Failoni introduced the violinist [Auguste-Joseph] Tolbeque* from the Opéra to me; he is the brother of the famous (or rather notorious!) arranger of all operatic quadrilles.[103] In the evening, at the Opéra, I heard an act of *La Bayadère amoureuse*, an opera by Scribe and Auber,[104] and then went on to a soirée at O'Reilly and Coste's, the editors of *Le Temps*, who receive on Tuesdays and Fridays. Many deputies were present, and I met the famous Dupin *ainé**. Cavé (the author of *Les Soirées de Neuilly*), whom I had already met at Boursault's,

**Example 33. Cabaletta from the act 1 [mezzo-]soprano aria
in Rossini's *La Gazza ladra*, quoted from memory**

was also there. He promised me to look for a subject for a romantic opera, and I undertook to lend him some volumes of Gozzi*.

Saturday 15 January. Today my dear little daughter is 6 months old. Wrote a few lines to Mme. Devrient in Valdes' letter which I sent in Türkheim's care.[105] Visits from Mme. Cinti-Damoreau*, Paul Duport, and Humboldt. I asked him to report to the king in Berlin about the situation concerning *Robert le Diable*, in the hope that he will pardon the delay. Humboldt promised to do this with all his usual kindness and friendliness, and it lay heavily on my heart that I had not made more of the presence of this influential man in putting my case to the king, in this way, perhaps, myself working for the expedition of my opera. This is another instance of me being my own worst enemy. At midday I dined with Scribe, where I found many theater poets. I asked Mélesville to write a libretto for me, and he agreed to come on Tuesday at 11 to propose various subjets.[106] Lesourd, who has become a very influential person with the minister of the interior, was also there. He gave me an appointment[107] for tomorrow in the ministry in order to present him with the circumstances surrounding *Robert le Diable* and Mme. Devrient.

Sunday 16 January. With Failoni to the former general Macdonald*, who is now an agent of the ex-queen of Naples (Murat)*, in order to present him with my five romances on her behalf. She now calls herself Comtesse Lipona and lives in Trieste. She was always very enthusiastic in her support of me in Venice, also when I produced the *Crociato* in Trieste. I furthermore knew her son. We did not find Macdonald at home. Called on Paul Duport, who proposed a number of subjects from which to choose a theme for an opera. None really appealed to me, even though there were some attractive ideas among them. Note to Lesourd that I will come tomorrow. Minna and I dined at Mother's at noon. In the evening I went with Mother and Tante Mosson* to an extremely tedious benefit concert for a Spanish family. Even Kalkbrenner was boring today. He played in a sextet for piano, harp, clarinet, horn, violoncello, and contrabass in one movement. It is one of his own compositions,[108] is both facile and uninteresting, and provides no opportunities for his great talent to shine. We went home after the first half.

Monday 17 January. Called on Lesourd, but did not find him in. Called on Herr and Madame Crémieux. I took the latter a copy of my five romances. Called on Gouin* at the post office.[109] There I met Dr. Rouvières, author of the famous *La Médecine sans Médecin*. He comes across as a strange, brusque fellow, an enthusiast of the Feydeau and Planard. In the evening to the Opéra Comique, where they performed *Les deux Familles,* which I heard again with great enjoyment. Labarre has a gracious talent, and one can discern a thorough harmonic training throughout. His first work is, moreover, scored with all the apparent experience and effectiveness of a seasoned master. But then who does not know how to score these days? The art of instrumentation has become a tart exposing her most private and tender charms, which everyone now knows, uses, and abuses. Afterwards to the Opéra for a moment, where I saw Lubbert, who told me that he has received permission from the Commissaires de la Liste Civile to pay Scribe his dues[110] for *Robert le Diable* and, at the same time, to hand over to him the commission and the assessment of the expenses for the opera.

Tuesday 18 January. Called on Armand Bertin early, since Duponchel had told me that he [Bertin] would be breakfasting[111] with Montalivet, so that I could explain my situation[112] and those of Mme. Devrient to him. He was still asleep, and I had to return at ten. He promised me his support. Long note to Humboldt, who wanted details of Taglioni's current contract. Long letter to Lesourd, who has undertaken to present it to Montalivet so as to expedite my opera and the engagement of Devrient. When I visited him, however, he said it would be better if I delivered the letter to the minister personally, so I took it away with me. I further learned that Armand Bertin had not been able to speak to the minister, so that my visit had been all in vain. Yet another day lost for my work and for my art. In the evening I took my wife and mother-in-law to the Vaudeville, where Gouin had lent us his box. They gave *Claire d'Albe*, a vaudeville in two acts by Bayard and Duport after the novel by Mlle. Cottin.[113] The scene in act 2, when D'Albe forces his wife to admit her lover in order to corroborate her guilt, is very impressive. Then *La Mendiante*, a vaudeville in two acts by Ancelot*,[114] even though Saint-Brice is advertised as the author. Ancelot had earlier intended this subject for an *opera semiseria* and had given it to Benoist* for composition, but then changed his mind. He was wrong, because the material would have made a fine opera, and if it were not for the fact that a German translation had immediately appeared, I would have made it into an opera for Germany. The subject is too risky for Italy.

Wednesday 19 January. Wrote the letter to Montalivet and sent it, courtesy of Failoni, to the ministry. Called on Casimir Delavigne, who told me that Saphir* has expressed the wish to visit me. Called on Börne*. In the evening to the Opéra, where they performed the ballet *Cendrillon* by Albert, with music by the Spanish guitarist Sor*.[115] It is a bad, boring work with uninteresting, dry, thinly scored music.[116]

Thursday 20 January. Called on Scribe, but did not find him at home. Called on Germain Delavigne and gave him Kotzebue's *Der arme Minnesänger*[117] for his inspection. On leaving, I met Mira*, who told me that the Theatre Commission has now been nominated, and Armand Bertin is a member. Wrote to Armand Bertin on the flimsiest of pretexts; this evening he is to introduce me to Montalivet. As for my resolutions of 1 January! Wrote a letter to Liebmann Schlesinger congratulating him on his birthday, thereby making up for the New Year's letter I never wrote. In the evening with Minna to the Théâtre Italien where they performed Rossini's *La Cenerentola*. There was outstanding ensemble work: the stretta of the first finale had an electric effect, thanks to Lablache's thunderous voice. Malibran was also excellent. Don Magnifico is Zuchelli's* best role, and Donzelli* is good. (I had already sent Mother the 18 fr. for the box, care of one of the servants.) In the theater I met German, the subprefect in Douay, who four years ago had been one of the editors of *La Gazette de France*. What a country of charlatans France is! However, he is a good man who rendered me many services in connection with the *Crociato*.

Friday 21 January. Called on Scribe in order to see whether he could prevent Hérold's opera *Zampa* (with libretto by Mélesville) from coming to performance. Otherwise, because the subject has close similarities with *Robert le Diable* (especially in the *couleur*), I would be preempted[118] in various musical effects that, in this genre, have not yet been heard on the French lyric stage. Since Scribe had also given Hérold an opera text a long time ago, he should request that the latter first complete and produce this work, and if he should refuse, to withdraw the libretto from him. If Hérold agrees, I would have the appropriate time to bring *Robert le Diable* to the stage, if he refuses and Scribe takes back his libretto, the latter has promised to give it to me, and I would at least gain a good opera text for myself. I am afraid that this means nothing less than a cabal, but the long period of care and concern that *Robert le Diable* is costing me exonerates my inner judgment (or should I say my conscience) from this selfish mode of behavior. Visit from Mélesville. He showed me the plans for two opera libretti (one of them being Musäus's* *Der geraubte Schleier*), both of which pleased me. He is going to write out the plan of the other one for me, and then we will decide. In the evening to the Opéra Comique: I saw *L'Illusion*, an opera in one act by Saint-Georges* and Ménissier, music by Hérold,[119] a neat, melodic work with occasionally piquant harmonies. More the pity that it is so full of reminiscences. Then I went for a while to O'Reilly and Coste, who entertain every Friday.

Saturday 22 January. Called on Duponchel. Wrote to Türkheim, enclosing the actress Miller's bill of exchange (she is from the Théâtre des Nouveautés). At midday I had both the Delavignes, Scribe, and Duponchel to lunch with me in order to discuss the new scene in act 3 of *Robert le Diable*.[120] This was the first time that I hosted a dinner in these quarters,[121] and I feared it would all go badly since the food had to be brought in (from the restaurant in the Hotel Wagram, where Mother is staying), but all turned out well. Indeed, my darling Minna supervised everything. In the evening to the Italian Opera, just in time for act 2 of *La Prova d'un opera seria*,[122] with music by Gnecco*. Lablache was endlessly entertaining.

Sunday 23 January. At last I have begun working on my music again, for the first time since the New Year. Admittedly it was only for an hour in bed, but at least it is a start. I revised the Buffo Duet in act 3 of *Robert*.[123] From four to six there was a big social gathering at the once-so-famous Mme. Récamier's where I was invited through Lenormand. Delphine Gay*, the well-known poetess (who so modestly[124] calls herself *la muse de la patrie*[125]) read a song from her big new epic, *Magdalena*, as well as several individual poems, one of which, "Les Adieux au Monde," is indeed lovely. At midday dined at Mother's with Börne. Minna then went with her mother to the Porte-St-Martin to see *Napoléon*,[126] and I to the Opéra Comique to hear *Les deux Familles*.

Monday 24 January. Did no work today. Read a lot of the *Corsaire Rouge*. With Minna, called on Mme. Cinti-Damoreau.* Visit from the singer Durand who was accompanied by a gentleman called the Chevalier Buquet. Borrowed 2500 fr. from Leo. In the evening I went with Mother to the Opéra to hear *La Bayadère amoureuse*. Adolphe Nourrit's* voice has deteriorated a lot (unfortunately for *Robert le Diable*). I saw many of my acquaintances, but heard nothing new about my opera, and came home early.

Tuesday 25 January. Called on Scribe, Duponchel, Germain Delavigne, Schlesinger, Lubbert. The latter proposed to me that, if possible, I should rewrite Dabadie's* role for Levasseur, and therefore allowed me to take my score home for a few days in order to think about it. This I have done, but actually because Mélesville has told me that the opera he has written with Hérold has many similarities[127] with *Robert le Diable* in *couleur* and dramatic situation. Hérold, as chorus master[128] at the Opéra, can go into the copyist's room[129] whenever he wishes and read my score, and should he want to, study my new instrumental effects like the four drums, the organ, the mixtures of woodwind colors, the harmonic combinations, etc., and since it seems that he will produce his work before mine, I would then appear to be the imitator even though I am the one who has been plagairized.[130] Indeed, he may well have accomplished this theft already,[131] since my opera has been with the copyist for the last two months, but better to take this precaution late rather than never. Visit from Herr and Madame Cherubini. I am always delighted to see the venerable Cherubini. He offered my wife and me places in his box. Madame Crémieux also called on Minna. Dined at Coste and O'Reilly's. Madame O'Reilly would appear to be sickly and overexcitable, but nonetheless very charming. There were many writers and journalists at this supper, and among others, I met Cavé's collaborator on the *Soirées de Neuilly*, Dittmer, as well as the young director of the Vaudeville, Étienne Arrago*. When I returned home towards midnight, I found poor Minna in tears and filled with consternation. Our beloved child had suddenly developed a dry, hollow cough, and since the malady of the lungs that carried off our other two angels began in just this way, her anxiety, as well as mine, was terrible. What made it all worse was that Minna had sent for our doctor, the famous pediatrician Dr. Guesait, only to find everyone asleep, and the porter[132] with instructions not to wake his master in the night. We went to bed in fear and anxiety only at two in the morning.

Wednesday 26 January. The child passed a peaceful night, thank Heaven, and the cough eased off considerably. The doctor, moreover, said it was not very serious. I wanted to see Schlesinger because of the unsatisfactory box I have at the Conservatoire concerts; not finding him there, I wanted to write him a note, but, on getting up from my chair, hit my head badly on a metal beam. So I went to Habeneck* about this box. In the evening to a brilliant musical soirée at Countess Merlin's: Lablache, Malibran, David, etc., sang and Rossini accompanied. Mother and Minna were placed[133] next to the charming Countess Saint-Aulaire, and Minna was able to make her acquaintance, something that has pleased me very much.

Thursday 27 January. Early in the morning I was eventually again able to work on the revision of *Robert* in bed. I heard that Fräulein Vespermann* has arrived here from Munich with a letter from Michael for me. Since she is leaving tomorrow for London, I called on her myself. She does not strike me as pretty—which amazed me somewhat, since she is the beloved of both the king and Prince Karl of Bavaria*. She told me many good things, on the king's behalf, about my *Schütz-*

enmarsch, and that he has ordered it to be performed this Lent. In the evening I again stayed at home and worked on *Robert*. The only problem was that I have become so unaccustomed to working, and so confused by the concerns and cabals in which the management of the Opéra so continually involves me, that I could not get into the swing of things.[134]

Friday 28 January. Wrote a long letter to Wilhelm with instructions about what to say to Devrient: at the same time I wrote to her. Together with Minna, chose a present for Mother's birthday (a writing set[135] from Picherot, in the Passage de l'Opéra, for 140 fr.). These two matters took up nearly the whole morning. When I returned home for lunch, I met Geraer (Schlesinger's cousin), who passed on the letter that Fräulein Vespermann had left behind for me. He was accompanied by the famous, or rather notorious, Saphir, whom he introduced to me, and who asked for permission to call on me. The meeting[136] was painful[137] for me: Saphir's character and antecedents[138] make any further acquaintance with him unpleasant, especially since he has written many bitter articles against Michael's plays and my operas. Whatever the case, the man's wit is too dangerous to alienate by contempt. I was therefore cold but polite, and replied with the commonplace that it would be a pleasure for me. In the evening at the Opéra I saw a few acts of Rossini's *Moïse*[139] in which Dorus[-Gras]* sang Cinti's usual role tolerably well. I then went to a soirée *(romantiquement littéraire)* at Antony Deschamps's*. He recited[140] two satires; his brother Émile,[141] a fragment from his translation of *Romeo and Juliet;* and Victor Hugo*, a *Préface à un volume de poésies politiques* that contained several wonderful individual poetic ideas. A young poet from Normandy also read a few poems. Then there was some awful music-making; I left after the first piece.

Saturday 29 January. Mother's birthday. May God preserve us this wonderful woman for years to come. I have, unfortunately, received news of yet another of Lubbert's intrigues. Les Commissaires de la Liste Civile, from whom he has to obtain authorization to mount new operas (on account of the costs that only they can provisionally approve), have written to him saying that, before they can authorize the production of *Robert le Diable*, they need to know what the costs will amount to. He has now artificially inflated the assessment to the region of 120,000 fr. simply so the commissioners will find the opera too expensive and therefore not authorize its production. In order to parry this blow, I had to pass the whole day making visits appropriate to this end, calling on Germain Delavigne, Armand Bertin, Lesourd. I further went to Leon de Wailly and [Giovanni] Glossop.[142] At midday I hosted a small dinner in honor of Mother's birthday: present were Mother, Tante Mosson, Koreff, Antoinette [Montalban]*, and Marie Patzig*. In the evening to the Opéra Comique for the first performance of a two-act opera, *Le Diable à Seville*. The words, after a Spanish sketch,[143] are by Cavé, I believe (I have mentioned him often already in my diary), the music by a Spanish refugee,[144] Gomis*. Without having heard a note of Gomis's music before (with the exception of a few choruses in the *mélodrame Aben Humeya* at the Porte-St-Martin), he has, in the artistic community anyway, acquired the reputation of being an original talent: so one looked forward to making the acquaintance of this piquant musical individuality. The libretto failed completely, but the music was successful, even if it did not live up to expectations. For my part, I was so drunk with sleep after the dinner that I could not allow myself an opinion.[145]

Sunday 30 January. Scribe invited me over to hear the libretto that he has taken back from Hérold to give to me (see 21 January). It pleased me extraordinarily, being tailored[146] to music better than any of Scribe's opera texts to date, full of dramatic pathos, as well as happy situations, with a wonderful role for Chollet*. The words of all the set pieces in the three acts have been completed, and I could begin composing immediately, except that some of the dialogue is still missing. Whatever is still unclear could be explained in a few hours by a prose summary of the scenes. We agreed that he should give it to me on the following conditions: I should undertake to complete the score in eight months (reckoned from 8 February), failing which I should pay him 6000 fr. However, I could then keep the work for another four months, with an extension should I move, or even travel out of France. But after twelve months I would have to be ready to produce the work at the Feydeau, provided that theater invites me to do so. Should I still not be ready, Scribe retains the right to entrust his poem to another composer, and would, moreover, receive another 6000 fr. as compensation for the twelve lost months. I further proposed, on concluding the agreement, to deposit 3000 fr. with him as a guarantee, should I have immediate access to his manuscript. He refused this as unworthy of me, but I insisted, in order, as I can confide in the secrecy of my diary, to bind him, since, with Scribe's uncertain and vacillating character, Hérold or Auber could perhaps persuade him, in a moment of weakness, to take the manuscript back from me. This deposited 3000 fr., however, binds the contract in iron. We agreed that I would have a formal document drawn up tomorrow and submitted to him for inspection. Afterwards to the Conservatoire, where the Société des Concerts are again giving a cycle of concerts, as they did last year.[147] We have fortunately again secured[148] our box no. 28, but for this particular concert Minna and I were in Cherubini's box, since he had specifically invited us. They performed Beethoven's *Symphonia Eroica*,[149] executed, as always, in an incomparable manner. This Société des Concerts is indisputably the most outstanding orchestra in Europe for the performance of Beethoven's symphonies—indeed, for any orchestral music. Each symphony is rehearsed with great care and many times, as opposed to the German practice of attempting the impossible by rehearsing a symphony only twice. Apart from the symphony there were also choruses and arias from *Euryanthe, Der Freischütz,*[150] *Guillaume Tell,*[151] etc. In the evening with Minna to Leo's.

Monday 31 January. Took the draft of the contract to Scribe, who approved it. We agreed that a duplicate of the fair copy would be written out and brought to him during the morning for his signature. To Lesourd, but I could not speak to him, since his antechamber was filled with solicitors.[152] In the evening to the Opéra Comique, where they performed *La jeune Femme colère*, an opera in one act by Étienne* with music by Boieldieu.[153] This is one of Boieldieu's most insignificant operas, meager and empty of ideas. The only piece that has any dramatic effect is a quartet in A major. The small trio in which the two old people take their leave of the irascible woman [of the title] is good, particularly in the scoring for clarinets and horns. This is particularly striking because the rest of the opera is so thin in woodwind writing. I have decided to compile an anthology of all the pieces I hear that either please me greatly or strike me by their originality of detail, so that I can remember to buy these pieces later. I will mark the passages where I discuss such pieces with a special sign (XAnth). This little collection should serve as an amusing source of reminiscence[154] and as valuable evidence and appendix to the observations in my diary. Afterwards they performed *Les deux Familles*. I found my earlier judgment confirmed. I heard the opera again with enjoyment, my admiration lessened only because the finish and skill evident in the best pieces can be ascribed to Labarre's teacher, Boieldieu, who collaborated on them. Leo has assured me of this, and indeed that the best piece in the opera, the buffo duet sung by Chollet and Mme. Prévost*, is altogether Boieldieu's work. In addition to the latter, what pleased especially was a small octet, made up only of one musical phrase, and even this only in four parts. Then, the duet that closes act 1 is also very good in its dramatic intention, declamation, and accompaniment. In act 2 what struck me particularly is the challenge (in the form of a romance) that Ponchard* sings in order to announce his presence to the enemy. It is very well written in this contracted[155] form, with striking instrumentation, even if very simple in the first half. Horns and bassoons hold the harmony, the timpani marking the rhythm of the larghetto with crotchet beats (𝅘𝅥 𝅘𝅥 𝅘𝅥 𝅘𝅥), and nothing else. Then in the act 2 finale there is a very moving dramatic phrase for the Father (Henri). In act 3 Chollet's aria is really charming. Finally, I very much liked the idea in Mme. Casimir's* cavatina *(larghetto),* when the reprise of the theme is accompanied by the other four voices in harmony.

Review of the month. Without exception, I kept to none of the resolutions undertaken at the beginning of the year, either as artist or as man, and there is no point in detailing everything I should have done and have not. The month has been completely wasted from the point of view of my art.

February 1831

Tuesday 1 February. Wrote out the two copies of the contract in neat hand for Scribe. This took until eleven-thirty, long past the time agreed for our rendez-vous. When I arrived, Auber was there. I did not have myself announced, but rather waited in the dining room until he left. During this time my heart was wildly beating. What if Scribe should have told Auber (his friend of many years)[156] about our contract, and Auber should fancy the subject for himself and ask Scribe to reserve it for him, and Scribe should agree? And if not that, what if he should have betrayed our dark secret about my position with regard to Hérold in the matter? Fortunately nothing like this happened, and when Scribe appeared, he assured me that neither I nor the opera had been mentioned. He read the contract, received the 3000 fr. guarantee, and signed it. I immediately took charge of the first two acts in order to have them copied. At home I again read through the libretto and was confirmed in my earlier opinion that it is outstandingly tailored for music, in fact a very interesting opera text; even if it contains only the simplest effects, the material can no doubt stimulate some striking music. There is only one regrettable aspect as far as my own particular talent is concerned, and that is the few and uninteresting choruses, but perhaps this could be remedied later? Called on Lesourd, but he was again unavailable.

Wednesday 2 February. The commission that will decide the fate of the Opéra has been nominated.[157] Fortunately Armand Bertin is among them. I therefore went to him and gave him my contract with the Opéra so that he can have the commission validate it. With Leon de Wailly to Madame Récamier (about the gathering to which she had invited us on 22 January). Fortunately, we found her alone with Chateaubriand*, and since I had never before spoken to this famous man, it was pleasant for me to observe him in the company of others.[158] To begin with, he was very taciturn,[159] and conversation faltered so often that I was obliged to think up fresh topics.[160] Later, however, he spoke of his stay in Berlin, the choral unions, the enthusiasm of the Italian public for music, and, when I brought the conversation round to his tragedy *Moses*, his opinion about the difficulties posed for a writer of prose handling French verse. The drama contains many choruses, but he does not want all of them sung. When I told him of Schiller's idea to have the choruses in *Die Braut von Messina*[161] spoken, he said that that was exactly what he also intended. Afterwards called on Madame O'Reilly, but did not find her at home. I left her a copy of my *Romances*. Dined with Mother. Then went with her and Antoinette to the Opéra Comique, where they performed *Le Diable à Séville*. The house was full and the music appeared to find great favor.

Thursday 3 February. Called on Casimir and Germain Delavigne. Today I was asked to dine with the minister of the interior, Montalivet, apparently at the instigation of my friend Armand Bertin, who very much wanted to gather together those who have an interest in asking the minister to expedite decisions about the Opéra. So, apart from me, Scribe, both the Delavignes, and Rossini were present. The minister was cold and stiff, anything but obliging. He spoke a few insignificant words to each of us, somewhat more attentively to Rossini, but still hardly encouragingly. The dinner was just as tedious. Afterwards several hundred people began gathering, since the minister receives every Thursday evening. Later I went to the Italian Opera, where I was just in time to see part of act 2 of Rossini's *Zelmira*.[162] Mme. Lalande* makes little impression in this role. In the foyer I saw Véron for the first time since I learned that he will probably be the future director of the Théâtre Italien. He spoke with greater freedom[163] and candor than I had thought possible of him, and offered to help me hinder Devrient from being engaged in Berlin.

Friday 4 February. I have engaged Wild to copy *Le Portefaix* in my lodgings. He asked me 10 fr. for a copy of all the lyrics contained in the two acts. Called on Tante Mosson. Went to the décor painter, Cicéri*, to discuss with him the proposals for the scenery in *Robert*. Germain Delavigne was also there, and we conferred for over two hours. On my return, I found Hiller waiting for me. Called on Mélesville. In the evening with Minna to a concert for the benefit of the actress Kirchheim from Breslau. Among the performers was a choral union of German amateurs, mostly workers,[164] who meet in their free time in the evenings to practice male-voice choruses instead of going to the taverns and other places of entertainment: most laudable. They sang well in parts; what pleased me most was a cobblers' chorus by a young musician from Offenbach called Schedel, who later also played a capriccio for piano of his own composition. This was bad, as was the execution. Afterwards I attended the usual Friday soirée at Coste and O'Reilly's.

Saturday 5 February. After riper reflection I find that *Le Portefaix* pleases me just as much as on the first reading, apart from there being so few prominent, detached[165] choruses, which is a pity for my particular talent. It occurred to me to insert[166] two piquant choruses: one in act 3 for the Alquasils, in which they would excuse themselves for slipping away from Margento and mendaciously describe how this has come about, and then an introduction to act 2, which would begin with a faint, voluptuous chorus of women, as if during a sirocco; they would then play and dance, in the middle of which they hear the angelus, and, as true Spaniards, interrupt their fandango to fall to their knees in prayer. This would better prepare the way for the prayer, which is already part of Scribe's text. I therefore went over to Scribe, who approved these ideas, significantly improved on the proposal for act 3, and promised to have them ready by the day after tomorrow. Wrote a note to Germain about the estimate[167] for the opera. Called on Glossop to inquire about Spanish melodies. With Minna, visited Madame Merlin. I stayed at home in the evening, reflecting and improvising on the introduction to *Le Portefaix*.

Then I read a brochure by Choron (which Hiller had left for me) in which he set out the reasons why he thought he should become a member of the Institut[168] in Catel's place. It is really quite interesting as a resumé of his musical endeavors, artistic activities, and various insights.[169] In the end it served him no purpose, though, because Paer was elected to Catel's place.

Sunday 6 February. To Lesourd. He assured me that he will present my letter for Montalivet to the commission, and will also tell them that Lubbert had deliberately[170] inflated the financial assessment[171] of the opera to 120,000 fr. in order to spoil its chances. Dined with Mother and Koreff. I stayed with Mother for the evening, and worked intensively on the aria "Pardonnez moi, ma jalousie" from act 2 of *Le Portefaix*.

Monday 7 February. To Scribe in order to fetch act 3 of *Le Portefaix*. He has completed all the set pieces in this act, apart from the finale. I now have the pleasure of seeing that the chorus of Alquasils, formerly missing from the libretto, and added at my suggestion, has become one of the most attractive pieces in the work. Then I went to Mélesville, with whom I had earlier arranged a meeting about a new opera text. We spoke much about Musäus's *Der geraubte Schleier* (which I would like to call *L'Étudiant d'Innsbruck*, and integrate aspects of student life, customs, and songs into act 2). I proposed that we should prepare it for the Opéra (actually so that he cannot be angry if I later make a debut at the Feydeau with *Le Portefaix*). To Mother; we dined at four-thirty because I wanted to secure good places at the Théâtre des Variétés with Tante Mosson and Minna. Fortunately, we succeeded in doing so. They performed a *drame vaudeville* in two acts, *Madame Lavalette*, by Barthélemy, Cheric, and Brunswick* which is about the liberation of Lavalette* from the Conciergerie by his wife.[172] It has a very impressive moment: the two Englishmen have promised to play her a special song on a hurdy-gurdy when her husband has successfully escaped, but after his flight the policeman[173] and jailer enter the prison too soon, recognize her, and pursue Lavalette—so that one fears he will be retaken. She is so frightened that she becomes delirious, but just then the hurdy-gurdy plays. Afterwards there was a new farce, *Madame Cagnard*, which was pathetically bad, followed by another new *drame vaudeville* in two acts called *L'Ange gardien*,[174] just as tedious. We returned home after act 1. To Pixérécourt.

Thursday 8 February. Visits from Léon de Boit, Failoni. In the evening stayed at home, since I have firmly resolved to work at least once in the day, and if the morning is wasted, then to make up for it in the evening. Today, however, my resolution came to naught because of one of Minna's little obstinacies. So as not to leave my mother alone, I decided to work in her apartments. Minna also agreed to spend the evening there, although not very happily. I therefore had the chest containing my work taken there. The only problem was that Minna decided to take a nap after dinner, something she never usually does, and stayed lying on the sofa a long time without a mention of going out. This hurt me inwardly, although I said nothing. Therefore, since I could not retrieve the chest until much later, because Joseph had gone for his meal, and I had to find something to do, I organized some notebooks for *Le Portefaix*. While doing this, I came across a packet of old sketches dating from my stay in Vienna (1813), and another from my time in Sicily and Italy (1816). To my amazement, I found myself quite happy with the first of these, which were fragments for an Italian opera, *Quinto Fabio*; however strange Italian song and form were to me then, I feel these sketches contain more natural lyricism and more traces of originality than those from 1816 (the beginning of my Italian sojourn) for a German operetta, *Gefehlt und Getroffen*,[175] and for an Italian rondo,[176] clumsy imitations of Rossini, facile ideas without spirit or invention. There is one piece in this file, the best of the sketches which, with improvements, could still be usable. I wrote it in February 1816 on the journey to Italy, between Paris and Lyons. It is a small instrumental piece called *Entr'acte*, skillfully built around the following theme [see example 34].[177]

**Example 34. Meyerbeer's theme for the
(lost) instrumental piece *Entr'acte***

I will remove it from this file of useless sketches and have it bound in my penultimate notebook.[178]

Wednesday 9 February. Worked a little on *Robert*. To Scribe to hear him read act 3. To Duponchel, but he was not at home. To Lubbert: a few days ago I asked him if I could take my score away with me to study possible role adjustments (see diary). Since the reasons for my doing so still make it inconvenient for me to return the score to him, I prevaricated, saying I had been unwell lately. I actually went to call him to account over another of his despicable actions,[179] which Scribe told me about today. In order to ingratiate himself with Armand Bertin (who is a member of the commission), he has apparently proposed[180] to mount[181] *Loup Garoux*, by Bertin's sister Louise, which was booed off the stage at the Feydeau.[182] He did not deny it, but maintained that he had understood *Robert* to be included in the proposal.

Thursday 10 February. Spent the whole morning walking around looking for libretti translated by Castil-Blaze, the rhythms of which could serve me as models
in the eventual adjustments to *Le Portefaix.* This is because I have promised Scribe
to ask for alterations only when I have finished the whole opera, and until then to
compose anything new using a so-called *monstre* (i.e., a pattern of any words
providing the desired rhythm). Visit from Anthony Deschamps and Léon de Wailly.
Dined at Scribe's where I found his little natural daughter by Mme. Grevecke.
Afterwards to the Italian Opera to fetch Minna and Mother. I was just in time to
hear a few pieces from act 2 of *La Cenerentola.* Today Joseph Herz* sent in the
accounts for the income from my houses for 1830, a clear profit of 3900 thalers.

Friday 11 February. To Armand Bertin to have news about the Opéra Commission, but he was not at home. The desire to find copies of Castil-Blaze's opera
translations has become an *idée fixe,* and will not leave me in peace. I therefore
walked for several hours in the region of the Odéon, looking for them. I found
two and will go later to Barba to buy the others at the current prices,[183] since I
will otherwise waste a lot of time. Compared[184] the copy of act 3 of *Le Portefaix*
with the original. Afterwards called on the Countess St. Aulaire with Mother and
Minna, only to find that she was not in. Then to Armand Bertin, who told me that
today Lubbert read a long *mémoire* to the commission in which he spoke very
badly about my opera. In the evening with Mother to the Opéra to see Rossini's
Moïse. Dorus sang Damoreau's role. Since yesterday we have begun using water
purer than the usual Parisian stuff (which is filtered through carbon), but even
this new source was so badly carbonized today that it upset my stomach; by evening
I felt really unwell.

Saturday 12 February. I felt so ill that I did nothing all day. In the evening with
Mother to the Italian Opera for Mozart's immortal *Don Giovanni.* Lalande had
the difficult task of replacing Sontag in the role of Donna Anna. Were she still in
possession of her earlier resources,[185] her method, declamation, and expression
would perhaps have been capable of it. But her voice is now so unsteady and
castrato-like[186] in the higher register, and she has to make such efforts in singing,
that today she made little impression, except in the recitative that precedes the
aria in act 1.[187] The other female roles were taken by Malibran (outstanding as
Zerline) and Tadolini* (very mediocre). The men were as last year: their effectiveness 100 percent less. Sontag's name was on everyone's lips in the foyer during the interval.

Sunday 13 February. Even though I usually note down the events of each day on
the following morning, I was so busy this morning[188] that I cannot remember all
that happened yesterday. I was supposed to meet Armand Bertin in front of the
Théâtre Italien, where he was going to attend a rehearsal of *Fausto,*[189] but I ar-

rived too late. He had already gone in, and I did not want to have him called out. Then with Antoinette to the Conservatoire Concert, since Minna did not feel well. I invited the wife of Germain Delavigne to join us in my box. They gave Beethoven's Symphony [no. 7] in A major[190] (divinely performed), then a bad, superficial duet from Carafa's *Jeanne d'Arc*,[191] followed by some very uninteresting violoncello variations. Next came the big aria from Boieldieu's *Les deux Nuits*,[192] which has not yet been staged here: it is a regular, cleanly developed piece of music, but monotonous and unimpressive. This was followed by the second finale from *Fidelio*,[193] but the performance was mediocre, and finally the overture to *Euryanthe*. At midday we (Mother, Minna, and I) were invited to dine with our ambassador, Freiherr von Werther*, who has not asked us for the last six months. In any case we were invited apparently only because Mother had sent him caviar. It was a very boring gathering. In the evening to Leo's, who gave a small ball. [*Tk:* Scribe the stretta of the first finale *(Portefaix)*. The scene in act 3 of *Robert*.]

Monday 14 February. I postponed my toilette until twelve, when the pedicurist Mr. Werner came and attended to[194] my nails (both hands and feet). Worked things out with Minna and accompanied her to the rue Richelieu. To Schlesinger. All this lasted until four o'clock, by which time it was too late to begin any regular work. Collated the rest of the copy of act 3 of *Le Portefaix*. In the evening to the Opéra Comique for the first performance of a one-act sentimental opera, *La Veillée*, with text by Paul Duport and St. Hilaire*, and music by Paris*. The text is rather boring and insignificant. The music is the first work of a so-called grand prix (as they call the pupil[195] of the Conservatoire who wins the first prize in the competition[196] and consequently is enabled to travel in Italy and Germany for five years at the expense of the government.[197] He is a pupil of Le Sueur*, and his work already reveals that experience of scoring and attack[198] that was once so arduous to attain, yet now is to be found in the first works of even pupils[199] (ever since Rossini turned it into a mechanical process).[200] There is an embryonic inclination to melodic phrases, but nothing more, no trace of anything special. I do not believe he has a future[201] as a musician.[202] The performance was not bad, but rather feeble.

Wednesday 16 February. To Scribe about the changes. To Armand Bertin.

Thursday 17 February. Dined with Spontini at Mother's, and spent the whole evening there. Took Spontini "Kennst du das Land"[203] [*Tk*].

Friday 18 February. In *Le Portefaix* a violent contrast between the Mardi Gras with all its masks, and the apparent collapse of a building with the people fleeing, will make for dramatic effect.

Sunday 20 February. In the evening worked on the transposition of Bertram's part [in *Robert le Diable*].[204]

Monday 21 February. Worked on the transposition and act 5. In the evening arranged and transcribed[205] the Buffo Duet.

Tuesday 22 February. Transposed act 3.

Thursday 24 February. Revised and altered the duet "Les chevaliers de ma patrie."[206] With Minna to Spontini. Dined with Börne at Mother's. Heard act 2 of *Masaniello*.[207]

Friday 25 February. Finished the duet at Mother's. Sketched a letter to Michael: he has unsuspectingly accepted[208] a conductor for the performance of the *Schützenmarsch* who, while apparently obliging, is more likely to ruin the work. I am also anxious about the choice of the four singers, that the wind instrumentalists should practice on their own first, and that there should be choristers for the performance in the amphitheater. At 10 fetched Paganini, to take him to Cherubini.

Saturday 26 February. Quartet evening at Baron X's, where Berlido[209] played Beethoven's big C major Quintet:[210] the last movement in fact gave me the idea for the dice-throwing figure in *Robert*. There are rumors that *L'Orgie*[211] will be given in May (but, it would seem, neither too early nor too late enough to warrant the transference of the première of *Robert* which is entailed in the agreements[212] and adjustments to the contract).

Sunday 27 February. After 12 with Paganini to Cherubini. Told Paganini that he is not dining with us on Monday, and also about Mme. Vaudemont [*Tk*].

March 1831

Tuesday 1 March. Worked a little on act 4.

Wednesday 2 March. [Received] the shocking news [that *Euryanthe* is to be given before *Robert*]. This report has made all work impossible for me. I hardly need say that if it were possible to mount *Euryanthe* before 30 March, I would go for it.

Friday 4 March. Armand Bertin will support the draft of the *contract supplémentaire* in the commission, and I wrote a letter about this ostensibly to him. Worked on the romance about the removal[213] to Sicily[214] (which I began on 2 March), the chorus and its conclusion, the second duet in act 3.[215] In the matter of the contract, I have partially made the unexpected friendship of M.,[216] whom many people regard as a friend of the new director (Véron, who was installed on 1 March).

Monday 7 March. Worked on the Duet of the Knights[217] in act 3.[218] Première of *Faust.* The transposition has spoiled the introduction and duet [in act 3],[219] which now have less impact. To Paganini concerning Mme. Merlin.

Tuesday 8 March. Worked for half an hour on the duet for Alice and Bertram ("Qu'as-tu donc").

Wednesday 9 March. At 9:30 took Paganini to the rehearsal.

Thursday 10 March. Conference with Scribe and Germain about the new scene. Count Moretti. From there took Paganini to Mme. Vaudemont before 9.

Friday 11 March. Worked a little on the chorus "L'honneur et la victoire." Heard at the Opéra that Véron does not want to engage Devrient.

Saturday 12 March. Worked for one and a half hours without particular success on the march and chorus,[220] and finale of the Bertram-Robert duet in act 3. Worked again in the evening somewhat perfunctorily on Bertram's march and chorus. The libretto was read to the commission with success.

Monday 14 March. Worked on *Robert* as confusedly[221] as ever.

Tuesday 15 March. Artists' dinner at the duke of Choiseul's, *chef* of the above-mentioned Commission for the Opéra. Worked on the stretta of the act 4 duet,[222] also in the evening. To Spontini.

Thursday 17 March. Worked on the stretta. In the evening I felt too unwell to work and accomplished little.

Friday 18 March. In the evening to Saphir.

Monday 21 March. Sent off the letter to Devrient today. To Damoreau. I hosted a dinner for Paganini. The guests were Boieldieu, Auber, Rossini, Bertin, Cherubini, Casimir and Germain Delavigne, Habeneck, and Count Moretti.

Wednesday 23 March. At 4 with Halévy to Schlesinger to discuss *Euryanthe.*

Saturday 26 March. At 9:30 to Cherubini. To Véron. [Wrote] to Levasseur. Wrote in reply to Michael about the *Schützenmarsch.*

Monday 28 March. Cinti-Damoreau came today.

April 1831

Friday 1 April. Once again I am forced to conclude a disgraceful settlement with my laziness. The many unannotated days awaiting completion have so accumulated that I can no longer remember enough to fill the gaps. And so as not to lose the habit of the daily entries, and in order to make a fresh start, I will sacrifice what cannot be saved, and begin the new month with fresh resolutions. Among the main events during this period from 5 March onwards was the tragic death of my cousin, relation by marriage, and playmate of my youth, Babette Eberty*; the weaning of my child (18 March); the performance of my *Schützenmarsch* (18 March), which, according to Michael's report, made little impression (apparently, he says, because the accompanying brass drowned out the chorus); a production of my *Crociato* at the Teatro alla Scala in Milan with the old tenor [Gaetano] Crivelli*, a great success;[223] a performance of Beethoven's giant symphony with chorus,[224] outstandingly played at a Conservatoire Concert (and which I heard for the first time); and an interesting dinner for artists and writers that I hosted in Paganini's honor. Among the new plays I saw was *Madame Dubarry*, a historical vaudeville in three acts by Ancelot that is very popular.[225] Today I composed and wrote out the new recitative to be interpolated into act 1 of *Robert*, "C'est qu'il est en notre village un beau tableau représentant."

Saturday 2 April. Because yesterday the Opéra copyist, Leborne, indicated to me that he has at last received instructions to continue with the copying, I busied myself with a revision of act 1 and took it to him. To Mother and Tante Mosson. The latter wanted to read the will of my blessed Grandfather, and wishes particularly that [Hermann] Eberty*, who has no means of his own and has always lived off Babette, should not, now that she is dead, be dependent on his children when they come of age. She appears to have the intention of leaving him the benefit of her entire personal fortune should she not be able to dispose of a portion of Grandfather's inheritance. Looking for the will among my documents wasted a lot of my time. In the evening I went to the Opéra to hear the dress rehearsal of *Euryanthe*, and attended act 2.[226]

Sunday 3 April. Worked on the new chorus in the act 2 finale, "À l'honneur à la victoire." Attended a performance of the Bohrer* Quartet; they played a beautifully constructed and tastefully developed quintet by Onslow*, then a wonderful violoncello sonata by Beethoven (in A major); the scherzo is elfin and ghostly.[227] Finally they played Beethoven's Quartet no. 12 in E-flat Major.[228] Since he wrote seventeen, this one of his last; the first movement is difficult to grasp, perhaps even incomprehensible. The scherzo that is part of the andante, is, however, splendid. Dined with Mother and then worked all evening in her apartments on the chorus from earlier in the day.

Points to remember:

I have an idea for a cantata, *Die Erfindung der Instrumente,* for the Société des Concerts at the Conservatoire that could provide opportunities for all their great virtuosi to shine.[229] The difficulty would be how the voice would be accompanied before and until the invention of instruments. Perhaps the gods could be brought in as teachers, or perhaps it could be partially conceived as melodrama in the manner of *Der Eisenhammer?*

I also have an idea for an Italian intermezzo for two or three voices with possible text by Körner, "Der Vetter aus Bremen," or "Das war ich" ("La servante justifiée"), or "Domestikenstreiche," or "Brelan des Valets."

Should I write an opera for Malibran, I think I will use a text by Gozzi, *La Figlia del aria.*[230]

I also have the idea for a small cantata, *Der Nebel* (based on an idea from an unpublished romance by Lamothe Langeon).

In the Berlin paper *Der Gesellschafter,* which appeared in the first half of 1830, there is a novella, *Die Marquisen von Manzara.* I would like to get hold of this and read it, since it apparently contains some very dramatic material that Blum arranged for the Berlin stage under the title *Friedrich August in Madrid.*

May 1831[231]

Tuesday 3 May. To Devrient.

7 May. To Failoni concerning Duke Visconti.

8 May. Wrote to Duke Visconti that I will definitely[232] send him written answer by 1 June.

[On 14 May Meyerbeer and Véron signed a contract that specified the details relating to the approaching production of *Robert le Diable.*][233]

24 May. Took Devrient the score of *Die Vestalin.*

June 1831

Friday 3 June. Today ———— came about the duet in *L'Esule di Granata* for London.

6 June. I wrote to Visconti and asked for respite until 1 July.

9 June. Today we moved to Auteuil.

22 June. To Devrient at 12:30. At 1:30 to the Opéra. Between 4 and 5 to Scribe. Took along Bellini's *Capuleti*[234] and *Sonnambula*.[235]

24 June. At 12 Habeneck, Halévy, and Schneitzhöffer*[236] came. To Véron concerning Devrient and Levasseur.

25 June. At 11 to Schlesinger about the copyist. Today we held the first choral rehearsal of *Robert*.

July 1831

Friday 1 July. Fetched act 1 from Leborne.

2 July. Ordered dinner in the Café de Paris. At 11:30 to the chorus with the score of act 1.

3 July. Wrote to Bohrer that Lindpaintner is coming at 12:30.

4 July. Lindpaintner came at 1:30.

6 July. At 1 with Lindpaintner to Rossini.

9 July. To Damoreau. To Véron with the contract. Wrote to Scribe that the reading[237] will take place on Monday.

13 July. Saw the bacchanal in *Les Danaides*,[238] *Achille à Scyros.*[239]

14 July. Sent Humboldt Heine's letter.

15 July. To Véron about the organ.[240] To Halévy to ask whether the pupils of the Conservatoire could also study the choral parts *en attendant*. Asked Véron whether the rehearsals will be in my residence. Checked whether [Filippo] Taglioni has a copy of the scene.

16 July. Yesterday (15 July) my beloved daughter celebrated her first birthday. *Aujourd'hui premier répetition des chanteurs de 'Robert'.*[241]

30 July. 4me répetition après 8 jours d'interruption.[242]

August 1831

[On 7 August and 20 August Filippo Taglioni called on Meyerbeer to hear the music he had written for the act 3 Ballet of the Nuns.][243]

Friday 26 August. Took act 3 from Leborne. Where possible I have added wind instruments where the solo voices sing without orchestra in the stretta of the act 4 finale. To Véron about the alteration in the act 2 finale necessitated by the *Pas de Cinq*.

29 August. To Cicéri.

31 August. Looked at the libretto of *Anna Bolena*.[244]

September 1831

Thursday 1 September. Germain must ask Cicéri about the *changement à vue* in act 3. To Taglioni. To Nourrit, as to whether Véron has spoken to him about Dorus.

5 September. My birthday.

6 September. Bought a diary. To Scribe after sending the answer. Ordered sixteen- and eighteen-line notepaper. Asked Habeneck if the clarinetists could change the C clarinets for B ones, and whether they have a very good trombone. To Duvernoy* to see whether they have *trompettes à piston* in C.

8 September. Rehearsal at 11. Must arrange[245] the passage [example 35] beforehand.

Example 35. Theme (1) from *Robert le Diable*

15 September. To Damoreau about the cadenza in act 4.[246]

27 September. Today the string rehearsals began.

28 September. Today we moved into the Hotel Wagram.

30 September. The organ must be demonstrated.[247] Sent the trumpet parts [in the act 5 trio] to Leborne.

October 1831

[*Thursday 6 October*. Taglioni's diary records the first rehearsal of the Ballet of the Nuns.]

Saturday 8 October. First orchestral rehearsal. Before the rehearsal I altered the passage "Console toi fais comme moi" [Bertram in the act 1 finale]. To Habeneck on account of the B horns.

11 October. Second orchestral rehearsal.

13 October. Rehearsal with the wind instruments of the stage band [in act 3]. Third *mise en scène* rehearsal.

15 October. Third orchestral rehearsal. [Taglioni presented his daughter Marie to Meyerbeer for the first time.]

17 October. *Mise en scène* of the Gambling Scene [act 1 finale], the rolling and appearance of the dice. *Mise en scène* of the falling asleep.[248]

18 October. Fourth orchestral rehearsal. To Prévot about the speaking-trumpets for the chorus [of demons] in act 3.

19 October. To Halévy about the bells [in act 5]. To Véron, to ask that Scribe should come to the rehearsal. Played through the third finale with Habeneck on account of the passage [see example 36].

Example 36. Theme (2) from *Robert le Diable*

To Habeneck, that Norblin should first play the violoncello theme alone.[249]

20 October. To Habeneck, that he take the following more quickly and *piano* [see example 37].

Example 37. Theme (3) from *Robert le Diable*

Had the *Valse Infernale* played twice so that I could hear it from the pit.[250] To Tulon[251] to see whether he has arranged[252] the will-o'-the-wisps.[253] Fifth orchestral rehearsal.

22 October. Aujourd'hui je dois commencer à travailler un nouvel air de Mme Damoreau.[254] To Germain about "ces épouses du Christ. Arrêtons, saissons. Ses yeux baissés sont vers la terre,"[255] "Des chevaliers de la Neustrie."[256] [Taglioni records rehearsing the Ballet of the Nuns with costumes, beginning with the entry of Nourrit.]

23 October. Check whether the organ will be ready tomorrow.[257] Correct[258] the changes to the trio in act 5 in the copyist's. In the copy "C'est à vous que je bois."[259]

24 October. To Germain: "dejà commencent les combats."[260] To Véron as to whether the Gambatis are coming.[261]

25 October. Sixth orchestral rehearsal. [In Véron's handwriting:] *D'aujourd'hui en 8 jours je compte d'après engagement sur le finale. L. Véron.*[262]

27 October. Seventh orchestral rehearsal. To Tulon, that he should look at the flute part[263] in the *Pas de Cinq,* and also the high stave[264] in the trio. To Halévy about a cut[265] in the organ piece, and to make the chorus easier in [see example 38]:

Example 38. Theme (4) from *Robert le Diable*

28 October. To Duponchel about the flying machine and Archangel Michael[266] in act 5; the conclusion of act 3 and the black gauze. Mobile doors for the organ.

29 October. To Habeneck, that the four timpani should practice together [in the act 2 finale].

[*31 October.* Taglioni began rehearsing the Seduction Scene with his daughter.]

November 1831

Tuesday 1 November. To Scribe on account of Schlesinger (price, what kind of installments for the payment, *arrangement en opéra comique*), extension of contract with the Opéra.

3 November. Eighth orchestral rehearsal.

5 November. Ninth orchestral rehearsal.

[*6 November.* Taglioni records the sixth rehearsal of the Ballet of the Nuns with Nourrit. "Marie wept because the rehearsal had overtired her."]

7 November. To Leborne: he should write the viola part of the trio on a separate sheet, since I am still not sure about it. Duponchel: blue lightning and will-o'-the wisps while Bertram is in Hell.

8 November. Tenth orchestral rehearsal. Duponchel: that the theater should be darkened after the Buffo Duet. Halévy: tam-tam in place of cymbals, or tam-tam at the breaking [of the magic branch]; that the tam-tam and thunder be tried out today. Urhan* and all the violas should try the trio in act 5. Véron: no people at the dress rehearsal. Duponchel: that there should be blue lightning and will-o'-the-wisps during the Devil's Aria.

10 November. Eleventh orchestral rehearsal. Habeneck: that the trio in act 5 be rehearsed with Urhan's viola. To Habeneck: four timpani with contrabasses, but without violoncelli.

12 November. Twelfth orchestral rehearsal. Rehearsed the timpanists in the two crescendi at the end of the *Prière* and in the andante of the trio in act 5. The old curtain[267] to be pulled further back. The appearance of the Mother at the end. Change the situation whereby one learns him to be the son [i.e., Bertram's] already in act 2.

15 November. Thirteenth orchestral rehearsal. To Leborne about the contrabasses with the four timpani, and the *grande caisse* in the trio. Cut to be made in the stretta of the finale [of act 4].

19 November. To Germain about my name in the book, and cuts[268] in the manuscript. That Michael should sit today with the *chef de claque*. Final dress rehearsal.

21 November. To Nourrit, Levasseur, and Habeneck with the alteration to the organ ritornello. That Michael should be allowed onto the stage. First performance of *Robert le Diable.*[269]

23 November. Rehearsal at 1. To Scribe. D'Ortigue, Humboldt, Berton*.

24 November. Rehearsal at 1. To Scribe about "Grâce, grâce."

25 November. Duponchel, that the devil's curtain[270] should stay during the overture.

26 November. Took the *Romances* to Edmond Blanc* and called on D'Argout.

28 November. Véron about Taglioni. [See the 2 December entry.]

December 1831

Thursday 1 December. At 10 to Edmond Blanc.

[*2 December.* Meyerbeer wrote to Véron insisting that Marie Taglioni, who had withdrawn after three performances, should be held to her contract and complete the scheduled 6.][271]

5 December. Duponchel. *Acte 3: indiquer les mesures où le théâtre s'éclaire après la Procession des Nonnes. Acte 1: mise en scène de la Sicilenne. Acte 3: après l'air de Bertram tonnerre et éclairs.*[272]

6 December. Cherubini—Le Sueur.

8 December. At 1 to Fétis.

[Undated entries at the end of the *Taschenkalender*.]
Dinner with Börne, Heine, Humboldt.—With Duponchel: to discuss the Resurrection of the Nuns, whether other dance options could be developed, e.g., something

Amazon-like, or dice-playing. How gambling could be expressed in dance. Whether or not other nuns should not first appear drinking, then behave badly in a way that disgusts,[273] but Lea [i.e., Hélène] does it with grace. Taglioni shines in all genres.—Whether Ferdinand Prévot or Hurteaux* should sing Alberti.—To Véron about Fétis, Devrient. Whether there should not be more painters, or whether he should propose a bonus[274] to Cicéri if he delivers within a definite time. To Armand [Bertin], that 80,000 fr. is not the most expensive opera by far, and that if I had not allowed *Euryanthe* [to be performed], they would have had to find the funds.—A glockenspiel newly invented by Drury in London (1830) is being used a lot in the intermezzos of melodramas. Write to Rossini.—*À Mr Leborne: double notes dans les chants: toutes les annotations de scène et d'expression. Notes changer dans la fin du 1er Finale dans les choeurs. Voir la partie du souffleur pour arranger les petits roles.*[275]

NOTES

1. Opera in three acts by Rossini (Luigi Balocchi and Alexandre Soumet, after C. della Valle, the Duca di Ventignano's libretto for the two-act *Maometto II* [Naples, San Carlo, 3 December 1820]; Paris, Opéra, 9 October 1826). This theatrically elaborate revision of the earlier Italian work marked Rossini's début at the Salle Le Peletier and appealed to a public inflamed by news of the Greek War of Independence.

2. A Parisian socialite.

3. The soprano-bass *Gran Duetto* ("Si mel credi") in act 2, created by Pisaroni and Lablache, is the vocal and dramatic high point of this opera, and was the only piece to enjoy some popularity. Ricordi published it as a separate excerpt (no. 1372).

4. This is the first mention of the opera. "It seems likely that it was Scribe who originated the idea of a libretto on the theme of *Robert le Diable*, and that the papers of the Scribe *Nachlass* permit the reconstruction of no less than eight levels in the composition of the libretto before 1827" (Mark Everist, "The Name of the Rose: Meyerbeer's *opéra comique, Robert le Diable,*" *Revue de Musicologie* 80:2 [1994]: 212). This article provides a comprehensive investigation of the origins and genesis of the opera. A similar survey of the process that transformed the *opéra comique* into an *opéra*, and a consideration of the ethos, meaning, and influence of this seminal work, are provided by Karin Pendle, "The Transformation of a Genre: Meyerbeer's *Robert le Diable,*" in *Eugène Scribe and the French Opera of the Nineteenth Century,* Studies in Musicology no. 6 (Ann Arbor, Mich.: UMI Research Press, 1979), pp. 427–55. Adolphe Jullien's comparison of the medieval mystery play *Robert the Devil* (founded on the romance, and edited by Edouard Fournier [1878]) with Scribe's libretto shows how carefully the material was adjusted to the sensibilities of the romantic age "*Robert le Diable,* le *Mystère:* L'opéra-comique avant l'opéra," *Revue et Gazette musicale* 46:48, 46:49, 46:50 [1879]). The legend has obvious affinities with the story of Faust and Mephistopheles. Other aspects of the plot were derived from German and English romantic sources: Christian Heinrich Speiss's *Schauerroman* (horror novel) *Das Petermännchen* (1791) (French trans. by Latouche, *Le petit Pierre* [1820]); Matthew Gregory Lewis's Gothic romance *The Monk* (1796); and Charles Robert

Maturin's Gothic tragedy *Bertram, or the Castle of St. Aldobrand* (1816). For a discussion of the sources, see Catherine Joint-Dieterle, *"Robert le Diable:* Le premier opéra romantique," *Romantisme: Revue de la Société des Études Romantiques* 28/29 (1980): 154–55.

5. A Parisian socialite.

6. This refers to the famous act 2 trio for three basses ("Quel parlar! quell'aria incerta") from *Margherita d'Anjou*, published as a separate excerpt by Ricordi (no. 961). The virtuoso piece, for coloratura *basso cantante, basso profondo,* and *basso buffo,* was created by Nicola Bassi, Michele Cavara, and Nicolas-Prosper Levasseur. It ends as it began, with the same staccato melody heard in the opening canon.

7. "I undertake to deliver to M. Meyerbeer *La Nymphe du Danube,* scenario and libretto[7] by the first of March at the latest. If by this date I have not kept my promise, M. Meyerbeer will be free to take the subject, the title, and the music already completed of this work to whatever author and theater are convenient to him."

8. A letter from Michael Beer to Eduard von Schenk suggests that even by this stage, Meyerbeer's interest in the project had waned at the advent of the potent new attraction of *Robert le Diable* (E. von Schenk, *Michael Beers Briefwechsel* [Leipzig, 1837], p. 9).

9. The first mention of one of the famous dinner parties Meyerbeer regularly held for colleagues or others associated with his artistic interests, especially members of the press and government.

10. It was announced in the *Journal de Paris* (19 April 1827, p. 4): "A few days ago the Comité de Lecture for the Théâtre Feydeau unanimously passed an *opéra-comique* in three acts, entitled *Robert le Diable,* on which the Administration is pinning great hopes. The words are attributed to two authors who have always collaborated successfully, MM. Scribe and Germain Delavigne. The music is to be entrusted to a composer, M. Meyer-Beer, who, having acquired a brilliant reputation in Germany and Italy, is extending it in our country, where several of his works have already been successfully presented."

11. "I am working without let-up on our *Robert le Diable* and have made great progress. Nevertheless, I would be obliged if I could delay my arrival in Paris by a month, that is, until the first of November instead of the first of October, as I had proposed. This delay is because my wife has miscalculated the time of her confinement."

12. *Dizionario e Bibliographia della musica* (Milan, 1826).

13. This aria from *L'Esule di Granata* was first interpolated into *Il Crociato in Egitto* in Trieste for Carolina Bassi (1824), and then for Giuditta Pasta in Paris (1825). It was thereafter regarded as part of the latter opera, and became the single most famous aria from Meyerbeer's Italian period. It was published as a separate piece in Paris by Pacini (no. 1099).

14. In 1827 Meyerbeer's birthday (6 *Elul*) fell on 19 September. By now he had begun celebrating his anniversary according to the Christian calendar.

15. This is the first record of Meyerbeer's visit to Spa, which would henceforth feature prominently and recurrently in his life. The town is almost the oldest watering place in Europe and, even though so close to the then-new industrial cities of Liège and Verviers (twenty miles away), remained free of the disfiguring influences of these manufacturing centers, with the beauty of its surroundings unimpaired. There are sixteen springs, the Sauvenière possibly the oldest. As early as Roman times the naturalist Pliny is thought to have been alluding to it when he says, "Tungri, a state in Gaul, has a remarkable bubbling fountain, giving forth a taste of iron." For a history of Meyerbeer's long and unique association with this town, see Albin Body, *Meyerbeer aux eaux de Spa* (Brussels: Veuve J. Rozez, 1885).

16. Grétry visited Spa in 1782 and was indebted to it for some of the impressions used in *Richard Coeur de Lion.*

17. The *Harmonicum,* December 1828, reported that "The celebrated Meyerbeer is at present in Spa."

18. *BT,* 2:76–78.

19. *C. F. Zelters Darstellungen seines Lebens* (Weimar, 1931), p. 284. See *BT,* 2:78.

20. For a list of the books and scores which Meyerbeer eventually sent to Paris, see *BT,* 2:591.

21. Bochsa was conductor at the King's Theatre, London, from 1822 to 1832.

22. This concerns the projected London production. For a revision of the text, Meyerbeer turned to Karl von Holtei.

23. Actually *Das Galgenmädchen,* a *Novelle* by Friedrich de la Motte-Fouqué. Meyerbeer had presumably suggested this work as the subject for a libretto. See the entry for 2 June 1855.

24. Tgb. *Teufelspuk.*

25. This presumably turned out to be *Le Dieu et la Bayadère,* which contains supernatural elements, i.e., a divine visitation by Brahma.

26. The success of *La Muette de Portici* (1828) had much to do with the vivid and imposing scenic effects by Cicéri and Daguerre. The new opera with its Oriental setting also provided scope for spectacle.

27. This subject had already been used by Coccia (1818) and Mercadante (1826).

28. *Angiolina, ou L'Épouse du Doge, drame* in three acts (Théaulon and M.-J. Brisset; Paris, Théâtre des Nouveautés, 22 June 1822) [Wicks 3142].

29. Paganini's European tour had brought him to Berlin. Renée de Saussine (*Paganini,* p. 120) reports that King Friedrich Wilhelm III "appointed him to be honorary first director of music. Spohr and Meyerbeer vied with each other in sharing his attentions."

30. Ponchard (Robert), Huet (Bertram), Mme. Boulanger (Alice), Mme. Rigaud (Isabelle).

31. Meyerbeer was accompanied by his wife and mother, and stayed at the Hôtel du Portugal. In order to thank the Société Grétry, which had conferred membership upon him, he presented it with several of his scores.

32. While working on *Robert le Diable,* Meyerbeer began to realize the impossibility of mounting the work at the Opéra Comique.

33. Presumably the new opera projected for Italy with text to be provided by Rossi.

34. King Ludwig I, himself a poet; Meyerbeer was setting his *Bayerischer Schützenmarsch* to music. His expression of admiration for the royal poem (with its celebration of "German freedom and German justice, fervent hatred for oppression and tyranny") and dedication to the king is contained in the letter of 30 September 1829 (*BT,* 2:83–85).

35. Meyerbeer appears to have kept his arrival secret for a few days.

36. In his *Taschenkalender* Meyerbeer noted down a few ideas as starting points for his discussions with Scribe and Delavigne: "Viganò's *Bianca di Messina* as [model for] a dance piece. Likewise a dance piece for Taglioni and Montessu as they struggle against the magic sleep in the act 2 finale and make powerful leaps in an attempt to revive themselves, and are the last to fall asleep.—In act 3 a big recitative for Bertram in which he recounts the story of his fall from heaven, etc.: it should include only a small arioso that recurs from time to time. Lots of rhythmical changes. Since it contains the whole of Robert's history, all the main themes of the opera must recur in the orchestra.—I must have Hartmann bring *La pachianella* (Sicilian dance) and other Sicilian melodies from my trunk; Michael must like-

wise write to Cattereau in Naples.—Fata Morgana—Wilhelm must take down all the data from Mödler.—*Bianca di Messina,* ballet by Aiblinger.—*Terzetto buffo* or quartet for Bertram, Alberti, and Raimbault instead of the quartet in act 2, in which the two curiously question Bertram, who mocks them.—Bertram has too little to sing.—Aria for Alberti.— The action happens in Sicily, and yet apart from the Princess there is not a single other Sicilian, not even a chorus to bring out the Sicilian *couleur.* The conspiracy must be different. There are no comic pieces, not even a comic chorus.—four acts—The opera is a little bare and people will say it has the *baguette en main* and does not know how to eat it. Perhaps Fata Morgana is therefore the solution. In act 1 after the quartet, a journey through the air. At the end of act 2 Bertram takes Robert through the air.—Alberti's role.—Perhaps one could see the procession to the tournament on horseback on the heights in the background, perhaps even a little of the tournament itself.—Perhaps in the conspiracy scene there could be a *conseil des diables,* as in *Manfred.—Pèlerinage de Sainte Rosalie.* Alice could be called Rosalie, or perhaps Robert's mother, and she must have been a Sicilian princess. Perhaps Alice is making the pilgrimage *en son honneur.* How could the devil hold his Sabbath in a place where it could be seen? Only by an independent coincidence (like Fata Morgana) could Alice interrupt the conspiracy without some *niaiserie* by the devil, but the crucifix would not be allowed. Already in act 1 and also in the new introduction the *maître des ceremonies* should have something to sing. The action should be shifted to Palermo. There should be demonic laughter at the words "hell is as bad as they say."— Flares in the *tableau des vices.*—One must speak earlier about the Procession of St. Rosalie. The whole of the Hell Scene must be without singing until he picks the branch that is attached to a solitary tree. Then the chorus comes in with *il est à nous.* The tree goes up in green fire."

37. "Would you . . . ask M. Pélissier if the manuscript of *Robert le Diable,* with the visa of the censor, is in the *carton de l'administration* of the Opéra Comique" (*BT,* 2:86).

38. Presumably the text of "Robert, toi que j'aime."

39. By now *Robert le Diable* was being redrafted as a *grand opéra.*

40. Narrative poem by Goethe, dating from 1797, the so-called *Balladenjahr,* when he and Schiller undertook the composition of a series of literary ballads. Meyerbeer was presumably assisting Scribe with materials for the libretto *Le Dieu et la Bayadère,* which the latter was writing for Auber. Cf. *BT,* 2:89–90.

41. A collection of lyric poems by Heine published in the *Buch der Lieder* (1827).

42. Presumably the *Sicilienne* "L'or est une chimère," which is the 12/8 rondo theme of the act 1 finale in *Robert le Diable.* This would constitute the first *monstre* that Meyerbeer provided for Scribe.

43. Meyerbeer informed Rossi that he would not be writing the opera for Italy. Rumors of the projected opera persisted all the same, as in the *Harmonicum* of January 1830: "16th. I read in foreign journals of three new Italian operas being in preparation: one by Meyerbeer, *La Donna Caritea,* for Malibran."

44. See Martine Kahane, *Robert le Diable: Catalogue de l'exposition Théâtre National de l'Opéra de Paris 20 juin—20 septembre 1985* (Paris: Bibliothèque National, 1985), p.14.

45. *Biographie W. A. Mozarts nach Originalbriefen* (Leipzig, 1828).

46. Meyerbeer had already met Count and Countess Appony during his stay in Rome (1817-18). See the references to the couple in Spohr's *Selbstbiographie.*

47. *Oberon, or The Elf King's Oath,* fairy opera in three acts (James Robinson Planché, based on W. Sotheby's translation of Wieland's poem *Oberon* [1780]; London, Covent Garden, 12 April 1826), was given in London thirty-one times during the first season and was

frequently revived. Its popularity during the nineteenth century was enormous and international. The English-speaking nations have consistently ignored it in the twentieth century, in spite of the revival at the Metropolitan in 1918 (in Bodanzky's famous arrangement).

48. This would be Meyerbeer's favored residence in Paris throughout his life. A description of the suite he regularly occupied over the years is provided by Johannes Weber, *Notes et souvenirs d'un de ses secrétaires* (Paris: Librairie Fischbacher, 1898), pp. 31–34. See also Renée de Saussine, who quotes from a letter of Paganini on the eve of his visit to Paris in 1831: "You had better address your letters to Paris to the Hôtel des Princes, rue de Richelieu No. 109. That is the address where all the great put up. Meyerbeer and his family are staying there" (*Paganini*, p. 128).

49. The "Ballade de la Reine Marguerite de Valois" appeared as no. 36 in the collected *Quarante Mélodies*.

50. This textual variant was not retained in the printed version.

51. *Euryanthe*, romantic opera in three acts (Helmine von Chézy*, after a medieval French romance; Vienna, Kärntnertor-Theater, 25 October 1823), was Weber's only opera without spoken dialogue. It was consistently performed during the nineteenth century all over Germany and Austria, and occasionally in France. During the twentieth century there have been regular revivals, but in spite of intense musical admiration, it has never established itself in the repertory.

52. A performance was projected for Paris.

53. In 1829 Thackeray was on a continental journey that took him, among other things, to Goethe's Weimar.

54. *BT,* 2:99. *Archives de l'Opéra, Registre de Correspondence, 592, 1830, No. 30, 10. Janvier*.

55. To the signing of the contract.

56. Scribe and Auber were working on *Le Dieu et la Bayadère*.

57. In spite of Rossini's apparent friendship for Meyerbeer, he appears to have evinced a hostile attitude in private. His famous quip about Meyerbeer and Halévy ("Let the Jews finish their Sabbath"), as an explanation for not writing any more operas after *Guillaume Tell*, probably carries more truth than intended. For a more reflective consideration of underlying aesthetic differences, see Herbert Weinstock, *Rossini* (New York: Alfred A. Knopf, 1968), p. 180.

58. On 7 September 1829 Meyerbeer had sent Pixérécourt three pieces from *La Nymphe du Danube* (*BT,* 2:89).

59. The Order of Pedro I was instituted in 1826 and bestowed only until his fall from power in 1831.

60. *BT,* 2:597.

61. "Another promenade, the Promenade des Artistes, passes along the brook Picherotte, which crosses the road from the Sauvenière to the Géronstère and touches the beautiful property La Havette. It is said that the celebrated composer Meyerbeer found in this spot the inspiration for *Robert le Diable* . . ." (*A Pictorial and Descriptive Guide to Belgium, the Ardennes, and Holland,* new and rev. ed. [London and New York: Ward, Lock, and Co., n.d. (c. 1898)], p. 166).

62. See Meyerbeer's letter of 20 July 1830 to Marie Patzig, wet nurse and nanny to Blanca, sent to Baden-Baden (*BT,* 2:104).

63. *Le Dieu et la Bayadère, ou La Courtisane amoureuse, opéra-ballet* in two acts, was produced on 30 October 1830. It achieved considerable success, being performed in Paris 146 times until 1866. The last German revival was in Hamburg (1881).

64. On 26 July the Opéra was closed because of popular disturbance in the streets. The so-called Les Trois Glorieuses followed (27–29 July), resulting in the proclamation of Louis-Philippe, duke of Orleans, as king of France. After the revolution, the Opéra was put under the control of the minister of the interior, who decided to return to the old system of directors directly responsible to him. The Opéra opened again on 4 August with a performance of Auber's *La Muette de Portici*. On 24 August the famous performance of this opera in Brussels ignited the Belgian Revolution.

65. *BT,* 2:107–9. She had already appeared in Paris at the Théâtre Allemand on 6 May 1830 with spectacular success.

66. Tgb. *de la réduire à sa plus simple expression.*

67. Opera in one act (Jules-Joseph Gabriel and Delabouillaje; Paris, Opéra Comique, 2 December 1830).

68. Tgb. *Rossiniert und Auberisiert.*

69. Opera in three acts (Jean-Baptiste-Charles Vidal and Paul Duport; Paris, Opéra Comique, 23 April 1830).

70. Opera in one act (Jules-Joseph Gabriel and C. Moreau; Paris, Opéra Comique, 11 December 1830).

71. Tgb. *redacteur de la.*

72. According to D'Ortigue, Jouy wished to work with Meyerbeer, but the composer always discouraged this because of the comparisons that would inevitably have been made with Spontini *(La Vestale)* and Rossini *(Guillaume Tell).* See *Journal des Débats,* May 1864.

73. *Charles VII chez ses grands Vassaux* (1831), the model for Donizetti's *Gemma di Vergy* (1834).

74. The drama *Le Maréchal d'Ancre* (Paris, Théâtre de l'Odéon, 25 June 1831) [Wicks 10960] was used by Prati for Alessandro Nini's *La Marescialla d'Ancre* (1839).

75. Tgb. *professeur suppléant.*

76. The first mention of Meyerbeer's alimentary complaint, which was to become chronic and worsen with age. It was probably a form of Crohn's Disease, a type of ulcerative colitis, a mysterious condition in which ulceration of the lining of the colon gives rise to frequent diarrhea with the passage of blood and mucus. The situation is compounded by the presence of germs in the bowel. It may well be autoimmune disease, whereby the sufferer rejects his own stomach lining. For further developments in the course of this condition, see 6–10 January and 24 September 1841, May 1844, July–August 1848, August 1850, August–October 1851, 31 August 1853, 22–23 July 1859, 2 August 1860, and recurrent references throughout 1861 (esp. 29 January, 25 August, 4 September, 9 November), 1862 (esp. July–September), 1863 (esp. February–April, 21 August, 7 September, 28 December), and 4 January 1864.

77. Cooper's novel *The Red Corsair* (1827) combines his naval experiences with his mythmaking love of adventure and romance.

78. *La Familie Riquebourg, ou Le Mariage mal assorti, comédie-vaudeville* in one act (Paris, Théâtre du Gymnase Dramatique, 1 January 1831) [Wicks 9101].

79. Tgb. *choquant.*

80. *Jeune et Vieille, ou Le premier et dernier Chapitre, comédie-vaudeville* in two acts (Scribe, Mélesville, and Bayard; Paris, Théâtre du Gymnase Dramatique, 18 November 1830) [Wicks 4574].

81. Giovanni Failoni was a friend of Meyerbeer who appears to have had a close knowledge of the social and musical scene in Paris. The composer had known him since his

earliest days in Italy. See the reference to the journey undertaken in his company with Michael Beer (31 December 1817) in the entry for early 1818.

82.   *Opera buffa* in two parts (G. A. Frederico; St. Petersburg, Ermitage, 10 October 1781). The text was first set by Pergolesi in 1733, and Paisiello wrote it to celebrate the name day of Grand Duke Alexander of Russia. It was revived constantly throughout the nineteenth century, and into the twentieth (Rome, 1927; Cairo, 1936).

83.   Lablache had just made his début at the Théâtre Italien on 7 November 1830 in Cimarosa's *Il Matrimonio segreto*.

84.   A civil servant.

85.   *Le Fils de l'homme, souvenirs de 1824, comédie* (Pittaud de Forges and Eugène Sue; Paris, Théâtre des Nouveautés, 28 December 1830) [Wicks 4223].

86.   See 7 February 1831.

87.   Actually *Le College de *** (Reichnau), Souvenirs de la Suisse en 1794, comédie-vaudeville* (Masson, de Leuven and Villeneuve; Paris, Théâtre du Gymnase Dramatique, 27 November 1830) [Wicks 3594].

88.   *Robespierre, ou Le 9 thermidor, mélodrame* in three acts (A. Bourgeois and Francis [Cornu?]; Paris, Théâtre de l'Ambigu-Comique, 16 December 1830) [Wicks 5643].

89.   This must correct Wicks [7552], who has the first performance at the Théâtre du Luxembourg in 1832.

90.   "Mère grand," *nocturne à deux voix* [sopranos] (text by A. Betourné), no. 11 in the *Quarante Mélodies*. The date of composition is unknown, but probably 1830.

91.   This subject has been closely researched in recent years. See Catherine Joint-Dieterle, "*Robert le Diable*," pp. 147–66; Hugh MacDonald, "*Robert le Diable*," in *Music in Paris in the Eighteen-Thirties,* ed. Peter Bloom, La Vie musicale en France au XIXe siècle, 4 (Stuyvesant, N.Y.: Pendragon, 1987), pp. 357–64; Rebecca Wilburg, "The *Mise en scène* at the Paris Opéra: Salle Le Peletier (1821-1873) and the Staging of the First French Grand Opéra: Meyerbeer's *Robert le Diable*" (diss., Brigham Young University, 1990).

92.   Tgb. *convenierten.*

93.   Tgb. *étude.*

94.   The salon of Mme. O'Reilly was frequented by many artists and writers.

95.   Tgb. *factum.*

96.   Humboldt came to Paris in September 1830 at the behest of Friedrich Wilhelm III in order to repair relations with the house of Orleans and to inform the king about events in the French capital. He returned to Berlin at the end of January 1831.

97.   This opera in three acts had its première at the Opéra Comique on 11 January 1831. The subject was drawn from the stories of El Cid, and the bass aria "Deux familles: non, de ma juste colère" became famous.

98.   The classic introduction to the Opéra and its complex relationship to the French government and its administration is William L. Crosten's *French Grand Opera: An Art and a Business* (New York: King's Crown Press, 1948; reprint, New York: Da Capo, 1972). His study centers on the high point of the Opéra's achievement during the 1830s (Véron's administration). A more modern work, covering the period from the late 1820s to the mid-1860s (and so the era of Meyerbeer's association with the house), and providing a sociopolitical context to the role of the Opéra in French society, is Jane Fulcher, *The Nation's Image: French Grand Opera as Politics and Politicized Art* (Cambridge: Cambridge University Press, 1987).

99.   Ballet in three acts (scenario Scribe, choreography Aumer; Paris, Opéra, 3 May 1830). The work enjoyed a moderate success, with forty-seven performances until 1832.

100.   Tgb. *appuyieren.*

101. Tgb. *ripieghi.*

102. Tgb. *entrainante.*

103. Jean-Baptiste Tolbecque.

104. The original title of *Le Dieu et la Bayadère, opéra-ballet* in two acts (Paris, Opéra, 13 October 1830). It was given in Paris 146 times until 1866. Performed also in German, English, Danish, Russian, Dutch, and Swedish, and revived in Hamburg (1881).

105. Türkheim was a banker.

106. Tgb. *subjet.* Knowing the libretto of *Zampa*, and perceiving its qualities, Meyerbeer no doubt also wanted to make use of Mélesville's abilities.

107. Tgb. *rendezvous.*

108. Op. 58.

109. Gouin was to become Meyerbeer's trusted friend and *homme de confiance* in Paris.

110. Tgb. *prime.*

111. Tgb. *dejeuniere.*

112. Tgb. *affaire.*

113. *Comédie-vaudeville* in two acts (Paris, Théâtre du Vaudeville, 25 December 1830) [Wicks 3564].

114. Wicks [11229] designates it a *drame* (Paris, Théâtre du Vaudeville, 15 January 1831).

115. While traveling from London to Russia, Sor stayed in Paris to attend a revival of his ballet, which had first been produced there on 3 March 1823.

116. It nonetheless had enjoyed great success, and was performed 111 times between 1823 and 1831.

117. Meyerbeer saw this play on 3 May 1812.

118. Tgb. *diverginiert.*

119. *Drame lyrique* in 1 act (Paris, 18 July 1829).

120. The Cloister Scene in scene 2. The idea, genesis, nature, and reconstruction of this famous and decisive scene of supernatural seduction, the first *ballet blanc*, and the archetype for all romantic ballets, are discussed at length by Knud Arne Jürgensen and Anne Hutchinson Guest, *Robert le Diable: The Ballet of the Nuns* (Amsterdam: Gordon & Breach, 1997). "With *Robert le Diable* the supernatural entered the Opéra, whence it was transferred to the ballet in such works as *La Sylphide*, . . . and ballet, under the direct influence of *Robert*, became the primary vehicle for this phase of romanticism on the French stage" (Pendle, "The Transformation of a Genre," p. 455).

121. Tgb. *quartier.*

122. Opera in two acts by Gnecco (text by the composer; Milan, La Scala, 16 August 1805). Loewenberg does not mention this particular revival (cf. *Annals of Opera,* col. 588).

123. No. 9 *Duo bouffe* ("Du rendez-vous, voici l'heureux instant").

124. Tgb. *modeste.*

125. "The nation's muse."

126. *Napoléon Bonaparte, ou Trente ans de l'histoire de France,* prose *drame historique* in six acts (Alexandre Dumas and A. Cordellier-Delanoue; Paris, Théâtre de l'Odéon, 11 January 1831) [Wicks 11616].

127. Tgb. *rapport.*

128. Tgb. *chef de chant.*

129. Tgb. *copesterie.*

130. *Zampa* was first performed on 3 May, *Robert le Diable* on 21 November. Not only was it very successful in Paris (694 performances until 1913), but all over the world, and revived in the twentieth century (Birmingham, 1922; London, 1983; Wexford, 1993).

131. Indeed he had. The unusually rich, even experimental, harmonies of Hérold's opera were ascribed to the influence of *Der Freischütz*, but perhaps the source was closer to hand. Certainly the use of the organ in act 3 was a flagrant instance of his borrowing from Meyerbeer.

132. Tgb. *portier.*

133. Tgb. *placiert.*

134. Tgb. *en train kommen kann.*

135. Tgb. *Schreibe Necessaire.*

136. Tgb. *rencontre.*

137. Tgb. *pénible.*

138. Tgb. *antecédents.*

139. *Moïse et Pharaon, ou Le Passage dans la Mer Rouge* (Balocchi and Jouy; Paris, Opéra, 26 May 1827). This was the French revision of *Mosè in Egitto* (1818).

140. Tgb. *recitierte.*

141. Émile Deschamps was to be of great importance to Meyerbeer in the creation of both *Les Huguenots* and *Le Prophète*. For an account of his life and works see G. Jean-Aubry, "A Romantic Dilettante: Émile Deschamps (1791-1871)," *Music and Letters* 20 (1939): 250–65.

142. English impresario of the Court theaters in Naples and Milan (1820s).

143. Tgb. *canevas.*

144. Tgb. *refugié.*

145. The impression must have remained very positive, because Meyerbeer was to recall this work years later on 29 July 1847.

146. Tgb. *coupiert.*

147. The orchestra and its famous concerts had been founded by Habeneck on 9 March 1829.

148. Tgb. *attrapiert.*

149. No. 3 in E-flat major, op. 55.

150. Romantic opera in three acts by C. M. von Weber (Friedrich Kind, after a tale in J. A. Apel and F. Laun's *Gespensterbuch* [1811]; Berlin, Schauspielhaus, 18 June 1821), the foundation stone of German national music, and one of the most successful of all operas, given in Berlin 852 times by 1937, and in Dresden 1,084 times by 1959. No other German opera had ever spread so quickly throughout the world.

151. Opera in 4 acts (V. J. Étienne de Jouy and H.-L.-F. Bis, based on Schiller's drama, *Wilhelm Tell* [1804]; Paris Opéra, 3 August 1829), Rossini's last and greatest work, the climax of his artistic career. After *Il Barbiere di Siviglia*, this was his most successful opera, given 868 times in Paris until 1912, with a reprise in 1932. Performed all over the world, and still occasionally revived.

152. Tgb. *solliciteurs.*

153. This 1-act *comédie* was premièred in St. Petersburg at the Ermitage on 18 April 1805.

154. Tgb. *revenit.*

155. Tgb. *retrecierten.*

156. Indeed, his closest collaborator, for whom he was to write thirty-eight libretti from 1823 to 1861.

157. The commission was made up of Le Duc de Choiseul (president), Royer-Collard, d'Henneville, Armand Bertin, Edmond Blanc, and Cavé (secretary).

158. Tgb. *en petit comité.*

159. Tgb. *taciturne.*

160. Tgb. *frais.*

161. Schiller's neoclassical play (1803) exploring the problem of human freedom and a Sophoclean notion of fate.

162. Rossini's last Neapolitan opera (A. L. Tottola, after P. L. de Buirette de Belloy's drama [1762]; Naples, San Carlo, 16 February 1822). This was the first of his operas that Rossini himself conducted in Vienna and London. It was only moderately successful by the standards of the composer's other mature works.

163. Tgb. *abandon.*

164. Tgb. *ouvriers.*

165. Tgb. *saillanter, detachierter.*

166. Tgb. *plazieren.*

167. Tgb. *devis.*

168. Tgb. *membre de l'institut.*

169. Tgb. *aperçu.*

170. Tgb. *à dessein.*

171. Tgb. *sous devis.*

172. Wicks [10747] describes this as a *drame historique* in two acts by L. Lhérie [= Léon-Lévy Brunswick], Barthélemy Thouin, and V. Lhérie; Paris, Théâtre des Variétés, 6 January 1831). The Conciergerie was a prison in Paris.

173. Tgb. *gendarme.*

174. *L'Ange gardien, ou Soeur Marie* (Dartois and H. Dupin; Paris, Théâtre des Variétés, 29 January 1831). Wicks [6425] calls this a *comédie-vaudeville.*

175. Presumably the same as *Robert und Elise.*

176. Presumably the aria written for Therese Grünbaum, "Perchè muni tiranni."

177. A. Pougin mentions a composition in the supplement to his *Biographie universelle* that would appear to be identical with this piece.

178. This sketchbook was lost with Meyerbeer's other papers *(Nachlass)* during World War II.

179. Tgb. *Miserabilität.*

180. Tgb. *propiniert.*

181. Tgb. *montieren.*

182. *Opéra comique* in one act (Scribes and Mazères; Paris, Opéra Comique, 10 March 1827).

183. Tgb. *au prix courant.*

184. Tgb. *collationiert.*

185. Tgb. *moyens.*

186. Tgb. *kastratenmässig.*

187. The recitative no. 10a, "Don Ottavio, son morta," followed by the aria no. 10b, "Or sai chi l'onore."

188. Tgb. *matinée.*

189. Opera in four acts by Louise-Angélique Bertin (text drawn from Goethe; Paris, Théâtre Italien, 8 March 1831).

190. Op. 92.

191. *Jeanne d'Arc à Orleans*, opera in three acts (Lambert and Théaulon; Paris, Opéra Comique, 10 March 1821).

192. Opera in three acts (Scribe, after Bouilly; Paris, Opéra Comique, 20 May 1829). Boieldieu's last opera.

193. *Fidelio, oder Die eheliche Liebe*, opera in two acts by Beethoven (Josef Sonnleithner, a German version of Bouilly's French libretto *Lénore, ou L'Amour conjugal* for Gaveaux [1798]; Vienna, Theater an der Wien, 20 November 1805). In 1806 the opera was altered and reduced from three to two acts by Stefan von Breuning, and given its final form in 1814 by Georg Friedrich Treitschke. This final version was produced at the Kärntnertor-Theater on 23 May 1814. The work is a distillation of Beethoven's humane passion, a glorious expression of faith in liberty and the repudiation of tyranny.

194. Tgb. *arrangierte*.

195. Tgb. *élève*.

196. Tgb. *concours*.

197. Tgb. *des gouvernements*.

198. Tgb. *coupe*.

199. Tgb. *élèven*.

200. Tgb. *procédé mecanique*.

201. Tgb. *qu'il y ait de l'avenir*.

202. Clément and Larousse concur rather witheringly: "la partition . . . ne doit être considerée que comme une de ces nombreuses épaves, de ces 'frutti di mare' des concours de l'Institut" [the score . . . can only be considered as one of those numerous bits of flotsam, one of those *frutti di mare* thrown up by the competitions of the Institut] (*Dictionnaire*, 2:1130).

203. Goethe's famous poem from *Wilhelm Meisters Lehrjahre*, when Mignon tries to recall her homeland in Italy.

204. For Levasseur.

205. Tgb. *arrangiert und transkribiert*.

206. No.14 *Duo*.

207. *La Muette de Portici, grand opéra* in five acts by Auber (Scribe and G. Delavigne; Paris, Opéra, 29 February, 1828). This was the composer's most famous opera, performed in Paris 505 times until 1882, and given all over the world throughout the nineteenth century. Commissioned for the Opéra, this work inaugurated a new era in the history of French *tragédie lyrique*, in which the fusion of powerful historical drama with substantial solo roles and an increased reliance on chorus, orchestra, ballet, and scenic effects set new standards in lyric theater. The example was of great significance for Meyerbeer's artistic development.

208. Tgb. *acceptiert*.

209. A violinist.

210. Op. 29 (1801).

211. Ballet in three acts by Carafa (scenario by Scribe, choreography by Coralli). It was eventually produced on 18 July 1831, and enjoyed moderate success (forty-seven performances until 1832).

212. Tgb. *démarchen*.

213. Tgb. *enlèvement*.

214. No. 2b, *Romance* ("Va, dit-elle, va, mon enfant").

215. No. 12, "Mais Alice" (for Bertram and Alice).

216. Charles Maurice?

217. Tgb. *des Chevaliers*.

218. No. 14, "Si j'aurai ce courage."

219. No. 9 "Ah! l'honnête homme."

220. No. 8, "Sonnez, clairons."

221. Tgb. *confuse.*

222. No. 18b, "Grand Dieu."

223. There is a review in the *Revue musicale* 9 (1831): 62.

224. No. 9 in D minor, op.125 *(Choral).*

225. *Comédie-vaudeville* in three acts, written in collaboration with Etienne Arrago (Paris, Théâtre du Vaudeville, 28 February 1831) [Wicks 10740.]

226. *Euryanthe* was produced in Paris on 6 April 1831 to a cool reception (*Revue musicale* 11 [1831]: 77). It was given only four times.

227. Op. 69.

228. Op. 127 (1824).

229. Tgb. *brillieren.*

230. *La Figlia dell'aria, ossia L'Innalzamento di Semiramide*, from a play by Calderón (Venice, Teatro San Salvatore, 1786).

231. In May 1831 Count d'Argout, the minister of trade, took over the direction of the Parisian theaters.

232. Tgb. *définitivement.*

233. *BT,* 2:613–15.

234. *I Capuleti e i Montecchi*, opera in 4 parts by Bellini (Felice Romani, modified for Bellini from his libretto for Vaccai [which was based on Matteo Bandello's ninth *novella*, which in turn drew on Foppa's libretto for Zingarelli of 1796, based not on Shakespeare, but on Gerolamo della Croce's *Storia di Verona*]; Venice, La Fenice, 11 March 1831). The opera enjoyed great success, confirming the international reputation Bellini had won with *Il Pirata* (1827).

235. *La Sonnambula*, opera in two acts by Bellini (Felice Romani, based on Scribe and Aumer's ballet pantomime *La Somnambule, ou L'Arrivée d'un nouveau seigneur* of 1827, in turn based on the *comédie-vaudeville La Somnambule* by Scribe and Delavigne of 1819; Milan, Teatro Carcano, 6 March 1831). In this elegiac rustic idyll, Bellini's melodic gifts reached a new maturity. The opera won enduring success all over the world.

236. Respectively conductor, chorus master, and musical assistant.

237. Tgb. *lecture.*

238. *Tragédie lyrique* by Salieri (François-Louis-Gand Lebland de Rollet and Louis-Théodore de Tschudy, after Calzibigi's *Ipermestra;* Paris, Opéra, 26 April 1784).

239. Ballet in 3 acts by Cherubini (scenario after Metastasio; choreography, Pierre Gardel; Paris, Opéra, 18 December 1804).

240. This was for the Church Scene in act 5.

241. "Today the first singers' rehearsal of *Robert.*"

242. "The fourth rehearsal after an interruption of eight days."

243. Taglioni's diary provides an important supplement to the composer's sparse observations during this period of preparation and rehearsal. The diary is kept in the Paris Opéra library [Fonds Taglioni R 25], and the passages relevant to the ballet are quoted by Knud Jürgensen in *Robert le Diable*, p. 8. On 20 August Taglioni observes that Meyerbeer "played me the music of the seduction scene of the nuns from Robert the Devil destined for my daughter; this music is charming."

244. *Anna Bolena, opera seria* in two acts by Donizetti (Felice Romani; Milan, Teatro

Carcano, 26 December 1830). This was the composer's first great tragedy and won him international recognition.

245. Tgb. *arrangieren*.

246. In no. 18c, *Cavatine* ("Robert, toi que j'aime").

247. Tgb. *demontiert*.

248. The Magic Slumber Scene (act 4, scene 2).

249. The prelude to no. 15c, *Récitatif* ("Voici ce lieu témoin d'un terrible mystère!").

250. Tgb. *parterre*.

251. Principal flautist of the Opéra orchestra.

252. Tgb. *arrangiert*.

253. Tgb. *feu follets*. The stage directions for the emergence of the nuns prior to their famous ballet: "Les feux follets paraissent et voltigent sur les tombeaux" [The will-o'-the-wisps appear and flitter on the tombs].

254. "Today I must begin working on a new aria for Mme. Damoreau." Perhaps this was a new version of Isabelle's act 2 aria, "En vain j'espère" (no. 4)?

255. Directions relating to the Resurrection of the Nuns (no. 15b).

256. The duet for Robert and Bertram no.14, changed to "Des chevaliers de ma patrie."

257. For the Church Scene in act 5, scene 2.

258. Tgb. *corrigieren*.

259. Robert's words in the opening chorus no. 1b ("Versez à tasse pleine").

260. Words to be changed in the act 2 finale (no. 8).

261. Trumpeter brothers working in London. They were brought to play the trumpet in the act 5 trio, the melody of the *Andante cantabile* "O mon fils."

262. "In eight days from now I reckon on receipt of the finale."

263. Tgb. *partie*.

264. Tgb. *ais*.

265. Tgb. *coupure*.

266. Tgb. *Archeange Michel*.

267. Tgb. *rideau*.

268. Tk. *coupure*.

269. *Robert le Diable* was one of the greatest successes in the history of opera. It was performed 754 times at the Paris Opéra until 28 August 1893 (there were performances every year apart from 1869, 1875, and 1880) and revived there in 1985. The opera spread to even the remotest corners of the world, including Dublin (1832), Calcutta (1836), Warsaw (1837), New Orleans (1840), Mauritius (1841), Odessa (1846), Valparaiso (1847), Batavia (1850), Rio de Janeiro (1850), Constantinople (1850), Mexico (1852), Corfu (1854), Buenos Aires (1854), and Melbourne (1866). It was performed 260 times in Berlin (–1906), 251 times in Brussels (–1913), 241 times in Hamburg (–1917), 111 times in Vienna (–1921), 83 times in Milan (–1886), 57 times in Parma (-1882), and 54 times in London (–1890). Since the Second World War, it has been revived in Florence (Maggio Musicale Fiorentino, 1968), Paris (Opéra, 1985), and New York (Carnegie Hall, 21 February 1988). A series of reviews are reprinted in *BT* (2:617–20), and by Marie-Hélène Coudroy in *La critique parisienne des "grands opéras" de Meyerbeer* (Saarbrücken: Musik Edition Lucie Galland, 1988) in the section devoted to *Robert le Diable*. Various arrangements of the airs from the opera followed, by Chopin, Herz, Adam, Thalberg, Kalkbrenner, Johann Strauss *(Vater)*, and Liszt, among others. The tremendous success and level of interest generated by the opera meant that it assumed an almost legendary mystique of its own, with stories about its origins, genesis, and production widely circulated in the German and French press, and establishing

themselves in the annals of theatrical anecdotes. A typical example is this little story about its rehearsal:

In October 1831 a small, elegant man arrived at a house in Paris in the vicinity of the Madeleine Church, and rented an apartment. He immediately paid the rent for three months and further tipped the concièrge handsomely, observing, "I will be working in my rooms for several hours each day. I am, moreover, expecting a visitor, a big man with rough voice."

The concièrge answered, "What will I do if I do not recognize him?" Whereupon the new tenant answered, "He will say to you: 'I want to talk to the devil.' After this discussion the porter and his wife felt very uneasy at the imminent prospect of observing the devil!

The next day the new tenant returned with a large box, annotated in black, and looking for all the world like a coffin. Two hours later the expected stranger arrived, and indeed asked to speak with the devil. Aghast, the concièrge and his wife listened at the door of the small apartment in order to find out what could possibly be happening inside, and overheard an extraordinary conversation. "Do you have the courage to play a real devil?" Then, "You will never be able to be the devil like that!" Further, "The devil is more attractive than you would imagine!"

Deeply shocked, the concièrge immediately hurried to the police and reported this bizarre scene which he had inadvertently overheard. When the police commissioner arrived and asked the men to identify themselves, he received the answer: the composer Meyerbeer and the first bass of the Paris Opéra, who were simply rehearsing the role of Bertram in the opera *Robert le Diable*. "We could not practice in the hotel because of the other guests, so we decided to rent this apartment for the purpose."

As a small compensation for the anxiety they had undergone, the porter and his wife received two complimentary tickets to the première of the opera on 21 November 1831.

From Günther Haensch, *Deutsche Texte zum Übersetzen* (Munich: Max Hueber Verlag, 1967), p. 103, trans. R. I. Letellier. Reference to Meyerbeer's observations on rehearsing in his rooms (15 July 1831), on moving into the Hotel Wagram (27 September 1831), and on his rooms in the rue Madeleine (27 and 28 November 1839) show that such stories in the papers were often based on fact.

270. Tgb. *Teufels rideau.*

271. Marie Taglioni danced the role 6 times and then withdrew, possibly because she had already begun rehearsals for her father's new ballet, *La Sylphide*, which was premièred on 12 March 1832. Her part was taken over by Louise Fitzjames*, a French ballerina, who was to dance it 232 times. Jürgensen discusses Taglioni's possible ambiguity regarding the role of Hélène, observing that "what this ballerina probably lacked most in the rôle was the kind of bizarre erotic charisma needed for this strange 'religious' female devil" (*Robert le Diable*, p. 8). Taglioni, however, did dance this role on later occasions, notably in Berlin at the Court Opera on 20 June 1832 (when Meyerbeer wrote additional music for her), and in Sweden (Royal Theatre, 20 September 1841).

272. "Act 3: indicate the bars when the stage is illumined after the Procession of the Nuns. Act 1. The stage directions for the scene of the *Sicilienne*. Act 3. Thunder and lightning after Bertram's aria."

273. Tgb. *degoutiert*.
274. Tgb. *prime*.
275. "To M. Leborne: breves in the singing parts; all the stage and vocal directions. Change certain notes in the chorus of the act 1 finale. See the prompter's book to arrange the small roles."

Section 2
1832

1832

January 1832

Wednesday 4 January. Today the engraver[1] received act 5.

[On 5 January a parody of *Robert le Diable* was given at the Théâtre de la Gaîté, taken over from the Vaudeville. On 10 January Filippo Taglioni gave a big dinner in honor of Meyerbeer and his brothers. Duponchel and Coulon were in attendance.]

17 January. At 11 to Scribe.

[On 19 January Meyerbeer was created a chevalier of the Légion d'Honneur by King Louis-Philippe.]

22 January. Places for Kalkbrenner.

[On 23 January an English parody, *Robert le Diable, the Devil's Son,* by E. Fitzball and J. B. Buckstone, was given at the Adelphi Theatre in London; it was billed as a "romantic and magical *burletta.*"]

24 January. At 4 to Scribe.

February 1832

Thursday 2 February. Soirée at Mme. Récamier's.

3 February. Dinner at O'Reilly's. Soirée at Countess Rumford's.

4 February. Today I sent off a letter to Count Redern*.

5 February. Soirée at Princess Vaudemont's.

7 February. Sent the dances to Humboldt.

14 February. Today the score was sent off to Redern, and I also wrote to Redern.

18 February. [Wrote] to Cherubini that I will fetch him at 2:30.

20 February. Felix Mendelssohn.

[On 20 February *Robert le Diable* was produced at the Drury Lane Theatre in an adaptation by Bishop entitled *The Daemon, or The Mystic Branch*; on 21 February the opera was given at the Covent Garden Theatre in an adaptation by M. R. Lacy entitled *The Fiend-Father, or Robert of Normandy*.]

27 February. At 2 to Felix Mendelssohn.*

March 1832

Thursday 8 March. Dined at the duke de Choiseul's. To Mme. Rumford and Heine.

13 March. To Scribe.

17 March. At 10 to Scribe. To Hiller. *Le 6 avril MM Scribe & Dumas ont promis de livrer l'opéra.*[2]

18 March. To Humboldt, to Dumas. At 12 Humboldt fetched me to Taglioni's.[3] [Wrote] to Gouin concerning Bamberg*.

20 March. Yesterday I wrote to E. de Sauvage in Liège.[4]

23 March. At 3 to Pixérécourt (discussed Bamberg with Gouin, Pixérécourt, and Paganini).

28 March. Paganini came at 12. At 3 to Dumas. Today the outbreak of cholera has been officially confirmed.

30 March. At one o'clock to Dumas.

April/May 1832

Sunday 1 April. At 3 to Dumas.

Monday 2 April. At 3 to Dumas.

Friday 6 April. At 11 to Scribe and Dumas.[5]

Monday 16 April. Departed from Paris. At three o'clock in the afternoon I left for London accompanied by my English teacher, Hampton. A boring route. The only friendly, attractive town is Boulogne-sur-Mer. The town is almost entirely populated by English families who choose Boulogne to escape the expensive resorts in England, but to stay as close to home as possible. Many of them are fleeing debts, or are gamblers, so Hampton says. At midday we dined very well in the Hôtel du Nord, everything tasting all the better since we had traveled through the night of 16 April into the morning of the seventeenth. A few hours later we arrived in Calais, where we stayed the night.

Wednesday 18 April. We made the crossing by the English packet-steamer *The Courier* in three and a half hours under such calm conditions that one could have imagined oneself on a river. Consequently I experienced no seasickness this time, even though I am prone to it. I nonetheless suffered from giddiness for the duration of the voyage. In Dover I had to pay two pounds sterling in duty on my manuscripts, in spite of Hampton's acquaintance with one of the customs officers, a Mr. Ward. We lodged in The Ship, which is reputedly the best tavern, but was nothing special.

Thursday 19 April. We traveled to London by diligence (stage coach) in nine hours. A lovely route: blooming, friendly countryside. We arrived at eight o'clock.

Saturday 21 April. Conference with Albert and Grieve*. Drury Lane should lend its chorus. Whether a performance in French would be allowed. The illumination should be slow. Opening of the graves. The moonlight should be represented by gas lighting. Transformation of the gravestones into grassy banks, rose garlands, then eventually ghosts and demons. Fountain[6] that eventually flows blood. The grave-clothes should fall off during the bacchanal. Finally when Bertram sinks down the devil's ladder with black wings, the Archangel Gabriel and the flaming sword. The appearance of Robert's mother.

Sunday 23 April–Wednesday 2 May. Again and again I have forgone my resolution to record even in summary the daily events of my life in my diary. The problem is principally the unfortunate circumstances in which I find my theatrical affairs[7] here. The performances in Covent Garden and Drury Lane have discredited the music of *Robert* in such a way that no one has much hope for the production at the Italian Opera.[8] Even the reception I have experienced here, from artists and the world at large, has been rather cool. No one has taken any trouble on my behalf, the newspapers have ignored my arrival, etc. The only sign of recognition that I have experienced has been a letter from the Philharmonic Society, of which I am an honorary member; they offered me free admission[9] to their concerts. Also, when I attended a rehearsal at the Italian Opera, and Mason* presented me to the orchestra, they received me with lively applause.[10] When I went to a rehearsal for the Philharmonic Concert, however, no one lifted a finger.

Monk Mason, the manager of the Italian Opera, a good but crazy man who is close to bankruptcy, so they say, has prepared nothing; the choral rehearsals have not begun, even though the opera is to be given in twenty days. We all wish, for various reasons, that the opera could be given in French, but permission for this can be granted only by the lord chamberlain, who does not seem to want to give it. In short it is complete confusion.

I have seen the following operas at the Italian Opera: Rossini's *Elisabetta*, for the debut of Tosti (who enjoyed only a *succès d'estime*); Rossini's *Il Barbiere di Siviglia* for the début of Lablache and Mme. Cinti (the latter proved very popular). Act 1 of Donizetti's *L'Esule di Rome*[11] was interesting: thoroughly old-fashioned ideas, but with interesting treatment of form, and deviation from fixed procedures,[12] from stereotyped structures, with good declamation and dramatic conception, and lovely harmonies and instrumentation. The closing trio of act 1 is a splendid piece of music that deserves its fame. The duet between the prima donna and the tenor is novel in form (at least by the standards of Italian music). Mlle. Brugnoli* sparkled in the ballet; she is certainly the second most brilliant dancer in Europe, with only Taglioni surpassing her in grace.[13] Lamenzo is also excellent.

Of the English theaters, I have seen only Drury Lane. Here I attended a performance of the tragedy *William Tell*[14] by Sheridan Knowles*, currently the most famous of English playwrights, particularly because of his new drama *The Hunchback,*[15] which has achieved great fame in Covent Garden. Macready* as Tell pleases me very much.

I have so far heard a concert in the Italian Opera House for the benefit of the fund[16] for destitute artists. Even though more than twenty pieces were performed, I found nothing particularly outstanding. Braham and Miss [Elizabeth] Inverarity sang, the first an adagio with violoncello obbligato (with outstanding cantabile playing by Lindley*) from *Judas Maccabaeus* by Handel.[17] One cannot judge a singer on the grounds of this aria, since the voice serves merely as a foil for the cello. Miss Inverarity sang the aria from *Der Freischütz*.[18] She is famous for her lovely voice, but on this particular evening the voice seemed toneless to me, and her delivery decidedly mediocre. Harper's* wind band, which also played, is very good, even though the tone of the normal trumpet in England is dull and, I could even say, slimy, because the mouthpiece is too narrow and the shaft too long. The bugle (a low trumpet with stops) plays well, but the quality of the tone does not appeal to me. I also heard one of the famous Philharmonic Concerts, where the orchestra unites all talents. The performance of the symphonies was precise and powerful, the counterbasses quite simply the best I have ever heard in my life (the famous Dragonetti* plays with them). The other string instruments are also good, but the wind instruments only average. All the tempi were sluggish, and there was moreover an overall heaviness and want of grace.[19] They performed Haydn's Symphony in D [see example 39] with its charming andante in G,[20]

Example 39. First theme from Haydn's Symphony no. 104 in D Major

Beethoven's *Pastoral* Symphony,[21] Cherubini's overture to *Der Wasserträger* [*Les deux Journées*], and Spohr's overture to *Der Berggeist*.[22] The latter, while brilliant and well orchestrated, was generally unremarkable. The famous John Baptist Cramer played in a quintet of his own composition, but both work and performance were so unexceptional that I was disappointed.[23] I experienced a similar disappointment[24] in the previous concert when I heard the famous Field* who played one of his own concertos: both composition and playing could have embarrassed even a student.

I have dined only with Moscheles and Latour*.

Until 11 May. The choral rehearsals have unfortunately still not begun, even though Mason has engaged the excellent chorus master, Harris, from Drury Lane for the purpose.

I have dined at Madame Flemming's[25] (cousin of the Gants), at Dr. Billig's, and, finally, at a public engagement arranged to endow a fund[26] for destitute writers.[27] Nearly all the writers in London were there, as well as all the journalists and many artists etc., a gathering of about two hundred to three hundred people. Here I experienced English dining conventions for the first time. The president was the duke of Somerset, and one of the secretaries the famous traveler Sir John Malcolm*. Each table had its steward in a long red robe. There was applause[28] mixed with ugly whistling when the king's health was drunk, since Lord Grey* has just tendered his resignation.[29] Then the *Benedicite* was sung in four parts with piano accompaniment, followed by *God save the King* with drinks between each so-called toast. Every toast is proposed in the following way: a specially chosen servant called the "toastmaster" climbs on a stool behind the president after he has knocked on the table, and calls out, "Gentlemen, fill your glasses to the brim." The secretary then reads a speech to the company in praise of the sub-ject proposed for the toast.

Wednesday 23 May. At nine rehearsed with the count. Before ten the trio in act 5 with the harp. At ten with the whole orchestra. Communicated the changes in "Sonnez clairons"[30] to Mapelien. To Mapelien: has he has copied the organ part? At three o'clock to Moscheles. Mendelssohn. To Mason about the *Pas de Quatre*. With Harris tried the organ of Covent Garden.

Friday 25 May. [Wrote] to Dumas, Schlesinger. At nine sent for places in the steam-boat. At ten the rehearsal, which I asked Mme. Damoreau to attend. At four-thirty dined with the musicians. Letter from Moscheles for Hamburg.

Saturday 26 May. To Mason about the overture. Embarked[31] from London at one o'clock in the morning.

Thursday 31 May. Arrived in Berlin.

June 1832

Sunday 3 June. To Taglioni. At 9 to Blume. At 11 Schätzel.* At 12 to Lichten-stein* about the organ.

5 June. At 8 to Patschke, the copyist. At 5 a choral rehearsal.

6 June. At 9:30 choral rehearsal.

7 June. At 9:30 choral rehearsal. At 11 rehearsal with the singers. At 2 the décor.

11 June. Today *Robert* was performed at the Italian Opera in London.

12 June. To Count Redern about the thunderclaps, evening lighting, cloister décor, machinery, gas lighting.

13 June. Lengthen the ritornello preceding the chorus "Accourez peuple fidèle."[32] Arrange[33] the abridgment[34] in the *Pas de Cinq* and the entr'acte to act 4.

17 June. Night, thunder, flames, chain-rattling, Bengal fire. [Test] the raising of the curtain in front of the church in act 5. [Arrange] a step for the two harps.

20 June. First performance in Berlin of *Robert der Teufel*.[35]

21 June. [Arranged] the recitatives in act 1, the recitative after Isabelle's aria in act 2, for the chorus to lead into the finale, the recitative in act 3 after the trio, a third reduction in the ballet, the entr'acte to act 5.

23 June. [Rehearsed] the chorus of demons under the stage.

24 June. A better bell. Fewer speaking trumpets under the stage. More Bengal fire. To Beutler* about the payment[36] of the chorus,[37] and strengthened the trumpets in the stage music in act 2.

July/August/September 1832.

1 July. Left Berlin.

7 July. Arrived in Baden-Baden. Minna.[38]

16 July. Departure from Baden-Baden.

23 July. Arrival in Bad Ems.

1 August. Arrival in Schwalbach.[39]

5 August. Began the corrections today (five pages).[40]

10 August. Today Minna finished her cure in Baden-Baden.

11 August. Minna arrived in Schwalbach to consult the doctors here.[41]

12 August. Minna left for Bad Ems.

13 August. Today I sent off the corrections of act 1 to Schlesinger.

18 August. Long letter to Schlesinger. Sent him act 2.

21 August. Saw Minna in Bad Ems.

22 August. Today Minna's cure ends. Today I sent off all the supplements to Schlesinger with an appended letter.

25 August. To Schlesinger, that he should send the answer to Mainz.

27 August. Today I sent off acts 4 and 5 to Schlesinger.

28 August. [Wrote] to Schlesinger and Michael, enclosing Scribe's letter.

2 September. Today act 3 was sent to Schlesinger from Frankfurt.

3 September. Left Frankfurt.

7 September. Arrived in Paris in the evening.[42]

October 1832.

Monday 1 October. Heine.[43]

2 October. To Fétis about old French music and the *traité du contrepoint.*

7 October. With Heine to the Café de Paris.

8 October. To Heine.

9 October. Contract[44] with Véron.[45]

11 October. French Bible from Leo.[46]

16 October. To Cherubini.

19 October. To Heine concerning Bohain*.

21 October. To Bohain (letter for Heine).

27 October. Dumas came at 11. Contract with Dumas.

November 1832

   Arrived in Frankfurt on 6 November. The *Crociato* has been given in Berlin at the Königstädter-Theater, where it apparently has caused a furore. Madame Kraus-Wranitsky starred as Palmide. In the space of a month it was given nine times, having come to the stage on 15 October. Traveled to Mainz in order to make the acquaintance of the composer Panny* from Vienna who was giving a concert. I traveled incognito but was recognized—how, I just do not know. Consequently, Kapellmeister Ganz*, Zulehner* and several others came to greet me, and I made myself known to Panny. He appeared to be very pleased and told me that he had seen me in Trieste together with Paganini when the *Crociato* was produced there. His compositions are very original and striking.[47] They are actually large choral songs with codas, but they are something of a new type and conception. But all the compositions are in this form and consequently strike one as very similar. I heard (1) a new table song,[48] (2) "Herbstfahrt auf dem Rhein,"[49] (3)"Fischer-Chor,"[50] (4) "Die Dampfschiffahrt auf dem Rhein" newly composed for this concert, (5) "Der junge Fischer," a Russian romance,[51] (6) "Wikingerbalk" (a fragment from the Frithjof Saga). "Die Herbstfahrt" and "Wikingerbalk" are the most interesting.

In the Museo in Frankfurt I heard a new descriptive symphony by Spohr that purports to express the emotions that he felt on reading the poem "Die Weihe der Töne" by Pfeiffer. It was preceded by a lecture on Spohr's characteristics and achievements, in which reference was made to all the composers of the last hundred years who have achieved any distinction; even Ries and Moscheles were among them, but my name was not mentioned, even though everyone knew I was present. The symphony[52] itself was divided by Spohr into the following four movements: (1) *Largo.* The stubborn silence of nature before the creation of sound. *Allegro.* Vigorous life after the latter. The sounds of nature (birdsong, etc.). Tumult of the elements. (2) Lullaby, dance, serenade. (All three of these different themes are counterpointed, although only two emerge clearly.[53] The third quite disappears and I could not recognize it when the three came together.) (3) Battle music. Departure for war. Feelings of those left behind. Return of the conquerors. Prayer of thanksgiving (which has the *Te Deum laudamus* as cantus firmus).[54] (4) Funeral music (which features[55] the chorale "Begrabet den Leib"). Comfort in sound.

Attended the Cäcilien-Verein founded by my friend Schelbe in the manner of[56] of the Berliner-Singakademie. In my honor he performed Mendelssohn's "Ave Maria," a motet for eight voices;[57] "Treu und sanft," also by Mendelssohn; a wonderful motet with instrumental accompaniment by J. S. Bach, "Gottes Zeit ist die allerbeste Zeit";[58] the *Gloria* and *Crucifixus* from J. S. Bach's big Mass [in B minor],[59] and another two of his motets, the better known of which is "Fürchte dich nicht";[60] also an agreeably effective choral song by Schnyder von Wartensee*.

Earlier I also attended a concert by Moscheles. He played his latest Concerto in C major, a thoughtful, well-developed and strikingly scored composition lacking only life and impetus. His playing, correct and elegant, was similarly cold. He then played a fantasy on two Irish national melodies, also charmingly composed, scored and performed. The two themes were very delicately counterpointed one against the other. In conclusion he performed a free fantasia on the *Andante* [= *Allegreto*] from Beethoven's Symphony [no. 7] in A major and "Escouto de Jeannetto" from *Die beiden Savoyarden* by Dalayrac. Here he also fused the two themes.

This November *Robert le Diable* was performed with great success[61] in Toulouse (at least according to *La Gazette du Théâtre*). Productions of this work with other singers in Rouen[62] and Liège have also turned out brilliantly. Finally

Robert was also given in Hamburg on 20 November.[63] According to letters from Heinrich and Wilhelm (since I do not yet have newspapers) it went down extraordinarily well. From the *Hamburger Correspondenten* I see that it was given four times in ten days. Moritz Schlesinger writes that *Robert* has also had great success in Poitiers.

December 1832

Frankfurt. Visited the writer Hofrat Döring*. The singer Schmetzer brought the young nineteen-year-old Vollweiler* to meet me. I knew his father many years ago. The young man has composed several very expressive songs in Schubert's* style.

On Wednesday 5 December I again attended the Cäcilien-Verein. In my honor, they performed the Gradual from Vogler's last Mass (composed in 1811), a simple, lyrical theme richly and wonderfully harmonized and developed. Then came the chorus from Handel's *Israel in Egypt*,[64] which is treated like a recitative: "Schwarze Nacht ist rings umher,"[65] a bold and marvelously executed idea. Bach is also supposed to have composed a fugue in this way. Afterwards came further pieces by Handel from *Samson*[66] and *Messiah*.[67]

On 6 December we dined with our Prussian ambassador, Nagler*. There I met the well-known journalist Durand, who formerly edited[68] *Le Journal de la Haye* and now *Le Journal de Francfort*. He appears to be a great partisan of my *Margherita d'Anjou*, and told me that *Margherita* is to be given in the French Theatre in The Hague on this very day.

Kapellmeister Guhr was with me today. In spite of my reasons against it, he is determined to perform *Robert* in concert on Christmas Eve. So I played him the first two acts regarding the tempi and other details.[69] Tomorrow I will go through the last three acts with him.

Hofrat Küstner* from Darmstadt, formerly a theater director in Leipzig, also called on me.

Today I received news from Gouin about the most recent performance of *Robert* in Paris (the fifty-fifth). On 2 December *Robert* was performed on a Sunday for the first time; the receipts were 7613 fr.

Review of the year 1832. We spent the winter in Frankfurt-am-Main. Since Kapellmeister Guhr was determined to perform *Robert* on 25 December in Frankfurt, completely against my wishes, and I did not want to attend it because I thought it would turn out badly, I went to Baden-Baden for ten days. However, the reports were good, and the reception favorable. A very positive review by Wilhelm Speyer* appeared in the *Didaskalia*, and a negative one by Hofrat Rousseau in the *Oberpostamtszeitung*, even though he does acknowledge the enthusiasm of the public and praises details.

In Karlsruhe I made the acquaintance of the theater intendant, Count Leiningen*, and Kapellmeister Joseph Strauss. Moritz Schlesinger writes that *Robert le Diable* has caused a furore in Dijon, and has been given with success in Poitiers, Nancy, and Metz. It is being rehearsed in Le Havre, Brest, and Marseilles. The Opéra in Paris ended 1832 (on 31 December) with the sixty-first performance of *Robert*. On the other hand, the opera found no favor in Weimar: by the third performance the house was apparently empty. The reviews in the *Leipziger musikalische Zeitung* and the *Zeitung für die elegante Welt* were written with such bitterness that, without fear of author's vanity, I must presume personal animosity on the part of the critics.

NOTES

1. Tgb. *graveur.*
2. "Scribe and Dumas have promised to deliver the opera on April 6." This was to be the abortive *Les Brigands.*
3. Filippo Taglioni was about to travel to Berlin with his daughter to assist at the première of *Robert le Diable* in the Prussian capital.
4. *Robert le Diable* was performed in Liège on 26 March with Mme. Ponchard (Isabelle). The décor and costumes were copied from the Opéra. In this Meyerbeer was fulfilling a promise made to the Cercle Grétry.
5. Meyerbeer, Scribe, and Dumas had regular meetings about the new libretto until 16 April.
6. Tgb. *fontaine.*
7. Tgb. *affaires.*
8. At the Haymarket Theatre.
9. Tgb. *entrée.*
10. Tgb. *applaudissement.*
11. Opera in two acts (D. Gilardoni, after Marchioni, based on the play by Caigniez and Debotière; Naples, San Carlo, 2 January 1828).
12. Tgb. *procédé fixe.*
13. Tgb. *grazie.*
14. London, 1825.
15. London, 1832.
16. Tgb. *fonds.*
17. Oratorio HWV 63 (words by Morell, after the Bible; London, 1 April 1747).
18. Presumably no. 11, "Leise, leise, fromme Weise."
19. Tgb. *grazie.*
20. Symphony no. 104 *(The London).*
21. No. 6 in F major, op. 68 (1808).
22. Opera in three acts (G. Döring; Cassel, 24 March 1825).
23. Tgb. *désappointiert.*
24. Tgb. *désappointement.*
25. The family Flemming belonged to Moscheles's circle of friends. They owned a country estate in Hampshire. (See *Aus Moscheles Leben, Hrsg. von seiner Frau*, 2 vols. [Leipzig: Dunker & Humbolt, 1872–73], 2:34.)

26. Tgb. *fonds*.

27. Tgb. *Littoraten*.

28. Tgb. *applaudissement*.

29. The Whig cabinet of 1830 tried for Parliamentary reform, which led to a crisis and Grey's retirement. He nonetheless became prime minister again in May 1832 and was able to carry through his reforms.

30. No. 8a, the opening chorus of the act 2 finale.

31. Tgb. *embarquiert*.

32. No. 6, *Choeur dansé* ("Accourez au devant elle").

33. Tgb. *arrangieren*.

34. Tgb. *coupure*.

35. The translation was by Theodore Hell and Meyerbeer himself conduced. He was called out to great ovation after act 3. In act 2 Marie Taglioni, in Sicilian costume, performed a *pas* especially arranged by her father.

36. Tgb. *gratification*.

37. The situation of the choristers at the Royal Opera in Berlin was extraordinarily bad, their monthly salary being only twelve thalers (cf. *BT,* 2:628). Meyerbeer was to concern himself greatly about the professional conditions of musicians in Berlin during his time as *Generalmusikdirektor*.

38. A letter from Scribe in Montalais dated 7 July 1832 contains mention of Meyerbeer's work on an adaptation of Scribe's play *Le Bachelier de Salamanque* (vaudeville written with H. Dupin and G. Delavigne in 1815) (see entry for 8 July 1815) (*BT,* 1:645, 2:205–6). The same letter makes the first mention of *Les Huguenots* ("[J]e ne vous parle de 'Huguenots' parce que probablement vous vous entendiez avec Véron . . .") [I will not speak to you about the 'Huguenots,' because you probably agree with Véron . . .].

39. On 1 August *Robert le Diable* was first performed in Strasbourg. On 11 August Wilhelm and Michael Beer traveled from Baden to attend a performance.

40. This was of the printed proofs of the score.

41. On 11 August 1832 King Friedrich Wilhelm III named Meyerbeer Prussian *Hofkapellmeister* (*BT,* 2:208).

42. On 18 September 1832 Meyerbeer wrote to Minna describing developments with Véron, and his first sight of *Les Huguenots*: "Nothing can come of the *Portefaix* because Véron will not give up on the five-act format, and Scribe can find no way of expanding the work without spoiling it. The day after tomorrow he is going to bring me the plan for a new five-act opera" (*BT,* 2:222). The result was a contract between Véron and Scribe, in which Scribe agreed to provide the libretto for a five-act opera entitled *Leonore* within two months (*BT,* 2:225–26).

43. Heine had published a political article in the *Augsburger allgemeine Zeitung* (13 April 1832) in which he reported on the success of *Robert le Diable*.

44. Tk. *traité*.

45. The contract with Véron was for *La Saint Barthélémy,* which would become *Les Huguenots*. It was signed on 23 October 1832, and stipulated a terminus of 15 December 1833, in default of which the composer would pay a fine of 30,000 fr. This huge drama was tangentially adapted by Scribe from Prosper Mérimée's *Chronique de Charles IX*.

46. Meyerbeer's visits to Fétis and Leo reveal his enthusiasm for the new libretto, with its underlying Reformation theme. This necessitated a deepening of his own perceptions of the subject. Indeed, a comparison of Scribe's adaptation of Mérimée (Scribe, *Œuvres complètes*, vol. 3, série 3 [Paris, 1874–85]) with the final form of the libretto "shows that

most of the vivid details, gleaned from every available document related to the time, were the composer's contribution to *Les Huguenots*" (Kathleen O'Donnell Hoover, "Meyerbeer," in *Makers of Opera* [Port Washington, N.Y., and London: Kennikat Press, 1971], p. 104).

47. Tgb. *frappant.*

48. Op. 37.

49. Op. 32.

50. Op. 30.

51. Op. 29.

52. Symphony no. 3 in C minor *(Die Weihe der Töne),* op. 78 (1828).

53. Tgb. *detachieren sich.*

54. This idea was not lost on Meyerbeer, and occurs in the act 1 finale of *Les Hugue-nots*, sung by Marcel under the quicksilver commentary of the guests at Nevers's party, who marvel at Raoul's call to Queen Marguerite de Valois.

55. Tgb. *figuriert.*

56. Tgb. *à l'instar.*

57. Op. 23, no. 2.

58. Cantata no. 106.

59. BWV 232 (1733).

60. No. 4.

61. Tgb. *succès.*

62. This took place in April 1832.

63. The opera was given in Dublin on 26 November 1832.

64. Oratorio HWV 54 (words from the Book of Exodus) (London, 4 April 1739).

65. No. 11, Chorus ("He sent a thick darkness").

66. Oratorio HWV 57 (words by Newburgh Hamilton, after Milton's *Samson Agonistes* [1671]; London, 18 February 1743).

67. See September 1818.

68. Tgb. *redigiert.*

69. Tgb. *details.*

Section 3
1833–1834

1833

[Undated entry.]

My will. Am I yet able to dispose of my grandpaternal inheritance? Should my wife and child later predecease me, would I then have natural heirs, and if so, who? Would I be obliged to allow them a share, and if so, how much? Should my wife marry again in the event of my death, do I have the right to instruct that my child be educated away from home? And if not, what is she entitled to claim by Prussian law and our marriage rights? Do I have the right to leave my wife only the interest from the capital due to her, or does she have the right to demand the capital itself? When there are children, how does one usually determine the proportion of parts between mother and children? I think a third should go to the mother if there are several children, and a half to her if there is only one, but on the condition that, in the event of a second marriage, she should consent to entrust the children to guardians outside the home. (Would she have to sign it jointly with me?) I further think that in such circumstances she should lose the right to her half or third, and that the capital should pass to my child or children after my death. Should my children die without attaining their majority, or having descendants of their own, my wife should enjoy the interest of my entire fortune, even in the event of a second marriage. However, after her death the capital should pass to my brothers or their heirs. A codicil should suffice to determine how the capital should be managed and safely invested during my wife's life. I have to decide how this is to be drafted in a foreign country.

January 1833

Schnyder von Wartensee, a Swiss, a learned theoretician, a fine composer of songs and composer of the operas *Fortunat* and *Estelle* (the latter has not yet been published); Wilhelm Speyer, a dilettante violinist, composer, writer, pupil of Spohr and André*; Rosenhain* from Mannheim, a young pianist and composer; Curländer, a Dane, and pupil of Aloys Schmitt: all are acquaintances I have made here, as is the popular novelist Legationsrat Döring. Called on the revitalized Aloys Schmitt, a composer and pianist; Schelbe, the director of the Cäcilien-Verein; Kapellmeister Guhr; Theater Intendant Grüner; Regisseur Ehlers; and our Ambassador von Nagler*, inter alia.

At the Cäcilien-Verein I attended a public concert of Handel's glorious *Samson*. I am always deeply moved by Samson's aria "Nacht ist umher,"[1] the six-part chorus ("Jehovah"),[2] and so many other wonderful pieces. This was preceded by Mozart's Symphony in D major, that of the two in D which is heard less frequently than the other.[3]

In the theater I was delighted by Dittersdorf's *Das rote Käppchen*,[4] which I heard for the first time, especially by the naïveté and intelligence of his melodies and striking comic declamation. My particular favorites are the introduction, the two arias for Hans Christoph, and the first finale.

March 1833[5]

6 March. Wrote an arietta, "Soave instante," for Giovanni Battista Rubini.[6] [*Tk*] [On the autograph is the inscription: *All Eco abbellito di Rubini; all Usignolo del Nord; alla soave speranza; Omaggio di Giacomo Meyerbeer Francoforte 6 Marzo 33.*][7]

Friday 22 March. Today my beloved brother Michael died in Munich. [*Tk*]

At the beginning of March we went to Baden. Here it was that I received a dispatch[8] that my beloved brother Michael had become ill in Munich with a nervous fever. I could not decide, without further urgency, to leave my wife and child Blanca alone, and therefore answered likewise by dispatch[9] to Bellile that he should notify me if the illness should take a turn for the worse, because I would then leave my wife and child to hurry to Michael. The answer came (again by dispatch) that the situation was indeed very serious. I left for Munich on the same day (Friday, 22 March), traveling by day and night. By the time I arrived, my noble, wonderful brother was already dead and buried. (He died on 22 March.) Had I not waited for the second despatch, I would have arrived one or two days before his death, and, should he have had any moments of consciousness, he would have had the joy of seeing his brother. Eternal reproach on me, for whom he did so much in his life. Agitated thoughts troubled me on the return journey, and I could not shake myself free of them. I met both my other brothers there, who had also traveled from Berlin and also arrived too late. I received a moving letter from Amadée Prévôt.

I returned to Baden on 30 March. Here I received the news from Speyer and Beurmann* of the brilliant success of *Robert* in Frankfurt-am-Main (first performance on 30 March). A few days later I received a letter from my brother Wilhelm in Berlin, describing our dear mother's tremendous grief over the loss of Michael, and asking me to come to Berlin to comfort her. I had De Saules von Neuchâtel come to keep Minna company, and set out via Karlsruhe, Frankfurt, etc., in spite of my antipathy to Fridays. I left for Berlin today (Saturday, 6 April) [and arrived there on Friday, 12 April].

June 1833

9 June. Searched for the music of *Die drei Pintos*. Called on Schadow and Schulze*. Wrote to Schadow. [Arranged] the modulation to E-flat for Mme. Grünbaum in the romance [in act 1 of *Robert le Diable*].[10]

20 June. Left Berlin today.

21 June. Arrived in Dresden. To Hofrat Winkler. In order to return the original sketches of *Die drei Pintos* [to Hofrat Winkler], I received copies in their place. Had the copyist check[11] that both tally, and prepared a letter of testimony. [Arranged] the changes in the Scene of the Nuns for Dresden, the times of the productions of *Robert* in Dresden and the casting. Scored Meyer's *ranz de vaches*. [Acquired] the vocal scores of *Colombo*[12] and *Rinnegato*,[13] yearbook of the German theater.

28 June. Today I met with Minna in Frankfurt.

30 June. Arrived in Wiesbaden. The *Crociato* [has been produced] in Florence and Dettmold, *Robert* in Vienna (20 June)[14] and Strasbourg (by the Augsburg Society).

July 1833.

Monday 1 July. Michael's manuscripts to Schenk. *Die drei Pintos.*

2 July. From today I rented quarters[15] in Schwalbach for three weeks (at nineteen gulden per week) at Die Beiden Indien.[16] Arrived in Ems.

4 July. Returned to Schwalbach this evening.

Monday 15 July. Celebrated my daughter Blanca's birthday in Ems.

Wednesday 17 July. In Wiesbaden heard Maurer's* *Aloysia*.[17]

19 July. [Wrote] to Speyer, enclosing the music.

30 July. Traveled to Ems.

August 1833

Tuesday 6 August. Today I visited Mother in Mainz. [Wrote] to Gouin, Winkler, Küstner, Gottfried Weber.

7 August. To Frankfurt to hear *Robert*.

8 August. This evening Maurice Schlesinger traveled to Paris from Mainz.

9 August. At midday I sent off the letters for Véron and Gouin (care of Schlesinger) from Mainz. [Wrote] to Heinrich, Minna, Winkler.

10 August. [Wrote] to Küstner.

11 August. Departed from Schwalbach.

13 August. In Darmstadt reconciliation with Gottfried Weber.

18 August. Received the first intimation from Schlesinger in Paris. [Wrote] to Schlesinger in Paris that he should answer positively.

23 August. [Wrote] to Gottfried Weber and Wilhelm from Karlsruhe. Arrived in Frankfurt today.

24 August. To Küstner with the *mise en scène*.

25 August. To Count Leiningen with the production-[*mise en scène*] book. Left for Mainz at six o'clock this evening.

29 August. Arrived in Paris at nine o'clock this evening.

[On 31 August *Robert le Diable* was performed in German at the Kärntnertor-Theater in Vienna.]

September 1833

Sunday 1 September. [Wrote] to Minna.

3 September. To Véron. At 11 to Bertin. At 12 to Scribe with the music.

11 September. Left Paris today.

12 September. Arrived in Dieppe.

13 September. [Wrote] to Schlesinger, Gouin, Scribe, that he should alter the trio in act 2 and the entry of the Page[18] in the finale [of *Les Huguenots*].

16 September. Returned to Paris this evening.

17 September. [Looked at] my *Canzonette* and the French romance "Charme de la vie (écho)" from the *Dictionnaire d'Amour*.

26 September. Herr Hiller came at 11.

27 September. To Victor Hugo between 10 and 11.

October/November 1833.

Tuesday 1 October. Today I left Paris.

3 October. Arrived in Baden this evening.

10 October. To Küstner. Today I heard *Robert le Diable* in Karlsruhe.[19]

14 October. In Karlsruhe. [Bought] Bach's chorales and André's book.[20]

17 October. To Theodor Hell.

20 October. Left Baden today.

21 October. Arrived in Basel late this evening.

25 October. Arrived in Lausanne at three o'clock.

27 October. Left Lausanne at twelve o'clock today. Stayed overnight[21] in Martigny.

28 October. Stayed overnight in Brig. [Wrote] to Gouin.

[On 28 October *Robert le Diable* was given in Danish in Copenhagen.]

29 October. Today passed through the Simplon. Stayed overnight at Domodollola.

30 October. Arrived late this evening in Milan. The libretto of *Il Furioso.*[22] Tosi, Artaria, Basily, Ricordi, Lichtenthal, Cernuschi, Mozart, libretti by Romani and others.

31 October. Checked on when the diligence to Verona arrives and departs. To Rossi.[23]

[In November Meyerbeer began a sojourn in Nice that lasted until early March 1834.]

Thursday 28 November. Today eight years ago (1825) at two o'clock I solemnized my marriage with my beloved Minna.

[On 15 December the contracted deadline for the completion of *Les Huguenots* passed without Meyerbeer's having finished the score. Véron demanded payment of the 30,000 fr. indemnity specified in the agreement, with 10,000 fr. to go to Scribe.][24]

1834

[On 25 January *Robert le Diable* was produced in Dresden. By 13 March Meyerbeer had left Nice and was in Milan[25] until late April 1834,[26] then in Florence from late April to early May. A letter of 14 May 1834 is written from Milan, but indicates (by directions for a *poste restante* in Baden-Baden) that he had returned to Germany.[27] Subsequently both Giacomo and Minna undertook water cures, he in Schwalbach and she in Bad Ems. On 2 July he wrote to Scribe from Baden informing him of his decision to abandon *Le Portefaix.*[28] On 24 July 1834 he attended a theatrical performance in Wiesbaden, and left Schwalbach only on Thursday 28 August 1834.[29] He traveled via Saarbrücken and was in Paris by the end of August. By 20 September he was in Boulogne, but back in Paris by the end of the month. On 29 October he was the witness at the marriage of Martial Célerier and Mlle. Gouin, daughter of his confidant, in the Église Saint-Eustache.]

November/December 1834

Saturday 1 November. At 12 Saint-Georges. At 11:30 to Scribe in Montalais. Dined with Deschamps.[30] *Droits d'auteur* from *Robert.* Middle tempo in the duet in act 4 [of *Les Huguenots*].[31]

7 November. At 6 Scribe came. Prepared the work for Émile [Deschamps].

8 November. Rehearsal of the Berlioz* concert. At 4 Émile Deschamps.

9 November. To Scribe. At 12 to Émile Deschamps.

10 November. At 10:30 to Émile Deschamps.

11 November. At 3 Émile Deschamps came.

12 November. At 10:30 Émile Deschamps came.

17 November. At 3:30 Émile Deschamps came. Dinner at the Prussian ambassador's.

18 November. List of the cities for Fétis.[32] At 2 to Émile Deschamps.

19 November. Fétis came at 9. Between 2 and 4 Émile Deschamps. Title for "Le Moine."[33]

22 November. Rehearsal of the Berlioz concert.

23 November. [Émile] Pacini at 11.

24 November. Stöpel* at 10.

25 November. At 11 Heine.

28 November. At 2:30 to Deschamps.

29 November. At 11 with Heine to Armand [Bertin]. Dined with Véron.[34]

30 November. At 12 to Damoreau with "La Mère Grand" and "Le Moine". At 4 to Émile Deschamps.

25 December. Left Paris.

[On 26 December *Robert le Diable* was given in Russian at St. Petersburg.]

30 December. Arrival in Baden.

[Undated entry.]
    Abréger la scène de Marcel,[35] *mettre sous la musique la poesie de l'introduction ou entre Marcel. Couper les recitatifs du 2e acte (en respectant le page), l'air de Mme Damoreau.*[36]
    Johann Sebastian Bach's cantata *Ein feste Burg ist unser Gott* for four voices

with orchestral accompaniment:[37] score from Breitkopf & Härtel; information on chorales with rules and examples for the correct performance of altar songs, etc., by Wilhelm Schneider* (Leipzig, Theodor Hennigs); *Die musikalische Liturgie* by Rohleder* (Glogau, 1831); *Graduel et Antiphonaire Parisien.*[38]

Notes

1. No. 13, Recitative ("Oh loss of sight!") and no. 14, Aria ("Total eclipse! no sun, no moon").

2. No. 26, Chorus ("Then shall thy know, that he whose name / Jehovah is alone").

3. No. 38, K. 504 *(Prague)* (without the minuet).

4. Opera in three acts (text by the composer, after Livigni's *Giannina e Bernadone* [1781]; Breslau, 26 May 1790). Frequently revived in Germany throughout the nineteenth century (Dessau, 1899).

5. During March 1833 *Robert le Diable* was produced in Geneva and Nîmes.

6. Unpublished.

7. "To Rubini's beautified echo; to the Nightingale of the North; to sweet hope; homage from Giacomo Meyerbeer, Frankfurt, 6 March 1833."

8. Tgb. *estafette.*

9. Tgb. *per estafette.*

10. The key of no. 3, "Va! dit elle," is E major.

11. Tgb. *collationieren.*

12. *Colombo, melodrama seria* in two acts by Morlacchi (Felice Romani; Genoa Carlo Felice, 21 June 1828).

13. Originally *I Saraceni in Sicilia, ovvero Eufemio di Messino, melodramma seria* in two acts by Morlacchi (Felice Romani; Venice, La Fenice, 28 February, 1828). It was called *Il Rinnegato* for the Dresden performance (Court Opera, 1832).

14. In German at the Josephstädter-Theater.

15. Tgb. *quartier.*

16. "The Two Indians."

17. *Aloysia, oder Aloise,* opera in two acts by Ludwig Maurer (Franz Ignaz von Holbein, after the novella by E. Wodomerius; Hanover, 16 January 1828), the most successful opera by the famous violinist.

18. Tgb. *entrée des pagen.*

19. On 28 October *Robert le Diable* was also produced in Brussels.

20. Johann Anton André wrote two volumes on harmony, counterpoint, canon, and fugue, entitled *Lehrbuch der Tonsetzkunst* (1832–43). Meyerbeer presumably bought the first of these volumes. Both purchases were part of the preparation process for the composition of *Les Huguenots.*

21. Tgb. *Nachtquartier.*

22. *Il Furioso all'isola di San Domingo, melodramma semiseria* in two acts by Donizetti (Jacopo Ferretti, after Cervantes; Rome, 1833).

23. During this visit to Italy Meyerbeer sought Rossi's secret help in redrafting Marcel's role in *Les Huguenots.* See Heinz Becker, "Meyerbeers Mitarbeit an den Libretti seiner Opern," in *Kongress-Bericht Bonn, 1970* (Cassel: Bärenreiter, 1973), pp. 155–60. He also heard a performance of Bellini's *Norma* that impressed him greatly, especially the

chorus "Guerra! Guerra!" in act 2, and served as an inspiration for the famous Blessing of the Daggers in act 4 of *Les Huguenots*.

24. Meyerbeer paid the fine, but was so angered that he resolved never to allow Véron to produce his work.

25. *BT,* 2:367.

26. On 7 April 1834 *Robert le Diable* was performed in Budapest for the first time, and on 20 April had its one hundredth performance at the Paris Opéra.

27. *BT,* 2:375.

28. After a silence of several years, Meyerbeer wanted to return to the theater with a *grand opéra* like *Les Huguenots*. It further seemed to him that there was no tenor in the troupe of the Opéra Comique capable of assuming the principal role as he envisaged it. (*BT,* 2:377–78). Scribe passed the libretto of *Le Portefaix* on to Gomis: it became the latter's most successful work (Paris, Opéra Comique, 16 June 1835).

29. *BT,* 2:385.

30. Émile Deschamps, the poet, had become a friend of the composer. He was deeply impressed by *Robert le Diable*: for him it put Meyerbeer in the same relationship to French romantic music as Delacroix to painting and Hugo to literature. See Henri Girard, *Émile Deschamps, dilettante* (Paris: Librairie Ancienne Honoré Champion, 1921), p. 56.

31. Meyerbeer turned to Deschamps for the additions to the duet which he wanted on Adolphe Nourrit's suggestion. Scribe, who often used collaborators, was happy for Deschamps to provide the extra verses and the modifications Meyerbeer always requested. During 1834 Scribe was also working with Halévy on *La Juive* and had little time to make minor changes in his libretti. The projected modifications to act 4 were discussed at length by Meyerbeer, Nourrit, and Deschamps before the actual text was written. The poet did not rewrite the entire act 4, but made revisions and additions to Scribe's text. He himself listed his work on the opera in a copy of the *Huguenots* libretto preserved among his papers:

    1. The entire role of Marcel throughout the opera [a translation of Rossi's words?].

    2. The Page's aria in act 1.

    3. Valentine's romance in act 4.

    4. The grand love duet that ends act 4.

    5. Raoul's aria during the ball in act 5.

    6. The grand trio in act 5.

He was also responsible for the elimination of the role of Catherine de Medici from act 4. See Girard, *Émile Deschamps, dilettante,* pp. 62-63. For a thorough analysis of the genesis of the opera and background to the libretto, see Karin Pendle, "The Technique of Grand Opera and the Transformation of Literary Models: Meyerbeer's *Les Huguenots,*" in *Eugène Scribe and French Opera of the Nineteenth Century* (Ann Arbor, Mich.: UMI Research Press, 1979), pp. 465-93.

32. Meyerbeer provided a list of the cities where *Robert le Diable* had been produced in the first two years of its history. This was later published in the *Revue musicale,* 1834, p. 372. *France:* Paris, Bordeaux (47 times), Marseilles (51), Toulouse (54), Lyons (32), Rouen, Nantes (27), Lille, Strasbourg, Brest (19), Metz, Nancy, Le Havre (21), Grenoble, Nîmes, Angoulême, Châlons-sur-Marnes, Bourg, Macon, Clermont, Amiens (14), Dijons (25), Poitiers, Angers, Douai, Clermont-Ferrand, Besançon, Avignon, Perpignan, Montpellier, Valenciennes, Bourges, Laval, Autun, Boulogne-sur-Mer, Montauban, Aix, Moulins, Gras. *German lands:* Vienna, Berlin, Munich Dresden, Hamburg, Cologne, Frankfurt-am-Main, Frankfurt-an-der-Oder, Weimar, Mainz, Wiesbaden, Hanover, Breslau, Glogau, Liegnitz,

Brunswick, Leipzig, Bremen, Stuttgart, Württemberg, Cassel, Freiburg, Lippe-Detmold. There were *further productions* in England, Belgium, Holland, Denmark, Hungary, Switzerland, and Russia. This comes to thirty-nine cities in France, twenty-three cities in the German-speaking lands, and seven other countries, a total of sixty-nine different theaters. The list can be further expanded chronologically: 1832 (London, Liège, Berlin, Strasbourg, Dublin), 1833 (Antwerp, Vienna), 1834 (New York, Budapest, Pressburg, St. Petersburg, The Hague), 1835 (Prague, Bucharest), 1836 (Basel, Calcutta, Laibach), 1837 (Warsaw), 1838 (Lisbon), 1839 (Stockholm), 1840 (New Orleans). Within eight years the opera had been performed in a total of 1,843 European theaters. The 1840s saw it triumph in Italy: Florence (1841, 1842, 1843), Padua (1842, 1844, 1845), Trieste (1842, 1844), Brescia (1843), Cremona (1843, 1844), Livorno (1843), Venice (1843, 1845), Milan (1844, 1846), Rome (1844), Verona (1844), Bassano (1845), Turin (1846), Bologna (1847) (thirteen cities in all).

33. Text by Émile Pacini (1834), no. 8 in the *Quarante Mélodies*. This dramatic monologue of a Capuchin friar's spiritual struggle became one of Meyerbeer's most famous songs. Liszt made a piano transcription of it (S. 416, 1841).

34. Perhaps the visit was an attempt at reconciliation. On 29 November Meyerbeer returned to Botté de Toulmont*, the librarian of the Conservatoire, a book borrowed from Philidor's collection "contenant des airs d'anciens ballets," suggesting his research of the atmosphere and style of old France (*BT,* 2:420).

35. Marcel's big act 3 monologue was omitted.

36. "Shorten Marcel's scene, position the words of the first scene where Marcel enters, under the music [suggesting a translation of Rossi's Italian text]. Cut the recitative in act 2 (belonging to the Page), Mme. Damoreau's aria."

37. Cantata no. 80 (1730). The chorale tune is used in various forms throughout the opera as a leitmotif of the Protestant cause.

38. Meyerbeer obviously made a careful study of sixteenth-century Huguenot musical and liturgical practice.

Section 4
1835

1835

January 1835

Wednesday 7 January. [Wrote] to Gouin and Maurice Schlesinger.

11 January. [Wrote] to Heine, rue des Augustins no. 4, Hôtel d'Espagne, to Gouin.

13 January. [Wrote] to Moritz Schlesinger.

15 January. Today I sent off the romances and a letter to Mother.

19 January. [Wrote] to Gouin and Schlesinger.

22 January. [Wrote] to Gouin.

25 January. [Wrote] to Gouin and Edmond Blanc.

28 January. [Wrote] to Gouin about the nomination[1] and *I Puritani*.[2]

29 January. [Wrote] to Schlesinger (about *I Puritani*, Saint-Georges, Bertin, "Le Moine"). To Speyer.

February 1835

Thursday 12 February. Traveled to Karlsruhe to hear *Fidelio*.

14 February. My beloved mother's sixty-eighth birthday.

4 March. [Wrote] to Gouin, Deschamps, Dumas.

April 1835

Thursday 23 April. Left Baden this evening. [Wrote] to Castelli, to Breitkopf.

24 April. Sent the letters to Schott and Beurmann from Strasbourg, care of Minna.

25 April. From Nancy [wrote] to Wilhelm about Beurmann.

27 April. Arrived in Paris this morning.

May 1835

Friday 1 May. Note to Duponchel.

2 May. At 10 to Scribe, to Véron and Duponchel.

3 May. At 11 to Cerfberr.

4 May. De 3 à 5 heures ou Mardi la matinée de Mr Scribe[3].Had the duet bound. Fetched the key and casket for the score from Munk.[4]

5 May. Delivered the score today: the [full] score, the libretto, the letter ostensibly for Crémieux, the contract.[5] Between 9 and 10 to Crémieux.

10 May. Moved into the Hôtel des Princes.

11 May. At 9 to Scribe.

15 May. Specht came at 4.

16 May. Nourrit came at 1.

18 May. At 3:30 Specht and Oettinger.*

20 May. Bull* came at 4.

21 May. Armand [Bertin], Haber,[6] Onslow, Heine.

25 May. To Géraldy* about Bull.

28 May. To Connery about C. M. von Weber.

30 May. Dined with Scribe.

31 May. At 11 Marmier* came.

June 1835

Monday 1 June. At 10 to Halévy.

2 June. First choral rehearsal of my opera.

6 June. To Schlesinger, that he should leave the article out of the newspaper.

15 June. Wrote to Hiller and invited him for Thursday.

18 June. Today Hiller dined with me. At 12 Scribe came.

19 June. At 4 to the [scene] painters. Scribe came at 5:30. At 1 to Halévy at the Opéra. Dined with Levasseur.

20 June. Today Hiller dined with me. At 12 first singers' rehearsal of my opera.

23 June. Children in the women's chorus.[7] Contract with Véron.

24 June. Berlioz and Léon de Wailly dined with me.

26 June. A second couplet for Nourrit's romance.[8] At 3:30 to Nourrit. Copy for Thiers. Arranged the vocal parts of the *Orgie*[9] in C and D. Tomorrow to Halévy precisely at 12 for the twelfth choral rehearsal. To Émile [Deschamps] about the Page.

29 June. At 10:30 met Deschamps about the second verse ("repaires impures").

July 1835

Sunday 5 July. To Halévy about Bois Rosé.[10]

6 July. Change "L'aventure est singulière."[11]

10 July. To Halévy about Falcon,* the women's chorus, rehearsal time.

12 July. The two Schlesingers dined with me.

16 July. To the duke of Choiseul. At 5 to Émile Deschamps.

17 July. Between 3 and 4 to Scribe in Montalais.

18 July. Rehearsal at 12. Émile Deschamps came before 4.

19 July. At 10 to the rehearsal at the Opéra.

20 July. At 4 Émile Deschamps came and I played him act 2 of the score, regarding the recitatives.

21 July. Played for Halévy.

22 July. In the morning to Scribe. To Émile Deschamps with the recitatives of act 2.

[On 24 July *Robert le Diable* was given in Prague in German.]

25 July. To Émile Deschamps before 10. To Duponchel. To Véron, that no one should attend the rehearsals during my absence. To Scribe in the evening.

26 July. With Duponchel to Benoist, and the poem for Émile. Leborne: remove "C'est Marguerite de Valois" from act 2, and the stretta of the act 3 finale. Act 3 for Dupont.

30 July. To Gouin. Name of a good doctor in Dieppe. The newspapers to be sent to me in Dieppe. Traveled via St. Germain.

31 July. [Wrote] to Scribe.

August 1835.

Saturday 1 August. Today to Dieppe.

12 August. Left Dieppe today.

14 August. Saint-Georges came at 3.

[On 16 August Duponchel succeeded Véron as director of the Opéra.][12]

17 August. At 11:30 to Halévy. At 12 Falcon. At 1 Nourrit.

21 August. At 12 Scribe (about Émile [Deschamps]), *l'ange,* etc., the swans,[13] *la barcarolle.*[14] At 7 to Deschamps.

27 August. To Scribe.

28 August. Chorus for Damoreau's aria.[15] I want to hear the *Serment*,[16] and Taglioni the Bathers' Chorus.[17]

September 1835

Saturday 5 September. To Armand [Bertin] about [Michael Beer's] *Die Paria.*[18] To Halévy about the chorus in Damoreau's aria; that Mlle. Bouvenne [a coryphée] should already begin learning her part in the aria ["O beau pays"]. The four *hommes d'armes.* The *Orgie* arranged for eight persons. The *Serment.*

7 September. To Halévy about the six newly invited members of the male chorus. Listened to the *Serment.*

10 September To Jules Janin* about *Der Paria.*[19]

13 September. To Habeneck about the violoncello solo chords[20] in the recitatives,[21] and the violoncello in Nourrit's romance.[22]

14 September. To Halévy, that Mlle. Laurent should take the second coryphée's part in Damoreau's aria, like Mlle. Bouvenne. The four *hommes d'armes.* The *Serment* by the chorus. Rehearsed act 3.

29 September. Bellini's monument.[23]

October 1835

Tuesday 6 October. 1er repetition de mise en scène au soir.[24]

14 October. [Asked] Deschamps for the last lines of the stretta in the act 1 finale.

23 October. Fétis came at 3.

28 October. At 3 the woodwind rehearsal. To Duponchel, that Nourrit should not go with the Guard on account of the rehearsal.[25]

November 1835

Tuesday 3 November. First string rehearsal.

5 November. Dined with Duponchel.

7 November. Rehearsal at 11:30.

12 November. At 12:30 to the first rehearsal of act 1. At 1:30 rehearsal of act 2. Letter for Émile [Deschamps]. The *traité* with Schlesinger.

15 November. At 6:45 to the prize-giving at the Conservatoire.

16 November. To Duponchel about *tableau du lever de rideau du 2me acte*,[26] and that [Marie] Taglioni above all should feature in the two choruses.[27]

17 November. Rehearsal at 12. To Leborne about the horn and clarinet parts in the romance.[28] To Habeneck about bass drum and side drum.[29]

18 November. String rehearsal of the finale and the new recitative for Falcon [= Valentine].

20 November. To Nourrit about Norblin—*a due* or cavatina? [Read] his prose alteration to act 4.[30] Abridgment[31] of act 5.

22 November. For the last fourteen days there have been rehearsals with *mise en scène*, but two were missed on Saturday, one on Sunday, and one on Tuesday [14, 15, and 17 November], i.e., four musical rehearsals without *mise en scène*. Tomorrow afternoon choral rehearsal of acts 4 and 5, and practice with the soloists.

26 November. Nine rehearsals have been missed because of *Le Siège de Corinth*.

27 November. Today was the first performance [of the revival of] *Le Siège de Corinth*.

[*Undated entries*.]
No rehearsal on Sunday [15 November?]. Who will sing the Gypsies?[32] Scribe's rehearsal at 12:30 so that I can hear act 4. Tomorrow evening acts 4 and 5 at 7 precisely in the Foyer des Rôles, the chorus also in their foyer. Is a string rehearsal necessary with the *mise en scène* tomorrow? Should the Opéra drummers for the *Rataplan* and the *banda* be at the *mise en scène* rehearsal? If several acts are generally[33] rehearsed, could one not have two rehearsals daily? The Opéra balls must be discouraged.

Orchestre: Two full rehearsals on the fourth, two full rehearsals on the fifth; one rehearsal of the ballet music; touching up;[34] *banda*; acts 1 and 2 *mise en scène* with orchestra, one rehearsal of act 3 (particularly for the double orchestra, one rehearsal of acts 4 and 5 (*banda* and harps in act 5), two rehearsals of the whole opera; three string rehearsals with harp and *banda* for acts 4 and 5. To Leborne about boxes[35] for the *banda* [to sit on?].

Recitatives in act 4, arrange the chorus "Honneur à la plus belle" as ritornello, "Noble dame" in act 3 [for Nevers], shorten the *a due* in canon for Nourrit and Falcon.

Valve horns[36] and harps to be muffled[37] and the timpani for act 1. The *Serment* in the finale to be rehearsed with and without chorus. Bathers' Chorus in act 2: one harp in the orchestra, one on the stage. Cuts[38] in act 1 in the chorus.

Projected abridgments and adjustments.[39]

Acte 1. 1) *Toute la petite scène "buvons à son tendre martyre."*
   2) *Aller de la fin du 1er Choeur de l'Introduction, au couplet de M. Alexis* [Dupont, in the role of Cossé] *"de ces lieux enchanteurs."*
   3) *Faire partir Mlle. Falcon après son 1er couplet sans l'entrée des choeurs dans la coulisse et le recitatif qui l'ensuit.*
   4) *Dans l'entrée de M. Nourrit dans l'Introduction ne dire qu'une seule fois (la dernière fois) "il n'est pas mal vraiment."*
   5) *Morceau bouffe. Les coupures de M. Leborne.*
Acte 2. 1) *Ôter tout à fait les Choeurs "Qu'elle est belle la fiancée."*
   2) *Une reprise du Serment* (or at least the whole second half).
   3) 1/2 coda and C variation: from the *Pas de Six.*
Acte 3. 1) *Ôter "Sur les bords de la Seine" et une reprise du "C'est le jour du dimanche."*
   2) *Un écho dans la danse des bohemiens.*
   3) *Resserrer le Septuor.*
   4) *Finale "Une seule fois je l'aime," et aller de suite à "J'aurai donc satisfait."*
   5) *Un couplet des Bohemiennes.*
   6) *Dans la stretta du Finale ôter le couplet "Plus de paix plus de trève."* [Not cut from the final version.]
Acte 4. 1) *Ôter le petit Duo entre Raoul et Valentine.*
   2) *Ôter la seconde fois reprise grand couplet "Si tu me quittes on t'immole."*[40]

In the greatest necessity also the following cuts: the whole of Falcon's romance;[41] the second couplet of Nourrit's romance;[42] the Quarrel Chorus by half.[43]

December 1835

Wednesday 2 December. Rehearsal of the *banda*. To Habeneck and Leborne about the harps in act 2, the harps in act 5. Whether the timpani play in F-sharp or C-sharp.

16 December. Rehearsal with the *banda* at 12. [Rehearsed] the entr'acte to act 3. The small linking piece[44] in the first tempo of the act 4 duet.

17 December. To Émile Deschamps. Must practice the drum[45] in the *Rataplan* with the chorus early on Saturday. With Scribe concerning the changes in act 3. To Habeneck that I want to send Mohr the music of the chorale in act 5. To Falcon, whether she wants to sing only one couplet, and whether one could then leave out "Bonheur de la table" and the following recitative. The bell in A for the Curfew.[46]

23 December. Cut the *Morceau d'Ensemble* in act 3.

24 December. In the rehearsal the omission[47] of the *Morceau d'Ensemble* in act 3.

26 December. To Leborne about arranging a link between the first and second scenes of act 4. "Et déja vers le ciel des anges m'ont porté."[48]

30 December. To E. Deschamps about the recitative ("Noble Dame").[49] To Habeneck about the harps, *banda* in act 5,[50] and fixing the dates [for rehearsals?].

[*Undated entries.*]
    Schlesinger, German romances. Leborne, about changes in the septet. To give the brass supplement for the trio [act 5] to Leborne so that he can arrange it, and have it copied soon. Played for Taglioni's *répétiteur* so that the tempi are not too slow. Rehearsed the drum in the *Rataplan*. Horn and bassoon[51] for Falcon's romance. To Dacosta about the trio. Remove the cries of the wounded[52] for the second sopranos. "Auras-tu ce courage" (Finale I). Recitative before Dorus's aria.—Because of Nourrit's new piece, the changes to act 3 can be ready only by Thursday, so rather a general rehearsal and act 4 tomorrow.—About the Opéra balls.[53]—Leborne "Si l'un de nous ose y porter atteinte" to be changed in the orchestra. Fix the canon in act 4.[54]— Link[55] between the andante and stretta in act 4.—Mlle. Flécheux* should not sing in *Robert.*[56] Cadence of the canon in act 4.— The conclusion of Dorus's aria, and the preceding recitative.[57]—A new conclusion to the entr'acte of act 3.—Have the harp part copied. Conclusion of Catherine's[58] recitative before the entry of the monks.[59]—Recitative for Laurent.—"Noble Dame," Taglioni, torchlight procession,[60] the drum on the bark frenzied[61] during the fanfare.[62] Habeneck (*banda*, bugle, orchestral trumpets).—Scribe (Fair Scene,[63] plan of the opera).—Crémieux. To Véron, that no one should speak of this because the ballet master will otherwise delay longer. Not to leave him any more time, since it must be settled in twenty-four hours.[64]

NOTES

1. The direction of the Opéra was open to change.

2. Opera in three acts by Vincenzo Bellini (Count Carlo Pepoli, after the play *Têtes rondes et Cavaliers* by Ancelot and Saintine, loosely based on Sir Walter Scott's novel *Old Mortality* [1816]; Paris, Théâtre Italien, 24 January 1835). The opera had just enjoyed its triumphant première with the so-called *Puritani* Quartet: Grisi, Rubini, Tamburini, and Lablache. Bellini's melodic inspiration was at a high point in this opera, which also showed the composer's awareness of musical developments in Paris by its rich orchestral textures.

3. "From three to five o'clock or on Tuesday morning with Mr. Scribe."

4. The score of *Les Huguenots* was about to be deposited with a lawyer.

5. Tgb. *traité*.

6. Luidel von Haber, a banker.

7. No. 8, *Choeur des Baigneuses* ("Jeunes beautés, sous ce feuillage").

8. No. 2, *Romance* ("Plus blanche que la blanche hermine").

9. No. 1d, *Orgie* ("Bonheur de la table").

10. A Huguenot soldier (a tenor *comprimario*) with an important solo part in the *Rataplan* Chorus (no. 14, *Couplets militaires des Soldats Huguenots*).

11. No. 5, *Morceau d'Ensemble* ("L'aventure est singulière").

12. See J. Fulcher, *The Nation's Image* (Cambridge: Cambridge University Press, 1987), pp. 86–88, for an account of the transition. One of Duponchel's first actions on becoming director was to refund Meyerbeer the 20,000 fr. indemnity that Véron had insisted on receiving. Duponchel thus won the composer's good will and secured the score of *Les Huguenots* for the Opéra.

13. Scenery for act 2, set in the gardens of the château of Chenonceaux on the banks of the Loire.

14. No. 7, *Air* ("O beau pays de la Touraine"), for Queen Marguerite de Valois.

15. Laure Cinti-Damoreau was to create the role of Queen Marguerite at this stage.

16. No. 12a, *Serment* ("Par l'honneur, par le nom").

17. Taglioni was preparing the choreography for the opera. The Bathers' Chorus is a *choeur dansée*.

18. Michael Beer's one-act tragedy, a parable on anti-Semitism, was first performed in Berlin in 1823 and in Vienna in 1827. Publication followed in 1829 [Richel 12]. Marmier's French translation appeared in 1834 in the *Nouvelle Revue germanique*.

19. Meyerbeer was perhaps negotiating a review of the French translation of his brother's drama.

20. Tgb. *accorde*.

21. This particular sound is tonally associated with Marcel.

22. Later changed to the viola d'amore.

23. Bellini died on 23 September 1835 of an abscessed liver, and was buried in the Père Lachaise cemetery. Chopin would be laid to rest next to him in 1849.

24. "First stage rehearsal in the evening."

25. In order to conserve his voice.

26. "the rising of the curtain in act 2."

27. In both the *Choeur des Baigneuses* and the *Scène du Bandeau* (nos. 8 and 9).

28. The accompaniment to Valentine's romance, no.22 ("Parmi les pleurs"), has prominent writing for clarinet, horn, and bassoon.

29. Tgb. *caisse et tambour.*

30. Nourrit suggested changes in the act 4 love duet.

31. Tgb. *coupure.*

32. Tgb. *Bohemiennes.*

33. Tgb. *généralement.*

34. Tgb. *raccord.*

35. Tgb. *carton.*

36. Tgb. *cors pistons.*

37. Tgb. *sourdinen.*

38. Tgb. *coupuren.*

39. For a survey of the cuts necessitated during rehearsals, see Sieghard Döhring's investigation of the composer's manuscripts of the four *grands opéras* held in Cracow, "Die Autographen der vier Hauptopern Meyerbeers: Ein erster Quellenbericht," *Archiv für Musikforschung* 39:1 (1982): 32–63.

40. Translation:

"Act 1. 1) The whole of the small scene 'Buvons à son tendre martyre.'

       2) Go from end of the chorus of the introduction to the couplets for Mr. Alexis [Dupont, in the role of Cossé] 'De ces lieux enchanteurs.'

       3) Mlle. Falcon [Valentine] should go after he first couplet before the entry of the chorus offstage and the recitative that follows.

       4) On the entrance of M. Nourrit [Raoul] in the introduction 'Il n'est pas mal vraiment' should only occur once (the last time).

       5) The comic piece. The cuts by M. Leborne [the copyist].

Act 2 1) Cut the whole of the chorus 'Qu'elle est belle la fiancée.'

       2) One repeat of the Oath (or at least the whole second half).

       3) The half coda and C variation in the *Pas de Six.*

Act 3 1) Omit 'Sur les bords de la Seine' and one of the repeats of 'C'est le jour du dimanche.'

       2) The echo effect in the Gypsy Dance.

       3) Tighten up the Septet.

       4) In the finale [cut] from 'Une seule fois je l'aime' to 'J'aurai donc satisfait.'

       5) One of the Gypsy Couplets.

       6) In the stretta of the finale leave out the couplet 'Plus de paix plus de trève.' [Not cut from the final version.]

Act 4 1) Remove the small duo for Raoul and Valentine. [Missing in the final version.]

       2) Take out the second repeat of the big couplet 'Si tu me quitte on t'immole.' [Missing in the final version.]"

41. Act 4, no. 22 ('Parmi les pleurs')—not eventually cut.

42. Act 1, no. 2 ('En m'écoutant')—not eventually cut.

43. Act 3, no. 20, *Choeur de la Dispute* ("Nous voilà, félons").

44. Tgb. *ventre.*

45. Tgb. *tambour.*

46. Act 3, no.17, *Couvre-Feu* ("Rentrez habitants de Paris").

47. Tgb. *coupure.*

48. The original text of the act 5 *Vision,* no. 27c ("Ah! voyez le ciel").

49. Nevers's words of greeting to Valentine at the commencement of the *Cortège de Noces* (act 3 finale, no. 21).

50. For the Chorus of Assassins.

51. Tgb. *corno e fagotto.*

52. Tgb. *cris des blessés.*

53. This was in order to avoid clashes with rehearsals.

54. In the *Andante amoroso* section of the *Grand Duo* (no. 24).

55. Tgb. *ventre.*

56. Louise Marie Flécheux created the role of Urbain (in place of Dorus-Gras, who had originally been intended), but took Cinti-Damoreau's place as Marguerite de Valois. Meyerbeer was obviously concerned to conserve her vocal energies for her new part.

57. No. 6b, *Cavatine du Page* ("Nobles seigneurs!").

58. Catherine de Medici was still a character in the opera at this point.

59. Tgb. *Entrée des moines.*

60. Tgb. *Fackeltanz.*

61. Tgb. *tambour de barque échelever.*

62. All details from the wedding celebrations that take place during the act 3 finale.

63. The opening of act 3, no. 13 ("C'est le jour du Dimanche").

64. Filippo Taglioni was presumably dragging his feet.

Section 5
1836

1836

January 1836

[*Undated entries.*]
Tell the singers that journalists will be present. To Brodt[1] about the machinery. Duponchel: that the bells should be repaired.[2] Cut the *Morceau d'Ensemble* in A-flat major in act 3 in order to give the chorus time to change. The same applies to the *Choeur de Dimanche*.[3] Rehearse with Mori*, Gras and Nau*. Dress[4] rehearsal of all three acts with illuminated décor in order to time the duration of the intervals,[5] and the general length. Halévy. Rehearse the *Litany*[6] this evening. Habeneck: when will we meet with Urhan concerning the romance? Duponchel about changes in the décor after the trio. Leborne: have the cuts[7] in the ballet been completed? Shorten the reprise of the last chorus, "Par le fer et par l'incendie."[8] Alteration in the piece for Serda* in act 4.[9] Falcon's romance.

Saturday 2 January. Delavigne, Heine, Curschmann*, Berton, Paer, Delavigne.

3 January. Heine 5 or 3 Cité Bergère.

9 January. Tenth orchestral rehearsal. Second of act 1, second of act 2, third of act 3, first of acts 1, 2, and 3 with the *mise en scène*.

11 January. Habeneck came at 11 about the overture.

12 January. To Habeneck and Halévy about the *cor anglais* and *cors pistons* for the rehearsal of act 4. Conclusion of the recitative before the *Entrée des Moines*.[10] The trumpets in the act 5 trio.

19 January. Scribe. Title.[11] *Tableau final*, that the trio should not come to a formal end. The breaking down of the doors of the church.[12]

23 January. Levasseur duet act 3 "À minuit."[13] In place of the ritornello, the trumpets in the orchestra should start the finale.[14]

24 January. Habeneck: do the brass[15] have enough intelligence to practice the alterations without having them written down? ditto the harp echoes. Should the bells in act 4 be loud or soft? Cuts[16] in act 4. Is Nourrit's cavatina too strenuous? Finale and alteration in the last chorus of act 5.

27 January. At 2 Habeneck came. Played the overture and *Air de Danse*, the altered chorus in act 3, discussed the bells.

29 January. Scribe, the title, "Noble dame,"[17] abridgment of the recitative in act 4, denouement, text for the recitative before the [ensemble] piece in act 4.[18]

30 January. Brodt's machinery. To Émile about the romance.

31 January. At 11 Serda came. To Émile about the recitative in the *Morceau d'Ensemble* in act 4. Serda: gave him the recitative. Rehearsal of the décor with the whole *equipage*. Mlle. Flécheux; Nau: rehearsal.

February 1836

Wednesday 3 February. Invited Scribe to hear Serda, also Nourrit.[19] Mlle. Nau, concerning Mlle. Flécheux who is ill,[20] concerning Serda. The barque[21] should be wider. All the machinery and *équipage* for Tuesday so that the length of the intervals can be assessed. To Émile about the romance and its preceding recitative.

4 February. After the rehearsal with Duponchel to Nau. To Halévy: this evening the *Litany* and Bouvenne's understudy[22] should be rehearsed, and also the act 2 finale. To Falcon with the changes in the act 5 chorus. An opening should be made so that the harps can be heard. Showed the harpists the changes. Positioning of the brass. Musket machines.

6 February. Punctuated Serda's role, and Falcon's phrases in the act 4 *Morceau d'Ensemble*. Because of *I Puritani*, must start act 3 tomorrow.

7 February. To Crémieux about the *Procureur du Roi*.[23]

9 February. 11:30 rehearsal. Take the flute and oboe out of Nourrit's cavatina. The two shooting-machines. To Habeneck the alteration in 3/4 where bells come in.

11 February. This evening [presided from] a piano in the orchestra.

14 February. Send the two verses of the romance. To Trevaux, that tomorrow Ferdinand Prévôt should also come to the rehearsal of the bells, and that the other bells should not be covered anymore. Brodt [should] make stronger shooting-machines.

15 February. Rehearsed the trio with Halévy and the chorus. [To] Leborne: have the trumpets and other instruments in the last act altered.

17 February. Duponchel: the three acts should be rehearsed in their proper order; whether an audience should be admitted to the dress rehearsal. At 12 with Scribe to the [scene-] painters. Shortened Dorus's ritornello before the ball game[24] [see example 40].

Example 40. Theme (1) from *Les Huguenots*

20 February. To Leborne: has he made the cuts in the act 3 stretta in Mohr's vocal part?

23 February. Auguste.[25]

24 February. To Duponchel about jumping with the torches.[26] Dress rehearsal with lighting. The monks in white.[27] Scribe wants a rehearsal with lighting. Abridgment[28] of the ball game.

26 February. Auguste about tomorrow. To Duponchel: a litter[29] with horses[30]. No public at the dress rehearsal. Lighting at the rehearsal.[31]

27 February. Ball at Cerfberr's. To Armand about the Court Concert and the dress rehearsal. Letter of thanks to the orchestra and chorus.

28 February. The new shooting-machine. Rehearsal at 1. Afterwards to Auguste.

[*29 February*. Première of *Les Huguenots*.][32]

March 1836

Tuesday 1 March. Brodt, that the organ should be tuned. That Mother should write to Wilhelm about the Berlin papers.

3 March. To Schlesinger *Chronique de Paris*. To the *Indépendant, Solitaire, France Juge*.

5 March. At 9:30 d'Ortigue came. *Constitutionnel*.

6 March. Henri Blaze*. To Armand about Janin's article.[33] To Scribe, that I will be with him at 12:30 with Taglioni. To Leborne about the cuts.[34]

7 March. [Tickets for] Berlioz. D'Ortigue with ticket, and wrote about the *Revue*. Fétis came at 4. Two tickets for Heine, one for Henri Blaze. To Émile. To Germain [Delavigne].

8 March. At 1 a rehearsal. At 10 to Fétis. Dinner with Bertin. Ticket to Buloz*. From Leborne act 4, the act 5 trio, introduction to act 1. Three places for d'Ortigue. About Panofka* and Falcon. Autograph for Mira. Schlesinger and Castil-Blaze. The abridgments[35] to Dorus.

10 March. To the *Revue de Paris* with a description of my career for Traxel*.

11 March. Tickets for Panseron*, Traxel, Panofka, Crémieux, Leo, Heine.

12 March. Emanuel with the *Ménestrel*. Dined with Véron. At 4 Henri Blaze came.

13 March. At 12 to the *Revue du Nord*.

14 March. Cherubini. Ticket for Stöpel. *Stalles d'orchestre* for Henri Blaze. Berton.

15 March. Dined with Duponchel. At 4 Henri Blaze and Royer* came.

17 March. At 3 Heine came.

[On 20 March Berlioz's famous critique of *Les Huguenots* appeared in the *Revue et Gazette musicale de Paris*.[36]]

22 March. At 3:30 to the artist [Maurin?] for my portrait.

Meyerbeer at the time of *Robert le Diable* and *Les Huguenots*. Lithograph by François Delpech, after a drawing by Antoine Maurin (mid-1830s).

24 March. George Sand*. Rothschild.*

25 March. At 4 corrections for the *Revue.* Box[37] for the *Revue du Nord.*

26 March. At 8:30 Schlesinger.[38]

28 March. To Heine (for Kaufmann).

29 March. At 10 Herr Lewald*.

31 March. At 11 Herr Lewald.

April 1836

Friday 1 April. The sketches of *Les Huguenots.* At 11 to the portrait artist. To Buloz about Lewald. Schlesinger: a piece from *Les Huguenots* for Lewald.

7 April. To Mme. Damoreau. Duet and aria from *Robert.* That Urhan should bring his viola and another accompany Lafont*.

9 April. At 3 to Heine.

10 April. At 12:30 with Schimon* to Cherubini and Kalkbrenner.

15 April. At 4 Heine. Gouin should allow Lapelouze* [a ticket] this evening. 1. Grillparzer*.[39] 2. Specht. 3. d'Ortigue.

16 April. At 11 to Dumas.

17 April. Heine, Sand.

19 April. Recital by Baillot. At 2 Heine came with Guerault.

20 April. Box for Heine and Guerault.

22 April. Box Heine two places. Two Dumas. Grillparzer.

24 April. [Grillparzer to dinner.]

29 April. Grillparzer. Dumas.

30 April. We hosted a dinner.

May 1836

Friday 5 May. The *Romances* for Mme. Fernemons.

7 May. At 12:30 rehearsal.

11 May. Score of *Robert*. Corrected the words for the end of the women's quartet.

18 May. Between 1 and 2 to Erard's* to hear Liszt*.[40]

21 May. [Wrote] to Minna.

28 May. At 5 Herr Liszt met me for dinner. Supper[41] at 11:30 at Dumas's.

June 1836

Wednesday 1 June. Translation of *Die drei Pintos*.

2 June. At 11:30 with Winkler to Scribe.

3 June. Winkler. Letter to the king of the Belgians.[42]

4 June. At 3 Hofrat Winkler came.

8 June. Left Paris early this morning and slept in Virtu.

11 June. Arrived this morning in Baden.

14 June. Today sent my letter to Gouin.

17 June. Today act 3 was sent off from Strasbourg.

20 June. [Wrote] to Gouin that Crémieux should send his observations about the ownership rights of composers to Werther.

22 June. [Wrote] to Breitkopf.

28 June. [Wrote] to Gouin. Sent the act 3 finale off to Schlesinger.

29 June. [Wrote] to Winkler in Dresden.

30 June. [Wrote] to Mme. Birch[-Pfeiffer]* about the *Crociato*.

July 1836

Saturday 2 July. Early today at 5 left for Paris.

3 July. Slept today in Ferchampenois (at Sauvage's). [Wrote] to Fétis.

4 July. Arrived in Paris this evening. To Schlesinger about Balzac*.

17 July. [Composed] "Les marguerites [du poète]" by Henri Blaze.

20 July. At 10 to Dumas.

21 July. Met Edmond Blanc at 3 to see whether one could put it in the newspaper, and where and when I could receive the patent.

22 July. That Halévy should take the chorale in act 5 more slowly.

30 July. Left Paris. Slept in Rethel at the 24 Posten. Good.

31 July. Slept in Namur.

August 1836

Monday 1 August. Arrived in Spa.[43]

2 August. To Dr. Beurmann.

3 August. [Wrote] to Gouin, Minna.

14 August. Sent Schlesinger act 1 of the vocal score. [Wrote] to Minna. Early today Mother left Spa.

21 August. [Wrote] to Gouin together with an enclosure for Schlesinger. Sent off the full score of act 1.

22 August. I want to write to Meyer [in Aachen][44] about Klopstock's *Messias*. [Sent] the *Geistliche Lieder von Klopstock* to Härtel*.

27 August. Today the packet containing acts 4 and 5 of the vocal score and the full score of the act 1 finale was sent off to Paris.

28 August. [Wrote] to Minna enclosing music for the album of Princess Labanoff.

September 1836

Thursday 1 September. Prague *Crociato*.

3 September. Today the packet containing act 3 of the vocal score and act 2 of the full score was sent off.

4 September. [Wrote] to the king requesting the order.[45]

5 September. My birthday. Sent Meyer in Aachen 17 fr. for the *Messias*[46] and acknowledged [the receipt] by letter. [Wrote] in answer to Minna's birthday letter.

9 September. [Wrote] to Minna about coming to Paris.

11 September. [Wrote] to Minna. Departure from Spa. Slept in Liège. [Heard] *L'Éclair*.[47]

12 September. Slept in Brussels. [Heard] *Guillaume Tell*.

13 September. To Antwerp.

14 September. Left Brussels and slept in Cambrai.

15 September. Arrived in Paris at 10 in the evening.

19 September. [Wrote] to Minna and Nonna that I will travel to Baden. *Les Huguenots*.

24 September. [Sent] the *mise en scène* [of *Robert le Diable*] to Küstner.[48]

28 September. Left Paris at 10:30, and slept in Sezanne.

29 September. Slept in Void.

October 1836.

Saturday 1 October. Arrived in Baden.

9 October. [Wrote] to Breitkopf enclosing the *Elégie* ["Le poète mourant"].[49] [Wrote] to Wilhelm together with indications for the décor in Leipzig. Left Baden with Minna. Slept in Saverne.

10 October. Slept in Nancy (*au* Petit Paris).[50]

11 October. Slept in St. Dizier.

12 October. Slept in Sézanne.

13 October. Arrived in Paris.

14 October. To Alexandre Dumas.

17 October. At 10 to Al. Dumas.

19 October. [Wrote] to Speyer.

22 October. To Dumas at three o'clock.

November 1836

Thursday 3 November. At 2 to Dumas. At 2:30 rehearsal of *Notre Dame.*[51]

[On 4 November *Robert le Diable* was given in Calcutta in French.]

5 November. To Dumas. George Sand.

6 November. George Sand.

7 November. To Dumas.

9 November. At 4 Savoye came.

10 November. 38 rue du Montblanc 9:30 Chopin*.

11 November. To Coste for Savoye.

12 November. At 3 Savoye came. To Coste.

13 November. To Dupré.

19 November. To Dupré.

19 November. Soirée at D'Argout's. Vocal score for Duprez*. Full score for Kastner.

December 1836

[*Undated entries.*]
Sum of pieces to be omitted:

Act 1: *Choeur* "Point de surprise."
Quintetto in the finale "C'est l'amour."

Act 2: *Choeur* "Quel belle la fiancée."
Pas de Cinq.

Act 3: Entr'acte.
Air de St Bris.
Scène et Choral Marcel.
Tempo largo in the finale.

Act 4: *Romance de Falcon.*
Cavatina "Tu l'as dit" and "Salut."[52]
Duettino for Nourrit and Falcon.

Act 5: Canon in the trio.

[On 4 December Berlioz gave a concert at the Conservatoire in which the first two parts of *Harold en Italie* and the *Symphonie fantastique* were performed: the enthusiastic applause was led by Cherubini and Meyerbeer.][53]

Friday 16 December. Made the drums optional again in the act 3 finale. Nohr should first try the cuts.[54] First [tried] the bells with Trevaux.[55] Habeneck should have the steps closed off in order to position[56]the harps. To Habeneck about the violoncello theme in the *Pas de Cinq*. Habeneck should not hurry the overture.

18 December. Positioned the chorus and the brass in act 3 on opposing sides. Fireworks[57] instead of the shooting-machine.

22 December. Duponchel should not allow anyone into the rehearsal. Habeneck must position[58] the eight harps well in the orchestra. Brodt should have a stronger shooting-machine, and place it more forward.

24 December. Leave the drum out of the *Rataplan*. A lamp [must be] placed in the corridor so that I can work in my box.[59] Leave the violoncelli out of Nourrit's "Je t'aime" in act 3. Triangle at the beginning of the theme in the *Danse des*

Bohemiens.[60] To Taglioni, that if the dancers have no *tambour de basque*, they must be given the rhythm. Rehearsal on Sunday [1 January 1837]. The harps behind the scene for the act 2 chorus. No drum in the *Rataplan*. Notepaper to record my observations. Rehearse the ballet piece for [Fanny] Elssler* between acts 1 and 2. The horn for the *Couvrefeu*.

NOTES

1. Stage mechanic at the Paris Opéra.
2. Tgb. *repariert*.
3. Act 3, scene 1—not eventually cut.
4. Tgb. *costume*.
5. Tgb. *entr'actes*.
6. No.14b, *Litanies* ("Vierge Marie").
7. Tgb. *coupure*.
8. No. 28, *Scène finale*.
9. Serda was to create the expanded role of St. Bris after the censor's refusal to sanction the appearance of Catherine de Medici on stage.
10. In the Blessing of the Daggers (act 4, scene 4—no. 23, *Conjuration et Bénédiction des Poignards*).
11. *Les Huguenots* instead of *St Barthélémy*. The remark indicates that both Scribe and Meyerbeer were uncertain about the title for their work. The *Revue et Gazette musicale* (21 February 1836) reports that *"Les Huguenots, tel est le titre véritable du nouvel opéra de M. Meyerbeer"* [*Les Huguenots*, such is the actual title of the new opera by M. Meyerbeer]. The alternatives, *Léonore* and *Valentine*, were used only in the first contract, and do not appear again.
12. In act 5, scene 2.
13. No. 18, *Scène et Duo* ("O terreur je tressaille").
14. The orchestra in fact does.
15. Tgb. *cuivre*.
16. Tgb. *coupuren*.
17. Act 3, scene 7.
18. No. 22, *Entr'acte, Récitatif et Romance*. The romance was replaced by an extended recitative.
19. This concerned the transformation of the role of Catherine de Medici into the bass part of St. Bris—as the result of the censor's objections to the portrayal of a monarch on stage.
20. Nau was to understudy Flécheux's role as the Page.
21. In the wedding celebrations in the act 3 finale.
22. Tgb. *doublure*. Bouvenne was presumably one of the *2 jeune Filles* who sing the solo line in the Litany.
23. Meyerbeer was seeking legal advice about the censor's intervention.
24. The games of the court ladies in the gardens in act 2.
25. The famous director of the claque at the Paris Opéra. For an account of his character, abilities, plotting of applause, and fees, see W. Crosten, *French Grand Opera* (New York: King's Crown Press, 1948; reprint, New York: Da Capo, 1972), pp. 41–48.

26. In the Wedding Procession of the act 3 finale.

27. Tgb. *les moins blancs.*

28. Tgb. *coupure.*

29. Tgb. *litière.*

30. For the entry of Queen Marguerite de Valois at the beginning of the act 3 finale.

31. This does not appear to have been usual.

32. Meyerbeer's most perfect and popular opera was performed 1,120 times at the Paris Opéra between 29 February 1836 and 22 November 1936. Only Gounod's *Faust* has been given there more often (2,336 times by 1959). It soon spread all over the world (e.g., New Orleans, 1839; Stockholm, 1842; Odessa, 1843; New York, 1845; Havana, 1849; Helsinki, 1850; St. Petersburg, 1850; Riga, 1850; Batavia, 1851; Lisbon, 1854; Barcelona, 1856; Dublin, 1857; Warsaw, 1858; Algiers, 1858; Sydney, 1863; Mexico, 1865; Constantinople, 1866; Malta, 1869; Cairo, 1870; Buenos Aires, 1870; Rio de Janeiro, 1870; Bucharest, 1876; Zagreb, 1878; Ljubljana, 1904; Sofia, 1922; Tallinn, 1924; Jerusalem, 1926; Kaunas, 1932). It became Meyerbeer's most performed work: 459 times in Hamburg (–1959), 394 times in Brussels (–1935), 385 times in Berlin (–1932), 249 times in Covent Garden (–1927), 247 times in Vienna (–1911), over 200 times in New Orleans (–1919), 118 times in Linz, 108 times in Milan (–1962), 75 times in Parma (–1927), and 66 times in New York (–1915). Postwar performances have been in Hamburg (1959), Milan (1962), Lille (1964), Rouen (1965), Barcelona (1971), Toulouse (1972), Leipzig (1974), New Orleans (1976), Sydney (1981, 1990), Berlin (1987, 1991), San Francisco (1990), and Montpellier (1990); concert performances have been given in Milan (1956), London (1968), New York (1969), Vienna (1971), and Paris (1976). See *BT,* 2:680–81, for a listing of reviews, also the section under *Les Huguenots* in M.-H. Coudroy, *La critique parisienne des "grands opéras" de Meyerbeer* (Saarbrucken: Musik Edition Lucie Galland, 1988), for reprints of contemporary critical reactions. Edouard Hanslick observed that a person unable to appreciate the dramatic power of this opera must be lacking in certain elements of the critical faculty.

33. This appeared on 7 March in *Le Journal des Débats.*

34. Tgb. *coupuren.*

35. Tgb. *coupuren.*

36. In a letter to his sister, Nanci Pal, Berlioz described the work as an "encyclopédie musicale dont le succès se rattache à tant d'intérêts d'art et de fortune" [a musical encyclopedia, the success of which is as much due to artistic interest as it is to good fortune]. F. Stoepel, writing in the *Allgemeine musikalische Zeitung* (20 June 1836, 269) observed that "the opera is one of the most admirable creations of the human spirit. It depicts the fine arts of poetry, of music, and of painting in enchanting effects with the rich life of scenic presentation, enhanced by the fairy play of the dance and the dazzling finery of the costumes, all in the powerful process of seductive illusion."

37. Tgb. *loge.*

38. The meeting presumably concerned the final details of the contract between Meyerbeer and Schlesinger for the publication of *Les Huguenots.*

39. The first meeting with Grillparzer took place on 5 April 1836 (see *BT,* 2:681).

40. Liszt had been in Geneva with Marie d'Agoult since August 1835.

41. Tgb. *souper.*

42. King Léopold I, the "Nestor of Europe."

43. He was accompanied as usual by Amalie Beer, and they once more stayed at the Hôtel de Tuileries. See A. Body, *Meyerbeer aux eaux de Spa* (Brussels: Veuve J. Rozez, 1885), p. 24.

44. A bookseller.

45. Presumably the Ordre pour le Mérite.

46. The famous religious epic poem by F. G. Klopstock, published 1748–73.

47. Opera in three acts by Halévy (Saint-Georges; Paris, Opéra Comique, 16 December 1835). This was the composer's most successful *opéra comique*, and appeared only a few months after his greatest *grand opéra*, *La Juive* (23 February 1835). It was given in Paris more than three hundred times until 1899, and was also a great favorite in Germany, revived in Berlin (1927), Neuberg (1980), and Freiburg (1991).

48. This concerns the Munich staging of *Robert le Diable*. Küstner had been the intendant there since 1832.

49. Text by Charles Millevoye (1836). No. 21 in the *Quarante Mélodies*. This extended lyrical *scena* was one of Meyerbeer's most popular songs, a dramatic monologue depicting the dying moments of a poet whose life passes before his eyes.

50. "at Little Paris."

51. *Esmeralda*, opera in four acts by Louise Bertin (Victor Hugo; Paris, Opéra, 14 November 1836).

52. The meaning of this entry is unclear.

53. See Martine Kahane, *Robert le Diable: Catalogue de l'exposition Théâtre National de l'Opéra de Paris 20 juin—20 septembre 1985* (Paris: Bibliothèque National, 1985), p. 24.

54. Tgb. *coupuren*.

55. An instrument maker.

56. Tgb. *placieren*.

57. Tgb. *pétarades*.

58. Tgb. *placieren*.

59. Tgb. *loge*.

60. No. 16, *Danse bohémienne*.

Section 6
1837

1837

January 1837

Friday 6 January. [Discussed] Zimmermann* with Habeneck; Faubel* and my place in the Conservatoire. *Allegro furioso* in act 4[1] [see example 41]:

Example 41. Theme (2) from *Les Huguenots*

7 January. At 12 Habeneck came. Inspected the carriage for the journey to Rouen. A doll for Levasseur's child. At 4 Lard and Devienne.[2]

8 January. At 8 Valentin. Pierre Erard. Musard*.[3] Spazier*. Habeneck. Mother's birthday.

9 January. Tadolini, Faubel, Detmold, Heine.

11 January. At 1 Fitzjames, 22 rue Grangebatelier. At 10 to Vigneron.[4]

12 January. At 3 Léon de Bast.[5] At 4 Kastner*. At 10 Grevedon.

13 January. Soirée at Merlin's. At 4 Guerra* came. Had to refuse Merlin. Ticket for Venedey*.

14 January. At 4 to Buloz.

15 January. At 12 Henri Blaze. To Rodrigues. Box[6] for Balzac. To Savoye. To A. Nourrit. Saint-Georges. Crosnier*.

19 January. At 4 Saint-Georges came.[7]

20 January. At 3:30 Léon de Bast.

[On 20 January Schlesinger published the second edition of the score of *Robert le Diable,* which coincided with the 160th performance at the Opéra.]

21 January. At 3:30 Nourrit came to Mother's.

22 January. At 4 the poet von Vestris came. At 10 Léon de Bast.

23 January. At 2:30 Herr Munk and General Debazet. At 4 to M. Schlesinger.

24 January. At 2 to Gérard*. To Arrago. To Ed. Blanc.

25 January. To Mlle. Falcon. To Ed. Blanc. Box[8] for Boieldieu. Seat for Spazier. Léon de Bast. To Gouin whether I should write to Merle about Théodore Anne*.

26 January. Between 10 and 11 to Grevedon. To Henri Blaze. To Spazier. Invited Duponchel and Gentil*.

27 January. To Gentil. To Worms.

[On 27 January act 5 of *Robert le Diable* was performed at the Opéra for Levasseur's benefit.]

28 January. At 5 to Ed. Blanc and Montalivet. Soirée at Liszt's. At 2 to Planard. To Kalkbrenner. At 10 a rehearsal. Dinner in my apartments.

29 January. At 10 the poet von Vestris came. 9:30 Léon de Bast. To Savoye. At 10 Faubel. Concert in the Conservatoire. At 11 Duvergier came.

30 January. At 11 Duvergier*. To Crémieux. Corrections for Léon de Bast.

31 January. 9:30 Léon de Bast. Soirée at Kalkbrenner's.

February 1837

Wednesday 1 February. Committee[9] in Cercles des Arts at six o'clock. Box[10] for Ed. Blanc.

2 February. Breakfast[11] in my apartments.

3 February. Soirée at Pinieux's. Soirée at Berger. Dined at Cerfberr's. To Lard that the stretta of act 4 is missing.

4 February. At 4 Devienne.

5 February. From 11 until 1 Spazier.

6 February. At 12:30 to Planard.

8 February. Soirée at Merlin's.

9 February. Breakfast[12] in my apartments. Merruau*. Mainzer*. Savoye.

10 February. At 9 Auguste. At 10 Gouin. Stalls[13] for Spazier, Mangold. Alary*. To Loewe-Weimars*. Custine*, Arrago, Legouvé*, Léon de Bast, Crémieux. Portrait for Duponchel. Schlesinger about Grevedon.

12 February. At 1:30 with Leo to the painter Lehmann*.[14]

13 February. Dined with Loewe-Weimars. *Les théâtres qui ne peuvent pas disposer d'un double orchestre pourront facilement faire arranger ce morceau de manière, à ce que les entrées et les repliques essentielles de l'orchestre sur la barque soient transportées dans le grand orchestre*.[15]

14 February. Dined with Crémieux. To Mme. Ries. To Léon de Bast. Legouvé. Arrago.

15 February. The bass clarinet[16] from Brodt and instructions on how to play it.[17] Drawing of the shooting-machine. Receipt[18] from Grevedon and Schlesinger. Duponchel's portrait. Musard. Jullien*. [Decided] on the title of the collected romances and "Le poète mourant."

16 February. Henri Blaze came at 2.

17 February. Whether Lyons and Toulouse [can acquire] the bass clarinet. From 2 to 3 Arrago.

18 February. At 10 Léon de Bast came. At 2 to Legouvé.

19 February. At 11 Calvi.

20 February. Abrantes, Merruau.

21 February. At 10:30 Iwan Müller with the new clarinet. At 11.30 Calvi, Abrantes, Loewe-Weimars, Crémieux, Ed. Blanc. Merruau.

25 February. To Armand. Merruau. To Ed. Blanc. At 10 to Schlesinger.

26 February. Soirée at Rodrigues's.

27 February. At 11 the sculptor Leguine.

28 February. Massol* came this morning. 2.30 the sculptor Leguine.

March 1837

Wednesday 1 March. Dined with Pinieux. Kaskel.* Léon de Bast.

2 March. In the evening at 9 to the Committee in the Cercle. Coste, Merruau, Mainzer, Savoye, Crosnier about Castil-Blaze.

3 March. At 2:30 the sculptor Leguine came. At 9:30 Léon de Bast. [Wrote] to Schlesinger about Grevedon. At 4 Kaskel at Mother's.

4 March. 9:30 Léon de Bast. Album for Kaskel.

5 March. At 1 Jules Lovy came. [Wrote] to Camille Pleyel*. To Ed. Blanc.

6 March. To Ed. Blanc. Falcon. Lovy.

7 March. At 9 Léon de Bast. At 9:30 Leguine. Dined with Pleyel.

8 March. Soirée Merlin.

9 March. 9:30 Leguine. Dined with Schlesinger. At 3 to Henri Blaze. Early to Ries, Mme. Berger. Nourrit.

[Caecilie Meyerbeer was born on 10 March at 49, rue St Augustin.]

11 March. At 9:30 to Leguine.

12 March. Early to Ries. At 4:30 Saint-Georges.

13 March. At 4 to Scribe. Germain Delavigne. To Ries with the libretto. At 1 to [Dr.] Guersent. [Wrote] to Schlesinger about Jullien.

14 March. 9:30 to Scribe.

15 March. Dined with Lusy and Gentil.

16 March. At 4 Nourrit.

17 March. At 9 Conservatoire. Scribe. Janin, Dumas, Specht, Coste. Crémieux.

18 March. At 3 Saint-Georges. Soirée at Taglioni's. Scribe.

19 March. At 12:30 to Henri Blaze. 2 Conservatoire Concert. Spazier. [Wrote] to Dumas. Crémieux. Coste. Batta*.

20 March. Soirée at Pinieux's. 12:30 Halévy and Habeneck. To Scribe. Ed. Blanc.

21 March. Between 1 and 5 Guersent. At 1 audition at Duponchel's. Scribe. Ed. Blanc. Letter to Lyons. To Ar. Bertin. Gouin.

22 March. At 3 H. Blaze and Duvailly came. To Charles Maurice.

23 March. [Wrote] to Schlesinger. Full score for Faubel. Émile Deschamps came at 10. At 5 to Ed. Blanc. Coste.

24 March. At 3 to Henri Blaze. [Wrote] to Savoye, Faubel, Ries. Concert in the Conservatoire. To Levasseur, Janin.

25 March. To Gasparin. [Wrote] to Nourrit. "Le Corsaire." The copper plates to Schlesinger. [Wrote] to Ries, to Savoye.

26 March. Matinée at Seghers's*, rue de Jardinet, no. 3. Matinée at Tremont from 2 to 4. At 10 to Ries. At 9:30 Liszt came. To Ed. Blanc.

27 March. 9.30 Schlesinger. [Wrote] to Ries, Ed. Blanc. Tremont. Sent to Faubel.

[Wrote] to Émile Deschamps. To Schlesinger. Letter to Speyer. Catalog of Weber's works.[19]

28 March. Dined with Ries and Schott* at the Hôtel des Princes. At 9 Crosnier. Soirée Girardin.

29 March. Ed. Blanc. Soirée at Mme. Merlin's. [Wrote] to Custine. Baermann. Küstner. [Sent] Schott the full score of *Les Huguenots* and *God save the King.*[20]

30 March. Dinner at Crosnier's. Had the romances copied for Mme. Falcon.

April 1837

Saturday 1 April. Munk. Sent to Gouin. [Wrote] to Nourrit[21] about Panofka. 8:30 Auguste. To Lard about Mme. Sand. *God save the King* for Schott. Baermann. Kastner. To Falcon. At 12 to Méry*. 2:30 Henri Blaze. Concert by Thalberg* at the Conservatoire.

3 April. Ed. Blanc. At 10 Panofka came. Coste and d'Ortigue. Crevel de Charlemagne*. Lovy. Arrago. Ries. Duponchel *Pas de Quatre.* Crémieux. Letter to Duplanty.

4 April. Soirée Beauregard*. Eight o'clock soirée Rodrigues. At 12 to Mme. Falcon. Letter and 40 fr. to Mme. Belgiojoso*.

5 April. Ed. Blanc. At 3 Crevel de Charlemagne. At 4 to Belgiojoso. At 10 Panofka. Sand. Mme. Falcon. Baron Strehlen, Rue de Marivaux, 9 Hôtel Richelieu.

6 April. To Scribe. Duprez.[22] Crémieux. [Wrote] to Mainzer about Strehlen.[23] From Leo 4000 fr.

7 April. [Wrote] to Wailly, and [sent] Blaze the rhythms. Concert at Mainzer's. Saint-Georges came at 4. At 11 Duprez.

8 April. 9:30 to Scribe. Beauregard. Soirée Crémieux. Duponchel. Taglioni *Pas de Quatre.*[24] Benoist. At 4 Merlin.

9 April. To Henri Blaze. To Ed. Blanc. Dinner at Duponchel's. [Wrote] to d'Ortigue.

11 April. At 11:30 Rastoul came to *déjeuner.* The libretto for Rastoul. *Pas de Trois.* Sauvage's *Les Boyards.*[25]

12 April. 9:30 [took] Guerra to Mme. Taglioni. [Wrote] to Custine. Soirée at M. D'Argout.

13 April. [Wrote] to Clerval de Charmagne. At 10 to Scribe. At 2 to Mme. Merlin.

14 April. At 11 Guerra. At 11:30 Th. Mundt*. At 1 Roger de Beauvoir*. At 3 Henri Blaze and Wailly came. At 4 to Mme. Merlin.

15 April. At 10:30 to Scribe. At 2 to Taglioni. At 5 to Mme. Merlin's. Dinner at Belgiojoso's.

16 April. At 11:30 to Mme. Dorus. [Wrote] to Trevaux.

17 April. At 1 to Henri Blaze. At 4 Trevaux came. [Wrote] to Beauregard. Panofka. [Wrote] to Crosnier. Germain Delavigne.

18 April. At 10 to Scribe. At 2:30 to Mme. Merlin. To Gouin about Charles Maurice.

19 April. At 10 to Scribe. At 4 to Cerfberr. [Wrote] a letter to the Conservatoire for Mundt.

20 April. At 10:30 Guerra. At 11:30 to Duprez. [Wrote] to Ed. Blanc. Sent a vocal score to the Conservatoire for d'Ortigue. To Girardin and Beauregard.

21 April. Ed. Blanc. At 4 Lard came. Programme for the solo instruments: how often the string instruments should be doubled. Mme. de Chambure.

22 April. At 2 to Mme. Merlin. To Mme. Belgiojoso. Today the letter to Stieglitz* was sent off.

23 April. Conservatoire. At 11 H. Vogel* came.

24 April. Mme. Chambure. Franchomme*. On Thursday practice the women's chorus.

25 April. Duponchel about the *Pas de Trois*. At 10 Wailly came. At 2:30 Duprez came. [Wrote] to Vogel and Wailly. At 4 to Mme. Merlin. [Wrote] to Beauregard.

26 April. To Duprez 10:30. At 12 to Mme. Merlin. That Joseph should take the orchestral parts to Mme. Merlin. At 4 to Delavigne.

28 April. At 8:30 to Habeneck (take the full score to him: if there are no more rehearsals, one harp will do). At 9 to Scribe with the manuscripts.[26] To Mme. Merlin about the programme.[27] At 11:30 to Duprez. At 7 rehearsal. The bassoon should be there.

28 April. At 2 to Scribe. At 3:30 to Mme. Merlin.

29 April. At 12 Möser came. At 12 to Mme. Merlin.

30 April. Soirée at Coste's. D'Ortigue. Beauregard. Falcon. Cerfberr. Girardin.

May 1837

Monday 1 May. To Duponchel. Falcon. E. Deschamps. Scribe.

2 May. At 11 Möser. At 12 Taylor. Dined at Custine's. At 4 Benoist came to fetch the *mélodie* for Buloz. At 9:30 in the evening to Duprez.

3 May. At 10 to Émile Deschamps. At 11 to Merruau. At 3 Henri Blaze. To Scribe.

4 May. To Nourrit at 10. To Duprez. The scoring of "Tu l'as dit."[28]

5 May. At 4 Henri Blaze came, and Benoist after the Cercle des Arts.

6 May. At 4 to Nourrit. At 9 in the evening soirée at Jourdan's, 10 rue Cadet.

7 May. At 4 Henri Blaze. [Wrote] to Émile Deschamps. Duponchel about the *Pas de Trois.* [Spoke] with Tulon about the *Pas de Trois* and Dacosta [about] "Tu l'as dit."[29]

8 May. At 10 to Nourrit.

9 May. To Traxel. 12:30 rehearsal.[30] 7:30 rehearsal. That there should be no public at the rehearsal.

10 May. 9:30 rehearsal. To Scribe. Berton. With Scribe from the *Pas de Trois* on. In the evening rehearsed the chorus of Duprez's aria.[31] The full score of the *Pas de Trois* for Habeneck, so that harps can be added.

11 May. At 4 Möser.

12 May. [Wrote] to Scribe, that there should be a rehearsal at 11. Cut the *Ronde des Bohemiennes.*[32] To Boursault.

13 May. [Wrote] to Boursault. Scribe to the rehearsal. At 4 [took] Benoist the manuscript *de la nouvelle chanson.* At 10 to Gentil. To Armand Bertin.

14 May. M. de Girardin. Rehearsed the duet with Falcon. Dined with Gentil and Lusy. About act 4. *Pas de Trois.* Antenor [Joly]*.

15 May. At 9 to Leborne. To Janin. Crémieux. Coste. *Traité* with Scribe.[33] [Wrote] to Duponchel about Duprez's costume, and that he should speak to Antenor about Falcon. To Falcon. [Wrote] to Armand Bertin. At 9:45 Kastner came.

16 May. Whether the dancers for the *Pas de Trois* have been engaged? Cut[34] in the *Ronde des Bohemiennes.* To Scribe. Falcon. Gentil. M. de Girardin. To Crosnier and Cerfberr about Möser.

17 May. [Wrote] to Habeneck. To Ed. Blanc. [Wrote] to Rodrigues, Merlin. At 9 Auguste. 9:30 to Gouin (Flécheux, Möser, *Pas de Trois*, stalls, *Robert*).

18 May. Massol, Levasseur, Habeneck, Duponchel, Gentil, Lusy, Duprez, Halévy, me, Gouin, Malençon.

19 May. Berlioz. At 2 to Damoureau. To Duprez (about lunch). To Bornstedt*. Henri Blaze. Girardin. Ticket for Specht. Pixis. Merruau.

20 May. At 10 Buloz came. At 11 Möser. At 12 Bornstedt. To Scribe. Merruau.

21 May. At 10 to Gentil. To Merruau. Armand Bertin.

22 May. At 4 Henri Blaze. 5:30 Montalivet.

24 May. At 3 Henri Blaze came. To Scribe.[35]

25 May. At 1 to Duprez. To Tulon. Ed. Blanc about Lehmann. The letters for Pixis. Ticket for Panofka.

26 May. Habeneck ("À vous et ma vie et mon âme").[36] "Laisse moi partir" again slower. Wait for the applause[37] before the chords preceding "Oh terreur l'ai-je dit." Not to take the stringendo in the stretta so fast.[38] With Schlesinger, Blanchard*, Berlioz to the Opéra. Algiers, fourth performance.[39]

27 May. At 11:30 to Scribe. Blanchard. To Besson.[40] D'Ortigue. At 2 met Berton at the Institut. To Ed. Blanc for Lehmann.

28 May. Today Minna left Paris.[41] At 12 to Falcon with Levasseur and Duprez.

29 May. Berton. With Schlesinger concerning Kalkbrenner. Mme. Stolz*. Roger*. Saint-Georges.[42]

30 May. Soirée at Turcas's*. Nourrit. *Die drei Pintos* from Gouin. Merruau, Beauregard, Mme. Stolz, Ed. Blanc. Botté de Toulemont.

31 May. Schlesinger concerning Mme. Stolz and Kalkbrenner. Dined with Kalkbrenner. At 12 to Mme. Stolz. At 4 Henri Blanchard came. The score of *Les Huguenots* for Batton*. To D'Ortigue. Ed. Blanc.

[Undated entries pertaining to events in May.]

[Wrote] to Richard Wagner* in Königsberg,[43] to Gottfried Weber about the Institut. Wrote to Castelli and sent him a score. [Wrote] to Baermann. The piece by Sand for the musical paper.[44] That Leduc should write out the receipts from *Les Huguenots*. Send [Louis] Viardot's* books back to him. Fetch the vocal scores from Mme. Merlin. From Andréoli the printed hymn from the *Crociato*.[45] Biography to Léon de Bast. Search out the Klopstock lieder for Schlesinger. Arrange "Le poète mourant." [Take] the stretta of Raoul's aria in act 5 to Gouin in case Nourrit wants it.

June 1837

Thursday 1 June. In the evening to Girardin. At 4 to Schlesinger about Schilling. *God save the King* for Schott.

2 June. [Wrote] to Ed. Blanc about the invitation, presentation, and the minister.

3 June. At 11 d'Ortigue. At 11 rehearsal.

4 June. At 10 to Planard, before 10 to Ed. Blanc. At 12:30 rehearsal.

5 June. At 11:30 to Scribe. [Wrote] to Scribe about the *Anabaptistes*.[46]

6 June. [Wrote] to Merruau. Duprez. At 10:30 to Halévy's, where I also found Habeneck.

7 June. [Wrote] to Ed. Blanc about the rehearsal in Versailles.[47] Joel.[48] Roger. Saint-Georges. Taylor* about Dettmoldt.

8 June. Dined at Coste's. At 11:30 rehearsal at Versailles. To Mlle. Valentin*.

[Wrote] to Taylor about Dettmoldt. [Sent] Mother a copper engraving for Dett-moldt. [Sent] Planard act 1.

9 June. To Duponchel about Merruau. To Buloz at 4. [Wrote] to Blanchard.

10 June. To Ed. Blanc as whether Chasles can come. To Botté [de Toulemont]. To Probst.[49] To Roger.

11 June. To Saint-Georges. [Wrote] to Taylor about Dettmoldt. The remarks[50] for Scribe. To d'Ortigue and Botté that they should come on Monday.

12 June. Before 10 Probst. At 11:30 d'Ortigue and Botté de Toulemont. At 12 to Crémieux. To Ed. Blanc. At 3 d'Ortigue, Botté. At 4 Buloz.

13 June. At 10 Alizard*. Dined at Rothschild's. Invited[51] Antenor Joly and his brother to supper. To Mme. Girardin.

15 June. At 9:30 Mlle. Serre. At 3 to Crosnier. Gave Crosnier the letter for Lablache. Copper engraving for Dettmoldt. Ed. Blanc. Gouin. Auguste.

16 June. Procura for Gouin.[52] Damoreau. After 12 to Duprez.

17 June. At 3 to Roger. At 4:30 to Cerfberr.

18 June. At 1 to Cerfberr. 2:30 Conservatoire. At 4 Saint-Georges came.

19 June. At 10 after the Cercle des Arts.

20 June. From 10 until 12 Traxel came. [Wrote] to Henri Blanchard. To Saint-Georges about "La Ronde." Cercle des Arts.

21 June. At 5 d'Ortigue to dine.

24 June. [Wrote] to Nougier, Scribe, Traxel. Rehearsal *Stradella*.[53] At 4 Martens came.

26 June. To Ed. Blanc. At 4 Henri Blaze came.

27 June. [Wrote] to H. Blanchard. At 3 H. Blaze came. Observations for Scribe.

28 June. At 4 Schlesinger. Merruau. This evening to Gouin on account of the supplement to *Les Huguenots*. [Discussed] the supplement to *Les Huguenots* and Schumann[54] with Schlesinger. To Barisel.

29 June. At 4 to Scribe. Write to Ed. Blanc. Barisel.

30 June. Dined at Coste's. At 3 to Saint-Georges.

July 1837

Saturday 1 July. At 4 Henri Blaze came. At 10 Castelli to Schlesinger. Dined with Mme. Dorus.

2 July. At 10 to Scribe in Montalais concerning his copy. *Traité*. Gouin.

3 July. At 9:30 Barisel came. Crémieux. *Procura* for Gouin. From 12 until 2 to Crémieux.

4 July. At 4 Henri Blaze came. *Norma* and *Anna Bolena*. At 3:30 Roger.

6 July. Between 3 and 4 Merruau came. To Paganini. To Coste. From 1 until 2 d'Ortigue.

7 July. [Wrote] to Crémieux. [Wrote] to Scribe. [Consulted] with Halévy about the third Monk[55] [see example 42]:

Example 42. Theme (3) from *Les Huguenots*

Schlesinger about the shooting-machine. At 5 Montalivet. At 1:30 Saint-Georges.

8 July. *"Le Clocheteur des trépasses": les paroles de cette ballade se trouvent dans la mémorial du Jongleur.*[56] At 1 [took] Paganini to Mother's.

9 July. The supplement for *Les Huguenots*. George Sand. To Ed. Blanc. To Crémieux.

10 July. [Wrote] to Benoist about the three Monks. Schlesinger [about] the shooting-machine. Schumann. [Sent] Roger the books. M. Duchesne*. Passport.

11 July. [Sent] the music back to Schlesinger, shooting-machines. George Sand. Fortepiano at Pleyel's for Duponchel. [Wrote] to Beauregard. Montalivet. Supplement to *Les Huguenots.*

12 July. Had Auguste come. At 10 Gouin came. Fifty-ninth proposal.

13 July. Today I left Paris. Good night's lodging at Sezanne.

14 July. In Ligny fairly good night's lodging.

15 July. In Sarrebourg.

16 July. In Bischofsheim.

17 July. Arrived early today in Baden. [Wrote] to Gouin. Charles Maurice.

18 July. To Mme. Vespermann.

19 July. Left Baden this afternoon. Slept in Bruchsal.

20 July. In Frankfurt. Speyer: bells, shooting-machine, bass clarinet, harps.[57]

21 July. Slept in Hanau.

22 July. [Slept] in Buttlar.

[On 23 July 1837 the first installment of Balzac's *Gambara*, containing a eulogy of *Robert le Diable*, appeared in Maurice Schlesinger's *Revue et Gazette musicale de Paris;* other installments followed until 20 August 1837.]

26 July. Arrived in Berlin.

27 July. Prof. Gans 31 Charlotten- and Bärenstrasse.

31 July. Began [drinking] the Spa water. Before 10 to Redern. From 11 until 1 Förster.

August 1837

Wednesday 2 August. With Buchholz about Giacomo.[58] Power of attorney for [Joseph] Herz. New Society contract. To Gotthold Schlesinger. Dined with Eberty.

5 August. At 10 to the Akademie.

4 August. Write to Gottfried [Weber] and the pieces for Monday eleven o'clock. To Humboldt, Werther, Dunker*, Buchholz.

5 August. The letters for Gans readdressed to Montpelier.

10 August. Mme. Löwe.

11 August. Between 12 and 1 Truhn*.

13 August. At 12 Fillon.

[On 16 August Scribe informed Meyerbeer of the delivery of the text for the last three acts of *L'Africaine*. He handed them in person to Gouin and asked him to send them on to Meyerbeer.]

20 August. [Met] Lichtenstein behind the Catholic Church.

21 August. Looked for the *Canzonette*, Sandfass.[59]

22 August. [Wrote] to Öttinger and H. Blaze.

23 August. At 11 to Lichtenstein. Herz about Hellborn.

24 August. Dubois's *Die Mexikaner.*[60] At 10 Buchholz, Humboldt, Heinrich.

25 August. At noon to Lichtenstein, Hofrat Kolzenbach for the passport. Bischofswerder. Princess Wilhelm[61] (about the duchess of Orleans). Score for the crown prince. Werther for permission to wear the Order.[62]

26 August. [Wrote] to the king. At 12 sitting in the Akademie. Charles Dubois (five o'clock).

27 August. Data for Baermann's letter. Score for the crown prince. The reorganization of Heinrich's allowance.[63] Today [wrote] to Öttinger.

28 August. Today [wrote] to Sachs and Henri Blaze, to Scribe, Musikdirektor Bach*, Baermann, Berlin letters.

29 August. [Wrote] to Baermann and Pastor Ohlenfeldt. Today left Berlin. Slept in Treuenbritzen.

30 August. Slept in Leipzig.

31 August. Slept in Weimar.

September 1837

Friday 1 September. Slept in Buttlar. [Wrote] to Speyer, W. Wagner, Beurmann, Gutzkow*, Durand.

2 September. Bells, shooting-machine, bass clarinet, harps, what has been omitted. Slept in the town Kreuznach, near Frankfurt.

3 September. [Wrote] to Beurmann, Winkler, Gouin, rosette (fifth act, why not the fourth?). *Pas de Deux* instrumentation ([wrote] to Taglioni about Princess Wilhelm). Letter to the duchess of Orleans.

4 September. Arrived in Baden today,

9 September. Left Baden. Inspected the translation for Gollmick*.[64]

10 September. Arrived in Frankfurt. Speyer: what the box[65] and letter cost. Notes for [W.] Wagner. Gollmick's altered translation. Schuster. Attended the rehearsal. Write whether my observations on tempi and acting have been useful, whether it was full, and what sort of reception. That Guhr should write.

11 September. 8:30 Speyer, Wagner, Gollmick. 9 Guhr, [Mme.] Kratsky.[66] 11:30 Dettmer. [Wrote] to Beurmann, Durand.

13 September. At 9 Dr. Beurmann.[67] Left Frankfurt. [Sent] Gouin *certificat d'origine* of the piano.

14 September. Arrived in Baden.

21 September. Wagner.

22 September. [Wrote] to Wagner, to Kaskel about Lyser*, Baermann.

23 September. [Wrote] to Speyer, Gouin . Concerning Lafont*, that she should not do the reprise of *Robert.* When is this to be? News about *La Muette di Portici.*[68] Why is Gentil angry with Halévy? Schlesinger in Brussels. Rossini.

24 September. [Wrote] to Guhr, to Speyer concerning what Beurmann has written to me, and Flersheim the *abonnement suspendu*. [Sent] the songs to the Berlin Schlesinger. [Wrote] to Ed. Blanc, Lüttichau*,[69] Lewald.[70]

27 September. [Wrote] to Wagner.

29 September. Schlesinger for Brussels. Fétis.

30 September. To Lobstein. [Wrote] to Speyer.

October 1837.

Sunday 1 October. [Wrote] to Guhr.

2 October. Send to Scribe.

6 October. [Wrote] to Lüttichau.

7 October. [Wrote] to Gutzkow.

10 October. [Conferred] with Halévy and Armand about *Robert*. H. Blaze in Brussels.

14 October. [Wrote] to Schlesinger in Berlin.[71]

16 October. [Wrote] a letter of recommendation for Gütkow to Wilhelm.

17 October. To Karlsruhe. To Otterstedt,[72] Leiningen, Haber, Haitzinger*.

20 October. [Wrote] to Traxel, Castelli. [Sent] the music to Haitzinger.

23 October. [Wrote] to Gottfried Weber.

28 October. [Wrote] Mme. Dorus-Gras, to Schlesinger in Berlin.

November 1837.

Thursday 2 November. [Wrote] to Gouin . Who is the new Italian tenor at the Opéra?[73] Has Demoiselle Pauline Garcia* been engaged?[74] Has he spoken to Armand Bertin? How successful has *Piquillo*[75] been? *Monde parisien. Traité*. Halévy's opera.[76] [Wrote] to Leiningen.

9 November. Today we moved into Blume's.

12 November. Today Tante Mosson left for Berlin.

18 November. [Wrote] to Gouin . [Sent] Schlesinger the proofs[77] of the "Poète mourant."[78]

29 November. [Sent] Schlesinger the second corrections.

30 November. [Sent] Gouin and Schlesinger the German songs.

December 1837.

Tuesday 5 December. [Meyerbeer stopped work on *Cinq Mars.*][79] [Wrote] to Schlesinger *(Revue des Théâtres).*

9 December. [Wrote] to Hell, Schwarz ("Poète mourant"). [Sent] Leiningen the libretto of *Les Huguenots.* [Wrote] to Winkler. [Gave] Otterstedt power of attorney. [Wrote] to Gouin.

11 December. [Wrote] to Gottfried Weber, Schwarz, Kastner, Baermann.

14 December. [Arrived in Paris.]

[On 16 December *Robert le Diable* was given in Warsaw in French.]

NOTES

1. The 6/8 stretta (C-sharp minor—E major, actually) of no. 23, *Conjuration et Bénédiction des Poignards.*
2. Lard and Devienne were proofreaders employed by the publisher Schlesinger.
3. In 1837 Musard took over direction of the balls held at the Opéra.
4. An artist.
5. A French journalist.
6. Tgb. *loge.*
7. Meyerbeer had begun the composition of a new opera, *Cinq-Mars,* to a libretto by Saint-Georges. The opera was never completed.
8. Tgb. *loge.*
9. Tgb. *comité.*
10. Tgb. *loge.*
11. Tgb. *déjeuner.*
12. Tgb. *déjeuner.*
13. Tgb. *stalle.*
14. The painter was a nephew of the banker Leo and recorded that he knew Meyerbeer "als einen intimen Freund der Familie häufig im Salon meiner Tante [Leo] begegnet" [as an intimate friend of the family, often to be found in the salon of my Aunt Leo].

15. "Those theaters not able to provide a double orchestra should simply arrange this piece in such a way that the entries and replies of the band on the bark are taken over by the main orchestra."

16. Tgb. *clarinette basse.*

17. This instrument was famously introduced into the orchestra by Meyerbeer in act 5 of *Les Huguenots,* where it accompanies the nuptial blessing in the hour of death (no. 27a, *Interrogatoire*). The composer's notes suggest that it was not used at the première, but rather at the reprise later in 1836. See Adam Carse, *The History of Orchestration* (1925; reprint, New York: Dover Publications, 1964), pp. 205–6, 253–54.

18. Tgb. *quittance.*

19. On 27 March 1837, act 5 of *Robert le Diable* was given at the Opéra for Levasseur's benefit.

20. Meyerbeer's choral piece *God save the King* for four men's voices was composed for Wilhelm Ehlers and performed in Mainz at Easter 1835. In 1837 this and the *Festgesang* for four men's voices and chorus for the installation of the Gutenberg Memorial in Mainz (1834) were published by Schott.

21. Adolphe Nourrit bade farewell to the Paris stage in a glittering benefit concert held on 1 April 1837 (24,380 fr.), and Duprez made his début.

22. Meyerbeer had begun coaching Duprez to take over the role of Raoul after Nourrit's departure from Paris. On 11 April Duponchel organized a soirée in his apartments to present the new star of the Opéra. Meyerbeer was present, as well as Princess Chimay, Prince and Princess Belgiojoso, Countess Merlin, the brothers Bertin, Rémusat, Mornay, Cuvillier-Fleury, Louis Viardot, Scribe, Gustav de Wailly, Cherubini, Auber, Halévy, Berlioz, Adam, Zimmermann, Niedermeyer, and Cicéri. Duprez sang two arias from *Le Muette de Portice* and "Rachel, quand du Seigneur" from *La Juive.* At the end of the evening Liszt improvised at the piano. (Martine Kahane, *Robert le Diable: Catalogue de l'exposition Théâtre National de l'Opéra de Paris 20 juin—20 septembre 1985* [Paris: Bibliothèque National, 1985], p. 24). Duprez made his début at the Opéra on 17 April in the role of Arnold in *Guillaume Tell.*

23. Baron Strehlen wanted to acquaint himself with Mainzer's singing school for workers in Paris.

24. Rehearsals of the ballet in act 3 of *Les Huguenots.*

25. A proposed libretto.

26. Of *L'Africaine* and *Le Prophète.*

27. On 29 April 1837 a charity concert for the poor of Lyons was held in the Salle du Vauxhall under the patronage of Mme. Merlin and other society ladies. It was directed by Meyerbeer, Halévy, Habeneck, and Trevaux.

28. The *andante amoroso* passage in G-flat major from the act 4 *Grand Duo.*

29. The clarinet features prominently in the *Grand Duo.*

30. For the reprise of *Les Huguenots.*

31. Meyerbeer had composed a special aria for Duprez. It is preserved in the British Library, and listed in Augustus Hughes-Hughes, *Catalogue of Manuscript Music in the British Museum,* vol. 2, *Secular Vocal Music* (1906; reprint, London: Trustees of the British Museum, 1966), p. 428: "**Egerton 2829**, ff. 6-9. Paper; A.D. 1837. Small folio: 'Air composé expressément pour le début de Duprez dans 'les Huguenots', par Meyerbeer, qui lui a envoyé, écrite de sa main, l'ébauche ci-incluse.—Cet air inédite a été chanté 10 fois par Duprez—en 1837—et supprimé comme inutile.' The above inscription is signed 'G[ilbert] Duprez'. The music was written for insertion in Act V of the Opera, as an alter-

native to the original setting of the scene beginning 'Il l'aura! oui. Courons aux armes', following the air 'A la lueur de leurs torches', as published in 1836. The melody only of the first part of the air is given, but the second portion of it has the pianoforte part written under it, in score, followed by a neat copy of the same."

32. No. 15, *Ronde bohémienne* ("Venez, vous qui voulez savoir d'avance").

33. Preparations were underway for the new contracts relating to *Le Prophète* and *L'Africaine*.

34. Tk. *coupure*.

35. On 24 May 1837 Meyerbeer signed a contract with Scribe for the libretto of *L'Africaine*. It was stipulated that he was to receive the completed text by the end of August and that he was to have finished setting it by 1840. The libretto was drawn partly from an unidentified German tale, partly from *La Veuve de Malibar*, a novel by Antoine Lemierre depicting the love of a Hindu girl for a Portuguese explorer, a theme already used by Spohr in *Jessonda* (1823) (see Kathleen O'Donnell Hoover, *Makers of Opera* [Port Washington, N.Y., and London: Kennikat Press, 1971], p. 105). Another point of departure was the poem "Le mancenillier" by Millevoye about a young girl who sits under a tree that gives out poisonous fragrances and is rescued by her lover (see *The New Grove Dictionary of Opera*, ed. Stanley Sadie [London: Macmillan, 1992], s.v. *"L'Africaine"*).

36. *Les Huguenots*, act 2, no. 10, *Allegro con spirito* (duet for Marguerite de Valois and Raoul).

37. Tgb. *applaudissement*.

38. All references to the *Grand Duo* for Valentine and Raoul (act 4, no. 21).

39. Of *Robert le Diable*.

40. Gustave-Auguste Besson was an instrument maker.

41. Minna Meyerbeer had decided that she did not want to live in Paris, but preferred Berlin. Her delicate health, and no doubt her mental condition, had been damaged by the loss of her first two infants, and from 1840 she would spend the winter at one watering place or another.

42. Weber's family was pressing Meyerbeer to begin the completion of *Die drei Pintos*. He turned to Saint-Georges and Roger de Beauvoir for a French reworking of the libretto.

43. The first mention of Richard Wagner. He is not to be confused with Dr. W. Wagner, who wrote a long and enthusiastic article on *Les Huguenots* in the *Didaskalia* 15:248 (9 September 1837) and 15:249 (10 September 1837).

44. During October 1836 George Sand, while visiting Geneva, had written her famous eleventh letter of the *Lettres d'un Voyageur* addressed to Meyerbeer, and discussing the aesthetic, social, and intellectual implications of the appearance of *Robert le Diable* and *Les Huguenots*. The collection was published in Brussels (Bonnaire) in 1837. For a translation, see Sacha Rabinovitch and Patricia Thomson, *Lettres d'un Voyageur* (Harmondsworth, U.K.: Penguin, 1987), pp. 275–91.

45. The *Scena ed Inno di Morte* from *Il Crociato in Egitto* (no. 15 in the Pacini vocal score) was arranged and printed as an organ voluntary.

46. The original title of *Le Prophète*. The libretto was based on ideas and information drawn from Voltaire's description of the Anabaptist revolt in chap. 132 of his *Essai sur les moeurs* (1754), an excerpt of which was printed in the first edition of the libretto. Other possible literary sources include a novel by Van der Welde, *Die Anabaptisten* (1826), and the article "Anabaptistes de Münster" in Jules Michelet's *Mémoires de Luther*, a collection of historical anecdotes, letters and documents (see *New Grove Dictionary of Opera*,

s.v. *"Le Prophète"*). It is likely that Schiller's *Die Jungfrau von Orleans*, containing as it does a confrontation between God's appointed servant and her doubting father, was another source of inspiration, as was the mixture of religion and politics in Sir Walter Scott's *Old Mortality* (see the notes appended to the end of the *Taschenkalender* for December 1838). Karin Pendle further draws attention to Henry Sutherland Edwards's thesis that *Le Prophète* is also based on the story of "the false Demetrius, who, when he had raised himself to the throne of Russia, was confronted with his humbly-born mother" (Edwards, *The Lyrical Drama* [London, 1881], 1:257). Scribe could have read of Demetrius in any history of Russia, and may well have known Pushkin's *Boris Godunov* (1831) which describes peasant revolts, fanaticism and a leader used as a tool by a revolutionary group, all themes that he used in his libretto (Pendle, *Eugène Scribe and the French Opera of the Nineteenth Century* [Ann Arbor, Mich.: UMI Research Press, 1979], p. 565).

47. The new Théâtre du Palais de Versailles was opened on 10 June 1837.

48. A tailor employed by the Opéra.

49. Heinrich Albert Probst was the Paris representative of the Leipzig publisher Breitkopf & Härtel.

50. Tk. *remarque*.

51. Tk. *invitiert*.

52. Gouin was given power of attorney to act on Meyerbeer's behalf in Paris.

53. Opera in five acts by Niedermeyer (E. Deschamps and E. Pacini; Paris, Opéra 3 March 1837). Based on episodes from the life of the famous singer-composer Alessandro Stradella, the opera was created by singers of great merit—Nourrit, Falcon, and Dérivis. One of the arias, "Ah! quel songe affreux!," became famous.

54. This concerns Schumann's negative reactions to the Leipzig performance of *Les Huguenots* on 20 April 1837, which culminated in the notorious polemic against Meyerbeer and his opera in the *Neue Zeitschrift für Musik* (5 September 1837). From then on he maintained a consistently hostile attitude towards Meyerbeer, doing the latter's long-term reputation in German aesthetic circles incalculable damage.

55. Tk. *le 3me Moine*. Three monks bless the weapons of the conspirators in the Blessing of the Daggers.

56. *"Le Clocheteur des trépasses*: the words of this ballad can be found in the memoirs of Jongleur."

57. Preparations for the Frankfurt performance of *Les Huguenots*.

58. Buchholz was a lawyer Meyerbeer consulted about the legal status of his italianized first name.

59. A barber.

60. This was a libretto proposed by Charles Dubois, a newspaper editor, and probably based on *Les Mexicains, ou L'Idole de Tlascala, mélodrame* in three acts (Duveyrier; Paris, Théâtre de l'Ambigu Comique, 15 May 1819) [Wicks 4934].

61. Princess Augusta* of Saxe-Weimar, the future queen of Prussia and empress of Germany, married King Friedrich Wilhelm III's second son, Wilhelm, in 1829. She followed artistic matters closely.

62. Presumably the Légion d'Honneur.

63. Heinrich Beer had probably overspent in pursuit of his collection of musical manuscripts. A letter of Amalia Beer to Meyerbeer of 13 September 1837 suggests that there were tensions between his brothers Wilhelm and Heinrich (*BT*, 3:63).

64. Meyerbeer had requested Gollmick to make some alterations to Castelli's German

translation of *Les Huguenots*, a task he attended to in a few days, returning the completed libretto to Speyer.

65. Tgb. *loge*.

66. A singer.

67. The several meetings with Beurmann in September indicate the importance that Meyerbeer attached to this journalist. In vol. 2 of his work *Brüssels und Paris* (Leipzig, 1837–38) he had already spoken very perceptively of Meyerbeer's importance for France.

68. Revived at the Opéra in 1837.

69. Winkler had already informed Meyerbeer of the plans to produce *Les Huguenots* in Dresden on 27 August 1837.

70. Probably an answer to August Lewald's open letter "An Herrn Meyerbeer, Baden 16 August 1837," *Europa* 3 (1837): 446–55), in which he reported on the performance of *Les Huguenots* in Baden, discussed Meyerbeer's stay in Paris and his French style, and concluded that, like Gluck and Mozart, Meyerbeer was a cosmopolitan, not a German, composer.

71. Heinrich Schlesinger had written to Meyerbeer on 24 September 1837, urgently requesting the composer to send him the songs intended for an anthology album he was planning to publish. It eventually appeared as *II. Album avec paroles françaises, italiennes et allemandes. Neue Original-Compositionen für Gesang und Piano von Carafa, Curschmann, Donizetti, Halévy, Huth, Kücken, Loewe, Mme. Malibran, Mendelssohn-Bartholdy, Meyerbeer, Panseron, Reissiger, Truhn*. It included Meyerbeer's songs "Hör ich das Liedchen klingen" (Heine) and "Menschenfeindlich" (M. Beer).

72. Freiherr von Otterstedt was the Prussian ambassador in Karlsruhe.

73. He was Giovanni Mario*, whom Duponchel was paying 200 fr. a month.

74. She was not engaged.

75. *Piquillo*, opera by Hippolyte Monpou (Alexandre Dumas and Gérard de Nerval; Paris, Opéra Comique, 31 October 1837).

76. Halévy was composing *Guido et Ginevra*, first performed on 5 March 1838.

77. Tk. *épreuves*.

78. On 8 November Maurice Schlesinger had requested permission to publish "Le poète mourant" together with Legouvé's translation of the *Hymne* in an album of Clapisson, Stuntz, and Panofka, and Meyerbeer agreed to this on 14 November. The publisher had to ask repeatedly for the proofs of "Le poète mourant" and eventually acknowledged receipt (25 November 1837).

79. The information that Meyerbeer stopped work on *Cinq-Mars* is based on an article by Reyer in the *Journal des Débats* (27 mars 1881) describing attempts to secure some of Meyerbeer's manuscripts from the estate of Ernst-Otto Lindner for the Paris Opéra Library. Reyer provided a description of the manuscript that concluded with the words "Baden-Baden, le 5 décembre 1837." (See *BT*, 3:63.)

Section 7
1838–1839

1838

January 1838

Friday 5 January. At 4 to Berton. At 12 Olivier* to Duponchel. [Discussed] Rosenhain and the contrabassist Müller* with Habeneck. At 2 M. Achille. Soirée at Beauregard's.

6 January. At 10 Alary. Charles Maurice. Berton for the Institut. 200 fr. Gallitzin*.[1] [Wrote] to Artaria.

7 January. Soirée at Janin's. To Scribe about Ries and the duet. At 3 Henri Blaze. [Wrote] to [Gottfried] Weber.

8 January. At 3 Alary. For Koreff to Ed. Blanc and Bertin. [Wrote] to Henri Blaze about *Die drei Pintos*.[2]

9 January. The essay to Weber.

10 January. At 9:30 to Crémieux. At 11 Alary came with Habeneck and Dacosta.

11 January. Soirée at Derbel's. At 10:30 Mme. Marx* came. [Wrote] to Rosenhain, Müller, Escudier*.

12 January. Today Gouin dined with me. At 2:30 Escudier.

[During the night of 13 January a fire destroyed the Théâtre Italien.]

14 January. Dined with Boursault. Soirée at Ekkard's. Concert Conservatoire. Waited for Alary until 11. At 11 to Duponchel.

15 January. At 2 Massol. At 3 to Duponchel.

16 January. At 3 Rastoul. To Scribe. At 12 to Merruau. J. Janin. Saint-Georges. Soirée Belgiojoso.

17 January. At 1 to H. Blaze. At 12 Candia[3] and Alary.

18 January. At 1 to H. Blaze. Merruau. Belgiojoso.

19 January. Rendezvous with Saint-Georges tomorrow at one o'clock. At 2 to Merruau.

20 January. At 3 Rastoul. At 10 to Scribe. At 12 to Merruau. Soirée Poisson. At 4 to Belgiojoso.

21 January. At 12 to Saint-Georges. Biography for Escudier.[4] To Coste. [Wrote] to Panofka. To Tremont. At 5 Panofka.

22 January. At 1:30 Saint-Georges. At 2 Rastoul. At 3 Candia. To Pacini about Rastoul. Coste. Biography. To Lusy.

23 January. At 2 Rastoul. At 3 M. Joel. To Demidoff*. Dantan*. At 3 Viardot. Gentil dined with me. Soirée Belgiojoso. For Koreff to Berlin.

24 January. At 3 music newspaper. Dantan has been paid. [Wrote] to Munk and Merruau.

25 January. At 3 to Crosnier. At 4 music newspapers. At 12 to H. Schlesinger.

26 January. At 2 Candia. Soirée at Schlesinger's. To Zimmermann about Frisch.

29 January. At 3 Candia. With Émile Deschamps "Inno di Morte."[5] Neukomm* and Chopin for Pacini.

30 January. At 4 Kastner (manuscript).[6] To Saint-Georges. To Gallitzin. [Sent] Émile Deschamps the "Hymne de Morte."

31 January. [Wrote] to Dacosta.

February 1838

Thursday 1 February. At 3:30 Saint-Georges came. At 4 Kastner. At 9:30 in the evening to Ed. Blanc's. [Discussed] Schlegel with Cherubini. The *chanson* for Buloz.

2 February. Demidoff.

3 February. To Kalkbrenner and Cerfberr.

4 February. *Déjeuner* Crémieux. Soirée at Janin's.

5 February. At 2 Candia came.

7 February. At 11:30 Saint-Georges came. At 1:30 Candia came. Today Lusy, Gentil, and Gouin dined with me. Took Prince Gallitzen to the theater. [Wrote] to Weber.

8 February. To Montalivet. At 11 Saint-Georges. [Wrote] to Schlesinger about Kastner's essay. At 9 Léon de Bast. To Berton. [Discussed] Mlle. Oliver with Halévy.

9 February. At 1 Candia came. Soirée at Schlesinger's. [Wrote] to Theodor Hell.

10 February. At 11:30 to Buloz. At 3 to Demoiselle de Pan.[7] Candia came at 1. Mainzer dined with me. Candia came in the evening.

11 February. Dined with Célerier. At 12 to Saint-Georges. At 2 Candia.

12 February. At 11:30 to Saint-Georges. At 2 Candia came. At 4 Schiansky[8] came. [Wrote] to Émile Deschamps.

13 February. At 3 to Mlle. de Pan. At 1 Saint-Georges. [Discussed] Schiansky with Duponchel.

14 February. In the evening to Mlle. de Pan. To Potienctef. [Sent] Schlesinger Weber's printed essay.

15 February. At 11 Mlle. Oliver should come to Cherubini. At 11 to Mlle. de Pan. Buloz, Leo *déjeuner*. Custine. To E. Deschamps. At 1 to Crosnier. At 2 Candia came. At 4 Castil-Blaze came.

16 February. At 12 to Mlle. de Pan. [To] Kastner about G. Weber's article. To E. Deschamps.

17 February. [Sent] Bordogni* the full and vocal scores.[9] Met Berton at the Institut.

Deschamps. [Wrote] to Pleyel. At 12 to Mlle. de Pan. At 11:30 to Crosnier. [Conferred] with Habeneck about the drumrolls. In the evening at seven o'clock to Leo.

18 February. At 12 Candia came. At 2 to Crémieux. At 11 Gouin came. To Mainzer. At 4 to Leo to Mme. Schebest*. [Sent] Crosnier the plan for Weber's opera.[10] To E. Deschamps. Pleyel. Morel*. To Beauregard.

19 February. At 12 to Duponchel. At 2 Candia. E. Deschamps. At 3 Heine. At 4 to Crémieux. [Wrote] to Bordogni.

20 February. At 2 with Gouin and to Mlle. de Pan. 3:30 Candia. E. Deschamps. Pleyel. To Berton. Probst. Letters for Bordogni and Candia. Heine.

21 February. At 4 Legouvé. To Armand Bertin. Letters for Crosnier and Bordogni. To Mlle. de Pan. Heine.

22 February. Heine. To Berton. At 11 Prussian ambassador, passport. At 1 to Schlesinger about Méry. Merlin. Ed. Blanc. To Mme. Schebest. [Wrote] to Pleyel that he should fetch the piano. At 10 in the evening departed from Paris.

25 February. Changes for Mme. Schneider. At 9 the régisseur. At 10:30 Wächter. At 4 to Arrigoni.[11] At 5 M. Devrient*.

26 February. Arrived in Baden.

27 February. [Wrote] to Winkler.

March 1838

Thursday 1 March. At 12:30 traveled from Baden.

5 March. Arrived in Dresden in the late evening.

7 March. At 9 Winkler came. At 10 to Tante Jette. To Kaskel. Klengel. At 4 to Reissiger*. Declined Devrient.

8 March. At 10 Zezi came. At 4 to Reissiger. After the rehearsal with Jeritzer and Winkler. At 3 Tante Jette.

11 March. Alterations in modulation for the bass clarinet. Bathers' Chorus. No aria in act 5. Bells. Schuster.[12]

12 March. Bass clarinet. Viola. Changes for Mme. Schneider. Aria in act 5. That the *banda* should rehearse *apparti*.

13 March. Cut in the Gypsy Dance. At 4 to Herr Tichatschek*. Bells. Side drum and bass drum in the Conspiracy Scene. [Wrote] to Winkler about Schuster and Fischer. Title. Low prices. The alterations for Lüttichau and Pathengesch.

14 March. At 10 in the theater. Abridgment in the act 5 aria and modulations for the bass clarinet. Changes for Schneider. Watzdorf*. Kaskel. Dessauer*. Tante Jette and Miltitz*. Hofrat Weigl*.

15 March. At 9 to the theater. Arranged the bells. To Fischer and Tante Jette. At 4 to the theater. At 5 to Mme. Devrient. To Winkler. Traveled from Dresden in the evening.

17 March. Arrived in Berlin. J. P. Schmidt. Bresson*.

18 March. To Heinrich. To Frau Mosson, Eberty, Spieker*, Redern and his mother, Humboldt, Geheimrat Schulze*, Bischofswerder, Victor Ebers*, Dunker, Lichtenstein, Esperstädt, Dr. Arndt, Fanny Ebers, Crelinger, Werther, Schadow, Tölken, Förster*.

21 March. At 4 dinner at Redern's. "Poète mourant" for Kaskel*. Major Serr. Sachs*.

22 March. [Justizrat] Bennewitz. Hellborn. The second letter to Gouin.

23 March. Schadow. Crelinger, Dunker, Werther, Bresson.

24 March. At 3:30 Gans met me.

25 March. At 12 Förster came. At 2 Nougier came.

26 March. At 2 Sandfass. At 11 to Schadow.

27 March. At 10 Löwe came with his daughter to sing. At 12 Hauck* came. At 2 Nougier came.

28 March. At 10 Herr Hofrat Förster. At 2 to Buchholz. Lichtenstein, Werther, Bresson, Gans, Humboldt, Varnhagen*, Fränkel.

31 March. To Countess Brühl. [Conferred] with Wilhelm about Heine.

April 1838

Sunday 1 April. 11:30 at Herr Musikdirektor Bach's. [Wrote] two letters to Küstner.

2 April. At 10:30 to Humboldt.

3 April. Had to inquire about Hellwig's canon from the steward Adler at the Opera House.

4 April. [Wrote] to Winkler.

5 April. [Wrote] to Kaskel, Pacini.

7 April. [Wrote] to Humboldt.

11 April. At 2 Justizrat Marchand came (to dine).

20 April. [Wrote] to Fétis.

22 April. At 2 *déjeuner* Dunker.

23 April. Book of stage directions[13] to Küstner.

24 April. At 7 to Geheimrat Lichtenstein. Gläser,* complaint.

27 April. At 10 rehearsal of *Belisario.*[14] Departed for Dresden.

28 April. Arrived in Dresden in the evening. Had the act 4 romance copied for Devrient.[15] Dr. Sachs (biography). Lyser.[16] Hofrat Pieritz.

29 April. Devrient (cadenza, Freimüller*).

30 April. Hofrat Pieritz. Morlacchi. Lüttichau. Dessauer. Left Dresden today.

May 1838

Tuesday 1 May. Arrived in Berlin today.

2 May. Humboldt.

3 May. The duet for Princess Wilhelm.

4 May. H. Schlesinger. C. M. von Weber's green book. Corrections of the collected songs, "Le Ricordanze."[17]

5 May. Dr. Sachs diploma. Departure cards. Gubitz account. [Wrote] to Kaskel, Miltitz,[18] Winkler, Lyser. [Sent] Schlesinger receipt and corrections.

6 May. Departed from Berlin.

9 May. Arrived in Frankfurt in the evening.

10 May. Returned the music borrowed from Breitkopf. Fétis, letter for Bériot*.

11 May. Arrived in Baden.

14 May. [Wrote] to Leiningen, Fétis, Baermann.

15 May. Left Baden this morning.

19 May. Arrived in Paris this evening.

19 May. Armand Bertin.

20 May. Halévy, Duprez, Armand, Mme. [Dorus-]Gras.

21 May. To Pleyel.

22 May. At 11 to Candia. At 12 to Taglioni. Dumanoir.* At 1 to Stolz. At 2:30 to Guyot. Bordogni came at 10 in the evening.

23 May. At 10 to Pleyel. At 11 to Candia. At 3 Merruau.

24 May. At 9 Pleyel. At 12:30 Bordogni. At 2:30 Mlle. Dorus-Gras. At 4 Crosnier. At 6 dinner Rocher de Cancale.

25 May. At 9 Sauton. [With] Dumas at 9:30 to Meyer. At 11 Riek. At 12 Hermann*. At 2:30 to Guyot.[19]

26 May. At 9 Hermann came. At 9:30 to Méry. At 3 to Duponchel.

27 May. At 9:30 Méry. At 12 Pacini.

28 May. At 9 to Guyot. At 12:30 Firmin. At 2 rehearsal in the Opéra.

29 May. [Sent] Duprez's music to Lyons. At 10 M. Barthélemi. 2:30 rehearsal at Duponchel's. Blanchard, d'Ortigue, Koreff, Merlin, E. Blanc. Schlesinger about M[aurice Charles?].

30 May. Today Henri Blaze dined with me. At 12 Commission des Auteurs. To Mme. Nau. Answered Leo and Léon de Bast. At 3 rehearsal at Duponchel's.

31 May. 2:30 rehearsal.

June 1838

Friday 1 June. Sent the packet to Duprez in Lyons.

3 June. At 1 rehearsal at Duponchel's. [Wrote] to Léon de Bast. Buloz. Castil-Blaze.

4 June. At 10 Crémont. Adalbert von Bornstedt. Émile Deschamps. Lapelouze.

5 June. At 3 rehearsal at Duponchel's.

6 June. Gail* at 10. At 11:30 Candia.

8 June. At 12:30 rehearsal in the Opéra. At 2 Commission des Auteurs.

9 June. At 9 Conservatoire. At 4 Bornstedt. Buloz. 4:30 Merruau.

10 June. To Ed. Blanc.

11 June. At 9 Conservatoire. At 2 Commission des Auteurs.

12 June. D'Ortigue to lunch. At 10 or at 3 Mlle. Lebrun.*[20] Audition of Mlle. Stuart. At 3 rehearsal at Duponchel's.

13 June. At 10 the painter came.

14 June. Between 10 and 11 Sauvage. At 11 the painter came. At 12 Méry. At 1 Mlle. Lebrun. Dinner Neuwall.

15 June. At 2:30 Commission des Auteurs. Heine. G. Weber's treatise for the Institut. Biography for Méry. Duponchel. Guests: Ed. Blanc, Ar. Bertin, Ed. Bertin, Habeneck, Gouin.

17 June. [Wrote] to Bornstedt. Dined at Bertin's.

18 June. At 11 to Méry.

19 June. To Ed. Blanc. A. Joly. Today Munk dined with me. At 4 Heine. At 10 Duverger* came.

21 June. Méry biography. Ed. Blanc. Berton. Crémieux, Candia.

22 June. 2:30 Commission des Auteurs. Today Gentil dined with me.

23 June. At 10:30 Gouin, Candia. [Wrote] to Berton. At 11:30 Heine. At 12 to Bornstedt.

24 June. Dined with Leo. Auteuil. To Scribe. To Mlle. Nau, Germain Delavigne.

25 June. At 10 M. Barthélemi, Antenor Joly. Bohrer's concert.

26 June. Dined at Beauregard's. At 11 Heine. At 3 rehearsal with Candia. At 4 Crémieux.

27 June. Dined at Ed. Blanc's. At 12 Candia came.

28 June. Between 9 and 10 E. Deschamps. Thursday at 11 Heine. At 1 Scribe came. At 3 to Ponchard. To Berryer*.

29 June. Antenor Joly. 2:30 Commission des Auteurs. Soirée Perthius. Saint-Georges, Roger, Ant. Joly and his brother, V. Hugo, Heine, Morel, Méry, Gouin, me.

30 June. At 10:30 to Heine. Dinner in my rooms. Perthius, Sand. [Wrote] to Minna (about Speyer).

July 1838

Sunday 1 July. At 10:30 Heine. Germain Delavigne. Stuart. Candia.

2 July. At 10 Hurteaux. At 3 Scribe came.

3 July. At 1 Mlle. Rieux.[21] At 10 Gouin with Thomas*. At 11 Heine. At 2:30 Mlle. Lebrun. Today Gentil and Lusy dined with me.

4 July. At 3 Mlle. Lebrun. *Séance* at Devéria's* at one o'clock. Dinner Ed. Blanc *à 11 heures chez Mlle. Gras.*

5 July. Dined at Berton's. Devéria one o'clock. At 3 Candia. Crémieux about Cherubini. Germain. Heine. Soirée Buloz.

6 July. To Mlle. Lebrun. At 12 to Duprez. At 2:30 Commission des Auteurs. Crémieux, Germain. At 5 to Bordogni.

7 July. At 11 or 1 to Devéria. At 12 to Duprez. Gail dined with me. 2:30 Candia. At 3 a rehearsal. [Wrote] to Cherubini. Crémieux. Dined at Colonel Dumas's. To Heine.

9 July. At 10 to Mlle. Philipp. Today Coche* came. At 12 Devéria. At 12:30 Candia. At 2 Mlle. Lebrun. M. Michel.

10 July. To Germain. Scribe. At 2:30 Commission des Auteurs. At 3 a rehearsal with Candia. At 7 rehearsal in the theater.

11 July. At 9 Commission des Auteurs. At 10 Barthélemi. At 11 or 1 Devéria. At 12 Duponchel. At 1 Candia. At 2:30 Commission des Auteurs.

12 July. At 12 Candia. At 1 to Saint-Georges. D'Ortigue and Danjou* dined with me. Antenor Joly.

13 July. At 1 Candia. 2:30 Commission Dramatique. Answered Mlle. Stuart. M. Edouard [Bertin]. Bohrer. [Wrote] to Wilhelm enclosing the transposition of the Page's role.

14 July. At 11 or 1 to Devéria. Today Henri Blaze dined with me. At 1 Candia.

15 July. At 1 to Candia. At 4 to Saint-Georges. To Ed. Blanc.

16 July. 11:30 Pinieux. At 1 Candia. To Heine. 2:30 Commission Dramatique.

17 July. At 10 to Antenor Joly. Romberg for Wielhorsky* and the Dresden book. 2:30 theater rehearsal or Candia. The things for Wielhorsky.

18 July. At 10 to Duponchel. At 10:30 Duprez. At 11 Ed. Blanc. At 12 Ed. Blanc. At 1 Habeneck came. [Wrote] to Cherubini about Beauregard.

19 July. Between 9 and 10 Ed. Blanc. At 12 to Mlle. Stuart. At 2 Mlle. Rieux came. Dinner Pleyel. Leo, Heine, Crémieux.

20 July. At 1:45 rehearsal. At 2:30 Commission Dramatique.

21 July. At 10 the singer Lomer. At 11 Barthélemi. At 12 Scribe came. At 2 Commission des Auteurs. At 3 rehearsal. 7:45 Barisel.

22 July. At 11 Mlle. Barthélemi. 12:30 Candia.

23 July. At 9 Ed. Blanc. At 12 Edouard Bertin came. Dined with Coste in St. Germain. 4:30 to Bordogni.

24 July. Dinner Montalivet (at five o'clock met Ed. Blanc). Rehearsal at 3.

25 July. At 11 Antenor Joly came. At 1 to Bordogni. At 1 Concone* came to go [with me] to Mlle. Mequillet.[22] Today Coste, Merruau and Gouin dined with me.

26 July. Heine. Today Hyp. Prévost* dined with me. At 12 Scribe. At 12 rehearsal.

27 July. At 2:30 Commission Dramatique.

28 July. Between 12 and 1 to Mlle. Drouart. At 3 Habeneck and Lebrun. Lusy. Anoillo dined with me. [Wrote] to Ed. Blanc about Schlesinger.

29 July. [Wrote] Heine a letter for Mlle. Olivier.

30 July. Candia. At 4 to Crémieux. Between 12 and 1 Scribe.

31 July. Duponchel (Gouin). Candia about Devrient. Schneitzhöffer. Neuwall. [Mlle.] Stuart.[23] German songs to Morel. Gouin about Berton.

August 1838

Wednesday 1 August. Between 9 and 10 Scribe came to breakfast.[24] Schneitzhöffer.

2 August. At 9 Scribe came.[25] At 4 Massol. Schlesinger About Horzalka*. Danjou.

3 August. Corrected Schlesinger's songs.[26]

4 August. At 9 Scribe came to breakfast. This evening I left Paris.

5 August. Slept in Verdun.

6 August. Slept in Homburg.

7 August. Arrived in Schwalbach.

21 August. Interrupted the [curative] drinking and bathing because of diarrhea. Went to Wiesbaden to hear Bériot and Mlle. Garcia.

24 August. Dresden book for Breiting*. Lyser. Whether Wilhelm has called on Frau Weber and Frau Schubert.

25 August. I want to write to Ganz about the contrabassoon.

28 August. [Wrote] to W. Wagner in Frankfurt-am-Main.

September 1838

[On 2 September *Robert le Diable* was given in Lisbon in Italian.]

Monday 3 September. Breiting's waltzes. [Sent] Minna the score for Breiting. She should have my letters to Küstner copied.

4 September. Today at 3 Ganz came to Schüztenhof with the contrabassoon. [Wrote] to Breiting in St. Petersburg. Today departed from Schwalbach, and slept in Mainz.

5 September. My birthday. Slept in Homburg.

6 September. Slept in Mars la Tour.

7 September. (Au Chateau) de Séricour par la Ferté sous Jouarre.[27] Slept in Epernay.

8 September. Arrived in Paris in the evening.[28]

11 September. [Wrote] to Scribe. Janin, Morel, Antenor, Armand, Mainzer, Berlioz, Candia.

12 September. At two o'clock Candia.

13 September. At 10 Mlle. Marx came. Dinner at the Belgian Ambassador's. At 3 Candia. 2 tickets for Berlioz's opera.[29]

14 September. Today Mainzer dined with me. At 3 Candia came with Duponchel from Mlle. de Pan.

15 September. At 3 Saint-Georges. Today Mother came. At 1 Candia came. The observations for Scribe.[30] At 4 Panofka. Oppenfeldt*.

16 September. At 10 Mlle. Untal. At 3 Candia came. Observations for Scribe.

17 September. Mlle. Stolz. Mlle. Stuart. Oppenfeldt. Humboldt. At two o'clock Scribe came to me.

18 September. At 1 Mlle. Marx* and [Major] Serr. At 3 Habeneck and Masset*. 3 people to the table d'hôte. [Wrote] to Wilhelm Lyser.

19 September. At 12 Scribe. At 2 Stuart. Armand Bertin. At 3:30 Candia.

20 September. Coste and Merruau (table d'hôte). To the Odéon. At 12:30 rehearsal. Fortepiano for me and Mother.

21 September. At 11 Marx and Serr. At 3 to Mlle. Stuart. Stolz.

22 September. At 12 Candia. At 2 Mlle. Stolz. At 4 Dr. Löwenthal and Schiansky.

23 September. With Mlle. de Pan to Duprez (at 12). At 1 Stolz.

24 September. At 3 Candia.

26 September. 80 fr. for St Denis. At 12 to Bornstedt. At 1 Candia. At 3 Schiansky.

27 September. At 1 rehearsal. At 4 to Bornstedt. [Wrote] to Henri Blaze. Savoye, Janin, A. Bertin, Zumpt, Eichhoff, Heine.

28 September. At 11 rehearsal in the theater. Between 1 and 2 to Henri Blaze. At 2:30 Commission des Auteurs.

29 September. 11 rehearsal. To Armand Bertin.

30 September. At 12 Scribe. At 3 Candia.

October 1838

Monday 1 October. At 3 Candia in the theater. At 4 Mangoldt.

2 October. [Wrote] to Armand Bertin. To Fould.

3 October. At 2 Commission des Auteurs.

4 October. At 12 Candia. Humboldt.

5 October. At 10 [took] H. Hahn* to Cherubini. At 12 Candia. At 2 Commission des Auteurs. Duponchel about Pougnard. Soirée for Candia.

6 October. At 10 [took] Hahn to Cherubini. At 11 to Saint-Georges. At 1:30 Candia. Scribe, Heine, Bornstedt. [Wrote] to Scribe.

8 October. At 3 Candia. Crémieux, Humboldt, [Elie] Furtado.

9 October. Dinner at Crémieux's. At 2 Candia.

10 October. At 1 Rubini and Candia. At 3 to Saint-Georges. Dinner Lusy.

11 October. Between 1 and 2 Rubini. At 3 [took] Furtado to Mother's.

12 October. At 12 rehearsal in the theater. At 11:30 to Bordogni. At 2:30 Commission des Auteurs.

13 October. Dinner at Antenor Joly's. At 1 rehearsal in the theater.

15 October. Bordogni. Humboldt. A child's bed for Caecilie.[31] Minna arrived in Paris this evening.

17 October. To Halévy, Duponchel, Charles Maurice. Savoye. Oppenfeldt. At 12:30 with Unald to Bordogni. At 1 Candia came. At 4 to Saint-Georges.

18 October. At 3 Candia.

19 October. At 10 Mme. Mabouty. At 12 Assemblée Dramatique. [Wrote] to Roger on Sunday. At 4:30 to Schlesinger.

20 October. From 10 to 11 Hédouin*. Habeneck.

21 October. At 3 Saint-Georges came.

22 October. At 11 rehearsal. [Wrote] to Bordogni about Unald.

23 October. At 9 Conservatoire. At 10 Hédouin. At 2 Candia. At 2 Commission des Auteurs.

24 October. Hédouin. Bornstedt. At 4 Bornstedt came. Today moved into the Hôtel de Paris.

25 October. At 4 Scribe.

26 October. At 9 I went to Hédouin. At 10 Mme. Mabouty. Took Mother to the rehearsal.

27 October. At 12 audition of [Mlle.] Rualz.[32] To Pleyel.

29 October. At 10 Blondeau*. At 12 Scribe came. At 3 Habeneck came.

31 October. Dinner at Edmond Blanc's. To Mlle. Garcia.

November 1838

Thursday 1 November. To Greville. Belgiojoso. Crémieux.

2 November. At 10 Mme. Mabouty. Dined at Crémieux's. [Wrote] to Schlesinger about Fétis's biography and Blondeau. Commission Dramatique.

3 November. At 10 H. Heller*.

5 November. At 4 Coralli.*[33]

6 November. At 11 rehearsal. At 4 Scribe. With Schlesinger to Théophile Gautier*. A. Clerc*. Returned Fétis's *Manus*. Pierre Erard.

7 November. At 4 Heller. To Charles Maurice. Gouin *France musicale* which D. has received. Present for Habeneck. Véron. *Huguenots* on Friday. Ed. Blanc. Humboldt. Burghersh.[34]

8 November. At 9 Émile Deschamps. At 11 to Delavigne. Lord Burghersh. Candia about Belgiojoso and the duet. Candia's costume. At 1 rehearsal. Janin.

9 November. At 9 Hahn. 9:30 Ettlinger. At 10 Mme. Biagioli. At 2 Commission Dramatique.

10 November. [Wrote] to Candia about Agouado*, Belgiojoso. To E. Deschamps. Cornelius*. [Wrote] to the Cercle des Arts. Levasseur. Stolz. At 5 rehearsal.

11 November. At 3 Habeneck. Duponchel and Gentil to dinner.

12 November. Schlesinger about Heine, Heller. At 4 Hahn. Levasseur. At 3 Lord Burghersh. At 1 to Mme. Stolz. To Levasseur.

13 November. Elssler.*[35] Burghersh. At 4 Candia. [Sent] the songs and duet to E. Deschamps.

14 November. At 12 rehearsal. At 2 Lord Burghersh. At 2 the Commission Dramatique. To Mlle. de Pan.

17 November. 10:30 Candia. At 1 rehearsal.

18 November. At 12 Etienne.

19 November. At 4 Savoye.

21 November. Dined with the Bavarian ambassador. [Wrote] to Victor Hugo, Scribe, Lord Burghersh.

22 November. At 10 Bornstedt. At 10 Duverger. At 4 Coralli.

24 November. To Gentil. Gouin. Habeneck. At 1 Coralli. Oboe in the *Huguenots* duet.

25 November. Took the proofs[36] to [Henri] Berthond myself. At 5 Stolz. Dined with Lavalette. Mainzer about Théophile [Gautier?].

26 November. To Gouin. [Take] Auguste with me to the rehearsal tomorrow.[37] Second aria. Abridgment in the *Pas de Deux*. Leborne. At 3 [with] Scribe [to the] rehearsal. To Stolz. [Sent] Brodt and Leborne the *Huguenots* duet. [Wrote] to Leborne about the trombones [see example 43];

Example 43. Theme (4) from *Les Huguenots*

To Norblin[38] about the violoncelli in the aria, to Habeneck that he should rehearse the aria twice.

27 November. Auguste and Gouin to the rehearsal. At 12 Théophile Gautier to breakfast. 2:30 Commission Dramatique. At 6:45 orchestral rehearsal.

27 November. At 9 Conservatoire. M. de Girardin. Janin. Merruau. At 1 Duponchel. At 2 Coralli. At 3 Candia and Girardin. To Armand Bertin. Charles Maurice.

29 November. At 12 Candia. Abridgment[39] of the *Pas de Deux.* Schlesinger about Albert Clerc*.

30 November. Géraldy. Charles Maurice. Heine. Abridgment[40] of the *Pas de Deux.* [Wrote] Coralli about the pages with armor during the aria. Reprise of *Robert.*[41]

December 1838

Saturday 1 December. [Wrote] to Armand Bertin about E. Deschamps.

2 December. To Janin. At 12 Crosnier. At 4 De Candia. To Mlle. de Pan.

3 December. [Sent] Leborne the cuts[42] in Candia's aria.[43] Auguste. At 10:30 Schlesinger.

4 December. Gouin, Dorus. What Candia and I [will give?] to Auguste. To Mlle. de Pan. Lehon. Janin. That there should be a report of the second performance. Benefit for Lafont.

5 December. Halévy about Charpentier. Habeneck and Leborne the orchestral parts[44] of the Vow[45] in *Les Huguenots.* Oboe in the act 3 duet.[46]

6 December. Candia about Auguste. Habeneck [about] the *Serment* in *Les Huguenots.* Friday *Huguenots.* Lafont's benefit. Ticket for Munk. Specht. [Wrote] to Heine. Boigne*.

7 December. [Discussed] Schiansky with Duponchel. Lafont's benefit. [Sent] the *Serment* to Habeneck. [Sent] Brodt the act 3 duet.

8 December. Berlioz. [Wrote] to Heine. At 3 Commission Dramatique. At 3:30 to Candia. Buloz about the song.

9 December. At 10 Schiansky about Duponchel. To H. Blaze. At 3 to Candia.

10 December. At 7 Humboldt met me. Gouin. H. Blaze. Candia. Lafont. [Received] permission from Duponchel for Humboldt.

11 December. At 4 H. Blaze. Crémieux. Merlin. [Wrote] to Cherubini.

12 December. [Wrote] to Candia about Auguste. At 1 or 2 Botté is coming. At 3 Commission des Auteurs. Schlesinger about Beauregard. My *Romances* for Lapelouze and Belgiojoso.

13 December. To Candia. Humboldt. Soirée at Gail's. Sent an answer to Savoye.

15 December. At 1 Henri Blaze came. At 2:30 to the Institut.

16 December. At 12 Duverger came.

17 December. At 12 Duverger. At 2 to Henri Blaze. At 3 or 4 Savoye.

18 December. At 3 to Henri Blaze. At 2:30 Commission Dramatique. Alphonse Karr*.

19 December. Alphonse Karr.

20 December. At 1 Henri Blaze. Kastner came at 2. At 3 to Crémieux. With Bordogni about Mlle. König.

22 December. Karr. Janin. Music for Lapelouze. *Stella*[47] and *La Fille du Danube*[48] from Leduc. Humboldt. Duprez. Opera tickets for Mainzer. Chopin. Botté (library).

28 December. Leave[49] from the Commission Dramatique. [Sent] Gouin the *Histoire de l'Opéra depuis 1830.*

29 December. Sand. Armand. Ed. Blanc. Bornstedt. Saint-Georges. Castelli. Breiting. Baermann. Küstner.

31 December. The letters for Munich with the scene arrangements, the Dresden *mise en scène* book. Answer from Zulehner.

[Notes on the empty facing page.]

Passport from Werther. Present for Minna. Heine. Rehearsals for Duprez.[50] Act 3 so that the ballet could be practiced.—What if Jean [in *Le Prophète*] seriously believed in his mission, and Massol [= Anabaptist] was the one who wrote the letter to the commandant of Münster? People should believe that the Prophet does not have human origins in order the better to motivate his horror at being recognized by his mother. "Vous ai trompé, ce ne pas mon fils!" The people "Miracle! Miracle!" Attend to[51] the poetry. From the beginning the peasants speak of Jean as a visionary. It would be more evocative if the coronation ceremony were to take place in front of the steps of the church, rather than have a corona-tion procession that would be too reminiscent of the cortège in *La Juive*.[52] Be brief, biblical language. Read W. Scott's *Puritans*[53] and Schiller's *Jungfrau von Orleans*.[54] Revise my rhythms. No fire-and-brimstone sermon. Massol the trea-surer [of the Anabaptists]: a trio in which he cheats the others in dividing the spoils.[55]

1839

[Neither *Tagebuch* nor *Taschenkalender* survives for the first half of 1839. Two contracts with Scribe (16 and 26 January, with a supplement of 27 March 1839) mark the progress of work on *Le Prophète*.[56] Carl Baermann's* diary, kept during a concert tour to Paris with his father Heinrich, throws much light on this period, and especially on Meyerbeer's home life.[57]]

[*Friday 14 December 1838*. Went to Meyerbeer, who received us with great friend-liness. In the evening we dined with him and made the acquaintance of his wife, who is extraordinarily affectionate, as are his children. Meyerbeer is a wonderful person, gifted with endless talent and genius, while nonetheless remaining lov-able and modest, and so loyal and friendly in his relations, that whoever has deal-ings with him is inevitably charmed and drawn to venerate him.

Sunday 16 December 1838. Dined with Meyerbeer, then went with his wife to *Robert le Diable*.

Monday 17 December 1838. In the evening Meyerbeer took us to Lafont.

Tuesday 18 December 1838. In the evening dined with Meyerbeer; he had also invited Habeneck, Kalkbrenner, Rosenheim, Heller, Panofka, Candia, etc. Then we played the duo for two clarinets. Meyerbeer had invited the foremost editors to this *diner* so that they could write about us in the public papers. We were very popular, and Meyerbeer was equally enthusiastic.

Wednesday 19 December 1838. Dined with Meyerbeer.

Saturday 22 December 1838. Called on Meyerbeer.

Monday 24 December 1838. In the evening we dined with Meyerbeer, and then accompanied him to the Opéra.

Friday 28 December 1838. Meyerbeer came to see us, and wanted us to play him a duet by Mendelssohn, which we did. In the evening we dined with Meyerbeer.

He really is a kind, cheerful man, full of spirit. He loves his children very much, who are, in any case, very lovable. Any father would have to be a monster not to love them.

Monday 31 December 1838. At nine o'clock we went to Meyerbeer and accompanied him to a soirée at Levy's. We made some very interesting acquaintances, most especially Alexander von Humboldt.

Tuesday 1 January 1839. Dined at Meyerbeer's.

Wednesday 2 January. In the evening we went to Meyerbeer's, where we dined, and then accompanied his wife to the Grand Opéra, where they performed *Les Huguenots.* Duprez was quite outstanding, totally involved in what he is doing, full of imagination. On the whole the scenery is simply amazing. The chateau in act 2 especially is depicted with endless verisimilitude much enhanced by the new mode of excluding the side-wings, and the use of gas lighting, which gives the clarity of daylight.

Friday 4 January. Early in the day to Meyerbeer, and accompanied him to Scribe, and from there to Hiller.[58]

Saturday 5 January. In the evening dined with Hiller at Meyerbeer's, where we also found the famous singer Mlle. Löwe*, from Berlin. Meyerbeer speaks of her talent with great enthusiasm.

Thursday 10 January. Went to Meyerbeer's who held a big dinner for us today. He had invited, among others, Berlioz, Halévy, Janin, Duponchel, Habeneck, Lüttichau (the intendant of Dresden), Mlle. Löwe, Dr. Koreff, Bertin, Coste. After supper, which lasted until 9:30 and was endlessly brilliant, we played, at pressing invitation, my Duo in E-flat, which was so popular that Habeneck immediately invited us to perform this Sunday in the first Conservatoire Concert.

Sunday 13 January. Attended a big dinner at Kalkbrenner's. (Meyerbeer and his wife were among the guests.)

Wednesday 16 January. Meyerbeer called on us. In the evening we dined with Meyerbeer, who was exhausted by the arrangements for our concert.

Thursday 17 January. Early in the day Father went to Duponchel with Meyerbeer and Schlesinger about the concert, but still had no results.

Friday 18 January. From early in the morning we were running around Duponchel.

Poor Meyerbeer had to do so much! He is really rather exhausted. When we arrived home, we found him sitting, worn out, on our sofa. He told us that we will
play on Monday in the Grand Opéra. He had just come from the theater, where
Les Huguenots had its ninety-seventh performance, with receipts of 8900 fr.

Saturday 19 January. Early in the day Meyerbeer fetched Father and took him to
Duponchel.

Tuesday 22 January. In the evening we dined with Meyerbeer, who was rather out
of sorts. In his opinion we played very well, and the public were very appreciative.

Friday 25 January. Went to Meyerbeer's, where we dined.

Saturday 26 January. At one o'clock with Meyerbeer to the Grand Opéra for the
dress rehearsal of the ballet *La Gypsy*.[59]

Sunday 27 January. After the concert we dined with Meyerbeer. Then we accompanied his wife to the theater. Meyerbeer is always pleased when we go to his
operas, and we must do what we can to make him happy.

Friday 1 February. Calls from Schlesinger, and later from Panofka and Meyerbeer,
who stayed with us for an hour. There was a very interesting conversation on
artistic matters, with some charlatanism from Meyerbeer who wrote down various ideas. So what, everyone has his weaknesses.

Monday 4 February. Went to supper with Meyerbeer. Since his wife is ill, we
dined at the table d'hôte of an excellent hotel, with Mainzer and Savoye. The
meeting had been arranged to persuade Mainzer to have his choir, made up entirely of laborers, appear in our concert.

Wednesday 6 February. I was with Meyerbeer's wife, who is suffering greatly,
and, I fear, is incurable. It seems to me that she is afflicted with a type of con-
sumption. I think the woman will have to endure a great deal, or rather he will,
since it would be better for her if she were called to a better life. It is such a
happy family that it would be tragic if their happiness were to be clouded by such
a terrible blow. They all love each other so much, the children the parents, and
the children each other, all in the most charmingly childlike way. It is a very moving
situation, and I wish them the greatest happiness.

Saturday 9 February. Called on Meyerbeer.

Sunday 10 February. I was at Meyerbeer's, where there was terrible confusion because of Schlesinger, who put Mario de Candia's name on our billboard when he is not going to sing. Meyerbeer has been greatly shocked because Mario has refused to sing in our concert, and I had to run immediately to the Conservatoire and cross his name off every one of the posters. Dined with Meyerbeer.

Tuesday 12 February. To Meyerbeer's, where we dined. In the evening we accompanied his wife to *Les Huguenots.*

Friday 15 February. Early to Meyerbeer, then a great deal of rushing around for the concert [17 February]. Dined with Meyerbeer in the evening. Madame is still suffering.

Sunday 17 February. Our ambassador, and therefore our compatriot, who should be the first to lend us a hand, returned to us the ticket for his box (which we had sent him) with the observation that Count Bondy, who has a subscription box, will take him, and that we should not forget to send a ticket to the Austrian ambassador. Meyerbeer, on the other hand, paid for the box (which cost 400 fr.) and wrote such an affectionate accompanying letter, that he increased the worth of the gift one-hundred-fold.

Monday 18 February. Went early to Meyerbeer and discussed many instructive things with him.

Tuesday 19 February. Meyerbeer called on me. Later we dined with him.

Friday 22 February. Dined at Meyerbeer's, with Schimon and Rosenhain, and there we met Herr Gouin. After the meal I played Meyerbeer my concerto (which I have dedicated to him), and which so pleased him, that he gave me the greatest praise by saying that he preferred it to Weber's concerto. Schimon also performed a very beautifully composed étude. Today Meyerbeer was so affectionate that my heart again went out to him. He is so modest and witty in his behavior that everyone should love him without prejudice. His wife and children were also particularly charming today. We really passed the most pleasant evening, which belongs among the most blessed of my life, with noble ingenious men who do not pursue the superiority of their convictions, but rather behave with salutary modesty.

Monday 25 February. Dined with Meyerbeer, and accompanied his wife to the tedious *Robert.*

Sunday 3 March. Went to Meyerbeer, who had Herr Giraldis sing us his *Mönch.* This is perhaps one of Meyerbeer's best compositions, full of poetic truth. Giraldis himself is an outstanding singer, and would have great success if he could be

Minna Meyerbeer, née Mosson, in earlier years. Engraving by Degener. (From A. Kohut, *Geschichte der Juden* [Berlin, 1898–99].)

persuaded to appear on stage. Dined at Meyerbeer's with Herr Gouin, and then accompanied his wife to the theater, where they were performing *Les Huguenots*. This opera again left a great impression on me. Meyerbeer would very much like to have me here [permanently], and if I could only support myself here, I would gladly stay.

Wednesday 6 March. Called on Madame Meyerbeer and had the most interesting conversation. This woman has great spirit. A little later Meyerbeer himself arrived, and I had the pleasure of an extremely fascinating conversation with him about Mozart, Rossini and other composers. We spoke much of his *Huguenots*, and he explained a great deal to me.

Thursday 7 March. Went early to Meyerbeer's, and again later. Found his dear wife ill once more, and cannot help feeling that she does not have long to live. Earlier I had the great pleasure of accompanying Meyerbeer to Scribe. Both masters are working regularly on their new opera [*Le Prophète*], and Meyerbeer is pleased with him and his efforts. He sets great store by this new composition, but complained to me about the trouble involved in the production of any new opera.

Monday 11 March. Breakfasted early with Meyerbeer, on oysters. Dined with Meyerbeer in the evening.

Thursday 14 March. Enjoyed a caviar *déjeuner* with Meyerbeer.

Friday 15 March. Went to Meyerbeer at four o'clock, and played for him.

Saturday 16 March. Received a farewell visit from Meyerbeer. Went once again to Madame Meyerbeer to thank her for all the love and kindness which she has shown me.]

[On 8 March 1839 Adolphe Nourrit committed suicide in Naples. On 10 May Berlioz was nominated a Chevalier de la Légion d'Honneur and chose Meyerbeer as his sponsor. *Robert le Diable* was performed in Stockholm in Swedish on the same day.]

June 1839

Sunday 9 June. A powerful coda after the second couplet would be good:[60] worked on it from 7 until 8:45.

Monday 10 June. From 7 until 8:45 began improvising aimlessly[61] on the conclusion of act 2. Receptions. Rehearsals of *Les Huguenots*. Returned Laube's* visit.[62]

Wednesday 12 June. At 8:45 scored Jonas's couplets for one and a half hours. A young musician came, Gold*, from Odessa. Changed the instrumentation of the Vow in act 2 of *Les Huguenots* at the wish of the singers who could not keep in tune. [Heard] *Guillaume Tell.*

Thursday 13 June. Improvised from 7 until 8:45 on Duprez's aria (conclusion to act 3): I devised an original, happy start to the stretta "Roi du ciel . . . comme devais ton serviteur." Partial dress rehearsal of *Les Huguenots* (début of Mlle. Nathan).

[In early July 1839 an anonymous brochure was circulated to the members of the Chamber of Deputies demanding the resignation of Duponchel and the appointment of a more capable director for the Opéra. Berlioz, writing to Liszt on 9 August, identified it as by Émile D. (presumably Deschamps).[63] On 7 August 1839 the 182nd performance of *Robert le Diable* took place, with Mario in the title role, singing the new *Scène de Prière:* "Où me cacher? . . . Oh! ma mère."[64] On 20 August 1839 Richard Wagner and his wife, Minna, arrived in Boulogne-sur-Mer.[65]]

October 1839

[*Undated page.*]
Richard Wagner 3 rue de la Tonnellerie. Dietsch* 14 rue de Helder.

Sunday 13 October. [Wrote] to Beauregard. Habeneck. Adam. Schneitzhöffer. Beauregard. Blanchard to lunch.

Monday 14 October. [Wrote] to Beauregard, to Kastner. To Adam.

Tuesday 15 October. At 3 a rehearsal with Stolz. Duprez and Moscheles.

Wednesday 16 October. At 4 to Kastner. At 4 rehearsal with Fitzjames.[66] Wagner. Hédouin. Moscheles. Benedict*. At 2 to Crosnier.

Thursday 17 October. Brockhaus*. At 4 Kastner. [Mlle.] Rieux.[67] [Wrote] to Crosnier, to Moscheles.

Friday 18 October. Awoke at 6:30. Corrected "Rachel à Nephtali"[68] for publication. [*Tk* At 10 Benedict *(Drei Pintos).* Duprez.]

Saturday 19 October. Improvised from 6:30 until 8:45 on the cavatina of Duprez's aria. The theme seems good to me ("Je t'ai perdu") (notes). I will shape the piece into a *rondo agitato*. Visits. [*Tk* At 1 Benedict.[69] To the table d'hôte with Benedict.[70] To Mme. Rieux. Nourrit's letter. [Wrote] to Schilling. Blanchard.]

Sunday 20 October. From 7:45 until 9:45 tried further to compose the *rondo agitato.* I am most demoralized by the continuing maligning of my artistic position here, which is evident to me in a thousand different ways. My spirits are constantly preoccupied by this, and cannot find the right reflectiveness so necessary for inspiration. I read an interesting article by Merruau in *Le Temps* about the triumphal progress of *Robert le Diable*. [*Tk* Wagner. Hédouin.]

Monday 21 October. At midday to Leo's: Chopin[71] played new mazurkas, wonderfully beautiful, and again the heavenly piece in A-flat, which I so love.[72] Then Chopin and Moscheles [performed] the latter's double sonata (for Archduke Rudolph), a truly classical work.[73] [*Tk* Dinner at Leo's. [Wrote] to Blanchard, to Schilling in Stuttgart, to Crémieux.]

Tuesday 22 October. In *Le Constitutionnel* [I read]: "Les partitions de M. Meyerbeer nous coûtent déjà la voix de Mlle. Falcon."[74] Things like this, which are now so frequently observed, rob me of all inspiration for hours at a time. At Crémieux's with Pauline Garcia, who appears to have no desire to enter the world of French opera. She complained about the failings of chorus and orchestra in yesterday's performance of *Les Huguenots*. [*Tk* At 10 Nourrit came.[75] To Merruau. [Mlle.] Dobré*.[76]]

Wednesday 23 October. Heine and Blaze to dine with me. [*Tk* At three o'clock Henri Blaze. [Wrote] to [Auguste] Nourrit, to Heine (about a meal), to Nagler (ditto), to Joly.]

Thursday 24 October. In the evening [heard] Garcia in *La Cenerentola*, outstanding, but, as I feared, her voice is too weak for the Opéra.

Friday 25 October. At 12 Herr Wagner met me at Joly's. At 1 Merruau came.

Saturday 26 October. At 10 Joly came. At 3 Nourrit met me. Moscheles, Rieux, Dobré, Rothschild.[77]

Sunday 27 October. Woke up in a good frame of mind. Completed the rondo and wrote it out. I wanted to begin the recitative when I received *La France musicale*: strong, mean-spirited attacks[78] à propos the article in *Le Temps* (of 20 October). I was incapable of even the least activity for the rest of the day. [Passed] the whole day alone in my room in indescribable agitation, and am still not recollected. [*Tk* Invited Nagler to lunch. At 4 to Kastner. Soirée at Géraldy's.]

Monday 28 October. At 1 Gail. At 4 to Kastner.

Tuesday 29 October. Punctuated the part of Valentine for Küstner. At 4 to Kastner. Jules Janin.

Wednesday 30 October. [Wrote] to Chabran about Wagner. At 2 Rieux. At 4 Kastner. Henri Blaze.

Thursday 31 October. 12:30 Rieux. At 1:30 Wagner met me at Brockhaus's. At 2 Henri Blaze. At 3 Mlle. Dobré. At 4 Kastner.

November 1839

Friday 1 November. At 10 Wagner met me with Chabran and Schlesinger. At 3:30 to Dobré. [Wrote] to Charles about the proofs[79] of "Rachel à Nephtali." Revision on account of Jähns*.

2 November. Commission Dramatique. 2:30 Rieux, Kastner, Merruau. 4:30 Saint-Georges.

4 November. At 11 H. Heller. Dined at Moscheles's. At 3 Dobré. At 4 Kastner. Cercle de St Cécile.

5 November. At 11 Rieux. At 2 Commission Dramatique. At 4 Kastner.

6 November. [Discussed] H. Kastner with Crosnier. At 2 Mlles Dobré, Rieux. At 3:30 Saint-Georges met me at Cerfberr's.

7 November. At one o'clock H. Hiller. At 2:30 to Kastner. At three o'clock Wagner and Schlesinger came.

8 November. At 11 with Wagner to Schlesinger. [Wrote] to Heine. To Gouin. Armand Bertin.

9 November. At 4 Saint-Georges. 4:30 H. Blaze.

10 November. 2 places for Laube. Wagner. Zeuner*, Moscheles, H. Blaze, Janin.

11 November. At 4 Mlle. Julian. At 2 Commission Dramatique.

12 November. Breakfast at 11. [Wrote] to Heine, Laube, and H. Blaze. Looked for Th. Gautier's poem.

13 November. Rieux. Searched on Jähns's behalf. Émile Deschamps. Soirée at Leo's.

14 November. Laube, Heine, H. Blaze dined with me at the table d'hôte.

15 November. Punctuated [the role of] Valentine for Küstner.

16 November. [Wrote] a letter to Chabran for Herr Wagner. [Wrote] to Pauline Garcia. At 2 to Schlesinger's concert. To Halévy and Berton about the Institut. Gentil dined with me.

17 November. [Wrote] to Halévy about Mlle. Marx.

18 November. Crosnier on Kastner's behalf. At two o'clock Commission Dramatique. At 4 to Crosnier.

19 November. At 11 Kastner. At 4 Gail.

20 November. Heinefetter*. Scribe. At 10 to E. Deschamps. 2:30 Gail. 3:30 with Kastner to Crosnier. 4:30 H. Blaze. The music for Gail and E. Deschamps. Called on Dr. Haller*.

21 November. At 11 to Crosnier. At 1 to Berton.

22 November. Wrote to Crosnier that I will come only at 4:30.

23 November. At 2 with Berton to the Institut. A. Bertin. At 9 Scribe. [Sent] Munk the contract.

24 November. To Armand Bertin. At 2 the concert. [Discussed] Schneitzhöffer with Monnais*. Dietsch.

25 November. At 12 Ed. Monnais. [Arranged] a rendezvous for Wagner with Joly.[80]

26 November. At 11 Ed. Monnais. M. David*. With Wagner to A. Joly. To A. Bertin.

27 November. To A. Bertin. Pack up 2 rue de la Madeleine (take some camphor). To Cherubini.

28 November. To Scribe. Cherubini. [Wrote] to Heine about his books. At 12 to Schlesinger. At one o'clock rue de la Madeleine.

30 November. Institut. [Sent] Berton 10 fr. At 9 Berlioz's rehearsal. At 4:30 Scribe. [Wrote] to Kastner for Saint-Georges. [Wrote] to Bertin for Heine.

December 1839

Sunday 1 December. Fétis's biography. Heine came. At 2 Berlioz's concert. At 5 to Scribe. [Wrote] to Mother and August Schmidt* in Vienna. [Sent] Heinrich the Dresden régisseur's book. [Sent] Minna the letters for Brunswick and [wrote] about the letter from G. Weber's widow.[81]

2 December. At 3 Wagner. Baron Koreff.

3 December. Letter to A. Joly for Wagner. Letter to Scribe.

4 December. Letter to Scribe. Gentil to lunch. Have the small piano tuned. At 3 rendezvous with Monnais. Heine. 3:30 Garcia.

5 December. To Scribe. [Wrote] to Valtier and Kastner asking them not to come tomorrow. [Wrote] to Mme. Dorus for Wagner.

6 December. At 11:30 to Heine.

7 December. [Wrote] to Kastner about my departure. To Scribe. At 1 rehearsal of Wagner's overture.[82]

8 December. At 12 to Heine. Yesterday wrote to Fischhof* in Vienna. [Sent] the letter for A. Joly to Gouin. [Discussed] Deschamps and Heine with Gouin.

9 December. Heine about Provence.[83]

10 December. Requested leave[84] of 3 months from the Commission Dramatique.

12 December. Today left for Baden. Slept in Sezanne.

13 December. Slept in Void.

14 December. Slept in Pfalsburg.

15 December. Arrived in Baden in the evening.

17 December. Sent Gouin the corrections of "Fantasie"[85] and "Allein."[86]

18 December. Sent the corrections of "Garten des Herzens,"[87] "Suleika,"[88] and "Chanson vendéens"[89] with Conrad.

22 December. Wrote to Millenet.[90] [Sent] Schlesinger "Rachel à Nephtali," and in what order [the songs] should appear.[91] The lithographs of "Floh,"[92] the trio for three tenors in *Il Pirata*.[93] Not to publish anything by me in the *Gazette* until he has something by Rossini. Third correction of Candia's aria.

23 December. Sent Millenet the music.[94] Changes for the Widow Weber.

24 December. I wrote to Gouin.

25 December. Wrote to Schlesinger and Gouin. Wrote out the corrections of the four romances. [Wrote] to Baermann, Seyfried, Castelli.

26 December. [Wrote] to the Widow Weber.

29 December. [Wrote] to Gouin (New Orleans).[95] Provence 33 [fr.]). [Wrote] to Jähns, to Türkheim together with Weber's songs for Jähns.[96]

30 December. Gotha. Vienna. Castelli. Agitated, could not work.

31 December. Awoke at 7. [Worked] until 8:30 on the stretta, from 10 until 11 on Fidès's solo in act 1. Tempo? Letter Gouin. Regli.[97] Wrote to Schlesinger. Worked a little. Gouin. Munk. Schlesinger. Monnais. Falcon. Order. Schlesinger. What is being said about *Les Martyrs*?[98] Schlesinger tells me nothing about this new opera. Humboldt. Brunswick, that they have nor understood my letter. Spontini. Princess Wilhelm. *Les Huguenots* in London.

[Undated entries at the end of the Calendar.]
[Sent] Ponchard the "Poète mourant." Biography and portrait for August Schmidt in Vienna in the Riedelschen Buchhandlung. Letters to Wagner, Garcia, Chabran. Mother's birthday will be on Monday 20 January.[99] Verdi's* opera pieces.[100] Monnais, that he should inform me who will be writing what after Donizetti.

[Appendix to 1839 written on the rubrics for 1–3 January of the 1840 appointment book.]
Gouin. Vienna. Falcon. Vocal score of *Les Huguenots* and *Gesammelte Lieder* for Mother. "Rachel à Nephthali"; the corrections[101] have still not been sent off. Mario must not [sing] in *Robert* at Elssler's benefit. H. Blaze. The *Geistliche Lieder*. That he can now issue them as a collection.[102] To Schlesinger with H. Blaze

about the title. The order of sequence. Verdi. See to the errors in "Rachel." E. Deschamps. The expression "sa grosse panse" in "Maître Floh." "L'ange déchu." H. Blanchard,[103] that he already has "Fantasie" and this will be given on 4 January. Wagner. Géraldy. Merruau. Benedict. Berlioz. Heller. H. Blaze. G. Sand. Kaskel. H. Blanchard. Fétis. Kastner. Morel. H. Prévost.[104] Corrected the aria for Haitzinger. The same in the evening. [Finished] the rest of Jonas's entry[105] [in *Le Prophète*].

NOTES

1. Prince Alexis Galitzin, a Russian diplomat, and musical dilettante.
2. Meyerbeer was planning to redraft the sketches of Weber's opera to a completely new French libretto.
3. Meyerbeer began coaching Mario in the role of Robert for his forthcoming début in *Robert le Diable*.
4. The meetings on 11, 12, and 21 January with the Escudier brothers marks the commencement of a difficult relationship between Meyerbeer and these publishers. Meyerbeer provided them with information about his career that was published on 28 January 1838 in *La France musicale* (no. 5). The Escudiers apparently did not make it clear that this was the beginning of a series of articles on Meyerbeer's operas which would appear over the next few months and, while containing many flattering observations, are full of trenchant criticism of his art and decidedly hostile in tone (*La France musicale*, nos. 7, 8, 20, 21, 22, 24). The policy of the Escudiers, as publishers of a new musical journal, appears to have been to win Meyerbeer's trust by their biography, without revealing their true attitude of inveterate hostility, which would henceforth characterize their dealings with him.
5. The *Inno di Morte* ("Tutto è silenzio") from act 2 of *Il Crociato in Egitto* (no. 15 in the Pacini vocal score).
6. Presumably this refers to a manuscript by Gottfried Weber, who had sent three MSS to Meyerbeer for submission to the Académie (see his letter of 12 December 1837, *BT*, 3:76).
7. A singer.
8. A stage designer from the Berlin Court Opera.
9. Of *Les Huguenots*.
10. *Die drei Pintos*.
11. Court Theatre painter in Dresden.
12. Karl August Schuster was a singer.
13. Tgb. *Regisseurbuch*.
14. *Belisario*, *opera seria* in three acts by Donizetti (Salvatore Cammarano, after Jean-François Marmontel's drama *Bélisare* [1776]; Venice, La Fenice, 4 February 1836). It was initially very successful throughout Italy and enjoyed an international reputation.
15. Meyerbeer traveled to Dresden for the last of Schröder-Devrient's performances in *Les Huguenots* on 29 April 1838. Her benefit concert that evening was a great personal triumph for the composer, who was crowned with laurels, received in the royal box, and later publicly serenaded (*Revue et Gazette musicale* 13 [1838]: 202).
16. Lyser published a review of the performance of *Les Huguenots* in the journal *Ost*

und West 50 (1838), and later an article entitled "Giacomo Meyerbeer," *Wiener allgemeine Musikzeitung* 154 (1842): 589–90.

17. Text by Gaetano Rossi (1833). No. 18 in the *Quarante Mélodies*.

18. Miltitz wrote a brief entry of twelve lines in the *Allgemeine musikalische Zeitung* (25 April 1838, 277), praising *Les Huguenots*, calling it "ein sehr grossartiges Werk, voll grandioser und origineller Ideen, in einer höchst wirksam Instrumentierung" [a great work, full of grandiose and original ideas, with most impressive orchestration].

19. Parisian lawyer in charge of Meyerbeer's royalties in Paris.

20. She sang the role of Valentine in the 1838 performances of *Les Huguenots*.

21. She sang the role of Alice in the 1839 performance of *Robert le Diable*.

22. A singer.

23. A singer.

24. On 1 August Meyerbeer and Scribe drew up a new contract for *L'Africaine*, postponing the termination date of composition from 24 August 1840 until 24 August 1842 (*BT* III, 681-82). The reason for the postponement is clearly stated in the preamble to the second contract signed on 2 August 1838: ."[L]a maladie prolongée de Mlle Falcon, qui devait jouer le rôle principal dans L'Africaine, et l'absence de toute autre cantatrice capable d'éxécuter ce rôle, ont forcé M. Meyerbeer à une nouveau traité . . ." [{T}he prolonged illness of Mlle Falcon, who was to have created the principal role in *L'Africaine*, and in the absence of any other singer capable of executing this role, has forced M. Meyerbeer to draw up a new contract . . .].

25. On 2 August 1838 Meyerbeer and Scribe signed another new contract setting out the conditions for cooperation on the new text, *Le Prophète*, which Scribe undertook to provide for Meyerbeer (*BT,* 3:682–84).

26. On 3 August 1838 Meyerbeer signed a contract with Heinrich Schlesinger for his two German lieder "Komm" (Heine) and "Scirocco" (M. Beer).

27. Meyerbeer must have visited Scribe at his country house, the Château Séricourt.

28. Meyerbeer appears to have returned to Paris especially to attend the première of Berlioz's opera *Benvenuto Cellini* (Léon de Wailly and Auguste Barbier, after the *Autobiography* of Benvenuto Cellini [1558–66]; Paris, Opéra, 10 September 1838), proof of the high interest in which he held the work.

29. *Benvenuto Cellini* had only four performances.

30. On the libretto for *Le Prophète*.

31. Caecilie Meyerbeer was born in 1837.

32. A singer.

33. Coralli choreographed a new version of the ballets in *Robert le Diable*.

34. The first reference to the earl of Westmorland, the English diplomat, composer and friend of Meyerbeer over many years.

35. Thérèse and Fanny Elssler had already made their début at the Opéra in the act 2 divertissement in *Robert le Diable* on 30 November 1834.

36. Tgb. *épreuven*.

37. Of *Robert le Diable*.

38. Cellist in the orchestra of the Paris Opéra.

39. Tgb. *coupure*.

40. Tgb. *coupure*.

41. Mario made his début at the Opéra in the role of Robert (ten performances).

42. Tgb. *coupure*.

43. Raoul's romance in act 1 of *Les Huguenots*.

44. Tgb. *orchestre.*

45. Tgb. *Serment.*

46. For Marcel and Valentine.

47. Opera by A. Lecomte (John Towers, *Dictionary Catalogue of Operas and Operettas* (Morgantown, W.Va., 1919; reprint, New York: Da Capo, 1967), 2:791.

48. Ballet in two acts by Adam (scenario Desmares, choreography F. Taglioni; Paris, Opéra, 21 September 1836). Marie Taglioni danced the leading role. The ballet was performed thirty-six times until 1844.

49. Tgb. *congé.*

50. Duprez had taken over the role of Raoul.

51. Tgb. *soignieren.*

52. The Entry of the Emperor in the act 1 finale of *La Juive.*

53. He means Sir Walter Scott's *Old Mortality* (1816), which in its story of the Old Covenanters in late-seventeenth-century Scotland has a similar theme of Protestant militarism and millenarianism.

54. Schiller's play (1801) is also about a visionary call to arms, and contains a public confrontation between the protagonist and her skeptical father.

55. This idea would eventually result in the *Trio bouffe* in act 3 of *Le Prophète.* According to Wilhelm Altmann's *Autographenkatalog No.25*, letter no. 167 from Meyerbeer to Scribe (30 November 1838) discusses textual changes to acts 1 and 2 of *Le Prophète.* Meyerbeer asked for a pastoral refrain in Jean's romance, and also for alterations in the *prêche pour la partie de Massol*, for which he recommended, as a model, the Sermon of the Capuchin in Schiller's *Wallensteins Lager* (the prologue to the *Wallenstein* trilogy of 1798–99, later also used in Verdi's *La Forza del Destino*). He also undertook to send a Protestant Bible to Scribe (who was traveling at the time), presumably to provide linguistic models.

56. See *BT,* 3:687-88.

57. Heinrich Baermann, accompanied by his eldest son, Carl, embarked on his eleventh concert tour in December 1838. He arrived in Paris in the middle of the month and lived in private lodgings found for him by Meyerbeer, who also invited the Baermanns to dine with him for the duration of their stay. Carl Baermann's diary, retained by his descendants, was never published, and is now lost. Fortunately, Heinz Becker was able to examine the diary and make excerpts of the pertinent passages in June 1952, sometime before the death of Georg Baermann in Munich-Pasing (*BT,* 3:688-92). At some point during 1839 Meyerbeer probably wrote his *Fantasie* for clarinet and string quartet for the Baermanns.

58. The interesting observations are continued in Carl Baermann's letter to his wife, Barbara, in Munich (autograph in the private ownership of Michael Obermayer in Munich; quoted by *BT,* 3:690).

Paris 4 January 1839

Dear Wife,

Meyerbeer treats us with unstinting affection, and is doing everything possible to promote our interests and success; indeed, he wants to compose a piece for us both (with solo voice) that would undoubtedly stimulate Parisian curiosity. We have already dined with him about twelve times, and hardly a day goes by when we are not together. All the rumors of his excessive luxury are completely unfounded. He is a simple, dear man, who, of course, has his weaknesses (don't we all!). He at least should be allowed some conceit when his *Robert* has been given 207 times (with hundreds of people unable to find seats), when the 91st performance of *Les Huguenots* has earned 10,000 fr., when his melodies are heard on all the streets, in every household, and at any social gathering. One can hardly be surprised if the composer is not a little affected who can say to himself: Paris does homage to you! You have brought pleasure to nine hundred thousand people! But he lives in such tranquil simplicity that he does not even have his own carriage . . .

59. Ballet-pantomime in three acts by Benoist, Thomas, and Marliani (scenario Saint-Georges, choreography by Mazilier). The premiere followed on 28 January 1839, and the work proved considerably successful, with forty-two performances until 1844. It marked the emergence of the young Ambroise Thomas* onto the Parian musical scene.

60. Meyerbeer had started composition of *Le Prophète*. The reference is to Jonas's couplets (later Zacharias's, no. 13, "Aussi nombreux que les étoiles").

61. Tgb. *vaguement*.

62. In his *Erinnerungen* (from *Gesämmelte Werke in 50 Bänden*, ed. Hubert Houben and Albert Hänel [Leipzig: Max Hesse, n.d.]) Laube described this meeting and left a vivid and thoughtful description the composer: ". . . I was sitting and reading one afternoon . . . when a small man came into the room. He was dressed very simply but tastefully, and inclined his head a little to one side. In a soft voice he asked if it was I: I replied in the affirmative, whereupon we spoke German. . . . He was overwhelmingly courteous, even though he had the performance of his new opera ahead of him, and a return journey to the home country to face . . . , and invited me to dinner in the Hôtel de Paris in the rue Richelieu where he was staying. . . . He was a very astute man, with unbelievable industry, and took unbelievable care of his work and its publication.

Artistically he was convinced that opera must have interest as a dramatic process, and that the indifference of German opera composers to the theatrical effectiveness of the text has had deadly consequences. He studied the theater like a dramatic poet, and turned to the most gifted of Frenchmen, Scribe, for his texts. . . . Meyerbeer was wealthy and, again, used his wealth carefully for his artistic and practical ends: he never used it sparingly. Nor did he save on time. The artistic aim had to be fully realized, fully worked out, even if this meant many changes or even rewriting.

So what did he make of life and all his many worries, in spite of all his wealth? It is difficult to say. He was a thinking person and had his opinions on everything. At the end of the day he was a Jew, and as a Jew remained doubtful about the durability of emancipation, this being why he favored the French. They are not suspicious of the Jew; to them he is a man like any other, he maintained. This is why he took part in all questions of liberalism, both small and great, but remained cautious, like a badger in his warren, preferring to question rather than talk himself.

Who was he actually? An artist, and one of great abilities. Of what kind? from where? His origins, his education, the religion of his fathers, are clearly discernible at the heart of his operas. The synagogue with its songs, which penetrate to the core, is clearly heard as soon as serious matters arise. The orchestral accompaniment of the wicked Bertram in *Robert*, Marcel and the fourth act of the *Huguenots*, the song of the Anabaptists in the *Prophet*, all spring from the synagogue. And this does not contradict what one calls Protestant in Marcel; a Lutheran, after all, holds fast to his Bible, and the Bible is of Jewish origin . . ." (pp. 399–400, translated by R. I. Letellier).

63. On 15 November 1839 Edouard Monnais became joint director of the Opéra with Duponchel.

64. This was inserted in act 2, and printed as a supplement in the Brandus vocal score.

65. For an account of Wagner's meeting with Meyerbeer, see Heinz Becker's article "Setkáni v Boulogne-sur-Mer: Wagner a Meyerbeer," *Hudebni veda* 21 (1984): 293–302 [with German abstract]. Meyerbeer furnished Wagner with letters of recommendation for Duponchel, Habeneck, and Antenor Joly, director of the Théâtre de la Renaissance.

66. Louise Fitzjames was dancing her famous assumption of the role of the Abbess in the Ballet of the Nuns. See the note on 2 December 1831.

67. Meyerbeer was probably coaching her.

68. This *chanson biblique* about forbidden and unrequited love (with words by Émile Deschamps) (1834) became one of Meyerbeer's most popular songs. No. 3 in the *Quarante Mélodies*.

69. Note by Wilhelm Altmann: Benedict, Weber's pupil, had been present at the composition of *Die drei Pintos* in 1821. He was amazed at the intractability of the sketches and examined them more closely, but retained no memories that could have helped Meyerbeer.

70. Berlioz, Hiller, and Moscheles were also invited to dine with Benedict (Altmann).

71. Chopin had spent the winter of 1838–39 with George Sand at the monastery of Valdemosa on Majorca, and the summer of 1839 on George Sand's estate at Nohant. He returned to Paris only in October.

72. Polonaise no. 6, op. 53 *(The Heroic)*. Meyerbeer held Chopin in high esteem, and there seems to have been a mutual cordiality, in spite of the popular myth of estrangement between them, born of Meyerbeer's famous criticism of Chopin's playing, in which he pointed out the rhythmic ambiguities of the latter's fondness for extreme rubato (see, for example, R. Jordan, *Nocturne: A Life of Chopin* [London: Constable, 1978], pp. 208–9, and J. Siepmann, *Chopin: The Reluctant Romantic* [London: Victor Gollancz, 1995], pp. 110–11). Meyerbeer himself observed that he once restored domestic peace, after a difference between himself and Minna, by sitting at the piano and soothing her with one of Chopin's nocturnes.

73. The Grand Sonata in E-flat, op. 47.

74. "M. Meyerbeer's scores have already cost us the voice of Mlle. Falcon."

75. This was Auguste Nourrit, brother of the famous tenor.

76. She was to sing Alice in 1842 and Marguerite de Valois in 1845, and was probably learning these roles as an understudy.

77. Note by Wilhelm Altmann: At the wedding of Mlle. Nathan, Meyerbeer heard discouraging reports about the latest performances of *Robert le Diable* and *Les Huguenots*.

78. Tgb. *attaquen*.

79. Tgb. *épreuve*.

80. Meyerbeer's intervention with Joly on Wagner's behalf was to lead to the acceptance of *Das Liebesverbot* for presentation at the Théâtre de la Renaissance in March 1840.

81. Gottfried Weber died on 21 September 1839 in Bad Kreuznach.

82. The *Columbus* Overture. For an account of its disastrous performance at the Conservatoire Concert of 4 February 1841, see Ernest Newman, *The Life of Richard Wagner,* vol. 1, *1813–1848* (London: Cassell, 1933; Cambridge: Cambridge University Press, 1976), pp. 283–85.

83. Meyerbeer's nickname for the Brothers Escudier.

84. Tgb. *congé*.

85. Text by Henri Blaze de Bury (1836). No. 39 in the *Quarante mélodies*.

86. "Menschenfeindlich" (text by Michael Beer, 1837); "Seul" in the French translation by Henri Blaze de Bury. No. 2 in the *Quarante Mélodies*.

87. Words by Wilhelm Müller (1839). No.9 in the *Quarante Mélodies*.

88. Words by J. W. von Goethe (1838). No. 25 in the *Quarante Mélodies*.

89. "Chant des moissonneurs vendéens" (words by Henri Blaze de Bury) (1839). No.
14 in the *Quarante Mélodies*.

90. Millenet, a schoolteacher in Gotha and director of the Duke's theater, was coor-
dinating the festivities planned there for the production of *Robert le Diable* early in the
new year.

91. At the beginning of March 1840 Schlesinger published a *Collection des mélodies
de Giacomo Meyerbeer*, containing twenty-two titles and richly illustrated by A. Devéria.

92. "La chanson de Maître Floh" (text by Henri Blaze de Bury; German translation
by Grünbaum) (1837). No. 23 in the *Quarante Mélodies*.

93. The Italian theater journal, not Bellini's opera.

94. The *Festlied* for Gotha.

95. Meyerbeer had heard of the plans to produce *Robert le Diable* in New Orleans
(November 1840).

96. On 11 January 1840 Jähns acknowledged receipt of a volume containing thirty-
two songs and other compositions in C. M. von Weber's original handwriting. Meyerbeer
had borrowed it to help him in his work on *Die drei Pintos*.

97. The founder and editor of *Il Pirata*.

98. *Grand opéra* in four acts by Donizetti (Scribe, based on Corneille's tragedy
Polyeucte [1641]; Paris, Opéra, 10 April 1840). Originally composed to an Italian text by
Salvatore Cammarano (*Poliuto*, in three acts) with Adolphe Nourrit in mind, it was rehearsed in Naples in 1838 with Duprez in the title role, but then banned by the censor.
Donizetti, as a consequence, left Italy to pursue his artistic career in Paris (see William
Ashbrook, *Donizetti and His Operas* [Cambridge: Cambridge University Press, 1982], pp.
131–32, 148–50). Meyerbeer was obviously interested in news of its rehearsal. The opera
was not a great success in Paris where it had only twenty performances, but was subsequently given in many other countries all the same. In Italy it was played mostly in the
Italian form as *Poliuto*. See entries for 29 and 30 March 1856.

99. According to the Jewish calendar.

100. Excerpts from *Oberto, conte di Bonifacio*, Verdi's first opera (Piazza, revised by
Solera, probably from the original text for Verdi's uncomposed *Rocester)*, was produced
in Milan at La Scala on 17 November 1839.

101. Tk. *épreuven*.

102. Tk. *en collection*.

103. Henri Blanchard reviewed Schlesinger's collection of Meyerbeer's songs in the
Revue et Gazette musicale de Paris 20 (8 March 1840).

104. These names were probably recipients of New Year's greetings from the composer.

105. Tk. *entrée*.

Index of Names

Names in square parentheses indicate the original spelling or variants, as found in the *Tagebücher* and *Taschenkalender*. Numbers in bold print indicate references to the Register of Names.

Index of Scholars
(Biography, Criticism, and History)

Index of Stage Works

Title, genre, and principal author are listed.